Also by JOHN R. ALDEN

JOHN STUART AND THE
SOUTHERN COLONIAL FRONTIER [1944]

GENERAL GAGE IN AMERICA [1948]

GENERAL CHARLES LEE [1951]

THE AMERICAN REVOLUTION: 1775–1783 [1954]

THE SOUTH IN THE REVOLUTION: 1763–1789 [1957]

A HISTORY OF THE UNITED STATES
[with Alice Magenis, 1960]

THE FIRST SOUTH [1961]

THE RISE OF THE AMERICAN REPUBLIC [1963]

PIONEER AMERICA [1966]

A History of the
AMERICAN REVOLUTION

A
HISTORY
OF THE
AMERICAN
REVOLUTION

BY JOHN R. ALDEN

JAMES B. DUKE PROFESSOR
OF HISTORY IN DUKE
UNIVERSITY

★ ★ ★ ★ ★ ★ ★
★ ★ ★ ★ ★ ★ ★

NEW YORK

Alfred · A · Knopf

1972

THIS IS A BORZOI BOOK

PUBLISHED BY ALFRED A. KNOPF, INC.

Library of Congress Catalog Card Number: 69-10201

Manufactured in the United States of America

Published February 3, 1969

Second Printing, September 1972

PREFACE

WERE excuse needed for writing this book concerning the American Revolution, I might plead that my version of that momentous convulsion differs from all those offered by other historians. It is now more than thirty years since I entered the highways and byways of the Revolution as a graduate student at the University of Michigan under the guidance of that most kind and most exacting scholar, Professor Verner W. Crane. During that long generation I have read many documents in diverse archives and libraries concerning the upheaval that ended with the founding of the American republic. I have inflicted upon scholars and the public several books about phases of the Revolution and individuals who played important parts in it. Not surprisingly, I have acquired some notions of my own about men and events. I venture to offer my views in the hope that they will not be found to lack merit.

There are other reasons for preparing this volume, among them the continuing importance of the Revolution, not merely in the minds of scholars, but also in the affairs of mankind generally. A special circumstance is the need for a modern and relatively detailed book devoted precisely to the era of the Revolution in America. Beginning with the origins of the Anglo-American troubles that came after the Seven Years' War and ending with the first inauguration of George Washington, the volume covers the tempestuous years in which the Thirteen Colonies separated from the British empire, in which the American union was founded. Still another reason for the appearance of this work is the need to bring together the results of recent and fruitful researches in the history of that era by American and British scholars, who have been delving most profitably into it since World War II.

I have striven to examine the Revolution from many vantage points, and I have dealt with things social, economic, political, military, and diplomatic. I have not slighted the War of Independence, which was, of course, central in the era. I have not neglected to narrate the campaigns

v

of that struggle, but I have emphasized strategy rather than the details of battle and have sought to interweave civil and military history. Nor are things and persons British hastily treated. Without some understanding of Britain, without information about British institutions and the shifting fortunes of George III and the British politicians with whom he toiled, the American Revolution is not understandable. Trying to describe its course, I have concentrated upon events and issues that seem to me to be the most important. I have not attempted to cover the years 1783 to 1789, interesting as they are, in detail, but to confine my treatment of that period largely to the development of the American union.

Bias is the constant companion of the historian; it is often apparent in writings about the Revolution. I have striven to restrain my prejudices. All my opinions will not please all professional scholars or all readers. It will be apparent that I believe that the Declaration of Independence was politically and morally justifiable; that the creation of the American republic was a long forward step not only for the Americans, but for mankind generally; and that the establishment of the stronger American union in 1789 was the crowning achievement of the Revolutionary generation. Such views do not require that I utterly condemn George III, Lord North, Loyalists, or Antifederalists. I have tried to do justice to all persons who were conspicuous upon the Revolutionary scene, but also to manifest that charity which should always be exercised when one limns fallible human beings engaged in tragic conflict. There are few villains in this work.

It will be obvious that I do not subscribe to geographic, economic, or institutional determinism. Nor do I believe that the War of Independence was dictated by the Deity or by Fate. The course of events in Britain and America during the years 1763 to 1789 might have been far different from what it was. The complexities of that turbulent period cannot be reduced to inexorable simplicities. Nor is it possible to offer a final assessment of the consequences of the Revolution. It is not even certain that the political separation of Britain and America which took place in the eighteenth century is a permanent one. Few will question that repercussions from the Revolution continue everywhere upon the globe two centuries after it began.

I have corrected some of those seemingly inevitable and annoying small errors that appeared in my earlier books. I hope that I have not committed many new ones. I am indebted to several persons for assistance, especially Professor Clarence Gohdes, Mrs. Vivian Jackson, Mrs. Martha C. Love, Mr. Howard H. Peckham, Dr. Mattie Russell, Dr. Wilcomb Washburn, Mrs. Alice B. Wells, Mr. William Wickham, and Mr.

Richard A. Winters. The Duke University Research Council generously supplied funds for copying documents and for typing.

I wish especially to acknowledge the profit that I have derived from examination of the notes and unpublished writings of the late Professor Fred J. Ericson, a devoted scholar of the Revolution and a longtime friend. His widow, Mrs. Vivian Ericson, graciously donated those papers.

John R. Alden

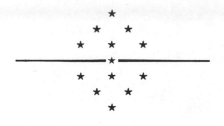

CONTENTS

CONTENTS

ILLUSTRATIONS

MAPS

A History of the
AMERICAN REVOLUTION

CHAPTER I

The American Colonies

IN February 1763, England was at a peak of magnificence. On the tenth day of that month at Paris representatives of the Bourbon Kings of France and Spain, Louis XV and Charles III, signed a treaty which officially ended the Seven Years' War. In that struggle England had won triumph after victory on land and sea over her traditional Bourbon enemies, and the treaty testified to the prowess of her soldiers and sailors. The French had been driven from India; they had suffered defeat after disastrous defeat in the New World. The first French empire had been virtually destroyed. Britain had established her supremacy over the entire eastern third of North America, from the icy shores of Hudson's Bay to the hot sands of the tip of the Florida peninsula, from the Atlantic to the Mississippi. Britannia ruled not only the waves, but also far-spread possessions—colonies and bases—upon four continents. Twenty years later Britain acceded to another treaty at Paris in which she acknowledged the loss of the most valuable of all her own dependencies, the Thirteen Colonies in North America. The United States of America entered the family of nations. In 1789 George Washington became the first President of a stable American republic. Seldom have the fortunes of empires and peoples so swiftly and so greatly altered. In barely more than a quarter century, in the era of the American Revolution, the greatest maritime empire known to man was gutted. It later revived, achieved new majesty and power, and spread over the globe. Even so, the Revolution vitally injured the European colonial system, and the emergence of the American republic was doubtless the most momentous political event of modern times.

One may not predict the ultimate destiny of that republic, but its appearance unquestionably marked the undertaking of a far-reaching human experiment. The Americans of the Revolutionary generation not only rid themselves of eighteenth-century European royalty and aristocracy, but undertook to destroy established churches and other institutions that cramped both body and mind. They executed an internal reformation, and they opened the way for further and vast changes. It is fitting, indeed, to think of an American Revolution that began with the founding of Jamestown in 1607, that gained powerful impetus in the last third of the eighteenth century, and that continued with vigor two centuries after America became independent.

Man is greatly tempted to see in past events the directing hand of God, or ineluctable Fate, or historical laws. The Americans were long inclined to believe that they were a chosen people, that they had a special mission, that the Deity guided them as He did the ancient Israelites. The historian, alas, must obtain his information from defective human records and remains. He cannot find the decree of the Divine declaring such to be His intention. The historian does not discover an ordinance from Providence asserting that the inhabitants of the Thirteen Colonies must achieve their freedom by force; he cannot read a ukase from Destiny proclaiming that Britain and America must separate, amicably or otherwise; indeed, he knows of no immutable law which describes the rupture between Britain and America in the eighteenth century as a permanent one. No thoughtful person could say almost two centuries after the Anglo-American divorce that remarriage was utterly impossible. Certainly few men believed in the year 1763 that the Americans would break loose from the British empire within two brief decades. They were quite loyal to Britain; they were proud to be British subjects; they were prosperous; and they were nearly as happy as a people might then be. They could look forward to a splendid future under the British flag.

One hundred fifty-six years after the founding of Jamestown in Virginia, 143 years after the planting of Plymouth in Massachusetts, the colonies that soon afterward created the American union were neither weak, poor, nor immature. More than 1.6 million people dwelled along the north Atlantic seaboard, their settlements stretching from the Maine district of Massachusetts to the Altamaha River in Georgia. Their number was rapidly increasing; it would reach 2.5 million before the colonists fell into armed clash with their mother country. Their harvests from generous fields, from thick forests, and from fish-filled waters were abundant. They had easy access to metals sufficient for their needs. They possessed many broad and navigable rivers, such as the Connecticut, the Hudson, the Delaware, the Susquehanna, and the James, and also fine harbors on the Atlantic that made easy the inlet and outlet of men and things. They were no longer confined to the immediate vicinity of the ocean. They occupied the coastal plain—the Tidewater; they also had spread across the Piedmont, to the foot of the Appalachian divide; and they were ready to move over the mountain wall. Their thirteen governments were both firm and respectable. They were not without laws, literature, or the arts; they were not, on the whole, a frontier people. By and large, the American society was both sound and wholesome.

There have been those who have seen weakness rather than strength in the Americans as they were in 1763. Thus it has been pointed out that their settlements were scantily spread out along the Atlantic seaboard for more than a thousand miles, hardly occupying more than the thin edge of a vast continent. But a casual inspection of a map of North America of that year deceives the observer; it does not indicate the essential solidity of the English colonies. It has been declared that all of the colonists of that time were fewer than the inhabitants of the borough of Brooklyn in New York City in the twentieth century. Such is the case. However, the population of all England in 1763 was less than that of New York City in the twentieth century, and all the people of the British Isles in 1763 were fewer than those of metropolitan New York in the twentieth century. Nor do the maps of 1763 indicate the fact that the Americans were constantly and rapidly increasing in number, in part because of accretions from Europe and Africa, in larger part because of a natural increase that was extraordinary.

For the Americans were doubling in number with every generation. There were few bachelors or spinsters among them; early marriages were the rule; and widows and widowers quickly remarried. Life for the unmarried was neither easy nor happy. Families lacking a father or mother were most uncomfortable. In a land of generous opportunity, in a land where possession of a farm or a thriving shop was within reach of nearly all white men, children were assets rather than burdens. Contraceptives were virtually unknown in America, and the social diseases were uncommon. The typical American family included a brood of children. Travelers observed that Virginia belles and the women of the frontiers produced progeny as rapidly as their Yankee sisters, even though the curious practice of bundling in New England should have increased the birthrate in that region. To be sure, disease carried off many infants and children. Even so, the increase in the American population was, had been, and would long continue to be geometrical rather than arithmetical. It was evident to Benjamin Franklin and to other thoughtful men that the Americans would become a numerous people, that they would probably surpass the British in number within a century.

That conclusion was buttressed by the signing of the Treaty of Paris of 1763, for it marked the conquest of ancient and formidable enemies in French Canada, the end of the French empire in North America, and the removal of the greatest obstacle to the expansion of the colonies into, and even beyond, the valley of the Mississippi. In that treaty, which brought to a close the long contest between Britain and France for supremacy in North America, the French monarchy acknowledged defeat and ceded Canada and all that part of Louisiana—except for New Orleans—lying eastward of the Mississippi River to Britain. In that treaty, Spain, having vainly tried to help France in the last years of the Seven Years' War, was forced to yield Florida to Britain, in order to secure the return of Havana, captured by the British arms in 1762. Thus all of the eastern third of North America became British soil. Moreover, during the negotiations that led to the treaty, France, choosing to liquidate her empire on that continent, gave New Orleans and the western half of Louisiana to Spain. French troops vanished from the valley of the St. Lawrence as well as that of the Mississippi, and the French Canadians, numbering about 60,000, became British subjects. French regulars and Canadian militia had wreaked havoc on the frontiers of the American colonies and had checked their westward advance. They would do so no longer. The only remaining bar against the spread of the Americans to the Mississippi was the Indians. They might, and did, delay the westward progress of the colonists. They could not permanently prevent it. Indeed, the way was opening for the Americans to push on across the Mississippi, even to the Pacific Ocean, for Spain could not resist as stubbornly in the future as France had in the past. Nor were the colonists then forced to fear the return of French or Spanish armies from Europe, so long as they were protected by the British navy, easily dominant on the Atlantic. Many Americans lusted for the lands east of the Mississippi abandoned by the French—longing for good earth would lead to the forming of American farms beside the Pacific within less than a century—but it cannot be said that the colonists lacked either space or natural resources in 1763.

To be sure, there were, east of the Appalachians, no far-stretching prairies of rich dark earth like those of Illinois and Iowa, nor a "Black Belt" like that of Alabama and Mississippi. Nevertheless, the colonists were exploiting very fertile lands in the Connecticut River valley, in eastern Pennsylvania, and elsewhere. The Thirteen Colonies also contained large quantities of not-so-rich soils that were suitable for raising grain, vegetables, fruit, and cattle. They gave forth much more food than the Americans could consume. The Americans exported grain and flour from the Middle Colonies—New York, New Jersey, Pennsylvania, and Delaware; and they shipped out rice from the far Southern Colonies—South Carolina and Georgia. Even New England, where stone was more abundant than fat earth, sent forth food, for the Yankees exported fish in large quantities. Virginia and Maryland supplied tobacco to smokers in the colonies, the British Isles, and northern Europe. South Carolina sent out blocks of indigo dyestuff. Furs and deerskins were loaded upon vessels in many colonial ports. Lumber, masts, and naval stores were shipped out from the Carolinas and from New England.

Too much may be made of the things sent to sea by the Americans. Foreign markets were important to them, but not vital. The typical colonist was a homestead farmer who lived well, with his family, in large part upon the produce of his own land. He did not send much to remote markets; he did not buy very much from distant manufacturers. He and his were, in the main, self-sufficient. He saved his money, acquired more land, and helped his sons to get farms. The industrious and thrifty farmer was commonly prosperous. Rainfall was normally sufficient, even abundant, everywhere between the Atlantic and the Appalachians. Complete crop failures were few. In the long settled parts of the colonies clapboard houses, together with some made of brick and stone, had replaced the huts and log cabins that sheltered the first colonists. Hearth fires helped ward off the cold winter. The farmer and his family were well clad, although their clothing did not meet the requirements of European fashionable circles. The materials of which it was made might be produced and processed on the farm. The food eaten by the family might be equally plain, but it was usually plentiful. Its members ate meat daily, once, twice, even thrice. The farmer and his sons often went hunting, bringing home ducks, turkeys, quail, geese, deer, bear, and opossum. They also caught fish in nearby lakes, rivers, and coastal waters. The males were taller and stronger than their relatives in the British Isles and northwestern Europe. The typical American household enjoyed homely comfort as well as freedom from want.

Not everyone who lived on the American land was a member of a family owning a homestead farm. Interspersed among such farms were estates in the Northern Colonies tilled by tenants and bond servants, and plantations in the Southern Colonies cultivated by Negro slaves. For America had her wealthy landowners, who possessed deeds to hundreds and thousands of good acres and who formed the body of an untitled aristocracy. The Schuylers, the Livingstons, and the Johnsons of New York, the Carrolls of Maryland, the Lees and Carters of Virginia, and the

7

Manigaults and Middletons of South Carolina, with other and similar clans, belonged to a patrician order. Their homes were often sufficiently large and elegant to be described as mansions rather than houses. The ladies of such families did not cook, and their men did not push the plow. A few of those families had their coaches. Happily, tenants were not numerous, and they could rather readily get land. They were not permanently condemned to an inferior status. Nor were the bond servants, who were persons legally obliged to work under the control of masters and mistresses during a period of four to fourteen years. Many of them had sold their services in return for transportation to the New World. Such individuals served for shorter periods. Others had been convicted of crime in England and had been permitted to enter into service in lieu of execution or other punishment. The convict was bound to toil for a period of either seven or fourteen years. As the War of Independence approached, about 1,000 convicts entered American ports each year. When the bond servant was released, he might become a tenant, and then a homestead farmer. The condition of the Negro was, of course, not temporary. He and his progeny, with exceptions, were, and remained, the property of white owners.

A surprisingly large minority of the Americans lived in cities and towns. By eighteenth-century standards the colonies contained as many as five cities, Philadelphia, Boston, New York, Charleston, and Newport. The largest of those cities—Philadelphia, Boston, and New York—were comparable in size to Bristol, Sheffield, and Leeds in England. There were in the colonies many towns with 1,000 or 2,000 inhabitants, and more villages and hamlets. One of every twenty Americans could be described as urban. In the cities and towns lived merchants, men whose transactions extended beyond the local, storekeepers in great variety, printers, physicians, lawyers, teachers, mechanics with diverse specialties, barbers, shipbuilders, household servants, and numerous laborers. No metropolis was to be found in America, no great capital like London or Paris. However, her "cities in the wilderness," as they have been called, were centers of thought and political action as well as commerce.

America had her social hierarchy, but it differed from those of England, France, Germany, and Spain. The lines between classes were not so sharp as they were in the British Isles. Moreover, the mass of the white colonists, on the land, in villages, and in cities was composed of middle-class folk. There was a thin upper layer in the colonial social structure of merchants, prosperous lawyers, and officeholders, together with the owners of landed estates and plantations. Such people were not usually distinguished from their fellows by a hereditary title or a coat of arms. Here and there a baronet could be found, but no American-born man was a baron, a viscount, or a marquis; nor was there an American countess. The line between Americans of the middle rank and those of the patrician order was not clearly marked, but it was nevertheless real. Fundamentally, the possession of wealth, particularly in the form of land, set the gentry apart from other Americans. Far below the patricians, and below the middle class, were the tenants, the bond servants, and the truly poor whites of the cities and of the country. Even such people could move upward in the colonial world, and they frequently did. The gentry contained men and women whose ancestors had been bond servants. Unlike Australians, Americans of the twentieth century do not boast about forebears who were convicts; it is nevertheless likely that criminals expelled from England produced progeny in America, and that the shadow of the gallows looms behind some lengthy American family trees. Below all the whites, however hopeless might be their condition, were the Negroes, whether free or slave. Nearly all of them were human property. A few of them were cooks, maids, footmen, butlers, carpenters, and masons. Most of them were field hands, valued for their muscles, their physical energies, and their ability to reproduce themselves. One of every five Americans was of African descent.

The colonists were divided from each other in various ways. They were a medley of peoples from the British Isles, northwestern Europe, and Africa, with a small contingent of Sephardic Jews. The English, together with the Welsh, the Scots, and the Scotch-Irish, were easily in the majority. Nearly all the New Englanders were of English stock. Persons of English ancestry were numerous in Virginia and Maryland; in no colony were they few. New Londons and Lancasters, Bristols and Bostons, Worcesters and Gloucesters, Northamptons and Southamptons, Deals, Dovers, and Durhams studded the American landscape. It is probable that one third of the population of Pennsylvania was German. There were settlements of the "high Dutch" almost everywhere south of New England. Some of them knew little or no English. The Scotch-Irish, putting themselves down to the westward of the Germans, were strung out from Pennsylvania to Georgia. Those aggressive Ulsterites supplied the third largest element of European descent in the colonies.

Nor were the colonists united in their religion. They sought to find God along all the Protestant pathways; a few of them searched for Him under the guidance of the papacy; some of them were Jews; some were heretics. The Congregationalists dominated New England, and their church was established there, except in tiny and anarchic Rhode Island. Their close religious relatives, the Presbyterians, were numerous in the Middle Colonies and in the interior of the Southern ones. Anglicans were plentiful on the Southern Tidewater; their sect was officially favored in all the Southern Colonies—Maryland, Virginia, the Carolinas, and Georgia —and in four New York counties. Quaker meetinghouses were a common sight in the region about Philadelphia. People implored the Almighty in Dutch Reformed churches in New York and New Jersey. Mennonites, Moravians, German Calvinists, and Lutherans made their prayers to Him in Pennsylvania. Here and there scatterings of Baptists and Methodists had made their appearance. There was a bewildering variety of sects in America; moreover, many of them were riven into two or more parts by theological disputes. Many Americans then belonged to no church, partly because it was difficult to secure membership, partly because expulsion for heresy or misconduct was frequent. Unitarianism and deism were making headway among the more sophisticated Americans. The colonists enjoyed a larger measure of religious freedom than any other people in the Western world. Nevertheless, church and state were utterly separated in no colony. In Maryland, founded by the Lords Baltimore, who were Roman Catholics, papists could not lawfully hold office. Legally supported in the South, the Anglicans suffered from discrimination in New England. Those who subscribed to the doctrine of the Trinity were everywhere favored as against others who admitted that they did not understand it. If the Americans were in large part unchurched, they were nevertheless a Christian people.

The Americans were separated, not only in God, but by nature. They were divided from each other by rivers, swamps, forests, and hills. Their roads were as yet wagon tracks and paths rather than highways. He who traveled by land crossed rivers by wading, by swimming, or by ferry. He was plagued everywhere on occasion by mud and sand; in winter the roads in the Northern Colonies were often covered with snow and ice. Taverns were not ubiquitous; sometimes they were iniquitous. The wayfarer who went by land from Boston to Savannah traversed a thousand arduous miles. It was easier for him to make his journey by sea. Mail service was also slow and uncertain, and expensive, even though it had been renovated by the efficient deputy postmaster general, Benjamin Franklin. Newspapers and news, except for wild rumors, moved slowly. Many of the Americans had never seen a city.

The colonists were also geographically divided by clashing economic and social interests. Those who lived to the north of the Susquehanna River, chiefly engaged in agriculture, also devoted themselves to commerce, and even, to a degree, to manufacturing. They owned few slaves, and the gap among them between the middle class and the gentry was neither wide nor extremely difficult to cross. The principle of aristocracy was not so firmly established in the Northern Colonies as it was to the southward. Four of the five American cities were located in the Northern Colonies; urban influence was stronger within them than it was in the South, where there was only one city, Charleston, South Carolina. The South was overwhelmingly agricultural and rural. Besides, the South had its special kind of tillage, the production of tobacco, rice, and indigo on plantations. There was as yet no difficulty between North and South because the one region contained few Negro slaves and the other contained many. However, the economic interests of the Southern planter were not identical with those of the Northern homestead farmer, nor with those of Northern merchants. Although the Southern social structure, except for the position of the Negro, was not rigid, the Southern aristocrats were prouder and more exclusive than their Northern counterparts. Seeds of discord between South and North existed; they would later come to flower. The names "North" and "South" were not much used before George Washington became President of the United States. The Mason-Dixon line, the boundary between Maryland and Pennsylvania, was not surveyed until 1767, but within less than two decades that line was recognized as one that separated two distinct parts of America.

Contest between North and South was potential rather than actual in the year 1763. Clash between East and West had long since produced violence, and it would soon lead to more bloodshed. The colonists of the interior, of the Piedmont, of the Old West, were often at odds with those of Tidewater. The inland people were rougher, less educated, poorer, more addicted to emotional Christianity, more democratic both socially and politically than those of the seacoast. The men of the hinterland were often financially in debt to those of Tidewater. They were commonly denied representation in the colonial assemblies in proportion to their numbers. They keenly disliked taxation, and Tidewater people sometimes used their political power to place a disproportionate share of public burdens upon the poorer folk of the interior. In the Southern Colonies the aristocrats, the plantations, and the Negro slaves were all located on the seaboard; the Old West was largely inhabited by white homestead farmers. The men of Tidewater were not exposed to attack by the Indians, and they were not eager to spend money for defense against them; those of the interior who suffered from the raids of the redmen on occasion begged in vain at the colonial capitals for help. From such cleavages arose Nathaniel Bacon's rebellion in Virginia in 1676. In 1764 Pennsylvania frontiersmen marched against Philadelphia, against Quaker pacifists who thought it unnecessary to wage war with hostile Indians. After 1765 the Carolinas were torn by strife between the Regulators of the interior and the Tidewater people. The Regulators of North Carolina took up arms in 1768, and they did not finally put down their weapons until they were crushed by militia in the pitched battle of the Alamance in 1771.

The Americans were divided in still another way, by rivalries and animosities between colonies. They lived under thirteen separate governments. They had their particularistic prides. They thought of themselves as Rhode Islanders, Jerseymen, Virginians, South Carolinians, and so on. Their governments quarreled over boundary lines; fought for advantages in both internal and external commerce; and debated about fair contributions to their common defense. The interests and the allegiances of the colonists were regional, continental, and imperial—and local. In the main, the loyalties of the colonials were as yet given to their respective colonies and to the British empire.

But the Americans were rapidly developing that community of sentiment upon which modern nations are based. It is tempting to magnify the differences and the controversies among them. They had much in common in terms of Old World heritage; they had experienced common difficulties in the New World; and they had common enemies. The ancestors of the colonists, except for the Negroes, were not utterly diverse; nearly all of them came from the British Isles and that part of Europe which lies north of the Pyrenees and west of the Elbe River. They were almost exclusively Protestant. With minor exceptions, they spoke English, at least an American variety of that language. Their institutions, their literature, their ways of thought, and their customs, were largely of English origin. They retained no affection for Holland, for France, or for any German principality. As settlers in the New World they had encountered similar trials in the conquest of American savannahs and wildernesses. They had fought together against the Indians, the Spanish, and the French. Their governmental systems were more alike than they were different. They had a common history of clash with British officials in America and with the British government in London.

By the year 1763 the colonists were becoming increasingly aware that they had much in common, also that they differed from their "cousins" of the Old World. They were employing the terms "America" and "Americans" to designate their settlements and themselves. In part, they used those words for convenience, as did the British. But it is clear enough that the names were increasingly adopted because the colonists realized that they had become a new and a distinct people. They saw themselves as Americans as well as New Hampshiremen, Pennsylvanians, and Georgians. They knew that they were not merely Englishmen who happened to live on the western side of the Atlantic.

12

I · The American Colonies

Let it not be thought that the colonists at that time desired to separate from Britain or to form their own union. Nevertheless, it was even then apparent to some informed and thoughtful colonials that the Americans were rapidly increasing in number; that they possessed a sound and burgeoning economy; that they were not without military power; that they would before long be able, if necessary, to defend themselves; and that they were sufficiently mature to govern themselves. The astute Benjamin Franklin was by no means the only American who knew that the American population, through generation and immigration, was doubling in every quarter century. And were they not a healthy, sturdy, and educated people? They were indeed so by the standards of their time. The beggars who infested the streets of London were unknown in America; the highway robbers who frequently relieved travelers of their money and their jewelry on the roads leading to and from the imperial capital were uncommon in the colonies. Prostitutes abounded in England; there were a few in American ports. A large fraction of the colonists was literate. In New England, where many elementary schools were maintained at public expense, the ability to read and write was common. The Americans were not an ignorant people. Many of them, being owners of property or taxpayers, possessed the right to vote, exercised it, and so played a part in public affairs. Colonial voters were often well versed in domestic questions. Nor were they entirely unacquainted with matters imperial and European.

Not that the colonists as a whole were sophisticated. They were as yet colonial in literature and the arts as well as in politics. Indeed, they would remain culturally colonial long after the creation of the United States. They had produced no philosopher of imposing stature, unless one chooses to assert that the Reverend Jonathan Edwards was the equal of John Locke and David Hume. No American Shakespeare had grown to manhood on the banks of Maryland's Avon River, or any other American stream. No majestic Milton had sprung from the New England Puritans; no Cavalier poet had arisen from the Virginia aristocracy. The first novel to be published by an American author would not appear until a generation had passed. The first truly gifted American painter, John Singleton Copley, had not yet become famous for his portraits. To be sure, America was not a cultural desert. Benjamin Franklin was already famous for his electrical discoveries. That versatile genius would soon indite his equally famous autobiography. Moreover, America was a nursery for political philosophers and craftsmen. These would before long lay the solid foundations of an enduring and great republic. No European nation possessed their equals. Before the end of the third quarter of the eighteenth century

Franklin was joined on the public scene by George Washington, Thomas Jefferson, John Adams, John Dickinson, John Jay, and many another man distinguished in the conduct of public affairs.

To point out that the colonists were not remarkably productive in literature and the arts is not to declare that well-educated men were not to be found among them. On the contrary, although they had produced few men who added to the rich stock of English literature or to the scantier body of English art or to the thin corpus of English music, there were many colonials who were well acquainted with Latin, Greek, Hebrew, history, poetry, philosophy, and law. Plato, Plutarch, Homer, Virgil, Cicero, Milton, and Shakespeare were not unknown on the western side of the Atlantic. The more prosperous Americans owned and read books other than the Holy Scriptures. Many a ship carried books from London or Bristol across the ocean. Nor were those colonists eager for learning always forced to master the ancient or modern classics without assistance. Girls did not usually receive instruction beyond the elementary, but the sons of prosperous and learned fathers commonly pursued more advanced studies under tutors and at college. The doors of Harvard, Yale, Princeton, and Columbia Universities, then only colleges, were open in the year 1763; those of Brown University, Rutgers University, and Dartmouth University soon would be; and the University of Pennsylvania, in the form of an academy for boys, was flourishing. The Southern Colonies contained only one institution of more or less advanced learning, the College of William and Mary, at Williamsburg, Virginia. However, young Southern males were not therefore denied access to knowledge. They had already found their way to the College of New Jersey at Princeton. Others were sent to England and the European Continent to complete their formal education. Southern youths enrolled at English private schools, such as Westminster; at the University of Edinburgh; and at the University of Leyden. A few studied in France and Switzerland. Many of the American leaders of the Revolutionary generation had either graduated from or attended a college or university of some sort.

Notable in that generation were lawyers, a few of them the products of the London Inns of Court, most of them men who had studied under the direction of practicing attorneys. Earlier, lawyers had been few in the colonies, but able men had increasingly found opportunity at the bar in a thriving economy and an increasingly more complex society. Lawyers in private practice have never been revered by laymen; litigious and pettifogging, they were not loved by those whom they harassed about private matters in the courts of eighteenth-century America. They were the more disliked because the colonists had managed to get along with only a few attorneys in the past. Justice too often fled when the lawyers approached; if it remained, it was submerged under legalisms, delays, court fees, and the charges of the advocates. However, it was otherwise in public affairs, for in that arena the interests of the younger lawyers were commonly those of the colonists as a whole. They were coming forward as more or less learned champions of American liberties. Among them was Patrick Henry, who had won acclaim in Virginia in the famous case of the "Parson's Cause." With fervid oratory he had persuaded a jury to bring in a verdict that deprived Anglican clergyman James Maury of a windfall that Maury sought at the expense of Virginia taxpayers. Similarly, James Otis, a Massachusetts lawyer, had achieved popularity. In 1761, Otis had denounced the use of general warrants in the enforcement of English statutes governing maritime trade as unconstitutional. He accordingly became a champion of American liberty against English aggression. Lawyers would fulminate both in speech and in print in behalf of American rights during the years between the Treaty of Paris and the Declaration of Independence.

Let it not be thought that the Americans had no leaders other than laymen. Her clergymen, many of them college-trained, were numerous and influential; not all of them lived in theological quiet. Less powerful than they had once been, the men of the cloth were less potent than men of money. Even so, laymen listened attentively to Congregational, Presbyterian, Baptist, and Lutheran exhorters, and the voices of the Anglican vicars were not always languid and ignored. Those who occupied pulpits did not confine themselves to things holy and eternal. Many of them forthrightly instructed their listeners about questions unholy and temporal. Political opinion often came forcefully from the altar, all the more effectively because it had at least a measure of sanction from the Divine.

At least as important as the clergy in the things of this world were newspaper publishers, merchants, planters, and militia officers who had been polished in the school of experience rather than by tutors and professors. Such men might be well educated as a result of wide reading, as Benjamin Franklin was. They were more often men of a practical stamp who had found out about the ways of mankind in the countinghouse, in the printing shop, in the management of plantations, in colonial legislatures, in campaigns against the Indians and the French. Such was George Washington of Mount Vernon, Virginia, no profound scholar, but a responsible, reliable, and redoubtable man. He and others like him might not be profoundly versed in philosophy or poesy; but they had the courage, the will, the information, and the ability to govern themselves and others. They, with their formally educated fellows, would prove equal to the heavy tasks of creating and forming an enduring nation.

In sum, the Americans in the year 1763 were a prosperous and mature people, a people capable of self-government, a people beginning to recognize their essential unity. External pressure—so we may say, with the advantage of hindsight—would drive them still closer together, and toward nationhood, if that pressure came from Britain. And it did.

CHAPTER II

Britain in the Year 1763

IF North America supplied the largest jewels in the British imperial treasury in February 1763, that treasury held numerous others. Britain was at a zenith of power and prosperity, the envy of Europe. The prestige of Britain had never been higher. Her monarchy was stable; her system of government seemed to be liberal and enlightened to European political philosophers such as Voltaire and Montesquieu; her public finances were not deranged; her navy was at least momentarily unchallengeable; her maritime commerce was extensive and growing; and her ladies and gentlemen lived in elegance. The Industrial Revolution had already begun in England and would add to British wealth and strength. But the prestige of Britain exceeded her power; her political and social systems were much less than absolutely admirable; and her men of public affairs were, with some exceptions, ill fitted to govern distant dependencies peopled by Englishmen.

The British empire was indeed impressive. In addition to the North American colonies and dependencies in India, it contained many bright, though smaller gems. Among them were Bermuda, the Bahamas, Jamaica, Barbados, Antigua, Montserrat, Barbuda, Tobago, Granada, Dominica, and other islands studding the Caribbean Sea. England had footholds on the coast of Central America. The English flag had flown over the rocky peninsula of Gibraltar and the Balearic island of Minorca for a half century, and the western Mediterranean Sea was in consequence almost an English lake—Minorca had been captured by the French during the war, but Louis XV had been forced to return it. Senegal had been seized from the French during that conflict, and had become one of the British possessions on the west coast of Africa. Newfoundland was English soil, and the English East India Company maintained tiny outposts on steamy Sumatra. The empire was vast and it seemed likely to expand rather than to diminish.

Not yet twenty-five years of age, the young George III presided over that variegated collection of territories. The prospect for him at home was as handsome as it was beyond the oceans. His great-grandfather George I and his grandfather George II were German rather than English, and many in England, Scotland, and Ireland had looked upon them as foreign usurpers of the throne. Adherents to the exiled house of Stuart had been so numerous as late as 1745 that Bonnie Prince Charlie, the Young Pretender, had been able to land in Scotland and to march with an army into England. But that uprising had ended in crushing defeat for the gallant prince and his followers at Culloden in northern Scotland in 1746. Thereafter the cause of the Roman Catholic Stuarts was hopeless. Broken in body and spirit, Prince Charles Edward at last became a pensioner of George III. A romantic and sentimental popular attachment to him and to his family endured for some years after the collapse of the rebellion of 1745. However, even in Scotland, where it was strongest, few were willing to fight for the Stuarts when George III ascended the throne in 1760. Indeed, the partisans of that family, especially those who were Scots, swiftly allied themselves to George III. Immediately after taking the Crown he formally declared, "I glory in the name of Britain," thus claiming that he, unlike his ancestors, was not German. Was he also hinting that he valued the English no more than he did the Scots? As soon as he could, he made John Stuart, Earl of Bute, a Scot, his prime minister; and he appointed dozens of men who came from beyond the Tweed to offices in London and in the British possessions overseas. Whatever else may be said about George III, it cannot be denied that he did much to cement the Anglo-Scottish union that had been created a half century earlier.

The throne of the youthful George III was safe from internal contest. Moreover, the British Isles were at least momentarily impregnable against assaults by European enemies, for the British navy was easily the strongest in the world. It was so powerful that it could hold its own against the combined fleets of France and Spain—this at a time when there was no other important European navy. In the Seven Years' War British fleets had prevented a French invasion across the Channel; had substantially protected the British merchant marine; had struck at the mercantile shipping of France and Spain; had prevented the Bourbons from sending reinforcements to their outlying possessions; and had taken part in the captures of Louisbourg, Quebec, Havana, Manila, and various other French and Spanish strongholds and territories. Early in the year 1763 the seas traversed by Europeans were almost as much British as the

18

shimmering lakes of Cumberland county, as the austere lochs of Scotland.

Nor was the power of Britain on land to be despised. Her regular army, compared to those of France, Spain, Frederick the Great of Prussia, and Empress Catherine of Russia, was small. Greatly enlarged during the Seven Years' War, it contained not many more than 100 regiments of infantry, and its contingents of cavalry and artillery were even less impressive in size. However, the British soldiers were as good as any in the world, and their power could be asserted, with the help of the navy, at critical and distant places. Sturdy recruits could be obtained in the home islands for wars against European enemies. Moreover, Britain's colonies in North America, with 1.6 million inhabitants, could easily, with the help of the navy, defend themselves against foreign attack. In fact, they could supply men, if needed, for asssaults upon the islands that France still retained in the Carribean and upon the bulky residue of the Spanish domains in the New World. So long as Britain remained mistress of the seas, so long as she retained the loyalty of her North American colonies, her land forces were more than sufficient for the defense of the home islands and her territories beyond the oceans.

To be sure, the population of the British Isles was then comparatively thin. At a time when France contained about 20 million people, there were some 6.7 million in England and Wales combined, fewer than 1 million in Scotland, and fewer than 3 million in Ireland. The Spanish were also then more numerous than the British. However, after generations of slow growth, the number of Englishmen was rising rapidly. That burgeoning was not as yet commonly perceived, in part because the English government would then undertake nothing so systematic as a census, in part because increase was regional rather than general.

The number of the British was growing, to a degree, because of minor advances in medicine and cleanliness, but in the main because of the onset of the Industrial Revolution, which was well under way in northern England. It was as yet an unappreciated phenomenon. Its consequences were not yet evident to inventors and manufacturers involved in it, certainly not to politicians. The now celebrated improvement in the steam engine wrought by James Watt in 1769 was not fascinating to most Englishmen at the time. Nevertheless, the makers of cloth, iron, and steel were adding to the prosperity of the nation. Beginning earlier in Britain than on the European Continent, the Industrial Revolution would at length bring almost startling riches. It was already supplying employment for thousands; it would later provide occupation and sustenance for millions.

If the informed observer in London was not fully aware in the early months of 1763 of the rise of British industry, he knew full well that the nation's maritime commerce was flourishing. It had suffered during the recent war from the attacks of enemy warships and privateers. They had captured some 3,000 English merchant vessels, the toll being moderately heavy because the French and Spanish had prudently preferred to assault unarmed ships rather than the royal navy. The navy and British privateers had seized not more than half as many French and Spanish merchantmen. However, the prizes taken by the enemy were comparatively numerous, in part because the French did not try to replace their losses since they declined to build new vessels that would very likely be brought captive into British ports. On the other hand, the British continued to send new merchantmen to sea. British traffic on the oceans was both vast and lucrative. Peculiarly valuable was the trade between Britain and her dependencies in North America, in which the mother country exchanged finished goods for raw materials. Those colonies supplied a splendid and growing market. In times past Britain had prized her possessions in the Caribbean above those she held on the North American mainland. But it had subsequently become evident that her territories on that continent were the most precious part of the empire, and that their value was swiftly increasing, not merely because they supplied markets for manufactures, but also because the subjects of George III there were multiplying and expanding their settlements.

All of which is not intended to suggest that the people of the British Isles were principally sailors, soldiers, merchants, clerks, and makers of finished goods. On the contrary, the majority of them were folk who lived in villages and hamlets and upon the land. London could boast of perhaps 700,000 inhabitants, and other cities had 25,000 or 35,000. However, the raising of crops and domestic animals employed more human energy than all other occupations. It was not then necessary for the British to send ships beyond the oceans for foodstuffs, or even to import them from Holland or Denmark. In that day the islands produced more grain than could be consumed at home, and some wheat was actually sold abroad. The British at home were rural rather than urban, parochial and provincial rather than imperial in their outlook. English farmers and villagers, Scottish Highland herders, Welsh miners, and even Irish tenants contributed physical power and courage to the British state. If they exhibited stolidity, they also contributed solidity to the body politic.

Although the majority of the British at home were plain and sturdy rather than sophisticated and cosmpolitan, it cannot be said that Britain did not excel in the domains of letters and the arts. True, British civilization did not flower in the third quarter of the eighteenth century as it had

20

in the age of the Renaissance, as it would during the reign of Queen Victoria. True, too, the advantages of formal education were still withheld alike from the common folk of England, Wales, Scotland, and Ireland. Many of them were utterly illiterate; and many could do no more than sign their names. There were good grammar schools for a few young males; "public" schools such as Eton and Westminster for a fraction of that few; and universities that offered instruction to very small bodies of youths. No provision was made for the education of females beyond the elementary; the belief prevailed that women, even ladies, did not need much learning. Nor was the advanced instruction given the males altogether splendid. It was ancient rather than modern, classical rather than liberal, narrow rather than broad. The colleges and universities of Scotland and Ireland were poverty-stricken; Oxford and Cambridge were by no means rich. Oxford and Cambridge had other great weaknesses. They admitted only young men who were members of the established Anglican Church. Many of their learned fellows and professors desired no disturbing light from science, no enlightenment from foreign history, no joy from French or German literature, no harsh exposure to economics. The two universities supplied quarters to professors who did not lecture, tutors who did not teach, and students who did not study. Even so, talent and genius bloomed, within and without the universities, and the annals of Britain in the first decades of the reign of George III are studded with the names of brilliant poets, historians, orators, dramatists, novelists, and artists. Interspersed among them were a few gifted politicians.

Merely to list the men who gave bright luster to that time in Britain would require pages. At the close of the Seven Years' War Laurence Sterne was basking in the richly deserved fame he had won with *Tristram Shandy;* soon he would write *A Sentimental Journey*. Thomas Gray, having indited the mournful and haunting cadences of his immortal "Elegy Written in a Country Churchyard," had not yet received his inappropriate reward of a professorship in modern history at Cambridge University. When the treaty ending the Seven Years' War was signed, young James Boswell, sorely wounded after an amorous campaign, was recuperating in his quarters in Downing Street. Dr. Samuel Johnson, having received a pension from George III, was talking with remarkable force and wit in London taverns, in coffeehouses, and at private parties. Boswell had not yet made the acquaintance of his great and good friend, but before long he would begin to collect data for his superb biography of Johnson. Within a few months after the war Edward Gibbon began to think about writing a history of the city of Rome. A quarter of a century later he would complete his *Decline and Fall of the Roman Empire*. That superb scholar, David Hume, who demonstrated as a philosopher that knowledge and logic rest firmly upon quicksands, who as a historian intelligently saw that effects proceed from causes, was still very much alive in 1763. Thirteen years later, in the year of the American Declaration of Independence, Adam Smith, another Scot, would proclaim in *Concerning the Wealth of Nations* that prosperity is nurtured by economic freedom.

One may continue lengthily to name the literary lights and scholars, to recall men as gifted as those who have been mentioned. There was Dr. Oliver Goldsmith, who found it possible to write touchingly in London about the charm and innocence of country life, in *The Vicar of Wakefield*, and also to plumb the special power of women over men in *She Stoops to Conquer*. There was the poet, William Cowper, whose liberal patriotism appeals even to those who are not English.

> England with all thy faults, I love thee still,
> My country! and while yet a nook is left
> Where English minds and manners may be found,
> Shall be constrain'd to love thee . . .

English painters, among them Sir Joshua Reynolds and Thomas Gainsborough, had at last achieved excellence. Richard Brinsley Sheridan, author of those sparkling comedies, *The School for Scandal* and *The Rivals,* was their contemporary. The oratory of William Pitt and Edmund Burke stirred, astonished, and delighted listeners who were not personally condemned by those two virtuosos in rhetoric. Their performances in the House of Commons matched those of that splendid actor, David Garrick, in the theater.

The British people in the eighteenth and nineteenth centuries were not renowned for their modesty. They had excuse to be proud at the close of the Seven Years' War, and they were then sufficiently vain. To them, Europe was the center of the world, and the British Isles were the heart of Europe. They would not have found fault with lines written by Wilfrid Scawen Blunt as he approached Gibraltar in 1875 en route to his English home:

> Our exile is accomplished. Once again
> We look on Europe, mistress as of yore
> Of the fair earth and of the hearts of men.

But even the lands beyond the Channel and their inhabitants were inferior to Britain and the British. An educated and prosperous Englishman of the eighteenth century believed that a town house in London was equal to a palace in Utopia. Excelling in everything, England was above all the sanctuary of freedom. Her citizens did not grovel under the rule of an arbitrary Bourbon, a brutal Romanov, or a Turkish sultan. Not a few Englishmen believed they had attained political perfection under an ideal constitution. To them James Thomson, the poet, told only the truth when he proclaimed that the Goddess of Liberty, having wandered during many ages from place to place, had found a permanent home in the British Isles before 1736. Nor did they condemn Thomson's "The Seasons" when he declared that Britain had progressed

> To this deep-laid indissoluble state,
> Where wealth and commerce lift the golden head;
> And, o'er our labours, liberty and law,
> Impartial watch—the wonder of a world!

To such men, Thomson was not ridiculous when he boasted in his "Rule Britannia" of 1740:

> To thee belongs the rural reign;
> Thy cities shall with commerce shine.
> All thine shall be the subject main,
> And every shore encircles thine.
> Rule, Britannia, rule the waves,
> Britons never will be slaves.

Not all the denizens of the British Isles conceived in pride that the power and the glory of the island state would be permanent. William Cowper knew that no breed of men is everlasting, that the finest creations of mankind must at last fade.

> We turn to dust, and all our mightiest works
> Die too; the deep foundations that we lay,
> Time ploughs them up, and not a trace remains,
> We build with what we deem eternal rock;
> A distant age asks where the fabric stood,
> And in the dust, sifted and search'd in vain,
> The undiscoverable secret sleeps.

Everything was not splendid and idyllic in the islands even in Cowper's own time. Wealth, opportunity, education, elegance, and power were reserved for a small minority. Humble English laborers could not rejoice in the glories of Gray's "Elegy." The Welsh miner never heard the name of Laurence Sterne. The servant in a ducal household did not read Gibbon, and he knew nothing about the destructive onrush of the

Germans across the northern frontiers of the Roman Empire in the fifth century of the Christian era. The tenants of the Duke of Bedford did not buy Sir Joshua Reynolds's paintings. The only real privilege possessed by many subjects of George III was that they could feel superior to foreigners—and American colonists. At the bottom of British society was a mass of folk who led a simple life in comparative and even absolute poverty, laborers, clerks, artisans, miners, sheepherders, tenants, owners of small farms, and fishermen who inhabited cottages and huts rather than castles or mansions. The beauty of Chippendale furniture was not for them. They did not eat much of that famed English roast beef. Their food consisted of bread and butter, cheese, beer, and a vegetable or two, with meat once or twice a week. If they resided near the seacoast, they had fish. Their clothing was plain; their manners were rough; their speech was unpolished. Moreover, there were wretches whose fortune was even harsher—shoeless and impoverished Scottish Highlanders, rootless beggars, orphan waifs who slept fitfully in London doorways and under London bridges, numerous unemployed in London and other ports, and an ample supply of wastrels and criminals. There were no slaves or serfs in the British Isles, but there was a great body of the poor and a contingent of outcasts. For the outcasts there was no hope, and not much for the respectable poor. Said Dr. Johnson, who knew from lengthy and disconcerting experience whereof he spoke:

SLOW RISES WORTH, BY POVERTY DEPRESS'D!

It was assumed by their betters that the humble, in the main, deserved their fate, indeed, that they were made of meaner stuff than ladies and gentlemen. Worse yet, ordinary folk very generally themselves admitted that they were formed from inferior materials.

Above the common folk was a substantial middle class of merchants, manufacturers, bankers, prosperous farmers, shopkeepers, and professional people. Above them was the aristocracy, titled and untitled, a few thousand persons of gentle birth, the peculiarly privileged of Britain, the nobles and the country gentlemen, with their consorts. Among them were lords and ladies, such as the Duke and Duchess of Portland and the Duke and Duchess of Devonshire, who owned tens of thousands of acres and who were made as comfortable as might be by hundreds of servants. Also in that aristocracy were squires who possessed only hundreds of acres, but who were nevertheless socially acceptable, even select. That aristocracy was not remarkable for its ancient pedigrees; its titles were derived from Stuart and Tudor monarchs rather than from Norman

Kings. It was not an utterly exclusive aristocracy, for it often acquired recruits from families of rich merchants. Intermarrying with the offspring of the aristocracy, the children of wealthy middle class families frequently brought physical and mental vigor as well as money into the nobility and the gentry. The sordid cash of men who lacked a coat of arms quickly became old and good money in consequence of such unions; and the children produced by such alliances were not despised by aristocrats who owned taller family trees. Daniel Defoe did not greatly exaggerate when he declared in "The True-Born Englishman" that:

> Wealth, however got, in England makes
> Lords of mechanics, gentlemen of rakes;
> 'Tis impudence and money makes a peer.

The gap between those of gentle birth and the lower ranks of society was not so wide in England as it was in France, Germany, and Italy. Even so, the British aristocracy was truly privileged. Nor was that aristocracy set apart from the ruck of the British branch of mankind merely because its members possessed lands, commodious homes, cash, more or less suitable lineage, and social prestige. Its young men had easy access to the immense benefits of advanced education and foreign travel. They were welcomed and given special favors at Eton, at Oxford, and at Cambridge. They obtained college diplomas with less intellectual strain than fellow students of baser stuffs and lighter purses. Commissions in the army and navy were usually given only to the young men of the upper class; thus they were tendered special opportunity for careers in the armed forces. If one of those select youths chose to enter the Anglican clergy, he became a dean or bishop without undue delay. If he decided to become a lawyer, he could afford to spend the necessary years of preparation in the Inns of Court in London—Dr. Johnson, son of a provincial bookseller, with a subtle intellect and lust for learning, was unable to stay long enough at Oxford to get his degree or to study law. With a contingent of bishops, hereditary peers filled the House of Lords. The House of Commons was largely composed of country gentlemen, courtesy lords, Irish lords who could not sit in the upper chamber, baronets, and knights, together with a few men of mercantile background. The offices of state in Whitehall, except for clerkships, were filled by the upper class. No son of a laborer or of a tailor was to be found in the King's privy council or in the ministry. The aristocracy also benefited from its association with the royal family, including the King. From the monarch its members received titles, orders, honors, pensions, and salaried appointments of various sorts.

So firmly entrenched was that aristocracy that its members were virtually assured of their position in society. An unfortunate or shiftless tradesman of that time was likely to end his life in debtor's prison, the almshouse, or the gutter. But there was special relief for aristocrats, both men and women, who had lost their money. For such people there were government jobs, with or without duties. Alternatively, the needy person of gentle birth might quietly be given a pension paid from the King's privy purse or from the Irish treasury. In effect, a member of the aristocracy possessed social security from birth to death. Sir Marmaduke Belford, Baronet, was quite sure of help in case of need, but not Martin Boggs, butcher.

Observing English society as it was in the third quarter of the eighteenth century, one is tempted to find deep-seated and widespread discontent in its lower ranks. It did not exist. The English were—and are—more like the Germans than they wish to admit; and they had great respect for tradition and the established order. If a laborer, clerk, or servant believed that he suffered from discrimination, he did not clamor for its destruction. Had not the Mordaunts and the Wentworths always been the superiors of the Higginses and the Joneses? Of what avail to challenge them, or the Anglican Church, or the monarchy with which they were allied? There were materials for social revolution in Britain, but there were few who would apply the torch. A demand for reform gained strength only with the coming of the American and French Revolutions.

Social and economic inequities were accompanied by political injustice, incompetence, and iniquities. The prime requisite for membership in the House of Lords, at that time a far more important body than it was in the nineteenth and twentieth centuries, was suitable birth. Most of the men who sat in that chamber inherited their seats. Others entered it through the favor of the Crown and fellow aristocrats. Nor was the house of Commons the citadel of democracy that it afterward became. The men who sat in that ancient assembly were elected, but the right to vote was confined to some 215,000 males, chiefly property holders, a small minority of the adult population. Moreover, the constituencies, whether county or borough, that sent men to Westminster were bizarrely unequal. Thinly peopled counties elected two members, and heavily peopled counties chose two members. Boroughs with few or no inhabitants sent one or two men to London, and certain cities were not specially represented. Many boroughs were controlled, even owned by aristocrats, and others were manipulated by the King and whatever ministry happened to be in power. Elections in the counties were dominated by the nobility and the gentry. The shires sent gentlemen to Parliament. So did Oxford and Cambridge. A few spokesmen for mercantile interests entered the House of Commons from London, Bristol, and other cities. In 1763 Britain was ruled by an agrarian aristocracy—together with the King.

Unlike his remote descendants on the throne in the twentieth century, George III was not a mere symbol, a gracious figurehead. Nor was he a divinely chosen and absolute monarch. He inherited substantial power from his grandfather in 1760, and he sought to increase it. When he became King, it was not an established principle that an English ministry, and the cabinet, composed of its key members, were responsible to the House of Commons. However, without a majority in the house, necessary to get money from Parliament, a ministry was expected to resign. On the other hand, its members were responsible in large degree to the monarch. Accordingly, ultimate power was not positively vested in the monarch, in the House of Commons, or in Parliament. In such a system, the King could dominate; or, if the ruler lacked vigor, one or more members of the ministry could seize the reins. George III, from the moment he ascended the throne, successfully asserted the royal prerogative. His great-grandfather, George I, and his grandfather, George II, had permitted aristocratic politicians largely to manage the domestic affairs of Britain. George I, knowing little English, was as much concerned with the affairs of the small German state of Hanover from which he sprang as he was with those of Britain. George II, also fond of Hanover, had not devoted much energy to British domestic questions. Both of those monarchs had been threatened by Stuart pretenders to the throne, and had needed the firm allegiance of the aristocracy. George III was not menaced by the Stuarts. He was determined to rule as well as reign, and he largely succeeded. The aristocracy was politically divided and venal; he won friends and allies within it; and he at length secured a ministry and a Parliament that satisfied him almost completely. In the 1760's men went in and out of high office almost as if they were playing a game of musical chairs, with the King supplying more and more of the music.

Had George III been opposed by a united British aristocracy, he would not have been able to restore the royal authority. But part of that aristocracy was imbued with a traditional loyalty to the monarch. Country gentlemen, Anglican clergymen, and various nobles, notably Scottish ones, gave to George III the fealty they had earlier offered to the house of Stuart. Such men at an earlier or later time would have been called Tories. There was then no organized Tory Party. There were many men who called themselves Whigs, but no one Whig Party. The Whigs claimed that they were devoted to English freedom as it was established by the Glorious Revolution of 1688, but they were not agreed upon a precise

definition of that freedom. Nor were they uniformly and exclusively motivated by principle. It is to be feared that many of them sought power,
position, and pelf rather than sacrifice in behalf of their country. Dominating the ministry and Parliament for many decades before the accession
of George III, they had split into factions. The largest of these was led
by the old Duke of Newcastle and the young Marquis of Rockingham;
another looked to William Pitt for guidance; a third followed the leadership of the Duke of Bedford; and a fourth gave its allegiance to George
Grenville. The King was able to take advantage of the divisions among
the Whigs. Besides, he was able to seduce Whigs of varying complexions
by gifts of offices, pensions, promotions, and honors. Gradually he developed a personal following known as the "King's Friends." He was a
potent force in British politics during the first decade of his reign; with his
adherents and allies, he was the master of Britain during the fateful
twelve years that followed, at the end of which Britain had to acknowledge the loss of her most valuable colonies. It is perhaps needless to say
that Britain then contained only a few republicans. Some "Common-
wealthmen" looked back to John Hampden and Oliver Cromwell for
inspiration. Their voices were heard, but almost ignored; Britain did not
desire another intestine struggle like that which had convulsed her people
at the middle of the seventeenth century.

George III did not corrupt an aristocracy renowned for unsullied
virtue. British patricians, titled and untitled, had long since become accustomed to sell their votes and their influence in Parliament for cash and
social credit. They frequently talked and wrote about their devotion to
principle and honor, but they eagerly sought to accumulate principal and
honors. Their morals, public and private, were not admirable when
George III inherited the throne. Their behavior did not improve. Becoming the font of public favors, the King used them to reward those who
bent to his will and to punish those who resisted it. To Colonel Sir
William Draper, who had behaved as the King wished and who had
gambled away his money, the King gave a pension of £1,000 per annum
from the Irish treasury. To the historian Edward Gibbon, who was a
member of the House of Commons and who indicated that he was turning
against the King's measures, the monarch presented a sinecure post in the
Board of Trade, and so secured Gibbon's loyalty. Thus the monarch
helped Gibbon to write his magnificent history of the fall of the Roman
Empire—and the scholar endorsed the mistakes which led to the collapse
of the first British empire. If a member of the House of Commons voted
so as to please the King, his brother might receive a colonelcy from
George III. If a brilliant lawyer desired an appointment on the bench and

failed to support royal policy, he was held unfit to be a judge. Contractors, generals, and admirals who sat in the House of Commons gained when they voted as the ruler desired. Many men in British public life not only had their price, but named it without much ado; if he could make a useful bargain, the King paid it. The use of patronage as a lever, it may be added, had its humorous side. In March 1763, it became known that government was about to make Hugh Elliot, ten years old, a captain in the army. The boy was a son of Sir Gilbert Elliot, an influential Scottish politician. The appointment was so outrageous that it raised a public outcry. The "infant captain" did not get his commission. Nor did he obtain it ten years later, when he again sought the appointment. George III would not give his consent to such rank favoritism. However, since Elliot had reached the age of twenty-one and had presumably acquired skill in statecraft, he was then named British minister to the German state of Bavaria.

Let it be repeated that the King did not create the corruption that existed in British public life—he merely made use of it and encouraged it. Even the Anglican Church was afflicted by abuses. It was a reformed church in great need of reformation. Its bishops were dependent upon the King and politicians for preferment. The income of one bishop might be ten times that of another. Lesser appointments in the church were commonly made by noblemen and country gentlemen who looked after their younger sons and the younger sons of their friends. A member of the clergy might hold three positions, and perform the duties of all three by deputy. An eighteenth-century Anglican bishop might well have expressed the same hope for his son that Bishop Richard Corbet voiced early in the seventeenth century:

> I wish thee all thy mother's graces,
> Thy father's fortunes and his places.

On the other hand, a lowly and poorly paid curate or vicar might be treated as a superior servant by an aristocrat who dominated his congregation, as the obsequious Reverend William Collins was by the haughty Lady Catherine de Bourgh in Jane Austen's *Pride and Prejudice*. There were clergymen who differed from profane, rakish, and dissolute laymen in no way except clothing. The Anglican Church contained learned and pious men, but it suffered from many of the same ills that existed in other British institutions.

Certainly the filling of offices with men of suitable family did not uniformly bring the best of men into public service. The lazy, the inexperienced, the incompetent, and the dishonest were to be found in the

House of Lords; in the House of Commons; in the ministry; in the cabinet; in the lower ranks of civil officials; in the army; in the navy; and among royal officials overseas. There were governors of British dependencies who secured their posts in somewhat the same fashion that Colonel Rawdon Crawley acquired the governorship of Coventry Island in Thackeray's *Vanity Fair*. The difficulties caused by the presence of drones, novices, and grafters in office were compounded by the evils of traditional and careless organization. Boards and bureaus were inherited from the past, not formed to do current business. Because the British empire had existed for only a century and a half, there was no one department specially and exclusively responsible for colonial affairs. It is notorious that the paymaster of the forces and the treasurer of the navy, supplied with funds for the armed services, were permitted to invest moneys not immediately needed, and if they wished to do so, to pocket the income. Those two men might hold public cash even after they had departed from their offices. The accounts of a military commander were audited five years, ten years, even fifteen years after he had spent the money. There was no boorish Prussian efficiency in London. Not the least of the weaknesses in the British political system was that it put government of an empire in the hands of men of the country rather than those of the city. Rural magnates, like Platonists and eunuchs talking about love, discussed and decided questions about manufactures, commerce, tariffs, and distant colonies.

Enviable though the situation of Britain was in the early part of 1763, it was neither ideal nor invulnerable. Her triumphs in the Seven Years' War did not proceed from the nature of things. During the crucial period of that conflict her military efforts had been directed by William Pitt, whose genius for waging war can be compared only with that displayed by Winston Churchill in the world struggle that began in 1939. If Britain took up the sword in 1770 or 1775, it could not be assumed that a Pitt or a Churchill would be available. In the Seven Years' War Britain had had a potent ally, Frederick the Great of Prussia. With the help of the British and a few German princes, Frederick had held his own against French, Austrian, Russian, and Swedish armies. But Britain had ceased to supply the warrior King with funds before the end of that conflict, and no help from him could be expected in the future. In fact, Britain could rely for assistance of any sort only upon Hanover and Portugal. Moreover, France and Spain had not been able to exert their full powers in the war just ended. The French state, even more riddled by favoritism, corruption, and incompetence than Britain, had not exerted its formidable strength. But new and abler men had come forward in both France and Spain.

They lusted for revenge, and they were already rebuilding the Bourbon armies and navies. Given opportunity, they would do what they might to reduce Britain and her empire. It would be peculiarly awkward for Britain if her American colonies, having given powerful assistance in the recent war, should rebel and secure the assistance of the Bourbons. That possibility seemed remote to most British politicians. In a time of triumph measures were taken in London which provoked an uprising in America, and Britain at length was indeed assailed by her old enemies when she was enmired in an American rebellion.

Immediately after news came of the signing of the Treaty of Paris, the London *Chronicle* smugly reported that "The French Court, sensible of the defects of their colony and plantation laws, proposed to form a new code, modelled on the laws of the British plantations." Did the British have a special genius for the governance of empire? If so, they would soon fail to make use of it. Within a few weeks decisions were taken in London that incited American revolt and led at last to armed clash between the mother country and her American colonists.

CHAPTER III

A Casual Empire

AFTERWARD, in bitter struggle with the mother country, the Americans declared that they wished to return to "the good old days" of 1763. So saying, they did not merely indulge in nostalgia, did not vaguely muse about a never-never time. For they were then pleased with their economic condition, at least temporarily relieved of French and Spanish menaces, and satisfied with the political machinery of the British empire. They possessed far greater freedom than colonials under French, Spanish, Portuguese, or Dutch rule, and their loyalty to Britain was beyond serious question. They were proud to be British subjects. Britain had generously and carelessly permitted them to participate in the conduct of their domestic affairs. They possessed the personal rights of Englishmen. Every one of the Thirteen Colonies, along with other British territories in the West Indies and Nova Scotia, had its own parliament. In each of those commonwealths there was an elective body that represented the settlers. Known by various names, such as the House of Burgesses, the Commons House, the House of Delegates, and the House of Commons, it resembled the British House of Commons. Those thirteen bodies had nought to say about the foreign affairs of the empire; they could neither declare war nor make peace, except insofar as the Indians were concerned; and they lacked authority over maritime commerce. However, they had become dominant on internal questions, to the satisfaction of the colonists. Not represented in the British Parliament, the Americans harbored no great grievances against that august assembly. It had never taxed them for revenue. It had regulated their oceanic trade and, to a degree, their manufacturing, but not in such a fashion as to create profound discontent among them. The Americans were fundamentally content with the constitution of the empire. They were gaining power within it. Some of them believed that their local legislatures ought, at least eventually, to be recognized as the equals of the British Parliament. Were there Americans who desired, consciously or unconsciously, independence from Britain? If such there were, they were few. The Americans not only declared their loyalty to Britain, they knew what they were saying; and they meant what they said.

One may not doubt that a principal reason for the happiness of the Americans within the British empire was the weakness of British officials within the Thirteen Colonies. Two of them, Connecticut and Rhode Island, under century-old charters, were virtually autonomous. In those two colonies, the lower house of the legislature, its upper house (called the council), together with the governor, judges, and other officers, were locally chosen. In Pennsylvania and Delaware the colonists were restrained to a degree by proprietors, the descendants of William Penn, their representatives, and their allies. The governor, chosen by the Penns, could veto laws passed by unicameral assemblies. The situation was similar in Maryland, where the Baltimore family still retained proprietary rights. There the governor and a council appointed by the head of the Baltimore family could, and did, check the popular branch of the assembly. In the other eight colonies British authority, at least in form, was more vigorously asserted, for each of them had a royally chosen governor, judges, and other officers. In one of those royal dependencies, Massachusetts, members of the council were chosen by the legislature and the governor; in the other seven, councilors were nominated by the governors and named in London. The consent of the royal governor and council was required for legislation in all of those eight colonies. Moreover, the British privy council could, and sometimes did, disallow, or veto, a law that had received the approval of a governor and a council. Besides, the privy council could reverse decisions made by the highest colonial courts. A royal governor looked like a homely viceroy supported by a retinue of less dignified appointees. Whether royal or proprietary, a governor always had a following of sorts among the colonists—a court party—for he could confer offices, social prestige, and economic favors upon his friends. And yet—royal and proprietary authority had waned, and would continue to diminish, unless Britain changed her colonial policy.

For the House of Burgesses and its counterparts had largely achieved their ambition to become local equivalents of the House of Commons. In British theory, even if such bodies were established in accordance with provisions of charters, they were municipal, or derivative, meeting only by British permission. Colonial charters, admitted to have legal status, were not looked upon as sacrosanct in London. There it was commonly assumed that the legislature met, at least ultimately, by British permission. However, the colonists believed that their representatives acted for them as a matter of right, in every one of the American commonwealths, whether or not they possessed charters, whether they were royal, proprietary, or corporate in form. They had had their way in practice; and it may be cogently contended that long-established practice settled the theoretical question. Moreover, emulating the British House of Commons, the elected chambers in America had successfully claimed the power to initiate money bills; had used their authority over finance to coerce royal and proprietary governors and councils; and had even wrested executive power from them. Some royal governors, judges, secretaries, and treasurers were dependent upon those elected chambers for payment of their salaries, and colonial Solons on occasion neglected to pay the salaries of officials who opposed their wishes. Gaining a concession from a weak or venal governor, they often managed to keep it permanently. Governors, usually mediocre men, came and went, but the lower house of assembly fought on, decade after decade. British governors were not Spanish viceroys in 1763. They were splendid in theory, and sometimes even in appearance, but they were on the defensive, and they were losing ground.

Engaging in chronic clash with champions of prerogative, the Americans as a whole desired neither independence nor the absolute equality of their assemblies with Parliament. They had not set precise political goals for themselves. There were indeed some among them who conceived that the colonies properly owed obedience only to the British Crown, and that their assemblies should sooner or later be recognized as the full equal of the legislature that met at Westminster. But such persons were as yet in a small minority. Those Americans who saw that they were gaining power within the empire were very generally satisfied with gradual change. One may not doubt that most of the colonists were pleased with political conditions as they were.

All of which is not to say that the Americans harbored no resentment against their parent state. The endless bickerings between British governors and American lawmakers left a residue of ill feeling. Besides, British schemes for federating the colonies aroused distrust among the colonials. Those schemes were not executed. To many thoughtful Americans, they were appealing. But most of the colonists suspected that proposals for centralization were intended, among other things, to restore, or at least to buttress, British authority. More important was the hostility created by the efforts of Parliament to regulate colonial commerce and manufacturing. American scholars have even contended, mistakenly, that British restrictions upon the American economy were the underlying and primary cause of the American Revolution.

For about one hundred and fifty years after the first colonists clambered ashore at Jamestown, Kings and other politicians in London normally did not bother themselves much with questions of colonial government. Their first goal was, of course, to secure and keep power in London. They gave attention to dispatches from Moscow, Munich, and Madrid rather than to reports from Boston, New York, and Charleston. They were much more familiar with the intricacies of diplomatic intrigue in western and central Europe than they were with political questions that constantly arose in British America. No King, no prime minister, no member of the cabinet went across the Atlantic to inspect the colonies. However, there was no lack of interest in London in things economic—although genuine competence in such matters was scarce among members of Parliament and ministers of state. Men at Westminster and in Whitehall eagerly sought to enhance the wealth and security of the home islands. Embracing the principles of mercantilism, they waged bitter economic warfare against France, Spain, and Holland. They looked upon the British empire as an economic rather than a political community. They valued colonies as producers of raw materials needed by the mother country, as consumers of British manufactures, as contributors to British wealth and material power. The welfare of the mother country came first, but they did not intend to reduce the colonists to poverty. It is a curious fact that they prized their island possessions in the West Indies—Jamaica, Barbados, and others—above those on the North American mainland until the middle of the eighteenth century. Until that time they preferred those territories that supplied needed raw materials to those that consumed British manufactures. And the islands gave forth cotton, indigo, tobacco, ginger, and, above all, sugar, things both needed and much desired in England.

In accordance with those mercantilistic policies England began to execute in the middle of the seventeenth century her famous Navigation Acts. At first primarily directed against the Dutch, but later also aimed at the French, they required after 1673 that all goods brought into American ports be carried in British (including colonial) ships. Those laws likewise demanded that exports from the colonies be carried in British (or colonial) vessels, and that certain "enumerated articles" intended for northern European markets be sent to and landed in England. The list, lengthening with the passage of time, included cotton, tobacco, sugar, rice, indigo, furs, and deerskins. In theory, American maritime trade was further confined by the Molasses Act, first passed in 1733, which placed a duty of sixpence per gallon upon all treacle brought into British ports on the North American mainland from foreign islands in the West Indies. That duty was intended to be prohibitive. Other Parliamentary laws limited American manufactures after 1699. The first of these restricted the size of establishments making woolen goods, and declared that they must not be sent beyond local markets. A law of 1732 placed limits upon the making of hats in the colonies. More important, the Iron Act of 1750 asserted that the colonists were not to build any more mills making finished iron products or steel. In the following year Parliament even undertook to limit paper currency put forth by the New England colonies—it forbade the issuance by them of paper money that had to be accepted as legal tender.

This list of Parliamentary measures intended in part to cramp the economic activities of the colonies could be much enlarged, and it is not at all surprising that at one time American scholars believed that the colonists suffered from a severe discrimination. However, the colonists had fewer and less substantial grievances than appears at first sight. It should be observed that the Navigation Acts fostered the colonial as well as the British merchant marine at the expense of foreign competition— more than one third of the vessels carrying the British flag were built in America, and one third of them were owned and used by Americans. It is also true that, when it suited them, American merchants ignored those acts, and almost with impunity, since enforcement of them was remarkably lax. Smuggling was no great crime in the eighteenth century, and the Americans, like the British, avoided customs houses and officers when it was sufficiently profitable for them to do so. British customs officers in the North American ports were few and not usually officious. Often they closed their eyes, after receiving a suitable present of a case of Madeira or port wine, to violations of the laws. They made no strenuous effort to collect the sixpenny per gallon duty levied by the Molasses Act of 1733. They accepted instead a penny or even a halfpenny per gallon, casually nullifying the purpose and the letter of the law. Nor were the restrictions placed upon American commerce and manufacturing so cramping as they seem, because they often required the Americans to do what they would have done in any case. They would have bought most of the British goods from British merchants without being forced to do so; and they would have sold large quantities of raw materials to them without being required to do so. American makers of woolens, hats, and iron were not badly injured by Parliamentary hindrances; they did not prosper mightily in the eighteenth century; but, for economic reasons, they would not have become rich in the absence of British restraints. The Acts of Navigation, and those that regulated American manufacturing, were in practice much less injurious than they were in the statute books.

There were Americans who were severely damaged by the British controls, for example, the tobacco planters of Virginia and Maryland. Their largest markets were in the northern parts of the European Continent. They were not permitted to send the weed directly to Holland, Germany, Scandinavia, or Russia. They were forced to send tobacco destined for those markets to England and to sell it to English merchants. A heavy tariff was levied upon it in English ports, and English middlemen profitably resold it to nicotine-hungry Dutchmen, Germans, Scandinavians, and Russians. Had the planters of the Chesapeake region been permitted to sell tobacco in the ports of northern Europe, they would have gained. We do not have in consequence the compelling reason why planters of Virginia and Maryland passionately defended American "rights" by word before 1775 and thereafter on the battlefield. It is beyond doubt that many aristocrats of the Chesapeake region were chronically indebted to the British merchants to whom they sold tobacco and from whom they purchased finished goods. Thomas Jefferson estimated that Virginia planters owed at least £2 million to British merchants in 1773. It has been contended—and denied—that the debts of the planters induced them to stand forth against British "tyranny." Surely their affection for the mother country was not enhanced in proportion to the sums they owed to British merchants. But, given direct access to markets in northern Europe, would they necessarily have secured freedom from those obligations? It is to be suspected that the planters, having incomes that fluctuated in accordance with yields of tobacco and prices, did not cut their expenses when crops were small or when prices were low. So they became indebted to the British merchants, who served as their bankers. Once in debt, it was not easy for the planter to pay off his obligations, with interest. Some of the Virginia and Maryland aristocrats undoubtedly slipped into economic difficulties by excessive purchasing of luxuries, lands, and slaves upon credit. It cannot be gainsaid that the aristocrats of the Chesapeake were in economic straits as much because of their own extravagance, carelessness, and recklessness as they were because of injuries inflicted upon them by British laws. One ought not exaggerate the difficulties of the planters. They might have been embarrassed for lack of cash and yet quite solvent. They had much to lose in a political upheaval. But it is hardly to be doubted that many embarrassed planters blamed Britain and British merchants for their woes.

It should not be forgotten that British laws conferred positive benefits upon the colonists. Not merely that they gave help to the colonial merchant marine. The English tobacco market was reserved for the Marylanders and Virginians—Englishmen were not allowed to grow the weed, and foreign tobacco was barred from British ports. Soon after 1700 England began to pay bounties to North Carolinians, New Englanders, and others who produced naval stores—tar, pitch, and turpentine. Before the middle of the eighteenth century England also began to pay a bounty upon indigo, making it possible for planters of the Low Country of the Carolinas and Georgia to reap that weed and lucrative profits.

In the main, Parliament, seeking to channel the efforts of the colonists into the production of raw materials and of processed goods not competitive with British manufactures, did discriminate against the Americans. It placed the economic interests of the colonists above those of foreigners; but it favored the economic interests of the mother country against those of the colonists. There were English politicians who thought it quite unnecessary to justify the special privileges given to inhabitants of the mother country at the expense of the colonists. After all, were not colonists inferior simply because they were colonists? It was commonly assumed in France and Spain, as well as in Britain, that Europeans born and reared outside the "metropolis" were inevitably inferior. In Britain those who believed it necessary to justify the favor given to the people of the parent state declared that they deserved it because they supported the British fleets and armies that protected the colonies against foreign attack. Did they take into account the military contributions of the colonists? In whose wars did both the British and the Americans fight?

Who can balance all these accounts and considerations? In any event, the Americans in 1763, even in 1773, did not see British restrictions upon their commerce and manufacturing as unbearable.

If the Americans were glad to be British subjects, if they were satisfied with their condition within the British empire, it is nevertheless true that the Treaty of Paris encouraged them to think about their rights rather than their duties as Englishmen. So long as they were menaced from Montreal and from New Orleans, they valued highly the protection given them by British tars and redcoats. The withdrawal of the French Bourbons from North America, the departure of the Spanish Bourbons from Florida, and the replacement of the French by the Spanish in western Louisiana, very largely relieving the Americans of fear of attack by their traditional white-skinned enemies, made it clear that they did not need British military help as they had in the past. In the immediate future, at least, they would be forced to defend themselves only against the Indians;

38

and the Indians, although they might raid and devastate settlements on the frontier, could do no more than vex and harass the colonists. The Americans felt themselves to be secure as never before, and they felt their own strength as never before. They were even less disposed to yield to British authority than they had earlier been.

On the other hand, British attitudes toward the American colonies also altered in consequence of the Seven Years' War. As it approached, authorities in London resurrected a scheme that had long possessed a charm for many minds, both British and colonial. Ought not the Americans to create a general council that could provide for the common defense against the French and hostile Indians, that could win friends among the redmen—and have the power to tax in order to raise funds for those purposes? With encouragement from London, colonials interested in the proposal met in the Albany Congress in 1754 and drafted a plan of union, largely the product of the fertile intellect of Benjamin Franklin. However, the Albany Plan was rejected by the colonies because of its novelty, colonial jealousies, and a fear that it would be used to buttress and even to increase British power in America. It was also set aside in England, in part because its execution might diminish that power. The British cabinet then took other steps toward achieving the purposes of the proposed union. It sent troops across the ocean to join small detachments of redcoats already stationed in America, established a regular army there, and placed it under a British commander in chief. It also provided for the appointment of two royal Indian superintendents, one of these to win friends and influence chiefs among the tribes resident to the northward of the Ohio River, the other to do likewise among the warriors who lived to the westward of the Southern Colonies, both men to serve under the direction of the commander in chief. These new officers—and troops —contributed heavily to the destruction of the French empire in North America. The commander in chief and the Indian superintendents exerted authority that had earlier been in the hands of colonial governors and legislatures. It is easier to create than to abolish offices; and an army established principally for one purpose is often found to be necessary for others. At the close of the long war, the British cabinet could not resist the temptation to maintain the regular army in North America under the commander in chief and to keep the two Indian superintendents in office. At that time General Jeffery Amherst presided over the army from his headquarters at New York City; Sir William Johnson watched over the northern Indian tribes from his home in the Mohawk River valley; and John Stuart kept an eye upon the southern Indians from his resi-

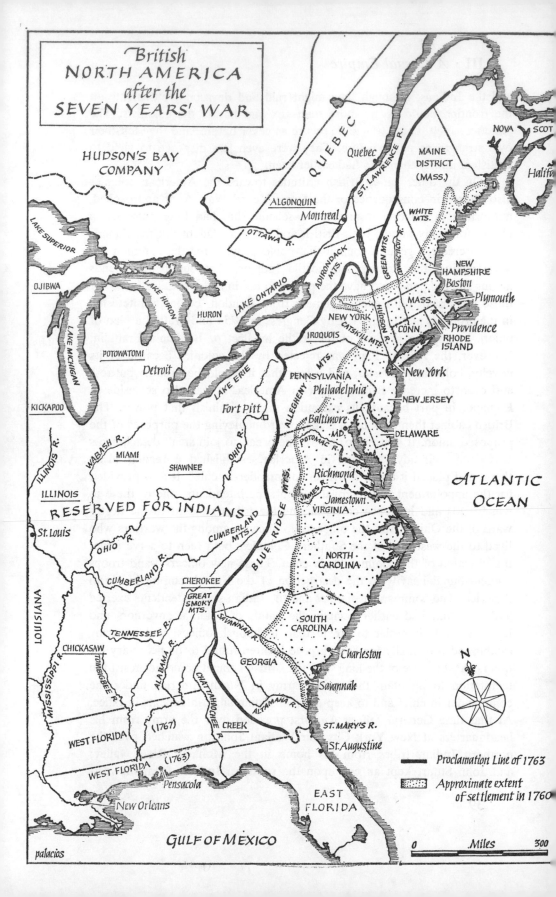

British
NORTH AMERICA
after the
SEVEN YEARS' WAR

HUDSON'S BAY COMPANY

QUEBEC

Quebec

MAINE DISTRICT (MASS.)

NOVA SCOT

Halifax

ALGONQUIN

Montreal

OTTAWA R.

ST. LAWRENCE R.

WHITE MTS.

LAKE SUPERIOR

ADIRONDACK MTS.

GREEN MTS.

CONNECTICUT R.

NEW HAMPSHIRE

Boston

Plymouth

DJIBWA

LAKE HURON

LAKE MICHIGAN

LAKE ONTARIO

NEW YORK

IROQUOIS

CATSKILL MTS.

HUDSON R.

MASS.

CONN

Providence

RHODE ISLAND

HURON

POTOWATOMI

Detroit

LAKE ERIE

PENNSYLVANIA

Philadelphia

ALLEGHENY MTS.

New York

NEW JERSEY

KICKAPOO

Fort Pitt

Baltimore

MD.

DELAWARE

WABASH R.

ILLINOIS R.

MIAMI

OHIO R.

POTOMAC R.

SHAWNEE

Richmond

JAMES R.

BLUE RIDGE MTS.

Jamestown

VIRGINIA

ILLINOIS

RESERVED FOR INDIANS

St. Louis

OHIO R.

CUMBERLAND MTS.

CUMBERLAND R.

NORTH CAROLINA

ATLANTIC OCEAN

LOUISIANA

CHEROKEE

GREAT SMOKY MTS.

TENNESSEE R.

SOUTH CAROLINA

CHICKASAW

ALABAMA R.

TOMBIGBEE R.

SAVANNAH R.

GEORGIA

Charleston

MISSISSIPPI R.

CHATTAHOOCHEE R.

CREEK

Savannah

ALTAMAHA R.

ST. MARY'S R.

N

WEST FLORIDA (1767)

St. Augustine

WEST FLORIDA (1763)

Pensacola

EAST FLORIDA

New Orleans

GULF OF MEXICO

Proclamation Line of 1763

Approximate extent of settlement in 1760

0   Miles   300

palacios

dence in Charleston, South Carolina. Let it be remembered that these men were instruments of the British Crown, that they were in no way responsible to colonial lawmakers.

After the capture of Quebec in 1759, imperial authority was also more vigorously asserted for purposes other than defense. It has been suggested, indeed, that in the later years of the Seven Years' War British colonial policy altered almost fundamentally, at least that British politicians displayed a disposition to fight for the rights of the Crown; and that their measures aroused serious discontent in the colonies. They strove to establish royal control over the period of service of the more important judges in the colonies; they engaged in a vexing contest with the House of Burgesses over the salaries of Anglican clergymen in Virginia; they became involved in a squabble with the Commons House of South Carolina; and the use of general warrants toward more effective enforcement of the Navigation Acts in Massachusetts aroused bitterness there. Denouncing those warrants, which gave royal officials excessive latitude for searches and seizures of smuggled goods, lawyer James Otis declared that they were unconstitutional, that is, that they violated the rights of Englishmen. He not only challenged the power of Parliament to permit the execution of such documents, but also urged that the use of them violated the natural rights of mankind. Afterward, indeed, John Adams asserted that the defiance of British authority by Otis marked the beginning of the clashes between Britain and America that ultimately led to the separation. Adams magnified the importance of the stand taken by his friend Otis. It can be said with confidence that the employment of the general warrants was not a sufficient grievance for rebellion, even in Boston, where zealous customs officers were by no means popular. Here was another irritation, one that contributed in small part to ill feeling between Britain and America.

It is doubtless true that the unwonted energy of British politicians after the conquest of Quebec caused some uneasiness among the Americans. A spurt of unusual activity by Anglicans on both sides of the ocean added to it. The Society for the Propagation of the Gospel in Foreign Parts, an organ of the Anglican Church, established a mission near Harvard College, not to win over men who knew no Christianity, but to win converts within one of the great citadels of the American Congregationalists. On the other hand, the English government refused to permit the Congregationalists to send missionaries among the Indians. Congregationalists and Presbyterians were given cause to fear that the Anglican Church would receive support in London for the establishment of an American bishopric—and then bishoprics. They did not quite believe that

41

every cathedral was a temple of the Devil, but they wanted neither bishop nor archbishop nor an excess of Anglicans in America. They were disturbed both by the exertions of the English Church and by the favor it received in London. Most British politicians were not disposed to do anything substantial in behalf of that church on the western side of the Atlantic. But who could say that they would continue to ignore pleas for support from the Archbishop of Canterbury, from the Bishop of London? Concern, jealousy, and fear persisted among the colonists. Benjamin Franklin might not think that America would be sorely injured by the appearance of an Anglican bishop in New York or Philadelphia. Devoted Congregationalists, Presbyterians, and Baptists remembered with enduring bitterness the persecution of their sects by Archbishop Laud and other Anglican divines in seventeenth-century England.

It is fair to say that Britain did not adopt a new colonial system during the Seven Years' War, but that the continuance of the old one was marked by an increase in chronic bickering over local and regional issues in which the mother country and her representatives in America had engaged with the colonists for several generations. Such quarrels would persist so long as the Americans remained within the British empire. For example, in South Carolina as the War of Independence approached, the Commons House not only bitterly denounced the council as a collection of British-born officeholders, but even issued paper currency without the consent of the council or of the governor. Those contests would exacerbate ill feeling that arose because Britain adopted measures in and after the year 1763 that provoked the colonists generally.

But it is also true that Britain began to turn away from a policy of "salutary neglect" as the French empire in North America tottered toward its fall. Endeavors on the part of politicians in England and of royal officials in America to defend—and to expand British authority—were sporadic and minor. They were signs, not noticed by most Americans, of great change soon to come. For alarm was growing in London lest the colonists seek to leave the empire. They vaunted their loyalty to the mother country—but could one believe their fervent declarations of devotion to Britain? Men in the imperial capital began to magnify the shortcomings of the colonists as the war progressed. The colonies spent large sums toward the winning of that conflict, and they put many thousands of men in the field. However, some of the Thirteen did not do enough, soon enough, in the common cause. Such delinquencies had occurred in earlier wars without important consequence. Much was now made of them in England, even though several of the colonies strained their resources toward the defeat of the French and the Spanish, a fact recognized by the generous-minded William Pitt, who arranged to repay them large sums they had expended for military purposes. Faultfinders among British army officers condemned colonial troops because they did not usually perform so well as regulars. It was not taken into account that the Americans were untrained and inexperienced. Much was made also in London of the assistance given the French by colonial merchants, who were not always as devoted to the empire in deeds as they were in words. At a time when the British navy was doing what it could to prevent the flow of troops and supplies to the French possessions in the New World—and with much success—certain American merchants of Boston, New York, and other ports saw a splendid chance to profit. They carried foodstuffs to neutral ports in the Caribbean for transmission to the French colonies. At least one American vessel went directly to New Orleans to unload a cargo, much to the pleasure of the French governor, who had earlier reported that he had not seen a French ship during a period of eighteen months of warfare. To be sure, French and English smugglers did not refrain from crossing the Channel in wartime in the eighteenth century. Nevertheless, the Americans who lucratively traded with the enemy were less than absolutely loyal. Their sins were magnified in Whitehall.

Certainly there were publicists in London in the later years of the war who were alarmed lest the Americans seek to leave the empire, who urged an extraordinary measure toward preventing their departure from it. After the capture of Quebec and of the French island of Guadeloupe in the Caribbean in 1759, London pamphleteers, upon the assumption that Britain could not keep both Canada and Guadeloupe at the end of the war, forcefully demanded that Britain keep Guadeloupe and permit France to retain Canada. They would have it that the sugar plantations of the Caribbean island were worth more to the empire than the snowbanks of Canada. Except for a few furs, they said, Canada held nothing of economic value for Britain. But their principal argument for giving Canada back to the French was that the presence of the French in the valley of the St. Lawrence had served as a constant reminder to the Americans of the benefits they received from their connection with Britain. So long as they were seriously threatened from Canada, they would hardly try to separate from the mother country. Relieved of the French menace, they would challenge British authority more sharply than in the past, would move toward an absolute separation. The fears of those pamphleteers were, in the main, warranted, but their Machiavellian argument did not persuade politicians in power. The conquest of Canada had cost so much in treasure and in blood. Relinquish the fruits of a hard-won triumph? Permit the French to entrench themselves again on the St. Lawrence? The

British cabinet preferred to believe that the Americans, after all, were not disloyal. The men who entered into the Treaty of Paris for Britain would have it that the safety of the British possessions in North America was enhanced by the departure of the French, and they secured the cession of Canada by France. And yet—might it not be prudent for Britain, after peace should be made, to reconsider her colonial policy?

CHAPTER IV

A New British Policy

WHATEVER may be made of the connection between the departure of the French from North America and the appearance of the American republic, it is beyond doubt that British politicians began to move swiftly toward a clash with the colonists soon after the signing of the Treaty of Paris. Those politicians were of that mediocre variety that confidently undertake to solve delicate and dangerous questions avoided by indolent and cautious men, questions carefully and generously manipulated by statesmen. Under the leadership of the Earl of Bute and George Grenville, two commonplace prime ministers, and a commonplace King, George III, they undertook to stop the colonial clock. It had been running toward greater American freedom within the empire. They intended, indeed, not only to arrest it, but to turn it back. They tried both to reduce the Americans to a proper obedience and to force them to carry more of the burdens of empire. They resolved to maintain a standing army in North America; emphatically to exert British authority over the Indians; to prevent, at least temporarily, the westward advance of the American settlements; to compel the subjects of George III in North America and the West Indies to pay the cost of those measures; and to restrain American commerce as never before, toward assuring the prosperity and power of the mother country. They intended to establish beyond cavil that Britain was the mistress of the empire, that she must be obeyed. Those politicians swiftly drove the inhabitants of the Thirteen Colonies into revolt.

It should be emphasized that George III was not personally and directly responsible for those clumsy and profoundly disturbing measures. They were, in the main, the products of his advisers. That monarch displayed no burning desire to dominate America during his first nine years upon the throne. In fact, he knew little about his domains and subjects in the New World, and he did not much concern himself with them. He permitted his ministers to do what they would about America, until it became evident that he might lose the most valuable of his possessions overseas.

No sinister tyrant carrying on, openly or secretly, a long campaign against American liberty, George III nevertheless had something to do, inevitably, with the onset of the American Revolution. He did not intend to be, and he did not become, a despot. He wished to be a "patriot king," a benevolent ruler, according to his lights. Which does not mean that he was determined to attack political, social, and economic corruptions and injustices in Britain. He sought, rather, to destroy the political factions that existed at the beginning of his reign, and to place power in the hands of ministers who would undertake to please the monarch. He did not insist that those men be utterly his servants. He permitted them to use their discretion in many matters; but he would not keep a minister with whom he seriously disagreed. He demanded that the ministry—and, of course, the cabinet—be responsible to him rather than to the House of Commons. Toward achieving his goal, he became, like Sir Robert Walpole and the Duke of Newcastle before him, a most energetic political manager. As related above, he soon developed a political following of his own, the King's Friends. But he did not get a prime minister and a ministry that pleased him for very long until 1770 when Frederick, Lord North became both prime minister and an obedient tool of the monarch. During the first decade of his reign George III had no fewer than six ministries, with men entering and leaving office with excessive celerity. Those swift changes caused confusion in policy, notably in colonial questions. Moreover, the men whom the King brought forward were often young and incompetent. They, even more than other British politicians, were not fitted for the tasks of governing a new, greater, and more complex empire. It follows, then, that in the first decade of his reign George III indirectly contributed to the loss of the most valuable part of that empire. Later, when tension between Britain and America became acute, he added direct contributions.

It should be added that George III could not himself supply highly intelligent leadership. Afterward Walter Savage Landor asked:

> What mortal man ever heard
> Any good of George the Third?

And American and British historians were long fond of describing the King as a tyrannical ogre grasping for power he was unfit to wield. But he had virtues, and even some graces. He was industrious and conscientious, after his fashion. He was courageous. He was never unfaithful to a homely German wife who was thrust upon him—royal protocol did not permit him to marry the beautiful Lady Sarah Lennox, with whom he fell in love soon after he became King. Unlike his grandfather and great-grandfather, he kept no mistresses. Pudgy and protuberant-eyed, he nevertheless possessed dignity; and he was a skillful dancer. He was a sincere Christian, but he disliked religious persecution. And yet, like so many royal majesties, he was unfitted to exercise great power in an intricate world. Had he been reared as a farmer's son, he would have been a good farmer; had he been the offspring of a tradesman, he would competently have kept shop. His intellectual endowment was modest. He received the poor education from tutors that is commonly given to royal princes. It is recorded that he was slow to learn to read and write, that he slept excessively as an adolescent. He outgrew some of his early shortcomings. However, he did not read widely—he could not appreciate the genius of Shakespeare. He did not travel as a young man, did not make the Grand Tour that English lords so commonly undertook in his time. Like all of his principal advisers, he never visited North America; his ignorance of the New World was great. Moreover, the King's mind was disorderly; at times he was incoherent. He labored under the strain of his royal duties. At last, after he had presided over the rupture of the British empire, he suffered from fits of insanity.

It may seem remarkable that George III, with talents so few and so uncultivated, could play such a large part in the British state. It must be remembered that his predecessors on the throne were not mere figureheads. He inherited power as well as prestige. The great William Pitt was not renowned for unsuitable modesty. The warning by John Donne that "no man is an islande" hardly applied to Pitt, for he thought of himself as a continent. Pitt might not admire the unimpressive royal person, but even he almost slavishly bent the knee to royalty. The kingly man could not but offer a measure of reverence to the undistinguished man who was King. Moreover, English politicians who stood forth against the monarch were divided among themselves even before the end of the year 1761. The King was able to make his former tutor, the Earl of Bute, first lord of the treasury and prime minister; and he kept that hollow and humdrum man in that high office as a "palace premier" until the spring of 1763, long enough for Bute to lead Britain to the edge of a colonial crisis. The King for a time adored his former mentor; his trust and affection were sadly misplaced. Bute collected flowers and dispensed offices to his fellow Scotsmen. He made many friends for George III in Scotland; he gained none for the King in America.

Although the Seven Years' War brought glory and power to Britain, it was not won without sacrifices. Indeed, because it imposed a strain upon Britain's resources, Bute, with the blessing of the King, eagerly offered small concessions to France and Spain in order to put an end to the conflict. The national debt had soared above £130 million, which seemed an immense sum to many politicians at the time. Both the army and the navy had been largely increased. Taxes had risen high, including one on land that was disliked by squires and noblemen. Before the war that tax was set at two shillings in the pound, at 10 per cent of the assessed valuation; during the war it had been doubled. With the war came also economic dislocation, which was followed at the peace by depression. Yet the economic situation was by no means desperate. It could be predicted that Britain would prosper in the future as never in her past. But there was clamor for lower taxes. What should be done?

Faced by a demand for reduction of the land tax, the Bute ministry could have undertaken to cut expenses by disbanding the bulk of the army and a part of the navy. Such had been the British practice in the past. In times of peace Britain had maintained only a small army, relying principally upon the navy for defense. Men of the Tory cast of mind had, in fact, been hostile to a standing army ever since the reign of William III. Some of its officers unhappily anticipated that the army would be cut in half. Officers of the newer regiments feared that those regiments would be disbanded, and that they themselves would be relieved of duty and placed on half pay. Many of them were pleasantly surprised, however. For the Bute ministry decided, for reasons not entirely clear, that it was unwise to send most of the redcoats back to civilian life. To be sure, it could be believed that the expansion of the empire made it necessary to maintain larger garrison forces than in the past; and General Jeffery Amherst was urging that an army of regulars was needed for the future defense of North America. Perhaps pride had somewhat to do with that decision. Would not a small army be inconsistent with the greatness of Britain? Whatever were its reasons, the ministry undertook to reduce the navy rather drastically, but to keep eighty-five regiments of infantry in service. Then, fearing that Parliament would refuse to support so many troops, the King's advisers determined to ask for permission to keep only seventy-five regiments.

The old Duke of Newcastle was shocked when he learned that the Bute ministry desired to maintain seventy-five regiments of infantry. But

IV · A New British Policy

William Pitt, always eager to maintain the grandeur of Britain and never niggardly with public funds, warmly endorsed the measure in the House of Commons. Moreover, that body was pleased to hear that the ministry did not intend to extract from British pockets all the money that would be required to support those regiments. On February 25, 1763, precisely fifteen days after the signature of the treaty of peace with France and Spain, Welbore Ellis, Secretary at War, made a pregnant announcement. That part of the army stationed in America was "to be supported the first year by England, afterwards by the colonies." With little ado Parliament gave its consent—and it is not recorded that any man in it rose to say that an attempt to force the colonists to contribute might have the most dangerous consequences. Would heed have been given to such a warning? The King's advisers had already resolved that Parliament must tax the colonists, must compel them to meet the costs of the redcoats on duty in America. They were busily creating a crisis that would rend the empire. In March 1763, that political chameleon, that astonishing marplot, Charles Townshend, then president of the Board of Trade, gave the House of Commons a glimpse of vicious policy and behavior to come. He urged that Parliament impose taxes upon the colonists for revenue. He did so without the consent of his colleagues in the ministry, irritating both them and the King. The monarch and his advisers had not yet decided precisely what tax or taxes they would impose upon the colonists.

The Bute ministry had reached the conclusion, however, that England must have a naval squadron in American waters as well as an army upon American land. In April 1763, Parliament gave its consent to the maintenance of a small fleet of eight warships and twelve armed sloops at Halifax, Nova Scotia. That squadron was not too large for the purpose of defense—and ships kept in commission had to be stationed somewhere. However, it was placed at Halifax not merely to serve against foreign enemies, but to assist British customs officers in the collection of duties and the enforcement of the Navigation Acts. Britain was moving toward more stringent curbs upon American maritime commerce.

Before the end of that April, after helping to lay the foundations for a crisis within the empire, the Earl of Bute retired to private life. His place at the head of government was taken by George Grenville. Not because, on second thought, the King and other politicians saw that they were slipping into a sea of colonial troubles. Bute departed from the British political scene because he could not stand against a storm of personal abuse. He was accused of attempting to expand the power of the King at the expense of Parliament, as an enemy of British liberty. But he was much more bitterly assailed because he was a Scot, and a Scot who gave as many public offices as possible to other Scots. Taking lessons in English, men from "that land of Calvin, oat-cakes, and sulphur" thronged into London when Bute was the chief minister. The influx of office seekers from North Britain inspired the famous remark by Dr. Samuel Johnson that "the noblest prospect which a Scotchman ever sees, is the highroad that leads him to England." Some of the Scots failed to get an appointment, and sadly returned home. However, many Mackenzies, Macleods, and Montgomerys were successful. The harsh manners, the Scottish brogue, and the sycophancy of those officeseekers exasperated Englishmen who readily forgave similar defects in other Englishmen; but they were offensive also to James Boswell, one of their countrymen and unsuccessful seeker for himself of a commission in the Guards.

It was not the shortcomings of the Scots that most deeply offended the English; even Dr. Johnson suggested that "Much may be made of a Scotchman if he be caught young." The great grievance against them was they competed only too successfully with the English for public jobs and honors. It was venomously asserted that the Scots, having failed to conquer England by arms under the leadership of the royal Stuarts, were trying to achieve the same end by means of sinister politicking as allies of George III. The enemies of the Scots found an exotic and erratic champion in cross-eyed John Wilkes, the famous rake and wit, who savagely attacked them in his weekly, *The North Briton.* Wilkes did not confine himself to the facts, which were sufficiently awkward for the sons of Caledonia. He dared even to suggest that the widowed mother of the King had been Bute's mistress. He fanned the flame of resentment against the Scots until the heat of it became unbearable for Bute. The Scottish nobleman became a sinister figure to many Englishmen. Long after he had left office, suspicion survived that he retained the ear and the confidence of the monarch. Actually, the King, discerning the weakness of Bute, soon began to ignore him. Many Scottish politicians continued to look to George III for leadership. But neither Bute nor the Scots were responsible for every untoward decision taken in London regarding America.

Whatever else he may have been, George Grenville, Bute's successor, was not a Scot or a friend of the American colonists. He was thoroughly English; his outlook was insular; he entertained lofty notions of British sovereignty; he knew almost nothing about the colonies; by no means an inveterate enemy of liberty in Britain, he could never quite believe that an American subject of George III was the equal of a British one. He was bold, brave, and stubborn, like that Sir Richard Grenville of earlier times who challenged a Spanish fleet with one ship and sank beneath the waves after a desperate struggle. In an age when British politicians were notoriously fickle and unreliable, he displayed loyalty to principle and to his partisans. A lawyer by training, a veteran office-holder, he was looked upon as a man of ability, especially in finance. Like so many public men, he was a windy bore. A brother-in-law of William Pitt, he possessed none of the genius of the "Great Commoner"; Pitt did not love him.

As prime minister, Grenville, who had held office under Bute, moved vigorously. He was in power only from the spring of 1763 to the summer of 1765. However, during less than twenty-seven months he and his colleagues executed the decision of the Bute ministry to place a large garrison force of British troops on the North American continent, demanded that the colonists provide quarters and supplies for some of those troops; attempted to curb the westward expansion of colonial settlements; gave greater authority over Indian affairs to British officials; sought vigorously to curb American seaborne trade; restricted American paper currency; and imposed taxes upon the colonists to compel them to contribute for the defense of the empire. In ignorance and in arrogance Grenville and his associates, encountering feeble opposition in Parliament and none from the King, drove the inhabitants of the Thirteen Colonies into revolt.

It is not meant to suggest that all of the gentlemen Grenville assembled about him were completely uninformed about America and that all of them looked upon the Americans as a people who must offer complete and unquestioning obedience to King and Parliament. William Petty, Earl of Shelburne, president of the Board of Trade, a committee that gathered information about the colonies and prepared reports about them, was something of a student. Besides, he was ordinarily cautious and conciliatory in dealing with the Americans. However, he exerted little influence upon Grenville, and he was driven from his office in September 1763. Much more knowing about things American at that time than any other member of the Grenville cabinet was George Dunk, Earl of Halifax, who served first as Secretary of State for the Northern Department, which was concerned with northern Europe, later as Secretary of State for the Southern Department, which looked after southern European and colonial business. A memorial erected to Halifax in Westminster Abbey says that he was known as the "Father of the Colonies." As Dr. Johnson once remarked, those responsible for such inscriptions are not placed upon oath. Nor is it required that they possess a nice historical judgment. Halifax was much better informed about colonial questions than any other important British politician except, perhaps, William Pitt; he was, however, neither fond of nor indulgent to British people in America. He behaved more like a stern stepfather than a true parent. Having been president of the Board of Trade for thirteen years, he had indeed acquired a fund of knowledge about the colonies. But he had not become either wise or benevolent. He had long favored British authority against American freedom; he had urged, as early as 1755, that Parliament tax the Americans; he had favored the founding of an Anglican bishopric in America; and he believed that colonial commerce should be closely channeled for the benefit of Britain. Informed about things American, he had learned little about the Americans. He lacked vision, and he could not compensate for Grenville's shortcomings. Indeed, he helped to create and to execute Grenville's disastrous designs.

George Grenville was not formed for great enterprises, but he did not lack confidence in his own powers. He tactlessly undertook to solve colonial questions that more prudent and wiser men had cautiously avoided. Did he wish to prove that he possessed the genius of his brother-in-law, Pitt? It has often been said that he was devoted to business and to economy. If so, he nevertheless executed the decision of the Bute ministry to maintain a large and expensive standing army. Moreover, he consented to the stationing of seventeen regiments of infantry, on paper about 8,500 men, on the North American continent and its adjacent islands.

Why place so many men beyond the Atlantic? To be sure, it was necessary to put them in one place or another. Presumably they were posted in North America so as to provide for defense against the Spanish from the south, to prevent possible revolt by the French Canadians, and to offer a shield against Indian assaults. General Amherst stationed regiments in garrisons on the northern shores of the Gulf of Mexico, and others in the St. Lawrence Valley. The remainder, except for small detachments, he scattered in small forts in the interior of North America. He dispersed his troops in most remarkable fashion, stationing companies and parts of companies at Fort Ticonderoga, Crown Point, Niagara, Detroit, Mackinac Island, Green Bay, Fort Pitt, and many another post in the hinterland of the Thirteen Colonies.

The decision to maintain that army in North America created trouble after trouble and induced British politicians to make mistake after mistake. The colonists were not asked whether they desired such protection; nor were they asked whether they were willing to pay for it. The forces under General Amherst were more than twice as large as those on duty in North America before the Seven Years' War, when the French were potent enemies. Thoughtful colonists wondered why so many more troops were needed, when the French menace had largely disappeared.

Was it, perhaps, intended that the redcoats serve as a reminder to the colonists that they owed obedience to Britain? Hints came from private persons in England in 1763 that the new army should serve to discourage the Americans from seeking independence. It is understandable that Americans soon began to suspect that the army might be used against them rather than for their protection. Their mistrust was justified. At least one associate of Grenville expressed the opinion that the redcoats should be employed to assert British sovereignty over the colonists. In September 1763, Grenville himself rather fancied that at least some troops should be moved into positions on the seacoast where they could render assistance to British customs officers. He did not try to translate the thought into action at that time. It is apparent, however, that British politicians had established a temptation for themselves. They now had troops at no immense distance from American towns and cities. Within a few years they succumbed to the temptation and sent redcoats into the settled parts of the Thirteen Colonies.

American agents in London—all of the American colonies had one or more representatives in the imperial capital—learned enough about the intentions of Grenville and his colleagues in 1763 to become gravely concerned about them. But one ought not to ascribe Machiavellian wiles to the prime minister and his associates. Had they been truly astute, they would have done as little as possible toward providing for the defense of the colonies, and would have needed little money for that purpose. They could have put a few troops in Quebec and Montreal to prevent an uprising by the French Canadians, could have placed a few in the Floridas to keep an eye upon the Spanish—compelling the Americans to defend themselves against the red men. Occupied and burdened by Indian troubles and wars, the Americans would have had less energy to spend toward undermining British authority, would have been more appreciative of the benefits they received from their connection with Britain. Such a policy had an added advantage in that the Americans knew more about Indian fighting than did British officers and soldiers.

Even as the Grenville people and General Amherst made their military arrangements for North America, it became sadly apparent that their planning was uninspired. The redcoats and the American frontiersmen paid bitterly for their mistakes. Amherst, endowed with no more subtlety than Grenville, despised Indians. Sprinkling his troops here, there, and everywhere, he exposed many of them to Indian attack. Moreover, having given the warriors liberal presents to secure their neutrality or help during his campaigns against the French, he reduced the flow of donations to them as soon as the French were defeated. Fickle, capricious, unsophisticated, the Indians understood that the withdrawal of the French was a blow to them. They had hitherto been able to play the French and the British against each other; they would thenceforth be compelled to deal solely with the British. And it seemed clear to those tribes residing north of the Ohio River that Britain would not be generous to them in the future. In the spring of 1763, one after another, they took to the warpath. Swarming around isolated British posts, they captured several of them. They besieged but failed to take Fort Pitt. However, their raiding parties brutally ravaged the frontier settlements of Pennsylvania, Maryland, and Virginia. An army under General Henry Bouquet relieved the garrison of Fort Pitt only after a desperate struggle at Bushy Run. Fortunately, by means of presents and guile, the two Indian superintendents, Sir William Johnson and John Stuart, managed to persuade most of the Iroquois confederacy and all of the southern Indian tribes to remain neutral. Even so, the attacking Indians, among whom the great chief Pontiac of the Ottawa was conspicuous, were formidable enemies. Furious and almost desperate, Amherst considered a scheme to strike at the hostile red men by spreading smallpox among them. It is probable that he ordered it to be executed. He called upon the colonies for help, and he went home to England, consigning the burden of the Indian war to General Thomas Gage, in the autumn of 1763. Gathering regulars and colonial militia, Gage sent them forward to attack the red men. Gradually the Indians, suffering from a shortage of guns and ammunition, lacking cohesion, and assailed by punitive expeditions, lost heart and abandoned the struggle. It continued however, with diminishing violence, until the fall of 1765. Before they laid down their tomahawks, the Indians had killed many hundreds of redcoats, militiamen, and civilians.

The American colonists were less than enthusiastic about the performance of the British army in Pontiac's War. Some of them were rather pleased that Amherst had lost reputation. The Americans were not particularly grateful for the measure of protection they had received from the redcoats. What is more, Pontiac's War persuaded Grenville and his associates to move swiftly in order to prevent such conflicts in the future— and so to protect the British garrisons. They issued the famous royal Proclamation of October 7, 1763, which added to colonial discontent. That executive decree contained far-reaching provisions. It established three new colonies in North America, Quebec in the St. Lawrence Valley, East Florida, and West Florida. However, the vast territories between the Appalachian Mountains and the Mississippi River were closed against occupation by white men. Thus the principal cause of warfare with the Indians—the seizure of their hunting grounds and villages by westward-moving colonists—would be removed. Further, the Proclamation recognized the red men as the communal owners of the lands they occupied, thus reserving additional broad areas east of the mountain divide for the Cherokee and Creek tribesman. Besides, the Indians were forbidden to sell their lands except at a public meeting presided over by a royal official. Presumably that official would be one of the Indian superintendents; it was tacitly assumed that Sir William Johnson and John Stuart would continue to serve in peace as they had in war.

Were those bars against American expansion merely a rather grandiose effort to avert Indian wars? If so, it could be defended because of its purpose, even though it proved unwise. But there is evidence that the Proclamation was designed, not only to placate the Indians, but to cramp the Americans and to protect British pocketbooks. At the time it was asserted by British politicians that the decree was intended to be a long step toward restoring and preserving peace with the savages. Later, however, some of those who helped to frame the Proclamation said that they had hoped to confine the Americans to regions adjacent to salt water; and that they had been opposed to settlements beyond the mountains in which the Americans would sooner or later begin to manufacture for themselves. They had desired that the Americans continue essentially to be producers of raw materials and consumers of British finished goods. It would not have been prudent, of course, to voice such thoughts in 1763.

In any event, the Proclamation was disliked by many Americans. By American standards, it was becoming difficult to secure good land east of the Appalachians. Tillers of the soil and their sons yearned for new farms beyond the divide. They saw the royal decree as a wanton and cruel blow to their chances of acquiring comfortable homesteads "on the waters of the Mississippi." Believing that it was capricious and unjust, they were tempted to believe that it also violated their personal rights. It was indeed of doubtful legality in that it was applied to some Virginians who had put themselves down in the Kanawha River valley as early as 1745. They had done so under Virginia law; they had been driven from their new homes by the Indians; they desired to return to their farms. They were told that they could not. They and other pioneers decided to ignore the royal decree, and hundreds of them crossed the mountains in 1764 and 1765. They put up log cabins in western Virginia and southwestern Pennsylvania.

The settlers were not the only Americans who determined to defy or circumvent the Proclamation. Land speculation was a favored American way to wealth. Planters, merchants, and lawyers had found it possible in the past to secure large grants of unsettled lands to the westward at several colonial capitals. They had been able to get them cheaply, and sometimes to hold them until the advance of settlements made them valuable. Such speculators, including Lees and Carters of Virginia and similarly prominent men of Maryland and Pennsylvania, had formed companies and were striving to establish titles to hundreds of thousands of acres beyond the mountains. Still other men of sanguine temperament were meditating such gambles in lands over the mountain wall, among them British merchants. The speculators could hardly hope for quick returns, but it was possible for them to create estates cheaply for their old age, for their children, or for their grandchildren. Like the pioneers, they denounced the Proclamation. It was unfair, and it was an unconstitutional infringement upon the powers of the colonial governments. They were men who did not lack influence. Again and again after 1763 the Virginia House of Burgesses demanded that all bars against the westward expansion of the Old Dominion be destroyed.

The Proclamation of 1763 and later British decrees that imposed less rigid restrictions upon the pioneers and speculators pleased the Indians, even though some of them, seduced by presents, rum, and sweet talk, sold hunting grounds to whites as they had in the past. It is not surprising that they very generally took up arms as clients and allies of George III in the War of Independence. Superintendent John Stuart, striving to retard rather than to prevent invasion of Indian lands, trying to placate both the Indians and the whites, nevertheless became unpopular both among pioneers and among politicians who gathered at Williamsburg, Charleston, and Savannah. The barriers erected by Britain against the pioneers and the speculators proved to be temporary and irritating, not permanent and exasperating. It cannot be said that they turned angry pioneers and American speculators into bitter enemies of the mother country.

Nor were British efforts to soothe the Indians by restraining white men who traded with them a prime cause of American discontent. It was never possible, so long as the Indians possessed lands desired by white men, to prevent the whites from taking those lands. Nor was it ever possible to compel traders who dealt with the red men to bargain honestly with them. Going into Indian villages in the distant wilderness, the traders exchanged guns, ammunition, tomahawks, knives, clothing, mirrors, rum, and other goods for furs and deerskins. They could, and did, frequently cheat their unsophisticated customers. It has been reported even that they bartered skimpy breechcloths for large deerskins. Several of the colonies had vainly tried to regulate the activities of the rascals, scamps, and irresponsible men among the traders, without much or enduring success. When they were cheated by traders, the Indians tended to vent their anger indiscriminately upon the whites, often attacking inoffensive frontier families rather than the swindlers. Seeking energetically to ward off Indian wars and to protect redcoat garrisons, the British Board of Trade prepared a "Plan for the Future Management of Indian Affairs" that would have placed control of the trade substantially in the hands of Sir William Johnson and John Stuart. That Plan was not adopted; it was set aside in the summer of 1764 because of the expense it would entail. However, Johnson and Stuart, supplied with funds by General Gage, were permitted to impose some healthy restrictions upon the traders during the four years following. Resentful traders communicated their vexation to the colonial merchants who supplied them, and the merchants conveyed their dissatisfaction to colonial assemblies. It is to be believed that the trammels placed by Johnson and Stuart upon private enterprise in the Indian villages served to make red-skinned friends for Britain, and perhaps a few white-skinned enemies.

We are by no means done with the consequences of the decision to maintain an army in North America. Backwoodsmen and their allies, held back only temporarily by the onslaughts of the Indians in Pontiac's War, planted themselves beyond the Proclamation line in northwestern Pennsylvania as soon as the warriors retreated into their forest fastnesses. The governors of Virginia and Pennsylvania—it was not then certain which colony had jurisdiction—ordered those venturesome pioneers to vacate their log cabins, to leave the Indian country. They refused to obey. Were they to be allowed to flout the authority of the Crown? In 1765 General Gage instructed the commanding officer at Fort Pitt to use force to drive out the offending settlers. Redcoats burned the cabins of some of the backwoodsmen and escorted the owners eastward. Within a few months they reappeared on forbidden ground, accompanied by other pioneers. By that time, however, the colonists were in revolt everywhere against Britain, and Gage prudently postponed further use of the troops. He did not wish to supply evidence to support an American denunciation of military tyranny. Defying civil and military officers, the frontiersmen clung to soil west of the mountains.

Other difficulties arose from the presence of small detachments of troops in New York City, Albany, and other colonial towns. During the war with France the redcoats had been welcomed in such places; and the colonists had quite willingly furnished quarters, certain provisions, firewood, and candles in accordance with the annual British Mutiny Act. After the removal of the French menace, American civilians began to encourage redcoats to desert, telling them that the British Mutiny Act, which annually gave British army officers their authority over their troops, did not extend to America, and that they could not be punished for leaving the colors. Some soldiers fled from the poorer pay and hardships of military life to freedom and civil opportunity. Colonial officials also began to display reluctance to obey the Mutiny Act. General Gage urged that Parliament revise the law so that it would unquestionably be applied to North America. It required that the colonies provide quarters—in public barracks, vacant buildings, or taverns—for troops located in the settled parts of North America; also that the colonies contribute cider or beer, firewood, candles, and other supplies for the redcoats. They were ordered in addition to furnish carts and wagons for military transport at fixed prices. In Parliament the revision of the Mutiny Act was mere routine. But that law forced the colonial assemblies to vote money for the army, whether they would or no, and it was soon assailed by many Americans as a violation of their rights as Englishmen. It was associated in their minds with the detested Stamp Act, which was passed during the same session of Parliament and which they considered to be utterly unconstitutional. The new Mutiny Act added fuel to flames of revolt.

Tempted in 1765 to employ the redcoats against pioneers in the western wilderness, General Gage—and his superiors in London—was confronted by a crisis on the Atlantic seaboard. Again the thought of using the troops was enticing. Neither Gage nor his employers succumbed to the temptation to resort to force on the seaboard at that time. But the presence of the army in America continued to seduce them toward exertion of armed might.

But it is now necessary to turn to other Grenville decisions and laws that stimulated revolt by the Americans, both on the seaboard and in the interior.

CHAPTER V

A Breach in the Empire

IF George Grenville possessed any important talents, they were in the realms of commerce and finance, not those of things military and political. It seems likely, however, that he knew little more about trade, taxes, and money than he did about civil and military strategy. He kept a diary while he was prime minister—a hint that he was fond of paper work and records rather than profound in intellect. Nor did Thomas Whately, Grenville's trusted lieutenant and a secretary of the treasury after August 1763, compensate for the deficiencies of his chief. One must praise Whately for his steadfast loyalty to Grenville in an age when fidelity was usually uncommon among public men in Britain. Unfortunately for Grenville, Whately had no great gifts. A lawyer, a landscape gardener, and a Shakespearean scholar, he contributed little to legal learning, horticultural design, or knowledge about Shakespeare; he had no more foresight than Grenville, but helped him to lay mines beneath the British empire. When Grenville left office in the summer of 1765, he bequeathed a crisis in America to his successor, the Marquis of Rockingham.

For all his energy, Grenville was unable to proceed with schemes to get money from the colonists toward the support of the army in America until the spring of 1764. He and his colleagues needed time in which to choose the means by which they would extract pounds, shillings, and pence from American pockets, also to frame laws for that purpose. Besides, they were involved in an embarrassing clash with John Wilkes. The passing of the Earl of Bute into private life did not satisfy that troublesome journalist. He assailed the Grenvillites as tools of Bute; he condemned George III as an enemy to English liberties; and he also published obscene and blasphemous writings that shocked men accustomed to strong and foul language. Undertaking to punish Wilkes, the ministry used vaguely worded general warrants to arrest him and other men who helped him publish his nasty effusions. Thus they violated the constitutional rights of Englishmen, and they were rebuked by an English court. Wilkes fled to France in December 1763, to escape punishment. However, the ministry barely escaped censure by the House of Commons in February 1764.

If the struggle with John Wilkes served to delay new laws to get money from the Americans, it did not prevent more stringent execution of old laws intended to cramp American commerce. It will be recalled that the Bute ministry, stationing a naval squadron at Halifax, ordered its commander to do all that he could to help customs officers enforce the laws restricting American maritime commerce. That instruction was not withdrawn by Grenville. On the contrary, during the summer and fall of 1763, colonial governors, customs men, and even army officers were commanded to do all within their power to execute those laws. Grenville also began to renovate the customs service in America. It had been remarkably inefficient; it was collecting no more than £2,000 in duties per annum; and its members cost the Crown £7,000 or £8,000 each year. More than one of the customs officers were absentees, Englishmen who did not leave England and whose work was done by deputies. Grenville commanded the absentees to go to their stations—a vicious blow to men from whom personal toil had not hitherto been required. It was made evident to all the customs men beyond the Atlantic that neglect of duty would be punished, and that all taxes that had been levied to regulate trade must be collected. Feeling the whip, customs collectors moved with unwonted zeal. Early in 1764 they created dismay in the Northern colonial ports. It will be remembered that they had been accepting a halfpenny or a penny in lieu of the sixpence per gallon duty levied upon molasses imported from the foreign islands in the West Indies. Forced to abandon their easygoing habits, they demanded every sixpence due under that statute. Colonial merchants protested vehemently, because exaction of the full duty would virtually have stopped the lucrative and most important trade they carried on with the French, Spanish, Dutch, and Swedish islands in the Caribbean.

Why did the importers complain so bitterly? Could they not simply pass the burden of the duty on to the consumers of molasses? The difficulty was that collection of the tax might destroy a great and profitable web of commerce. The planters of the foreign islands could and did produce sugar cane and molasses abundantly and cheaply. The sweet fluid was much wanted on the mainland, partly because the poorer Americans used it in place of more expensive sugar, partly because molasses was the principal ingredient of rum. That beverage was important to the Americans. It was a favorite tipple among the colonists; the Indians gladly bartered furs and deerskins for it; and it was exchanged for Negro slaves in unhealthy ports on the west coast of Africa. The foreign islands of the West Indians were also of impressive importance to the Americans as markets for lumber, grain, and rice, and especially for inferior fish that could not be sold on the mainland. If merchant captains from Boston, Newport, and Philadelphia did not buy molasses from the foreigners, they could hardly hope to sell to them. The sixpence duty would presumably compel American merchant captains to purchase molasses in the British islands of the Caribbean, and so would bring profit to British planters. But those planters did not even produce sufficient molasses to satisfy American needs. The sixpence duty, inflicting heavy blows upon the commerce of the Americans, would also injure them by depriving them of currency. Since the Americans were debtors and the British were their creditors, sterling money tended to flow from the colonies to London, Bristol, and Liverpool. The colonists suffered from a chronic shortage of British currency. This was alleviated by the importation of foreign money, especially Spanish dollars, from the West Indies, because American merchant captains sold more than they bought in the Spanish and French possessions. It is clear enough that collection of the sixpence duty would damage the economy of the Americans, both directly and indirectly, in several ways. Hence their outcry against it.

The Molasses Act was to expire in the fall of 1764, but the Americans could not hope that it would be permitted to lapse. It would undoubtedly be continued by Parliament, if only to please some dozens of its members who owned estates in Jamaica, Barbados, and other British islands in the West Indies. However, American merchants did hope to secure a reduction in the duty upon molasses. They urged that it be set at a halfpenny or penny per gallon. The traffic, they said, would not bear more. Their wishes were expressed in London through some of the colonial agents resident in the imperial capital. Thus they encouraged the Grenvillites, who needed no encouragement, to proceed with schemes to tax the colonists for the support of the army in North America. Did those Americans know what they were doing when they petitioned for a smaller tax upon molasses that would not hurt their commerce? If the duty was too low to serve as a device to control trade, would it not be a tax for revenue? And if Parliament could impose such a levy merely to get funds, why could it not impose other and larger taxes for the same purpose? At least two Americans, Benjamin Franklin and Chief Justice Thomas

Hutchinson of Massachusetts, saw clearly that American acceptance of bearable duty upon molasses would establish a precedent for unbearable taxation by Parliament. Such a duty, observed Hutchinson, was unconstitutional, for it would violate the right of an Englishman not to be taxed for revenue without his consent. However, Hutchinson did not raise an alarm. Nor did Franklin. Writing from Philadelphia to his friend, "Omniscient" Richard Jackson, in London, Franklin merely said that Britain could not both choke American trade and extract large sums from the Americans through taxes. At that time the Philadelphian was not a militant and passionate defender of American rights. As deputy postmaster general in America, he held a royal appointment, and his illegitimate son, William Franklin, had just become royal governor of New Jersey. The prudent Franklin was still an Englishman as well as an American. At length, he would become utterly American.

It is doubtful whether George Grenville as prime minister cared very much what the colonists felt or thought. By March 1764, he had determined that they must contribute toward the maintenance of the army in America, which cost between £200,000 and £400,000 annually, and also that Parliament must tax the Americans to get the money. In the middle of that month he introduced a far-reaching revenue bill, which encountered little opposition and which became law within less than three weeks. It was of such great consequence to the colonists that it has been called the American Act. It struck hard against the colonists. Among other things, it provided for an admiralty court to sit at Halifax in Nova Scotia and to function without a jury. Thereafter Americans accused of violating the maritime trade laws could be tried in that distant town before a British judge without American jurors. The duties upon port and Madeira wines brought into American ports were increased, to the discomfort of colonial gentlemen who preferred wine to rum. Much more injurious was a threepence per gallon duty placed upon molasses. Moreover, that levy was quite forthrightly declared to be one to secure revenue, not to regulate American commerce. And worse, for the colonists, was yet to come. Even before he introduced the American Act, Grenville announced that he was considering the imposition of stamp duties upon the colonies, an announcement that was quite acceptable to Parliament.

The American Act could not but create American discontent. And almost simultaneously Parliament passed a Currency Act, which restricted the supply of colonial paper money. The assemblies of New England, it will be recalled, had been forbidden, since 1751, to issue paper money that could be used to pay all debts. There was talk in Virginia and North Carolina of printing such legal-tender bills. British merchants, fearing that debts owed to them by Virginians and North Carolinians would be paid in depreciated money, had asked for protection against their debtors. They received it. The law of 1751 was applied to all of the colonies. It added a minor injury to major ones. How far was the supply of currency in America to be reduced?

But the heaviest of all the blows that Grenville aimed at the Americans was the notorious Stamp Act. He did not bring it before the House of Commons until the spring of 1765. He pretended for many months that he was willing to consider an alternative method to secure more money for the support of the army in America. He said that he was willing to do as much as he could to please the Americans, but also that they must assume part of the burdens of empire. Britain was in financial straits; her public debt was high; and the British people were paying very heavy taxes. On the other hand, the colonists were not weighed down by huge public debts and onerous taxes. (It may be worth remark that Britain never secured much tax revenue from America; and also that the nation remained solvent despite the expensive War of Independence and the long wars waged against the revolutionary French republic and Napoleon.) Ideally, Grenville told several of the colonial agents in London in May 1764, the colonies ought to ask Parliament to impose upon them stamp duties such as had been collected in Britain for several decades. That suggestion was, of course, preposterous. Did he think that they would respond favorably to it? If so, he was hopelessly ignorant about America and the Americans. Nor was he really interested in any arrangement by which the colonial assemblies might supply funds. He did not set a quota for each of the colonies—and a colonial assembly could not act without such a quota. In fact, Grenville did not even officially ask them to help the mother country financially. It would have taken time to create a system by which the Americans would contribute through their legislatures. Grenville wanted money, and some of it in the near future; he intended that Parliament should levy the stamp duties, whether or not the Americans humbly asked for them.

The colonists did not graciously request Parliament to tax them. The assembly of Massachusetts vainly considered a proposal to vote money toward the defense of the empire. It could not act, for its members did not know how much Massachusetts should offer, nor how much her sister colonies would supply. In the main, the Americans responded angrily to the news that the American Act had been passed and that they would in all likelihood be commanded to pay stamp duties. Individuals, committees, and assemblies voiced a pervading unhappiness, discontent with British measures already taken, and alarm concerning those to come. A British army was not needed in North America; it did not give proper protection against the Indians; the Americans had not been asked whether they wanted it; and it would have been better to let the colonists defend themselves against the savages, as they did before the Seven Years' War. Britain was choking the flow of American commerce and currency. Americans were deprived of their right to trial by jury in the new admiralty court established at distant Halifax. The new duty upon molasses was injurious and iniquitous. It also was denounced as unconstitutional, as taxation without representation, by the assemblies of New York and North Carolina. But the new duty upon molasses, if it put an end to trade with the foreign islands of the West Indies, could be considered as a levy to regulate trade, like the duty that it replaced—even though Parliament had made it quite clear that the new tax was intended to secure revenue. Most of the colonists did not protest very violently against it. Many of them were confused by the issues presented by the threepence per gallon levy; protests against it from Massachusetts indicated that a lower duty would be acceptable in New England. The tax would not hurt as much in the Southern Colonies as it would in New England. Perhaps their inhabitants were not eager to squabble about constitutional right in connection with a tax that would not severely injure them. The situation was quite different with the proposed stamp duties. The levy upon molasses would hardly take more than £30,000 or £40,000 from American pockets. The stamp duties would extract at least £40,000, perhaps £100,000, from American purses—and they would take money from almost every adult American. The colonists were not rich. Britain could save much money by abolishing sinecures and unearned pensions. Nearly every American who voiced an opinion said that the duties would be unjust, wicked, and unconstitutional; that the Americans elected no members of Parliament; that an Englishman could be taxed only by a legislature in which he sat or was represented; and accordingly that stamp duties could be imposed upon them only by their own assemblies. Their argument appealed even to some royal governors in America. Such officials did not clamor against the proposed duties. But petitions and protests against them from several American legislatures poured into London.

Confronted by the complaints from America, Grenville might still have drawn back. A wiser, a more prudent, even a more timid man would certainly have given more thought to the stamp duties. Other British politicians before him had considered such duties, had foreseen that they might produce more trouble than money, and had cautiously set them aside as a tempting but risky way to get money from the British dependencies beyond the Atlantic. But the remonstrances from America persuaded Grenville that it was necessary to impose the duties, not merely to gain revenue, but to assert most emphatically the right of Parliament to do so. There could be no better device to proclaim the sovereignty of Britain in general and of Parliament in particular. The colonists must be taught to obey. Continuing to proclaim the poverty of the mother country, he nevertheless insisted upon making a prideful pronouncement of British power.

In February 1765, Grenville was given a last chance to avert a clash with the Thirteen Colonies. Conferring with several of their agents in London, he asked again and again whether they could offer a substitute for the stamp duties that would please the Americans. They proposed that the several colonial legislatures be requested to supply funds. It was certainly doubtful that those bodies would consistently and generously vote the money that Grenville desired. Grenville, politely but steadily, refused even to test that scheme. Nor did he discern the merit of an alternative quietly presented to him by Benjamin Franklin, who had recently returned to London as an agent for Pennsylvania. Franklin suggested that Parliament create a bank in America, one that could issue paper money and make loans to the colonists. The Americans would profit by getting a sufficient supply of money, and the interest from the loans made by the bank could be used for the support of the British troops in America. Franklin's substitute was most ingenious. It was even a better one than he realized, for he mistakenly believed that it would fasten a tax upon the Americans. Anyway, Franklin was too late. A stamp bill had been prepared, chiefly by Thomas Whately, and Grenville had presented it to the House of Commons. Indeed, debate upon the measure had already begun.

The bill brought forward by Grenville, applied to all of His Majesty's possessions in North America and the West Indies, levied stamp duties that could hardly be avoided by an inhabitant of those regions. Newspapers were taxed heavily, at a halfpenny per copy, and a franchise as much as £6. The payment of duty was required upon many and diverse legal papers and commercial documents; also upon pamphlets, almanacs, playing cards, and dice. Those who refused to pay the duties, as well as officials who did not insist upon collection of the tax, were exposed to severe penalties. In the main, the measure was modeled upon the British Stamp Act. It was to go into effect on November 1, 1765.

The consequences ought to have been exhaustively debated within and without the halls of Westminster. The bill was, in fact, assailed by many Englishmen, including merchants, who desired to please the Americans and who wished to avert any disturbance that would hurt their businesses. But most Englishmen either casually favored it or were indifferent. England contained but one man who might have challenged Grenville with any chance whatever of success. That man was William Pitt. He believed that the stamp duties were both unjust and unconstitutional. He was ill with gout, and he was absent from his seat in the House of Commons. It is doubtful, however, that even a healthy Pitt, with his vast prestige and compelling oratory, could have checked Grenville. Grenville had too much to offer—the maintenance of a British army largely at the expense of the prosperous Americans, and the hope that British taxes could be reduced in better times soon to come. The stamp bill was peculiarly pleasing to the many country gentlemen in Parliament; they yearned for a lowering of the taxes upon their lands. Most of those who sat in the House of Commons, and in the House of Lords, like Grenville scoffed at the notion that Parliament lacked constitutional power to take American money without American consent. They could not believe that its dominion over America was less than its authority over Britain. They tended to assume that the rights of Englishmen in America were not equal to those of Englishmen at home. A few members of the House of Commons spoke emphatically against the bill, declaring that it was unfair and unwise. At least one, the rich William Beckford of London, a follower of Pitt, said that it was also unconstitutional. Another Pittite, Colonel Isaac Barré, who had served in America, predicted in a flight of fervid oratory that the Americans, being sturdy sons of liberty, would be driven into revolt. At least one member of the House of Lords said that the bill was unconstitutional. However, there was a majority of 5 to 1 in favor of it in the House of Commons, and the Lords overwhelmingly endorsed it. It became law on March 22.

When Colonel Barré prophesied that the Americans would struggle for their liberty, was he merely indulging in lofty rhetoric? Immediately after the passage of the Stamp Act there was little concern in London lest the colonists revolt. Their agents in the imperial capital did not expect tumult in America. Assuming that his fellow Americans would not defy the mother country, Franklin, comfortably established in London, advised friends in Philadelphia to practice economy, so that they would not so severely feel the weight of British taxes—to make a merit of their misery. Franklin and the other American agents were doubtless influenced by the opinions and sentiments of the English people among whom they lived. So little did Franklin anticipate trouble to come that he secured an appointment as stamp distributor in Pennsylvania for his political ally, John Hughes of Philadelphia. Making a mild gesture toward pleasing the Americans, Grenville let it be known that he was disposed to name Americans as stamp distributors. There was to be at least one such officer in each colony; and his duties would be light, his pay good. Asked by Thomas Whately to nominate suitable persons, Franklin endorsed Hughes—to the later sorrow of that man. Despite his advice that the Americans yield to British authority, Franklin afterward managed to establish a reputation as a defender of American liberty. His fellow agent, Jared Ingersoll, who represented Connecticut, did not fare so well. Ingersoll accepted appointment as stamp distributor for his colony—and thereby virtually ruined a promising career. Neither Hughes nor Ingersoll was able to sell stamps. Both were forced to abandon their new offices in haste and in turmoil; later they obtained other British appointments; but they lost and never regained the confidence and respect of their American neighbors.

In the late spring of 1765 the news reached America that the Stamp Act had actually been passed. According to the Maryland *Gazette,* the colonists were "THUNDERSTRUCK." They were put to the test. It was one thing to inveigh against the Stamp Act before it was sanctioned by Parliament, quite another thing to resist its execution. Richard Henry Lee, a member of the distinguished Lee clan of Virginia, who afterward won enduring fame as the man who introduced the resolution in the Continental Congress that declared American independence, had helped to frame an ardent denunciation of the stamp duties late in 1764—and had almost simultaneously applied for the post of stamp distributor in the Old Dominion. Obviously Lee was not then certain that the Americans would rebel against the mother country. If they yielded to imperial authority, he personally might have the solace of an easy and profitable appointment. Had he secured it, he would hardly have become known as a great American patriot. (It was sufficiently embarrassing for Lee when it was revealed that he had vainly applied for the post.) There were unquestionably many Americans who hesitated to challenge Britain after the passage of the Stamp Act. In what manner could the colonists resist? And if they did stand forth against British authority, did they not risk subjugation by His Majesty's army and navy? Never before had colonists in the Americas of Britain, France, Spain, or Holland successfully defied the power of their parent state. The severed heads of men who had taken part in the rebellion of 1745 in behalf of Bonnie Prince Charlie were still on public display in London. A thoughtful colonist might well hesitate to throw down the gauntlet to Britain.

However, passion mounted swiftly in the Thirteen Colonies. Grenville might think that Britain was merely asserting her unquestionable dominion, but informed Americans saw in the measures of Bute and Grenville a pattern of tyranny. The Americans were to be required to support an army for which they had not asked; they were forbidden to expand into the interior of their continent; their maritime commerce was to be crippled by rigid rules, British customs and naval officers, hostile and arbitrary judges, and excessive taxation; their supply of currency was to be severely restricted; and they were to be compelled to pay heavy stamp duties that violated their rights as Englishmen. Their scanty supplies of cash would flow into the hands of British officials. If they meekly bent their knees beneath the shower of woes aimed at them, would not even worse befall them in the future? If they humbly paid the stamp duties, would not Parliament inflict others upon them? They were threatened with slavery. It may be asserted that Grenville did not intend to create a design for despotism. It is only too evident that he lacked the information, the vision, and the generous spirit of a statesman. The colonists did not err—whatever may be said in his behalf—when they concluded that their prosperity and their freedom were fundamentally threatened.

Who would be bold enough, rash enough, to raise the standard for resistance? Patrick Henry, a country lawyer who had hitherto played an important role in the hamlet of Hanover in Virginia, came forward. Self-taught and briefly taught, he was no legal luminary. He had turned to the law after failing in other occupations. He was not intellectually gifted. In American folklore of the nineteenth century he was a demigod; at least one American scholar of the twentieth century has described him as a mere demagogue. He was neither the one nor the other. His abilities and his shortcomings should not be assessed in the strong and passionate language that he himself employed. However his merits may be weighed, he was, as Lord Byron said, a "forest Demosthenes." If he appealed to the emotions rather than to the intelligence of his listeners, he was nevertheless a superb orator. Elected to the House of Burgesses, he took his seat in that body in May 1765 at Williamsburg. A few days later he delivered a speech that made him an American immortal.

Most of the members of the House of Burgesses had already gone home—did some of them prefer to be absent when the news came that the Stamp Act had indeed been passed? Certainly Henry was not prudent. He swiftly introduced a set of seven resolutions. These declared that Parliament did not have power to tax the Virginians when they first settled in America; that the Virginians had never been taxed without action by their representatives in the Burgesses since the founding of the Old Dominion; that Parliament had not acquired power to impose levies upon them; and that the Stamp Act violated the rights of the Virginians as Englishmen. The last two resolutions offered by Henry urged that the Stamp Act be flouted, and declared that anyone who advised obedience to it was an enemy of Virginia. In behalf of those trenchant declarations Henry, on May 30, delivered a stirring speech in which he did not hesitate to remind George III of the fate encountered by tyrants Tarquin, Julius Caesar, and Charles I. He was interrupted by a cry of "Treason!" Precisely what Henry replied to that charge is uncertain. He may have offered a polite apology for extreme language; he may have retracted nothing. In any event, after sharp debates, he secured approval by the Burgesses of the substances of his first five resolutions. Riding his horse back to Hanover, he left a rising flame behind him.

The fire kindled by Henry spread swiftly through the Thirteen Colonies. It was reported, erroneously, that the Burgesses had endorsed all of Henry's resolutions. Counterparts of the House of Burgesses throughout the old English colonies in the North American mainland hastily adopted similar resolutions. Demand after demand went to London that the detested stamp duties be repealed forthwith. Moreover, nine of those colonies, with Massachusetts leading the way, sent delegates to the Stamp Act Congress—others would have appointed deputies, had their assemblies been in session. Meeting in New York in the autumn of 1765, twenty-seven delegates to that body sent petitions to the King and to the House of Commons and a memorial to the House of Lords. Speaking for America, they specifically pronounced the stamp duties to be unconstitutional, because the Americans were not represented in Parliament. Nor could they be so represented. The delegates also condemned deprivation of the right of trial by jury in admiralty courts as a violation of the rights of Englishmen. They said that the threepence duty upon foreign molasses was injurious and vicious. Accordingly, they urgently requested changes in the American Act and revocation of the Stamp Act.

The Americans did not confine themselves to verbal objections. The Stamp Act was executed, despite grumbling, in Canada and in the Floridas, where there were few civilians of English descent and where regiments of redcoats were stationed. Nor did the planters of the British West Indies defy Britain. It was otherwise, however, in the Thirteen Colonies. A few stamps were bought in Georgia, because of special circumstances in that province; not a single one was purchased in the British dependencies stretching from South Carolina to the district of Maine. Georgia was scantily settled; the colony received a subsidy of more than £4,000 yearly from the British treasury; and its people could not logically complain that the Stamp Act did them economic injustice. Besides, the governor of Georgia, the able and determined James Wright, could call upon two troops of rangers in British pay for help; and there were many British sailors in the ports of Georgia. Even so, the stamp distributor for Georgia, who was not an American, served very briefly. Encouraged by Wright, he sold a few stamps that were affixed to the clearance papers of vessels in Savannah Harbor. Wright would not permit the ships to sail without stamped clearances. But the distributor hastily left the colony. A storm of protest was rising within it, and the governor prudently decided that it was unwise to continue his efforts toward collection of the duties. No other governor in the Thirteen Colonies made a serious attempt to enforce the law. To the northward of Georgia no stamp distributor ever opened his office, and no stamps were ever offered for sale.

For the Americans generally, indeed almost overwhelmingly, detested the stamp duties. They resolutely and angrily followed in the wake of Patrick Henry. Delegations—and mobs—waited upon men who had accepted appointment as stamp distributors, or who were about to receive appointment. Such men were informed that they would not be permitted to serve His Majesty. They must refuse to accept office; if they had already been appointed, they must resign. The distributors and would-be distributors were threatened with social ostracism, economic reprisals, and even violence. Most of them quickly, all of them eventually, yielded to intolerable pressure. To make sure that the duties would not be collected, the Americans, again in delegations or mobs of "Sons of Liberty," also proceeded against the stamps and stamped paper that were sent across the ocean in the fall of 1765. If they reached land, might not governors and other officers try to sell them? Enterprising citizens in American ports boarded vessels carrying them, seized them, and destroyed them. One consignment was landed at New York City, but it was placed in the care of the city council with the stipulation that the papers were not to be sold. The Americans circulated newspapers without stamps; they usually accepted the validity of legal documents lacking the stamps required by the British law; and their ships went to sea with clearance papers unsoiled by stamps.

In several of the colonies the courts were closed. Judges declined to make use of unstamped legal documents that were illegal. Doing so, they injured some colonists, but also some British creditors. For American debtors put off payment of their obligations to British merchants, and could not be coerced when the courts were not open. Indeed, the colonists demanded that British merchants and manufacturers use their influence to secure the cancellation of the Stamp Act. Delaying discharge of their debts, they also largely reduced their orders for British goods. And the pressure they exerted upon the makers and sellers of these goods was effective.

Defying British authority, the Americans, especially muscular mechanics and strong sailors, did resort to physical violence. The records do not show that they killed anyone, or even that they maimed anyone. Nevertheless, mobs of them destroyed the property of some would-be stamp collectors and of others who tried to defend British authority. They also frightened those men and their families. On August 14 an unruly throng of Bostonians proceeded against Andrew Oliver, secretary of the province of Massachusetts, a gentleman who had been appointed stamp distributor. The mob destroyed an office belonging to Oliver, broke the windows of his house, invaded it, and destroyed his furniture. Fortunately for Oliver, he was not in the house. He announced the next day that he would make no attempt to collect the stamp duties. Two weeks later another gang of Bostonians ransacked and severely damaged the homes of William Story, Benjamin Hallowell (a customs officer), and Lieutenant Governor Thomas Hutchinson, three men who believed that the colonists ought to abide by British law. Two nights afterward another mob moved against Martin Howard and Dr. Thomas Moffatt in Newport, Rhode Island. Those gentlemen were also known to be supporters of British authority; their houses were looted and wrecked. On November 1 an enthusiastic crowd of 2,000 men and boys of New York City built a bonfire within sight of a small British garrison in Fort George, and burned a coach and other vehicles belonging to Lieutenant Governor Cadwallader Colden. Colden was within the fort.

Why was it those mobs were not dispersed? The truth is that they were encouraged by politicians, lawyers, and even by clergymen, by men with claims to education and gentility who would not personally threaten or despoil their fellow citizens. Here and there a merchant, a planter, or even a tradesman raised his voice against needless violence and robbery, in vain. In that time both Americans and Englishmen were less sensitive to brutality than they were in later generations, and mob action was common on both sides of the Atlantic. Many Americans, deploring the extremes to which the mobs proceeded, nevertheless believed that the stamp distributors and their few friends deserved at least part of the indignities and losses they suffered. It was useless to ask the town watch, the constable, or the sheriff to intervene. Often, as Americans, they did not wish to act; in any event, they could not stop the mobs. Nor could the governors who, except for James Wright, did not have reliable forces of police at their disposal. They could call the militia into service. Of what avail, since it was composed of Americans, from whom obedience to orders could not be expected? The usual methods of maintaining and restoring order could not be employed.

Helpless and exasperated, governors loyal to Britain inevitably considered appealing for help to General Gage and the British army in North America. Three of them did actually ask him for assistance. One of them, William Franklin of New Jersey, soon withdrew his request; on second thought, he concluded that troops were not so much needed in New Jersey as they were elsewhere. Governors Francis Bernard of Massachusetts and Horatio Sharpe of Maryland urged the general to use his forces. But Gage, a sensible though not a clever man, prudently declined to put the troops in motion on his own authority. He would do what he could against a rebellion, for such was his duty. However, there was no armed uprising. The suppression of rioters was quite another matter. Gage reminded Governors Bernard and Sharpe that under English law a magistrate could employ troops to quell disorder. He would supply the soldiers. He authorized Sharpe to bring a contingent of redcoats from Fort Pitt to Annapolis. Sharpe decided not to use those troops. Bernard was unable to act, for he could not proceed without the consent of his council, which its members, being Americans, refused. The redcoats did not move against the turbulent mobs. In any event, the general could not do much for many months, since his men were few and far distant. Gradually he gathered about 450 soldiers in and near New York City. There he hoped, in the event of open rebellion, to make a show of resistance.

Behaving circumspectly, Gage avoided a clash with the Americans in New York City, and elsewhere. Nor did British warships fire their guns at targets in the colonial harbors. For the time being at least, the Stamp Act was a law only on British paper. A crisis had been created. What would King, Lords, and Commons do about it? The colonists, governors, military officers, and all concerned waited with patient impatience for their decision until the spring of 1766.

CHAPTER VI

Britain Retreats

THERE are those who believe that events make heroes and villains, but that individuals do not make great events. Surely history is not exclusively composed of the shadows of a few figures that tower above a faceless mass of mankind. Even so, it cannot be denied that the presence or absence of a particular person in a special time and place may be of the first importance. Had George Grenville been His Majesty's first minister when the news came across the Atlantic that the Americans defied Parliamentary—and British—authority, warfare would probably have begun between Britain and America a decade earlier than it actually did. For Grenville was convinced that Britain must exert any necessary force to impose her will upon the colonists; and they would surely have taken up arms rather than yield. One may speculate about the outcome and consequences of a struggle beginning in 1766 rather than in 1775. However, for reasons that had nothing to do with America, Grenville was not first lord of the treasury when the surprising news from the New World poured into the imperial capital. He had been replaced by Charles Watson-Wentworth, the young Marquis of Rockingham, a collateral descendant of that Earl of Strafford who had firmly and sternly served King Charles I against Parliament and Puritans and who had gone to the executioner's block for his "thorough" efforts. However, Rockingham, youthful and rich, but modest, was not quite as obsessed by notions of British—or Parliamentary—grandeur as Grenville. Surprisingly, with the help of William Pitt, Benjamin Franklin, and George III, he sought and secured an accommodation with the colonists. Britain rescinded the hated Stamp Act.

Until late in the eighteenth century it was vastly difficult for Europeans to concede that persons born outside Europe were their equals. It was assumed, alike by Englishmen, Frenchmen, and Spaniards, that they alone resided in the center of civilization. People who lived beyond the Mediterranean Sea, people who dwelled on the far side of the Atlantic, even people who inhabited the plains of Poland and Russia, were inferior. They were culturally deficient. Europeans who migrated beyond seas somehow also deteriorated, and their descendants declined still further in quality. Europeans carelessly, even unconsciously, looked down upon natives of the Americas, whether they were of black, brown, or white skin. In the eighteenth century there were even scientists who asserted that European animals were superior to their American counterparts. If an inhabitant of the New World was not rendered soft and slothful by tropical suns, he became heavy and lethargic in consequence of harsh North American winters. The notion, advanced by Jean Jacques Rousseau, that primitive man was noble, did not destroy that widespread belief in the inferiority of the people of the New World—although many Frenchmen in the late 1770's began to look upon the Americans as akin to "noble savages." British aristocrats and intellectuals, together with others who possessed neither lofty social stature nor sophistication, found it difficult to concede that their American brethren were their equals, even fundamentally. Many of the Americans were not of British stock. And those of British descent—were they not the offspring of Puritans, laborers, tenants, and ne'er-do-wells? Were not many of them transported convicts and the children of debased people sent across the ocean from English jails? In the main, the British were not quite so certain as were the French and Spanish of the inferiority of colonists. At least, their colonists were of a better breed than French and Spanish ones. Not very many Englishmen accepted Dr. Samuel Johnson's statement that the Americans were "a race of convicts" as a complete and impartial description. It was not universally assumed in Britain that the departure of convicts for America improved both countries. It is nevertheless true that there were Englishmen, as Benjamin Franklin observed, who placed themselves on the throne beside George III and talked about "our subjects."

Of such was Grenville at the time of the Stamp Act crisis. But in July 1765, George III decided that he wanted Mr. Grenville neither on the throne nor near it. Not that the King was unhappy because that gentleman had aimed so many blows at the Americans. The monarch was as yet not vitally interested in American questions. He was then willing to let his ministers form and execute colonial policy. He would not, however, have a prime minister who failed to display profound respect for the royal person and the royal opinions. Grenville had courage and assurance beyond his talents. He had the reckless complacency of the narrow-minded man of virtue. He did not even pretend to be humble before the monarch, and he bored the King with disquisitions upon public affairs. Besides, when the King was ill, when a council was established to act for him in the event that he was more or less permanently incapacitated, Grenville did not insist that the King's mother be a member of it. George III was offended, for he believed that it was Grenville's duty to assert the rights of the Queen Mother as well as those of the King. While conceding the genius of William Pitt, the monarch was not eager to have that imperious man as prime minister. But why should he put up with Grenville? With the support of Pitt, he dismissed Grenville, giving his place to Rockingham, who formed a ministry that included the prudent old Duke of Newcastle.

Out of power, Grenville was fatuously convinced that time would bring him both "honor and reputation." He continued utterly to reject the "new fangled and desperate doctrines" of the Americans. They claimed that as Englishmen they could not be taxed by Parliament because they were not represented in it. Did they not have spokesmen in that body in exactly the same fashion that most Englishmen did? The number of Englishmen who could then vote for members of the House of Commons was, as noted above, about 215,000; and electoral districts were remarkably unequal in population. Nevertheless, the British people who could not vote had their deputies if for no other reason because the men who sat in the House of Commons acted, not in behalf of those who elected them, but for all Britain. Surely the Americans, like voteless citizens at home, were "virtually" represented in Parliament. The argument was fallacious. Americans pointed out that many members of the House of Commons could and did defend the interests of their districts as well as those of the British nation, and that all Englishmen—or nearly all of them—lived in counties that sent men to the House of Commons, among other things, to levy taxes. American counties did not elect men who could speak at Westminster for the inhabitants of those counties. It was therefore farcical to talk about "virtual" representation so far as the colonists were concerned. They did send deputies from those counties to their own assemblies, and those bodies were, for local purposes, basically the equivalent of Parliament to Englishmen.

Grenville was forced to admit that his reasoning in behalf of "virtual" representation was not convincing. Afterward he and others toyed with the thought of arranging for American members of the House of Commons. It was even suggested that a few Americans should be made British peers. However, neither Grenville nor any other Englishman carried on a campaign to bring Americans into either chamber at West-minster. True, if the colonists had their spokesmen in the House of Commons, they would not be able to contend that taxation by Parliament was unconstitutional. But the scheme posed obvious difficulties. Would Parliament accept American members? How many should there be? And should they be permitted to debate and vote upon issues that were not strictly American? A delegation of Americans might take advantage of political divisions in Britain and create commotion, as the Irish Home Rulers afterward did. Moreover, as the Stamp Act Congress had indicated, the Americans did not wish to send men to the House of Commons. They did not desire to be completely united with the British people under a common legislature. They were moving away, culturally, emotionally, and politically, from the British, and they continued to do so.

Although Grenville relinquished his argument for "virtual" representation, although he played with the notion of actual American representation in Parliament, he never conceded that Parliament could not impose taxes in the absence of American spokesmen in the House of Commons. Instead, he retreated to stronger ground, taking a position that has been described as almost impregnable by some British and American scholars. He urged that Britain and her empire had been governed in the past by the King in Parliament; that the Crown had not been, and could not be, separated from Parliament; that the King in Parliament had possessed complete sovereignty over the colonies; it had not been fully exerted in the past; but it was in no way diminished.

Many British politicians, including King's Friends, gladly accepted Grenville's constitutional theory. They brought forward instances of taxes imposed upon Irishmen, inhabitants of the island of Jersey, and even Englishmen by Parliament without the consent of their direct representatives. The power to tax, they said, could not be separated from the power to govern. All the links of that chain of reasoning were not indestructible. The House of Commons had indeed as a representative body specially asserted its control over taxation. There were precedents enough to support the American position, which appealed to William Pitt—and even to that champion of privilege, James Boswell. John Locke had said, "They must not raise taxes on the property of the people without the consent of the people or their deputies." Moreover, the argument on behalf of Parliamentary power to tax ignored a formidable fact. That power—or the lack of it—could not be established merely upon the basis of the more or less ancient history of the British Isles. Neither Parliament nor the King in Parliament had tried to tax the colonists in North America for revenue during the 157 years between the founding of Jamestown and the passage of the American Act in 1764. Constitutional practice was utterly contrary to the mature Grenville theory. That difficulty had been explained away by Charles Townshend in Parliamentary debate before the enactment of the stamp duties. Britain, said Townshend, had tenderly nourished the colonists when they were weak and poor, had generously refrained from putting burdens upon them. But neither Townshend nor anyone else could produce convincing evidence of the loving kindness of the mother country to the colonies, except for Georgia.

Angry and stubborn—and consistent, except in the finest points of British constitutional law—Grenville steadily called in the last days of 1765 and the early weeks of 1766 for the use of force to put down the American "rebellion." On February 7, 1766, he formally asked the House of Commons to vote for coercion, but his motion was defeated by a handsome majority of 140. Why did the House refuse to follow that true-blue Englishman?

In part, Grenville failed to bend either Parliament or the Americans to his will because he encountered passionate and eloquent resistance offered by William Pitt, still the "Great Commoner," who disliked both Grenville and his policies. Expressing contempt for those whose opinions differed from his, Pitt proclaimed that taxation without representation was indeed unconstitutional. "I rejoice that America has resisted," Pitt fulminated. He was delighted that the colonists had prevented the execution of the Stamp Act. He had few followers in Parliament—haughty, he inspired respect rather than affection. He was, however, the most admired man in Britain. He served as a counterbalance to the aggressive Grenville. He urged swift repeal of the odious stamp duties.

Pitt expressed disdain for the Rockingham ministry as well as contempt for the Grenville people—even though the ministry contained some of his own followers. Nevertheless, he made it possible for Rockingham and Newcastle to seek an accommodation with the colonists, as they desired to do. Those two noblemen did not doubt that Parliament had the power to tax the Americans, but they and their friends had consistently contended that the power, if exercised at all, should not be employed without the substantial consent of the Americans. Faced by a crisis they had not created, the Rockingham people declined to use force against the colonists, and undertook to revoke the stamp duties. The tumults in America persuaded them to send a warship to Annapolis, Maryland, and quietly to add a regiment to General Gage's army, but they would not let the army and navy take the offensive. Instead, Rockingham, well aware that repeal would be bitterly contested, began to mobilize, toward the end of 1765, for a great struggle to secure it. He asked the merchants and manufacturers of London and other English cities for their help, and he obtained it. Britain had not yet recovered from the recession that followed the Seven Years' War; English businessmen were in distress because American orders for goods had diminished, and also because Americans had put off payment of their debts; and there were English mercantile men and industrialists who disliked the stamp duties on principle. Responding to Rockingham's appeal, they massively petitioned for the erasure of the duties. Rockingham was thus enabled to say that he sought repeal, not principally to placate the Americans but to foster the prosperity of Britain.

In February 1766, the Rockingham ministry was ready to move. Presenting much evidence about the crisis, it urged Parliament to pass a Declaratory Act and to cancel the stamp duties. The Declaratory Act was carefully drawn so as to soften those who wished to maintain the duties —and at the same time to satisfy Pitt. It proclaimed that Kings, Lords, and Commons "hath and of right ought to have, full power and authority to make laws and statutes of sufficient force and validity to bind the colonies and people of America, subjects of the crown of Great Britain, in all cases whatsoever." The Duke of Newcastle believed that it was not wise to make any statement about the powers of Parliament. Rockingham considered that it was necessary in order to secure repeal of the stamp duties. Pitt clumsily and vainly made an effort to amend the wording of the act so as specifically to recognize American freedom from British taxation. The Declaratory Act was endorsed by large majorities in both houses of Parliament, with the understanding that it proclaimed the powers of the legislature to be as ample over America as they were in Britain. Even so, Grenville and those who agreed with him were not at all satisfied. It remained doubtful during long evenings of debate at Westminster that the stamp duties would be withdrawn. Many of the King's Friends agreed with Grenville. Some of them privately sought advice from their royal master. The King hesitated. Was it not possible to make some compromise with the Americans? Informed that the King was wavering, Rockingham sought an audience with him and demanded that the monarch support his ministers. The King then told his personal followers that they could follow their consciences, if they had not been given office by the ministry. Those holding offices under it must be loyal to it. As for himself, the King would stand with Rockingham. His behavior puzzled the confused and swaying members of Parliament. Did the monarch really desire repeal? About fifty men who were under special obligation to him and who looked to him for leadership declared themselves, in the end, against repeal. The King did not help Parliament to reach a decision.

Neither did Charles Townshend. Speaking in the House of Commons, he offered argument both for maintaining and for rescinding the Stamp Act. He probably voted for repeal.

Ultimately, Rockingham was victorious. His cause gained strength because of a misunderstanding of American sentiment, a mistake that was nourished by Benjamin Franklin. Reports from America did not make it clear that the colonists believed that import and export taxes imposed by Parliament for revenues and collected in their harbors to be unconstitutional. If they were willing to accept such taxation, why, they were not utterly unreasonable, after all. Moreover, remarks made by Pitt in disorderly debate were interpreted to mean that he too distinguished between internal and external levies to secure revenue. And Franklin, appearing as a witness at the bar of the House of Commons, put on a remarkable performance in behalf of repeal. In order to put the Americans in the best possible light, he prepared suitable questions and arranged to have friends in the Commons ask them. Then he gave suitable answers. Besides, when asked by hostile members whether the Americans objected constitutionally to external taxes for revenue, he indicated that they did not. Did he misjudge American sentiment? More likely, he was so eager to resolve the crisis, so anxious, that he defined American views to please himself and his listeners. It was all important to get repeal of the stamp duties. The House of Commons, after a long meeting, reached its decision at two o'clock in the morning of February 22, the birthday of George Washington. By a vote of 275 to 167 it gave its consent to repeal.

The bitter struggle was then virtually ended, although the House of Lords had not yet acted. If there was anything resembling a representative body in Britain, it was that of the Commons. Even at that time, the peers did not lightly challenge its will. Nevertheless, before and after the House of Commons voted, many noblemen strenuously and bitterly defended the stamp duties and the power of Parliament to impose them. Lord Camden, Chief Justice of the Court of Common Pleas and an adherent of Pitt, cogently expressed the sentiments of his leader. Very few peers found his argument acceptable. The Lords, in the main, liked an analysis of the British constitution offered by Lord Mansfield, Chief Justice of the King's Bench. That jurist, born William Murray in Scotland, had won acclaim as a scholar at Oxford and had gone on to London to seek his fortune at the bar. He had succeeded remarkably, partly because he was intelligent and studious, partly because he was one of that detestable breed of men who are polite to the powerful and who deal harshly with the weak. He was also one of the most hated and despised men in England. He was as skillful as any lawyer in the nation in finding those precedents, however remote, that justified authority against liberty, privilege against justice. He was no less a royalist than George III himself. Mansfield not only pronounced "that the British legislature, as to the power of making laws, represents the whole British Empire, and has authority to bind every part and every subject without the least distinction," but also "that the colonists, by the conditions on which they migrated, settled, and now exist, are more emphatically subjects of Great Britain than those within the realm." And, continued that legal luminary, "when the supreme power abdicates, the government is dissolved." According to this curiously expressed chain of reasoning, the more certain it was that a man was a British subject, the fewer were his rights. Mansfield would have it that the authority of Parliament was even greater in America than it was in Britain, and that it must be asserted. Lord Temple vehemently aligned himself with George Grenville, his brother, and Mansfield. He and several other peers proclaimed that the authority of Parliament, if not firmly supported in America, must become "contemptible." Temple said that the stamp duties would take only one shilling per annum from each colonist. He did not point out that the duties would fall unequally upon the Americans, nor that such a contribution by every colonist would save every Englishman only threepence per annum. On the decisive vote concerning repeal the Rockingham ministry was able, however, to get a majority of 34.

On March 18 the King solemnly signed both the bill repealing the stamp duties and the Declaratory Act. If many lords sullenly accepted defeat, merchants, workmen, and sailors in London celebrated victory. They hoped for better times; and there were many among them who believed that the cause of English liberty had triumphed. It was not commonly observed that the Americans had gained only a qualified victory.

For the Rockingham ministry, seeking to avoid an ultimate clash with the colonists, was nevertheless determined to give the Americans no more than they absolutely demanded. They had not unequivocally denounced the constitutionality of the threepence per gallon duty imposed upon foreign molasses by the American Act—and had not those colonies most interested in commerce with the West Indies indicated that they would not object to a penny per gallon duty? The ministry saw the gap in the American defenses against Parliamentary taxation, and plunged into it. Presumably the Americans would not like, but would not rebel against, a low duty upon molasses, even one collected for the purpose of securing money. Accordingly, in the Revenue Act of 1766, passed in May without a struggle by Parliament at the behest of the Rockingham ministry, the tax upon molasses was placed at a penny per gallon, but was applied to all molasses imported by the Americans, whether from British or foreign

West Indian islands. That measure had been urged by a committee of London merchants who carried on trade with North America. Did those men of business realize that the tax, since it did not discriminate between British and foreign molasses, bore a very strong resemblance to one intended to get money from the colonists? Certainly the politicians of Westminster must have understood that the new duty looked very much like a tax for revenue. Britain had not positively abandoned power to tax the colonists either in theory or in minor practice. And even Pitt and his followers failed to denounce the new duty on principle.

Many members of Parliament went home in a bad mood when it was dismissed in the late spring of 1766. Those who wished to reduce the Americans to complete obedience even vainly asked that Parliament remain in session indefinitely, so that it could move swiftly if the colonists strenuously objected even to the weak-kneed, too-lenient measures taken by the Rockingham people. They were embittered and truculent. And would the middle-of-the-road Rockingham policy satisfy the Americans?

The news that the Stamp Act had been repealed put an end to the crisis in America. It was received everywhere in the Thirteen Colonies with great joy. Laborers, seamen, and artisans celebrated by drinking barrels of beer; planters and merchants consumed wine and toasted William Pitt and George III at great banquets; and clergymen offered prayers of thanksgiving. Newspapers happily trumpeted the triumph of the colonists. Merchants hastily ordered British goods, and it may even be that some American debtors quickly undertook to pay their British creditors. There was a general relaxation of tension. Colonists, royal officials, and British military officers breathed easier. Many Americans were eager to "let bygones be bygones," and to avoid new troubles. Men of wealth and high social standing, remembering the riots of 1765 and alarmed lest laborers and mechanics push hard against their betters, were especially anxious to avoid further commotion. Many merchants of New England paid the penny per gallon tax upon molasses without complaint—indeed, the Americans generally did not make a constitutional protest against that duty. It was collected, not without grumbling on the part of those who had to pay it, until the outbreak of the War of Independence.

It would be wrong, however, to conclude that the colonists were truly satisfied. They sent formal messages of thanks for the repeal of the Stamp Act to the King, and a statue of George III was erected in New York City in his honor. But no likeness of Rockingham made its appearance anywhere in America. The House of Burgesses voted to raise a statue of the monarch; it neglected to supply the necessary funds. The Commons House of South Carolina arranged to erect the figure in marble of William Pitt in testimony of its "great veneration and respect" for that person; but a motion to put up a replica of the King did not receive even a second. The "Great Commoner" was acclaimed everywhere—without full understanding of the position taken by that remarkable man—as the mighty champion of both American and British freedom. There was some suspicion in the colonies that George III was a champion of neither British nor American liberty.

The colonists raised no great uproar over the Declaratory Act, which, after all, did not specifically deny the validity of their argument against taxation without representation. Moreover, it was merely a statement of constitutional principle; it neither took nor immediately threatened to take their money without their consent. In the main, they ignored it. But, not pursuing their arguments against Parliamentary taxation to their logical conclusion, they made it clear enough that they did not intend to accept any new and substantial tax for revenue. The House of Representatives of Massachusetts and the House of Burgesses—Massachusetts and Virginia were steadily in the forefront in the defense of American freedom both before and during the War of Independence—did not fail to warn Britain against further efforts to tamper with American liberties. In Massachusetts the lower house balked when it received a "requisition," in accordance with an act of Parliament, from Governor Francis Bernard for money to compensate those whose property had been damaged in the riots of 1765. That house, reluctantly arranging to supply the funds, insisted that the governor could ask but could not demand that the house vote money. In Virginia, because Lieutenant Governor Francis Fauquier did not call it into session until the autumn of 1766, the Burgesses were unable for many months to speak for the Old Dominion. A polished and amiable gentleman, Fauquier hoped that the passage of time would cool tempers in Virginia, and that the Burgesses would dutifully declare their obedience and gratitude to the mother country that had kindly and affectionately redressed all their grievances. Instead, the house responded to Fauquier's plea in firm, even militant language. Its members were grateful to "the best of kings" because he had graciously assented to the repeal of the Stamp Act; they expressed a wish that "no future accident" should ever "interrupt" the union between Britain and the colonies; "we hope," they said, that Parliament acted in the spirit of "fellow subjects"; and they hinted that the Virginians would, if necessary, take up arms for the "preservation of their rights and liberties." Fauquier was shocked. He sent the defiant pronunciamento of the Virginians on to London. They had served notice as plainly as might be that it would be unwise to trifle with them.

There was other evidence that the Americans were less than utterly satisfied. In Massachusetts James Otis sought to establish the control of the House of Representatives over the upper house of that colony. He was successful. In New England generally there was unusually strenuous opposition to customs officers. Ships seized by them for violation of the Navigation Acts were recaptured by sailors and workmen.

Most of the Americans undoubtedly wished to find evidence that the campaign opened against them by the Bute and Grenville ministries had been permanently abandoned. They wanted an end to tumult and trouble. But they were not permitted to relax. Suddenly, almost unbelievably, the mother country again undertook both to tax and to coerce her mature and lusty offspring. Charles Townshend came forward through the confusion of British politics to resume the untoward labors of Grenville and to provoke a second crisis between Britain and America while the wounds of the first one were still unhealed.

CHAPTER VII

The Second Challenge from Britain

WILLIAM Pitt was not such a good friend of the Americans as they believed him to be. Nor was he, as a champion of liberty, a dauntless and inveterate enemy of George III. He was no republican, no reformer eager for political and social revolution, either in America or Britain. He had immense confidence in himself; he was impatient with lesser men; he retained great respect for the British throne; when in the mood, he could even play the part of a servile courtier before George III. In the summer of 1766 the two men became political allies. Neither of them held a high opinion of Rockingham; both of them believed that Britain ought to have a "broad-bottom" ministry that could command wide support from British politicians. Accordingly, the King dismissed Rockingham, and Pitt framed a "ministry of all the talents." The young Duke of Grafton was placed at its head. There was no truly gifted man in it, except for Pitt himself. Included in it were followers of Pitt, adherents of the King, a lieutenant of Rockingham, and Charles Townshend. Pitt gave it little guidance from its beginning, and at length withdrew entirely from it. Townshend, Chancellor of the Exchequer, came to the fore. Daring the colonists to resist, he pushed through Parliament new taxes that disturbed them profoundly; he undertook to buttress the authority of British civil officers in America; and he goaded the Americans into a second revolt. Having done almost as much mischief as a man might, he died. However, the King's Friends in that hybrid ministry—with help from Bedfordites who joined it—pursued Townshend's repressive policy. Yielding to the temptation to use the army and the navy to impose their will upon the colonists, they further exasperated the Americans. The "ministry of all the talents" created a second colonial crisis.

Collecting men for that ministry, Pitt ignored political principle as well as past political affiliation. It is apparent that he did not think it important to select persons who saw England and America as he did. Early in 1766—at the very time when Lord Temple was most strenuously struggling against the repeal of the stamp duties—Pitt, trying to form a new ministry, had proposed that Temple take a post in it. When Pitt assembled "all the talents," he did not exclude men because they did not agree with him about America. Nor did he try to secure the services of the ablest Englishmen. He was of such a temperament that he could not accept other men as his equals. He intended personally to supply all the genius needed to manage Britain and her empire; his colleagues would be his satellites, shining from the light he threw upon them. He would not even accept the office of prime minister—of first lord of the treasury. Instead, he accepted a peerage as Earl of Chatham, abandoning his seat in the House of Commons and taking an appointment in his ministry as lord privy seal, one that had no specific duties. Above the trifles of politics, he would be the guiding elder statesman. As a step toward maintaining his own authority, he did take the precaution of placing two of his younger followers in key governmental posts, making the Duke of Grafton prime minister and the Earl of Shelburne Secretary of State for the Southern Department. Shelburne thus became immediately responsible for colonial policy. But Chatham—as Pitt must now be called—also brought into office the unpredictable and unscrupulous Charles Townshend as Chancellor of the Exchequer, who would have something to do with American affairs. Did Chatham believe that he could control Townshend? The latter had already become a force in the House of Commons. It turned out that no one could restrain Townshend.

That Chatham, like Pitt, did not see eye to eye with the Americans soon became evident. It also became clear that Shelburne was not an unqualified friend to the colonists. In the weird world of British politics in the early years of the reign of George III he had been a "liberal" disciple of the Earl of Bute, and had then forsaken Bute for Pitt. Neither he nor Chatham displayed a liberal and broad understanding when they were confronted by a delicate and awkward question that had arisen in the colony of New York. Shelburne, a young Irish nobleman, has been attributed by at least one American historian a genius and vision that he did not possess. He was a collector of documents rather than a man of penetrating intellect, and could not make up for the deficiencies of Chatham. It is true that he tried to get information about America and that he sought to penetrate into American thinking, but without remarkable success.

The Mutiny Act of 1765 was ill received in New York, for the burdens of quartering and supplying troops it placed upon the Americans were heavier in that province than they were elsewhere. Because the headquarters of the British army in North America were in New York City after 1763—its supply depot was on Governor's Island—some troops were almost constantly present in the city and also at Albany, which was a way station between headquarters and garrisons in the St. Lawrence Valley and the region of the Great Lakes. During the Seven Years' War the province welcomed the redcoats as they went forward to fight against the French and hostile Indians. So long as that conflict endured, the New York assembly readily, if not joyously, furnished barracks for the soldiers, and officers were given private quarters. But the revised Mutiny Act raised a constitutional issue. The legislature had hitherto complied with requisitions; it had not been forced to do so by Parliamentary law. Now Parliament was attempting to compel it to build or maintain barracks, and also to supply foodstuffs, beverages, fuel, and candles for the troops. New Yorkers concluded that Parliament was trying to take money for those purposes from their pockets without their consent. They contended that only their own legislature had the power to decide whether or not they should be taxed for those purposes. When compliance with the new Mutiny Act was demanded from that legislature in 1765 and again in 1766, it rebelled. The lower house of New York, fearing that large sums of money might be needed, was reluctant to vote funds, and it refused to act under Parliamentary duress. It would consider requests for money; it would not promise to honor every request.

The outcry from New York against taxation forced by Parliament exasperated Chatham and Shelburne, along with Charles Townshend. Feeling against the contumacious New Yorkers rose the higher in London because scores of merchants of New York City simultaneously petitioned for removal of restrictions upon their maritime trade, including the penny per gallon duty upon molasses of 1766. Chatham and all his colleagues, except for General Henry Seymour Conway, a Rockingham man, resentfully concluded that New York must be taught a lesson. Not grateful for the repeal of the stamp duties, that province was behaving outrageously. Was it true, as General Gage had written in a "private" letter to Viscount Barrington, the Secretary at War, that "the colonists are taking large strides toward independency; and that it concerns Great Britain by a speedy and spirited conduct to shew them that these provinces are British colonies dependent on her, and that they are not independent states"? Had the Americans in general, and the New Yorkers in particular, gone mad? The rich merchant William Beckford, an ardent supporter of Chatham, urged him to do nothing rash, to "recall your troops from the old provinces in America, where they are not wanted, and the cause of anger, hatred, and malice is removed." Instead, after a formal meeting of the cabinet, the men of "all the talents" asked Parliament in May 1767 to forbid any other action whatever by the New York legislature until such time as it should comply with the Mutiny Act. That harsh measure was opposed in the House of Commons, but chiefly because it was not sufficiently severe. George Grenville desired to add a requirement that every member of every American legislative body be compelled to pronounce his allegiance to the principle of Parliamentary supremacy enunciated in the Declaratory Act. The restraining law was passed in the late spring of 1767.

In that same spring of 1767 the New York assembly voted £3,000 for the purposes described in the Mutiny Act. There was therefore no need to enforce the restraining law. No serious trouble arose from it in America after 1767, although the quartering provisions remained in the Mutiny Acts until the War of Independence. The assemblies of New York and of several other colonies voted money without sharp protest. However, neither the legislature of New York nor any other American legislature ever admitted that it was constrained by the Mutiny Act. Once and again the lawmakers of New York declared that they were merely making generous responses to requests submitted by the governor of the province. They continued to assert their right to vote or not to vote money for the benefit of the British army.

If Chatham was much less than an absolute champion of the Americans, Charles Townshend was their enemy. At first Townshend was not even a member of the cabinet. He successfully insisted that he be admitted to it and soon became a great power. Chatham fell gravely ill. He discovered anew that Townshend was unreliable. He thought that Townshend ought to be forced out of office, but he was too infirm to act. Townshend plunged into a political vacuum created by the enforced absence of Chatham from the helm of government. Taking advantage of rising hostility in Parliament toward the Americans in the early months of 1767, he used all his talents to drive the colonists into revolt.

What was wrong with Chatham? It was gout, that agonizing disorder that afflicted so many English gentlemen in the eighteenth century, a vexing illness from which Americans, including Benjamin Franklin, were not exempt. The malady has given rise to much humor, but it was, and is, painful and enfeebling to those who suffer from it. In the eighteenth century it chiefly struck men of means, those who could afford a diet rich in proteins. It may be that the courses of British and American history were altered because that ailment—aggravated by the consumption of too much wine—reduced Chatham for many months to chronic invalidism and occasional hysteria. Gout has an affinity for gifted and sensitive men. It frequently drove Chatham to distraction. It also drove him from London to Bath toward the end of 1766. There he "took the waters." He remained away from the imperial capital for many weeks but never fully regained his health. At Bath he would not, at times could not, give attention to public affairs.

The Duke of Grafton, had he been a man of parts, might have filled the gap created by Chatham's illness. But Grafton was not fitted for high office. His most laudable quality was his modesty. Only thirty years of age, he had been pushed into office as prime minister against his will by Chatham, though he had quite correctly contended that he was unequal to that august appointment. A descendant of King Charles II, he was, like that monarch, no paragon of sexual virtue. He had won a certain renown as a rake, and as the lover of the beautiful and notorious Fanny Parsons, a demi-mondaine who graced London for some years. Intending to do well—at least in public affairs—Grafton nevertheless lacked ability, experience, and force. Nor was Shelburne able to take up the reins. Shelburne was accustomed to play his own game; he was not open and frank; he did not have the trust of his colleagues; he did not have the complete confidence of Chatham. The way opened for Townshend, who had abilities, of a sort; who did not lack assurance; and who was nearly as bold as Chatham himself.

The British aristocracy produced some extraordinary men in the eighteenth century, but none more remarkable than Charles Townshend. Ten years older than Grafton, he had long been a man of mark in British public life. There were those who believed that he was the equal of the towering Chatham. He was much admired as a speaker in the House of Commons. He was a tall, heavy man with a loud voice, a modicum of wit, a gift for mimicry, and a penchant for abusing all and sundry, whether friend or foe. He was famous for his effrontery. In an age when British politicians were constantly inconstant, he shifted his allegiances so swiftly that he was noted for his fickleness. Behind a façade of health and vigor, he was both physically feeble and psychopathic. He was also financially dishonest, in a time when it was not easy for a man in British public life to be worse than an "honest grafter." Moving from an appointment as paymaster of the British army to that of Chancellor of the Exchequer, he accepted a reduction in salary. However, following the careless British custom of that time, he retained unexpended army funds, investing them and pocketing the income from the investments. Doing so, he committed no crime in an age when British public moneys easily and almost casually found their way into the private accounts of privileged persons. But Townshend also used public funds to buy stock in the East India Company, exerted his influence as Chancellor of the Exchequer to enhance the value of his shares, and then disposed of them at a profit, perhaps as much as £7,000 in all.

That strange, unscrupulous, and irresponsible man was entrusted with the task of preparing the British budget. It seems that he voted to rescind the stamp duties; if he did so, it was with great reluctance. Was there not some way to move part of the burden of taxes borne by British taxpayers so that it would fall upon the prosperous Americans? Were they not paying a duty for revenue upon molasses? Could not more money be secured by imposing more duties for revenue upon other goods as they entered American harbors? Had not Benjamin Franklin and other Americans, separating external from internal duties, admitted that Parliament could constitutionally impose import and export duties for revenue? And had not Chatham himself taken that position? Townshend answered all those questions in the affirmative. With impudent and contemptuous disregard for the opinions and wishes of his colleagues, he embarked upon a campaign to bring the Americans to heel.

As early as January 1767, if not before, Townshend was meditating the imposition of taxes upon tea and other goods entering the American ports, and also the formation of a Board of Customs in America to make sure that those taxes and all other earlier external duties levied by Parliament were collected. Thus he was preparing to assume the role formerly played by George Grenville. On January 26, 1767, in the House of Commons, Grenville, doggedly insisting that Britain ought never to have yielded to colonial resistance, urged that the expenses of the army in America be cut in half, and that they be paid by the inhabitants of the Thirteen Colonies. Moving the adoption of those proposals, offensive in both form and content to most members of the Grafton ministry, Grenville encountered overwhelming defeat. However, in the course of debate, Townshend made a remarkable speech in which he ridiculed Chatham, declared that he agreed with Grenville in principle, and promised that he would offer a method to get money from the Americans. Shortly afterward, censured in the cabinet for his insolence and his disloyalty to his colleagues, Townshend outrageously defended himself by saying that he had merely expressed the true will of Parliament. Shocked, Shelburne wrote to Chatham at Bath, informing him of Townshend's extraordinary behavior and intentions. That sick gentleman—was he utterly against Townshend and Grenville?—did not protest.

Then Townshend took wing. Privately, with the help of two cronies of questionable character—one of them, John Huske, having embezzled public money, later fled to the Continent to escape punishment—he developed his scheme for American import duties. Publicly, he consorted with Grenville. For several weeks the House of Commons, chiefly because of loyalty to the ministry, continued to vote against motions by Grenville that called for taxation of the colonists for the support of the army in America. Sentiment in Parliament was doubtless with Grenville. In any event, taking encouragement and ideas from Grenville, Townshend did what Grenville could not do. On March 12, at a meeting of the cabinet, he delivered an ultimatum. To reduce expenses, the army in America must be concentrated on the Atlantic seaboard; and the cost of maintaining it must be borne by the Americans. If the cabinet refused its consent to those propositions, he would resign. Dismayed, Shelburne and Grafton appealed to Chatham, but he would not, perhaps could not, interfere. The cabinet weakly submitted to Townshend, giving him permission to speak for it upon all American questions.

Townshend drove on. Exploiting his triumph, he assured the House of Commons early in April that he was preparing a plan for taxing the Americans that "might in time ease this country of a considerable burden." On May 8 he amazed and delighted that body with an oration that has often been called his "champagne speech." He was apparently not drunk with wine, but with power. With wit and mimicry he stabbed at Grafton, Shelburne, and others; he expressed his contempt for those youthful politicians; he and other men of "rank, ability, and integrity, and experience" must take the lead in restoring the majesty of Britain; if a report of his speech is correct, he even delivered a stroke against George III, saying that the prime minister ought to be responsible to the House of Commons rather than to the monarch. He was wildly applauded. A few days later Townshend began to put his American measures before Parliament. He was not yet able to offer a plan for the disposition of the army in America. He did, however, propose that duties be levied upon tea, paints, paper, lead, and other items imported by the colonists. He made it clear beyond doubt that he sought to buttress British authority in America as well as to secure contributions from the Americans toward meeting the expenses of the army. He declared that the proceeds from the new duties would be devoted, first, to paying the salaries of certain royal governors and other royal officials who had hitherto been dependent upon colonial assemblies for their pay; second, to support, in part, the troops. Since the proceeds would hardly be more than £40,000 per annum, it is apparent that much of the money was to be used to assert British sovereignty rather than to relieve the British taxpayers of an intolerable burden. Further, he asked that a Board of Customs Commissioners be established in America. That board was to see to it that the new duties, together with others already upon the statute books, were paid. His proposals were received with pleasure by Parliament. So few men opposed them that it would have been idle to ask for votes upon them. They became British law in the early summer of 1767.

It cannot be gainsaid that the capricious, reckless, and willful Townshend, standing forth for the cause of Old England, appealed successfully to more than politicians who repented the repeal of the Stamp Act. The City of London, doubtless quite unaware that his measures would shake the empire as had the stamp duties, gave him a formal vote of thanks for his services to the British state. Such as they were, they were almost ended. Late in that summer he fell into a fever, and he died before the results of his folly became only too evident.

But the spirit of the headlong and heedless Townshend lived on long enough to permit the adoption of two basic parts of his American scheme that he left unfinished. He had been planning to establish new admiralty courts in America to supplement the unpopular one created by the Grenville ministry at Halifax. The tribunal at Halifax had injured the colonists in theory rather than in practice, for it did little business. In 1768 the Grafton ministry set up three similar courts, at Boston, Philadelphia, and Charleston. Many American merchants were forced to appear in the new courts, which rigidly enforced the Navigation Acts. The Americans had good reason thereafter to protest against trial without jury, before judges who were determined to enforce the Navigation Acts to the last oppressive comma. In the spring of 1768 the cabinet also issued momentous orders for the concentration of the army in America along the Atlantic seaboard that had been demanded by Grenville and Townshend.

Two King's Friends who entered the Grafton ministry helped to make the decision regarding the army. One of those men was Frederick, Lord North, a friendly and likable gentleman of thirty-five who was to hold office under George III for fifteen disastrous years. He succeeded Townshend at the exchequer. Eldest son and heir of the rich Earl of Guilford, North was sent to Eton, and thence, like so many of the British politicians who appear in these pages, to Oxford. At Oxford he was a respectable scholar. There he acquired a useful smattering of Latin, but no information about Britain's American empire—American history would be completely ignored at Oxford until the twentieth century was well under way. Leaving the university and going on the Grand Tour of Europe as befitted a nobleman's son, North studied German and law on the Continent—but, again, nothing American. His private life was blameless, like that of George III, to whom he bore a striking physical resemblance. Like the King, he was tall, heavy, big-nosed, and pop-eyed. (Not surprisingly, in that age of scandalous conduct by monarchs and nobles, it was suggested by enemies of the two men that they had a common father, and that North's quite respectable mother was not so good as she should have been.) Endowed with a constantly sweet temper, gifted with a gracious sense of humor that appealed alike to sophisticated men and to plain country gentlemen, North was a most popular member of the House of Commons. He was not a brilliant debater. His tongue was too big for his mouth, and his speech was blurred. However, he was usually sensible. He was a devout Christian, and he was nearly as honest about public money as an aristocrat might be in his time. As he grew older, he often snoozed during debates in the House of Commons, thus amusing and annoying his political enemies. But he was industrious nevertheless, and intelligent as well. He had a defect, however, that ruined a most promising career. He was weak of will, and he was often to yield to dominating and less capable men, including George III. Because North had a large family, because his affluent father would give him little money, North needed the salary he drew as Chancellor of the Exchequer to maintain himself, his wife, and his children in modest luxury. The condition of his private finances, together with his lack of assurance, help to explain his notorious subservience to George III, the font of offices and favors. North obtained several appointments from the King for his own relatives. And finally, during the War of Independence, the monarch gave him £20,000 for services rendered. North had voted against cancellation of the stamp duties. Unlike Grenville and Townshend, he bore no enmity against the Americans. He hated neither Englishman nor colonist, yet he could never quite understand the Americans.

The name of Wills Hill, Earl of Hillsborough, is not blazoned upon historical pages like that of Lord North. No one has written a biography of that young Irish nobleman. Even so, the entrance of Hillsborough into the Grafton ministry was a most important event, because it portended the execution of the Grenville-Townshend plan for moving the redcoats from the interior of America toward the Atlantic seaboard. For, in January 1768, Hillsborough was given a newly created office, that of Secretary of State for the Colonies, being entrusted with American affairs that had been under the hand of the Earl of Shelburne. The latter had not been eager to move the army from the forts in the American hinterland. In fact, Shelburne had favored the occupation of the interior by settlers rather than withdrawal from it; he had proposed that three new colonies be founded in the valley of the Mississippi; and he had entertained a vain hope that the Crown might gain revenue by collecting quit rents upon lands sold in those colonies, rather than from taxes levied upon the Americans. But Shelburne was deprived of authority over America. The Duke of Grafton disliked him intensely and would not support him. A courteous and undistinguished gentleman, Hillsborough was disposed to exert British authority, and he followed in the wake of Grenville and Townshend. With him came into office two Bedfordites who saw America as he did. Disgusted, Shelburne resigned from the cabinet not long afterward, and Chatham also soon formally retired from office. Their departures were preceded by that of the Rockingham man, General Henry Seymour Conway, who resigned at the time when Hillsborough was appointed. Grafton's reconstituted ministry would not have been too distasteful to Charles Townshend, so far as America was concerned.

With Hillsborough in direct charge of American business, the Grafton cabinet swiftly moved to relocate the army in America and to devise arrangements for the territories beyond the Appalachians consistent with withdrawal of the troops from those regions. It would have been prudent at least to delay action, for ships entering English ports from America were bringing in disturbing reports. It was evident that the colonists were deeply offended by the Townshend Acts. It was likely that they would again resist British authority. However, the disquieting news from America actually induced the cabinet to proceed rather than to defer its decision. If the colonists were in a rebellious mood, the presence of troops in their midst would remind them of their duty to Britain. In April 1768, the cabinet announced its intentions. A new boundary line running to the westward of the Appalachians was to be established between the colonists and the Indians. The Americans were to be permitted to settle beyond the mountains, but most of the lands beyond the divide were to be reserved for the red men. To save money, the burden of regulating the Indian traders was returned to the several colonies. Almost all of the posts in the American interior were to be abandoned. Three regiments of redcoats were to be permanently stationed in the Middle Colonies—in New York, New Jersey, and Pennsylvania. Other important detachments were to be placed at Halifax and at St. Augustine in Florida, from which locations they could speedily be carried into the Thirteen Colonies. These arrangements, Hillsborough informed General Gage, would enable the army "to serve effectually upon any emergency whatever." Did it occur to His Majesty's confidential adviser that removal from the forts in the interior deprived the colonists of at least part of the protection against the Indians for which Britain was trying to force them to pay? The phrase "any emergency whatever" undoubtedly included the contingency of American revolt. Certainly, the concentration of the army on the seacoast was not necessary for defense against the French or Spanish. So placed, it would be able to move more rapidly against French and Spanish possessions in the Caribbean Sea. Whatever its reasoning, the cabinet erred. To demand that the colonists support the army and to post substantial detachments of it among them—the cabinet was stimulating revolt. Less than two months later it ordered two regiments to Boston to protect the King's servants in that city.

Pushing his program through the House of Commons, Townshend had publicly dared the Americans to resist. They accepted his challenge.

CHAPTER VIII

The Townshend Crisis

IF the Rockingham ministry grudgingly conceded no more to the American colonists than was necessary to placate them, it was nevertheless possible for them wistfully to believe that Britain, having thoughtlessly embarked upon a tyrannical course, had repented; that the American policy of Bute and Grenville was an aberration; and that "the good old days" of bickering good will between Britain and America would sooner or later reappear. The memory of economic distress exacerbated by the Stamp Act crisis lingered; also of its riots. Merchants and other men of substance and high social standing, fearing "leveling," were disposed to avoid future contest with Britain. Nevertheless, after the fateful year 1765, there was a body of Americans that suspiciously examined every British measure affecting the colonies. They saw in the program of Townshend and Grenville the same design for oppression that they had discerned in that of Bute and Grenville. The Stamp Act, they concluded, was not an accidental and unfortunate deviation. The Rockingham people had arranged to rescind the stamp duties because they had felt compelled to do so. It was the true intent of those who dominated Britain, not only to take money from the Americans without their consent, but to buttress and even to increase British dominion in America.

Not that the Townshend duties created among the Americans the almost universal anger they had exhibited two years earlier. In many American minds they were momentarily confused, like the molasses duty of 1766, with British taxes used to channel the maritime commerce of the colonists. Even that ardent defender of American rights, Richard Henry Lee of Virginia, did not immediately perceive that the new levies were in no way constitutionally different from the stamp duties. Moreover, the new taxes could be evaded by refusal to buy the goods upon which they were imposed. The Americans could not quite stifle their desire for tea, a beverage almost as popular among them as coffee at that time. However, they could easily get their tea leaves without paying duty upon them, for Dutch teas could be smuggled into American harbors. Returning prosperity among the Americans also contributed to their reluctance to engage the mother country. Merchants were especially disinclined to embark upon a sea of troubles.

Nevertheless, clamor began among the Americans against British tyranny, and it increased. John Dickinson of Pennsylvania satisfactorily explained to them why they must resist. A wealthy lawyer and gentleman farmer, he was an honest, dignified, and trusted man. In a series of *Letters of a Farmer in Pennsylvania* widely published in the American newspapers, Dickinson logically extended the constitutional argument against the stamp duties to cover the Townshend taxes. There were, said he, three kinds of taxes—internal ones for revenue, such as the stamp duties; external duties for revenue, such as the Townshend taxes; and external levies used as instruments to control commerce. The constitutionality of a tax depended upon its purpose. Import duties for revenue, like the stamp duties, violated the principle of "no taxation without representation." The external levies imposed to restrict commerce were often onerous; they were not unconstitutional.

Condemning the Townshend duties because they violated the rights of Englishmen, Dickinson also pointed out that the proceeds from them would be used only in part to defray the costs of defense in North America. Indeed, all of the money might be used to pay the salaries of royal governors, judges, secretaries, and other officials in the colonies. It was therefore obvious, said the Pennsylvania farmer, that the primary purpose of Britain was to strengthen her hold upon America, not to compel the Americans to assume their fair share of the burdens of empire. If those officials were paid with money derived from the new duties, they would not be dependent upon colonial assemblies for their salaries, as they had been in the past. Many of them had been constrained to yield to assemblies because of their desire for their pay. Assured of it, they would more vigorously defend the authority of Britain. Hence, the established system of government in several of the royal provinces would be subverted. Dickinson voiced no pity for royal officeholders who had had to bargain with the colonists for their salaries. Nor did he express fondness for Townshend's Board of Customs Commissioners, which began its labors at Boston in November 1767.

It should be observed that Dickinson, appealing to the constitutional rights of Englishmen, extended the American argument against taxation by Parliament just far enough to cover the Townshend duties. He was no rabblerouser; he was a sensible, cautious, and legal-minded man. He admitted the right of Parliament to put limits upon American commerce and manufacturing. Even so, his writings were accepted by most Americans as constitutional Gospel, and as a sufficient statement of American liberties within the British empire. With Dickinson they demanded the repeal of the Townshend duties.

There were defects in the argument advanced by Dickinson. According to his reasoning, the sixpence per gallon duty levied by the Molasses Act of 1733, because it was intended to prevent importation into America, was constitutional; however, the one penny duty of 1766, designed for revenue, violated the rights of Englishmen. That amusing discrepancy was not a serious defect in his reasoning. But Dickinson's argument was fundamentally faulty in that he carried it just far enough to demonstrate that the Townshend Acts were unconstitutional, in that he conceded to Parliament power to stifle American commerce and manufacturing. Relying heavily upon law and custom, he did not build an impregnable fortress against British oppression. Perhaps he was not aware that Britain was embarking upon a campaign to enforce the Navigation Acts in all their rigor and to collect every penny of duty levied by Parliament.

Accepting the Dickinsonian argument as sufficient for the principal evil of the day, the Townshend duties, the majority of the colonists not only demanded that the taxes be rescinded, but found ways and means to exert pressure upon Britain to achieve their purpose. Their chief weapon was a boycott—the word had not yet been coined—of British goods, together with efforts to stimulate American manufacturing. Gradually, during the years 1768 and 1769, the colonists established committees from the district of Maine to Georgia that enforced the boycott. So-called "non-importation agreements" became the orders of the day, and they were zealously executed by forthright defenders of American liberty. Some recalcitrant merchants, threatened by ostracism and even with physical violence, had to yield to the general will. Imports of British goods sank remarkably. Moreover, Britain gained only a trifling revenue from the Townshend duties—none at all in the Middle and Northern Colonies. The colonists consumed tea as usual, but they obtained its chief constituent from ships that brought in tea leaves illegally from Dutch ports. Since such Dutch teas, smuggled, were cheaper than English teas, the colonists were not forced to abandon one of their favorite beverages. They hoped, of course, that their boycott would persuade British merchants and manufacturers to request the erasure of the Townshend duties, in the same fashion that they had urged the repeal of the Stamp Act.

The increasingly effective economic warfare carried on by the colonists against Britain was sufficiently extraordinary, but it was not the only way in which the Americans displayed their anger. The cautious John Dickinson might acknowledge that Parliament possessed the power to restrain American commerce and manufacturing. He would not resort to physical violence. However, more and more Americans—including sophisticated ones—defined American liberties more and more generously as the Townshend crisis proceeded; and anti-British sentiment rose among the less educated colonists. Some informed Americans, urging the absolute equality of their assemblies with Parliament, began to challenge the right of the British legislature to ruin their commerce and manufacturing. Moreover, some of them were turning away from appeal to their rights as Englishmen to argument for the natural rights of mankind. They demanded, not only their rights upon the basis of law and precedent, but justice as an irrevocable gift from the God of Nature. What these men thought, more and more of the less educated Americans felt. These looked upon British customs officers, British naval officers, and judges of the admiralty courts who enforced British laws as enemies. Many American merchants, suffering from rigorous execution of the Navigation Acts, shared this hostility toward British officials. American mobs more and more frequently offered physical resistance to the servants of the King.

Almost inevitably, because the new Board of Customs Commissioners was established in Boston, that city became the principal center of strife between muscular and vigorous Americans and the King's men. Civilians and British soldiers exchanged insults and blows on the streets of New York, but their clashes were only occasional and did not lead to killing. It was otherwise in the New England city. There, violence became chronic, mounting at last to the "Boston Massacre."

The new customs commissioners, from the moment they began their labors in Boston, were socially ostracized. John Hancock, a young and rich merchant who had inherited a business and a fortune from an uncle, is reported to have said that he would not permit them to interfere with his enterprises. Soon, underlings of the board, including paid informers, began to suffer verbal and physical abuse. Sailors and workmen eager for action joyously pummeled the minions of the Crown—they could vent their anger against the disliked customs men and at the same time serve the cause of American liberty. After some weeks the commissioners themselves became uneasy. On March 4, 1768, a mob gathered ominously around the house of one of them, William Burch. He was not actually attacked. However, Burch and his colleagues became alarmed, perhaps needlessly. They asked Governor Francis Bernard what protection he could offer them in the event that they were assailed. He answered that he could not protect them. He could not get help from General Gage, for his council would not let him ask for it. Two weeks later another mob celebrated the anniversary of the repeal of the Stamp Act by hanging upon a Liberty Tree in the city effigies of commissioner Charles Paxton and customs inspector Williams. The commissioners then begged Commodore Samuel Hood, who commanded the British squadron stationed at Halifax, to send a warship to Boston to protect them. Hood promptly ordered the *Romney* to proceed to Boston Harbor. The commissioners also wrote to London. They said they were threatened by an insurrection, and Governor Bernard endorsed their plea for military aid. Both they and the governor declared that the civil officials of Boston and Massachusetts either could not or would not protect the customs officers.

The appeals from Boston for armed assistance arrived in London amidst protests from colonial assemblies against the Townshend duties. These had already created wrath in the imperial capital. Moreover, the House of Representatives of Massachusetts had added to that anger by sending out, in February 1768, a circular letter to the elected lawmakers in the other colonies inviting them to join in forming a united front against British tyranny—to arrange for a general congress. The Earl of Hillsborough had castigated the emission of the circular letter as a "seditious" attempt to form "unwarrantable combinations" and "to excite an unjustifiable opposition to the constitutional authority of Parliament." Partly because of intervention by Hillsborough, it was not possible for the Americans to hold the congress that Massachusetts desired. Hillsborough had found in the Americans "a malevolent and ungrateful disposition." He had expressed his "contempt" of those who challenged the sovereignty of Parliament. The British cabinet, sharing his vexation, authorized him to employ the army to defend the customs commissioners. It will be recalled that the cabinet had already decided to concentrate the army in America upon the Atlantic seaboard. On June 8 Hillsborough wrote a "secret and confidential" dispatch to General Gage, telling him to put one or more regiments immediately in Boston to protect the commissioners. The cabinet intended to cow the Bostonians into submission.

General Gage did not receive the order to place redcoats in the capital of Massachusetts until the end of August. Meanwhile, the customs commissioners, even though they had claimed to be in dire danger, continued to do their duty as they saw it. On June 10 they ordered the seizure of the sloop *Liberty,* the property of John Hancock. It has been urged that the *Liberty* had been used for smuggling. It has also been asserted that Hancock had committed no serious violation of British law, and that he was the victim of a frame-up. Certainly the commissioners were determined to make an example of Hancock. They had the *Liberty* towed out into Boston Harbor and anchored near the warship *Romney,* to discourage ardent defenders of American rights from trying to recapture Hancock's vessel. There was an immediate uproar in restless Boston. Employees of the commissioners were assailed with strong language and stones by mobs. The homes of two of them were damaged by rioters. Amidst much excitement, town meetings of Boston demanded both the cancellation of the Townshend duties and the removal of the customs commissioners. On June 13 four of the commissioners fled from the city, taking refuge on the *Romney,* and later in Castle William, a fort on an island in Boston Harbor. There they were safe enough.

From their asylum in Castle William the four commissioners sent out a second series of letters begging for armed protection. Since Governor Bernard could not request General Gage to send troops—the governor was not eager to act, it may be added, because he believed that the British cabinet would eventually take the responsibility for the employment of force—they appealed directly to the general on June 15, telling him that tumult was rising in Boston, "even to open revolt." The general replied that he was unable to act, since there was not a rebellion in Boston; nor did he find merit in a suggestion from Bernard that he put a force in Boston upon the pretext of routine quartering. However, Commodore Hood, responding to the petition of the commissioners, sent additional warships into Boston Harbor. Moreover, a second request for help sent by the commissioners to the treasury in London brought a swift answer from the British cabinet. It ordered two regiments of the garrison troops in Ireland, together with two warships, to proceed as swiftly as possible to Boston. On July 30 the Earl of Hillsborough wrote to Gage to tell him that the redcoats and the ships were being sent to support and protect "the civil magistrates and officers" of Massachusetts in the discharge of their duty and to induce "a due obedience to the laws of this kingdom."

Both Governor Bernard and General Gage desired the presence of troops in Boston after the rioting that followed the seizure of the *Liberty.* But neither man would assume the responsibility for introducing them into the city. Neither wished to be assailed for establishing a military tyranny in that troubled port. Were the commissioners seriously threatened? Probably not. However, they certainly could not do their duty if their underlings were prevented by violence from obeying their instructions. The state of affairs in the city may, perhaps, be deduced from the results of a poll of his council taken by Bernard late in July. He asked every member of it, in confidence, whether he should officially ask the general for troops. Not a single man replied in the affirmative.

In 1768, as in 1765, Gage refused to move upon his own authority to deal with mobs. If Bernard asked for men to suppress rioting, he would send them. If there was a rebellion in Boston, he would strike against those who took up arms against Britain. But there was no rebellion. Even so, he, too, unquestionably believed that military coercion was necessary in Boston. In a "private" letter to Viscount Barrington, the Secretary at War, who would not fail to relay its contents to other members of the ministry, Gage declared that his superiors in London must recognize that the situation in the city was ugly and that they ought to adopt "warm and spirited resolves with speedy execution in consequence." Gage also told Barrington that "the noble spirit of the New-Englanders" ought to be crushed. If Britain followed a policy of "moderation and forebearance," there would be "an end to these provinces as British colonies."

Resorting to the use of force, the Grafton ministry assumed that the Bostonians would become orderly—and that their fellow Americans would learn that it was imprudent to question the authority of Britain. The ministry took a great risk. For there was danger that the presence of troops in the city would incite the rebellion they were sent to prevent. The news of their coming aroused passions among the more forthright defenders of American liberty in the city. Ardent spirits among them talked about meeting force with force. The redcoats should be kept out of the city. They ought to be greeted with gunfire as they sought to enter it. A Boston town meeting was held on September 11 and 12 to consider what steps should be taken. Samuel Adams, Dr. Joseph Warren, and other zealous champions of American liberty were reluctant to submit tamely to the planting of troops within the precincts of the city. It may be that they were willing to take up arms. However, James Otis, then at the very height of his influence, intervened. Did Adams and Warren wish to begin hostilities, when the Bostonians could not expect help from other Americans? Otis, Adams, and Warren agreed that the town meeting must not issue a call to arms. Under their guidance, on September 12, the town meeting reminded every citizen that he was required by law to keep a musket—there was danger of war with *France;* hinted that the future might bring another upheaval like the Glorious Revolution of 1688 that had put an end to the tyranny of James II; and asked all the towns in Massachusetts to send delegates to a "Committee of Convention," which should consult upon the "peace and safety" of Massachusetts. Otis believed that even the call for the meeting of deputies from the towns was extreme. Ten days later representatives from most of them came to Boston. At first Otis would not even go to the "Committee of Convention." However, persuaded to attend it, he saw to it that the meeting did nothing rash. A majority of the delegates did not lust for battle. The convention merely drew up a list of grievances, and then permanently adjourned. It was apparent that Boston, undertaking to resist the British troops, could not rely upon help even from her sister towns of Massachusetts.

General Gage, informed that the army was likely to meet resistance in Boston, scoffed. He believed that the Bostonians would "shrink on the day of trial." "They are a people," he said, "who have ever been very bold in council, but never remarkable for their feats in action." Had he forgotten that they—and almost all the New Englanders—were of that stuff from which Oliver Cromwell had created an army that was the terror of Europe? The general would later change his mind about the fighting qualities of the Yankees.

The Bostonians might not be valorous, but Gage did everything possible to assure the safe landing of two regiments that he ordered, in accordance with his instructions from the ministry, to go from Halifax to Boston by sea. The 14th and 29th regiments were escorted into Boston Harbor by a naval squadron furnished by Commodore Hood. On October 1 Hood covered the passage of the redcoats from their transports to the shore with a ship of the line and seven frigates. His vessels were in battle array, ready, if necessary, to fire. There was no fusillade of bullets from stores and warehouses along the wharves. The soldiers went ashore amidst a quiet that was sufficiently ominous. Gage was able to say that the troops would encounter more opposition from "law & gospel, than sword and gun." Joined by the 64th and 65th regiments from Ireland, the redcoats made themselves as comfortable as possible in the city. It was soon made clear to them that they were not welcome. Governor Bernard was pleased to have them in town, and so were the customs commissioners, who returned from Castle William to resume their duties. But Bernard's council flatly refused to supply foodstuffs, fuel, candles, and quarters in the city for the troops. There were barracks on Castle Island. Let the redcoats occupy them. Some of the soldiers were forced to camp for a time on Boston Common, until Gage came to Boston from New York and rented buildings for them at His Majesty's expense.

Covered by the guns of the troops, the commissioners of the customs were indeed able to execute the British laws affecting the maritime commerce of Boston and to collect the duty of 1766 upon molasses. In fact, after 1768 the British customs service everywhere in North America, with the help of the new admiralty courts established in that year, functioned with great efficiency. So much so that it collected many thousands of pounds annually thereafter.

And yet General Gage was most unhappy as a result of the course of events in both London and Boston. Before the last of the troops arrived in the capital of Massachusetts—they had been delayed by a great storm—the British cabinet began to give ground in consequence of American resistance. The boycott of British goods was less effective than it had been in 1765, for Britain, having recovered from the depression that followed the Seven Years' War, was prosperous again. Nevertheless, British merchants were asking that the Townshend duties be rescinded. Was it sensible to risk an American rebellion in order to collect those taxes? Had not too much been hazarded by putting troops in Boston? A new Parliament elected in 1768 seemed to be determined to bring the colonists into proper subjection. It adopted an address to the throne which endorsed the coercive policy of the cabinet and which urged punishment of those men of Massachusetts who were chiefly responsible for the calling of the "Committee of Convention." Were they not guilty of treason? The cabinet ought to execute an old statute of the time of Henry VIII which provided for the trial and execution in England of persons who had committed treason elsewhere. However, the cabinet failed to move against those wicked conspirators. Even Lord Hillsborough, who was not remarkably fond of the colonists, thought it unwise to seek out and punish traitors. Indeed, since the "Committee of Convention" had not advised resistance against the redcoats, who had committed any deed that could be considered treasonable?

In February 1769, Hillsborough submitted a scheme for resolving the American crisis to the cabinet. He also, as a loyal King's Friend, gave it to George III, so that he and his colleagues would have the full benefit of the royal wisdom. Hillsborough proposed that every colony which made permanent provision for paying its royal officials be relieved of the Townshend taxes. However, he also urged that the colonies must furnish quarters and supplies for the redcoats stationed among them. If they failed to do so, the troops would be placed in taverns and even in private homes. To deal with Boston and Massachusetts, the colonial secretary offered another mixture of harshness and lenity. He advised, to please the recalcitrant Yankees, that a portion of the troops in Boston be withdrawn immediately, that the remainder be removed from the city as soon as conditions there permitted. Since Governor Bernard had become extremely unpopular in his province, Hillsborough suggested that the governor be given a leave of absence to come to England and to receive a baronetcy for his labors. However, Hillsborough also urged that the council of Massachusetts be royally chosen in the future—and that the charter of Massachusetts, in force since 1691, should be automatically rescinded in the event that an official protest came from the province against changing the method of selection of the council. Several members of the cabinet believed that Hillsborough's proposals were too stringent. The King himself said that tampering with the council of Massachusetts in violation of its charter was dangerous. Otherwise, he found no great fault in Hillsborough's scheme, except that he desired maintenance of the Townshend duty upon tea as a means of asserting the right of Parliament to tax the colonists. The monarch was willing to let them know "that there is no inclination for the present to lay fresh taxes upon them, but I am clear that there must always be one tax to keep up the right, and as such I approve of the tea duty."

Neither the Hillsborough plan nor the Hillsborough plan as amended by the monarch pleased the Duke of Grafton or Lord Camden, or Sir Henry Seymour Conway. Those men had hitherto been swept along by Townshend and his allies. Now they called for the complete repeal of the Townshend taxes. They had friends in the House of Commons. They might have had their way, except for the influence of the King, whose first important venture in the making of American policy was most unfortunate. It is reported, upon doubtful authority, that the cabinet formally voted in May 1769 upon the issue of total repeal of the Townshend duties as against rescinding all except that upon tea, and that the King's opinion carried the day—or night—by the narrow margin of 5 votes to 4. If so, Britain made a fateful decision by the narrowest of margins, since Parliament would doubtless have accepted the guidance of the cabinet. Had the monarch called for complete erasure of the detested duties, both the cabinet and Parliament would almost certainly have followed his leadership. As things were, the cabinet officially declared in that month of May that it would ask for the repeal of the taxes, except for that upon tea, in the following year; also that no new taxes were contemplated. With that announcement went instructions to Francis Bernard to return to England to accept his baronetcy, and others to General Gage. The commander in chief was told to remove half of the troops in Boston immediately, and to take the other half out of the city as soon as conditions permitted.

The program worked out in the cabinet in May 1769 was executed —by Lord North—in England. For the King had at last found the man who would be, like Bute, *his* prime minister. In January 1770, North replaced Grafton as first lord of the treasury. He would hold that office for twelve eventful years, until the first British empire was destroyed. He also continued to serve as Chancellor of the Exchequer, for he had acquired some little skill in governmental finance. As the head of a ministry dominated by the King's Friends, North asked Parliament, on March 5, 1770, to set aside all the Townshend taxes, except for that upon tea, not because the Americans protested against them, but because they were uneconomic, a burden upon British exports. The King and Lord North had their way. William Beckford, Chatham's "tribune" in the House of Commons, objected. Thomas Pownall moved that the duty on tea be also wiped out. His motion was defeated, 204 to 142. Alderman Barlow Trecothick of London likewise displayed better judgment than the King or the prime minister. He moved in April that the duty upon tea be re pealed. His motion was lost by a vote of 80 to 52. On May 9 Edmund Burke, the brilliant orator from Ireland who served as the spokesman for the Marquis of Rockingham in the Commons, offered a series of resolutions that condemned attempts to tax and to coerce the colonists. They were set aside by a large majority. That great master of polished invective, *Junius,* who was carrying on a private war against his enemies in government and was unmercifully castigating the Duke of Grafton and various other politicians in the London newspapers, aptly, ironically, and vehemently declared that "the parliament have done every thing but remove the offence. They have relinquished the revenue, but judiciously taken care to preserve the contention." The retention of the duty upon tea was "an odious, unprofitable exertion of a speculative right." It affixed "a badge of slavery upon the Americans, without service to their master." *Junius*—whose identity remains uncertain, although it is generally believed that he was Sir Philip Francis—was often unjust to those whom he attacked. But his assessment of the incomplete repeal of the Townshend duties as ridiculous and pregnant with future trouble was only too correct.

If the decisions reached by the cabinet and King in May 1769 displeased Grafton, Camden, and Conway because they were too harsh, and *Junius* because they were stupid, they exasperated Gage because they were too lenient. He believed that the leaders of the malcontents in Massachusetts should have been impeached; that the council of that colony should have been royalized; and that the government of Boston should have been altered to make its seditious town meetings impossible. Moreover, he claimed in the spring of 1769 that the presence of the troops in the city had usefully restrained its citizens. He, of course, obeyed his orders. However, troops remained in Boston for another year, until March 1770, with momentous consequences. Gage immediately withdrew the 64th and 65th regiments from the city. But Governor Bernard insisted that the 14th and 29th regiments remain within it. Without them order could not be preserved in Boston. Then Bernard departed for England, leaving many enemies behind him. The Massachusetts House of Representatives asked that he be dismissed—after it had been determined in England that he should be rewarded with a baronetcy. Later, he was buried, ironically, at Boston in England. A memorial placed over his grave declares that he was the last royal governor of Massachusetts. He was the last but two. Lieutenant Governor Thomas Hutchinson, who succeeded Bernard in fact immediately and later in title in Boston, Massachusetts, also pleaded that the two regiments were indispensable for the maintenance of authority in the city. Gage reluctantly agreed to let them stay. Accordingly, they continued on duty there until after the Boston Massacre, which occurred on the very day that Lord North introduced his bill to rescind the bulk of the Townshend duties, on March 5, 1770.

If Gage at first fancied that the presence of the troops in Boston was salutary, he learned before many months had passed that there was danger of a bloody clash between the redcoats and aggressive citizens of that excited city. Fracas between soldiers and civilians could not possibly be prevented, in an age when resort to fisticuffs was the usual method of settling disputes among common folk. Brawls in taverns and on the streets between drunken redcoats and workmen over the favors of a barmaid or a prostitute, for there were such women in Boston, could not be avoided. Indeed, fights inevitably occurred because of differences of opinion over trifles. Such quarrels were exacerbated by cultural differences between the participants and onlookers. The soldiers were English and Irish; they despised Yankee sailors, workmen, and shop apprentices. Harshly disciplined, they were not mild and temperate when they were off duty. Nor were their antagonists normally the best behaved of the Bostonians. There was even economic contest between the redcoats and civilians. British soldiers were then permitted to work in their spare time, to augment their meager pay, and they competed for jobs when employment was not easily obtained because of the American boycott of British goods.

The conduct of the soldiers on duty was also offensive to civilians, who resented challenges by sentinels, and the beating of the drums as guards were changed during religious services on the Sabbath. Army musicians enjoyed playing "Yankee Doodle," then a song that derided rather than pleased New Englanders. The mere sight of the redcoats was enough to inflame hot-headed young men of the town. On the other hand, the troops, unable to interfere when a crowd forced a merchant to comply with the Boston non-importation agreement, watched with an anger they could hardly control.

Such troubles might not have blossomed into tumult, since the British officers imposed ever more stringent discipline upon their men. However, ardent defenders of American rights not only encouraged physical attacks upon troops, but bedeviled them with propaganda. They were assailed by local officials, newspapers, and broadsides as instruments of vicious oppression. On the basis of letters from Gage sent to London and returned by friends of America a Massachusetts grand jury indicted the general for slandering the colony. It is to be suspected that Samuel Adams, Dr. Joseph Warren, and others deliberately carried on a campaign of abuse against the soldiers, not only to make them unpopular, but to widen the gap between Britain and America. They surely had somewhat to do, as Governor Bernard surmised, with the *Journal of the Times,* an extraordinary publication that first appeared in October 1768 and continued to plague both British officials and troops for more than a year. Composed of supposed Boston news items, it was sent from Boston to New York, and was published first in New York, later in Boston, other American cities, and London. The *Journal* offered authentic news, fabricated reports, and much anti-British preaching. It described John Hancock as the victim of a frame-up by haughty and corrupt commissioners of the customs. Governor Bernard was tyrannical and deceitful. Boston was a city of decent and law-abiding folk dominated by brutal and immoral soldiers, who should have been off on the frontier fighting Indians. The *Journal* related incident after incident in which an innocent lady had been attacked by a redcoat ravisher or ravishers and had been rescued by a worthy and courageous citizen or citizens. The *Journal* stung both officers and men, who were commonly quite innocent of wrongdoing, as James Otis himself afterward testified.

With the passing months tension rose in Boston. Two successive British commanders there, foreseeing an ugly outbreak, asked to be relieved, and managed to secure Gage's permission to depart for calmer scenes. The third officer to be placed over the troops, Colonel William Dalrymple, was not so fortunate. On September 5, 1769, after publishing a violent attack upon Governor Bernard and the customs commissioners as vilifiers of the people of Massachusetts, James Otis imprudently visited a coffeehouse frequented by the commissioners. There he quarreled with John Robinson, one of them, and was so severely beaten about the head that it was necessary to carry him to his home. Otis forgave Robinson. Was Robinson responsible for the fact that Otis not long afterward became insane? Perhaps not, since there is reason to believe that Otis had long been a manic depressive. In any event, Robinson was not forgiven by every defender of American liberties. On October 26 a mob attacked a British guard as it went off duty. One soldier was struck in the mouth, and

Captain Molesworth was hit in the head by a stone. A redcoat accidentally discharged his musket, hurting no one. The mob did not disperse until the soldiers affixed bayonets to defend themselves. Captain Molesworth and his men were charged with a breach of the peace, but they were acquitted, for Otis, who was not yet completely insane and who represented the city, pointed out that the troops had been wantonly attacked. On November 4 a mob celebrated Guy Fawkes Day by tarring and feathering a customs informer. The same evening another mob attacked John Mein, a newspaper publisher who had printed customs house facts and figures which suggested, unfairly, that certain ardent defenders of American freedom were secretly importing British-taxed goods. Mein managed to hold off his assailants with a pair of pistols, and escaped to the British main guard. The men who composed it were kept under arms all night to ward off an attack. They were not assailed. But Mein had to leave Boston for safety in England.

At last, in February 1770, came the first slaying in the American Revolution. On the nineteenth of that month Colonel Dalrymple informed General Gage that his men were being constantly waylaid in the streets, but that he had ordered them to refrain from violence. On February 22 a mob gathered about the home of Ebenezer Richardson, a notorious customs informer. Threatened, Richardson appeared with a musket and demanded that his tormentors leave him in peace. When they refused to disperse, he fired, fatally wounding Christopher Snyder, a boy of eleven who had come out to share the fun. Richardson was lucky not to be lynched. Carried off by the crowd, he was sent to jail, and later convicted of murder. He did not suffer the extreme penalty, since it was only too obvious to judges, if not to jurors, that he had acted in self-defense.

Eight days after the shooting of young Christopher Snyder there was a fight between soldiers and workmen, which was broken up before they could injure each other. However, they agreed as they were forced apart that they would meet on March 5 to resume their contest. Excitement mounted as that day approached. Lieutenant Governor Hutchinson was urged to arrange to send the troops out of the city; refusing to do so, he said they were obviously needed to maintain order. Mobs of men and boys went through the streets on March 5, looking for trouble. Late in the day it came. A mob of fifty or sixty had gathered about a sentinel in front of the customs house in King Street. He called for help, and Captain Thomas Preston sent a file of seven men from the British main guard to support him. Then Preston himself went to the scene. The mob would not disperse, pressed the captain and his men back against the customs house, and belabored the troops with oaths, icy snowballs, stones, fists, and clubs or sticks—"clubs" according to the later British version of the incident, "sticks" according to the American one. A soldier was knocked down. Someone, apparently one of the troops, shouted "Fire!" The men, one by one, discharged their muskets with fearful results. They killed five civilians, and wounded six more, most of those killed being innocent observers behind the mob.

The news spread swiftly through the city. Men talked openly about attacking the British detachments. Hutchinson managed to avert an immediate and bloody struggle by promising that Preston and his men would be brought to trial for murder. They were put in jail. Soon afterward, it became evident that the troops must leave the city, if peace was to be preserved. A Boston town meeting demanded that they be evacuated, and so did Hutchinson's council. Hutchinson reluctantly requested Colonel Dalrymple to remove the troops to Castle Island, and Dalrymple reluctantly complied. They did not return to the city, for Gage consented to their evacuation as an accomplished fact. One regiment remained on Castle Island, where it did not offend the eyes of the Bostonians.

The departure of the redcoats from the city did indeed bring a relative quiet to Boston. However, the fate of Captain Preston and his men remained uncertain over many months. Samuel Adams, John Hancock, Dr. Joseph Warren, and others like them were determined to punish the redcoats. They published masses of affidavits and statements that portrayed Preston and the soldiers as cold-blooded murderers, and accused British sympathizers of shooting into the mob from the windows of the customs house. Adams and Warren invaded the superior court room at the head of a crowd, demanding immediate trial. Fortunately, the magistrates of Boston, supported by Hutchinson, insisted that legal proceedings be put off until autumn, until public excitement had died down. In the meantime Hutchinson was able to inform his superiors in London of the unhappy incidents and to secure their consent to the use of the pardoning power to prevent any miscarriage of justice.

It was not necessary for the governor to offer executive clemency. Late in October Preston was tried before a blue-ribbon jury. He was defended by Thomas Auchmuty, also by John Adams and Josiah Quincy, Jr., two men unquestionably devoted to American liberty who were not enemies of justice. At least one of Preston's men claimed that Preston had given an order to fire into the mob. However, it became evident that he had not done so, and he was acquitted. Released, Preston was hurried off to England, where George III gave him a pension of £200 per annum to compensate him for his sufferings. Toward the end of November, Auchmuty, Adams, and Quincy defended Preston's men. Since they could

109

not claim that the soldiers had discharged their guns in accordance with an order from Preston, they relied upon a plea for self-defense. It was an effective plea. The jury, acquitting six of the soldiers, found two of them guilty of manslaughter, the man who had fired the first shot and another who had previously threatened to kill a civilian. The two men were able to read and write. They successfully sought the special privilege of benefit of clergy, were burnt in the hand, and were released. A third trial, of the men accused of firing into the mob from the customs house, was a farce. There was no evidence worthy of the name against them, and the members of the jury voted acquittal without leaving their seats.

The victims of the Boston Massacre were long looked upon as heroes in America, and one of them, Crispus Attucks, a mulatto, acquired fame as a Negro who sacrificed all in defense of American freedom. For many years the anniversary of the "massacre" was celebrated in Boston, with an orator depicting the victims as martyrs. However, more than a century later, descendants of American patriots in the Massachusetts Historical Society protested against the placing of a memorial to the slain at the place where the "massacre" occurred. It was nevertheless voted by the Massachusetts legislature—which by that time contained many men whose ancestors had suffered grievously under British rule in Ireland. Dr. Samuel Johnson's famous remark, that lapidaries carving inscriptions upon tombstones are not required to take an oath, again comes to mind. It is not demanded that those who vote for monuments to public heroes be sober scholars, or that they demonstrate beyond doubt that those they wish to honor are worthy beyond doubt.

The outcome of the trials in Boston was possibly affected by a change in the mood of the Americans, not only in Boston and Massachusetts, but everywhere in the colonies. For the repeal of the Townshend duties, though incomplete, and the withdrawal of the troops from Boston soothed American discontent in the summer of 1770. There was a clamor for putting an end to the boycott against British goods. Had not Britain substantially yielded to the colonists? Samuel Adams and many another American contended that it should be continued, at least until the British tax upon tea was erased. But just as many colonists, like the British, were not eager to fight on. Merchants very keenly desired public peace and the resumption of business. At length the colonists found a middle way. In port after port it was agreed that the boycott should thenceforth be limited to taxed tea. Even that proscription was not rigidly maintained. And the North ministry declined during three years to make American purchase or non-purchase of British tea an issue. Before the end of the year 1770 the colonies were generally quiet and prosperous again, and they remained so until Lord North once more put them to the test.

CHAPTER IX

A Decade of Westward Advance

IT was suggested in an earlier chapter that the American Revolution was not confined to Tidewater and Piedmont, that British efforts to prevent warfare between whites and Indians, to protect the lands of the Indians, to regulate their trade, and to restrain the westward advance of the Thirteen Colonies had aroused serious colonial discontent as early as 1765. During the following decade Britain withdrew most of her troops from the interior of America, returned responsibility for maintaining order in the Indian commerce to the several colonies, and grudgingly permitted the expansion of American settlements far beyond the Appalachian Mountains. The savages, resenting the westward rush of American pioneers, learned to look upon King George as their great and good friend. However, the pioneers, together with American land speculators and other Americans sensitive to exertions of British authority, continued to see the King and his advisers as hindrances to the exploitation and occupation of virgin and rich lands on both sides of the Appalachians. Attempts by the British government to promote the peopling of Canada, East Florida, and West Florida, the new colonies established by the Proclamation of October 7, 1763, largely failed. Despite obstacles erected by Britain, the Americans poured on westward after 1765. They saw in the valley of the Mississippi a collection of new Canaans that God had not reserved for red-skinned heathen. Before the beginning of the War of Independence, buck-skinned pioneers were firmly established in Kentucky and Tennessee. They would form the Patriot rearguard in that struggle; and they would even go in hours of crisis to the assistance of their fellow Americans east of the mountains.

It was not possible to convince many Americans, or many British, or many Europeans during the years between Pontiac's War and the War of

Independence, that Quebec or Nova Scotia had much to offer to the emigrant. Canadian winters were known to be long, and Ontario, "the Garden of Canada," was Indian country, beyond the southern boundary of Quebec, until 1774. Projects to mine coal on Cape Breton Island and to plant English settlers on Prince Edward Island remained projects. Nova Scotia continued to be a thinly populated province until after the War of Independence. Some hundreds of "old subjects" of George III made new homes for themselves in Quebec, chiefly at Montreal, after its seizure by British—and American—arms. Those "old subjects," entering the province from England and from the Thirteen Colonies, were chiefly traders and merchants. The wide regions to the northward of the Thirteen Colonies continued to be occupied very largely by French Canadians until the end of the War of Independence. British governors who also, under General Gage, commanded redcoat garrison forces, ruled over Quebec.

If Canada was cold and not very attractive to emigrants, East Florida was warm but not much more seductive to settlers. It included the peninsula discovered by Ponce de León and stretched westward to the Apalachicola River. It would not become an enticing winter resort until the twentieth century. It had not flourished under Spanish rule; indeed, the Spanish had made no great effort to populate the peninsula. They had valued their province of Florida chiefly as a barrier against British attacks upon the more valuable Spanish possessions in the Caribbean Sea and along the western and southern shores of the Gulf of Mexico. Even St. Augustine, its capital, though founded in 1565, was little more than a military outpost when the dons evacuated it at the end of the Seven Years' War. With the Spanish troops went the few Spanish civilians who had lived at St. Augustine and other smaller posts. Except for the Seminole—bands of Creek Indians who were moving toward independence from the Creek confederacy—East Florida was almost uninhabited when Colonel James Grant arrived in St. Augustine as its first British governor. The Seminole claimed that they owned almost all of the peninsula.

Colonel Grant was a respectable and competent governor. He did all that he could to develop his colony. He had enough faith in it to invest his own money in its future, and others for a time sanguinely dreamed of getting easy wealth from the new colony. British noblemen and other men influential in London, hoping for fat returns far beyond their investments, cheaply obtained grants of thousands of acres of land in East Florida. They were disappointed. Settlers moved southward into East Florida from South Carolina and Georgia, but not in large numbers, for one could not profitably raise rice and indigo in the province. An enterprising speculator, Denys Rolle, brought English debtors and beggars, together with

112

Negro slaves, to Mount Pleasant on the St. John's River. But his Rolles-town did not become a city. Dr. Andrew Turnbull, believing that the shores of Ponce de León Inlet were ideal for the production of semi-tropical products, imported Mediterranean workers—Greeks, Italians, and Minorcans—for that purpose. Turnbull's trees and vines did not flourish; nor did his settlement of New Smyrna. Many of his laborers sickened and died. East Florida acquired a dismal reputation for heat, mosquitoes, swamps, disease, and lack of economic opportunity. Gover-nor Grant, with the help of Superintendent John Stuart, managed to keep on good terms with the Seminole warriors, partly because few settlers desired the lands of those Indians. Grant and his successors did not labor entirely in vain, but East Florida contained almost as many troops as it did civilians until it became a refuge for Loyalists who fled southward during the War of Independence. There were finally enough people in the colony, in 1781, to warrant the election of a legislature. But most of the Loyalists departed soon afterward, and all British officials went with them, for the Spanish regained their ancient dependency at the end of the War of Independence.

The British colony of West Florida also endured for only twenty years. Included in it were the southern parts of the modern states of Alabama and Mississippi, together with Pensacola. Mobile was its princi-pal settlement. It contained some splendid land, on the eastern banks of the lower Mississippi River, and it was more attractive to settlers than its sister province. Men seeking to acquire farms and plantations came down the great river. A report of 1774 has it that 2,500 whites with 600 slaves were then located on the lowlands in the western part of the colony. A few French settlers remained after the departure of the French troops. British garrisons at Mobile and other smaller posts stimulated commerce, and merchants established themselves at Mobile and Pensacola to carry on trade with the Indians to the northward, the Creek, the Choctaw, and the Chickasaw. The colony was at first badly managed, by Governor George Johnstone, a verbose and contentious Scot who had learned about politics in the royal navy. Even so, it was possible to establish a lower house of assembly as early as 1766. The recall of Johnstone in the following year was of service to the colony. It was disturbed by threats of war from the aggressive Creek warriors, who deeply resented intrusions upon their lands, but it prospered moderately until the later years of the War of Independence. Then it became a scene of warfare. Mobile and Pensacola were captured by the Spanish, and at the end of that conflict the province—at least most of it—became Spanish territory.

The Americans, as they spread from the Atlantic to the Pacific, normally moved westward, rather than northward or southward. So it was during the decade before the War of Independence. Yankees from New Hampshire and Massachusetts pushed into Vermont; Connecticut families made their way into northern Pennsylvania; Pennsylvanians, Marylanders, and Virginians poured through the region south of the Ohio River; Virginians and North Carolinians settled in the valley of the Tennessee River; and South Carolinians and Georgians advanced toward the ridges of the southern Appalachians. Those westward movements did not take place without clash and commotion.

There was trouble in Vermont. Yankees who advanced into the Green Mountain country in the 1760's and 1770's at first assumed that they were under the jurisdiction of New Hampshire. Ethan Allen, his cousin Seth Warner, and other "Green Mountain Boys" were most unhappy when New York laid claim to Vermont and began to grant lands the Yankees desired for themselves. Feeling rose high in Vermont between Yankees and Yorkers. Attempts by governors of New York to establish their sway over the region were checked by armed New England settlers, not without a few casualties. In 1773 and 1774 New York vainly asked that British troops be sent into the region to establish order—and a régime suitable for its exploitation by New York land speculators. Few Yorkers actually put themselves down in Vermont. Ethan Allen, a bold, bombastic, and profane frontiersman, with Seth Warner and others, at last decided that Vermont must be formed into a new colony—and state. They did not achieve statehood until 1791; but the Vermonters quite successfully ran their own affairs after the Declaration of Independence.

There was uproar in northern Pennsylvania. Men from Connecticut moved northward into Vermont, but others from that seemingly crowded colony sought new homes beyond the Delaware River in Pennsylvania. Land-hungry citizens of Connecticut organized a Susquehannah Company before the Seven Years' War to form settlements in the Wyoming Valley. They had no intention of paying the proprietors of Pennsylvania, the Penn family, for the lands they intended to occupy; nor did they propose to pay Pennsylvania taxes. They had the support of the government of Connecticut, which asserted claim to the valley and adjacent territory by virtue of a provision of the charter of Connecticut of 1663, which could be construed to say that the colony extended westward to the Pacific Ocean. The Susquehannah Company bought the lands it desired from the Six Nations, who claimed to own them, at the Albany Congress in 1754. After the Seven Years' War Yankees made their way in numbers into the Wyoming Valley. Pennsylvania, not without reason, declared that any claim possessed by Connecticut to the Susquehanna region had long since lapsed or had been destroyed. But attempts by Pennsylvania to establish its authority over the "intruders" from Connecticut met armed resistance. More than one "war" was waged between the Yankees and the Pennsylvanians, and there were a few killings. Raids by Tories and Indians during the War of Independence helped to solve an ugly problem. Many of the Yankees were slain or driven away. At last, after that war, the remaining Connecticut men agreed to accept titles to their lands from Pennsylvania, and also to accept the jurisdiction of that state. It may seem that the Yankees gained little by their "invasion" of Pennsylvania. However, the state of Connecticut, abandoning its claim to part of Pennsylvania, was rewarded elsewhere. The Congress of the United States permitted Connecticut to establish the Western Reserve for its citizens in northern Ohio; and that rich country on the southern shores of Lake Erie later became the home of many thousands of Yankees seeking farms and opportunity beyond the Appalachians.

There were equally curious incidents, though less bloody ones, on the borders of South Carolina during the decade before the War of Independence. A reservation was established in 1764 for the Catawba Indians along the northwestern frontier of that colony in 1763. The lands of the Catawba, long allies of South Carolina, were coveted by white men. They were unable to buy those lands, because private purchases of Indian territory were forbidden by the Proclamation of October 7, 1763, and also by a law of South Carolina, passed in 1739. In 1773 William Henry Drayton, a wealthy young aristocrat of that colony, sought to secure a lease upon their lands from the Catawba—to prevent, so he said, unscrupulous men from buying the lands in defiance of the British and South Carolinian governments. Did it occur to the virtuous Drayton that he might establish a moral claim to the reservation that he would later exploit? Indian Superintendent John Stuart saw to it that Drayton did not get his lease. Other inhabitants of South Carolina attempted to get lands beyond the western settlements of the colony, to the westward of a boundary laid down between the colony and the Cherokee tribe in 1765. Some Cherokee warriors tried to give a tract in the valley of the upper Saluda River, in the country reserved for their nation, to a half-breed son of Alexander Cameron, Stuart's deputy among the Cherokee. Those who desired to make the present contended that the Proclamation of October 7, 1763, and the law of South Carolina forbidding private sales of Indian lands did not apply to a gift to an Indian. Stuart suggested to Alexander Cameron that the transaction ought not to be permitted. It was abandoned. Two Indian traders, Richard Pearis and Edward Wilkinson, employed a different tactic; they accepted lands from the Cherokee in exchange for the cancellation of their debts. Many Cherokee were indebted to them. Superintendent Stuart was able to quash those titles by invoking the South Carolina law against private purchases of Indian lands. Pearis was fined for violating that law, but did not fail utterly. Later, as a Loyalist, after the War of Independence, he secured compensation from a generous British government for land he did not own. It was difficult to prevent aggressive and ingenious white men from taking advantage of the red men.

Stuart was able to retard the westward advance of the South Carolinians, but he could not restrain the expansion of Georgia. By 1771 the Cherokee were in debt to many traders, and those traders owed money to merchants who supplied them with goods. Why not settle accounts by a cession of Cherokee lands to the traders—and their merchants? The Cherokee accordingly ceded a large area on the south bank of the Savannah River. Stuart objected, among other reasons because the Cherokee sold territory claimed by the Creek. The Creek warriors had long been restless, and he feared that they might take the warpath. But Governor James Wright was eager to do everything possible to promote the growth of Georgia. With his blessing, traders to the Creek, and the merchants who supplied those traders, cancelled Creek debts in exchange for a cession of the same tract of land, plus some claimed by the Cherokee. Stuart was unable to check Wright, who was respected and popular in London. Had not the governor restrained rioters in Georgia during the Stamp Act crisis? Wright went to London, was knighted, and personally secured endorsement by government of an official bargain with the two Indian nations. It was consummated at a great Congress at Augusta in 1773. Thereby Georgia acquired two million acres of land, the so-called "New Purchase." Neither the Cherokee nor the Creek were ultimately pleased with the transaction. They had acquired a new grievance against rapacious colonists who wanted land and more land. Would they ever be satisfied?

By far the most massive thrusts of the colonists toward the setting sun were in the regions immediately south of the Ohio River. It will be recalled that pioneers were established beyond the Appalachians in southwestern Pennsylvania and in Western Virginia—a few Virginians had planted themselves on the east bank of the Kanawha River—by 1765. After 1768 those pioneers were joined by thousands of backwoods people. Moreover, Virginians and North Carolinians moved into the valley of the upper Tennessee River, into the northeastern part of the state of Tennessee, in 1768 and 1769. Before the War of Independence, indeed, pioneers were settled on both sides of the lower Kentucky River, and

116

the city of Louisville was founded. The Old Southwest began to emerge.

Why did the surge of pioneers take place on the southern rather than the northern side of the Ohio River, so that the Old Southwest was occupied by the Americans before the Old Northwest? They did not throw up log cabins on the right bank of the Beautiful River until 1788, when Marietta, Ohio, was founded. In the main, the answer is that the Seneca tribe of the Six Nations, the Shawnee, and other warlike Indians who lived between the river and Lake Erie, constituted formidable barriers against the advance of the whites. The villages of those tribes were located in that region, and they were strong enough to offer desperate resistance. It was otherwise on the left bank of the Ohio. No powerful Indian nation resided in the great expanses where the states of West Virginia and Kentucky afterward appeared. Large parts of those wide spaces were claimed by the Cherokee, by the Shawnee, and by the Six Nations. However, they were used by the Indians almost entirely for hunting, and they formed a "neutral ground" between the northern and southern tribes. That neutral ground invited occupation. Moreover, it could be reached rather easily. During the Seven Years' War one road, or track, had been built from Cumberland, Maryland, to Fort Pitt, and another from central Pennsylvania to the same place. From Fort Pitt settlers could float down the Ohio River. It was also possible for Virginians and North Carolinians to push westward through passes in the Appalachians, especially Cumberland Gap, and they did.

The fact that the Old Northwest was relatively inaccessible to settlers during the decade before the War of Independence did not, of course, destroy all interest in that region. After 1765 two firms of Pennsylvania merchants sent agents into "the Indiana country"—the present day states of Indiana and Illinois—to buy furs from the red men. The two companies did not make huge profits. With equal optimism land speculators formed companies to develop large tracts of land in the same region. Indeed, such speculators cast covetous eyes upon many parts of Trans-Appalachia, and companies to exploit its rich lands blossomed almost amazingly. Their rosters included British politicians and army officers as well as American merchants and planters. But those new companies sent no settlers either into the Old Northwest or the Old Southwest.

Most famous among these combinations of speculators was the Grand Ohio Company, which was formed in 1769. It will be recalled that the British cabinet decided in the spring of 1768 to establish a new Indian boundary line to replace that laid down by the Proclamation of October 7, 1763. The new line was to run along the Allegheny and Ohio Rivers to the mouth of the Kanawha River, thence southward to the

Savannah River. All existing American settlements beyond the Appalachians were made legal, so far as Britain was concerned. It was the duty of Indian Superintendents Sir William Johnson and John Stuart to secure the consent of the Indians to the new boundary. However Johnson, himself a most successful land speculator in New York, disobeyed his instructions in the spirit, if not in the letter, in order to encourage westward expansion by the Virginians. At a great Indian Congress at Fort Stanwix in New York in the fall of 1768, Johnson bought from the Six Nations and several tribes subsidiary to them all their "rights" to land lying south of the Ohio River as far west as the mouth of the Tennessee River. Settlers immediately poured into southwestern Pennsylvania and the adjacent part of Virginia; and speculators immediately assumed that all Indian claims to the lands south of and adjacent to the Ohio River had been erased by the sale—or that they soon would be. Indian traders led by George Croghan, a deputy superintendent of Sir William Johnson, actually secured a deed from Indians at Fort Stanwix to a large tract in what is now the state of West Virginia in compensation for trade goods supposedly destroyed by the red men during and after the Seven Years' War. The hopes of the members of Virginia's Ohio Company, who sought land in the same region, revived. However, Samuel Wharton of Philadelphia, with Thomas Pownall and various other prominent Americans and Englishmen organized in the Grand Ohio Company, decided in 1770 to ask the Crown to sell them a large tract of land in a new colony to be called Vandalia, with boundaries roughly the same as those of the modern state of West Virginia. They secured the consent of Croghan's "suffering traders" and Virginia's Ohio Company by promising them subgrants.

The Vandalia scheme almost succeeded, despite the opposition to the colony of the Old Dominion—Virginia continued to claim that her territory extended to the Mississippi—and of the Earl of Hillsborough. Wharton and his partners exerted powerful influence in the imperial capital. Hillsborough at first favored the Vandalia project. Later, observing that it must produce many troubles, perhaps including an Indian war, he turned against it. His colleagues in the Grafton ministry, probably because they were eager to oust him from his post as Secretary of State for the Colonies, refused to support him. In August 1772, he therefore resigned. He was replaced by the Earl of Dartmouth, a stepbrother of Lord North, who was disposed to be of assistance to the Grand Ohio Company. Dartmouth was neither hostile to American expansion in particular, nor to the Americans in general. The British privy council formally endorsed the Vandalia enterprise in 1773; but it finally failed. General Gage spoke emphatically against it after he arrived in England that year upon leave of absence. Edward Thurlow, the British attorney general, and Alexander Wedderburn, the solicitor general, made legal difficulties. Benjamin Franklin became most unpopular in the British cabinet, and dislike of Franklin was doubtless transferred to the company in which he was a partner. Came the War of Independence, and Vandalia died, so far as Britain was concerned.

The Vandalia project alarmed and exasperated most Virginians. Was the Old Dominion, claiming to extend from sea to sea, or at least to the Mississippi, to be cut off on the west by a new colony? The House of Burgesses protested again and again against the Vandalians. Moreover, it demanded again and again that Indian barriers against the westward spread of Virginia settlements be removed. Two royal governors of Virginia after 1768, Lord Botetourt and Lord Dunmore, gave their support to the Burgesses. Botetourt was a courtier who was eager to please them; and Dunmore dreamed of securing estates beyond the Appalachians for his five children. Both governors would get generous fees if they could make grants of land across the mountains. Virginia not only survived the threat posed by Vandalia but secured cessions by the Indians that opened the way for the expansion of her settlements even to the Mississippi River.

One of the obstacles faced by Virginia was the claim of the Cherokee nation that its hunting grounds extended on the north as far as the Ohio River. There were no Cherokee villages within the boundary of Virginia, but the Cherokee were alarmed after 1768 by advances toward their homes both from the east and from the north. They saw that their independence, even their existence as a nation, was menaced. They sought to restrain the surge of the "longknives." John Stuart feared that rapid encroachment upon the hunting grounds of the Cherokee might drive them to take up arms. He was the more worried because Virginia frontiersmen had wantonly killed ten Cherokees in 1765. The murderers had never been punished; and the Cherokee yearned for revenge. Indeed, Stuart was concerned lest the onward rush of the American backwoodsmen bring on an Indian war as bloody as that waged by Pontiac and his allies. Stuart had once been a prisoner of the Cherokee, and he had been fortunate to escape burning at the stake. Moreover, Stuart, unlike Sir William Johnson, would do nothing to alter the boundary line laid down by the British cabinet in 1768 without the consent of his superiors in London. However, under pressure from Virginia, Stuart indicated that he was willing to accept changes in that line, provided that the Virginians did not approach the Cherokee towns too closely. His masters in London followed Stuart's lead. Accordingly, in a series of agreements negotiated

119

by Stuart and representatives of Virginia with the Cherokees during the years 1768 to 1772, the Cherokee abandoned their claim to lands adjacent to the Ohio River as far west as the Kentucky River.

The Shawnee were as warlike as the Cherokee, and they, too, saw the advance of the Virginians—together with Marylanders and Pennsylvanias—as a menace to their independence. Their towns were located not far north of the Ohio River. From their principal settlements at Chillicothe and Piqua they watched the thrust of the American pioneers along the southern bank of the Ohio with dread and anger. They would soon be unable to cross the river to hunt. After 1769 emissaries and wampum belts from the Shawnee, and from the neighboring Delaware nation, went from tribe to tribe, to the Six Nations, to the Cherokee, to the Creek. The Shawnee and Delaware urged that all Indians endangered by the onrush of the whites take up arms in defense of their homelands. Johnson and Stuart found it difficult to keep their charges quiet. The Shawnee made occasional isolated attacks upon white hunters and pioneers south of the Ohio. In May 1774, frontiersmen responded by brutally killing some Mingo Indians, neighbors of the Shawnee. The Mingo, placing the blame upon Virginians, began to make sporadic assaults upon settlers from the Old Dominion. They were joined by the Shawnee and a few of the Delaware. Lord Dunmore raised Virginia militia with almost astonishing celerity, and took the field. One force of Virginians destroyed some Shawnee and Mingo villages in July 1774. On October 10, Colonel Andrew Lewis with somewhat more than one thousand men fought a desperate battle against the hostile Indians under Chief Cornstalk at Point Pleasant on the Ohio River. Lewis was able to hold the field of battle. Meanwhile, Dunmore himself led a force across the Ohio into the heart of the Shawnee country. The Shawnee and Mingo became discouraged. Johnson had persuaded the Six Nations to remain neutral, and Stuart had seen to it that the Cherokee did not enter the conflict. The Shawnee and Mingo sued for peace. In November 1774, in a treaty dictated by Lord Dunmore, they abandoned all claim to lands south of the Ohio River.

Lord Dunmore gained no great credit from the war to which his name is attached; he did not crush the Shawnee, who remained powerful and dangerous. Nor did he or his children acquire money in consequence of his efforts to expand the settlements of Virginia. He was to be the last royal governor of the Old Dominion, and driven from his post. The man who profited most from Dunmore's successful labors to open Trans-Appalachia to Virginians was probably George Washington. As a colonel of the Virginia militia in the Seven Years' War Washington was given thousands of acres of land beyond the mountains; he acquired more thousands of acres by purchasing the rights of officers and men who had served under him and who were given smaller tracts. He was able, through agents, to select good lands on and near the south bank of the Ohio in southwestern Pennsylvania and the northern part of the state of West Virginia. Washington made no quick profits, but his Western lands mounted in value after the War of Independence. He still possessed more than 40,000 acres of land, chiefly beyond the mountains, when he died in 1799.

There was one body of Virginians who settled in Trans-Appalachia, who received no help from Dunmore, and who did not need his assistance. They were the families of Virginians who settled in the valleys of the Watauga, Holston, and Clinch Rivers in and after 1768; they put down in that part of North Carolina that later became known as northeastern Tennessee, and were joined by North Carolinians. Their new homes were in territory reserved for the Cherokee. They could not buy the lands they occupied, because of the Proclamation of October 7, 1763; giving suitable presents to some Cherokee, however, they secured a lease that would achieve the same purpose as a purchase. John Stuart informed the interlopers that their lease was an empty subterfuge, and that they must leave the Cherokee country. They ignored him, for he could command no force sufficient to remove them. They established a local government for themselves, and their settlements expanded. The main body of the Cherokee resented the intrusion of the Wataugans and their neighbors, but did not quickly take up arms to expel the whites. However, the Cherokee continued to nourish their hatred of the venturesome pioneers —and took up the hatchet against them when the War of Independence gave the opportunity.

Lord Dunmore had more to do with the founding of the first American settlements in Virginia's Kentucky than he did with the establishment of the first communities in Tennessee. By the year 1774 Virginians were floating down the Ohio and throwing up log cabins as far west at Louisville. But the first residents of Kentucky included North Carolinians as well as Virginians, and Richard Henderson of North Carolina was a principal architect of the later commonwealth of Kentucky.

No land speculator of the decade before the War of Independence was more astute or more resolute than Richard Henderson. It became apparent after 1768 that part or all of the Cherokee, however much they might later regret their action, could be persuaded to sell or lease their lands—and the lands of other Indians—in exchange for guns, tomahawks, knives, clothing, mirrors, rouge, and rum. Henderson knew that the Cherokee would not refuse to bargain with him. A judge, he also

121

knew of a British legal opinion offered by Lord Camden and Charles Yorke, which supported the validity of purchases of land by private persons from native rulers in India. He concluded that he could buy a vast domain in Kentucky and Tennessee from the Cherokee, despite the Proclamation of October 7, 1763. He did not consider a statute of North Carolina, which forbade private purchases from the Indians without the consent of her governor and council, an insurmountable obstacle. Nor did the fact that a large part of the land he intended to buy lay within the boundaries of Virginia stop him. He proceeded with his scheme, and neither Lord Dunmore, John Stuart, or Governor Josiah Martin of North Carolina was able to prevent him from executing it. In August 1774, at Hillsborough, North Carolina, he founded the Louisa Company, which five months later became the Transylvania Company, consisting of Henderson and eight partners. Stuart urged the Cherokee to be sensible, to avoid negotiations with Henderson, in vain. Governor Martin ordered the Transylvania Company to obey the laws of North Carolina. Henderson ignored the governor. At a meeting with the Cherokee in March 1775, at the Sycamore Shoals in the Watauga River settlements, the Transylvania Company bought a vast area stretching from the Kentucky and Ohio Rivers to the southern watershed of the Cumberland River. The company also purchased a corridor of land from the Watauga River to the Cumberland Mountains, so that its settlers could proceed westward without invading the hunting grounds of the Cherokee. It has already been suggested that the transaction was dubious on several grounds. It was of doubtful validity in still another way. Did the Cherokee own all the lands they had sold? Stuart scolded the Cherokee for selling a large part of their country. Lord Dunmore declared that the treaty of Sycamore Shoals was illegal, so far as Virginia was concerned. Henderson paid no attention to Dunmore. The Transylvania Company sold land to pioneers who soon appeared on the banks of the Kentucky River. The famous frontiersman, Daniel Boone, was Henderson's agent. The titles to lands in Kentucky given by the Transylvania Company to pioneers were later adjudged to be defective, and Henderson and his partners were forced to accept a small tract in Kentucky in return for abandoning their huge claim there. However, Henderson played a great role in the establishment of American settlements far beyond the Appalachian ridge and helped to place the boundary of the emerging American republic at the Mississippi River.

To what extent were the British measures restricting American exploitation of the lands south of the Ohio River grievances that contributed to colonial unrest and to the coming of the Revolution? Many American scholars born and educated on the Atlantic seaboard have written about the Revolution as if it were almost entirely confined to the regions east of the Appalachians. Some American historians of Midwestern background have urged that British policy concerning the Old West angered land speculators, pioneers, and colonial lawmakers jealous of the exertion of British power; and that it was a major "cause" of the Revolution. There can be no question that the Proclamation of October 7, 1763, vexed many colonists. However, George Washington saw as early as 1767 that it would not permanently prevent American expansion. It is to be believed that other land speculators, like Washington, expected that the Proclamation would be altered. It could also be circumvented. Moreover, most of the speculators put very little money in their schemes and had little to lose if those schemes failed. Benjamin Franklin did not turn against Britain because the Vandalia project did not prosper. Nor were settlers seriously restrained by the Proclamation. It will be recalled that much new land was opened to them by the establishment of the Indian boundary line of 1768; that they pushed far beyond that line, almost to the Mississippi; and that they were not driven back. Surely the short-lived British efforts to put the Indian trade in order did not create widespread and deep dissatisfaction among the colonists. Hence, it would appear that British policy regarding the West irritated, but did not exasperate, many Americans.

It follows that the boundary provisions of the famous Quebec Act, passed in the spring of 1774, did not constitute an American grievance of massive proportions. That law, offensive to the colonists on other grounds, pushed the boundaries of the province of Quebec southwestward to the Ohio and Mississippi Rivers, except "that nothing herein shall in any wise affect the boundaries of any other colony." The principal reason for the extension of Quebec was doubtless to meet the need for establishing civil government over the several villages of French Canadians in the Old Northwest—Detroit, Kaskaskia, Vincennes, and others—that had no formal government beyond supervision by British military officers after the conquest of Canada. Was it also intended to serve as a bar against exploitation by the Americans of the Old Northwest? Certainly, if the lands north of the Ohio were granted at the city of Quebec rather than Williamsburg, Boston, or Hartford, the inhabitants of the Thirteen Colonies would have less opportunity to secure those lands than inhabitants of Quebec. Moreover, Virginia claimed all of the Old Northwest, under her charter of 1609; and Massachusetts and Connecticut could assert claims to parts of it by their charters. Were their rights cancelled by the Quebec Act? The new boundary of Quebec, it should be observed, did not specifically destroy such rights; it did put them in question. Thomas Jefferson and other Americans vigorously condemned the extension of Quebec. However, the Americans were suspicious of every British measure by 1774. They found many other grievances in the Quebec Act that lacked substance. It is doubtful that all of those grievances were heartfelt. The Americans could believe that the extension of Quebec to the Ohio and the Mississippi—if that extension was intended—would not prevent their entrance into the Old Northwest. They were already planted in Kentucky, despite earlier British restrictions.

And yet—did not Jefferson and other Americans who condemned the new boundary of Quebec have reason to suspect that Britain was seeking new and more effective ways of curbing American expansion? In February 1774, the royal governors in America were ordered to sell public lands only by auction, to multiply the existing very low minimum price by five, and to double the quit-rent rate. They were also to reserve to the Crown all mines of gold and silver, and all precious stones. Ever since the founding of Virginia, the Crown had demanded only one fifth of those valuables. It is not surprising that British policy created uneasiness in the minds of Americans interested in the occupation and development of the West.

In that same February of 1774 Britain and America were entering a third crisis. The burning issues that created it had to do, not with the West, but with the East. British policy concerning the West exacerbated that crisis.

CHAPTER X

The Tea Troubles

THERE was no true meeting of British and American minds in the year 1770, no peace, only an uneasy truce. Indulging in half measures, George III, Lord North, the British cabinet, and Parliament met just enough of the demands of the colonists to secure a political relaxation. They did not satisfy the Americans. The chasm that had been opened between the mother country and her dependencies in 1765, which the Rockingham people did not completely close, had widened again. Indeed, Britain and America were farther apart at the close of 1770 than they had ever been, except at the height of the Stamp Act crisis. If the empire was to escape more and greater turmoil, even to endure, it was necessary that those who ruled in Britain should recognize that it would be increasingly difficult to please the colonists. With many others in London, Lord North failed to see the perilous state of colonial affairs. In 1773 he carelessly endorsed a scheme to persuade the Americans to buy Townshend-taxed tea in large quantities. So he revived the almost dormant issue of British taxation versus American rights; the colonists indulged in some "tea parties," including one at Boston; and Britain undertook to punish Boston and Massachusetts for disobedience.

It is not easy to assess the intensity and incidence of public passions of times gone by. Newspapers are especially bad guides to sentiment, for they dote upon extremes and feed on fighting. They were not fundamentally different in 1770 from what they would afterward become. One could easily bring forward quotations from British and American newspapers of that year and of the years immediately following to prove that the two great bodies of English-speaking people had come to detest each other most thoroughly. Such was not yet the fact. American sentiment

125

toward Britain was much mixed. There were still many colonists who were fond of the "old country," colonists whose loyalty to it could hardly be shaken; and there were many others who were less devoted to Britain, but who were not eager to quarrel with the parent state over issues that appeared to them to be less than ultimate. And yet—it cannot be doubted that the troubles of the years 1767 to 1770 hardened the hearts of hundreds of thousands of Americans against Britain and also stimulated the growth of an incipient national spirit among them. Anglo-American contests were no longer confined to laws, words, resolutions, and economics, with minor violences. American blood had been shed in quantity, and six Americans had been slain in Boston. After the passage of many generations, it is possible for the Americans generally to concede that Ebenezer Richardson and the soldiers who pulled triggers in the Boston Massacre were not wanton murderers—that they responded to gross provocation. But at the time they were, to unsophisticated Americans, brutal killers, minions of a British government disposed to establish arbitrary rule over the colonies. They were such even to certain educated men of Massachusetts like Samuel Adams and John Hancock. And few Americans, however well-informed and judicious they might be, could, even in an era when men of the Western world were not remarkably sensitive to pain, disease, wounds, and death, coolly set aside the Boston Massacre as an unfortunate incident of no importance.

Nevertheless, there were learned and thoughtful men in the colonies who did not enlarge their definitions of American rights, either because of the "massacre" or because of the Anglo-American contest of which it was only a bloody part. John Adams, a Harvard graduate, a rising lawyer, a man of studious habits, counsel for the defense in the trials after the "massacre," temporarily drew away from the world of politics. It is apparent that he did not quite approve of the behavior of his cousin Samuel Adams, that he could not join Samuel in passionate denunciation of British tyranny. John Adams resolved to devote himself to his legal practice. For a time he kept that resolution. He even drank tea, as he himself recorded, without trying to find out whether the leaves from which it was made were virginally Dutch in origin or contaminated by British taxation. Nor was George Washington, that level-headed Virginia planter, moved to enlarge his definition of American rights. He drank British-taxed tea. Was it worthwhile to squabble over every trifle? John Dickinson remained satisfied with the view of the nature of the British empire he had put forward in his *Letters of a Farmer in Pennsylvania*. At length even John Hancock, tiring of constant bickering in Massachusetts, forsook the arena of public affairs. The fortune he had inherited from his uncle was diminishing, and he answered the call of his business for attention. He parted from Samuel Adams, who continued to find irrefutable evidence of tyrannical intent in every British measure, however trifling, however innocent it might seem to a temperate observer.

Even so, there were other sufficiently sophisticated Americans who did expand their interpretations of American rights, among them Thomas Jefferson. Pondering over Richard Bland's *Enquiry into the Rights of the British Colonies*—with its appeal to the natural rights of man—the writings of John Locke, and those of other political philsophers, Jefferson, a young Virginia planter and lawyer, learned to estimate the rights of the Americans in terms of those of mankind rather than merely in those of Englishmen. The colonists had been endowed with life, liberty, and property by the Creator of the universe, not by English statutes, decrees, and customs. Government must concede and protect that endowment, must not attempt to reduce it. Oppression by lawful rulers would justify, even demand, their overthrow. He increasingly doubted that Parliament had ever possessed authority over America as a matter of right; he also came to believe that the sovereignty of the British Crown in America was neither absolute nor indestructible. Tyrannical exercise of the powers of the monarch might even force the Americans to rebel in defense of the rights given them by the God of Nature. By 1774 Jefferson had emerged as a thoroughgoing champion of American freedom in Virginia.

Benjamin Franklin, in London, also defined the liberties of the colonists more and more generously, even anticipating Jefferson in point of time. He, too, seems to have derived inspiration from the arguments advanced by Richard Bland. During the Anglo-American contest of the years 1767 to 1770, Franklin committed himself ever more positively to his native country. He ardently and cogently defended the colonists in letters published pseudonymously in English newspapers. He urged his fellow Americans to boycott British goods. In fact, he even advised them to continue to refuse to buy British wares until all the Townshend duties were rescinded. Meditating about the government of the British empire, he reached the conclusion as early as 1770 that Parliament possessed no valid authority whatever over the colonies. He would not even concede that the British legislature could rightfully restrict the maritime commerce of the Americans—although he was as yet willing to let Parliament do so. Franklin envisioned a noble empire of the future based upon recognition of the Americans as the equals of their British brethren. The two peoples —he was well aware that they differed from each other—would be united only by a common Crown. He even contemplated a time, not remote, when America, becoming richer and more powerful than Britain, might be the center of that glorious and enduring empire. Such thoughts the Philadelphian kept pretty much to himself, for few Englishmen would then have been able to see that his scheme of a mighty commonwealth was derived from a sense of justice and from the wisdom of a far-sighted political philosopher. Indeed, even though Franklin tried to avoid giving offense, he became the object of ever greater suspicion among the English. By 1770 he had become an agent for Georgia, New Jersey, and Massachusetts as well as Pennsylvania, and the principal spokesman for America in London. Almost an American envoy, he had to defend his constituents, and he could not do his duty to them without irritating, without arousing the anger of Englishmen who could not conceive that the Americans were their equals either politically, socially, or intellectually. To such men in London Franklin was a spy in their midst. Because he was polite, he was named "Dr. Doubleface" in London newspapers. They also called him a "Judas," for his letters to his employers in America were secured and scanned by British officials, who reported that he was even less devoted to Old England than he appeared to be, that he encouraged American resistance against British authority. One suspects that Franklin, cool as he was in temperament, resented such epithets, and that the abuse heaped upon him turned him more and more against Britain. He had loved that country, and some of its inhabitants. He would be driven at length to recognize that he could not be both an Englishman and an American.

And what were the opinions and feelings of Samuel Adams, who had succeeded James Otis as the leader of the malcontents in Massachusetts? He did not possess the versatile genius of Franklin or Jefferson, or even the solid abilities of his cousin John. Nevertheless, for about five years Samuel Adams played a great role in the Anglo-American world. Not that he had ever visited Old England. He was a New Englander to the core, a devout Congregationalist, and a Harvard graduate. He had failed as a businessman. During most of his adult life, he chose to devote himself to politics. Like Patrick Henry, he was not a statesman. Unlike Henry, he was not a compelling orator. But he was a propagandist extraordinary. He was also a remarkably skillful manipulator of Massachusetts committees and town meeetings. He was a truly gifted and most determined politician—in the vulgar sense of that word. His cousin John had complete faith in his integrity. Those attacked by him said that he was cunning, hypocritical, and less than fond of the truth. He did certainly on many occasions misrepresent the intentions of Britain; and just as surely, he portrayed the servants of the mother country in America in darker colors than they deserved. It is possibly a charitable judgment that he was merely a sincere and excessively prejudiced champion in the cause of American freedom. No one can doubt his utter devotion to that cause. It has been said that he sought separation from Britain as early as 1768, also that he did not desire American independence until 1775. Perhaps he did not know whether or not he desired America to leave the British empire until British regulars and American militia clashed in battle. It is clear enough, in any case, that he assailed Britain at every opportunity after 1768, and that he was emotionally prepared for a final separation well before the shooting began. With allies who shared his distrust of Britain and the British, he did all that he could after 1770 to drive Massachusetts—and America—into struggle with Britain.

In April 1772 General Gage declared that America was in a state of "profound tranquillity." So it was, but not because Britain and America had resolved their differences. The relationship that had existed between them in 1763 had not been restored. The attempts of Britain to alter it had been checked in large degree by American resistance. Nevertheless, those efforts had brought important changes. In 1772, Britain, continuing to assert her right to impose taxes for revenue, was collecting money from the duty upon molasses and small sums from that upon tea; she was rigidly regulating the maritime commerce of the Americans in reality as well as upon paper; and garrisons of British troops, supported in small part by the colonists, were posted in New York, New Jersey, Pennsylvania, and Massachusetts. Britain was also restraining, without much vigor or success, the westward expansion of the colonies. But she could undertake no more adventures toward getting money from the colonists or toward asserting her sway over them without encountering rebellion. Indeed, it is evident that many Americans, including Samuel Adams, were disposed to struggle toward restoration of the imperial system as it had been in 1763, and that more and more American leaders were inclined to believe that they were entitled to even greater freedom within the empire than they had enjoyed at the close of the Seven Years' War. If Britain desired a permanent accommodation with the Thirteen Colonies, it was necessary that she be most careful not to offend her restive offspring.

With the wisdom of hindsight it is clear that Lord North, if he desired the peaceful and healthy continuation of the British empire, would have done well to move toward a reconstruction of that empire upon the basis of political equality between Britain and America. But neither North nor any of his colleagues nor George III possessed the wisdom of Dr. Franklin. They did not even make a great effort to secure authentic, full, and unbiased information about the colonies. North would have done well to make a personal inspection of America, at least to send a cool and competent man of imposing stature across the ocean. But it did not occur to North or to his associates or to the monarch that it would be prudent to take such an unprecedented step until Massachusetts was actually in rebellion—and even then they did not act. They might, as a less suitable alternative, have consulted, soberly and lengthily, the agents of the colonies in London, including Franklin. Instead, listening to those agents upon occasion, and reading reports from the servants of the Crown in America, they muddled along in insular ignorance.

The advice that was received in London from British officials in the colonies was not helpful. The reports of royal governors and customs men inevitably praised the devotion and services to Britain of the writers and magnified the formidable and vexing opposition they frequently encountered as they loyally did their duty. Nor did the dispatches from New York of General Gage, or his "private" letters to Viscount Barrington—these being sent to Barrington's home in Cavendish Square rather than to the War Office—temperately assess men and conditions beyond the Atlantic. Gage was a "good fellow," and an honest and brave officer. He had married an American woman, Margaret Kemble, daughter of a respected citizen of New Jersey and a cousin of various dignified Schuylers, Van Rensselaers, and Van Cortlandts of New York. But Gage had remained a true-blue Englishman with the narrow notions about America of George Grenville. Continuing to despise the colonists as soldiers, he—an Anglican—also disliked Congregationalists and Presbyterians. He regretted that Britain had yielded to the colonists by repealing the Stamp Act, and he regretted even more that Britain had given way a second time by rescinding almost all of the Townshend duties. And he said so to Lord Barrington. Britain should have used force to crush the colonists in 1766; she should have used force to reduce them to obedience in 1770. Twice challenging the colonists, Britain had twice meekly refused to support words with deeds. She had thus actually stimulated the Americans to make greater demands. His criticism, from the traditional point of view of a European toward empire, was quite warranted. Continuing to urge that Britain act vigorously to preserve her empire, before it was too late, he gave Barrington forthright and stern advice. He declared that "democracy is too prevalent in America, and claims the greatest attention to prevent its increase, and fatal effects." Since quiet reigned in the colonies, Britain should take advantage of it not only to "assert, but also support that supremacy which she claims over the members of the empire, or she will soon only be supreme in words, and we shall become a vast empire of many parts, disjointed and independent of each other, without any head." Did he believe that Britain could so assert herself without raising a storm

130

in America? Gage also urged that the mother country, "as far as it can be done prudentially," do everything possible to cramp American commerce and industry—he was jealous for Britain of the growing wealth and prosperity of America.

That Britain could hardly move against the colonists without creating commotion was demonstrated even before the end of 1772. In March of that year Lieutenant William Dudingston of the royal navy, in command of the *Gaspée,* began to patrol the waters off Rhode Island, searching for American smugglers. He was zealous, and he was arrogant, offensive alike to smugglers and to law-abiding merchants and the captains of their vessels. If a ship seized by the navy was condemned in court, it could be sold, with the commanding naval officer receiving a share of the proceeds. On June 9, pursuing an American packet, the *Gaspée* ran aground not far from Providence. Four years earlier Rhode Islanders had destroyed a royal ship that had been excessively active. Informed of Dudingston's plight, John Brown, a prominent merchant of Providence who bore no love for customs or naval officers, hastily formed an expedition of armed men to put an end to the *Gaspée* before it could be floated. Late in the evening they rowed out to the helpless ship in eight longboats. One of them shot and wounded Dudingston. He and his men were forcibly removed from the schooner, and their vessel was set afire and burned to the water's edge. Dudingston and his crew were put ashore. Neither the governor of Rhode Island nor a sheriff could find the culprits, although most of them were well known in Providence. The British cabinet then undertook to bring the offenders to justice. The privy council appointed a board of inquiry to investigate the incident and offered a reward of £500 for information leading to the conviction of the criminals. Beginning hearings in Rhode Island in January 1773, the board was unable to secure evidence that could be used against them. However, the very appearance of its members in the colony was condemned throughout America. For Parliament, in March 1772, had made it a crime, punishable by death, to set fire to a naval vessel, and had also made it possible to bring a person to trial in England for such an offense committed in American waters. Was it not the right of an Englishman to be tried by a jury of the "vicinage," by a jury composed of men who lived in his district? Americans clamored against another invasion of their personal rights. Did Britain intend to enslave them?

A minor step taken by Britain in Massachusetts in 1772 similarly led to outcries of intended despotism. It was announced in the autumn of that year that the judges of the superior court of Massachusetts would be paid henceforth from customs house receipts rather than from the funds of the colony. Town meetings in and outside Boston immediately proclaimed that such provision for the magistrates was another step toward the establishment of a system of slavery for America. Precisely how judges paid by the Crown rather than by the colony would be so very much more dangerous to liberty was not explained. But feeling was sufficiently aroused to enable Samuel Adams, Dr. Joseph Warren, and James Otis to persuade a Boston town meeting, early in November, not only to appoint them, with eighteen other men, as a committee of correspondence, but to adopt a far-reaching pronunciamento, drafted by that committee, of "the rights of the colonists, and of this province in particular, as men, as Christians, and as subjects." So began a network of such committees in Massachusetts, and in New England, for other towns quickly copied Boston and set up such political engines. Thus developed a far-flung machine by which the towns could and did act in concert against Britain. Moreover, in their declaration of American rights, the men of the Boston committee forthrightly asserted that they were based upon the laws of Nature as well as the British constitution. They condemned Parliamentary taxation of the Americans; the commissioners of the customs; the courts of vice-admiralty; restrictions upon American manufacturing; deprivation of trial by jury; and the sending of troops and sailors into Massachusetts to support unconstitutional officers in executing unconstitutional laws. They hinted that Parliament actually possessed little if any rightful authority over America. They did not make their list of grievances as short as possible. They expressed suspicion that Britain had meditated, and was meditating the foundation of an Anglican bishopric in America. Had not the ancestors of the people of Massachusetts fled from England to escape the "prelates"? Endorsed by towns outside Boston, that declaration angered Governor Thomas Hutchinson, and he unwisely undertook to refute its charges before the General Court of his province, which he called into session to hear his defense of Britain.

Hutchinson sincerely believed that Massachusetts was in a most happy state, and that he might be able to convince its legislature that such was the fact. For he lacked good sense. Historians have not been unkind to him, if for no other reason because he shared their craft. He wrote a respectable history of Massachusetts—one need not be sensible to indite good history. Also in his favor among historians is the fact that he was a descendant of Mrs. Ann Hutchinson, who suffered persecution for her religious views in seventeenth-century Massachusetts. A Harvard man, a scholar, a proud Congregationalist, and a gentleman, he was a bit of a snob and an inveterate collector of public offices. As a pluralist, he would have been more at home in Old England than in New England. He assiduously sought and received appointments for his relatives as well as for himself. In his climb to power in Massachusetts he had managed to secure the chief justiceship of the province, even though it had been promised to the father of James Otis by two governors, and even though Hutchinson had no legal training. It was said by the enemies of Otis, and it may be believed, that Otis and his relatives, including Dr. Joseph Warren, never forgave Hutchinson. The governor was much respected for his intellectual powers; he was very popular among the many men of Massachusetts who deplored public tumult and who yearned for peace and profits. But he was heartily disliked as a person by many in Massachusetts who had not engaged in rivalry with him for offices and honors as an aristocrat, as an enemy of popular government, and as a champion of Britain.

Addressing the General Court, Hutchinson displayed both his scholarship and his lack of understanding. Praising the British constitution as suffused with the spirit of liberty, he flatly declared that "I know no line that can be drawn between the supreme authority of Parliament and the total independence of the colonies." That statement was politely challenged by the Massachusetts council, was rudely rebutted by the House of Representatives in a paper polished by John Adams, a better scholar than Hutchinson. The lower house asserted that Parliament had not possessed sovereignty over Massachusetts when the colony was founded and had not afterward acquired it. If there could be "no line between the supreme authority of Paliament and the total independence of the colonies," it followed "either that the colonies are the vassals of Parliament, or, that they are totally independent." It could not be argued, said the house, that the colonies possessed no rights whatever as against the British legislature. Hutchinson's contention therefore indicated that the colonies were independent. The house would not go so far—nor would it seek to draw a line between Parliamentary power and American rights without the consent of the other American colonies given in a congress. Hutchinson never had a chance to win the debate, in that the finest statement that might have been prepared in defense of Britain would not have convinced the majority of his listeners.

Let it not be thought that eagerness to struggle with Britain and her servants in America was confined to Rhode Island and Massachusetts in the early months of 1773. The tobacco planters of Virginia were among the few people in America who were not prosperous at that time. The tobacco market was so poor that George Washington had turned to hemp and wheat. In March of that year the House of Burgesses, perceiving the usefulness of the local committees of correspondence in Massachusetts, established one of its own and urged the lower houses of the other colonies to do likewise. All of them responded before the following autumn. Thus an intercolonial web of communication was created that fostered American unity and stiffened American resistance to all British measures. Upon the Virginia committee were such ardent defenders of American freedom as Patrick Henry, Richard Henry Lee, Richard Bland, and Thomas Jefferson. When it was founded, they had some difficulty in finding a burning issue to justify it. They chose the British law which made possible the trial in England of the burners of the *Gaspée* as a desperate act of tyranny. It is not recorded that they urged the people of Providence to refrain from destroying His Majesty's vessels. But they would soon be given better reasons to complain; and the network of committees of correspondence that Massachusetts and Virginia had initiated would make the most of those reasons and would help to lay the foundation for an American republic. Lord North was embarking upon a campaign to persuade the colonists to buy more taxed tea, supplying the great grievance for which Samuel Adams had vainly sought for so many months.

Before the sinister quality of Lord North's scheme was known in the colonies, the ardent champions of liberty in Massachusetts again took the offensive. In June 1773, the House of Representatives of that province published "the Hutchinson letters" and petitioned the Crown for the removal from office of both Governor Hutchinson and Lieutenant Governor Andrew Oliver. As an agent of that body Benjamin Franklin was assigned the task of presenting its demand in London. The consequences were melodramatic and important. The petition was inspired by receipt in the house of thirteen letters sent to Thomas Whately by Hutchinson, Oliver, and other defenders of imperial authority during the years 1767 to 1769. At that time Whately was not in office, and the letters were ostensibly private; but they dealt with public business; they had been examined by several English public men and at least one of them had been inspected by George III himself. Writing to Whately in January 1769, Hutchinson had declared, "There must be an abridgement of what are called English liberties" in Massachusetts. He had asserted doubt that a colony 3,000 miles away from the parent state could have all its freedoms. He had expressed a wish that Britain place "some further restraint" upon the province to prevent its separation from Britain, since he believed that independence would be disastrous for Massachusetts. Those imprudent statements, even though they had been written several years ago, even though they were not much stronger than others that Hutchinson had made publicly, condemned him in the eyes of the house. In the petition

Oliver was assailed as Hutchinson's ally in a "conspiracy" to bring soldiers and sailors into Massachusetts and to overthrow its system of free government under its charter of 1691.

In asking the Crown to deprive Hutchinson of his post, Franklin had to perform an awkward and unpleasant duty. For it was he who had secured the letters and sent them back to Boston. That indiscreet action would cost him dearly. He had urged that the letters be kept confidential, that they should not be published. He had hardly expected that they would be both published and used to create a furor, but they were. Samuel Adams was then clerk of the House of Representatives, and Adams knew persuasive propaganda when he saw it. Precisely how Franklin obtained the letters remains a mystery. He was forced to announce his responsibility before the privy council officially acted upon the petition from Massachusetts. Thomas Whately was dead. Whately's brother William, his executor, accused John Temple, who had served as a commissioner of the customs at Boston, of stealing the letters. It is indeed likely that Temple had something to do with the passage of the documents into Franklin's hands. Temple denied the accusation of William Whately, who demanded satisfaction on the field of honor. The two men fought a ludicrous duel, in December 1773, in which neither man was killed or desperately hurt. However, it became known to Franklin that Whately was considering a second challenge to Temple. To prevent another and perhaps fatal contest, Franklin announced publicly on Christmas Day that he was the person who had obtained and forwarded the letters to Boston.

When Franklin appeared before the privy council at the Cockpit in Whitehall on January 29, 1774, he was in a most embarrassing position as a gentleman, a British postal official, and a spokesman for the Massachusetts House of Representatives. In that time the contents of letters were not so sacred as they afterward were—Franklin's own letters had been examined by hostile eyes for which they were not intended. Nevertheless, a gentleman was supposed to have scruples in such matters. Moreover, Franklin was still British deputy postmaster general in North America, and presumably should have been more scrupulous than other gentlemen. What was even worse for Franklin, news had reached London of the Boston Tea Party, and sentiment was running hot and high against America and Americans. Every member of the privy council who could be present attended the meeting, and spectators came in numbers, for it was certain to offer a great show. In the crowded gathering were Lord North and General Gage, who was in England upon leave of absence. Franklin himself did not speak. Two lawyers in his behalf soberly urged the removal of Hutchinson on the simple ground that it was desired by the people of Massachusetts. The request could not possibly win the sanction of the privy council, and it might have been denied without much ado.

However, in defense of Hutchinson appeared Alexander Wedderburn, who was the British solicitor general, one of those disgraces to the legal profession who believe it to be their privilege to abuse all and sundry. In private life Wedderburn could be charming, and he would later become lord chancellor and an earl. Renowned for political treachery, he had been forced to leave Scotland because he had failed to control his tongue in the courts of his native country. Moving to London and learning better English, he now proved that he was a master of invective. In a long speech he savagely and wittily assailed Franklin, much to the amusement and joy of privy councilors and spectators, many of whom laughed aloud at his sallies. "Hear him! Hear him!" they cried. He did not scruple to apply the Latin word for thief to his victim. Lord North—he must have known that no good could come from Wedderburn's performance—did not join in the laughter or the applause. But Wedderburn went on and on. He closed by charging that Boston was the center of a conspiracy not only to oust Hutchinson, but to create an independent American republic, and that Franklin, a Bostonian by birth, was a party to it. What a spectacle it was—a dignified scientist and philosopher almost seventy years of age, one of the greatest men of the century, being pilloried by "Sawney Weatherbeaten," a windy and unscrupulous lawyer. In the audience were Dr. Joseph Priestley, the great chemist; Edmund Burke; Charles James Fox, an orator who could rival Burke on occasion; and the scholar, Jeremy Bentham. What did they think of Wedderburn's histrionics?

When Wedderburn had finished, Franklin, who had not said a word officially, shook hands with his lawyers and walked out of the room. Soon afterward he was deprived of his appointment as deputy postmaster general, and the petition of Massachusetts against Hutchinson was formally rejected. He was innocent of the charges that Wedderburn had brought against him; and he had rather deplored the aggressiveness of Samuel Adams and his like in Massachusetts. There were certainly Englishmen, including the Earl of Chatham and the Earl of Shelburne, who regretted that he had been a target of Wedderburn's philippic. He would talk to them and to others in England about ways and means to secure an Anglo-American accommodation as relations between the mother country and the colonies became ever more strained. Was his heart in those conversations? His dream of a magnificent Anglo-American empire had faded. Becoming utterly an American, he would thenceforth be unwilling to make any great concession to Britain to restore peace within the empire. He stayed on in London for about fourteen months, until the War of

Independence was about to begin. Returning home to Philadelphia, he was acclaimed as a hero. Old as he was, he would have as sweet revenge as a man might gain for the castigation he had received from Wedderburn. On that January day in the Cockpit he wore a brown coat of Manchester velvet. On February 6, 1778, he put on that coat in his lodgings at Passy, near Paris, and went forth to affix his signature to two treaties between France and the United States of America that assured American independence.

It is doubtful that Franklin would have been so nastily pilloried by Wedderburn, had not Britain and America been in the midst of a crisis. But they were pitted against each other for the third time, principally because Lord North tried in 1773 both to help the East India Company and to induce the colonists to buy more taxed tea. So he supplied an issue that would stimulate American feeling against Britain to fever pitch.

Early in 1773 "John Company" was in financial straits. Its condition was of great importance to Britain, since the company was the instrument of British government in India, and also to many influential Englishmen who were stockholders. It had assets that could be turned into cash. Its warehouses in Asia contained fifteen million pounds of tea, and more of the aromatic leaves were en route to those warehouses. Officers of the company urged Lord North to help them. It had been compelled in the past to unload and sell in England tea that was destined for the American market. English merchants who sent the tea across the Atlantic added their costs and profit to its price, and it was Townshend-taxed in American ports at threepence per pound. It was therefore more expensive than leaves smuggled into America from Dutch sources. The company asked permission to send tea to America in its own ships, and relief both from all duties in England and from the Townshend tax. North was quite willing to help the company, but he would not consent to the removal of the Townshend duty. Accordingly, he secured the passage by Parliament in May 1773 of a Tea Act that authorized the company to ship tea to America without paying any duty in England. The Tea Act was not strenuously opposed in Parliament. Yet it was pregnant with trouble, as John Norton, a London merchant, pointed out to officials of the company. They would be able to undersell Dutch tea in America, even though their product was Townshend-taxed. The colonists would certainly conclude that they were being offered cheap English tea in order to persuade them to pay the Townshend duty. They would see the Tea Act as a sinister device to weaken their stand against Parliamentary taxation. Lord North had indeed laid a trap for the colonists; and he could hardly have done it in ignorance, even though one may believe that he was giving troubles in America far less study than they deserved. It must be concluded that he expected the Americans to make a constitutional concession that might be vital and permanent merely for the sake of cheap tea. The indolent and easygoing North made an extraordinary blunder.

To that immense mistake North added another. American merchants had commonly been reluctant to quarrel with Britain. Businessmen in the ports of America engaged in maritime commerce had often stood out against boycott of British goods as long as they dared. There is reason to believe that many of them would have been pleased to handle British tea in quantity—if they could do so without bringing down upon themselves the wrath of other colonists. The company planned to send many millions of pounds of it across the ocean. But North permitted the East India Company to sell its tea exclusively to certain American merchants, so that only a few favored ones in each colony might profit. Thus five men of Massachusetts were tendered a monopoly in that province. Two of the five were sons of Governor Hutchinson, one was his nephew, and the other two were his friends; and, since Hutchinson himself was engaged in trade, it was inevitably suspected that he personally was one of those who was pleasing to the East India Company. Such an arrangement could not fail to offend all those American importers who were denied opportunity to buy and sell the tea. It was especially odious in that, if it succeeded for tea, it could be applied to other goods brought into American harbors. It certainly irked John Hancock that he was omitted from the list of monopolists, and that the Hutchinsons and their friends were preferred to him. He had broken with Samuel Adams. When he learned that he had been excluded, he made up his quarrel with Adams. Thenceforth he was an unwavering and most forward champion of American liberty. No great man, he would again be a most valuable ally of Adams.

Leaders of the colonists saw clearly that the Americans were being offered a poisonous potion in the form of a cheap and comforting beverage. They had not complained bitterly against the British duty of a penny per gallon upon molasses, collected ever since 1766; and they had not become excited because of occasional importations of Townshend-taxed tea. But it was something else again to pay the Townshend duty upon vast quantities of tea. And if the colonists did so, how could they logically protect against other and more burdensome Parliamentary levies in the future? The Americans very generally resolved, with many merchants giving tacit and even enthusiastic support, somehow to thwart the insidious and treacherous scheme concocted in London to strike at American liberty.

But how could the British strategem be countered? If the East India

Company's tea were landed and offered for sale, it was quite certain that it would be purchased by some because of its low price, and it was likely that other colonists would soon follow the example of their thrifty neighbors. The colonists found answers to their problem. They should prevent landing of the tea; if any were landed, they should prevent the sale of it. They executed a series of "tea parties" in American harbors.

The first of these festivities took place in Boston, because Boston was nearer to England than the other major American ports. Ships owned and leased by the East India Company and laden with tea sailed across the Atlantic in the fall of 1773; and other vessels carrying consignments of it followed. Three of the ships, one after another, sailed into Boston Harbor in November and December. Samuel Adams, John Hancock, Dr. Joseph Warren, and other champions of American liberty acted. They asked that the consignees refuse to accept the tea sent to them; the consignees, undoubtedly encouraged by their relative and friend, Governor Hutchinson, insisted that they would receive it. After a series of meetings, Boston town then declared that the tea must not be landed and demanded that the governor arrange to send the ships back to England. He would not do it. He could legally prevent them from leaving the harbor, since their cargoes had been entered at the customs house, and he did so. Those responsible for the vessel did not dare to unload it and pay duties. The customs officers made ready to seize the first of the ships—also quite legally—with the intention of selling the tea it carried, in order to collect the duties due. It was to be feared that people would buy some of that tea, thus paying the Townshend tax upon it. They were saved from temptation. There had been muscular men in Boston willing to exert themselves in behalf of American freedom ever since 1765. On December 16, bands of them dressed like Mohawk Indians paraded down to the docks, boarded the three vessels swinging idly at anchor, and tossed about 340 chests of tea worth more than £9,000 into the harbor. Samuel Adams did not dress himself up as a Mohawk chief leading his braves to battle. But it cannot be doubted that he played a large part, with Dr. Warren, in planning the affair.

Less forthright action served to ruin North's scheme in other American ports. Everywhere except in Boston their fellow citizens persuaded and bullied until the consignees agreed not to accept East India Company tea. A ship carrying 257 chests of it arrived in the harbor of Charleston, South Carolina, early in December. Christopher Gadsden, merchant and planter, "the Samuel Adams of South Carolina," mobilized men who demanded that the tea be returned to England. The captain of the ship could not easily comply. At length a compromise was reached. The tea was landed on December 22, but it was stored under lock and key, not offered for sale. Many months later a Revolutionary government of South Carolina sold the tea, using the proceeds in the cause of an American rebellion. Three days after the settlement at Charleston, on Christmas Day, a vessel carrying British tea appeared in the Delaware River below Philadelphia. Going into the city, its captain was informed that he would do well to take the tea back to England. He did so. New York was not put to the test until April 1774, when two ships appeared. A small consignment of tea in one of them was seized by "Sons of Liberty" and thrown into the harbor, and the chests that contained it were used to make a bonfire, by way of celebration, in the streets of the city. The captain of the second vessel prudently set sail for England. The last of the "tea parties," a curious affair, took place at Annapolis, Maryland, in the fall of 1774. An attempt by a merchant company of that town to bring in a consignment of more than 2,000 pounds of tea was foiled. The tea and the brig that carried it were destroyed, with the extorted consent of the owners. Nowhere in the colonies was the East India Company able to dispose of its surplus tea for cash.

It was known in London in January 1774 that Massachusetts was again in commotion. There were those in the imperial capital who said that steps had to be taken to reduce Boston, and the province of which it was the center, to obedience. Then came reports of the Boston Tea Party. Thereafter, it was generally agreed in London that repressive action must be taken. Alexander Wedderburn's onslaught against Benjamin Franklin was the signal that government was determined to do something about Boston, Massachusetts, and America. Reports of the other "tea parties" did not diminish that determination.

CHAPTER XI

Rebellion

A S the news of the American "tea parties" came into London, indignation arose among the British people. The colonists had not merely resisted government; they had wantonly destroyed private property. They must be brought to heel, and those who had lawlessly ruined so much good tea must be brought to the bar of justice. It was not easy to find ways and means to proceed against the Americans. At length the government undertook to vent its wrath upon Boston and Massachusetts, to make examples of them, so that all the colonists would learn that they could not flout the will of Britain. The steps which it thoughtlessly took were looked upon by many cool-headed men in London as "mild" and "moderate," and they were condemned by relatively few Englishmen in public life. They were not "mild" or "moderate" to the Americans; and they were downright stupid. Britain closed the port of Boston; tried to change the political system of Massachusetts in violation of her charter; and sent troops a second time into the province. Massachusetts rebelled, and all America rallied behind Massachusetts. At last, the British cabinet ordered General Gage to put his troops in motion, and the War of Independence began.

Unfortunately for the North ministry, it was not possible to move directly against those Americans who had most flagrantly defied British authority, the men responsible for the Boston Tea Party. On February 4, 1774, after considering a body of papers concerning that affair which the Earl of Dartmouth had collected, the cabinet resolved to ask Attorney General Edward Thurlow and Solicitor General Wedderburn to consider the evidence and to issue warrants for the arrest of all persons involved in it who had committed treason. A week later Thurlow and Wedderburn reported that certain Bostonians, including Dr. Joseph Warren, Dr. Benjamin Church, and William Molineux, had indeed been guilty of treason —they did not find evidence to support charges against the principal leaders of the malcontents in Boston, Samuel Adams and John Hancock. Moreover, the two lawyers absolutely refused to issue warrants for the arrest of those against whom there was evidence. It was doubtful that they could be convicted. Besides, whether the prosecution failed or succeeded, Thurlow and Wedderburn would have been assailed both in America and in England as cruel minions of an arbitrary government; and Thurlow, if not Wedderburn, seems to have feared that the ministry would draw back when public uproar came. According to the later recollection of William Knox, who was an undersecretary for the colonies at the time, Thurlow declared that he and Wedderburn would be "damned fools" to assume the responsibility for signing the warrants; and that, if they had been asked to do it by George Grenville, "who was so damned obstinate that he would go to hell with you before he would desert you there would be some sense in it." That profane man did indeed have reason to be wary, for neither North nor Dartmouth lusted for battle with the colonists—or with any other persons. The cabinet finally decided that it was necessary to secure more evidence before moving against the perpetrators of the Boston Tea Party, against the men who planned it as well as those who flung the chests of tea into the harbor.

But it remained most doubtful that the guilty individuals could be apprehended and convicted. Was there not some way in which Britain could immediately impose punishment? The answer seems to have been supplied by John Pownall, like William Knox an undersecretary for the colonies. It is said that he brought forward instances in which British cities had been forced to pay for damages inflicted by their riotous citizens. In any event, Lord North and his colleagues foolishly decided to exact payment from Boston for the deeds of some of her citizens. On March 14 the ministry introduced the extraordinary Boston Port Bill in the House of Commons. It provided that the harbor of Boston was to be closed to commerce until "peace and obedience to the laws" should be restored in the city, so that "the trade of Great Britain may be safely carried on there, and his Majesty's customs duty collected." The privy council would decide when that time had arrived.

The Port Bill was denounced in Parliament. It was sensibly suggested during debate that Boston be given an opportunity to pay for the tea that been destroyed in its harbor before severe penalty should be inflicted upon the city. Such was also the opinion of the Earl of Chatham, even though he believed that the destruction of the tea was "certainly criminal." A few of Chatham's followers, a few of the Marquis of Rock-ingham's friends, expressed dismay. It was dangerous to punish all Bos-tonians for the deeds of some Bostonians, to strike at the innocent as well as the guilty. George Johnstone, the former governor of West Florida, warned in the House of Commons that the bill would produce in America a "general confederation, to resist the power of this country." The predic-tion was wiser than the man. Johnstone was a windy and quarrelsome braggart, and he had little influence. On the other hand, that same Colo-nel Isaac Barré who had won the gratitude of the colonists by his fight against the Stamp Act voted for the Port Bill as a necessary corrective. Such was the belief also of overwhelming majorities in both houses of Parliament. In the House of Lords Lord Mansfield asserted that the at-tack upon the tea ships was "the last overt act of high treason." No formal vote was taken in either house, for it was obvious that the enemies of the bill could not defeat it. It was signed by the King on March 31, 1774.

So much specifically for Boston. But there was much more to come for the city as a part of Massachusetts, since the North ministry pushed through three more Coercive Acts. It asked Parliament to remodel the government of that province, as Sir Francis Bernard, Thomas Hutchin-son, General Gage, and the Earl of Hillsborough had long since urged. A bill introduced for that purpose on April 15 was drastic indeed. It called for the establishment of a royally chosen council in Massachusetts; for the appointment by the governor of all provincial judges and of all the sher-iffs, together with various other officers concerned with the enforcement of law; and for the selection of jury panels by the sheriffs. Except by special permission of the governor, each town was to hold no more than one meeting each year. The ministry desired to limit "democracy" in Massachusetts and to increase British authority in that troubled colony. The bill obviously violated the Massachusetts charter of 1691. Lord North declared in the House of Commons that the charter could not stand against the sovereign power of Parliament. He asked, "will this country sit still, when they see the colony proceeding against your own subjects, tarring and feathering your servants; denying your laws and authority; refusing every direction and advice you send?" He would not concede that Massachusetts was even entitled to a hearing before her charter rights were set aside. He demanded prompt action. The bill was condemned by Rockingham and Chatham men not only because it encroached upon the rights of the people of Massachusetts under the charter, but also because they were not given an opportunity to defend those rights. It will be recalled that George III in 1769 had thought it imprudent to tamper with that charter. But the King had obviously changed his mind; there is no doubt that he supported the ministry. Members of the Opposition in the House of Commons, including Burke, Sir George Savile, a highly respected Yorkshire gentleman, and Thomas Pownall, a former governor of Massachusetts, warned that the measure was pregnant with disaster. Even Colonel Barré, after giving his consent to the Port Bill, declaimed against trying to change the political system of Massachusetts. "The question now before us is," he said, "whether we will choose to bring over the affections of all our colonies by lenient measures, or wage war upon them." Having correctly predicted that the Americans would resist the stamp duties, Barré again prophesied accurately. For the bill was passed by both houses of Parliament by very large majorities, and Britain did at length wage war against the colonists. A small minority in the House of Lords formally and solemnly protested, but in vain. The law was sanctioned by the British public, and by the British monarch. But one petition was received against it—and that came from a few Americans resident in London who declared that their people were threatened with political slavery, that they would not accept that condition without a struggle.

North introduced two more bills to deal with Massachusetts that also swiftly became law, despite criticism from his English enemies. One of these made possible a change of venue for any person accused of crime in Massachusetts in the course of striving to execute British law. For it had been decided to appoint General Gage as governor of Massachusetts, to send British troops there, and to support them with a naval squadron. If Gage believed that such a person could not get a fair trial in Massachusetts he was authorized to move the trial to another colony or to England. The fact that Captain Preston and his men had received justice after the Boston Massacre was ignored. Another law, a special Quartering Act, was passed in an effort to help Gage house and supply his troops.

Did Lord North think of an effort to please as well as punish Massachusetts? Lord Shelburne declared in the spring of 1774 that repeal of the Townshend duty on tea was being considered by the ministry. The erasure of that tax would have taken much of the sting from the blows aimed at Massachusetts, would have been received with great pleasure in the other American colonies. It would have been wise to put an end to the issue of Parliamentary taxation. Perhaps North did canvass that possibility. If so, he rejected it—he continued to demand that America contribute money for the defense of the empire until the War of Independence was well under way. The wisdom of repealing the Townshend tax was evident to Lord Chatham and other political foes of North. A bill to cancel it was offered in the House of Commons on April 19, and Burke brilliantly debated in behalf of it. The Irish orator cogently condemned British efforts to exact a revenue from America. He declared that "in time of peace you flourished in commerce, and when war required it, had sufficient aid from the colonies, while you pursued your antient policy." He asserted that the revival of the issue of Parliamentary taxation by the Townshend duties "has produced the very worst effects," and that "partial repeal has produced not partial good, but universal evil." However, adherents of the ministry refused to be convinced. To revoke the duty, they said, was to abandon utterly Parliamentary supremacy over the colonies. Alexander Wedderburn proclaimed that "if you give up this tax . . . you will be required to give up much more, nay, to give up all." The bill was defeated by a vote of 182 to 49.

Before the last of the Coercive Acts was signed by the King, General Gage had reached Boston, on May 13, and had assumed his new duties as governor of Massachusetts. The appointment of the commander in chief of the army in North America as the civil executive in Massachusetts requires explanation. Thomas Hutchinson, tired and no longer young, had become so unpopular in the province that he could achieve nothing for Britain and had asked for leave of absence to permit him to go to England. It was believed in London early in 1774 that the lieutenant governor of Massachusetts, Andrew Oliver, was dying. Accordingly, granting Hutchinson's request, the British cabinet had to find at least a temporary replacement for the governor. Gage was its choice, not merely because he was a military man, although there was obvious advantage in combining the governorship with the command of the army in North America. Governor Gage would certainly be in a stronger position than his predecessors in Boston, for he would have no difficulty in getting troops from General Gage. There was another reason for selecting Gage. He was respected and liked by many in Massachusetts, despite the fact that the troops who had sojourned in Boston from 1768 to 1770 had been under his command. He was not yet hated there—he soon would be. He was obviously familiar with the American troubles. Moreover, Gage was willing to serve, and he heartily endorsed the measures adopted by the North ministry to bring Boston and Massachusetts to heel. In an audience with George III on February 4, 1774, he offered to return to America immediately to do what he could to execute those measures; and he told the monarch that four regiments would be sufficient to keep order and compel obedience in Boston. He was commissioned as governor on April 7; authorized to place as many troops as he thought necessary in the city; instructed to try to bring the leaders of the enemies of Britain in Massachusetts before the bar of justice; and given a complete pardoning power, which could be

145

used to protect the servants and friends of Britain and perhaps also to win over less courageous defenders of American freedom. Since the Port Bill was to go into effect on June 1—the other Coercive Acts at later dates— he hastened across the ocean.

According to George III, Gage told him in February in London that the Americans would be "lyons, whilst we are lambs," and that they would be "very meek" when faced by a resolute Britain. Did Gage indulge in a bit of soldierly braggadocio? Or did he tell the monarch, as courtiers do, what the King wished to hear? Gage was not an astute politician, but he surely knew, before he departed for the New World, that he would be confronted by awkward decisions. And if the Americans did not yield to the mother country, he could expect no lavish gratitude from those he served, no matter how loyally, no matter how energetically he did his onerous duty. Landing at Castle William for conferences with Thomas Hutchinson before proceeding into Boston, he did not learn that the situation in Massachusetts had altered greatly, that his tasks would be easier than he had expected. After giving Gage as much information as he could, Hutchinson sailed for England. He never returned. He died in England six years later a disappointed expatriate, for, whatever his faults, he loved his native Massachusetts. In Boston the new governor was honored by a traditional banquet in Faneuil Hall on May 17. It was suggested to him even on that festive occasion that he might not leave the city with a similar celebration. The name of Hutchinson was mentioned, and it was hissed.

Gage immediately began his labors and almost as quickly encountered disappointments. The Boston Tea Party shocked many Americans as well as Englishmen. Benjamin Franklin believed that the East India Company should be paid for the tea that had been destroyed, and several prominent men of Boston announced on May 18 that they would contribute to a fund for that purpose. Later, in an address to the new governor, 130 Bostonians declared that they would pay their share. These men and others urged both that the city compensate the East India Company and that the aggressive Boston committee of correspondence be abolished. They fought hard for their program in a series of town meetings, but they were unable to muster a majority. The closing of the port of Boston, on June 1, together with news from England that other punitive laws were moving through Parliament, ruined their cause. There were Bostonians who would have fought in any case against taking steps toward reconciliation with Britain. Angry resentment aroused by the Coercive Acts turned others against efforts to secure an accommodation. After a series of town meetings, the city decided, before the end of June, to do nothing toward

146

paying for the tea and to maintain its committee of correspondence. Boston chose, despite the wishes of a large minority, to fight.

So did the House of Representatives of Massachusetts. Committees of Correspondence of the province went into action even before Gage reached Boston. They urged resistance against Britain, a boycott of British goods, and the calling of another assemblage to speak for America like that at New York which had so forthrightly condemned the Stamp Act in 1765. They helped to circulate a "Solemn League and Covenant," which pledged all those who signed it to refuse to buy British wares after October 1. On June 7, in accordance with his instructions, Gage called the legislature into session at Salem. If he entertained hope that the House of Representatives would undertake to pay for the Boston Tea Party, that it would make even a gesture toward reconciliation with Britain, he soon abandoned that hope. The house refused even to consider the offering of compensation to the East India Company, and quietly began to prepare a call for a Continental Congress. Learning about its proceedings, Gage hastily issued a proclamation dissolving the legislature. But he was too late. Before he could act, the house endorsed an invitation to its counterparts in all the colonies to send delegates to a Congress to begin at Philadelphia on September 1.

Gage encountered other disappointments. He was assured of the support of Anglicans in Massachusetts, and he hoped to find allies among the Baptists, they being restive under Congregationalist hegemony; but the Baptists turned against Britain. He tried to obtain more evidence against those responsible for the Boston Tea Party and to initiate prosecution against them. His attorney general advised him to put off action against them to a more propitious time. He struck at John Hancock by depriving that vain gentleman of the colonelcy of a company of cadets that paraded in Boston on official occasions. The cadets immediately disbanded in protest. It is reported that he made an effort to bribe Samuel Adams, and that his overture was virtuously and indignantly rejected.

Feeling against Britain mounted in Massachusetts, especially in Boston. Deprived of its maritime commerce, the city suffered. Its sailors and workers, losing jobs, clamored against the cruelty of the mother country. Nor did the coming of redcoats into the city, which began in mid-June, make for tranquillity. Regiment after regiment made its appearance. The very presence of the soldiers in the city was galling to a majority of Bostonians. On July 14, writing to General Frederick Haldimand, who commanded at New York in the absence of Gage, the harried governor declared, "We are threatened here with an open opposition by arms every day, but tho' I don't credit it, I would be prepared against it." He ordered more troops to join him. With the redcoats came a naval squadron under Admiral Samuel Graves, which made evasion of the Port Bill impossible and further exacerbated restless citizens of Boston.

The "open opposition" against which Gage prepared soon came, but in such form that he could do nothing against it. At Salem, early in August, he began to reconstruct the government of Massachusetts in accordance with British law. He created a new royal council, swearing into office twenty-four men who had been selected because they were known to be completely loyal to Britain. With their consent he issued writs of election for a new House of Representatives, and called a meeting of the General Court of the province for early October. Suddenly, violence erupted outside Boston. The presence of the troops prevented an outbreak in the city, but outraged citizens hastened into action elsewhere. They would not permit Britain to change their government without a struggle. They pounced upon new "mandamus" councilors outside the city, threatening them with ostracism and violence and demanding that they either refuse to accept appointment or resign. The harrassed councilors, some of whom were manhandled, either complied, or fled into Boston. Farmers and villagers asserted that they would not permit judges and sheriffs named by Gage to function. They began to gather arms, and they said they would use them if the redcoats marched out of Boston. Before the end of August British authority was collapsing outside Boston. Gage himself prudently removed from Salem to the city. There he remained until the autumn of 1775.

Writing home on August 27, before he retreated to Boston, Gage declared that the situation was ominous. The remedy for it was further and thoroughgoing coercion. Britain must continue to use the whip and, if necessary, resort to the sword. There would be no peace in Massachusetts until its rebellious leaders were arrested for treason and sent to England for trial and punishment. Their arrest would quite likely be the signal for armed clash in Massachusetts. It would be no brief or trifling affair, he said, for he would be forced to contend with all of New England, not merely Massachusetts. He had learned to know the Yankees. They were not to be despised as soldiers. He then thought that the Middle Colonies would not rush to help New England, and he believed that the people of the Southern Colonies would be able to give little support. They "talk very high," he said, but "their numerous slaves in the bowells of their country, and the Indians at their backs will always keep them quiet." He was convinced that the "motley crew" who were about to form the First Continental Congress at Philadelphia would be unable to wage more than economic warfare against Britain. He had become acquainted with

148

the Yankees; he did not yet understand their fellow Americans. But it would require a year or two, he said, to overcome the New Englanders alone.

Back in Boston, Gage briefly meditated a march with part of his troops to Worcester to support judges friendly to Britain in that village and to enable them to hold court. He refrained, for it was only too likely that he and his men would be attacked. They might be surrounded and forced to surrender before help could come from Boston. He prudently decided to gather as many troops as possible in the city, and to make it a stronghold for Britain and her American friends.

That the Yankees were indeed ready to exchange gunfire was demonstrated beyond doubt at the beginning of September. On the first day of that month, fearing that they would seize 125 barrels of gunpowder stored in a powderhouse at Cambridge, Gage sent out a detachment of 250 troops to bring the gunpowder, most of which belonged to the province of Massachusetts, into Boston. The redcoats accomplished their task. As governor, Gage could legally move the property of the colony. However, the march of the soldiers aroused the whole province, for rumor expanded their mission into an invasion of the countryside. On the following day thousands of armed men converged upon Boston to confront the British aggressors—only to learn that they were not yet needed. In the excitement aroused residents of Cambridge, which had been quiet, seized three "mandamus" councilors who had hitherto escaped molestation and forced them to resign. They also chased Benjamin Hallowell, one of the commissioners of customs who had happened to enter Cambridge at an unfortunate time for him, into Boston.

On September 3 Gage began to fortify the city, which was then connected with the mainland of Massachusetts only by a narrow isthmus, or neck. Building entrenchments across that neck, he made Boston almost impregnable against infantry attack from the mainland. Committees of Bostonians, including passionate defenders of American liberty such as Dr. Joseph Warren and Dr. Benjamin Church, urged the general to desist. There was, they said, no intent on the part of the people of Massachusetts to assail the troops. Gage listened politely, but continued to strengthen his position. Had he not done so, he would have failed to do his duty. He could not be sure that his army was exempt from assault. He also brought still more troops into the city; built barracks; and prepared for a long stay. His meager army was as safe as might be, protected by fortified barriers on Boston neck against frontal attack and by the naval squadron against assault from the sea. He would not take the offensive without orders from London. He did what he could to make ready for war.

It became increasingly obvious that the precautions taken by Gage were warranted. As September wore on, the Patriots—as we may now designate the defenders of American rights, who often referred to themselves as Whigs—talked about restoring government in accordance with the charter of 1691, even in consonance with the charter of Massachusetts Bay of 1629, under which the Puritans had had virtual autonomy during a large part of the seventeenth century. Outside Boston villagers and farmers collected arms and carried out military drills. Shrewd Yankee politicians, circumventing the prohibition of town meetings, convened a gathering of citizens of Suffolk County, which included Boston. On September 9 the Suffolk County Convention declared that force must be used, if necessary, to defend American freedom, and even hinted that the safety of Massachusetts might require her people to take the offensive. A few weeks later Massachusetts began to form a revolutionary régime. Gage cancelled the call he had earlier issued for election of a new House of Representatives. The voters ignored him, and chose delegates as usual. These gathered at Salem on October 5. Gage would have nothing to do with them. Thereupon, they immediately formed themselves into a Provincial Congress, and undertook to serve as a government for Massachusetts. They made John Hancock president of the Congress. On October 26 that body, after learning that the First Continental Congress had pledged the assistance of all America in the event of British aggression, established an executive committee of safety. Later it formed another committee to gather military supplies; took over the command of the provincial militia; and appointed a receiver general to accept tax payments and to disburse public funds. Massachusetts was committed to open rebellion and began to emerge as an independent commonwealth. The rebels managed without courts for some time. When the courts again opened, American-chosen judges presided over them.

During the last four months of 1774 Gage assured all and sundry Americans, including the president of the First Continental Congress, who asked about his intentions, that he was not meditating offensive action. It was for his superiors to decide what to do about the darkening American crisis; and he did not learn their wishes until April of the following year. Reinforcements arrived at Boston, until his army mustered about 4,000 men. He kept his troops under tight rein, lest there be a second Boston Massacre. Many of the inhabitants of the city, especially the unemployed, were restive, and Gage's soldiers also became irritable from tedious duty and boredom. Gage could not entirely prevent altercations. Some of his troops put a coat of tar and feathers upon an American who imprudently tried to persuade them to desert. Threats and blows were exchanged by troops and civilians in the streets. The incident of March 5, 1770, was not repeated.

Carefully keeping the peace in Boston, Gage did not urge his masters in London to follow a pacific course. In a letter to the Earl of Dartmouth of September 25 he told the minister that it was no longer possible—had it ever been possible?—to arrest the principal opponents of Britain in Massachusetts without bringing on hostilities. He suggested to Dartmouth that the Secretary of State examine a letter sent by Gage to Thomas Hutchinson on the seventeenth. In it the general proposed that government suspend the Coercive Acts and request Massachusetts to send emissaries to London. Meanwhile, it should hire Hanoverian and Hessian troops, if it proposed to impose its will upon America. For the New Englanders would unquestionably fight. In later reports, sent to London as the year 1774 drew to an end, Gage told Dartmouth that he ought to have 20,000 men, including cavalry, if he were ordered to take the field. For he no longer believed that Jerseymen, Marylanders, Virginians, and Carolinians would stand idle while he subjugated the Yankees. The small force he then had in Boston did not frighten the Americans; it merely provoked them. He suggested an alternative and cheaper method of coercion—a naval blockade of the American coast, coupled with a complete withdrawal of British troops and officials from the colonies. It was for government, of course, to decide what to do. In "private" letters to Barrington, Gage even more emphatically declared that he ought to be heavily reinforced, if he were instructed to take the offensive. Early in October he asserted that he should be given 20,000 men, including picked German troops, Canadians, and three or four regiments of cavalry, together with field artillery. On November 2 he urged Barrington that "if you resist and not yield" to the Americans, "that resistance should be effectual at the beginning." If government thought 10,000 men sufficient, it ought to supply 20,000; if it proposed to spend £1 million upon coercion, it should expend £2 million. "The crisis is indeed an alarming one, & Britain had never more need of wisdom, firmness, and union than at this juncture." On December 14 the general opened his heart fully to Barrington, telling the Secretary at War that Britain ought to employ military power and that he favored the use of the army as the principal instrument of coercion. "I hope you will be firm, and send me a sufficient force to command the country, by marching into it, and sending off large detachments to secure obedience thro' every part of it; affairs are at a crisis, and if you give way it is for ever."

With the increasingly ominous dispatches from Gage, many reports of alarming tenor poured into London from America during the latter part of 1774. For the Americans very generally rallied beside their brethren of Massachusetts. They agreed with the men of Massachusetts that the punitive laws applied to their colony were unconstitutional and tyrannical. Who could say that the treatment given Massachusetts would not soon be extended to Virginia or South Carolina? Moreover, all the colonists found an added grievance in the summer of 1774 in the Quebec Act, which became a British statute almost simultaneously with the Coercive Acts. They lumped it with those detested laws, and labeled all five measures "intolerable."

That the Quebec Act was intended as a blow, even in part, against the Americans, remains doubtful. It has been mentioned that it aroused people in Virginia, Connecticut, and Massachusetts because they saw discrimination against them and in favor of the inhabitants of French Canada in the extension of Quebec southward and westward to the Ohio and Mississippi Rivers. The law was also widely condemned in the Thirteen Colonies because it granted religious freedom to the French Canadians and permitted their Roman Catholic Church to collect tithes. Was it just, asked jealous Americans, that an English government supporting Anglicans against Congregationalists, Presbyterians, and Baptists, should be so generous to the official church of the traditional enemies of both Britain and America? Placing power in the hands of an appointed governor and council, the act did not provide for an elected assembly. Were British subjects—almost entirely French-speaking folk who had no experience with such a body—to be governed arbitrarily? A system of law partly English, partly French, was established. Why were the Canadians denied benefits of English law—to which they were unaccustomed? The Americans disliked the Quebec Act because it was indulgent to the French Canadians and because it was unjust to the French Canadians.

Whatever the intentions of the framers of the Quebec Act, they could hardly have drawn up a law that would have escaped censure by the inhabitants of Britain's old colonies. Among them were many who doubted that the Intolerable Acts were truly wicked, many who desired to avoid a fatal clash with the mother country, and some who spoke out forthrightly against resistance to Britain. But an overwhelming majority of the Americans—perhaps a majority in every colony except Georgia— saw the British attempt to bring Massachusetts to heel as a dire threat to America as a whole. Passion rose among them everywhere along the Atlantic seaboard. Virginia moved swiftly to the side of Massachusetts. On May 26 the House of Burgesses proclaimed June 1, when the Port Bill became effective, a day of fasting. The Earl of Dunmore, governor of the Old Dominion, promptly dissolved the Burgesses. Most of its members declined to submit tamely. They gathered at the Raleigh Tavern at Williamsburg, and they arranged to send letters circulating throughout the colonies suggesting that they ought to form a Continental Congress to meet annually and to maintain a solid front in defense of American freedom. Their invitation actually preceded that extended by the Massachusetts House of Representatives. Later, in August, the Burgesses formed themselves into a convention; called for economic warfare against Britain until American grievances had been redressed; and chose delegates to the Congress. That convention became at length a Revolutionary legislature. A similar body made its appearance in North Carolina, another in South Carolina. Every one of the Thirteen Colonies save Georgia sent to Philadelphia delegates chosen either by a convention or the lower house of the legislature. In Georgia opinion was badly divided, and Governor Sir James Wright was able to stop the election of delegates and also to prevent resolutions demanding economic warfare against Britain. But such resolutions were adopted in several colonies, cities, and towns. Before the First Continental Congress convened in Carpenter's Hall in Philadelphia on September 5 it was evident that it would resort to economic weapons to defend American liberties.

The fifty-six Americans who gathered in the capital of Pennsylvania in the first of many "Continental" meetings were a distinguished body of men informed about and experienced in public affairs. Many of them were college graduates; not a few were lawyers; and nearly all had acquired a sound schooling in politics in colonial assemblies and offices. A decade of controversy with Britain had polished their wits. They were not dominated by emotion. Among them were Samuel and John Adams from Massachusetts; Patrick Henry, Richard Henry Lee, and George Washington from Virginia; John Dickinson and Joseph Galloway from Pennsylvania; John Jay and James Duane from New York; and Christopher Gadsden, John Rutledge, and Edward Rutledge from South Carolina. They and their fellow delegates, as the Earl of Chatham recognized, were men fit to rule.

Some members of the Congress were more determined than others to assert American rights. No delegate favored obedience to Britain at any cost. There were many colonists who desired to yield to Britain rather than to assert American rights and risk war and tumult. There were even colonists who gave unwavering allegiance to Britain, who believed that Britain had behaved neither arbitrarily nor tyrannically. Such men were not represented in the Congress. But it did contain delegates of various other opinions. The Adamses and Gadsden were disposed to fight rather than to give any ground whatever to Britain, and they were not without allies. Dickinson, Duane, the Rutledges, Galloway, and others looked upon the Adamses and Gadsden as extremists and sought to restrain them. The two Adamses desired that the Congress take steps to prepare for armed hostilities, but they did not quite dare to propose them. They did secure a declaration that in effect declared aggression by Gage against Massachusetts to be aggression against America. With Gadsden, they were eager to condemn British regulation of American maritime commerce, but they could not persuade the Congress to go so far.

Working in secrecy into October, the Congress did nevertheless move most vigorously. It adopted a Declaration of Rights, which demanded recognition by Britain of American liberties based upon "the immutable laws of nature, the principles of the English constitution," and the several colonial charters. In that declaration they specifically condemned as unconstitutional many laws passed by Parliament after 1763, including all those intended to secure revenue; those that extended "the powers of the admiralty courts beyond their ancient limits" and deprived "the American subject of trial by jury"; all the Coercive Acts; and the Quebec Act. They called for the repeal of all such laws that had not been rescinded. Asserting "that the keeping a standing army in several of these colonies in time of peace, without the consent of the legislature of that colony in which the army is kept, is against law," they maintained that the British troops should be removed from American settlements. From "the necessity of the case, and a regard to the mutual interest of both countries," they "cheerfully" accepted Parliamentary channeling of American external commerce. They wanted a return to the "good old days" of 1763—according to their view of that happy time. To compel Britain to go back to that halcyon year, they announced that they would create a Continental Association to prevent both consumption and importation of British goods and also exportation of American products to Britain.

The Congress sent the Declaration of Rights to London, together with a petition to the King and an "Address to the People of Great Britain." Significantly, it ignored Parliament. It also issued a manifesto to the Americans, and an appeal to the Canadians to join in the Continental cause. On October 20 it laid down rules for the Association, which was to be executed by local and provincial committees. Goods from Britain, India, and the British West Indies were not to be imported or consumed after December 1, 1774; nor were Negro slaves to be brought in after that day. If the boycott of British wares and slaves did not persuade Crown and Parliament to alter their ways, the Americans were, after September 10, 1775, to cease to export to Britain and her West Indian possessions—

154

except that rice-growers, who must suffer severely from such an embargo, would be permitted to send forth their product for European consumption. Before adjourning, the delegates issued a call for another Congress, to meet in May 1775 and consider further action.

One may believe that nearly all the members of the First Continental Congress desired to remain within the British empire, and that the great majority of them would have been pleased to secure an accommodation with Britain upon the conditions defined in the Declaration of Rights. Some were undoubtedly willing, in order to restore tranquillity, to accept less than was demanded. It is doubtful that even Samuel Adams consciously wished for independence. Nevertheless, it is apparent that most of the delegates were disposed to think of the Americans as one people and of the British as another. The Congress claimed for the colonists not merely their constitutional and charter rights, but those of mankind. And the doctrine of natural rights could be used to justify separation from Britain. Certainly there was no pervasive passion in the Congress for a closer political relationship between America and Britain. It considered an ingenious scheme offered by Joseph Galloway to prevent future disputes between them. In a "plan of a proposed union" between Britain and the colonies, Galloway urged the creation in America of a Grand Council, composed of delegates from the several colonies, to wield full powers in all matters of general American concern. Britain was to appoint a President General who could veto all measures of the council. The President General and the Grand Council would form "an inferior and distinct branch of the British legislature," which was also empowered to set aside acts of the American delegates. On the other hand, no Parliamentary act concerning America would be valid without the consent of the Grand Council. Under the Galloway Plan the Americans obviously could prevent new Parliamentary taxation without their consent. But the Congress voted against it by a narrow margin—and then expunged the tally from its minutes. The delegates, in the end, preferred looser ties with Britain to tighter ones. Did the delegates expect, or merely hope against hope, that Britain would give them what they desired? It was not likely that the mother country would accede to the demands of the colonists. Delegates might wish for an accommodation, but they displayed that "firmness," which, being opposed by "firmness," has so often led politicians and peoples into armed hostilities. The more astute, the more sensitive men in the Congress knew in their hearts that Britain would in all likelihood resolve to make full use of her army and navy to crush "rebellion."

Some members of the Congress were appalled by that prospect. Most were not. Certainly there were ardent spirits in Philadelphia, and elsewhere, who were quite willing to fight and who would hardly be satisfied with anything less than complete separation from Britain. Among them in Philadelphia were Dr. Benjamin Rush, who had become a republican by conviction as a medical student at the University of Edinburgh; Thomas Mifflin, a rising man in Pennsylvania politics; and Colonel Charles Lee, a British army officer on half pay, a restless devotee of the Goddess Liberty who had crossed the Atlantic in 1773 in search for her. As the end of the year 1774 approached, American militiamen drilled with unaccustomed energy. In mid-December several hundred men seeking to gain possession of 100 barrels of gunpowder stored in Fort William and Mary at Portsmouth, New Hampshire, attacked the fort. It was garrisoned by British Captain John Cochran and five soldiers. Cochran and his troops fired a cannon ball or two and a few musket shots before they surrendered their charge. Cochran was slightly wounded. The powder passed into the possession of men who preferred that it be used in behalf of American freedom rather than British authority.

As it became more and more likely that Britain and America would clash on the battlefield, more and more colonists drew back. There had been, ever since the beginning of the Anglo-American troubles, men who gave unswerving loyalty to the mother country. Now they were joined by many who felt that they had to choose between Britain and a mild tyranny on the one hand and American freedom and tumult on the other. A Loyalist, or Tory, party began to appear. Other colonists maintained, or adopted, a neutral position, for diverse reasons. Loyalist writers pleaded for the British connection in pamphlets and newspaper essays published in Boston, and in New York, where the clever printer, James Rivington, opened the columns of his *New York Gazetteer* to all shades of opinion. In Massachusetts lawyer Daniel Leonard as "Massachusettensis" emerged as a champion of Britain. In New York several Anglican clergymen thundered against wanton opposition to a beneficent mother country. John Adams as "Novanglus" challenged Leonard, and a host of writers, including Colonel Charles Lee, denounced the defenders of Britain in New York. The Loyalists gained little by resorting to the press.

Both the Loyalists and the neutrals struggled against the Association. But no edict of the autocratic Frederick the Great of Prussia or of the imperious Catherine the Great of Russia was better executed, after December 1, 1774. America both declared and effectually waged economic warfare against Britain—an extraordinary spectacle. There were merchants who disliked the Association, not only because they could not import British goods, but especially because they could not sell British wares they had on their shelves—as they had profitably done during

156

earlier boycotts. Loyalists and neutrals occasionally encouraged such merchants to refuse to sign agreements pledging them to execute the Association. However, its supporters were easily in the majority, and they were organized. Their committees rigidly enforced both non-importation and non-consumption. Those who strenuously resisted their decrees suffered indignities. More than one Loyalist was tarred and feathered. Others fled from their homes to escape brutal abuse by "Sons of Liberty" who would not grant freedom to the friends of Britain, or even to neutrals.

At the end of the year 1774 the champions of American rights were in almost complete control of the colonies. The British army held Boston. Georgia, a frontier province assisted by the British treasury and menaced by the Creek warriors, was not yet fully committed to the American cause. In New York Loyalists, neutrals, and others who feared that America had gone too far were striving to check the more ardent champions of American freedom. However, passion and time were with those Americans who were determined, even eager, to fight rather than give way to Britain. Before many months had passed, they would dominate New York and Georgia as thoroughly as New Jersey and South Carolina. Patriot militia would stand guard on Staten Island and on the wharves of Savannah as well as in the streets of Worcester and Williamsburg.

CHAPTER XII

Britain Chooses War

I N the early months of 1775, in both houses of Parliament statesmen probed into the American crisis and offered generous solutions that might have preserved the British empire into the distant future. The oratory of the Earl of Chatham and Edmund Burke evoked admiration, but won few if any votes. George III and his Friends were firmly in the saddle. They were quite unfit to guide the British ship of state in a mighty storm. They did not recognize its magnitude. They refused to accept the counsel of Chatham and Burke. Nor did they follow the advice of General Gage. Warned that the British army in North America, even with the help of the navy, was far too small to subjugate the colonists, that the Americans would fight and fight well, and that France and Spain would seize an opportunity to strike at Britain in distress, they nevertheless chose to wage war against unruly subjects who resided beyond the Atlantic. They intended to save the empire in their own short-sighted way. They sent orders to Gage which quickly brought on hostilities and then an ever-widening conflict that raged for eight years, ending in disastrous defeat for Britain.

Whatever may be said about the wisdom, or lack of it, of the King and his cohorts, the North ministry was even stronger in Parliament in the winter of 1774–5 than it had earlier been. If the complexities of governing an empire were too much for Lord North, he was sufficiently familiar with the highways and by-ways of British politics. As the autumn of 1774 approached, as grim news from America was pouring into London, the prime minister suddenly and shrewdly moved to consolidate his forces— before the public learned of the emergency growing beyond the Atlantic. The last Parliamentary election had taken place in 1768, and another had to be held, under the Septennial Act, by 1775. North foresaw that a contest at the polls might be embarrassing in 1775. On September 30, 1774, the King formally called for the election of a new House of Commons, to convene at Westminster on November 29. The monarch supplied funds for the campaign, and the holders of royal offices were told to exert themselves. Both George III and North were pleased by the outcome. They were assured of a handsome majority in both chambers.

Not that the King's Friends formed more than half of the House of Commons. But they had acquired recruits, including former Grenvillites and Bedfordites, and they constituted a large and mobilized minority which offered loyalty to the monarch and to North, in part from conviction, in part for pelf. No fewer than 170 members held either a governmental appointment or contract. Several dozen army and navy officers sat in the House of Commons. If such men failed to prove their gratitude for past favors, they could expect none in the future. For the King and North kept watch upon their followers. Any man who voted against the ministry was punished. He might be deprived of an office; he might be refused one. North was thus assured of the support of a phalanx of members. He could rely almost as surely upon the independent country gentlemen, about 150 in number, who sat in the house. They liked the friendly, good-humored North as a person. He was an Anglican, a man of the country rather than the city. He had reduced public expenses, and he had tried to shift part of their tax burdens to the shoulders of the colonists. They felt no sympathy for the Americans, about whom they knew little. They could not consider the colonists to be their equals. And there were other men in the house, followers of noblemen allied to the King's Friends, upon whom North could depend for votes. The House of Commons was securely in his grasp—and he was in the hands of George III.

Nor did North need to be too concerned lest the Lords oppose him, if for no other reason because seventy of the peers held government appointments. The majority of the nobles of Britain, like the independent country gentlemen, assumed that the Americans were their inferiors, and that they should be and could be held in a subordinate condition. Some of the peers offered an almost feudal fealty to the monarch. Others were jealous of his power, but were aware that their interests and those of the King were intertwined, that they and their ruler had common enemies. And nearly all the Anglican bishops, as usual, faithfully supported the head of the English Church. The Lords would do what North asked them to do about America.

Unfortunately for the British empire, George III, Lord North, the King's Friends, and their friends were indeed quite unfit to govern that

159

most valuable, that very special part of the empire inhabited by the Americans.

Having sought to become the head of the British state in reality as well as in form, George III had achieved his goal. Some of his fellow rulers—Frederick the Great, Catherine the Great, Charles III of Spain, Habsburg princes, and others—were striving to be "benevolent despots" on the European Continent. George III was not a despot, and he did not wish to be one. He could be benevolent to individuals whom he knew personally, who did not challenge his authority. He liked Britain, with minor exceptions, as it was. The British throne was occupied by a political boss of limited ability who lacked imagination. He possessed neither sympathy for, nor understanding of his American subjects. They were farmers, laborers, clerks, and artisans rather than nobles and gentlemen. They had somehow prospered. It was bad enough that there were those in England—Pittites, Wilkesites, and others—who clamored against him, men who denounced him as an enemy of liberty, who demanded change at home. He would not truckle to such Englishmen; nor would he permit the upstart Americans, who already possessed too much freedom, to dictate the terms upon which they would remain within the empire. The King believed that he had been patient with the colonists, and that his royal lenience had been abused. It seemed to him that his adversaries in Britain encouraged his refractory subjects beyond the Atlantic. He would yield neither to the one group or the other.

The followers and allies of the King were not much more enlightened than he. They, too, were content with conditions in Britain. They were accustomed to servants, to respectful tenants and tradesmen, to notions of their own superiority. They tended to despise commercial men—unless such men were rich. God in His wisdom had created their inferiors in Britain; and he was doubtless responsible for the colonists as well. The Americans had not kept their place. There were doubtless gentlemen, and even ladies, among them, perhaps not quite equivalent to English gentlemen and ladies. Most of them were common folk who had become restless and arrogant. Too many of them were Congregationalists, Presbyterians, Baptists, and Quakers who did not revere the Anglican Church. Were they not new Cromwellians? They prated about liberty. Did they not keep slaves? The noblemen, baronets, knights, and untitled gentlemen who dominated rural England, even those who were products of Eton and the English universities, commonly remained parochial in their views. Few of them were infected either by "leveling" or fanatical republicanism. The generals and admirals who gave their votes to the King and to North, whether in the House of Commons or in the Lords, had not

160

gained proficiency in statecraft as a result of their experiences, either in war or peace. The lawyers who sat beside them, constrained by ancient precedents, too often gazed at America through legalistic and short-sighted eyes. Merchants who held government contracts, if they had a better understanding of commerce and distant peoples than their political associates, were not free to dispense their information. Anglican bishops who gave their allegiance to government were not devoted to a social gospel, whether for Englishmen or Americans. They would not change England. So far as the colonies were concerned, they needed less freedom, more Anglicans, and at least one bishop.

To men of such limited outlook, proposals made by Dr. Josiah Tucker, Dean of Gloucester, a freak among Anglican clergymen, seemed ridiculous. Tucker was as loyal to his church and to his King as a man might be; and he harbored no affection for Britain's obstreperous colonists. Nevertheless, coldly considering the state of the empire in a tract entitled "The True Interest of Great-Britain set forth in Regard to the Colonies and the Only Means of Living in Peace and Harmony with Them," he displayed the genius of a philosopher and the wisdom of a statesman. The Americans, said Tucker, could not be held in permanent subjection. All subjects beyond seas of European monarchs would eventually seek and gain their independence. The Americans were moving more rapidly toward that goal than other peoples in the New World because they had enjoyed greater liberty than French and Spanish colonials. They were not ungrateful; they were merely like all peoples, seeking to foster their own interest. England should avoid the horrors of war with the colonists. Even if they could be temporarily subdued by force of arms, hatred of the mother country would increase among them, and they would sooner or later demand and secure complete separation. They were daily becoming richer and more powerful. It was not possible for Britain and America to form a closer union. Foreseeing the future greatness of America, he could not accept removal of the imperial capital to Philadelphia or New York and government of Britain by an American viceroy. He therefore urged that Britain of her own volition declare the Thirteen Colonies to be independent. He would maintain a military alliance between Britain and America, to protect America against the Bourbons and other enemies. Britain would not suffer as a result, for she would retain her all-important trade with her former colonies. How right he was about that commerce. It was valuable to both Britain and America—it did not continue because it was channeled by the Navigation Acts; it survived even the deep bitterness aroused by the War of Independence; and independent America long supplied the principal market for British goods. Tucker exhibited sagacity both in his analysis of the troubles of the empire and in his solution for those difficulties. He was not utterly ignored. A few writers in London newspapers perceived his wisdom and endorsed his remedy for the ailments of the empire. But Tucker's solution was not acceptable to George III, Lord North, the Earl of Chatham, or Edmund Burke. Not one of those men was willing even to consider the repeal of the Navigation Acts. They would compel the Americans to trade as they would trade, in the large, without compulsion.

That the King, North, and the coalition they led were less than enlightened does not prove that all those Englishmen who opposed them were informed, altruistic, and far-sighted men who sought to create an ideal society in Britain and a noble and enduring empire. There were a few republicans in the British Isles, the best known of them being Mrs. Catharine Macaulay Graham, who had won temporary fame for her history of England in the seventeenth century; no avowed republican sat in Parliament. After 1769 there was a Radical movement in England. The Radicals demanded reform of the House of Commons, toward making it more representative of the English people; denounced the King because he used part of the £800,000 granted him annually by Parliament to influence elections; attacked him because he gave pensions and sinecure appointments to aristocrats while deserving workmen were in want; assailed the aristocrats because they eagerly sought and secured the pensions and sinecures, and because they too manipulated elections; condemned government because it denied freedom of the press; and censured judges who deprived Englishmen of their traditional rights in the courts. They looked upon the Americans as fellow worshippers of liberty. The iniquities and inequities in England against which they struck were only too real. Merchants, newspaper publishers, tradesmen, and artisans joined the Radical camp. However, it was largely confined to London until the War of Independence was well under way, and it lacked a capable and responsible leader. The principal figure in it for some years was John Wilkes, whose political idealism and abilities were much less than absolute. Returning from France in 1768, he had suffered imprisonment for his scandalous publications. Elected four times to the Parliament of 1768 from the county of Middlesex, which included London, he had been four times denied a place in the House of Commons. After the last of those elections the house had gone so far as to seat his defeated opponent. Wilkes thus continued to be an abused hero. He was admired by London mobs. Americans contributed money to pay his political expenses and his private debts, and they named cities and villages after him. Elected mayor of London in 1774 and sent to the new Parliament with three other

162

Londoners pledged to seek the repeal of the Coercive Acts, he was not again denied admission. He would speak stirringly in behalf of the colonists; but he and his fellow Radicals commanded very few votes in the House of Commons.

The principal opponents of George III and Lord North in the new Parliament were, as might be expected, the Marquis of Rockingham, the Earl of Chatham, and their followers. Let it not be thought that either Rockingham or Chatham was in full sympathy with Wilkes or with the Americans. They, too, assailed corruption of Parliament by the King; they demanded that the monarch tell precisely what he did with "secret service" money included in the funds given him by Parliament; and they too thundered against sinecures and secret and undeserved pensions. But it is apparent that the Rockingham party, including Edmund Burke, desired no fundamental changes in the British political system. The Whig nobles who formed its spine desired above all to regain the power they had lost to the monarch. They would wield it to foster British commerce and to placate the Americans. It is to be feared that at least some of the Rockingham faction were not utterly hostile to sinecures and pensions upon principle; that they merely sought sinecures and pensions for themselves. It is only too likely that some of the Rockingham people favored conciliation of the colonists, not only because of principle, but because of the fact that George III and Lord North preferred coercion. Nor were the Chathamites entirely unaffected by lust for power, position, and pelf. If Chatham was less averse to great changes in England than Rockingham, he did not crusade for them. But he had a gift for understanding men, including colonials, and he made a magnificent effort to save the British empire.

Chatham did not obtain an opportunity to speak in the House of Lords on the colonial crisis until the year 1775 was well begun. The ministry did not receive reports about the First Continental Congress until December 13, 1774. Parliament was then in session, but North declined to present papers about America to the House of Commons until January 19, after the customary long Christmas holiday. On the twentieth Chatham, feeble in body but masterful in spirit, delivered a remarkable speech. He castigated the North ministry for a vindictive effort to punish Massachusetts; he praised the people of that province because they had defended their rights; and he declared his admiration of the First Continental Congress. Promising that he would soon present a plan for an enduring reconciliation between Britain and America, he asked that the Lords request the ministry to send General Gage orders to remove his troops from Boston as soon as possible. Rockingham supported

163

Chatham, to no avail. Other peers defended the repressive measures of the past, and made it clear that they favored use of greater force in the future. The motion offered by Chatham was defeated, 68 to 18. He persisted. He did not think it beneath his dignity to consult Benjamin Franklin. He invited Franklin to his home, and then visited him in his lodgings. On February 1, with petitions from the British business community pouring into Parliament and calling for conciliation, he proposed "a provisional act" for settling the Anglo-American quarrel. His plan declared that the American colonies must remain "subordinate" to Parliament as well as dependent upon the British Crown. Eight years earlier Chatham had given his assent to the Townshend duties; if he remembered that decision, he had learned to repent it. Now he proposed that Parliament should concede that it lacked the power to tax the Americans for revenue and should repeal or suspend all the laws passed after 1763 to which the colonists objected, except for the quartering provisions of the Mutiny Act of 1765. The Crown would retain the power to send troops into any colony—Chatham would not admit that he had erred in 1767 when he used extreme pressure to force New York to comply with the Mutiny Act—but the soldiers were never to be employed to deprive Americans of their liberties. Parliament was also to retain its authority over American maritime commerce. The Second Continental Congress should be authorized to meet, and it should be asked to develop a scheme whereby the colonies would freely contribute in proper proportions to a permanent revenue for the defense of the empire. Chatham was prepared to go very far toward meeting the demands of the First Continental Congress. The man who had done so much to expand the British empire was quite willing to make concessions in order to preserve it. He was utterly opposed to American independence. He did not insist that every part of his plan be adopted. He urged that action be taken, before it was too late.

It was already too late. The Earl of Dartmouth was impressed, and he asked that Chatham's scheme be considered. But Dartmouth, even though he was Secretary of State for the Colonies and Lord North's stepbrother, did not speak for the majority of the ministry. The cabinet had already decided, a week earlier, to order Gage to move against the rebels in Massachusetts. Two members of the cabinet, the Earl of Sandwich and Earl Gower, immediately denounced the plan. Sandwich, first lord of the admiralty, declared that he could not believe it "to be the production of any British peer." He hinted that Franklin, present as a spectator, "one of the bitterest and most mischievous enemies" England had ever had, was its real author. Franklin had the consolation of the high

164

praise that Chatham offered in rebuttal. Chatham said that the American was a man to be ranked with England's Boyles and Newtons, "an honour, not to the English nation only, but to human nature." Both Sandwich and Earl Gower asserted that the First Continental Congress was a traitorous assembly, and that it would be absurd to negotiate with that body. Chatham's plan was endorsed by 32 peers, but it was set aside, for 61 voted against it.

Petitions from British merchants, tradesmen, and manufacturers urging an accommodation with the Americans continued to reach Parliament during February. They were stimulated in some part by a desire to reopen American markets, closed tightly by the Association. But it is also true that industrial and commercial folk in Britain, together with urban workers, were averse to war against the Americans. So were several orators in the House of Commons who became ever more alarmed as it became increasingly evident that Britain was about to wield the sword. They said that America would fight, and perhaps successfully, against British troops. It was to be feared, they asserted, that France and Spain would come to the aid of the colonists. Young Charles James Fox, then rising to fame as a speaker, predicted that the employment of the army would lead to "defeat on one side of the water, and ruin and punishment on the other." John Wilkes became a prophet. If war broke out in America, "Who can tell, sir, whether . . . in a few years the independent Americans may not celebrate the glorious era of the revolution of 1775, as we do that of 1688?" On March 22 Edmund Burke delivered perhaps his most famous speech, in behalf of a plan to conciliate the colonists that was somewhat less generous to them than the proposals of Chatham, but liberal nevertheless. Perhaps because he was Irish by birth, rather than English, he was able to see the colonists as they were, as a proud and freedom-loving people. It was essential, he contended, that Parliament continue to control their maritime commerce, but Britain ought not quarrel with America over Parliamentary taxation. His magnificent presentation has aroused the admiration of those who have read the speech; it did not convince the House of Commons of the wisdom of his plan; it was quickly rejected by a massive majority. Britain was plunging into war. The orders to General Gage that provoked it were en route on the ocean to Boston. Other speakers in the Commons continued to urge an accommodation with the Americans, vainly. The orders to Gage went on to their destination.

There never was much doubt that Britain would respond to the rebellion in Massachusetts and the demands of the First Continental Congress by appealing to force of arms. As early as November 18, 1774, before he knew about the proceedings of that Congress, George III informed Lord North that "the New England governments are in a state of rebellion," and that "blows must decide whether they are to be subject to this country or independent." There is no evidence that he ever changed his traditional mind. That same day he ridiculed General Gage's suggestion that Britain suspend the Coercive Acts, gain time by inviting Massachusetts to send commissioners to London, and prepare for war in earnest. To set aside the Coercive Acts, even temporarily, would be to admit weakness. He told North that "we must either master" the colonists, "or totally leave them to themselves and treat them as aliens." Such, too, was the temper, except for Dartmouth and North, of the King's confidential advisers. They considered with the monarch a scheme to send a viceroy to America. Had they dispatched a prudent and thoughtful man with great powers at an earlier time, he might have succeeded in reconciling the colonies and Britain. They decided not to appoint a viceroy. It was just as well, for the person they had in mind for that high office was Lord George Germain, a haughty man who was detested on both sides of the Atlantic. The Earl of Dartmouth and John Pownall suggested that commissioners be sent across the ocean to look into American grievances, but they set aside that contrivance also. To do so, said George III, was to suggest that the mother country was "affraid." The King believed that no good could come from appointing commissioners. In the end he and his Friends decided to make a gesture toward satisfying the colonists upon the score of taxation, but to rely upon the armed forces of Britain, especially Gage's army, to solve the imperial crisis.

Strangely, most of the men round George III believed—or professed to believe—that it was not necessary to send large forces across the ocean to subdue New England, even all of America. To be sure, a foolish notion was current in England that the Americans were not a fighting people. It was publicly declared by the Earl of Sandwich and by General James Grant early in 1775 that they would not stand against British troops. As late as September 6, 1777, six weeks before a British army under General John Burgoyne laid down its weapons at Saratoga before ranks of tall, sturdy patriot soldiers, General James Murray asserted, "The native American is an effeminate thing, very unfit for and very impatient of war."

Gage had warned that neither the New Englanders in particular, nor the Americans in general, were to be taken lightly; and he had asked for powerful reinforcements, if it were decided that he was to take the offensive. The King's followers refused to accept his advice. Indeed, they accused him of timidity and incompetence. As early as November 1774, the Earl of Suffolk declared that Gage was "too far gone to be recovered." Attorney General Thurlow and Solicitor General Wedderburn condemned the general because he had not suppressed the "mobs and riots" in Massachusetts. He should have arrested the leaders of those "mobs," said Wedderburn. Had Thurlow and Wedderburn forgotten their refusal to begin prosecution of those same leaders? Undersecretaries of State for the Colonies John Pownall and William Knox also condemned Gage for inactivity and irresolution. By December 18 the King and his advisers had decided that Gage was responsible at least in part for their troubles and that he ought to be replaced. They desired to send out General Sir Jeffery Amherst as commander in chief. However, the King refused to dismiss Gage outright—it was not decent to recall him in disgrace. Before the end of January 1775, George III had worked out a method to remove Gage from his command. He would be continued as governor of Massachusetts, with Amherst taking over his military duties; and the government would announce that the appointment of Amherst as commander in chief was necessary because Gage was needed in Massachusetts. But that arrangement fell through, for Amherst declined to serve. Why he did so is not known. Perhaps he knew that the commander in chief in America faced an ugly task; perhaps he saw that a government that would remove Gage without good reasons might dismiss Amherst for equally little cause; perhaps he had his doubts about the American policy of the King and his Friends—he had risen to fame as one of William Pitt's young generals in the Seven Years' War. In any event, Gage remained at the head of the army in America for many more months. To assist him—and to infuse spirit into him?—the government did arrange to send three major generals, William Howe, Henry Clinton, and John Burgoyne, to Boston. Before they reached that city, hostilities had begun.

Thomas Hutchinson, watching the course of events in London with the keenest interest, kept a diary that reads fascinatingly. He recorded that Lord Dartmouth told him on January 25, 1775, that "measures were now determined with respect to America." Certainly the most important of all the decisions taken by government early in 1775 concerning the colonies was taken that very day. There was a meeting of the cabinet, and it adopted instructions to Gage. They were embodied in a "secret" dispatch from Dartmouth to the general dated January 27. It was a long letter. In many words Gage was told to move against the Massachusetts rebels, and quickly. Since the people of that colony had displayed a resolution "to commit themselves at all events in open rebellion . . . force should be repelled by force." More troops would soon be on the way to Boston. "It is hoped that this large reinforcement"—much smaller than Gage had requested—"will enable you to take a more active and determined part." Gage ought to raise a corps of Loyalists. Since the people of three New England colonies had apparently resolved "to cast off their dependence upon the government of this kingdom, the only consideration that remains is, in what manner the force under your command may be exerted." Gage did not need the many soldiers for which he had asked, before moving decisively. Said Dartmouth, "a smaller force now, if put to the test, would be able to encounter them with greater probability of success than might be expected from a greater army, if the people would be suffered to form themselves upon a more regular plan, to acquire confidence from discipline, and to prepare those resources without which every thing must be put to the issue of a single action." Dartmouth also informed Gage that the cabinet desired him "as the first and essential step . . . toward reestablishing government" to "arrest the principal actors and abettors in the Provincial Congress," even though "such a proceeding should be, according to your own idea of it, a signal for hostilities." Declared Dartmouth, "it will surely be better that the conflict should be brought on, upon such ground, than in a riper state of rebellion." Dartmouth left no doubt regarding the wishes of the cabinet. Gage should have moved against the rebels without waiting for instructions; now he must—in military parlance —"do something."

Those orders to Gage meant war, as Dartmouth, Hutchinson, and others well knew, and principally war on land. Whatever may be said about the political thought that inspired them, they were, as the event would demonstrate, militarily unsound. The cabinet erred sadly when it rejected Gage's advice to put off hostilities on land until it could put a large army in the field. It would have done well to rely instead upon a naval blockade, as Gage had alternatively suggested. Edward Harvey, the British adjutant general, was opposed to employment of the army until it was greatly enlarged. So was Viscount Barrington. He urged that Britain resort to naval blockade. But the opinions of Harvey and Barrington, like those of Gage, were set aside. It would seem that the first lord of the admiralty, the Earl of Sandwich, preferred to place the burden of suppressing the American rebellion largely upon the army.

Those pregnant instructions to Gage remained in England for forty-five days. It may be that the cabinet postponed their departure until it was assured beyond doubt of the support of Parliament. It may be that Lord North desired to wait until he could send word to Gage that Parliament was disposed to conciliate as well as to subdue the Americans. It may be that Dartmouth was granted a little time in which to pursue last-minute negotiations with Benjamin Franklin. On Saturday, February 11, the

London *Chronicle* announced that "On Thursday a messenger was sent to Falmouth with dispatches for General Gage at Boston, to be forwarded by a packet boat detained there for that purpose." However, Dartmouth was able to send, with the "secret" dispatch, papers describing events in the imperial capital on February 22.

Merchants and London city folk, together with aristocratic factions, might desire reconciliation with America, but Parliament insisted, by majorities of two to one, that the colonists submit. During February and March 1775 it declared Massachusetts to be in a state of rebellion, endorsed the sending of the three major generals to Boston, and gave its approval to enlargement of the army in America. It gave its assent to a bill which confined the maritime trade of New England to Britain and the British West Indies, and also barred the Yankees from fishing on the Grand Banks of Newfoundland—Britain, too, could wage economic warfare. The House of Commons did briefly balk when Lord North brought forward his Conciliatory Resolution, on February 17. That curious document had been framed by the cabinet in December 1774 and January 1775. If the cabinet really desired to reach an understanding with the colonists, the resolution ought to have been revised. For it seemed to offer a solution of sorts to the problem of Parliamentary taxation; but the mechanism for achieving that solution was utterly unacceptable to the Americans. The resolution was so phrased that the Americans could not believe that North was sincere. It was addressed through the governors in America to important persons in each of the several colonies. They were to be urged to use their influence to secure action by their assemblies. If any colony voted its fair share toward the defense of the empire, and if it provided for the support of its own civil officers and judges, it was to be exempted from Parliamentary taxation. Moreover, such a colony would be credited with all sums collected within its borders incidental to Parliamentary regulation of trade. It should be observed that North's offer was not directly addressed to the Continental Congress, but indirectly to the thirteen American assemblies; that it did not establish a quota for each colony; and that a colony must either tax its inhabitants for the defense of the empire, or accept taxation by Parliament for that purpose. The resolution was attacked in the House of Commons by Rockingham and Chatham men because it did not concede enough to the Americans. It was also condemned by supporters of the ministry who said that it conceded far too much. North won them over by hinting that it would divide "the reasonable from the unreasonable" colonists. It was passed on February 20.

It should be said that Lord North was not fond of warfare, even of

169

the political variety. Lord Dartmouth, it would appear, was eager to reach agreement with the Americans. Very likely, the Conciliatory Resolution was the most that the stepbrothers could extract from their colleagues and the King as a gesture to please the Americans. Their sentiments were not similar to those of "Terrae Filius," who asserted in the *Public Advertiser* of February 14 that "should we see the heads of some of those rebellious Americans on Temple-Bar, we might lament their folly, though we should applaud the deed." Dartmouth had voted for the repeal of the Stamp Act; and he did not hate the colonists. He was in touch through several intermediaries with Benjamin Franklin in January and February. He could not offer enough to satisfy Franklin, who must have been somewhat amused to receive overtures from a high official of a government that had permitted, even encouraged, Alexander Wedderburn to abuse him. The negotiations collapsed, on March 1. Soon afterward Franklin set out for America. His wife had recently died in Philadelphia; he could accomplish nothing more in England. Had he remained three months longer in London, he would hardly have escaped imprisonment.

It is likely that Dartmouth's last efforts to bargain with Franklin were undertaken in desperation, while storms prevented the departure of the "secret" dispatch for America. Certainly bad weather in early March delayed its transit. Thomas Hutchinson, to whom the dispatch was read by William Knox on March 22, knew that it must bring the gravest of consequences, and inquired about its progress. He learned that it was sent out from London in duplicate; that the original of the dispatch was placed on board H.M.S. *Falcon,* bound for Boston; and that H.M.S. *Nautilus,* sailing for the same port, carried a copy of the instructions to Gage. He was informed that, because of bad weather, the *Falcon* was still at Torbay on March 12, and that the *Nautilus* was at Plymouth. On March 13 the *Nautilus* set sail, and arrived in Boston after a swift voyage on April 14. Two days later Captain John Linzee brought the *Falcon* into Boston Harbor. Massachusetts newspapers quickly announced the arrival of the two ships and of orders to General Gage from London. After a long period of anxious waiting and preparation for warfare, Gage learned that his military advice had been rejected, that he must act with the troops he had in America.

During the early months of 1775 Gage continued to believe that Britain must use force against the colonists. He had served in many battles. He had fought at Culloden in 1746 against Bonnie Prince Charlie, the Young Pretender; he had displayed staunch courage on the ill-fated Braddock expedition against Fort Duquesne in 1755; and he had taken part in the several later campaigns in North America that forced the

French to surrender Canada. He was about fifty-five years of age, and did not lust for more combat. On February 10 he believed, partly on the basis of letters from Viscount Barrington, that he would be ordered to prepare for war and to move from Boston into the interior of Massachusetts. He was then hopeful—against hope—that the result would be less dire than he had earlier predicted. He was grasping at straws. He detected a shrinking away from hostilities among the Americans as war came closer. Informed that many men in the New York assembly were reluctant to execute the program of the First Continental Congress, he wishfully thought in the last days of January and during most of February that New York might prevent the establishment of a united American front against Britain, that New York might become "the loyal province," that the members of her assembly might become "the Saviours of America." Perhaps the Americans would resist less violently than he had earlier expected. But he really knew, or learned, that New York would not stand out against her sister colonies. There could be no serious doubt that the Americans would fight. On March 6 Bostonians celebrated the anniversary of the Boston Massacre at a meeting in the Old South Church, and Dr. Joseph Warren thundered against British tyranny in the very faces of forty redcoat officers who went to the proceedings. It was only too evident that the Yankees—and the Americans in general—were a stiff-necked people. On March 8 Gage predicted that the use of armed force by Britain would very likely be followed by the "horrors of a civil war." However, he continued to believe that Britain could not draw back. On March 28, in the last "private" letter he wrote to Barrington before the outbreak of that "civil war," he declared, "It's beyond my capacity to judge what ought to be done, but it appears to me that you are now making your final efforts respecting America; if you yield, I conceive that you have not a spark of authority remaining over this country. If you determine on the contrary to support your measures, it should be done with as little delay as possible, and as powerfully as you are able, for it's easier to crush evils in their infancy than when grown to maturity."

Gage did what he could to make ready for a struggle. He warned British civil and military officers throughout North America to expect the worst. He instructed the Indian superintendents, Colonel Guy Johnson— who had succeeded his uncle and father-in-law, Sir William Johnson, in 1774—and John Stuart to prevent the rebellious colonists from making friends among the Indians. They should do everything possible to assure the loyalty of the savages to King George. Johnson and Stuart should see to it that the Indians were ready to move against the frontiers of the colonies, in the event that the King asked for their help. Captain William

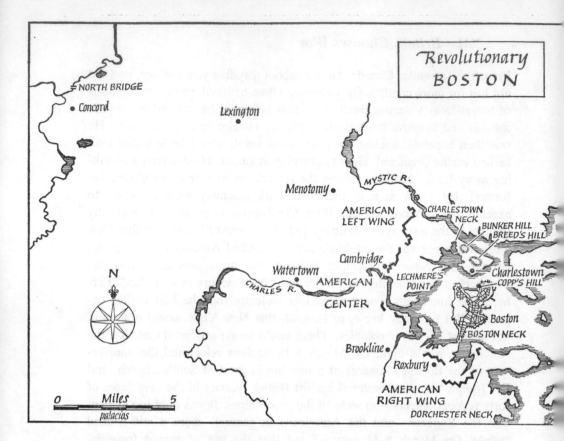

NORTH BRIDGE

• Concord

Lexington

MYSTIC R.

Menotomy •

AMERICAN
LEFT WING

CHARLESTOWN
NECK

BUNKER HILL
BREED'S HILL

N

Watertown
CHARLES R.
Cambridge

AMERICAN
CENTER

LECHMERE'S
POINT

Charlestown
COPP'S HILL

Boston
BOSTON NECK

Brookline •

Roxbury •

AMERICAN
RIGHT WING
DORCHESTER NECK

0   Miles   5

palacios

De la Place, commandant at Fort Ticonderoga, had observed that American civilians were displaying much curiosity about that post. It contained cannon, and it guarded the passageway between New York City and Canada. Gage told De la Place to watch out for a surprise attack.

Gage also gave his troops as much occupation as possible, both in and near Boston, to prepare for action. Late in January he sent 100 men to Marshfield, to defend Loyalists of Marshfield and Scituate who had begged for protection. The troops were not attacked. On February 26, having received instructions from Dartmouth to prevent the rebels from receiving arms from abroad, and having obtained information that cannon had been landed at Salem, he sent Lieutenant Colonel Alexander Leslie with 200 men to that village to seize the guns. Leslie was confronted there by Patriots who made it quite clear that further advance on his part would bring shooting. Learning that Gage had been misinformed, that there were no artillery pieces in the village, Leslie, avoiding a clash, turned and marched back to Boston. Thereafter Gage sent out detachment after detachment from Boston to march through the adjacent countryside. The soldiers did not go more than eight miles from the city. Gage made it plain that they were merely carrying on training exercises, and

172

they were not molested by angry citizens. But the general was getting his men ready for longer marches. Anticipating that he would be ordered to take the field, Gage even sent out officers in civilian clothing as far as Concord to gather knowledge of the terrain. On April 5 he asked Admiral Graves to help him find the best way to move troops across Boston Harbor for a swift advance into the interior of Massachusetts. A route was selected, and the admiral promptly put small boats in the water, ready for use.

Further, Gage kept close and successful watch upon the Provincial Congress of Massachusetts. That rebellious body met at Cambridge in February, and later convened at Concord. On March 12 it set a day of fasting and prayer, and invoked the blessings of God upon the British empire, George III, and the British royal family. But the Congress had not become convinced of the virtue or necessity of passive obedience. Two weeks later, its president, John Hancock, declaring that the people of Massachusetts were threatened by a powerful army, formally called upon them to prepare to defend themselves to the uttermost. Certain units of the Massachusetts militia were designated as minutemen, and instructed to go into swift action in the event that Gage's troops came out of Boston on the offensive. Military supplies were gathered at Worcester and Concord. Gage knew all about the arrangements made by the Congress and its committees, for he had at least two spies at or near Concord, about twenty miles from Boston. One of them may have been Dr. Benjamin Church, who had been a most passionate defender of American rights and who was high in the councils of the men gathered at Concord. Certainly Church, having accepted British money, was later an agent of Gage. Whoever they were, Gage's informers told the general that some light artillery, together with muskets, gunpowder, pork, and flour and other military stores, had been collected at Concord, and gave their precise location. Gage also knew in advance that the Congress would disperse on April 15.

Fortunately for Samuel Adams and John Hancock, they were beyond Gage's reach immediately after April 14. For they were the two men whose arrest the British cabinet desired above all. Early in February, indeed, they, with other principal leaders of the Provincial Congress, had been declared guilty of treason by Lord Chancellor Thurlow and Attorney General Wedderburn. Had they fallen into Gage's hands, they might well have suffered the supreme penalty in the Tower of London. However, Adams and Hancock removed after the adjournment of the Provincial Congress to a farmhouse near Lexington; and the general probably did not know where they were. Moreover, he had no cavalry, and he could not hope to catch them with infantry. They had their friends in and out of Boston who informed them of every British movement, and they would almost certainly learn about a march of British footsoldiers toward Lexington in time to seek safety by flight. Among their friends in the city was Dr. Joseph Warren. Gage made no effort to seize him, even though Warren remained in Boston until late in the day of April 19, many hours after British troops and American militiamen had engaged in combat.

Compelled to act by the "secret" dispatch from Dartmouth, Gage quickly decided to send a detachment to Concord to destroy the military supplies gathered by the rebels in that village. His instructions did not mention those stores because the British cabinet did not know about them when the dispatch was written. He had to move; and he had no promising alternative. On April 15 he ordered several companies of light troops, smaller and more active men, together with some grenadiers, larger and stronger men, to be set aside for special maneuvers. After nightfall on April 18 about 700 of those troops were ferried across Boston Harbor, landed at Lechmere's Point, and began to move by a side road toward Lexington. They were preceded by British officers on horseback who were familiar with the terrain west of Boston. A signal from the city informed Gage's enemies on the mainland that the redcoats were advancing. As they walked in disciplined procession through the dark night, Paul Revere and William Dawes, trusted couriers of the Patriots, rode on horseback before them into Lexington, warning the countryside that the British were coming. Revere also advised John Hancock and Samuel Adams not to loiter in their temporary lodgings near Lexington; they were not in great danger, but they prudently moved away from the British line of march. Revere and Dawes, with Dr. Samuel Prescott, who joined them to help spread the tidings, went on toward Concord. They were intercepted by mounted British officers, but Prescott was able to make his way into Concord with the alarming news. Revere, later an American folk hero, was captured, but released. He was of no importance to the British.

Before the British detachment reached Lexington, the soldiers saw lights appear in farmhouses adjacent to their line of march. They heard the ringing of churchbells, the beating of drums, and the sound of shooting. A British observer afterward related that one shot was harmlessly fired at the troops as they moved toward the village. Certainly the minutemen, and other militiamen, were turning out. They carried muskets, squirrel guns—whatever they had in the way of weapons. Soon after midnight 130 of them under Captain John Parker gathered at Lexington. It was a cold night; the British did not come; many of Parker's men went home. Before dawn the word came that the soldiers were approaching on a road that ran beside the green. Parker drew up 60 or 70 men in two lines on the green. Others—many of them unarmed—stationed themselves nearby to watch the proceedings. The British advance guard, led by Major John Pitcairn, commanding officer of the marines in Boston, came on into the village in bright morning. Some of Parker's men began to fall back; it was obvious that the British could not be resisted. But Parker insisted that they stand their ground. Pitcairn formed his soldiers, advanced toward the militiamen, demanded, perhaps profanely, that they lay down their weapons and disperse. They did not put down their guns, but many of them began to move away from the troops. A shot was fired, then others, then many by the troops into the retreating militiamen, despite efforts by Pitcairn to restrain his troops. The redcoats charged. The Patriots discharged a few guns at the soldiers as they fled for safety. Later, the Americans would have it that the British began the unequal struggle; later, it was claimed in behalf of the British that the shooting was begun by Americans who had placed themselves beside the green. It matters little who fired the first gun. Parker would not run. He and seven of his men were killed, and ten others were wounded. One British soldier was hit in the leg. The long-anticipated war had begun.

The British soldiers did not immediately feel regret over the encounter. As the main body of the British detachment approached, the advance guard fired a volley and gave a great cheer. Wild with excitement, the troops rejoiced that at last they were able to strike at the Yankees. Lieutenant Colonel Francis Smith, who commanded the expedition, was perhaps not quite so happy. It was obviously somewhat risky to proceed to Concord. But he had his orders, and he obeyed them. The British column moved on westward toward Concord and reached it without further incident. Forewarned, the Patriots had removed part of their military equipment. The British destroyed what they could find. But, before they could turn back, 300 or 400 militiamen engaged a covering party of redcoats at the North Bridge, and both soldiers and Patriots fell to the ground. A young Patriot killed a wounded soldier with blows from a hatchet. The troops would not return to Boston without casualties.

Meanwhile, militiamen in scores and hundreds converged upon the road that Smith had to follow back toward Boston. Soon after the British column left Concord, Patriots began to fire into it from houses and barns, from stone walls and orchards. Soldiers slumped to the road and died. Smith sent out flanking parties to clear his path. They shot and bayoneted a few militiamen; they set fire to buildings used by the Americans for cover; they began to loot. But there was no real respite for the troops, weary from their long march, and assailed by more and more Patriots as they approached Lexington. The British detachment was barely able to reach that village. It was saved—most of it—by a rescue column of 1,200 men under Earl Percy that Gage had prudently sent out from Boston to Lexington. Moving back toward the city, the combined British forces were soon in great trouble. Percy had brought two fieldpieces with him, and they were useful in pushing back the militiamen who swarmed about his troops. Patriot officers managed to gather a mass of them to defend a bridge at Cambridge that Percy had to cross in order to reach Boston. It became doubtful that he could cut his way into the city. He eluded most of his enemies by turning to the left and marching across a narrow neck to Bunker Hill on the peninsula of Charleston, north of the city. There, at the end of a long and dismal April 19, with his flanks covered by the British fleet, he was temporarily safe from attack.

It was a bloody business. The British had 73 killed, 174 wounded, and 26 missing. Of the Americans, 49 were slain, 41 wounded, and 5 missing. It was only too apparent to Gage that the Yankees, aroused, would fight desperately. Had they been disciplined, had they been under a unified command, Earl Percy would hardly have escaped from them. On April 22 Gage sent home a brief and somber report about the running battle. He would have more bad news for his superiors. Militiamen from all parts of New England were gathering beyond his lines. Soon he and his troops—including Percy's men, brought back into Boston—were invested in the city by a motley army of 15,000 Patriots. Governor Jonathan Trumbull of Connecticut, hoping to prevent more fighting, asked Gage to help arrange an armistice. Certain New Yorkers made the same request. Gage replied that the Patriots could prevent further hostilities by laying down their arms. Thereafter, there were many efforts to bring the war to a halt, America remaining within the British empire. They all failed.

CHAPTER XIII

The War Spreads

THE advice given by General Thomas Gage to the British cabinet, to prepare for warfare on land before beginning it, the advice that his superiors refused to take, proved to be judicious, but he derived little pleasure from his foresight. He and his army were invested in Boston for many months. That army won a bloody and fruitless victory at Bunker Hill. Gage was relieved of his command and returned to England, a most unhappy general. He was succeeded by General William Howe at Boston, who remained there with the army until March 1776, then retreated to Halifax. The Patriots, taking advantage of Britain's unreadiness for war, not only drove the British from Boston, but from the Thirteen Colonies. They were still in complete control of the colonies on the morning of July 2, 1776, the day they declared their independence from Britain.

Although Gage refused after the Battle of Lexington and Concord to consider an armistice, he did not put his troops in motion again for nearly two months. He had too few to risk a general attack upon the investing Patriot militia; and if that attack were successful, he could gain little from it. His army was far too weak to venture into the interior of Massachusetts. Indeed, Gage believed that he could not afford even to try to make his position in Boston impregnable. Immediately after the running battle of April 19, Admiral Samuel Graves urged the general to forestall artillery bombardment of Boston and the British fleet from hills on the Charlestown peninsula north of the city or from Dorchester Heights south of Boston. Why not burn the village of Charlestown and cover Bunker Hill and Breed's Hill with Earl Percy's men? Why not seize and burn Roxbury? From that place Dorchester Heights could be dominated by cannon. But an attempt to take Roxbury would inevitably have led to a struggle with the Patriots. The Americans had no heavy guns, and would probably have none for many months. Gage decided instead to concentrate in Boston and to remain quiet until he received help from England. He strengthened his entrenchments across Boston Neck. He entered into an agreement with the selectmen of the city by which Patriots were allowed to leave it and Loyalists to come into it. Thus he opened a refuge for the friends of Britain and at the same time secured the departure of enemies within his lines—he forced them to give up their muskets and other weapons before they left—who might have taken up arms to help the Patriots outside the city. He tried to raise a force of Loyalists, but secured very few enlistments.

In his embarrassing situation at Boston Gage would have welcomed good news from other parts of America. He received none. On the contrary, he learned during May that Fort Ticonderoga had been captured together with many heavy cannon, by the Patriots on the tenth of that month. It would be most awkward for him if the Americans managed to transport some of those guns to Boston. He learned also that the Patriots were seizing power everywhere in the Thirteen Colonies, that royal and proprietary governors were being expelled or reduced to helplessness. Patriot assemblies, considering Lord North's Conciliatory Resolution, denounced it as a deceitful subterfuge intended to divide and to injure the Americans, not to serve as a means of securing reconciliation between Britain and the colonies. If such was not the fact, why had Gage put his troops in motion? The Patriots prepared more diligently for war.

Gradually, Gage obtained help from England. Detachments of marines, infantry, and artillerymen landed at Boston. Before the middle of June he had about 6,000 men ready for service. He also received new instructions, on May 25, from the Earl of Dartmouth. Composed after the British cabinet had learned of the Patriot arsenals at Concord and Worcester, but before the news of Lexington and Concord had reached London, those orders commanded Gage to destroy the arsenals. Again Gage was told to seize the Patriot leaders. He was advised to issue a proclamation offering pardon to all rebels, except for their most malignant leaders. Dartmouth blandly said, "it is imagined that by the time this letter reaches you, the army under your command will be equal to any operation that may become necessary."

The cabinet still declined to believe that Gage could be in serious trouble in Boston. It was sending four regiments to New York. However, if Gage believed that he needed those regiments, he could order them to proceed to Boston. Gage hastily asked Admiral Graves to intercept the transports carrying those troops and to see to it that they changed their course for Boston. The four regiments could accomplish nothing at New York, and the commander in chief wanted them badly at Boston. But he felt strong enough before their arrival to undertake to occupy the Charlestown and Dorchester peninsulas, as steps toward making Boston impregnable.

The orders that reached Gage on May 25 came on H.M.S. *Cerberus,* a ship associated with great events in the history of the British empire. Its captain, James Chadds, had carried General James Wolfe to Quebec in the *Cerberus* in 1759, and he had borne the body of Wolfe to England after the capture of the city. Chadds brought to Boston three major generals, William Howe, Henry Clinton, and John Burgoyne, who did not win undying fame. He did not take any of those officers home as a dead hero. He did convey to London on his return voyage the bad news of the empty and costly British victory at Bunker Hill.

Precisely what Gage thought of the three generals, at the time that they disembarked or later, is not known. It is certain that he disliked an order he had received to pay each of them £500 for military gear. For it had been decided in London that the three men ought not be forced to pay from their own pockets for the equipment they would need in America. Gage immediately asked for a similar sum for the same purpose. He had served for twenty years in America, and *he* had never been given money to buy a military outfit. It is equally certain that he would have preferred the help of 3,000 additional troops instead of the three generals. On June 12, writing to Dartmouth, he declared that he would need 32,000 men, including French Canadians and Indians, to conquer New England. On the same day, in a "private" letter to Viscount Barrington, he both defended his own conduct in the past and insisted that Britain must put large forces in the field in the future. Had he moved against the rebels in the fall of 1774, he would have been crushed. The Patriots had become powerful. Government must remember that fact. It should raise large bodies of troops; it should hire, if necessary, Russians, Hanoverians, and Hessians; it should employ Indians, and perhaps even Negroes.

On that June 12 Gage also issued a proclamation declaring martial law and offering pardon to all rebels who laid down their arms. He made exceptions of Samuel Adams and John Hancock, who were beyond the pale of forgiveness. Adams and Hancock were in any case at Philadelphia and beyond his reach, at least for the time being. Patriots nearer Boston did not hasten to the British lines to take advantage of Gage's offer. Rather, they made fun of the general's proclamation. It had been composed for Gage by Burgoyne, who had a literary reputation, and it was a pompous, bombastic, and silly document. The Patriots outside Boston did not lay down their weapons. Instead, they moved to occupy Bunker Hill.

The Patriots decided to send a detachment to occupy and to hold Charlestown peninsula in order to wrest the initiative from Gage. On June 15 gossip spread through Boston that the British would take the offensive in a few days. The talk was well founded on fact. Gage, Howe, Clinton, and Burgoyne had agreed that the British army had become strong enough to seize and hold both the Dorchester and Charlestown peninsulas. News of their plan leaked out, in part at least because Burgoyne failed to keep silent about it, and it quickly reached the Americans outside the city. The Patriot generals decided to send troops to Bunker Hill to forestall the British. They could not make immediate and good use of that eminence, since they had no heavy artillery, but they would not let the British take it without a struggle. During the night of June 16 parties of militia began to throw up fortifications on Charlestown peninsula.

The Patriots were numerous rather than efficient. Their commanding officer, insofar as they had one, was Artemas Ward, senior officer in the Massachusetts militia. A graduate of Harvard and a veteran of brief service in the Seven Years' War, Ward was more of a scholar than a soldier. Under him was General Israel Putnam, a New England hero who was brave rather than competent; Colonel William Prescott, an able and valiant man who was not familiar with the roar of guns on the battlefield; and sundry other officers of limited experience and diverse talents. The men commanded by those officers numbered about 15,000, based upon Roxbury and Cambridge. A British ship's surgeon described them as "a drunken, canting, lying, praying, hypocritical rabble without order, subjection, discipline, or cleanliness" that would "fall to pieces of itself." They were certainly not disciplined; most wore civilian clothes; and they were armed only with muskets of various vintages. Housed in tents and huts for many weeks, suffering from lack of medical service, short of ammunition, they did not constitute the best army in the world. They did have enough to eat. There is little doubt that Gage could have driven them from Roxbury and Cambridge. But what would be the profit, since such a victory could not be exploited?

As it happened, Gage attacked only a part of that homely army, with the most unpleasant consequences for the British troops engaged and for him. At dawn on June 17 observers on British ships in Boston Harbor saw Patriot soldiers building a redoubt on the crest of Breed's Hill. Militia under Israel Putnam had been instructed to seize and fortify Bunker Hill, nearer to the mainland and to the American army, but Putnam had successfully and unwisely urged that they proceed eastward and concentrate upon the more exposed Breed's Hill. There the battle of Bunker Hill was fought. Soon after sunrise British warships opened fire against the redoubt, without much effect, except that the noise of the cannon frightened Patriots unaccustomed to the roar. The guns of the ships could not reach the redoubt. Gage conferred with the major generals who had recently come from England. All agreed that the Patriots must be attacked. Clinton, the cleverest of the three, suggested that Gage send a detachment ashore on the south side of the Charlestown peninsula behind Breed's Hill. The approach of the troops could be protected by the fleet. With their rear threatened, the Americans on the hill would probably soon take to their heels. However, Clinton's proposal was set aside. Instead, Howe, as the senior major general, was ordered to take 1,500 men across the harbor, to land on the northeastern tip of the peninsula, and to advance along its northern shore. The militia were not entrenched there, and Howe could outflank the redoubt. The British generals expected no serious trouble. Howe's men carried provisions for three days, since they would stay on as a garrison force after they had pushed away the Patriots.

But all did not go smoothly for the British. Howe did not hurry across the harbor, did not disembark upon the peninsula until after noon. In the meantime, the Patriots strengthened their redoubt. Besides, realizing that it might be surrounded by the redcoats, they formed defensive lines of fence rails and other odds and ends on both sides of it. About 1,200 of them, under Colonel Prescott, faced the British. There were more militia behind them, chiefly on Bunker Hill; some of them later came forward to assist Prescott. Howe, observing that the Patriots had strengthened their position, did not like what he saw; he called for and obtained reinforcements. British ships cannonaded Charlestown, on the American right flank, and set it afire; they also threw shot on the narrow neck connecting the peninsula with the mainland, making it awkward for the Patriots to bring up more men from the mainland. At length Howe attacked the American left flank. The result shocked him. From their makeshift defenses the militia there drove back the redcoats with heavy musket fire. Shaken, Howe ordered a second assault, concentrated against the redoubt. The British regulars moved up Breed's Hill through long grass in splendid order. They were forced back by deadly fire from the militia; their ranks were decimated and shattered. Said Howe afterward, "there was a moment that I never felt before." Whatever his faults as a general—and they were many—Howe was as brave as might be. Standing among the slain and the wounded at the bottom of the hill, he re-formed his men. Clinton hastened from Boston to help him. Howe again advanced against the Patriot center. Once more the militia fired volley after destructive volley into the charging ranks of redcoats and marines. But the British troops came on. The militia ran out of ammunition, and many of them began to flee. However, others covered their retreat to the mainland. The Americans suffered their heaviest losses as they fled. The British had gained the peninsula. They did not venture to attack the bulk of the American forces beyond it.

Britain could not afford to win many peninsulas at similar cost. Immediately after the battle, the Patriots in their camp were downcast. They had been defeated, even though they had—at least part of them—fought with great resolution. They had lost Dr. Joseph Warren, who had served as a volunteer in the redoubt and who was killed when it was finally taken by the British. His death deprived them of an ardent, able, and generous-minded man who would have been most valuable in war and in peace. About 140 of the militia were killed; nearly twice as many were wounded; a few were captured. But the Patriots learned that their defeat was virtually a victory. Of about 2,200 men who had fought under Howe, Gage counted 1,054 casualties, of whom at least 226 were slain.

Some British companies that took part in the battle were destroyed, and many British officers were killed or mortally wounded, among them Major John Pitcairn. Howe declared that his success was "too dearly bought." To him June 17, 1775, was "this unhappy day." His losses filled him "with horror." Nor were the reports sent by Gage to London cheerful. He made no effort to conceal the fact that the victory was extraordinarily expensive. The Patriot militia had fought bravely. Those in London who believed that the Americans would not fight must alter their mistaken opinion. He again called for large forces to subdue the rebels. If they were not supplied, Britain must resort to a naval blockade as her principal weapon. He knew that he would be censured because he had achieved so little at so great cost. He doubtless expected to be replaced as commander in chief. In a letter to Viscount Barrington he expressed his disappointment in bitter language. Boston had become hateful to him. He wished that "this cursed place was burned."

The shock of Bunker Hill was so great that Gage put off the occupation of Dorchester Heights. After all, the Americans still lacked heavy artillery, and were unlikely to get any in the near future. Not long after the battle Gage received an important reinforcement, the four regiments that had originally been ordered to New York. His army then became somewhat stronger than it was before Bunker Hill. However, it seemed to him prudent to avoid any further adventure of importance at Boston until the British army became powerful enough to strike decisively. He also reached the conclusion that the task of conquering the Patriots required that the bulk of that army be based upon New York, the strategic center of the colonies, insofar as they had one. Accordingly, he must remain as quiet as possible in Boston until his superiors decided what they would do in consequence of the events of the spring and summer of 1775 in America.

Gage was given additional reason for remaining on the defensive. The forces opposing him were "adopted" and strengthened by the Second Continental Congress. Convening on May 10 at Philadelphia, that body undertook to speak and to act for America. George Washington and other Continental officers appointed by it appeared outside Boston, also several companies of riflemen from Pennsylvania, Maryland, and Virginia.

The Second Continental Congress was composed substantially of the same men who had gathered in Philadelphia in the fall of 1774. It contained one very important new face, that of Benjamin Franklin, a delegate from Pennsylvania. Later, Thomas Jefferson came on from Virginia. Still later, deputies appeared from Georgia, so that all of the Thirteen Colonies were represented in it after the autumn of 1775. The Congress quickly assumed general direction of the Patriot war effort. Like other Patriot gatherings, it condemned Lord North's Conciliatory Resolution. There could be no accommodation with Britain on the basis of the prime minister's plan. It was a snare. Britain, if she desired reconciliation, must offer more precise and more generous terms. Eventually, early in July, the Congress did send the Olive Branch Petition to the King. But that document offered no concession to Britain. It merely asked George III to provide some means for negotiation with his "loyal subjects"; and it was endorsed by many delegates only as a last, polite, and futile gesture. However, the members of Congress unanimously and quickly agreed that the Patriots must protect themselves against the British army and navy. The New Englanders around Boston were fighting for an American cause. The Congress must assume responsibility for the defense, not only of Massachusetts, but of all America.

Accordingly, the Congress decided to appoint a commander in chief and other officers to direct the Patriot forces. Who should be commissioned for the supreme command? General Artemas Ward was a possibility. He was at Boston. But it was apparent that he was not a military genius. Moreover, he was a Yankee; and it seemed desirable, in order to secure unity among the Patriots, to choose a man who was not a New Englander. The Yankees had been too forward, too aggressive in asserting American rights, in the opinion of some Patriots of the Middle and Southern Colonies. They had aroused jealousy and suspicion southwest of the Hudson River. Afterward, John Adams recalled that John Hancock desired the appointment, or at least the refusal of it. But Hancock was not seriously considered. He was even less suitable than Ward—he was a New Englander, and he had never served in a military campaign. Lieutenant Colonel Charles Lee, a veteran British officer who had cast his lot with the Patriots, was available. He had several admirers in the Congress. However, he was ruled out for various reasons, including the fact that he was English-born. The commander in chief must be an American.

There was a member of the Congress who seemed suitable in almost every way, George Washington. He was obviously willing to serve in some military capacity, for he appeared at the Congress in the uniform of a Virginia colonel. As a young man Washington had taken the field under Generals Edward Braddock and John Forbes in two campaigns of the Seven Years' War. He had also commanded a regiment of militia on the Virginia frontier during that struggle and had displayed bravery on the battlefield. He had won the esteem of Braddock and of Gage. He was only forty-three years old, physically powerful, and unquestionably devoted to the Patriot cause. It was in his favor that he was a Virginian. He had not been among the most vociferous defenders of colonial rights before 1775; he had not been slow to come forward as a champion of those rights; he had shown neither unbridled passion nor timidity. He inspired respect and trust. He would not abuse the authority of the commander in chief nor seek to become a dictator. He was a wealthy man; he would not try to enrich himself at public expense. Nor would he use power entrusted to him in order to achieve social and economic leveling. His fellow delegates observed that he was not much given to talk, but that he spoke very sensibly when he did speak. On June 15 Washington was unanimously chosen as the head of the American army. He immediately accepted the appointment, declaring that he would take no pay.

The "Father of His Country" did not possess all the virtues, nor did he lack every fault. His ancestry has been doubtfully traced to the English Washingtons of Sulgrave Manor, but the first Washingtons in Virginia were middle-class folk. He had moved upward into the gentry, in part through ability, in part through his marriage of convenience to a wealthy widow, Mrs. Martha Custis. As a young man, he was befriended by Lieutenant Governor Robert Dinwiddie of Virginia, who opened up a military career for him. Apparently, he was not so grateful to Dinwiddie as he should have been. He was not a well-educated man. He had had little formal schooling; nor had he taught himself, as Benjamin Franklin did, by extensive reading. He was a country squire who set a proper value upon money and land, a careful planter who paid his debts and insisted that his debtors pay him. The tall Virginian was ordinarily sober, even dull, in maturity. He was not witty; like most men of his time, like

Franklin, he enjoyed an earthy anecdote. In his middle and later years he did not often pray for divine guidance; he was not an ardent Christian, though formally an Episcopalian. He liked flattery as well as most men. He was as sensitive to censure as most men. When things went wrong, he quite humanly ascribed shortcomings to others rather than to himself. He would tell Congress on more than one occasion that it had not done its duty toward its commander in chief. Intellectually, he was slow and solid rather than quick and brilliant. Above all, he was reliable.

Washington was neither a Caesar nor a Napoleon. Even so, Congress could not have found a better man. Consider the abler officers of high rank who served in the American forces in the War of Independence. There was not one who was his equal. Nathanael Greene was bold, enterprising, ingenious—and interested in making money. Fat Henry Knox was a fine artillery officer, and nothing more. Anthony Wayne was a splendid fighting man, but not an astute commander. Charles Lee, intellectually gifted, was temperamental, quarrelsome, and unsteady. Horatio Gates was an intriguer, and not very astute. Philip Schuyler, John Sullivan, and others too numerous to mention were defective in one way or another as generals. It should go without saying that the intelligent, bold, masterful, mean, and treacherous Benedict Arnold was not fitted to lead the American forces, despite his achievements.

Faults have been, and can be, found in Washington as a commander. He did not have the advantages of a good military education. He did not know, and he never quite learned, how to discipline and to drill his men. He was not a consistently brilliant strategist or tactician. He has been described as an American Fabius, as if he secured advantage over British Hannibals by avoiding battle. Actually, he was quite willing to fight when the odds were not too heavily against him. He retreated only when he was compelled to do so, during the campaigns of 1776 and 1777. Even in those years, he struck back at the British as soon as he possibly could. On occasion he was perhaps too venturesome. His generalship improved as the war continued. However, his defeats in the field were more numerous than his victories; and he had to share the laurels of his great triumph, at Yorktown, with the French. If Washington had his shortcomings as a strategist and as a tactician, he nevertheless performed superbly under the most difficult conditions. He gave dignity, steadfast loyalty, and indomitable courage to the American cause. There were American officers, including General Charles Lee and Lieutenant Colonel Alexander Hamilton, who found serious defects in their commander in chief. A few members of Congress, after the campaign of 1777, were momentarily disposed to put General Horatio Gates in Washington's place. His employers refrained from making that mistake. Indeed, the Congress supplied historians with convincing evidence of Washington's greatness. It not only appointed him as commander in chief, but maintained him in that post year after year, in victory and defeat, in prosperity and adversity, until the war was won.

When Washington was put at the head of the Continental army, most of the delegates in Congress believed that the help of experienced British officers would be useful, even indispensable, to him, at least for a time. The claims of General Artemas Ward to high rank could not be ignored; and he was commissioned as a major general in the Continental forces. However, Charles Lee was given similar status. Only Washington and Ward were placed above him. When Ward resigned from the service, a year later, Lee became the second ranking officer in the Continental army. He would indeed be useful to the Patriots; he would also be the source of much trouble for them. Why did Congress place so much faith in him?

Of the same age as Washington, Lee was an extraordinary man in appearance and also in substance. Washington would have been a conventional figure in the streets of London or the fields of Lincolnshire; Lee was an exotic wherever he went. Lean, aquiline-nosed, homely, slovenly, he was trailed about by dogs who accompanied him everywhere he went. Did he imitate Frederick the Great, whom he had met? He was a celebrated celibate, at least a bachelor, except possibly for a brief unofficial marriage in his youth to a Mohawk "princess." Born in Chester, England, he may have been distantly related to the Lees of Virginia, among whom he had made several fast friends. His family belonged to the English gentry: his mother was the daughter of a baronet. He was a hard-bitten soldier who had taken part in many campaigns in North America. He had fought with distinction in Portugal against the Spanish; he had watched warfare between the Russians and the Turks in eastern Europe. Beginning military service as an ensign in the British 44th regiment, then commanded by his father, Colonel John Lee, he had attained the rank of lieutenant colonel. He had also been given honorary appointments as a colonel in Portugal and as a major general in Poland. He knew his military business. He was brave, arrogant, profane, and brutally frank in speech and in writing. His career was studded by quarrels.

But, surprisingly, Lee was also a scholar, an idealist, and a propagandist. While his fellow officers in the British army spent their many leisure hours in gambling and drinking, Lee studied. He became familiar with Plutarch, with Shakespeare, and with Jean Jacques Rousseau. He adored Rousseau. He became a seeker for liberty, for an ideal society. At one time he devised a scheme for a Utopian colony in the Mississippi Valley. Possessing a satirical wit, he published a savage attack upon George III in a London newspaper in 1771. It has been suggested, erroneously, that he was *Junius.* On half pay after the end of the Seven Years' War, he returned to America in 1773, promptly espoused the cause of the colonists, and passionately defended it, as *Anglus Americanus,* in the newspapers. He made friends among the militant colonists, including Dr. Benjamin Rush and Thomas Mifflin in Philadelphia. Sojourning in Philadelphia during the sessions of the First Continental Congress, he helped to prepare one of its pronunciamentos, the appeal to the French Canadians.

A few men in the Congress in 1775 doubted that it was wise to place Lee high in the hierarchy of Continental officers, at least partly because he was an Englishman. Time proved their judgment to be correct. He was to be among the first and most vociferous clamorers for American independence; nevertheless, he did not become an American at heart. His idealism was intermingled with and corroded by personal ambitions. He had turned to Rousseau and to dreams of an ideal society because he was a social misfit. His denunciation of George III was not entirely based upon principle; Lee believed that he had not been promoted with sufficient rapidity in the British army. What was worse, he was mentally unstable. He suffered from the gout and, like the Earl of Chatham, had fits of hysteria that carried him close to madness. He was, as he himself said, an odd creature. There were men who served under him and who gave him enduring admiration and affection. He was gentle and generous to those who looked to him for leadership, who did not challenge his superiority. Others would find him to be haughty, self-centered, harsh, fickle, treacherous, and subject to bouts of insanity.

The Congress also gave a plum to Horatio Gates, another Englishman, who was tendered an appointment as brigadier general. Lee came from the British aristocracy; Gates's father was an upper household servant who ministered to the wants of a part of that aristocracy, the family of the Duke of Leeds. Normally, a man of such parentage would not have become an officer in the British army. Gates managed not only to secure a commission, but to climb to the rank of major before he resigned from that army in 1772. He served in many campaigns of the Seven Years' War in North America and the West Indies, without distinguishing himself remarkably. He was somewhat older than Washington and Lee, a kindly, good-natured, convivial man. It is to be suspected that he rose in the world not because of his ability, but because of his amiability. He made influential friends among his superior officers in the British army.

He was neither formally nor informally an educated man, nor was he intellectually gifted. He was appointed adjutant general under Washington because he had experience in army paper work. He was later an ardent seeker for rank and duties in the Continental army beyond his capabilities. Gates was to win lasting glory in one campaign, to suffer a most humiliating defeat in another. There was a firm limit to his intrigues. Emigrating to a plantation in Virginia in 1773, he threw in his lot with the Patriots, declaring that he was willing to give his life for "the liberty of the western world." A convinced republican—one may imagine that he, the son of a servant, had met with slights from some of his fellow British officers—Gates gave unwavering loyalty to the American cause. Like Charles Lee, he was one of the first to urge that America declare her independence. He did not die for America. He suffered much from dysentery during the War of Independence, but lived on to old age as a respected citizen.

Washington, Lee, Gates, and other new Continental officers proceeded promptly to the American lines outside Boston. Washington took command apparently without ceremony under the "Washington elm" or another tree. He did not hear and see what a Southern rifleman heard and saw a few days later, "such sermons, such Negroes, such colonels, such boys, & such great great grandfathers." Washington liked the appearance of the New England militia. He soon instilled a measure of discipline among them and established a system of command. He also soon began to think about assaulting the British. If he could drive them from Boston, the Patriot cause would gain enormously. In council of war he considered an attack in the summer, and again in the fall. He did not order his men into battle, for the British positions were virtually impregnable so long as he did not have heavy cannon. The British remained quiet, for equally good reasons. Weeks and months passed without much fighting. As the end of 1775 approached, Washington was faced by a crisis. The terms of service of the militiamen were expiring. They could hardly find enough wood to burn so as to keep warm in winter weather and wanted to go home. Many of them did so. However, Washington was able to secure the enlistment of many thousands of Yankees in Continental service for a period of one year. In consequence, his army actually gained in stability and strength what it lost in numbers. He also acquired, from various sources, a supply of gunpowder.

The British in Boston continued to have their troubles, which were not helped by the departure of General Gage for England on October 10. He was ordered home, ostensibly to help make plans for the campaign of 1775. General Howe was given command temporarily of the British troops in the Thirteen Colonies. Howe was instructed to hold on as best he could in America until large reinforcements came from England. He held on, until the end of winter. Food and ammunition arrived from England—although some of the transports carrying supplies were captured by Patriot cruisers. Fresh meat was brought in from Nova Scotia and the West Indies, and the Boston town bull was slaughtered for beef. The British soldiers cut down trees and tore down houses for wood to keep warm. They suffered from dysentery and boredom. Their officers were also unhappy. After Bunker Hill, they resigned in numbers. Asked by a Scottish friend whether he could help obtain a commission for a young man named Sutherland, James Grant responded, "If this business continues I could provide for all the Sutherlands in the country." Before he departed, Gage quarreled hotly with Admiral Samuel Graves. Burgoyne let it be known in England that Gage had serious shortcomings. Charles Stuart, a son of the Earl of Bute, informed his father that Howe was less than superb. "I hope to God," said Stuart, "that they will send some generals worthy the command of a British army from home."

In February 1776, the situation at Boston suddenly altered in favor of the Patriots. Colonel Henry Knox returned from a journey to Fort Ticonderoga with heavy guns that he had managed to transport over ice and snow on sledges. Rejoicing, Washington immediately undertook to make use of the cannon. He quietly placed some of them, together with a garrison, on Dorchester Heights during the night of March 4. The following morning Howe discovered that he was in an ugly predicament. He must then have wished that he had occupied those hills. The Patriot guns could throw shot down upon both the British fleet and the city, could make Boston quite untenable for the British. Howe and Admiral Molyneaux Shuldham, who had succeeded Graves, tried to bombard the heights with artillery. Their guns could not reach the top of the hills. Howe then swiftly issued orders for an assault upon Dorchester Heights. On second thought, he decided that it was imprudent to risk another Bunker Hill or worse, in order to remain a little longer in Boston. Washington was ready, not only to defend Dorchester Heights, but to mount an attack upon the city. A tremendous storm gave Howe an excuse for abandoning the enterprise. Instead, he chose to evacuate Boston. He reached an informal agreement with Washington which permitted him to leave without molestation by the Patriots, provided that he did no further damage to the city. He had acquired enough transport to carry his army to Halifax, and he embarked on March 17. With him went 1,100 Loyalists who would not remain in Boston at the mercy of the Patriots. Most of those Loyalists went on to England and exile. Howe and his troops spent the spring of 1776 in Nova Scotia. The main British army had been expelled from the Thirteen Colonies. It would return.

The triumph of Washington at Boston was accompanied by victories of the Patriots in the Southern Colonies. They were physically and seriously challenged neither by British soldiers nor by Loyalists in the Middle Colonies until the summer of 1776. Gage had withdrawn all the British troops from New York City, New Jersey, and Pennsylvania in order to hold Boston; and the Loyalists in those regions did not dare to take up arms. It was otherwise to the southward. Lord Dunmore was not driven from Virginia without a struggle; Loyalists took the field in North Carolina; and a British fleet and army appeared at Charleston, South Carolina. But the results were not happy for Britain.

Whatever were the faults of Lord Dunmore—he became a hated man in Virginia, where he was looked upon as "that bloody butcher"—he did not lack courage or energy. There were few Loyalists in Virginia, chiefly Scottish men of business. Nevertheless, as the war began, Dunmore neither fled to England nor remained quiet. On April 21, 1775, he seized Virginia's store of gunpowder at Williamsburg. Forced to flee from Williamsburg, he established himself aboard a British cruiser in Chesapeake Bay. He collected a handful of Loyalists; he secured the help of a few British warships in the bay, together with marines that they carried; and he obtained the assistance of some redcoats from St. Augustine. He promised freedom to all Negro slaves who would join him, and so managed to gather 200 or 300 "Loyal Ethiopians." He even sought, vainly, to bring down Indians upon the northwestern frontier of Virginia. Forthrightly proclaiming all Patriots to be traitors, who could be deprived of both life and property, Dunmore waged war as ruthlessly as his motley forces permitted. Ravaging the coasts of Virginia, he at length felt strong enough to send his "army" against Virginia Continentals and volunteer riflemen who collected to oppose him. On December 9, 1775, in the battle of Great Bridge, south of Norfolk, Dunmore's forces encountered a crushing defeat. The governor retaliated by bombarding and burning most of Norfolk. His artillery destroyed the houses of Patriots rather than Loyalists. The Patriots completed the destruction of the town by setting fire to the homes of the Tories. Dunmore could do little more. Unable to establish and maintain a base on land, he remained in Chesapeake Bay for many months. His "army" dwindled. At length, in the summer of 1776, he sent his Negro troops off to the West Indies—and back to slavery. He, himself, with the remains of his white-skinned contingents, sailed off to join a powerful British army gathering at New York.

Josiah Martin, the last royal governor of North Carolina and a former army officer, also was forced to seek safety aboard a British ship, and Loyalists who answered his call to arms encountered crushing defeat. There were many Tories in North Carolina, among them a body of Scots, including Highlanders who had recently crossed the Atlantic and had settled in the southern part of the colony. The most famous of those Highlanders was a woman, Flora MacDonald, who had achieved romantic glory in 1746 by saving Bonnie Prince Charlie from the pursuing troops of George II after the battle of Culloden. The Highlanders had been forced to leave Scotland because they could not afford to pay the high rents extracted by the Scottish lairds. Nevertheless, Flora MacDonald and her fellow emigrants had feudally transferred their affection to George III; and they gave to him the same loyalty they had formerly offered to the exiled house of Stuart. Learning that a British army and fleet would soon appear off the coast of North Carolina, Martin, on January 10, 1776, called upon all men faithful to Britain to take up arms against the "traitorous" rebels. The Highlanders, with a few other North Carolinians, responded. Gathering near modern Fayetteville in February, more than 1,700 Loyalists began to move toward Wilmington to join the British. The expected fleet and army were not at Wilmington, and the Tories did not reach that town. Their way was barred at Moore's Creek Bridge, over which they had to pass, by 1,000 Patriots who had ripped the planks from the floor of the bridge. Other Patriots were near at hand. The Loyalists charged across the bridge on February 27. They were driven back and routed by a Patriot counterattack. On the following day more than 850 of the Tories, almost encircled by oncoming Patriots, surrendered. Thereafter, the Loyalists of North Carolina were prudently quiet for several years. Martin never was able to resume his authority.

The British squadron and army with which Martin had hoped to restore royal rule in at least part of North Carolina arrived tardily at Cape Fear. General Henry Clinton, who had been sent from Boston to command the army, arrived with a few troops on March 13. But the fleet, and the bulk of the army—about 2,500 men sent out from Ireland—were delayed, partly by storm at sea. Commodore Sir Peter Parker, with most of the fleet, reached Cape Fear on May 3. The last of his vessels did not appear there until May 31. Parker commanded ten warships, including a 50-gun ship and five frigates. Parker and Clinton had been given a special assignment—Clinton and the troops were later to join General Howe at New York, but it was hoped in England that the admiral and the general could first inexpensively strike at the Southern Colonies before Clinton had to depart for New York, that they could enspirit and assist the Southern Loyalists. In fact, they found that they could accomplish little in

North Carolina. For a time Clinton favored an attempt to establish a British base between Chesapeake Bay and Albemarle Sound. However, the two British officers decided instead to proceed to Charleston. They learned that the Patriots were building a fort on Sullivan's Island in Charleston Harbor, but were making slow progress. They might secure and keep possession of the fort and the island at small cost. Charleston itself might later be seized.

The British expedition was off a bar across the mouth of Charleston Harbor as early as June 1. Its appearance caused alarm in the South Carolina capital. The Patriots there feared that the British intended to seize both the fort, commanded by Colonel William Moultrie and later named after him, and the city itself. The fort was unfinished, and work upon it, by Negro slaves, was going on very slowly indeed. Moreover, help expected by the Patriots from Virginia and North Carolina had not arrived. General Charles Lee, placed by Congress in charge of the defense of the Southern Colonies, had not known where to go to meet the British threat. He was on his way to Charleston with troops. "For God's sake," wrote John Rutledge, leader of the Patriots in South Carolina to Lee, "lose not a moment." Lee entered the city, together with several thousand Continentals and militia, before the British were able to attack.

Clinton and Parker were vexed by bad weather, and their assault was long delayed. They did not enter the harbor until June 7. Two days later Clinton put 500 men on Long Island, adjacent to Sullivan's Island. However, Parker and Clinton did not attack until nearly three weeks more had passed. In the meantime Lee infused energy into the Patriot forces, which increased to perhaps 6,500 men, of whom about 435 were stationed upon Sullivan's Island. Lee doubted that the Patriot fort could be held against British bombardment. He believed that the Americans should concentrate instead upon the land defenses of the city. But the South Carolinians insisted that the fort must not be given up without a struggle. Reluctantly agreeing to try to defend it, Lee spurred on the men who were building. The fort was still unfinished—the western side of it was open—when the British began their assault. The incomplete walls were made of palmetto logs. The fort contained only twenty-one usable pieces of artillery, and only thirty-five rounds of ammunition for them; altogether, it seemed most unlikely that it could withstand bombardment by the British fleet. Lee was less worried about Clinton's troops. He placed nearly 800 men on the northern end of Sullivan's Island to deal with the redcoats. He also made ready defenses on the mainland against a thrust by Clinton.

On June 28, Lee received a pleasing surprise. The British fleet went into action. Clinton considered an attack upon Sullivan's, or a crossing to the mainland. But he did not put his men in motion. They could not take the offensive across water with any chance of success unless the guns of the British ships reduced the American fort, at least not until they had frightened the American defenders of the island into a panic. But the fleet failed to destroy the fort; nor did its guns daunt the garrison. Late in the morning nine British ships anchored in front of the fort and began to throw shot and shell at it. The response was deliberate and accurate fire. Three of the smaller vessels then tried to change their position so as to bombard the unfinished part of the fort. All three ran aground on a shoal, and two of them fouled each other. Only one of them, after repairs, was able to take further part in the battle. Another ship, used to throw shells, had to withdraw because of mechanical troubles. The Patriot garrison concentrated its fire upon Commodore Parker's flagship, the 50-gun *Bristol,* and the frigate *Experiment.* Both vessels suffered heavy damage, and many sailors aboard them were killed or injured. Meanwhile, by a strange chance, the garrison fared much better. Palmetto wood is soft. The British cannon shot did not break or splinter the log walls; often they merely embedded themselves in the wood. The men in the fort could feel it shake, but they continued to fire slowly and methodically. After several hours of fighting they ran out of powder. But Lee sent them a new supply, and they resumed the struggle. The losses of the British increased. At last, at night, Parker abandoned the contest and withdrew. The following morning the British had to destroy one of the vessels that had run aground. Parker's killed and wounded were four times those of the garrison. The British stayed on in the harbor for three weeks. However, they could accomplish nothing, except to repair their ships, and at last Parker and Clinton departed for New York. Parker did not return to Charleston, and Clinton did not reappear there until more than three years had passed.

Four days after the battle of Sullivan's Island the Congress declared the independence of the United States of America. The good news from Charleston delighted the delegates, all the more because an attempt to seize Quebec had failed and because the British were about to descend upon New York City in great force.

CHAPTER XIV

The Invasion of Canada

FROM the period of the Revolution until the early years of the twentieth century there were always some Americans who desired that their union be truly Continental. In the first year of the War of Independence the Patriots made a remarkable effort to conquer the province of Quebec and to make of it a fourteenth colony—and state. They failed, in part because Quebec was inhabited by Frenchmen rather than Englishmen. They also strove, at the close of the war, to secure all of Canada by diplomacy. Again they failed. Canada remained a British possession. Indeed, the War of Independence ultimately solidified the hold of the British upon Canada, for many thousands of Loyalists who settled in the Maritime Provinces and Ontario at the end of the war offered a specially fervent fidelity to Britain. So did their descendants, for many generations, to a large degree because both the Loyalists and their progeny detested and feared the United States. Driven away from the St. Lawrence River in 1776, the Patriots did, however, profit from their defeat. Their invasion of Quebec persuaded Britain to establish two commanders in chief in North America and to send reinforcements to Quebec as well as to the Thirteen Colonies. That division of the British army and of its command helped the Patriots to win the fateful Saratoga campaign, an alliance with France, and independence.

Striving to found a Continental union in 1775 and afterward, the Patriots made no serious effort to win friends in Nova Scotia. Part of the population of that colony was of Yankee origin. However, the Nova Scotians were few in number, and were not eager to make common cause with the Patriots. Conquest of Nova Scotia would bring only small benefits to the Americans. Moreover, the province could not easily be captured, if for no other reason because the British navy maintained a base at Halifax, the only important settlement in the province. Indeed, after 1776, when Halifax became a place of refuge for fleeing Loyalists, the Patriots could hardly attack Nova Scotia with any hope of success. They were drawn instead toward the St. Lawrence, toward the old French province of Quebec.

Did the Americans intend to bring the blessings of liberty to Quebec? They said that such was their purpose, and one ought not doubt their sincerity. However, in sending troops northward toward Montreal and the city of Quebec in 1775, they had other reasons. They needed whatever help they could get from the inhabitants of Quebec, and they hoped to secure substantial aid from the French Canadians, restive under British rule. If they could not obtain active assistance, they might nevertheless be able to deprive Britain of Canadian allies. The Americans had suffered much from the attacks of French Canadian militia in earlier wars. The aid of that militia would be most useful; even the neutrality of the French Canadians would be valuable. Patriot control of the St. Lawrence Valley would bring other benefits. If the British were driven out of it, they would be denied easy access to the northern Indian tribes. It was to be feared that the British, if they retained possession of Quebec, Montreal, and Detroit, would supply the Six Nations and other savages with weapons and would encourage them to attack the American frontier settlements. Even if an invasion of Canada failed, was it not preferable for the Patriots to fight as much as possible on the St. Lawrence rather than in the midst of their own homes? The Patriots had still another reason for moving northward in 1775. By concentrating his army in Boston, General Gage had been unable to strengthen the British forces in Canada. There were only four scanty regiments of redcoats, together with four companies of artillerymen, in the province of Quebec, and they were scattered from the city of Quebec to distant outposts in the region of the Great Lakes. As the War of Independence began, the Patriots had an opportunity to strike, before Britain could send reinforcements across the Atlantic.

It will be remembered that the Americans asked for the help of the inhabitants of Quebec as early as the fall of 1774, in an address sent to them by the First Continental Congress. The French Canadians were invited to choose delegates to the Second Continental Congress. They did not respond, in part because the royal governor of the colony, General Guy Carleton, prevented wide circulation of the Patriot appeal. During the winter before the outbreak of the war American agents, including John Brown of Massachusetts, who was commissioned by the Boston committee of correspondence, made their way northward. Traveling as far as Montreal, Brown brought back encouraging information—and opinions. He found friends among the "old subjects," the English and American merchants who had settled in Montreal and other towns after the collapse of the French régime in Canada—but only some, for those who had been born in Britain tended to give their loyalty to the Crown. Brown was received with sympathy by those English-speaking inhabitants of Quebec who had migrated northward from the Thirteen Colonies, and he was assured that they would support the American cause. However, there were only a few hundreds of them; and they were counterbalanced by those "old subjects" who clung to the King. Brown also learned that the French Canadians, who formed the great bulk of the population of Quebec and who numbered possibly 80,000 in 1775, were not, in the main, enthusiastic supporters of Britain. A few at least were pleased with British rule; more were disposed to help the Americans. The mass of the French Canadians would not assist the British; they might be won over by the Patriots. Brown also discerned the weakness of the British forces on the St. Lawrence. He was told by the Green Mountain Boys that they would seize Forts Ticonderoga and Crown Point, both posts containing small garrisons, in the event that Britain and America engaged in hostilities. It became apparent that the capture of these two forts would open the way for the advance of an American army over Lake Champlain and down the Richelieu River valley to the St. Lawrence, Montreal, and the city of Quebec.

General Gage and General Carleton—Carleton was both governor of Quebec and commander, under Gage, of the troops in the province—were well aware of the importance of the two forts, especially Ticonderoga, the stronger one. The two posts guarded the Hudson River–Lake Champlain–Richelieu River passageway between New York City and the St. Lawrence Valley; Ticonderoga was momentarily all the more valuable because of its stores of artillery. In March 1775 (as already described), Gage warned Captain William De la Place, commandant at Ticonderoga, to prepare against a Patriot attack. On the day of Lexington and Concord Gage hurried off a letter to Carleton, instructing him to send one of his regiments southward to protect the two forts. Gage's fears were only too well founded. The forts fell into the hands of the Patriots before Carleton could act upon his orders.

Soon after the beginning of hostilities, not only the Green Mountain Boys but many other New Englanders prepared to move against "Ti" and Crown Point. The bold Benedict Arnold, who had taken part in the investment of Boston as an officer in the Connecticut militia, eagerly sought and obtained a commission from the Massachusetts committee of safety to lead an expedition westward. He began to gather troops from Connecticut and Massachusetts. However, eighty of the Green Mountain Boys had collected at Castleton, Vermont, on May 7, under the leadership of Ethan Allen, before Arnold could bring up his men. When Arnold appeared there, he claimed command of any and all Patriot forces that were to march against the forts. Allen would not accept Arnold as his superior officer. At length, it was agreed that Allen, with his men, and Arnold, without any men, should serve as joint commanders. Allen and Arnold might debate hotly about their respective powers; they did not disagree about the need for swift action. They moved quickly across Lake Champlain and, reaching Fort Ticonderoga well before dawn on May 10, demanded its immediate surrender.

There were fewer than fifty redcoats at "Ti," many of them invalids unfit for active service. Its walls were incomplete. Indeed, the fort was not defensible against assault. Moreover, De la Place and the garrison were surprised. Allen, Arnold, and the Green Mountain Boys, dealing roughly with two sentries who offered resistance, were within one of the doors of the fort before De la Place could be roused from sleep. He was offered a choice between surrender and a hopeless struggle. He chose to avoid serious bloodshed. Allen reported to the Congress at Philadelphia that his boys took the fort "by storm," although not a man was killed on either side.

Both Allen and Arnold claimed credit for the taking of Ticonderoga, and both tried to exploit the victory—separately. Crown Point fell easily. With men of his own, Arnold captured a small British garrison at Fort St. John's on the Richelieu River. He fell back when a body of redcoats sent forward by Carleton approached that post. Allen and his followers briefly engaged those redcoats, and then retreated. Before long most of the Green Mountain Boys went home, carrying loot they had obtained at Ticonderoga. But the Patriots had won "Ti" and Crown Point, and soon they placed garrisons of New England militia at the two posts. Both Allen and Arnold promptly began to clamor for an attack upon Montreal. Allen said that he could take the town with 1,500 men and some cannon. He did not think that the city of Quebec was beyond the reach of the Patriots. Arnold, a trifle more modest, believed that he could accomplish as much as Allen, with 1,700 men. But neither of those aggressive officers was entrusted with the army he desired. In fact, Arnold, who assumed the title of commander in chief at Ticonderoga, was soon superseded there by Colonel Benjamin Hinman of Connecticut. Arnold then turned toward a scheme to assail the city of Quebec by way of the forests of Maine.

197

The Patriots did not immediately take advantage of the successes of Allen and Arnold. The news of the capture of Ticonderoga was not received with unalloyed pleasure in Philadelphia. In May 1775, the Congress desired to wage only defensive war. It even ordered that the fort be evacuated and that the dozens of cannon captured with it be safely stored away until they could be returned to British hands. Fortunately for the Patriot military effort, the commands of Congress were not executed. It desired the friendship and help of the Canadians, but was utterly opposed at that point to sending troops into their country. On May 29 the Congress sent a second appeal to the Canadians for support. Parliament could deprive the French Canadians of freedom to practice their Roman Catholic faith. Were they not alarmed? They ought to want their own legislature; their fate was intermingled with the destiny of the Protestant Americans. The appeal was not a potent piece of propaganda. The French Canadians had never had an elected assembly, and they felt no urgent need for one. They knew very well that they had been granted freedom of worship by the Quebec Act, and also that the Americans had resented British generosity to them in the matter of religion. And the Americans had not been remarkably kind to Roman Catholics in the Thirteen Colonies. On June 1 the Congress, still relying upon persuasion that could not fully persuade, flatly resolved that it was opposed to any expedition by any Patriots against or into Canada.

But the Congress changed its mind. Patriots of the Northern Colonies urged that advantage be taken of a great and passing opportunity. An attack upon the British troops in Canada would not be an onslaught against the civilians of that province. Would not the presence of Patriot soldiers within Quebec encourage the French Canadians to stand forth against Britain? The news of Bunker Hill undoubtedly swayed Congress. That grim and bloody struggle would surely lead to others. The Patriots could not afford to make nice distinctions between defensive and offensive war. On June 27, the Congress issued orders to Major General Philip Schuyler to assume command at Ticonderoga and Crown Point. Moreover, if he also considered that a successful march into Canada was quite possible and that it would not be "disagreeable" to the Canadians, he was to march forward to the St. Lawrence.

The delay imposed by Congress injured the chances for success of an expedition into Canada, and those chances were further diminished by entrusting to Philip Schuyler a task that called for energy, celerity, and audacity. For he was not a James Wolfe—or a Benedict Arnold. Descended from a Dutch family long settled in New York, he was a prosperous country gentleman who lived in a commodious and comfortable farmhouse near Saratoga. His military experience was largely confined to service as a supply officer during the Seven Years' War. He was cautious and patient rather than impetuous and enterprising. He was not physically vigorous, and he lacked confidence in himself. He had other defects. He was courteous, even gracious, to those he considered his equals; but he was also snobbish to those he fancied to be his inferiors. He was not liked by Yankees, whose help he needed. Many of the New Englanders even doubted Schuyler's devotion to the Patriot cause.

Schuyler lingered at Ticonderoga for many weeks, collecting men and supplies, building vessels to traverse Lake Champlain, and gathering information about conditions in Canada. He would not go forward without careful preparation. Indeed, he was not at all eager to act. He rather hoped that he would receive orders to remain at Ticonderoga; none came. There can be no question that he had many obstacles to overcome, but he made too much of his troubles. He did not take into full account the fact that he was giving General Carleton time to prepare to defend Canada. Moreover, it was at least highly desirable that the Patriots achieve their goal before the onset of the cold Canadian winter. At last, Brigadier General Richard Montgomery, second in command under Schuyler, forced him into action. While Schuyler was at a conference at Albany, Montgomery, observing that delay was becoming increasingly costly, embarked on Lake Champlain for Canada with 1,200 men, on August 28. Schuyler soon joined him. They proceeded to the Richelieu River, where they were confronted by Fort St. John's, garrisoned by more than 700 men, of whom nearly three quarters were British regulars, under Major Charles Preston. The Americans fared badly in the preliminary skirmishing that accompanied their approach to the fort. Schuyler decided to erect defenses against the British. However, more Patriot troops came up, and Schuyler again assumed an offensive posture. Then he fell ill and left for Ticonderoga on September 16, abandoning leadership of the army to Montgomery. It was placed in good hands. With a heterogeneous collection of 2,000 Yankees, New Yorkers, and Green Mountain Boys Montgomery promptly surrounded and besieged Fort St. John's. Suddenly, the British hold upon Quebec was gravely endangered, for the redcoats at Fort St. John's formed the largest contingent of redcoats in the province. What was worse for the British, a second Patriot force under Benedict Arnold was moving through the woods of Maine toward the city of Quebec.

Guy Carleton had done everything possible to provide for the defense of Canada, except to call for the help of the Six Nations. Those tribes were largely under the domination of Indian Superintendent Guy Johnson and of Sir John Johnson, the son of Sir William Johnson. However, Carleton, a high-minded man, refused to employ large numbers of savages, because of the barbarities that would inevitably follow. The six Nations remained quiet, much to the relief of Schuyler and Montgomery. Carleton did enlist some "old subjects" recently arrived from Britain, including a few retired soldiers, together with several hundred French Canadians. Even so, his forces were small, and the French Canadians who responded to his call for service were not very reliable.

Carleton was in himself a source of great strength. He was a veteran of many campaigns. He had taken part in the British captures of the city of Quebec in 1759 and of Havana in 1762. It cannot be said with certainty that he was either a brilliant, a mediocre, or an incompetent general. His service at the head of an amy was limited. However his qualities as a military commander may be assessed, he was a brave Irish-born soldier and a gentleman in action as well as birth. He was, though, less aggressive than Montgomery, who was also Irish-born and who had served in the British army. Cold, reserved, and austere, but dignified and magnanimous, Carleton perhaps contributed more to the defense of Quebec as a governor than he did as a general. For he had ruled well over the province for almost a decade. If he had not won the affection of the French Canadians, he had gained their enduring respect. They would not rise against him in his hour of trial because he seemed to them to be a tyrant. He would also gain the esteem of the Americans with whom he came into contact.

Most of the French Canadians remained quiet as the Americans poured into their country. A minority of them did greet and help the Patriots as oppressed fellow colonials. But the great majority of the French Canadians were content to let the British and the Americans settle their differences by themselves. The Americans were their traditional enemies. Why did they so suddenly claim to be brethren? The British were not so bad as the Patriots said they were—and it was likely that they would ultimately crush the Americans. If most of the French Canadians would not fight for the British, neither would they join the Patriots. The Quebec Act, framed in part in accordance with advice from Carleton, served Britain well. That law pleased the Roman Catholic bishop and clergy of Quebec, not only because it made their faith legal, but also because it gave them authority to collect tithes. It was likewise gratifying to the *seigneurs,* the aristocratic landowners of Quebec, whose titles to their estates were confirmed. The law offered much less to the *habitants,* the numerous peasants of the province. However, they were not too well informed about the quarrel between Britain and America, and they tended to follow their traditional leaders, the clergy and the aristocracy. Neither the British nor the Americans received enough active support from the French Canadians to affect the result. Hundreds of them joined the Patriots, but soon deserted; hundreds of them rallied behind Carleton, but quickly departed for home. A few fought valiantly for Britain, a few for America.

Major Charles Preston and the garrison of Fort St. John's obstinately held out against the Patriots for more than two months. The place was so strong that Montgomery could not carry it by storm; nor did he have cannon powerful enough to destroy its defenses. Had the Patriots arrived a month earlier, the fort must have fallen quickly to them, but the British had had time to enlarge its garrison and to improve its works. Cutting off Preston's supply lines, Montgomery sought to starve the British into submission. They held on desperately, week after week. The Patriot general had his own troubles. His troops suffered from rain and cold. For a time his men were on half-rations; then Philip Schuyler sent forward supplies of food and ammunition. Montgomery's men were contemptuous of discipline; he had to persuade rather than to order. Militia came to join him, militia went home. But Montgomery did not abandon the siege.

Meanwhile, he also sent parties northward to recruit Canadians and to clear the way for an advance against Montreal, where Carleton was trying to raise forces to relieve Preston. Joining together two of those parties, Ethan Allen, who served as a volunteer under Montgomery, impetuously marched against the town. A body of British soldiers and volunteers moved out to face him. Allen then fled, but was captured with forty men. However, Carleton was unable to gather sufficient strength to move forward to Preston's assistance, and the defeat and capture of Allen were more than balanced by a successful Patriot attack upon Fort Chambly, a major link between Fort St. John's and Montreal. That post was not stoutly built and was vulnerable to the artillery possessed by the Americans. Patriot militia, with the help of a contingent of French Canadians, surrounded it. Fort Chambly was occupied by nearly ninety British regulars. When the walls of the fort began to collapse under American bombardment, the garrison surrendered. The way to Montreal was open to Montgomery—if he could take Fort St. John's.

At last, after a siege lasting for fifty-five days, during which Patriot guns made no impression upon his works, Major Preston saw that further resistance was hopeless. If the siege continued, he and his men would starve. Montgomery offered him generous terms. If Preston's men laid down their arms, the French Canadians among them would be allowed to go home, and the British troops would be permitted to embark for England. On November 2 Preston capitulated.

Montgomery did not fail to exploit his victory. He advanced as rapidly as possible to the St. Lawrence and against Montreal. That town could not be defended; Carleton had no more than 150 British troops there. He might have fled westward to safety, but his only real choice was to try to make his way to the city of Quebec, where he could make a last stand. Gathering his men in a flotilla of small craft, he began to sail down the St. Lawrence. He continued to encounter ill fortune. He met contrary winds and was delayed. His little fleet was bombarded by Patriot shore batteries and attacked by Patriot armed vessels. Nearly all his boats were captured, together with his troops, and Carleton himself narrowly escaped from his enemies. He slipped through them in a small boat propelled by muffled oars, and made his way into the city of Quebec. As he entered it, he learned that Benedict Arnold had appeared outside the city with a second American expeditionary force. Indeed, he had passed that force on the river. He would thus have to defend the city against the combined troops of Montgomery and Arnold.

In the preceding August, when all was quite quiet at Boston, Washington had had time to think about Canada. There were troops that he could spare. He concluded, on the basis of slender and inaccurate information, that a Patriot expedition could make its way up the Kennebec River, across the divide between Maine and the province of Quebec, and down the Chaudière River to its junction with the St. Lawrence near "the Gibraltar of Canada." There was an excellent chance, Washington believed, of seizing the stronghold of Quebec while Carleton was defending Montreal; Carleton would not be able to repel simultaneous thrusts at the two places. Benedict Arnold was at Washington's camp. He was available; he was also eager for action. When Washington offered him command of the expedition with the rank of colonel, Arnold immediately accepted the appointment. Washington gave him full authority, funds, and 1,050 good men, consisting of Yankee musketmen and three companies of Pennsylvania and Virginia riflemen. Among the riflemen was the redoubtable Daniel Morgan of Virginia, a semi-literate and most valuable officer. Several young men joined Arnold as gentlemen volunteers, among them Aaron Burr and Eleazer Oswald. Like Arnold and Morgan, they would overcome any and all hardships and dangers to achieve success.

Washington could hardly have found a more suitable commander than Arnold, then thirty-five years of age and strong enough to endure great physical trials. No man is better known as a traitor than Arnold. But his loyalty to the Patriot cause was unquestionable in the summer of

1776; almost three years would pass before he opened those negotiations with the British which led him to indestructible disgrace. He was of respectable Yankee ancestry—he had even more respectable descendants —but he was not born to the colonial purple. Not liberally educated, he was a Connecticut merchant when the War of Independence began. He had served as a youth in the Seven Years' War, and he was an officer in the Connecticut militia. He had displayed celerity in answering the call to arms after the battle of Lexington and Concord as well as vast energy in the capture of Ticonderoga. Even in the summer of 1776 it was obvious that Arnold was ambitious, proud, and disposed to assert most emphatically his claims to superiority. Washington knew other officers who lusted for promotion, who were not modest, and who insisted that their merits were greater than those of their fellows. But he could not lay his hands upon a man who excelled Arnold in courage, coolness, determination, and audacity. Much time would pass before Arnold's selfishness led him into treachery.

Arnold was competent in military business as well as brave and bold. He was able to sail with his men soon after the middle of September to the mouth of the Kennebec River. He had arranged for the building there of 200 bateaux, which were to carry his force up the Kennebec and down the Chaudière. The bateaux, of necessity hastily made, were more or less ready, but were roughly constructed, in part of green wood. Arnold inspected them, saw that they were not satisfactory, but characteristically decided that he would nevertheless proceed. He ordered twenty more of them made. He did not know that those heavy boats could hardly be carried across the many portages in his path. Indeed, he was not aware of the numerous portages. According to his maps, he and his men could travel almost entirely by water. Arnold would also learn that the distance between the mouth of the Kennebec and the city of Quebec was much greater than he supposed.

Arnold made his way easily enough up the Kennebec as far as modern Augusta. Then came the portages around rapids and falls in that stream. Moving forward in four divisions, the expedition was soon in difficulties. Arnold's men could carry the bateaux and their supplies across the portages only with extreme effort. The bateaux began to give way. Rain drenched the Patriots as they slowly advanced northward. Things went from bad to worse. Most of the bateaux had to be abandoned as useless; some sank with provisions on board. Food became scarce, at times unobtainable. Shoes wore out, and could be replaced only by moccasins or cloth. So great were the hardships that officers of the two rear divisions turned back with 350 men. But the rest plunged on through

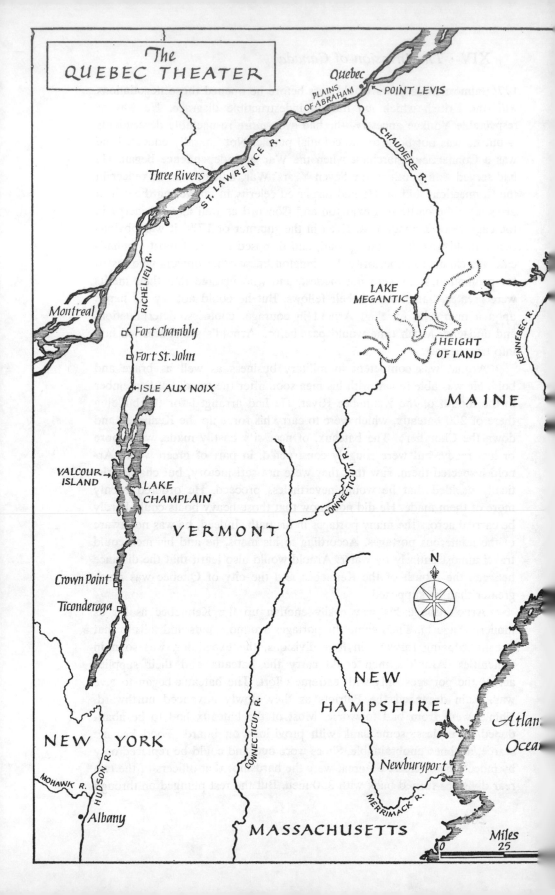

The
QUEBEC THEATER

Quebec
PLAINS
OF ABRAHAM ← POINT LEVIS

CHAUDIÈRE R.

ST. LAWRENCE R.

Three Rivers

RICHELIEU R.

KENNEBEC R.

LAKE
MEGANTIC

HEIGHT
OF LAND

Montreal

Fort Chambly

Fort St. John

MAINE

← ISLE AUX NOIX

VALCOUR
ISLAND

LAKE
CHAMPLAIN

CONNECTICUT R.

VERMONT

N

Crown Point

Ticonderoga

NEW
HAMPSHIRE

Atlan
Ocea

NEW YORK

CONNECTICUT R.

MOHAWK R.

HUDSON R.

Newburyport

Albany

MERRIMACK R.

MASSACHUSETTS

Miles
0   25

a forbidding wilderness, overcoming almost incredible obstacles. Some of them became lost; some died; all who could, struggled forward. Arnold, his remaining officers, and his volunteers set a splendid example. The stronger men helped the weaker. After a month of desperate effort, 600 scarecrows of men straggled into a camp on the headwaters of the Chaudière. There, at the beginning of November, they had their first good meal in weeks, food purchased by Arnold from astonished French Canadians. There they were allowed to rest briefly. Then they moved down the Chaudière and marched overland toward the city of Quebec. On November 9 they appeared at Point Levis on the south side of the St. Lawrence opposite the fortress. Collecting small craft, Arnold crossed the river on November 14, occupied the famous Plains of Abraham where James Wolfe had defeated the Marquis de Montcalm, and made ready to attack. Arnold and his gaunt ragamuffins had done all that mortal men could do, but they were too late, perhaps only by hours.

Learning that the Americans were at Point Levis, Hector Cramahé, who as lieutenant governor of the province of Quebec was preparing the city for defense, despaired of holding it. He had collected a supply of foodstuffs and a heterogeneous garrison that included 70 British regulars, 200 British "old subjects," 300 French Canadians, some cannoneers, and nearly 400 marines and sailors from British war vessels and transports that lay in the river. The guns of two of those vessels might also be of some help. However, Cramahé doubted the loyalty of his French Canadians, and believed that his forces were too few to man the long walls of the fortress. He feared that the city would fall quickly to the Patriots. Fortunately for him, before Arnold could cross the river from Point Levis, Lieutenant Colonel Allan McLean, a veteran British officer, came to Cramahé's assistance. Commissioned by Carleton to enlist Scots in the province and to help relieve Fort St. John's, McLean had been unable to do anything to aid Major Preston. It was otherwise at Quebec. Entering the city with eighty Scots, McLean energetically assumed responsibility for its defense. When Arnold demanded its surrender, twice, he was answered by gunfire. It was apparent that the garrison would fight. Even the intrepid Arnold did not quite dare to venture an assault against forces so superior in numbers, protected by strong walls, and possessed of artillery. In fact, fearing that he would be surrounded and attacked, Arnold moved up the St. Lawrence and awaited the arrival of Montgomery. As he went, Carleton came down the river and entered the city.

On December 2 Montgomery and Arnold joined forces twenty miles above Quebec, and Montgomery, as the senior officer, assumed command. He had a small but well-equipped army of men who had been tested to the utmost. He had brought cannon with him. He had dressed his 300 troops in winter uniforms of British regulars that he had captured at Montreal, and he was able to supply clothing for Arnold's contingent. Arnold's men, fed and rested, were ready for action. On December 5 Montgomery moved toward Quebec and put it under siege. From the Plains of Abraham he sent a message to Carleton asking its surrender. Carleton replied that he would not parley with rebels. Montgomery sent Carleton a second demand. He said that Carleton could not hold out with his motley and unreliable forces against his own troops, hardened by their trials and stimulated by the righteousness of their cause. If Carleton insisted upon fighting, Montgomery must take the city, and he feared that he would not be able to control his angry men. The governor did not bother to answer. If the Americans wanted Quebec, they must capture it.

Unfortunately for the Patriots, McLean and Carleton had had time to make ready for a determined defense. They had collected more men, and food enough to last for months; and they had done what they could to repair the walls of the city and to guard them with artillery. The garrison was nearly twice as large as Montgomery's army, even though some French Canadians and Indians appeared in the Patriots' camp. Moreover, time and weather favored Carleton. If he could hold out until spring, he would certainly receive help from England, and almost certainly more help than the Patriots would get. He and his men were protected against the harsh Canadian winter. Montgomery could not profitably carry on a long siege. His army must suffer from cold. Besides, the period of service of some of his New England musketmen would expire at the end of the year 1775, and they would very likely insist upon going home. He came to the conclusion that he must try to carry the city by storm. His decision was buttressed by an exchange of fire between his artillery and the guns of Quebec. Batteries erected by Montgomery threw shot into the city and inflicted casualties. However, cannon fire from its walls severely damaged the batteries. It was impossible to reach the walls by slow approaches under cover of entrenchments, for the ground was frozen. Montgomery laid plans for an assault.

There were delays. Some of the Yankee officers under Arnold declared that they would not serve under him any longer. They said he had behaved arrogantly. Montgomery persuaded them to resume their duties. The general and his officers devised a scheme for an attack, but it was revealed to Carleton by a deserter. The Patriot leaders revised their plan, and waited for a dark night on which to execute it, for they wished to move against the walls of the city as inconspicuously as possible. A tremendous snowstorm that began at sunset on December 30 and continued through the following night was the signal for action. At 2:00 A.M. on the last day of 1775 the Americans gathered at their assigned places; two hours later they advanced against the city. They were to make two feints, and two assaults, the one led by Montgomery, the other by Arnold.

Alas for the Patriots, their sham attacks did not deceive Carleton in the least. The defenses of Quebec were weaker in its Lower Town, and the British general foresaw that the Americans would concentrate against that part of the city. They did so. Montgomery with 300 men tried to break into the Lower Town from the south, while Arnold led 600 troops against it from the north. The two forces were to meet, and were then to take the Upper Town. Montgomery did not reach the rendezvous. The garrison was on the alert. Pushing his way forward along the northern shore of the St. Lawrence, Montgomery was confronted by a fortified house containing four pieces of artillery. With his advance guard, the Patriot general charged along a narrow street against the house. Its defenders waited until the Americans were near, then raked them with cannon and musket fire. Montgomery was instantly killed, and almost all of the Patriots in the advanced guard were either slain or wounded. Montgomery's men, lacking their dauntless leader, retreated in the face of seemingly insurmountable obstacles. Meanwhile, Arnold's contingent forced its way into the city. Arnold himself, however, in front of his troops, was wounded in the leg at the first British barrier, and was compelled to abandon command. His men rallied behind Daniel Morgan. The Virginian led some of them over the barrier and reached the place where he was to meet Montgomery. He halted briefly, waiting for all of his men to come up, and also for the appearance of Montgomery. Meanwhile, relieved of the menace of Montgomery, Carleton sent more troops, including British regulars armed with bayonets, against Morgan and dispatched a force to cut off Morgan's retreat. The Virginia rifleman fought on desperately, but he and many of his men at length had to lay down their arms. Nearly half of the Patriots engaged were killed, wounded, or captured. Only five men in the garrison were slain. The death of Montgomery was an especially heavy blow to the Patriots. They had lost one of their very best generals. Taking into account character as well as courage and ability, one may hazard the opinion that the Americans were never able to find his equal for command in the northern theater of war.

Not that Benedict Arnold displayed any deficiency immediately after the Patriot defeat. Despite his wound, he assumed direction of the remains of the American army, perhaps 600 men. He did not flee up the St. Lawrence; he planted more guns on the Plains of Abraham; and he maintained a blockade of Quebec. He dared Carleton and winter to do their worst. Carleton prudently remained in the city. He had the advantage in a contest of endurance; but his forces lacked cohesion, and failure in an attack upon the Patriots would probably mean the loss of the city. Reinforced by only 180 men, Arnold clung to his position through three months of winter. Even an outburst of smallpox among his men did not persuade him to abandon his camp. At last help came.

The news of the defeat and death of Montgomery had shocked Congress, Washington, and the Patriots generally. They had confidently expected that Montgomery and Arnold would continue to achieve miracles and that Quebec would fall. Instead came appeals for help from Arnold, who urged that General Charles Lee be sent northward with troops. Lee was appointed to the command of the American troops in Canada, but Congress then changed its mind and sent him southward. However, it responded vigorously to Arnold's call for aid. It sent a commission consisting of Benjamin Franklin, Samuel Chase, Charles Carroll of Carrollton, and Father John Carroll—two Protestants and two Roman Catholics—to win over the *habitants* to the Patriot cause. With the help of the Northern Colonies it also put thousands of troops of one sort and another in motion toward Canada. Had half so many been placed in the field in 1775, Quebec would surely have fallen into American hands.

As it was, the Patriots made a great effort too late. General David Wooster, taking over command of the American camp before Quebec from Arnold early in April, was able at one time to muster 2,000 men there. He bombarded Quebec without important result. A month later he was superseded by General John Thomas, who could count 2,500 troops there on one occasion. But the American militia came and went; many of them were struck down by hardship and smallpox; and Thomas could not strike. At the beginning of May large bodies of Patriots were pushing northward from Ticonderoga. They would have enabled Thomas to assault the city. Before they could join Thomas, however, the relieving force so long awaited by Carleton appeared in the St. Lawrence from England. He was rescued by a formidable army of British regulars and Hessians under General John Burgoyne. The very sight of the fleet carrying Burgoyne's troops created panic in the American camp. Thomas could not even muster enough men to check a sortie by 900 men from the garrison of Quebec. His army fled up the St. Lawrence in wild disorder.

Two months of disaster for the Patriots in Canada followed. The commission sent northward by Congress had not succeeded in winning the affections of many of the *habitants*. The arrival of Burgoyne definitely persuaded most of them to remain quiet. Retreating as far as the Richelieu River, Thomas died of smallpox on June 2. The remainder of his army was a disheartened, sickly, and disorganized mob. General John Sullivan came on from the south with reinforcements, so many that the number of the Patriots in Canada mounted over 8,000. Sullivan sent a body of his men to attack Three Rivers, the principal settlement between Montreal and Quebec. He even hoped to lead the Americans back to Quebec itself. To their surprise, his troops were confronted by the bulk of Burgoyne's army at Three Rivers. They were driven back and routed. Carleton and Burgoyne had as many British regulars and German troops as Sullivan had green and discouraged soldiers, and the two British generals steadily pushed forward. The dispirited Americans fell back and back. Even Benedict Arnold acknowledged that the only course open to the Patriots was to retreat. They abandoned Montreal and fled up the Richelieu River to Lake Champlain. At last, in the first days of July, the remains of Sullivan's army found a temporary refuge at Crown Point.

The Patriots continued to think about adding Canada to their union. During the remainder of 1776 and all of 1777 they were on the defensive in the northern theater of the War of Independence. However, after the destruction of Burgoyne's army in the Saratoga campaign and the entrance of France into the war, their hopes revived. In the spring of 1778 they began to plan a second invasion of Canada under the command of the Marquis de Lafayette. They believed that an expedition led by a French officer in American service and endorsed by France would receive the support of the French Canadians. The British forces in the province of Quebec were not large after the defeat of Burgoyne. But the Six Nations and other warlike Indians had taken up arms in 1777 and offered an additional obstacle; the Patriots could not spare enough men and supplies from other areas to enable Lafayette to move forward; and the scheme was set aside. Lafayette later attempted to resuscitate it. In the following winter Congress again considered an invasion, but turned against it upon the advice of Washington. At that time Washington was concerned lest the conquest of Quebec be followed by the resurrection of French rule there. In the Franco-American alliance of February 6, 1778, France had forever renounced all claim to Canada, but the general did not quite trust France to keep her word. Later his fears abated, and Washington twice projected an attack upon Quebec from the sea. In 1779 General Frederick Haldimand, then entrusted with the defense of the colony, was so alarmed for its safety that he begged that reinforcements be sent him from the principal British army at New York in order to check an American invasion. The troops actually embarked, but were driven back by a storm. They were not needed. Washington was never able to send Patriot soldiers and French warships up the St. Lawrence, and the war ended with British troops still in control of Quebec and Nova Scotia. During the peace negotiations at the close of the war the Americans tried to secure by diplomacy what they had failed to get by force, the inclusion of the two provinces within the boundaries of the United States. They did not succeed. In the Articles of Confederation, the first constitution of the United States, completed by Congress in 1777 and put into effect in 1781, there was a provision for the entrance of Canada into the American union. It was never used.

Had Quebec been long peopled by colonists of British descent at the beginning of the War of Independence, like Massachusetts and Virginia, it very likely would have become part of the American republic. The province—and Canada—paradoxically remained British because its inhabitants were then French. Moreover, the settlement of Loyalists in Nova Scotia and Ontario during and after the war assured that Canada would continue to be British into the distant future.

Were, then, the sacrifices made by the Patriots in their attempt to conquer Canada in vain? Did they merely accomplish the destruction of a few British regiments at excessive cost to themselves? The answer is that they reaped indirect and important benefits. Their invasion of Canada forced Britain to send an army to the St. Lawrence, thus dividing her forces in North America. Moreover, on the ground that Carleton was needed in Canada, the temporary separation of authority between Carleton and Howe arranged in 1775 was confirmed in the spring of 1776. Thus Britain created two distinct military commands in North America. That arrangement encouraged some very bad British planning for the campaign of 1777, planning that made it possible for the Patriots to deal severely with the army of General John Burgoyne on the Hudson River while the main British army was busy in Pennsylvania. It follows that the disastrous invasion of Canada in 1775 had somewhat to do with the Patriot triumph at Saratoga. And Saratoga led to the signing of the Franco-American alliance that ultimately assured American independence.

CHAPTER XV

Britain Prepares for War

ON May 26, 1775, George III adjourned Parliament for its customary long summer holiday. Three days later news reached London of the battle of Lexington and Concord. It was followed by reports which left little doubt that Britain was faced by an uprising of massive proportions. The King and Lord North did not hastily agree, even after they learned about Bunker Hill, to reconvene Parliament and to ask it for funds and help to meet a crisis. Instead, they put off a meeting of Parliament until October 26. That body was not in session for five months, during which the American rebellion became ever more alarming. The North ministry was not, however, entirely idle until autumn. It sent available troops, supplies, and warships across the Atlantic; and it dismissed General Gage. It made no overtures toward conciliating the Patriots. After November 1775, the ministry moved with greater energy. Lord George Germain was brought into office as colonial secretary to direct the suppression of the rebels. The King officially withdrew his protection from the colonies, and they were declared to be under naval blockade. Thousands of Hessians were hired to fight in America. They and other thousands of British troops were sent across the ocean in 1776. All those measures were firmly endorsed by Parliament. The command of the British fleet in American waters was entrusted to Richard, Viscount Howe; of the army in the Thirteen Colonies to General William Howe; of the army in Quebec to General Guy Carleton. The Howe brothers were also given power to negotiate with the Patriots. They appeared at New York early in the summer of 1776 with formidable forces and sweet words.

The first tidings of the battle of Lexington and Concord to reach

London—in a version hastily and obligingly sent across the ocean by the Patriots that put them in a most favorable light—created excitement. Could they be true? They could not be entirely false. A report from General Gage that arrived on June 10 confirmed the news—in a laconic British version. The response of the British public was diverse. There was no overwhelming outburst of feeling against the Patriots, no closing of political ranks for an immense and united effort to crush them; nor was there an overpowering demand for the resignation of the North ministry, immediate cessation of hostilities, and an accommodation with the colonists. In the main, those who had favored a policy of coercion called for greater coercion; those who had opposed the use of force continued to condemn it. The British people remained, insofar as they had opinions, divided. When John Horne Tooke, a Radical, began to collect funds in London for the relief of the widows and children of the Patriots "murdered" at Lexington, he was incarcerated for his impudence; he was not rescued by an insurrection. As information reached England of more fighting in America, sentiment in favor of repression grew stronger, for the continued shedding of English blood inevitably stimulated a desire for revenge. There never was any great doubt that Parliament would support the ministry in an effort to crush the Patriots.

The North ministry also continued to be divided. For Lord North himself and the Earl of Dartmouth, regretting that the dispute between Britain and the colonies had been transformed into military contest, refused to abandon their policy of adding an attempt to conciliate to the use of the army and navy. But the King was disposed to rely upon the exertion of force, and they remained in a minority among his advisers. The dominant opinion among them was ungrammatically but clearly expressed by the Earl of Rochford, Secretary of State for the Southern Department, in a letter to the King on June 11. Rochford did "not a bit despair of the news from America. The Rubicon is passed, & if pursued we must get the better." The principal remedy for the defeat of the British troops was to send more troops and warships across the ocean. By June 20 the cabinet had decided to dispatch to America six regiments of redcoats from Gibraltar and Minorca, with others drawn from garrison detachments in the British Isles; to enlist Scottish Highlanders and Irishmen for service beyond the ocean; to authorize Guy Carleton to raise 2,000 French Canadians; and to augment the fleet in American waters.

The aggressive advisers of George III, continuing to assert that force was the proper medicine for the ills of the empire, were compelled to admit that application of it had not hitherto been successful. Almost inevitably, they contended that their remedy had not been properly ad-

ministered by General Gage. He could hardly escape being a scapegoat—
even though he had not been given sufficient power to do anything substantial. It will be recalled that the cabinet had meditated replacement of
Gage before the beginning of the war. Within hours of the battle of
Bunker Hill, Lord George Germain, who then held no office but was
persona grata to at least some members of the ministry, urged that it
dismiss Gage upon the score of incompetence. When Gage's report upon
the battle reached London, there was an immediate outcry among politicians associated with the King's Friends for his removal. For Gage not
only related his costly victory, but declared that nothing could be
achieved in America without large reinforcements, as he had so often
asserted before the beginning of hostilities. He did not win friends among
his superiors by reminding them that his judgment had been correct, that
they were fundamentally responsible for the awkward situation in America. Among those who denounced Gage was Alexander Wedderburn, who
condemned both the general and Admiral Samuel Graves for the "present
bad posture of affairs in America." According to Wedderburn, Gage was
peculiarly at fault, and he urged Lord North to remove Gage from his
command. At the time it was believed that Lord Mansfield led Scottish
politicians in a campaign against Gage. It is possible that such was the
fact. Some years earlier Gage had deprived one Thomas Mills, a favorite
of Mansfield and rumored to be his illegitimate son, of a military appointment because Mills had another post which prevented him from doing his
duty to the army. But there were Englishmen as well as Scots among the
King's supporters who insisted that Gage must go. The King quickly
agreed, but declared that Gage must not be brought home in disgrace. On
August 2 the general was ordered to return to London to give information
toward planning the campaign of 1776. When he reached the imperial
capital, he was graciously received by George III, but he was never given
another command in the field.

It is apparent that Gage was not a masterful general. If those who
deprived him of his post had their faults, they also had sufficient reason
for replacing him—if they promptly put his command in the hands of a
better man. They did not do so. There was no commander of ability and
the highest rank in England who could be sent across the ocean. The
logical successor to Gage was Guy Carleton, who was the senior British
major general in America and who would inherit Gage's office in the
normal course of military promotion. Indeed, in the spring of 1775, after
much loose talk in London about appointment of Sir Jeffery Amherst or
William Howe as commander in chief, George III had taken the precaution of sending an assurance to Carleton that he was to replace Gage in

case of need. At that time Carleton was outranked in America by General Frederick Haldimand, who was acting commander in chief in North America during Gage's absence in 1773 to 1774. However, Haldimand was a Swiss by birth, and the King and his advisers had sensibly decided that a foreigner must not be entrusted with the task of suppressing a rebellion of British subjects. To avoid complications that might arise from the presence of Haldimand in America, he was ordered to England. Carleton therefore had good cause to expect that he would be the first choice for Gage's office. However, Carleton was obviously needed in Canada. Yet his claims could not be set aside. It seemed prudent to put off a final decision, all the more so because Gage had many supporters in and out of Parliament. Declared Lord North, "Gage has many friends, and is generally esteemed. The public, though satisfied, perhaps, at his recall, would not have approved of its being done harshly and with circumstances of disgrace." Accordingly, Gage was allowed to hold his commission for many months, but was deprived of authority; Carleton was given temporary appointment as commander in chief in Canada; and Howe was tendered a similar post in the Thirteen Colonies. That arrangement, even though it was not permanent, could not please Carleton. Aware that he would be dissatisfied with a less important assignment than that given to Howe, the King made sure that Carleton was informed of the reason for keeping him temporarily in Canada. The task of filling Gage's place remained. It was not accomplished until the spring of 1776; and it was then botched.

Lord North and the Earl of Dartmouth unhappily continued to seek a political accommodation as well as a military triumph. Britain had an opportunity, after August 21, 1775, to open negotiations with Congress, for its Olive Branch Petition was sent to Dartmouth's office that day by Dr. Arthur Lee of Virginia and Richard Penn, the latter a liberal-minded member of the proprietary family of Pennsylvania who had brought the document to England. North's Conciliatory Resolution had failed, in part because it was not addressed to Congress. Was it not worthwhile to swallow pride and to bargain with that body? Richard, Viscount Howe, older brother of the general, was eager to go to America and to negotiate for Britain with the Patriots. An admiral in the navy, Lord Howe had participated in the last-minute bargaining between the ministry and Benjamin Franklin before the outbreak of the war. Dartmouth believed that the American petition could be used to open discussion with the colonists. But the mild stepbrothers did not insist upon taking advantage of the opportunity extended by Congress. Eventually, Lee and Penn were informed that the King would not officially receive the petition and that no answer to it would be given. Afterward, in the House of Lords, Dartmouth asserted that "the softness of the language" in the petition "was purposely adopted to conceal the most traitorous designs." However, a reply of sorts was made as early as August 23. On that day a royal proclamation formally declared that, "Whereas many of our subjects in divers parts of our colonies and plantations in North America . . . have . . . proceeded to an open and avowed rebellion," all loyal citizens should help to suppress it. Military men were urged to do their duty, and others were asked to supply information about the conspirators responsible for the uprising and about all those English persons who were in correspondence with the conspirators.

Another answer to the Olive Branch Petition was given on October 26, in the King's speech at the opening of Parliament. Declared the monarch, "The rebellious war now levied, is become more general, and is manifestly carried on for the purpose of establishing an independent empire." It would be both wise and ultimately kind, he asserted, "to put a speedy end to these disorders by the most decisive exertions." The enemies of government immediately began an attack upon its American policy and demanded that conciliation be substituted for coercion. There followed many weeks of angry debate in both houses, with the Rockingham and Chatham factions, together with the Radicals, striving desperately not merely to check the North ministry, but to destroy it. They could not shake it. Indeed, as time went on, its majority in both houses increased. The war might be unpopular in the many quarters of the nation; it was not so in Parliament.

The sentiments of the British legislature quickly became evident. The enemies of the ministry demanded in both houses that Parliament condemn the King's speech. In the upper chamber Lord Lyttleton urged the repeal of all the British laws passed after 1763 that offended the Americans. Dr. John Hinchcliffe, Bishop of Peterborough, sensibly declared that the Olive Branch Petition offered a chance for negotiation. He believed, correctly, that most of the Americans did not yet desire independence. The Earl of Coventry asserted that the colonists could not be reduced to subjection and that Britain's choice lay between conciliating them and expelling them from the empire. He preferred an accommodation. In the House of Commons John Wilkes assailed the ministry for beginning a war that was "unjust, ruinous, felonious, and murderous." To General Henry Seymour Conway the war was "cruel, unnecessary, and unnatural." But, replying to the King's speech, both houses, by votes of more than two to one, pledged their full support to the British military effort. The Americans were condemned for seeking independence; they must be brought to heel. Nineteen of the Lords formally protested. They not only solemnly contended that continuance of the war would be ruinous for Britain, but assailed the ministry as "in every degree unworthy of public trust."

Conscious of their numerical weakness, the adversaries of the King and North sought to prove that the nation shared their dislike of government. They brought in petitions from London, Bristol, and other English cities that urged a compromise with the Americans. But the ministry was able to present memorials from English cities—merchants and manufacturers were profiting from orders for military supplies—that promised loyal support to help crush the rebels.

The minority fought on. At the beginning of November the opponents of the war found a promising issue. To free British troops for service in America, the ministry proposed to bring Hanoverian soldiers to Gibraltar and Minorca. Its plan was denounced both as a manifestation of national weakness and as a violation of law. It was even hinted in the House of Commons that the Hanoverians might be used to fasten tyranny upon Britain. To no avail. Britain needed soldiers; the German troops went on garrison duty in British fortresses. On November 15 the Duke of Grafton, who had finally resigned from office in the ministry because of its American policy, forthrightly denounced "this unnatural war." He said that victory would be even worse than defeat, for the "liberties of America once gone, those of Britain will not long survive them." On November 16 Edmund Burke presented a new plan to settle the quarrel between Britain and her colonies. Burke proposed to concede more to the Americans than he had been willing to offer in the spring of 1775. He urged that Britain abandon efforts to tax the colonists for revenue; that money collected in consequence of taxes used to regulate American trade be given to the colonies; that the Townshend tax upon tea and the Coercive Acts of 1774 be repealed; that amnesty be given to all those who had rebelled against Britain; that Britain recognize and negotiate with the American Congress. The House of Commons rejected Burke's scheme by a vote of 210 to 105.

The British enemies of George III and the North ministry continued to struggle into the spring of 1776. Britain could not win the war, asserted several members. General Henry Seymour Conway predicted that the Americans would prove to be excellent soldiers, and that their ardor would compensate for their inferior discipline. He went so far as to assert that they would be equal, man for man, to the British troops. John Wilkes and David Hartley more cogently contended that a British triumph would be an empty one. They said that the Americans could not permanently be kept in subjection, even by a very large garrison army. Wilkes pointed out that the Americans were rapidly increasing in number, that Britain was not keeping pace with America in population. Wilkes called for the impeachment of the officers of state responsible for beginning the war. He said they had caused the loss of "half our empire." But was not the public doctrine of Wilkes as desperate as his devotion to private pleasure? Lord North scoffed at him. A Parliament containing one Wilkes, declared North, had one too many. Hartley, who gloried in championship of the Americans, insisted not only that Britain could not permanently subjugate them, but that they would rise to great power. "The new world is before them. . . . When the final period of this once happy country shall overtake ourselves . . . may another Phoenix rise out of our ashes."

The minority had another and potent argument against the war, one which should have impressed Lord North and George III. Hartley and George Johnstone had expressed alarm in the spring of 1775 lest France and Spain take advantage of conflict between Britain and America. It was indeed likely that the Bourbons would strike at a Britain embarrassed by a war within her empire; they would hardly ignore a splendid opportunity to gain revenge for their losses in the Seven Years' War. Speakers in both houses of Parliament, Lord Effingham, the Duke of Grafton, the Duke of Manchester, and Henry Seymour Conway, warned against the Bourbon menace. The King and the ministry preferred to believe that the colonists could be conquered; that France and Spain would not intervene; that if they took up arms, they would act too late to affect the result.

If, as George Johnstone claimed, the bulk of the most perceptive men in Britain were against the war, it is nevertheless true that the North ministry acquired strength as the debates continued and that it was easily able to secure the consent of Parliament for its measures to prosecute the struggle. The strictures of its enemies were obviously motivated, to a degree, by partisanship. Moreover, their predictions that America must have her way, however well founded in fact and logic, did not please country gentlemen and others who could not conceive that British power was less than overwhelming, who gave an unswerving loyalty to old England. Besides, Britain was already committed to war—a war that was going badly, to be sure. How could she honorably make peace with the rebels? The war, as wars do, tended to feed upon itself. The ministry also gained new solidity and power by a shake-up in November 1775. It was the duty of Lord Dartmouth as colonial secretary to direct the war effort; and he was neither fitted for the task nor eager to perform it. He moved from his post to another in the ministry, and he was replaced by Lord George Germain. This change, with others, infused the counselors of the

King with added determination to fight. Not that Germain was superbly fitted to be a war minister. He would not perform in the War of Independence as Pitt had done in the Seven Years' War. But he was not so hopelessly incompetent as historians once thought him to be. He was, at least for a time, energetic; however, he displayed no genius in choosing commanders. Moreover, he was despised and hated. As Lord George Sackville, he had held important commands in the British army in the early years of the Seven Years' War. However, serving in Germany, in 1759, he misbehaved on the battlefield of Minden, declining to obey repeated orders to lead a cavalry charge. Why he failed to do his duty remains unknown. He was usually brave enough. Censured by fellow officers and civilian gossip, he demanded a court-martial. The result was catastrophic for him. He was found guilty of cowardice and was declared to be unworthy "to serve His Majesty in any military capacity whatever." The sentence was confirmed by King George II. Germain could not hold a command in the armies that he directed. He was also somewhat handicapped by ugly and probably well-founded rumors about his private life. However, Germain was acquainted with military business. Moreover, he was convinced that the American rebellion could be and must be suppressed. He insisted that Britain must wage war as harshly as might be necessary to achieve success. Here was an opportunity to cleanse his reputation. He was accustomed to slights—he was often dubbed the "Minden Hero" in hostile English newspapers—and he would not quail because he was attacked in Parliament. A tall, heavy, arrogant, and obstinate man, he brought added resolution into the North ministry.

The King, his Friends, and their allies not only defeated all efforts on the part of their British enemies toward securing an accommodation with the colonists, but easily persuaded Parliament to adopt their own measures. One of these was the Prohibitory Act, which became law three days before the Christmas of 1775. Repealing and replacing the Boston Port Bill and other laws passed in 1775 to restrain colonial commerce, it formally withdrew the King's protection from the inhabitants of the Thirteen Colonies and forbade all trade with them. The colonies were declared to be under naval blockade, and the ships and cargoes of those who violated it were made subject to seizure and forfeiture. The crews of such vessels could be impressed into the royal navy. In effect, the law asserted that a state of war existed in America. The law also made provision for the return of peace. The Crown was authorized to appoint commissioners with power to pardon persons and groups of persons; to restore the King's protection in colonies or parts of colonies that had ceased to oppose Britain; and to remove the blockade from those areas.

Introducing the Prohibitory Act, Lord North said that he was willing to "suspend every exercise of the right of taxation," if the Americans would assume their share of the costs of defense of the empire.

The Prohibitory Act was hotly assailed. It was denounced in the House of Commons by the young Charles James Fox, who now maturely exhibited his oratorical talents, and by David Hartley, who urged that Britain abandon hostilities immediately and content herself with asking the colonists to supply funds for defense. In the Lords the Duke of Richmond described the law as "most unjust, oppressive, and tyrannical." He did not consider the Americans to be rebels, but as men "resisting acts of the most unexampled cruelty and oppression." The Earl of Shelburne also said that the Patriots were not rebels; they had taken up arms, he protested, to protect "their just, their inalienable and constitutional rights." The law was passed by overwhelming majorities in both houses of Parliament.

Nor were the adversaries of the ministry able to prevent the hiring of German troops to serve in America. During the late summer and autumn of 1775 it became painfully evident to Lord North and his associates that they must ship to America many more troops than they had arranged to send in the early summer; also that they could not raise large forces in Britain. Conscription for service in the army overseas was a practice unknown in Britain at that time. Enlistments were difficult to secure except when the nation was engaged in struggle with its traditional European enemies; and the American war was by no means popular. The Earl of Effingham had resigned from the army in protest against it; so many officers in regiments stationed in Ireland but destined for service in America had resigned and sold their commissions that it was necessary to put a stop to all such transactions; and Admiral Augustus Keppel had declared that he would not accept a command in America. Recruiting parties had so little success that General Jeffery Amherst undertook to try to enlist convicts in 1776. The ministry was compelled to seek troops abroad to augment the army. Such was Britain's awkward situation, even though Germain asserted in the House of Commons on November 16, 1775, that "Such forces as are necessary to restore, maintain, and establish the power of this country, will not be wanting." There was a brigade of Scots in the service of the Dutch republic. An attempt to secure it failed. The Empress Catherine the Great of Russia had many thousands of veterans available. A six-year war she had waged against the Turks had ended in 1774. Would she sell soldiers to Britain? On being approached, she did not answer quickly. When she did reply, "Sister Kitty" rudely refused to help brother monarch George. Almost in desperation,

Britain turned to the princes of western and southern Germany. Several of them were willing to sell soldiers to Britain, if she would pay enough for them. She would pay. Treaties of alliance were signed in January and February 1776, by which Britain bought the services of 4,300 men from the Landgrave of Hesse-Kassel. Other later treaties enabled Britain to put about 30,000 German soldiers in the field before the end of the War of Independence. In all, the Landgrave of Hesse-Kassel supplied 17,000 troops, and the ruler of Hesse-Hanau 2,400—hence the application of the term "Hessians" to all the mercenaries. Brunswick furnished altogether some 6,000 troops; Anspach-Bayreuth about 2,400; and the rulers of Waldeck and Anhalt-Zerbst 2,400 men each. Those wretched transactions in human flesh have been sufficiently reprobated. But it may be worth recalling that the German rulers received a bonus for every man killed—and that three wounded men were counted as one slain.

The treaties made with the Prince of Brunswick and the Landgrave of Hesse-Kassel in the early weeks of 1776 were bitterly condemned in both houses of Parliament. It was both humiliating and wicked, said enemies of the ministry, to employ foreigners to subdue British subjects. The German troops would certainly commit barbarities. David Hartley asserted that the decision to employ the Germans was the very worst of many vicious ones made by the government. The answer to his reproaches and all others was that mighty Britain had no choice. Soldiers could not be obtained at home; they had to be bought abroad. Nevertheless, the first sordid engagements with the German princelings were endorsed by votes of three to one in both houses of Parliament—and other later bargains with them were approved by the British legislature.

It has been urged that the thinking of British politicians was so thoroughly cramped by British institutions that policy regarding America had to be what it was—that George III, Lord North, the King's Friends, and their allies could do no other than plump for repression. Such may indeed be the case. And yet—there were noblemen and many others in Britain who were able to free themselves of the past and to see clearly the present and the future. Condemning the treaties with the German rulers in particular and the American war in general, the Earl of Coventry urged, in the House of Lords, that the nation accept the validity of the proposals advanced in 1774 by Dr. Josiah Tucker. It was apparent, said that peer, that the Americans, becoming ever more numerous, richer, and more powerful, could not be permanently held in subjection. Accordingly, Britain ought to treat America as a friend, enter into an alliance with her, and continue to profit from lucrative trade with the Americans.

Instead, with Lord George Germain supplying determination, Britain made a great effort to win the war. Emptying arsenals of cannon, muskets, gunpowder, and military paraphernalia stored after the end of the Seven Years' War, stimulating the production of more armament and equipment, the ministry sent large and well-supplied forces across the Atlantic in 1776. The fleet in American waters was strengthened. The Hessians were hurried, with British troops, to Quebec and to New York. By autumn there were about 45,000 royal troops in America, perhaps 10,000 in the Canadian theater, approximately 35,000 in the Thirteen Colonies.

Who was, who were, to lead those soldiers was a question that was long unanswered. General Gage continued to hold his title as commander in chief in North America for many months after his return to England. His friend Viscount Barrington urged that Gage be given another appointment. It was suggested that he be made commander in chief of the British army. That lofty office, usually occupied by a most distinguished officer, was vacant. But Gage had not earned it, and he did not get it. It was proposed that he be entrusted with the defense of Gibraltar; he was not given that appointment. At last, in April 1776, he was summarily dismissed from the North American command—he was allowed, as a sop, to keep his office as governor of Massachusetts. It was then logical to offer Gage's post to Guy Carleton. It could not be contended in 1776, as it had been in 1775, that his continued presence in Canada was essential. However, Carleton's claim to succeed Gage was not recognized. Nor was another man tendered Gage's authority. Instead, the temporary division of power established in 1775 was confirmed. Carleton was made commander in chief in Canada, William Howe commander in chief in the Thirteen Colonies. The man primarily responsible for that step was undoubtedly Lord George Germain. Carleton had been associated with the Rockingham faction. Was his political affiliation held against him? He had been a protégé of the Duke of Richmond, who had served at Minden and who was at least a political antagonist of Germain. It may be significant that Carleton never favored the employment of Indians against the Americans, that he treated the Americans with all the respect and kindness that the exigencies of war would permit. Whatever was Germain's motivation, Carleton, deeply disappointed, became an open and ferocious enemy of the colonial secretary. Perhaps Carleton was not eager to serve against the Patriots. But was it just that he should not only be denied Gage's place, but given a less important appointment than Howe? Had he not successfully defended Quebec with small forces? And had not Howe, his junior, been driven from Boston? Whether Carleton would have performed better than Howe in the Thirteen Colonies, no one can say. But it is beyond doubt that the splitting of authority on the basis of geography between the two men, especially between two men who had reason to be jealous of each other, was militarily unwise and expensive to Britain. It is also clear that Howe was much less than a great general. Moreover, he lacked zeal.

If the business of command of the land forces in America was not well executed, it cannot be said that the ministry compensated for its errors in that respect by superior performance in the selection of a new admiral for the fleet in America and of peace commissioners under the Prohibitory Act. Viscount Howe was entrusted with the fleet. He was also chosen as the principal peace commissioner; and at his insistence, his brother, the general, was appointed as a second commissioner to assist him in bargaining with the Americans. The Howe brothers were thus given four high offices in America. They were not suited to any of their duties, partly because they were deficient in ability, partly because they were at political odds with their employers. Richard Howe was a great admiral, but he was not eager to crush the rebels; William Howe was neither truly competent nor utterly determined to shatter the Patriots; both brothers were unfit for delicate negotiations.

The Howes were remarkable men. They were two of the nine children of the second Viscount Howe of Langar in Nottinghamshire, who went out to Barbados as governor and died there in 1735. He was related to various aristocratic English families. But the lineage of the mother of Richard and William was far more important historically than that of their father. For she was Sophia Charlotte Mary, daughter of a favorite of King George I, the Baroness von Kielmansegg, known in England as the Countess of Darlington. It is commonly said that she was the illegitimate daughter of George I. She was indeed illegitimately descended from the house of Hanover; but it would appear that her mother was the illegal offspring of the father of George I. In any event, the Howe brothers were, as King William IV said afterward, "a sort of connexion" of the English royal family and were recognized as such by George III. The second Viscountess Howe gave her sons much more than Guelf and Stuart blood. Compelled as a widow to rear her large brood, she saw to it that her children were well educated, and she strove to mold her sons into heroes. It was said that she desired to bring them up as Romans; it is perhaps more accurate to say that they were trained as Germans. She did not labor in vain, so far as Richard was concerned; her toil was, at least in part, wasted upon William.

The second Viscountess Howe brought up at least two splendid sons: George Augustus, who became the third Viscount, and Richard, who was the fourth man to hold the family title. George Augustus went from Westminster School to the army, Richard from Westminster and perhaps Eton into the navy. George Augustus performed brilliantly. He early attained the rank of brigadier general. Killed near Ticonderoga in the Seven Years' War, in 1758, he was mourned by all who knew him; and the province of Massachusetts spent £250 to erect a monument to his memory in Westminster Abbey. He was, said General James Wolfe, who knew him well, "the bravest, worthiest, and most intelligent man among us." He was, perhaps, more important in death than he was in life, for he was idolized by Richard and William, who valued highly the tribute paid to him by Massachusetts. Richard also quickly made a name for himself. Born in 1726, he fought in all of England's wars with France during a period of sixty years, always with success. As a captain he fired the first English shots of the Seven Years' War on the Atlantic—and captured a French vessel; in 1794, as the trusted admiral of George III, he defeated the French in his last battle, that of the Glorious First of June. George Augustus had possessed charm as well as intelligence. Richard was less gifted intellectually, was reserved and not much given to talk. He was, however, utterly brave, studious, and devoted to duty. Sturdy, dark-visaged, he gained respect rather than affection. He won the sobriquet "Black Dick." He was a splendid fighting admiral; neither facile nor subtle, he was not suited for the intricacies of politics. He did not know at the beginning of the War of Independence—if he ever knew it—that he was a man of war, not a man for statecraft.

William seemed, for many years, to be as worthy as his two older brothers. Born in 1729, he attended Eton, went into the army at the age of seventeen, and made a fine record as a young officer. He served under James Wolfe in the taking of Louisbourg from the French in 1758, and he commanded the advanced guard that climbed to the Plains of Abraham in 1759 and opened the way for the capture of Quebec. He was in his youth something of a scholar as well as a fighting man. Wolfe, admiring George Augustus and Richard, believed that William was following in their footsteps. Wolfe said that he was "modest, diligent, and valiant," that there was "not a better soldier" in the English army in the Louisbourg campaign. Wolfe bequeathed £1,000 to him. William not only took part in the final defeat of the French in Canada, but served in the expedition against Belle Isle, off the coast of France in 1761, and in the one that captured Havana in 1762. In 1764 he acquired a colonelcy, was given the keys of the city of Dublin as a tribute to his brothers and himself, and married Frances Conolly, daughter of a rich Anglo-Irish aristocrat and of Lady Anne Wentworth, a member of the distinguished Wentworth family. In due course, William became a major general, marked for high command. Hence his appearance at Boston in 1775.

Did James Wolfe observe that William Howe was not the equal of George Augustus and Richard? He did not praise William in the ecstatic terms he employed for his brothers. Certainly, William ceased to be a model of propriety. He became fond of the bottle and of gambling, given to pleasure. After they had achieved high place, Richard and William became the subjects of essays in the British *Town and Country* magazine, a publication that thrived upon scandal. Nothing seriously to the discredit of Richard was offered, but it was otherwise with William. He was said to have been one of the many lovers of Signora Campioni, a singularly beautiful Italian opera dancer who spent some years in London in the 1750's, and of other demi-mondaines. The magazine also asserted that Howe kept a mistress, one Charlotte Vaughan, offered an engraving of Miss Vaughan, and declared that she had borne him a child. While details in *Town and Country* are not to be accepted as gospel, it is likely that William was not badly abused by scandal mongers. It may be significant that in 1778, at a time when General Howe had much to say about military appointments, one William Vaughan was commissioned as an ensign in a regiment serving under Howe at Philadelphia. The general afterward told James Boswell that the best husband was one who, after extramarital affairs, preferred his wife and returned to her. Why dwell upon his private life? Not because the pleasures of the general were unusual in his time. However, it is clear enough that William in maturity did not bear out the promise of his youth; that he was no longer devoted to lofty ideals; that the gallant captain and colonel had become a commonplace general who did not lust for noble fame and achievement. William resembled Richard in appearance, but was unfitted for any command that required imagination and celerity.

The Howe brothers belonged to a close-knit family that was sentimentally attached to the Americans. Richard and William had idolized George Augustus Howe—William did not eat for two days after learning of his death. They nourished a fondness for the Americans, because they had paid tribute to George Augustus. Indeed, with their sister, Mrs. Caroline Howe, who had married a cousin of the same name and who held an official appointment at the court of George III, they hoped that the rebellion could be put down without much fighting and with as little injury as possible to the Americans. The admiral and the general were not of the same stripe as Lord George Germain, the Earl of Dunmore, or Admiral Samuel Graves, under whose orders Falmouth, Maine, was bombarded and burned in the fall of 1775. Mrs. Howe, a strong-minded, bulky woman, had assisted the admiral in opening negotiations with Benjamin Franklin before the outbreak of hostilities. The politics of the brothers would clash with their military duties. The general had run into difficulty on that score as early as 1774, when he was forced to run for re-election to the House of Commons—he held a seat in the Commons from Nottingham after 1758, in succession to George Augustus. Many of his constituents demanded that the general declare himself against the use of force to quell the Americans. He complied, and was elected. He neverthe-less later agreed to serve against the Americans, because, as he said, his military honor demanded that he do so.

The Howe brothers were at military cross-purposes with their em-ployers even before they assumed their new duties. Richard Howe, ac-cepting command of the fleet in American waters, received instructions to assist his brother and most rigorously to enforce the British blockade of American ports established by the Prohibitory Act. Neither he nor the general had an inclination to wage a harsh war, but he did not refuse to serve.

The brothers were also at odds with their superiors on the question of making peace with the Patriots. The admiral desired full power to bargain with them—he had excessive faith in himself as a negotiator. He did not obtain the authority he desired. He and the general were indeed permitted to pardon Patriots at their discretion. However, they could not treat with the Americans about things political until the Patriots had put down their arms, until British governors and other British officials had been reinstated in their offices. After peace had been restored, they were authorized to promise the Americans freedom from Parliamentary taxa-tion, provided that they formally undertook to pay from 5 per cent to 10 per cent of the cost of defending the British empire—an elaboration of Lord North's Conciliatory Resolution. The ministry also sought to change the corporate colonies of Connecticut and Rhode Island into royal prov-inces. Let it be emphasized that the Howes were forbidden to publish these peace terms until Patriot resistance had ceased. They could not offer enough to satisfy the Patriots, and they could offer nothing specific save pardon until the war was ended. That Admiral Howe agreed to serve as peace commissioner, with such instructions, suggests that he was much less than a profound politician.

The Howe brothers, desiring to rely in large part upon conciliation, were not given power sufficient to negotiate; not wishing to wage war harshly, they nevertheless accepted commands from men who mistakenly relied upon them to use their forces to whatever degree necessary to suppress the American rebellion.

225

CHAPTER XVI

The Declaration of Independence

FOR more than fourteen months after the battle of Lexington and Concord the Patriots fought, so they said, for their rights within the British empire. Then, in the early summer of 1776, they formally announced that they would accept nothing less than absolute independence from Britain. On July 2 of that year the Continental Congress asserted that all ties between the Thirteen States and the mother country were severed. Two days later the delegates, in the Declaration of Independence, told the world why the Patriots had chosen to separate from Crown, Parliament, and the British people. That immortal document became an inspiration not only to Americans but to humanity. It has been excessively praised; it has been harshly condemned. It has been examined minutely, frequently, and exhaustively. Scholars have said that it is inaccurate historically, that the political theory which it voices is defective. Its very meaning has been endlessly debated, in part because the Americans and others have used it as an arsenal of sacred ideas, have sought to find within it authority for their own political and social notions. It continues to be a convincing apology for separation from Britain; it has not ceased to encourage faith in and to supply guidance toward a nobler human order.

The Patriots forswore their allegiance to the British empire not much more than a year after the beginning of hostilities. The fact has not gone unobserved, and it has given rise to questions. Can one believe their fervent protestations of loyalty offered as late as 1775? Can one even accept as sincere the expressions of attachment to Britain so frequently voiced by the defenders of American rights in 1765? And if the colonists meant what they said when they announced their affection for Britain

226

before 1775, were they not unconsciously disposed to accept nothing less than a final divorce from the parent state? Did not the American Revolution begin in 1607, when Englishmen and colonists began to pursue separate courses, as John Adams suggested after America had become free? And was not the Revolution consummated, as Adams said, in the minds of the Americans long before its appearance?

At long last, in the twentieth century, informed Americans have conceded that George Washington, being human, did not invariably tell the whole truth. One ought not accept statements made by the fallible Adams as if they were Holy Writ. Moreover, it is apparent that his declarations have been misconstrued. It is not to be denied that the colonists became less like the English with every passing day after the founding of Jamestown. It could not be otherwise. Unquestionably there was a wide gap between the Englishman and the American as early as 1763, and that gap grew thereafter. But it does not follow that many Americans, consciously or unconsciously, desired separation from Britain in 1763, or 1765, or 1775. As late as January 1776, Adams himself, not the least forward of the Patriots, asserted that he did not wish America to leave the empire. It is to be believed that he knew his own mind, and that he was not eager for separation from Britain only six months before the Patriots cut the last political tie with the empire—even though he thought it necessary to declare American independence. It must also be assumed that most other Americans of the Revolutionary generation were acquainted with their own desires, that they knew substantially what they wanted, and that their assertions regarding their political goals are largely to be trusted. To be sure, prudence, and even policy, probably did persuade some persons, especially as armed clash approached, to utter statements of loyalty to Britain that concealed a wish for divorce from the mother country. It was not safe for a citizen of Massachusetts in 1774, or in the early months of 1775, to proclaim that he desired American independence. Indeed, nowhere in the colonies could a man do so without fear of punishment. Other Americans who did not declare their sentiments doubtless kept silence because they feared that anti-British words would be followed by British deeds. Moreover, the expression of a wish for separation might lead to economic and social ostracism. Nevertheless, it must be concluded that the champions of American liberty, in the main, meant what they said, and that the bulk of them did not seek to leave the empire on the day of Lexington and Concord; that they would have been satisfied had Britain met the demands of the First Continental Congress; that, in fact, they would have accepted less than complete compliance with those demands rather than pursue their quarrel with Britain to a military decision.

If it be true that the great majority of the Patriots sought less than separation from Britain on the day of Lexington and Concord, it is indeed appropriate to ask why the Americans changed their minds so swiftly that their goal became independence only fourteen months later. Now, dependence and independence are not necessarily absolute opposites. The one may merge almost imperceptibly into the other. And it will be recalled that the champions of American liberties defined their rights within the empire in handsome terms a half year before the armed clashes outside Boston. The First Continental Congress claimed for the colonists, not only freedom from taxation for revenue, but power to manage their domestic affairs, subject only to veto by the Crown. Moreover, that body did not admit that Parliament could rightfully limit American maritime trade. It merely said that it "cheerfully consented" to the exercise of Parliamentary authority over American overseas commerce because of "necessity" and "a regard to the mutual interest of both countries." Even so, the change in the Patriot position, from a demand for a very large measure of freedom within the empire to the assertion of complete independence, was not trifling politically, and it was vast sentimentally. But that shift is not beyond explanation.

In some part, the Patriots increasingly turned against Britain because they resented new political and economic blows directed against them by the mother country during the later months of the year 1775. It should be remembered that they were formally denounced as rebels by the King in London on August 23. Moreover, the ban placed upon the overseas commerce of New England early in the year was extended to cover all the colonies. It was one thing for the defenders of American liberty to wage economic warfare against Britain; it was quite a different matter when Britain brandished an economic club. The Prohibitory Act of November created indignation in America. It authorized the seizure of American ships whose captains tried to take them to sea, also the detention of their crews. Further, following an ancient formula, it formally withdrew the protection of the King from his refractory subjects beyond the Atlantic. It will be recalled that the law likewise provided for the sending of peace commissioners to America who could restore that protection. Many Americans were not eager to listen to the commissioners. Sophisticated men among them, like John Adams, pointed out that protection by the King and allegiance to him by his subjects were reciprocal. Accordingly, since the monarch had withdrawn his sheltering arm, the Patriots owed no duty to him. Less scholarly Patriots saw themselves labeled as outlaws. They must defend their property and their lives as best they might. Would they not be safer as citizens of an independent nation?

XVI · *The Declaration of Independence*

If the British and the Americans grew apart slowly during the long decades before 1763, if the gap between them, in consequence of sharp debate and minor physical contests, grew more rapidly during the twelve years before the battle of Lexington and Concord, if it increased because of political and economic measures directed against the American after the beginning of hostilities, it widened speedily because of the bloody struggles that occurred during the early months of the war. Wounding words and economic blows do aggrieve, but killing, maiming, and plundering create deep and enduring rancor. The American militiaman who killed a redcoat at Bunker Hill and who fled to safety before royal troops wielding bayonets, found it difficult to continue to look upon the British as affectionate cousins. The widows, the children, and the brethren and friends of slain and wounded Americans began to look upon the British as ferocious enemies rather than troublesome fellow subjects. The cool historian of after times does not see the tears of the orphans of war; he does not hear the wailings of the widows or the curses of bereaved fathers and brothers. He may permit his penchant for using documents to turn him from passionate realities. Those Americans whose property was seized or plundered by the soldiers of George III—and the relatives and associates of those who suffered from robbery and looting—learned to see the King, his forces, and citizens of Britain as hostile strangers. Patriot women ravished by redcoats lost affection for the mother country—and so did the kin and intimates of those women. Irritation tended to become hatred. The Patriots were vexed, even exasperated, by British measures directed against them before 1775; many of them were maddened after the outbreak of the war by its inevitable cruelties and barbarities. Every blow struck by the royal troops against the Patriots increased the hostility they felt against Britain. Need it be said that the British troops, not gently treated by the Americans, began to think of them as traitors, even as hostile aliens, and to act accordingly? Blows begot blows, and hatred fostered hatred. More and more Patriots, considering scenes of carnage, of wanton destruction, of abuse of civilians, decided that they were willing to risk their property, their personal freedom, and their lives for the sake of independence.

The wrath of the Patriots was increased by British enlistment of Loyalists and Hessians. The raising of Tory contingents by Lord Dunmore, Josiah Martin, and General Gage turned neighbor against neighbor, even brother against brother. Many Patriots looked upon Loyalist troops, even Tories who did not take up arms, as traitors within the fold, and they transferred rancor which they felt toward the Loyalists to the British. The news that the mother country would use German soldiers in America also drove the Patriots on toward separation. In the eighteenth century it was not uncommon for a European ruler to hire foreign troops for service against foreign enemies. The Pope and the King of France had their Swiss guards. Nevertheless, kings did not usually employ mercenaries to subdue their own subjects. To the Patriots, the British use of German troops meant that Britain intended to treat the Americans as aliens. They were to be assailed as if they were strangers to the British state. Why should they not divorce themselves from that state? Reports of the coming of the Hessians were the more infuriating because it was to be expected that the Germans, in the fashion of European troops of the time, would maltreat civilians.

Nor was the affection felt by the Patriots for Britain nourished by British employment of Negro slaves as military laborers and occasionally as soldiers. Accepting, even soliciting, the help of the slaves, the British infuriated the Southern Patriots and won no friends among their Northern brethren. Soon after the outbreak of hostilities, unhappy and venturesome slaves began to flee from plantations and shops to royal camps and ships. Others fell into British hands or were seized in consequence of British raids and campaigns. Eventually, as a result, the Patriots lost many thousands of their blacks. The offer of freedom in exchange for military service issued to the slaves by Lord Dunmore, and a similar appeal to them made by British officers on the coast of Georgia early in 1776, especially exasperated the Southern Patriots, not the least because braver and badly treated Negroes responded. The owners of the absconding blacks thought unhappily about vanishing property. All masters became concerned lest they lose their slaves. What was much worse, all Southern whites feared that they would be forced to face servile insurrection. As it turned out, relatively few Negroes carried arms for the King. General Gage suggested that the aid of the blacks should be sought, but the commanders in chief who succeeded him did not eagerly entreat the slaves to fight for their freedom; they did employ thousands of slaves as military workmen. Most of the slaves continued with their customary tasks, remained loyal to their masters and mistresses. They proved to be an asset to the Patriot cause. Not a few slaves, not a few free Negroes, fought against the British. It is nonetheless true that the overtures made by the British to the Negroes after the battle of Lexington and Concord stimulated alarm among the Patriots.

Nor did Britain endear herself to the Patriots by her efforts to gain the liking and the help of the Indians. The Americans were the first to ask and secure aid from the red men—there were a few half-tamed Stockbridge tribesmen in the army that invested Boston in 1775. However, the

Patriots could not hope to get much assistance from the most powerful and warlike Indian nations, and sought only to persuade them to be neutral. Most of the aborigines were inclined to favor the Crown. It was the colonists who deprived them of their lands, who threatened to destroy them. Had not the servants of George III, especially John Stuart, striven to protect them against the onward rush of the American pioneers? The warriors, and even their chiefs, were often naïve. They could be cajoled by smooth talk, alcohol, and presents into acting against their own best interests. Nevertheless, the Patriots could not expect to secure many allies in the Western forests. Indeed, they wanted none—except to serve against Indians assisting the British. Even before the beginning of hostilities they dispatched emissaries to the red men to urge them to refrain from taking part in a family quarrel among the whites. After the battle of Lexington and Concord the Continental Congress and several colonies sent out commissioners with presents for that purpose. The Patriots also did what they could to interrupt the passage of gifts and supplies from Britain to the red men. Fearing the influence of John Stuart, they tried to arrest him. When he fled from Charleston to St. Augustine and safety, they held his wife during many months as a hostage for his good behavior. They also seized members of the Johnson clan in the Mohawk Valley, releasing them only upon paroles that required the Johnsons to remain quiet. But Stuart correctly concluded that the Patriots would not harm his wife, and the Johnsons eventually found excuse for violating their paroles. While the war was still young, it became evident to the Patriots that they would be forced to fight redskins as well as redcoats. Stuart urged the southern Indians to remain quiet until British troops should appear. Familiar with the barbarities of Indian warfare, he also urged his superiors in London to use Indian allies only in conjunction with white troops and under white commanders. General Guy Carleton believed that it was both inhumane and unwise to bring the Indians into the conflict. However, Lord Dunmore tried to bring savages down upon the frontiers of Virginia. Moreover, the efforts of other British officers and officials to maintain royal influence among the Indians were construed by suspicious Patriots as attempts to persuade the red men to take the field immediately. Warriors in great numbers did not assail the Americans until they were about to declare their independence. But the Patriots knew that the aborigines would sooner or later move against them in formidable force as allies of Britain. They themselves had earlier encouraged Indians to attack the French in Canada and Louisiana—and the French had sent Indians against them. But the colonists had sought the help of the warriors only against foreigners. Now Britain was preparing to use the red men against the Americans as if they were strangers. If Britain incited attacks by shrieking devils upon the American frontiers, surely George III and his ministers, nay, the whole British people, were Satanic. Why not recognize them as the cruel and mortal enemies that they were?

There is a cherished belief in North Carolina that citizens of her Mecklenburg County, learning about the running fight that took place in Massachusetts on April 19, 1775, met at their courthouse on May 20 and ceremoniously signed a document announcing their independence from Britain. Many myths have arisen among the Americans concerning their early history, not a few of them concerning the Revolution. Historians have searched in vain for authentic evidence that there was a Mecklenburg Declaration of Independence. Before the end of that month of May angry residents of the county did solemnly assert that they would refuse obedience to British laws and officials—for the time being. Nor did any body of Americans anywhere, either in 1775 or in the early months of 1776, proclaim a final separation from Britain.

Instead, amidst turbulence, the Patriots moved gradually, unevenly, and haltingly, step by uncertain step, toward absolute rupture. Looking back, Americans of later generations were tempted to see the severance of ties between Britain and the colonies as inevitable, almost as the work of God; and even historians, forgetting that the past is not inexorable until it is examined from the future, have been tempted to consider the progress of the Patriots toward independence as destined. Nevertheless, all the wise men among them did not foresee in the summer or autumn of 1775, or even in the spring of the following year, that they would before long divorce themselves from Britain. Again, they did not advance toward independence in smooth and orderly fashion; nor was the process invariably majestic. In several colonies representatives of the Crown were driven off soon after the first clash of arms; in others, they remained unmolested at their posts into the year 1776. In some of the American commonwealths Revolutionary assemblies rapidly seized power; in others, legislatures that had been elected in response to proclamations by British governors continued to act until that year was well begun. Here the Patriots were passionately active; there they moved cautiously. It must be believed that many Patriots vacillated. Indeed, not a few at last chose to continue their allegiance to the empire rather than to seek liberty outside it. Loyalists became ever more numerous as the day of independence approached.

The New Englanders and the Virginians were in the Patriot vanguard. They continued to lead against Britain, as they had before the outbreak of the war. Were they impelled, beyond other colonists, by economic grievances? Perhaps. The Yankees and the white inhabitants of the Old Dominion were very largely of English stock. Were they more disposed to go to the extreme in defense of their rights because of their heredity—with the mixed population of the Middle Colonies lagging behind? Hardly. Did they behave as they did because Virginia and the New England commonwealths had been the first to be settled—because the Virginians and the Yankees had been longer exposed to the influence of the American environment? In the large, they had not been in the New World very much longer than their fellow colonists of European rather than English descent. Assuredly, battle explains in part the forwardness of the New Englanders and the Virginians. Struggling against General Gage and Lord Dunmore, they were the first to feel the shock of combat. One observes that the Patriots of North Carolina similarly responded to warfare and the menace of British arms. After the battle of Moore's Creek Bridge, after receiving news that a British fleet and army were approaching their shores, the Patriots of that colony swiftly resolved that they were ready to assert American independence. Those of the Middle Colonies lagged behind their brethren at least in part because they were not seriously threatened by the British until the early summer of 1776. When they learned that they would soon be assailed by the Howe brothers, they too resolved that they would be satisfied with nothing less than the sundering of all bonds with Britain.

It is true that the Patriots did not move toward separation merely because they increasingly detested Britain and the British. At least some of their leaders came to believe that it was impossible to secure reliable safeguards of American rights within the empire. It became ever less likely that Britain would offer satisfactory definition of those rights. Moreover, could Britain be trusted to execute an agreement? What one British government gave, another might take away. If the Patriots, accepting terms offered from London, laid down their weapons, would they be able to unite and to contend successfully against British oppression in the future? Sophisticated and less informed Patriots alike more and more reached the conclusion that they could most effectively defend their rights, their property, and even their lives by leaving the empire.

They saw other advantages to be derived from independence. Released from Britain, they would escape from the shackles imposed upon them by the acts of trade and navigation. They would be able to manufacture as they pleased, to buy goods freely in Europe, to sell their own products as they pleased in the ports of that continent. Independence would enable them not only to protect their wealth, but to enhance it. Moreover, as citizens of a new nation, the Americans would not be dragged willy-nilly into wars declared by the British Crown to defend purely British interests in Europe, Asia, Africa, and the Caribbean Sea. Might not a liberated America, protected by the Atlantic, be able to avoid entanglement in the chronic and brutal wars of the Old World?

There was still another potent reason for proclaiming independence. Patriots unacquainted with the great world might believe that they could, unaided, withstand all the forces Britain was mustering, including Hessians, armed Loyalists, Negroes, and Indians. A stupid Patriot might even think that it would not be difficult to stave off assaults by Britain and her allies. Those conversant with the affairs of men and of states knew very well that they would be harshly tested, that, indeed, they might be crushed. Hence, the help of a foreign power—of foreign powers—was much to be desired. Military intervention by France, or by France and Spain, would reduce the vigor of British thrusts, might even be essential to successful defense. However, eager as many men in power in Paris and Madrid were to strike at Britain, they could not be expected to challenge her without assurance that the Americans were determined to struggle rather than accept compromise, to fight rather than yield. Accordingly, if the Patriots hoped to secure potent aid from the Bourbons, they must give proof of their resolution by declaring their independence.

If rage and reasons drove the Patriots on and on, other sentiments and other reasons restrained them. The fondness which they felt for Britain did not vanish with their first bloodshed, nor did their reverence for George III disappear forthwith. They had prized their British citizenship; they had shared in the glories of the empire; they had mourned the defeats of the British state; they had sacrificed life and treasure in common with their British "cousins" against foreign enemies in war after war. They had long venerated the British King. If the fealty they had given him was mystical and undeserved, it was nevertheless real and warm. Such strong and ancient ties did not snap straightway.

Moreover, every thoughtful Patriot had to consider what would be the political condition of America when separated from Britain. Independence without an American union could hardly be more than momentary. Was it possible to bring together under a common and enduring government mariners of Maine with tobacco planters of Maryland, South Carolina aristocrats with Pennsylvania German farmers, Yankees with Dutch New Yorkers, proud Anglican gentlemen of Virginia with equally proud Rhode Island Baptist traders? Surely the Americans could be neither safe nor prosperous as citizens of thirteen distinct and quarrelsome commonwealths. It would be preferable to remain within the empire rather than to fall into internal strife and anarchy.

Indeed, were the Americans generally determined to form a central government for themselves, could they do it? They must form a republic. Erecting an American throne, they would not be able easily to select an occupant for it. Many of them, in fact, would accept no King whatever to replace George III. If one desired an American monarchy, where was a ruler to be found? It would not do to substitute another scion of the house of Hanover for George III. Nor was it prudent to import a royal family from the Continent of Europe. Such a family might be far more hostile to American liberty than that which ruled over Britain. There was no American who could ascend such a throne with common consent. The colonists could hardly do other than to try to form a republic. But could they create a stable and lasting one? The republic established in England after the execution of King Charles I in 1649 had swiftly become the Cromwellian dictatorship. True, the Dutch maintained order and prospered on their flat lowlands without a crowned head—with the house of Orange supplying leaders who were almost monarchs. True, the Swiss, in their Alpine fastnesses, lived and flourished in their kingless cantons. But most European men of affairs, and even political philosophers who saw that Europe was in sorry condition, believed that Holland and Switzerland did not offer examples which could be followed. The virtuous and informed citizens of those small countries might be able to dispense with royalty. A hereditary monarch then presided over every large European state, over nearly all of the many smaller ones. Thoughtful Europeans—not excluding famous *philosophes* such as Montesquieu, Diderot, and Voltaire, who desired far-reaching reforms—conceived that a republican system could not then succeed in a great nation. They doubted that the masses of the French, British, and Spanish possessed sufficient character and capacity to wield authority wisely and well. In fact, they feared to place unchecked power in the hands of lawyers, merchants, tradesmen, and farmers. Many skeptical Patriot leaders similarly lacked faith in the ability and probity of their followers.

Not a few Patriots were reluctant to shake off the embraces of Britain because they dreaded social revolution. Would ignorant, poorer, and envious Americans be content with the shattering of British authority? Would they even be satisfied if they gained the right to vote? Was it not to be feared that they would rise against property rights, established churches, aristocracy, and domination by their American betters?

And was it safe to call upon the Bourbons for help? The Patriots had learned to look upon France and Spain as inveterate enemies. They had wrestled with hated French and Spanish papists in war after war. They had been at peace with those ancient antagonists not much more than a dozen years in the past. It was difficult for them to think of the Bourbons as friends, even as allies. Were they to be trusted? If French armies came to America and assisted the Patriots in driving off the British, might they not remain as oppressors far more malignant than the British? The inhabitants of England, deserted by the Roman legions, had implored the aid of the Anglo-Saxons against the wild Picts, had secured it—but had been subjugated by their allies. The Dutch, struggling for their freedom against Spain, had summoned a French prince to their assistance—and he had tried to conquer them. French rulers would join religious persecution to political tyranny. Better by far to endure the yoke of the British, galling as it was, then to slip under odious Bourbon sway.

Such doubts and alarms, coupled with the survival of traditional loyalty to Britain, persuaded many of the more cautious Patriots that America ought to remain within the empire. They became, of course, Tories. Others continued to think, or came to believe, that a declaration of independence ought not be too hastily issued. But more aggressive Patriots, setting aside misgivings, pressed on toward final separation. Even before the end of 1775 several of the officers holding high commands in the army that invested Boston asserted their willingness, even eagerness, to proclaim American freedom from Britain. Among them were Generals Charles Lee, Horatio Gates, and Nathanael Greene, and Colonel Thomas Mifflin. Washington himself had long since abandoned hope of reconciliation with Britain, and was ready to abjure all connection with the mother country. Those soldiers found it difficult to see their enemies within Boston as brethren. However, they did not publicly clamor for separation. The decision must be made by civilians.

A civilian appeared to voice their wishes. In January 1776, an extraordinary pamphlet entitled "Common Sense" was issued from the press in Philadelphia, which passionately urged the Patriots to divorce themselves from Britain and to stand forth as champions, not merely for American liberty, but also for the rights of mankind. It was quickly circulated throughout the colonies. Tens of thousands of copies were printed. It created furor. Reading it, many Patriots announced that its arguments were irrefutable, that the Americans must form an independent republic without delay.

The author of "Common Sense" was not immediately known, since he did not put his name upon his remarkable production. It was momentarily believed to be the work of Benjamin Franklin, of Dr. Benjamin Rush, of some other literate and devoted Patriot. Later it became known that the writer was Thomas Paine, a hitherto obscure Englishman who had crossed the Atlantic and had settled in Pennsylvania in 1774. How did it happen that such a recent immigrant became a spokesman—the spokesman—of the American Patriots?

Thomas Paine was no ordinary man. Born at Thetford, Norfolk, in eastern England in 1737, he was not yet thirty-nine years of age when "Common Sense" made its sensational appearance. He was of humble origins. His father was a Quaker, a corsetmaker who owned no acres. After a brief schooling, Paine himself turned to the construction of corsets for a livelihood. Then, reading widely and earnestly, he became an English revenue officer. For a time he taught school, but he was a failure in England and made little progress up the economic ladder. Death took his first wife; he separated legally from a second one. Returning to the revenue service, he was discharged from it in 1774 because he publicly and forcefully demanded better pay for himself and his fellow workers. He was then barely able to pay his bills and to escape imprisonment for debt. Clearly, there was no future for him in England. He had doubtless imbibed a Quakerish desire to do good; he had studied Newtonian science; and he had become a Deist. Observation and his own sad experiences convinced him that England was permeated by political and social injustice as well as religious ignorance and hypocrisy. Making the acquaintance of Benjamin Franklin, he secured from him a letter of introduction and sailed for Philadelphia. He carried with him little in the way of worldly goods, but he had learned to use the pen. He was a superb propagandist, and in Philadelphia he soon began to write in behalf of liberty for the Patriots, for enslaved Negroes, for mankind generally. It has often been said, by those who find his political and religious notions distasteful, that Paine was not profound. True enough. General Charles Lee remarked that there was "genius in his eyes." One cannot deny that he possessed intellectual ability, a singular gift for persuasive argument, and a noble compassion. Theodore Roosevelt once described him as "a dirty little atheist." Roosevelt often made unkind and unjust remarks about persons he disliked. Paine was remarkable for the cleanliness of his person; he was tall; and his belief in a Divine Being was similar to that of John Adams, of Thomas Jefferson, of George Washington, of many another distinguished Patriot of unquestioned virtue.

Whatever may be said about the personality of Paine, he offered most appealing propaganda in "Common Sense." He rehearsed, for calculating Patriots, the benefits that would be derived from independence. But, more important, in language suffused with emotion, he vehemently and cogently attacked monarchy in principle, the English Kings in general, and George III in particular. Government was at best "a necessary evil," "a badge of lost innocence." Government by monarchs was worse than any other. They claimed to rule by hereditary, even by divine right. But the first King in every royal line was doubtless "nothing better than the principal ruffian of some restless gang," who excelled his fellow rascals in savagery or subtlety, who forced "the quiet and defence-less to purchase their safety by frequent contributions." If that founder of a dynasty was to a degree deserving of reward for services rendered to the public, certainly his progeny were not entitled, merely because of hered-ity, to be masters unto the end of time. The English people owed nothing either to the bastard William of Normandy who conquered them or to his arrogant descendants. It was claimed that the orderly passage of power from King to King in consequence of blood relationship gave stability to the body politic, that it reduced domestic strife for power. Not so, con-tended Paine. Was not the history of England studded with civil wars waged for possession of the throne? It was contended that the British monarchy, being limited, differed from those of France and Spain, that Britain had found an ideal political balance that guaranteed the liberty of her people. Absurd, said Paine. Assailing George III, he declared that "the crown has engrossed the Commons." Contradicting himself, he in-correctly asserted that the King had little more to do than to wage war and to distribute offices. He was determined to find no virtue in George III. "A pretty business indeed for a man to be allowed eight hundred thousand pounds sterling a year" and to be "worshipped into the bargain! Of more worth is one honest man to society, and in the sight of God, than all the crowned ruffians that ever lived." George III was merely a "royal brute."

Nor would Paine admit that the Americans owed anything to the English people. If the English had in the past assisted or protected the Americans, they had done so because they profited thereby. They bore no love for their transatlantic kin. "Every thing that is right or reasonable pleads for separation. The blood of the slain, the weeping voice of nature cries, "TIS TIME TO PART'." The Americans could found an enduring republic—Paine offered a plan for federation of their commonwealths. They could not only establish and protect their own liberties, but offer a haven and an example for all humanity. "O! ye that love mankind! Ye that dare oppose not only the tyranny but the tyrant, stand forth! Every spot of the old world is overrun with oppression. Freedom hath been hunted round the globe. Asia and Africa have long expelled her. Europe regards her like a stranger, and England hath given her warning to depart. O! receive the fugitive, and prepare in time an asylum for mankind."

There were Patriots, like the acid-tongued Landon Carter of Vir-ginia, who considered Paine's arguments to be puerile. Nor was John Adams, jealous of the fame quickly won by Paine, profoundly impressed. Other Patriots, including Abigail, the intelligent wife of John Adams, declared that Paine had convinced them that it was both necessary and wise to proclaim independence. The vast circulation of "Common Sense" testifies to the potency of its influence. Professorial and literary men disposed to assess the power of the pen above that of the sword have been tempted to find in Paine's pamphlet a mighty force, to believe that it decisively altered the opinions of a multitude of Patriots. No one can weigh with precision the efficacy of his arguments, the impact of his eloquent phrases. It is not known that Paine converted any Tory. One may not doubt that he convinced some Patriots who had clung tightly to the British connection that it must be severed. He unquestionably gave voice, fluently, vividly, and fervidly, to opinions and feelings which many Patriots entertained, but had been unable to express for themselves. He both revealed and stimulated a tide flowing toward independence. Before the appearance of "Common Sense" few Patriots openly and unequivocally demanded final separation from Britain; after it came from the press, Patriots throughout the colonies demanded that every remaining bond with her be broken.

If the Patriots were to proclaim their freedom, it was necessary that they act in unison. Accordingly, the great debate concerning dependence versus independence had to be resolved in the Continental Congress. That body could not destroy the last links with Britain without general consent of the Revolutionary assemblies in the several colonies. Delegates to the Congress could not make such a momentous decision without instructions from home permitting them to do so. The representatives of Massachusetts were given sufficient authority to act as early as January 1776, those of South Carolina on March 23, those of Georgia on April 5. The North Carolina Revolutionary convention took a long forward step on April 12. The North Carolina Patriots had crushed a Tory uprising; their leaders learned that a British fleet and army threatened the colony; they specifically authorized its deputies in Philadelphia to vote for independence. On May 15 the Revolutionary convention of Virginia went further; it ordered the delegates of the Old Dominion to introduce a resolution calling for a formal separation from Britain. By that time the delegations of all the New England commonwealths were prepared to endorse such a resolution. It became apparent in early June in Philadelphia that the tide toward independence was rapidly rising. The Congress was keeping pace with the local Patriot assemblies. It had opened American harbors to the commerce of all nations save Britain, on April 6; it had counseled the Revolutionary legislatures in the several colonies to maintain or to found governments of their own, on May 10; it had urged destruction of all royal authority, on May 15.

Nevertheless, the Congress hesitated before taking the final plunge.

It contained men who were still opposed to independence upon principle, who urged delay, who hoped that the Howe brothers were bringing suitable terms for an accommodation with Britain. Other members pleaded for postponement until an American federation had been formed, until French aid was assured—voicing an opinion that was held by many cautious Patriots, even by some very warm ones, including Patrick Henry. Still other delegates were unable to vote for a divorce from Britain because they were curbed by instructions from home. Principal among those who demanded that a decision be deferred was the respected John Dickinson of Pennsylvania. He was stoutly supported by delegates from the Middle Colonies and from South Carolina. He and they were able during several weeks to restrain the advocates for immediate separation, to the distress and vexation of John Adams, Richard Henry Lee, and a growing party of delegates who clamored for swift and absolute sundering of all ties with Britain.

The struggle in the Congress began formally on June 7, when Richard Henry Lee submitted three resolutions. The first of these redundantly but emphatically asserted

> that these United States are, and of right ought to be, free and independent states, that they are absolved from all allegiance to the British Crown, and that all political connection between them and the state of Great Britain is, and ought to be, totally dissolved.

Lee also called for the founding of an American confederation and for attempts to secure allies among the rulers on the European Continent. Lee's first resolution led to an immediate debate. It was informally endorsed by seven delegations; it was opposed by six. Its supporters, aware that the Congress ought not proceed without unanimity—at least not without the appearance of unity—consented on June 10 to put off further discussion until July 1. However, that same day the delegates agreed to the appointment of a committee to prepare a document that would justify the resolution, should it be adopted. The Congress was thus half committed to positive action. Benjamin Franklin, John Adams, Robert Livingston, Thomas Jefferson, and Roger Sherman, named to the committee, began their work.

Resuming the dispute over Lee's resolution on July 1, the Congress heard a final impassioned appeal for delay by John Dickinson. However, in committee of the whole, nine delegations endorsed the resolution. It was opposed by those from Pennsylvania and South Carolina; two men from Delaware canceled each other's vote; and the spokesmen for New

York, instructed not to act, abstained. Then, suddenly, the champions of independence won a complete victory. The South Carolina men decided to join the majority; the arrival of a third delegate from Delaware, Caesar Rodney, changed the vote of that colony to the affirmative; and John Dickinson and Robert Morris withdrew from the Congress, so permitting Pennsylvania to signify her consent. On July 2 the Congress, by the unanimous vote of twelve colonies, with the delegation from New York silent but satisfied, solemnly sanctioned the resolution. America was to go her own way.

Why is it that the Americans do not, and never did, handsomely celebrate the anniversary of July 2, a day of so great importance in their history? Because, in faulty memory, they afterward recalled that the Patriots tore free from the shackles of tyrannical George III on July 4. On that day the Congress—with the New York delegation again consenting but abstaining; the New Yorkers were able later to vote in the affirmative —formally approved the famous document that has come to be known as the Declaration of Independence. It repeated and defended the Lee resolution in such extraordinary fashion that the decision taken two days earlier was forgotten. The recollections of the ablest of men, even those concerning the most momentous events, are not to be trusted. The author of the Declaration of Independence, Thomas Jefferson himself, later remembered July 4 as the day on which America announced her freedom.

It was, indeed, Jefferson who composed that noble pronunciamento —we may set aside an absurd claim that the first draft of the document was indited by Thomas Paine. Only thirty-two years of age, Jefferson had already won fame among the Patriots as a polemicist by publishing "A Summary View of the Rights of British America" in 1774. As a member of the committee given the task on June 11 of preparing a Patriot apologia, Jefferson was urged by his colleagues to compose it, and he did so. It is the judgment of all good and wise men that Franklin, John Adams, Livingston, and Sherman did not err when they selected the young Virginia planter to frame the Patriot justification. Putting down, as he afterward said, the "common sense" of the Patriots, he drew up a most uncommon proclamation. Franklin and Adams suggested several minor changes that Jefferson incorporated. Presented to the Congress, it was further and more substantially amended by that body. It removed a passage that condemned George III for defending the oceanic slave trade—denunciation of that commerce struck tender chords in delegates from the Southern States and from New England; and it deleted another which linked the "Scotch" with "foreign mercenaries"—a reference that

241

would have offended many Patriots of North British descent. Improved by various changes, the document was nevertheless very largely the work of Jefferson.

The Declaration of Independence is couched in solemn, dignified, felicitous, and mellifluous language that remains impressive and alluring. Assuming that Parliament never possessed authority over the colonies as of right, it offered argument to justify destruction of royal power. Parliament is mentioned only as a British assembly that assisted the "present king of Great Britain," by "pretended legislation," to commit numerous deeds of tyranny. The King—the Crown is consistently personified in the Declaration, in the same fashion that important acts of British ministers were always performed in his name—had indeed held lawful dominion over the colonists, under compact with them, but he had violated it. Accordingly, the Americans were released from all obligation to him, and so became an independent people.

To prove that it was just and proper to destroy the authority wielded by George III, the Declaration appealed to doctrines of natural rights and political contract laid down by Algernon Sidney, John Locke, and other British and European philosophers. Men in a state of primeval nature were "created equal" and "endowed by their Creator with certain unalienable rights," among them "life, liberty, and the pursuit of happiness"—Jefferson preferred "pursuit of happiness" to John Locke's "property." Government was instituted to protect those rights. A contract was made between those who were ruled and their ruler or rulers. Subjects owed obedience to government in return for protection of their natural rights. But if a government, by "a long train of abuses and usurpations," offered proof of intent to form an "absolute despotism," then it was the unquestionable right, even the duty, of the governed to rebel, to annul the contract.

To vindicate destruction of the authority of the King it was then necessary only to demonstrate that he had insistently sought to establish despotic rule over the colonists. He had done so, asserted the Declaration. "The history of the present King of Great Britain is a history of repeated injuries and usurpations, all having in direct object the establishment of an absolute tyranny over these states." A long list of those misdeeds was submitted to a "candid world." The colonists had often sought redress, but had been turned away. They had also appealed to the British people, in vain. Accordingly, their contract with the King was now dissolved, and the British people were henceforth foreigners, to be considered with "the rest of mankind, enemies in war, in peace friends."

The Declaration and its author have been condemned as well as praised. John Adams, jealous of the fame it brought to Jefferson, afterward asserted that Jefferson had offered nothing new. "There is not," he said, "an idea in it, but what had been hackneyed in Congress for two years before." Jefferson never claimed that his handiwork added magnificently to the corpus of political philosophy. He had merely expressed the sentiments of the Patriot leaders—but he had put them in elevated and moving language such as no other Patriot could employ. A better scholar than Jefferson, but a stodgy writer, Adams could not appreciate the achievement of his colleague. The theories of natural rights and compact contained in the Declaration, widely accepted by thoughtful men in the eighteenth century, have not withstood the tests of time and modern sages. It is doubted that men in a state of nature were free, even that they were "created equal." Does it matter whether or not they were actually free? They ought to have been, ought to be, free to form governments. It is urged that compacts between rulers and the ruled are also unhistorical. If so, it should not be denied that the conception of compact is sound and essentially equitable. Surely, no person solicitous for the welfare of the race will assert that mankind does not possess a moral right to rise against and to overthrow tyrants. Was George III, were George III and his advisers, striving to establish tyranny in America? It has been pointed out that all the charges against him and them cannot be proved, that some of them are without warrant. Quite true. The Patriot leaders made their list of accusations as long as possible. They put their charges in such form that they seemed to indict the King for the acts of his ministers. Assuming sinister intent in many measures taken by the monarch and his ministers before the beginning of hostilities, they did not do cool justice to those admittedly defective men. In their list of injuries perpetrated they included acts committed against the Patriots after they themselves had taken up arms. One may find many faults in the document, in form and in content. Nevertheless, in the large, the Declaration of Independence was, and is, morally valid.

The Declaration has supplied inspiration and an arsenal of arguments ever since 1776 to men seeking to create a better human order, not merely in America, but over the planet. However, although the delegates in Congress pledged "our lives, our fortunes, and our sacred honor" to the cause of independence, there were Patriots at the time who neither looked upon the document with reverence nor considered separation from Britain as irrevocable. Thus Robert Morris, later so famous as a manager of American finances, continued for a few weeks to hope that the Howe brothers would still be able to patch up the Anglo-American quarrel. Nor did the Declaration convince George III, Lord North, or their British supporters that they were tyrannical. The King continued to pray to his God for victory over his ungrateful and rebellious subjects. The body of Loyalists in America did not diminish. Rather, it grew. A small number of colonists contended for their rights against Britain until independence approached, then drew back as if from an abyss. Thus Johann Joachim Zubly, delegate in the Continental Congress from Georgia, at last discovered that he preferred British monarchy to an American republic. Such men, together with those few always faithful colonists who had defended British authority during the Stamp Act troubles, and with those more numerous colonists who had rallied to the cause of the mother country during the decade before the beginning of hostilities, formed a large minority that desired the downfall of the Patriot majority. Perhaps as much as a quarter of the white population of the Thirteen Colony-States sooner or later became Loyalist. Ardent defenders of American rights everywhere joyfully celebrated when they learned that the Congress had proclaimed independence. They had not yet been forced to face truly formidable British armies. They would be compelled to struggle desperately with their Loyalist and Indian neighbors as well as the troops and sailors of George III. It long remained uncertain whether the signing of the Declaration of Independence was a dramatic episode in an unsuccessful rebellion or signaled the birth of a new nation.

CHAPTER XVII

The Opposing Forces

MANY historians of the nineteenth century and the early part of the twentieth century, entertaining exaggerated notions of British power and American weakness, found it difficult to explain Britain's failure to crush the American rebellion. They could not understand how the Patriots withstood British offensives during the years 1776 and 1777; and they could not quite believe that Britain was not strong enough to defeat the Americans after 1778, when the Patriots had powerful aid from France. American historians, afflicted by ancestor worship, were tempted to enhance the achievements of the Patriots by magnifying the might of their enemies. It was forgotten that the Britain of 1775 did not possess the strength of the Britain of 1875. Striving to explain the successful resistance of the Patriots, the chroniclers offered various and curious reasons. It was urged that George Washington was a military genius and that the generals who opposed him were fabulously incompetent. The American historian, George Bancroft, believed that God interfered at critical moments in behalf of the Patriots. It was also asserted that the Howe brothers, more particularly the general, overswayed by friendship toward their antagonists, did not desire to destroy the Patriot forces. Some narrators even suggested that William Howe, as some embittered Loyalists insinuated, deliberately betrayed the trust placed in him. Actually, if one sets aside intervention by God or by Fate, if one does not inflate the strength of the British state, it will appear that the Patriots did not struggle against overwhelming odds. It is even quite possible that they would have gained their independence without the help of the French—and Spanish—armies and navies.

To be sure, the Patriots could not hope to challenge the British navy.

More powerful in 1763 than those of France and Spain combined, it became comparatively weaker during the fifteen years that followed. For the Bourbons renovated and increased their navies, while that of Britain suffered somewhat from economies imposed upon it, especially by Lord North. Moreover, the supply service of the British navy was riddled with inefficiency and corruption. Nor was the Earl of Sandwich, first lord of the admiralty, who was specially responsible for the direction of the British war effort on the oceans, a great man. He is better known for his exploits as a young rake than as a master of naval procurement, strategy, or tactics. He is more favorably remembered for his invention of the form of food named after him than for his selection of admirals to lead the British squadrons into battle. He has been described as unbelievably incompetent; a juster estimate is that he did not shine in a ministry not famed for the talents of its members. Several of the admirals in that navy were unimpressive, and many of the seamen had been pressed. Officers were almost invariably of "good family." Captain James Cook, whose father was a laborer, was a striking exception. Cook was so obviously a splendid man that he was able to overcome his handicap. Not limited by humble parentage, men such as Samuel Graves, Sir Peter Parker, and Marriot Arbuthnot became admirals, but not admirable.

Service for the ordinary and able seamen in that navy was so unpopular that it was necessary to resort to informal conscription—impressment—in order to get full crews for His Majesty's ships. An ordinary seaman was paid 19 shillings per month, an able seaman 24 shillings. Officers could take with them upon voyages hams, fruit, wine, and other delicacies. The men received an allowance of rum, and, at the best, monotonous and badly cooked food. Not infrequently they were served ship's biscuit containing weevils, and meat infected with maggots. Scurvy struck the men rather than their officers. Moreover, discipline was harsh. The lash was constantly used to compel obedience. A sailor who committed a serious offense might be given dozens of strokes with the whip. Casualties from hardship and disease were constant and numerous. It is reported that 1,512 British seamen were killed in action during the Seven Years' War, and that 133,708 died of disease or were missing. There was no specific period of service, and a man was discharged when it pleased his superiors; nor was he entitled to a pension that would maintain him in his old age. Unable to secure enough recruits by appeals to patriotism and cajolery, the navy resorted frequently to the press gang. Such groups forcibly enlisted men in English ports, and occasionally in colonial ones. It is not surprising that British sailors often displayed a rebellious spirit. There was much flogging on the *Cerberus* during its voyage to Boston in the spring of 1775. Both the later mutiny on the *Bounty* and the one at the Nore during the war of the French Revolution arose from conditions that were almost unbearable. The British navy was recruited by seduction and abduction, and its discipline was maintained by severity and brutality.

In the coffeehouses of London after 1775 there might be much talk about the invincibility of numerous British naval squadrons, but not so many war vessels were at sea. The French and Spanish navies had become dangerous—Britain had not set and preserved a "two-power standard" on the sea. But, despite its shortcomings in ships, supplies, admirals, and recruiting practices, the British navy remained formidable. In case of need, it could send dozens of massive ships-of-the-line to sea, and even more frigates. It was accustomed to victory over the Bourbon fleets. Its seamen were experienced and skillful—and not all of its admirals were incompetent. Ship for ship, and man for man, the British navy was definitely superior to those of Spain and France. And the Patriots could not hope to challenge the armed might of Britain upon the oceans. It was not possible for them quickly to build 64-gun ships and 74-gun ships to send against British vessels carrying as many or more pieces of artillery. Nor could they expect to match the British frigates in numbers. They could and did send dozens of cruisers to sea to attack British merchant vessels, and not without effect, but they could not put a battle fleet in commission. Nor could they prevent Britain from blockading their coasts, interrupting their overseas commerce, and curtailing the flow of weapons and military paraphernalia from the European Continent. That Britain could have compelled the Americans to lay down their arms solely by means of a long-continued and close blockade must remain very doubtful. In fact, intercourse between the Patriots and the outside world could not be completely cut off, because of the long American coastline on the Atlantic and its many harbors. Moreover, access to foreign lands, though important to the Patriots, was not vital. They were able to feed and clothe themselves, and also, if necessary, to make essential weapons. Unable to close all the American ports, the British could and did create shortages of goods in America and inflict hardships upon the Patriots. The British navy, until the French intervened, was also a potent force in that it could and did freely move troops from one American harbor to another. On occasion, its guns could support the troops. Further, it was able to interrupt internal American lines of communication, such as those that ran across the Hudson River.

The British army was relatively far weaker than the British navy. The "thin red line" existed long before that term became famous. At the beginning of hostilities the army probably contained not much more than 50,000 men fit for service, many fewer than it possessed on paper; and, because garrison forces were needed in the home islands, in the West Indies, and other places, only a part of that army could be employed in North America. Nor was it possible to use all of that part against the Patriots, for it was necessary to maintain garrisons in the Floridas and Canada. The burden placed upon the army by the decision to employ it as the primary instrument for the suppression of the American rebellion was a heavy one. Hence the need for hiring the Hessians, since it was impossible to raise large numbers of men in Britain to fight in America. Without the German troops, Britain could not have placed sufficient men in the field in America to move against the Patriot armies.

Which is not to say that the Hessians were of the same quality as the British soldiers. Some of them were well trained, but some were conscripts. All of them served in a war that was not their own. They had no reason to feel loyalty toward Britain, except for the pay that they received. Accordingly, as the war continued, many of them deserted, emerging at the end of the struggle as American farmers and artisans. Nevertheless, they were well equipped and harshly disciplined, and they added to the striking power of the British army. However, their very presence in that army stiffened American resistance. They were not only foreigners, but foreigners who began to loot as soon as they landed in America and never ceased to plunder. They were accustomed to brutal warfare in Germany, and they did not fail to commit rape. British generals could not keep the Germans under tight rein, partly because they lacked the power to impose the death penalty upon the Hessians.

The British troops were as good as any in the world. They might have been even better than they were. For their ranks were not filled by the physically and mentally superior of British youth. Service in His Majesty's regiments was by no means attractive to the common soldier. Pay was very low; discipline was severe; promotion from the ranks was almost unknown; and provision for retirement was meager. Many a soldier was a country boy who was plied with liquor at a tavern by a smooth-talking ensign or sergeant, and who discovered when he regained his senses that he had enlisted for service during the King's pleasure. Others were ne'er-do-wells who preferred the hard life of the soldier to misery and starvation. Some entered the army to escape punishment for crime. On occasion a man was forcibly inducted into it by zealous recruiters. Not infrequently a nobleman serving at the head of a regiment was able to enroll young men from the families of his tenants and from the village near his estate. From such disparate sources were molded, surprisingly, many fine regiments. The redcoats, serving for long periods, even for decades, became professional and proficient soldiers. They possessed the traditional British courage; and not a few regiments were imbued by splendid traditions stretching back to Minden and Culloden, even to Blenheim and the battle of the Boyne. The army was not remarkable for its efficient artillery, nor for cavalry, of which it had little; Britain relied upon her infantry, and with good reason. In the conventional warfare of Europe her regiments of foot soldiers were unexcelled. Armed with the musket and the bayonet, they were formidable on both the defensive and the offensive. They could repel attack by cavalry, and their own charge, with the bayonet, was fearsome.

It cannot be said that the British regiments were led by better men than they deserved. There was no special school in England for the instruction of officers, except for engineers. Accordingly, officers uniformly began their careers as amateurs. Nor were the young men who received appointments in the army necessarily talented. The lowest rank among the officers, that of ensign, was filled by youths whose parents or friends could afford to pay a substantial sum for their commissions. The senior ensign in a regiment, if he had the necessary funds, could buy a vacant lieutenantcy. And so on, up to the rank of lieutenant colonel. Accordingly, regimental officers were normally members of "good families," at least of families possessing money. They were presumably gentlemen. There were exceptions to the rules. Noblemen invariably advanced much more rapidly than commoners. In 1769 General Sir William Draper could not recall a single nobleman who had obtained a colonelcy by seniority— at a time when many titled men commanded regiments. Occasionally a "gentleman volunteer" was given a commission solely for valor on the battlefield. There was even one British general of the eighteenth century, James Robertson, who began his career as a common soldier. But commissions in the British army below the rank of colonel were almost always pieces of property that could be sold as well as bought. Accordingly, the army did not want men who somehow or other became ensigns without cash. They would be unable to secure promotion, and they would inevitably be dissatisfied. There were lieutenants of long and valiant service who saw young men become captains and majors.

It would be a mistake to conclude that officers who were not formally trained and who received advancement in part through influence and cash were uniformly incompetent. There were among them men like Lord Elcho, who declared upon being appointed to a colonelcy, "Be in no apprehensions ever about me. I shall always, I hope in God, do my duty as an officer, but not one step will ever I stir as a volunteer." There were among them men who preferred the powder on the cheeks of ladies to gunpowder. Gamblers, rakes, drunkards, and brutes were not lacking. Tedious garrison duty often brought out the worst rather than the best in the officers; they did not usually turn to military studies—or to study of any kind—to pass time. Between wars many of them were placed on half pay and reduced to a meager standard of living. One officer placed on half pay complained in the British *Gentleman's Magazine* in 1749:

> Curs's on the star, dear Harry, that betray'd
> My choice, from law, divinity, and trade
> To turn a rambling brother of the blade.
> Of all professions, sure, the worst is war;
> How whimsical our fortunes, how bizzare!
> This week we shine in scarlet and in gold,
> The next, the sword is pawn'd, the watch is sold,
> This day, familiar with my lord, we dine,
> The next his grooms our company decline,
> Like meteors, rais'd in a tempestuous sky,
> A while we glitter, then obscurely die.
> Of such disgrace must heroes still complain,
> And curse an honourable peace in vain?

The army contained officers like George Wickham in Jane Austen's *Pride and Prejudice,* that wastrel for whom Mr. Darcy bought a commission in order to persuade him to marry Miss Lydia Bennet, and so to save the Bennet family from wretched disgrace. It doubtless had many officers like George Osborne of Thackeray's *Vanity Fair*. But there were other and splendid men who were honorable, utterly brave, and even competent; men who had learned about war both in peacetime maneuvers and upon battlefields. The British army had in its regiments experienced officers who were equal to their counterparts in any European service.

It has been said with some justice that the British army was really only a collection of regiments. Colonelcies were often honorary; and their possessors had opportunities for graft that many of them did not fail to seize. There was no general staff, and the army was not staffed by great generals. Its field commanders obtained their appointments by influence as well as experience and performance. Moreover, their experience was primarily gained in European warfare, and did not fit them to deal with an American rebellion. They were trained to fight the French in Flanders or Germany rather than Americans who employed unorthodox tactics at unusual times and in strange places. They were not accustomed to swift movements or to warfare in winter. Even those, such as William Howe and Guy Carleton, who had served in North America, had had no opportunity to learn how to suppress a massive rebellion of British subjects. The British generals, on the whole, were not remarkably efficient by the standards of the European Continent; they were also ill fitted for warfare in the colonies. Declared a Hessian officer, "I readily concede, that Howe is no Caesar, and is not the greatest general of his time, but for an American war, he is a good enough general." He was not "good enough" for the War of Independence.

Praising the fighting quality of trained British troops, one ought not undervalue the Americans who served in the ranks. Declared "An Officer" in the London *Public Advertiser* (January 1775), "The Americans, though in general of our stock, appear to me to have for the most part degenerated from the native valour as well as robust make of the men of this country." The American militia, he predicted, would not be able to withstand British regulars. A Mr. Wombwell said in the House of Commons in October 1776 that the Americans were "bragging, cowardly banditti." British officers who had served in North America in the Seven Years' War, with the striking exception of Colonel Isaac Barré, did not admire the American militia who fought with them against the French. At the beginning of the War of Independence William Howe believed that one British soldier was more than equal to two American ones on the battlefield. His judgment, if properly qualified, was doubtless defensible in 1775 or 1776. It is surely true that the British regulars could then overcome double their number of undisciplined militia in fighting upon open ground. Indeed, since the American militia were sometimes poorly armed and were subject to panic, they were less than the equals of British regulars in such combat at the end of the war. It does not follow that the militia were to be despised. They were called into active service by the colony-states chiefly in emergencies and usually for fixed periods of time that might expire at a critical moment. But they often remained in the field when they might legally have returned to their homes. Their performance improved as they acquired experience. They could not be trusted to repel a bayonet charge by British veterans. Nevertheless, those part-time soldiers were brave enough; and when led by a Benedict Arnold, they could make a formidable attack. Afterward, American professional soldiers, insisting that their nation must not rely upon militia for its defense, easily demonstrated that they were less than utterly reliable in the War of Independence. Even so, outpourings of militia made possible a brilliant counteroffensive by Washington late in 1776; helped to defeat General John Burgoyne's army in 1777; destroyed a Loyalist army at King's Mountain; and assisted the American regulars on many a battlefield. Their shortcomings have been sufficiently described. Let it be remembered in their behalf that General Sir Henry Clinton, sadly contemplating the military scene in America after the battle of Yorktown, described the New England militia as "warlike," numerous, and formidable.

Moreover, the British had to face more than militia. For the American forces acquired a "hard core" of Continental troops, of regulars, that became firmer with the passing years. The Continentals, enlisted for only one year in 1775, served for three years or the duration of the war after the end of 1776. As the conflict progressed, they became ever more proficient and were inferior in no way to British veterans in its last years. Not that every Continental private soldier was a splendid physical and moral specimen. Alexander Graydon, a Continental officer, relates that a Mr. Heath helped him to secure a recruit. According to Graydon, Heath said that the fellow "would do to stop a bullet as well as a better man," that "he was a truly worthless dog," and that "the neighborhood would be indebted to us for taking him away." There was many another "worthless dog" in the Continental ranks. The forces raised by Congress did not form a Cromwellian New Model Army. Continental service was hard, and pay was often in the form of inflated paper money. Desertion was frequent—the British were able to form a corps of "Volunteers of Ireland" largely composed of men who had enlisted in Patriot regiments and had changed their allegiance. Nevertheless, the Continentals were in the main of good stuff, men who resolutely endured great hardships and continued to fight in seemingly desperate circumstances. They believed in their cause. Perhaps half of them were sturdy Yankees; among them were tall and vigorous Virginians; Delaware and Maryland supplied some excellent troops; indeed, every colony-state furnished fine men to the Continental regiments.

It ought not be forgotten that the forces which fought against the Patriots were heterogeneous and less numerous than the Patriot troops. The Hessians were obviously not the equals of the British; and they deserted in large numbers in the later years of the war. The Indian allies of the British were fickle and unreliable; moreover, their atrocities steeled Patriot resistance. As the war went on, more and more Loyalists took up arms. Trusting to British arms for victory at the outbreak of hostilities, they were slow to take the field. Later they formed "provincial" contingents and enlisted in British regiments. Like the Patriot troops, the Loyalist ones acquired proficiency as the struggle wore on. However, the Tories never joined the British in masses. There were perhaps three Patriots for every Tory; some of the Loyalists were Quaker pacifists; and many of them prudently remained quiet in districts dominated by the

Patriots. The Tory contingents that served with the British were sometimes impressive on paper rather than in the field. The Patriots exceeded the British and their allies in numbers in almost every major battle of the war. How many Continentals and Patriot militia served in the contest no one can say with assurance, but the total certainly ran to many scores of thousands. American losses could be, and were, replaced without excessive strain. On the other hand, it was difficult for the British to fill depleted ranks. It is not too much to say that every regiment was precious to the British. They could not suffer many defeats and continue to attack. The onslaughts of disease and desertion hurt the British far more than the Patriots. The red lines of the British were, in the end, too thin for the tasks imposed upon them.

Nor were the American regimental officers inferior to their British counterparts. Soon after taking command at Cambridge, Washington saw to it that several Yankees who held militia commissions were cashiered for misconduct. It is well known that he then expressed a low opinion of New England officers who were not gentlemen, who fraternized with their men, who could not maintain strict discipline. It has often escaped attention that the Yankee officers improved with time and experience. It is even true that one New England cobbler served steadily and valiantly as a Continental officer during five campaigns. The men who led the American militia often secured their appointments because they were locally popular; but they were almost as often liked and respected because they were men of ability who possessed the qualities of leadership. The strains of war weeded out the incompetents and brought forward the brave and enterprising, even in the militia. The officers in the Continental regiments were, of course, superior to those in the militia. Indeed, it seems fair to say that Continental lieutenants, captains, and majors were as good officers as the British who held the same ranks. Initially they lacked experience. However, they were the flower of American youth; and their zeal compensated for their deficiencies in training. General Howe, telling Lord George Germain in January 1776 that the Patriots should not be scorned, gave a special reason. He declared that the best of young American manhood was joining Washington. And so it was. The sons of the Southern planters, of New England merchants, of the country magnates of the Middle Colony-States hurried to secure commissions and careers in the Continental army. Among those eager and valiant youths were Samuel Shaw of Massachusetts; Eleazer Oswald and several Trumbulls of Connecticut; Alexander Hamilton, John Lamb, and Jacob Morris of New York; Alexander Graydon of Pennsylvania; Henry ("Light-Horse" Harry) Lee, James Monroe, and John Marshall of Virginia; and John

Laurens of South Carolina. Intelligent, informed, ardent, ambitious, lusting for glory, such men were willing to make every sacrifice.

The senior American officers were less fitted for their more difficult duties. At the beginning of the struggle they knew even less about the techniques and art of war than the British generals. Some of them hastily perused the treatises upon strategy and tactics that were then available in America. Charles Lee and Horatio Gates were looked upon as military oracles. None of the Patriot field commanders rose to the level of the mature Caesar or the young Napoleon. Lee and Gates, useful in the early years of the war, proved to be less than superb generals. Moreover, Lee's loyalty became questionable. But Washington and Nathanael Greene became competent, equal to the best of the British commanders; Henry Knox performed splendidly as an artillery officer; and "Mad Anthony" Wayne, rash rather than insane, Daniel Morgan, and Benedict Arnold were able, bold, and successful leaders of smaller Patriot forces. Other American commanders, such as Philip Schuyler and John Sullivan, were less capable, perhaps less fortunate. In any event, the Patriot generals were not excelled by Howe, who lacked intelligence and imagination; by Clinton, who was thoughtful, quarrelsome, and excessively cautious as a commander in chief; nor by Lord Cornwallis, who displayed no intellectual gift for warfare, who was no more than a fine fighting man. Had the British possessed a commander in chief with the popularity of Howe, the insight of Clinton, and the audacity of Cornwallis, the Patriots must indeed have been hard pressed.

Paradoxically, the Patriots drew certain profits from the lack of professional training among their commanders. When winter approached in northern Europe, just as admirals sought a port before a storm, generals took their men into towns and forts to keep warm. In the eighteenth century, in that region, fighting began in May and ended in November or early December. Officers and men were accustomed to a period of rest and relaxation in winter, and they looked forward to it. The British soldiers sang:

> And when in quarters we shall be,
> Oh! how I'll kiss my landlady.

The Patriot commanders, not enslaved by such tradition, attacked in winter, as did Montgomery and Arnold at Quebec, and Washington at Boston and again at Trenton in 1776. Hence, in part, Washington achieved surprise and victory at Trenton. European military protocol gave Washington a second advantage at Trenton, for it required that

Hessians rather than British troops be entrusted with its defense. It also demanded that unsuitable dismounted Hessian cavalrymen in their clumsy boots be sent through the woods against the Green Mountain Boys at Bennington in 1777 to overwhelming defeat. Professional habits and rules prevented the best use of the forces under the British commanders. On the other hand, Patriot generals, less trammeled by orthodoxy, sometimes gained greatly by doing what well-trained commanders would not attempt. In the main, to be sure, they were handicapped rather than helped by their inexperience.

The Patriots were afflicted by many weaknesses, aside from their lack of practice in warfare. One of those was political. Britain had but one monarch, one cabinet, and one legislature, and a long-established government. America had fourteen lawmaking bodies, and thirteen separate executives, all of them hastily formed at the beginning of the war. The Continental Congress, with its committees, supplied leadership for the emerging nation, but often needed help from the colony-states to execute its decisions. The result might have been chaos. Actually, the Patriot cause did not suffer too severely. The exigencies of the war almost compelled the Americans to combine their efforts. Common fears and enthusiasm compensated in large degree for faulty system. It is to be doubted that Britain possessed a great governmental advantage, since unity in London was more apparent than real. The various departments and offices in Whitehall did not work in unison. Incompetence and corruption plagued the British war effort. Britain did not have an overwhelmingly powerful and smooth machine for waging war.

It is also obvious that the Patriots lacked both money and industrial power. They had no stores of gold. They were forced to print money; and the Congress and the colony-states issued it in vast quantities. The Congress put forth more than $200 million in Continental bills, all of which steadily became less acceptable and at last became worthless. Both the Continentals and the militia were often paid in paper that had very little value. The Patriots, at the beginning of the war, were unable to make muskets, cannon, gunpowder, and uniforms. Even in the early years of the conflict there were Continentals wearing "breeches that put decency to the blush." A wit suggested in 1776 that the Americans must win the struggle if it continued to the end of the year, for the British troops, forced to fight naked men, would be terrified by the novel appearance of their enemies. Later, a Tory referred to Washington's army as "Falstaff's soldiers, poor and bare." The Continentals did not usually wear the handsome uniforms designed for them. However, they were not always half-naked and shoeless. The Patriots made hunting shirts and pants that substituted for buff-and-blue uniforms; they manufactured shoes, ammunition, rifles, and shot. Moreover, they brought in from Europe large quantities of muskets, cannon, tents, blankets, and other military paraphernalia. A belief exists among the Americans that the sufferings of the Patriot troops at Valley Forge in the winter of 1777–8 were typical. Such was not the fact. Indeed, the Patriots endured a more trying winter afterward in quarters at Morristown, New Jersey. Actually, the American army at Valley Forge was in a state of prosperous though harsh adversity. The Patriot forces usually began a campaign well, if not handsomely, clothed and well armed. But shoes and uniforms wore out, and were not easily replaced while the troops were in the field. As winter approached, they might seem to be half-starved ragamuffins. The Continental forces, like the armies of General Robert E. Lee afterward, in the Civil War, tended to diminish remarkably in winter, only to reappear vigorous, refreshed, and numerous in the spring.

It should be emphasized that neither the British nor the Patriots enjoyed any remarkable and enduring superiority in weapons, and that the musket was the gun upon which both sides relied. A persistent myth would have it that the Patriots, being armed with Pennsylvania rifles, held a great advantage over the British, equipped with inefficient muskets. Many companies, and even regiments, of Americans did carry rifles. It is also true that riflemen with their long-barreled weapons could bring down a man at 200, even 250 yards. They could aim at individuals; and they could concentrate upon slaying British officers. The rifle was, however, of limited use. It was most effective in skirmishes and in forest fighting. It was thus more useful against Indians than it was against formations of British regulars in combat on open ground. The rifle was less formidable than the musket when discharged at a mass of men at close range. It required twice as long to reload; and a rifle bullet, being half the weight of the heavy one-ounce missile discharged by the musket, did not do as much damage as the pellet from the musket. The musket bullet could smash as well as penetrate. The value of the rifle in such combat was seriously limited in another way. The musket was equipped with a bayonet; the rifle was not. Accordingly, riflemen, after discharging their weapons once or twice, were exposed to "the white weapon," to bayonet charges, which they could not hope to withstand with clubbed rifles, hatchets, or knives. Since the Americans, if only to maintain morale, felt forced on many occasions to face their enemies in large numbers on relatively open battlefields, they had to learn to check British attacks with musket fire and the bayonet. Many of the Continentals did learn that hard lesson. They, of course, were the élite of the Patriot armies, the men in whom Washington and other American commanders placed their final trust. Too often the exploits of the riflemen are glamorously reported; too often the deeds of the most essential part of the Continental armies are forgotten.

It is apparent that Britain, unlike America, possessed cash, generous credit, and factories sufficient to pay and equip her army and navy. Her resources were not inexhaustible, but Britain was not so poor that she needed to extract a revenue from the colonies in time of peace, was rich enough to maintain large forces in America during several campaigns without great strain. Even so, the war was increasingly burdensome for Britain, all the more so because her lucrative commerce with the Americans was brought to a halt. In fact, the Patriots were perhaps as able to carry on a long war as were the English.

For the Americans, without the command of cash and credit possessed by Britain, had many resources beyond their numerous soldiery. They could arm, feed, and equip their armies. It is true that it was not easy for them to convert their wealth to use, also that they encountered difficulties when they sought to establish systems of supply. Nevertheless, America could easily produce enough grain and animals to nourish her troops, enough cotton and wool to clothe them, enough iron and lead to arm them. It is well known that both the Continentals and the militia suffered at times from lack of food and clothing; it may be forgotten that it never became necessary to disband the Patriot troops. It may be worth recalling that the collapse of the Continental currency, complete by 1780, did not cause absolute starvation or nakedness in the American forces. The states were weighed down by the financial burdens of the war. They had collected property and poll taxes from their citizens; they had borrowed money at home and abroad, straining their credit; and they had been compelled to pay ever higher prices for everything needed to wage war. But they came to the rescue with supplies sufficient to permit the continuance of the Patriot war effort.

It should also be remembered that the British could not easily supply their armies. They were often able to buy cattle and grain with cash in America, but not enough to maintain their troops. They had to send large quantities of food and equipment across the Atlantic. British contractors were renowned neither for honesty nor for efficiency. They were not above sending rotten meat to His Majesty's soldiers and sailors. A Hessian reported that on the voyage to America he consumed "old hard bread or zwieback, stale water stinking like a barnyard puddle, pork preserved with saltpeter, musty peas, and a bit of smelly butter." Even when food was as well preserved and packed as might be in that time, it was likely to spoil during the long passage across the ocean. If it was good enough to eat when it was unloaded in an American harbor, it did not survive carriage to troops serving in the American interior. Some transports went down in storms; others were captured by Patriot cruisers. The British had to secure vegetables in America for their men, and forage for their horses. Their armies were unable to move at times because they could not feed their horses. When British troops marched inland, it was very difficult to transport their supplies in wagons and carts over rough roads and across frequent streams and rivers. The farther the British advanced into the interior, the greater became the problem of furnishing their soldiers with food and equipment. The damaging defeats that they encountered when they fought at a distance from salt water arose in part from long and precarious supply lines.

Distance, bad roads, slow sailing ships, and weather also created serious communications difficulties for the British. It was awkward enough for their generals and admirals to keep in touch with each other within the large theater of war. The Patriots had similar troubles. However, the British were also forced to exchange information and to decide upon strategy by means of messages carried across the Atlantic. Even with good weather and favorable winds, sailing ships needed a month to journey across the north Atlantic. Two, three, or four months might be required for the voyage; and ships did not even attempt to cross the ocean in January or February. The captain of a packet carrying dispatches for a British admiral might be forced to search for him in the broad stretches of water between Rhode Island and Jamaica. Accordingly, it was necessary for the British to give a large measure of freedom of action to their commanders in chief and admirals serving in America. On the other hand, the ministers of George III, particularly Lord George Germain and the Earl of Sandwich, could not evade responsibility for the outcome of the war; they possessed information denied to British leaders across the Atlantic; and they had to do what they could to assure unity of action among those leaders. Accordingly, British plans were made by several men much separated by space and time, often upon the basis of data that had lost validity because of the changing course of events. Hence arose in part the defective strategy that brought disaster to British arms in the campaigns of 1777.

The Patriots had other advantages. The British had to take the offensive, had to crush Patriot resistance; the Americans had only to keep the field until Britain should tire of the struggle. It was not required of the Patriots that they drive their enemies into the Atlantic to win the war; but the rebellion would continue so long as the Americans were able to fight effectively in any part of their territory. It was even conceivable that, being driven to the Appalachians, they would carry on the war from fastnesses in and beyond the mountains.

Not the least of the British difficulties was the American terrain, vast, forested, intersected by swamps, rivers, hills, and mountains, traversed by few and poor roads, and devoid of a strategic center. It was not possible to crush the Patriots by seizing their capital. If they had a capital, it was Philadelphia. However, the Continental Congress and its few servants could easily evacuate that city and carry on elsewhere—and did so when the British marched into it in 1777. Philadelphia was not to the Americans what Paris was to the French. Nor did seizure of any other American city, or of all five of them, assure a British triumph. Since the Patriots were not dependent upon foreign trade for their subsistence, since they were able substantially to arm, clothe, and feed themselves, even a complete closure of all the American harbors, which could not be and never was achieved, would not have compelled them quickly to yield. The British could interrupt the internal communications of the Patriots. A British post at West Point, together with British warships in the Hudson River, would quite effectively have separated the Yankees from their brethren. The British might similarly have established a military barrier between the Patriots on the Delaware River, on the Susquehanna, or on the Potomac. But the separation of the Patriots by such means could not be achieved by small bodies of men; nor is it at all certain that the results would have been decisive, even in the long run. Maintenance of such a barrier would have required so many men that the British would hardly have had sufficient other forces to strike at and to subdue completely any large territory isolated by it. In time, such a barrier, especially on the Hudson, must have embarrassed the Americans. Fortunately for them, the British did not occupy and fortify West Point.

Unable to achieve victory by capturing and holding a few key positions, the British were nevertheless compelled to maintain and to garrison bases. Had the Americans been willing to fight to a decision on the shores of the Atlantic, the British would doubtless have regained their colonies. The Patriots did indeed suffer by attempting to hold New York and Charleston against superior forces. However, they usually withdrew from the sea when pressed. In consequence, it was necessary for the British commanders who pursued them to leave part of their own troops behind to protect their lines of communication. Thus, as soon as General Howe seized New York in 1776, he had to fortify it and put a garrison of several thousand men in the city before he could follow a retreating Washington—without those men. When he captured Philadelphia in

1777, he was similarly embarrassed because of loss of striking power. Had the Loyalists been numerous enough to garrison key positions captured by the British—so preserving British strength for further offensives —the result of the war would very likely have been different. Commander after British commander hoped for such Loyalist help, at Boston, at New York, at Philadelphia, in South Carolina, but it never came. The Loyalists were too weak everywhere even to hold down disarmed Patriots. Accordingly, the British armies became weaker as they penetrated into the American interior—while the Patriot forces often gathered strength as they retreated.

To these assessments of forces and frailties, let it be added that the Americans in general and their leaders and generals in particular had more at stake than their enemies. It mattered little to the Hessian whether Britain won or lost the war. Nor was the outcome vital to the redcoat; were the Americans victorious, Britain would still be unconquered. The Loyalist, to be sure, risked everything, if he fought or was otherwise active in behalf of the empire. He hazarded his property, his home, and even his life. But so did all the Patriots. True, as the war continued, Britain was quite willing to pardon all the Americans in order to persuade them to lay down their arms. However, the Patriots were long unaware that such was the fact, and their leaders not unreasonably feared that military failure would lead them to the traitor's block or to the hangman. Indeed, even if the British kept their promises of amnesty, the Patriots would still have been exposed to the vengeance of the Loyalists. It could hardly be expected that the Tories, suppressed and maltreated by the Patriots, would be as generous as the British. The Loyalists managed to create a legislature during the war, in Georgia, under the protection of British troops. It immediately declared the property of the Georgia Patriots to be subject to confiscation. It is clear enough that the Americans had much to fear, and that fear steeled them to greater efforts. It is also true that they had much to gain from victory. Many of them sincerely believed that they were fighting, not only for their own freedom, but also for the rights of mankind, for a better world.

Attempting to weigh persons and things almost unweighable, one must say that the outcome of the struggle, if it were confined to the British and to the Patriots, was unpredictable. At the end of the year 1777 it had become evident that the Patriot armies were formidable. Would the Americans, suffering economic distress, have been able, without the help of French troops and ships, to overcome their antagonists? Probably not. Nor is it likely that secret aid from France and Spain, which began to reach the Patriots in the early months of 1777, would have enabled them ultimately to drive the British before them. Which is not to say that the Patriots could not have won their independence. For they might well have been able to carry on hostilities until Britain tired of the struggle. As it was, France and Spain did enter the war; and French fleets and armies ultimately assured the triumph of the Patriots.

CHAPTER XVIII

From Brooklyn to Princeton

THEY entered New York Harbor in scores, the tall-sailed warships of Admiral Howe and the humbler transports carrying the troops of General Howe. From Manhattan, week after week in July and August of 1776, General Washington watched the British forces grow. The Patriots had resolved, if possible, to defend the city, and Washington had collected a large army there. At last, when all was ready, General Howe moved to the attack. He routed one third of Washington's troops in the battle of Long Island; he seized the city; he pursued Washington to White Plains and defeated him there; he easily captured Fort Washington and its large American garrison; and he drove the Patriot general across New Jersey and the Delaware River. He won a chain of victories in the late summer and autumn of 1776, and the Patriots seemed to be in the direst distress. But the British had not conquered, as they had planned to do, New England. And suddenly, as winter came on, Washington struck back. He overcame a Hessian garrison at Trenton, defeated a British detachment at Princeton, and went into secure winter quarters, early in 1777, at Morristown in the hills of New Jersey. When weariness, cold, and snow forced both the British and the Patriots to remain quiet, Howe held only New York, Long Island, Newport, and eastern New Jersey. Guy Carleton and his army were still in Canada; and the Patriots had survived the first powerful British onslaughts.

Whatever may be said about the wisdom, or lack of it, displayed by the British government in its choice of commanders and its peculiar arrangements for making peace with the Patriots, one may not say that the British erred in choosing their principal objective in 1776. They decided to concentrate their forces against New England. General Howe was to take New York and Newport and to proceed eastward and northward into the Yankee country. He was to be assisted by his brother. Meanwhile, after driving the Patriots from Canada, Carleton was to recapture Fort Ticonderoga and then to penetrate into New England. The two British armies, it was expected, would both regain Boston and crush all resistance in that region. If New England, the great American stronghold, fell, the British would later be able to advance southward. Indeed, Lord George Germain even hoped that the conquest of New England would break the morale of the Americans and that the rebellion would be put down in one decisive campaign. He belittled the numbers and enthusiasm of the Patriots, magnified the Loyalist party. The Howes, too, set store upon help from the Loyalists, although the general knew long before he left Boston that he could expect little aid from the Tories of New England; and they hoped, against any reasonable hope, that the Patriots would find acceptable the terms of peace which the brothers carried but could not reveal. Germain put his faith in the harsh exertion of force; the brothers erroneously believed that they could erase the rebellion by persuasion as much as by power.

It was obvious to the Patriots that Guy Carleton would press southward from Canada in 1776 and almost equally certain that William Howe would appear at New York. They undertook to check both the British generals. Early in 1776 Washington began to prepare to defend New York. He sent General Charles Lee there. Lee told Washington that Manhattan could not be held indefinitely, if for no other reason because the British possessed massive naval power. He informed the commander in chief that the British could be forced to fight for the city, without undue risk to its defenders. To keep it as long as possible, Lee and other Patriot generals fortified Manhattan; to prevent the British from approaching the city by way of the East River, they also established batteries of artillery on the heights of Brooklyn and entrenchments to cover the batteries. Further, they placed cannon on both sides of the Hudson River to prevent British ships from going up the river, or at least to hinder their progress.

Washington was acutely aware of the strategic importance of the city and of the Hudson. He said that New York was "the place that we must keep from" the British. "For should they get that town, and the command of the North River, they can stop the intercourse between the northern and southern colonies, upon which depends the safety of America." They would also gain easy access to Canada. It was therefore of "infinite importance" to defend the city. The Continental Congress agreed with Washington that everything possible should be done to prevent the British

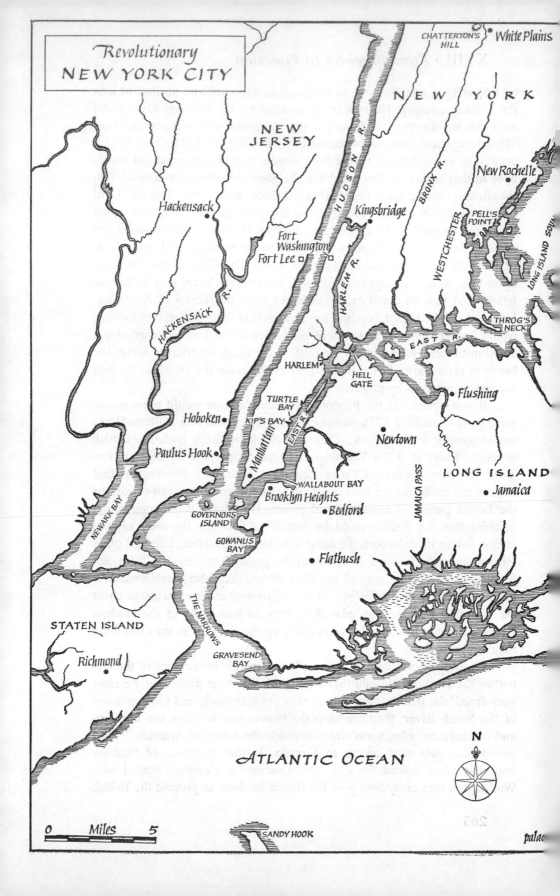

Revolutionary
NEW YORK CITY

NEW YORK

CHATTERTON'S HILL

White Plains

NEW JERSEY

HUDSON R.

New Rochelle

Hackensack

Kingsbridge

BRONX R.

PELL'S POINT

Fort Washington

Fort Lee

HARLEM R.

WESTCHESTER

LONG ISLAND SOUND

HACKENSACK R.

THROG'S NECK

HARLEM

EAST R.

HELL GATE

TURTLE BAY

Flushing

Hoboken

KIP'S BAY

Manhattan

EAST R.

Newtown

Paulus Hook

LONG ISLAND

WALLABOUT BAY

Jamaica

Brooklyn Heights

GOVERNORS ISLAND

Bedford

JAMAICA PASS

NEWARK BAY

GOWANUS BAY

Flatbush

THE NARROWS

STATEN ISLAND

Richmond

GRAVESEND BAY

N

ATLANTIC OCEAN

0   Miles   5

SANDY HOOK

from taking Manhattan, and undertook to raise large numbers of troops for the purpose. The general moved from Boston to New York and spent the spring and most of the summer making ready for the British onslaught. He finished the fortifications begun by Charles Lee, and he collected the largest army he ever commanded, about 29,000 men on paper, doubtless fewer in fact. Many of them were militia, and his Continentals were not yet veterans.

General Howe did not move against the rebels with undue haste. British officers and men who arrived early in New York Harbor enjoyed its beauty for several weeks. Meanwhile it became increasingly evident that it would be risky for the Patriots to try to hold the city. On July 12 two British warships, the *Phoenix* and the *Rose,* made their way up the Hudson as far as Tappan Bay. They suffered little damage from American shore batteries; the roar of the British guns impressed Washington's raw recruits; and it became apparent that the Patriots did not and could not control the lower stretches of the broad river. General Henry Clinton, having gained a little experience in island warfare at Charleston, had an inspiration. The only good exit from Manhattan to Westchester and the mainland was at Kingsbridge. He urged General Howe to take advantage of his brother's fleet and to place a detachment of troops on the heights at the northern end of Manhattan to threaten that exit. It could, perhaps, be closed. However, at that time the bulk of the Hessians who were to join Howe had not yet made their appearance, and the commander in chief declined to act until he had acquired strength definitely superior to that of Washington. He was not disposed to attempt any bold venture, however great its rewards might be.

The Hessians did not arrive until August 12. Meanwhile, the Howe brothers sought to open negotiations with Washington. For that purpose, on July 14, they sent a letter into the Patriot lines to "George Washington, Esq. etc., etc." The American commander refused to receive the message, on the ground that the letter was improperly addressed. Soon afterward a British officer was received by Washington. He explained to the Patriot general that "etc., etc." was intended to cover all of Washington's titles. The Virginian did not bother to say that it was easier to write "General George Washington" than to use the address employed by the brothers. The officer told Washington that the Howes were eager to reach an accommodation with the Patriots. The general declined to meet them, or either of them. Did they have power to pardon? They were obviously not instructed to bargain. In any event, he could not discuss terms with them; he had not been given authority to do so by his employers, the Continental Congress. But the overture made by the Howes was not without result. Many of the Patriot troops wishfully believed that a liberal offer of reconciliation had been made. Washington felt forced to tell his men that the Howes had not made any specific proposals for a peace.

Having extended an empty hand of friendship, the Howes then struck with a mailed fist. By mid-August all the troops assigned to General Howe, except for 5,000 men still en route across the Atlantic, were in New York Harbor and ready for action. His army was superior to that of Washington in almost every respect, perhaps even in numbers. Under the protection of the British fleet, he sent the flower of his soldiers ashore at Gravesend Bay on Long Island on August 22. Washington had put as many as one third of his troops on Long Island. They were separated from Manhattan by the East River, part of them within a fortified line between Wallabout and Gowanus Bays, the bulk of them stretched out on another line along a ridge to the southward that ran from west to east. Commanded by General Israel Putnam, the American forces on Long Island were not strong enough to sustain attacks by Howe, even though Washington sent additional troops when he saw that the British general was concentrating there. The Patriots had no safe avenue of retreat. Moreover, the American outer line was not anchored on its eastern end; it merely stopped, in relatively open country. Putnam had neglected to guard against a flanking movement around his left wing and Washington, inspecting Putnam's defenses, had not observed the weakness. Putnam had merely posted five mounted sentinels behind that wing to give warning if the British marched around it. Howe learned from Tories that the American left wing rested upon nothing whatever, and he took advantage of the negligence of the American commanders. He moved into position to attack on August 26. During the following night he sent a powerful force through the Jamaica Pass, and around the American left wing. The Patriot horsemen stationed behind it to warn of the approach of the British were captured before they could give the alarm. In the morning of the twenty-seventh the British struck. Assailed both in front and from the rear, the American left wing, under General John Sullivan, stood for a time. Then, facing British bayonet attack, it crumpled. On the Patriot right wing, outnumbered Maryland and Delaware Continentals under General William Alexander, the so-called Earl of Stirling, for a time withstood assaults by General James Grant. At length they too were driven back. In great confusion the bulk of the Patriots fled into their second line of defense. Howe might swiftly have pursued them into those entrenchments. So doing, he might have killed or captured all of the Patriots stationed on western Long Island. He preferred not to risk an immediate assault upon the second, shorter, and stronger American line.

Momentarily, the Patriots were permitted to rest. However, their position on the hills above the East River was precarious, since they could flee only across the river to Manhattan; and it was to be feared that Admiral Howe would close that route of escape. They could not indefinitely fend off General Howe's superior forces. Washington sent aid to Putnam on the day of the battle, and then personally assumed command within the American works. On August 28 he brought more troops over from Manhattan. But the Patriot general was not entirely unaware of the peril to which a large part of his army was exposed. Among the detachments he ordered to Brooklyn was a body of fishermen from Marblehead, Massachusetts. Washington obviously had it in mind that it might be necessary to abandon Long Island entirely—the fishermen could manage the small craft in which the Patriots must flee across the East River. Before that day ended, Washington saw that Howe was preparing to renew his attacks. After a council of war in the evening, Washington resolved to evacuate. Having chosen his course, he moved with celerity. Collecting a fleet of small craft, he called upon the Marblehead men, commanded by John Glover, one of his most reliable officers, and others familiar with boats, to ferry his troops and as much equipment as possible to Manhattan during the night. He posted a rear guard under Thomas Mifflin to protect his fleeing troops against British attack. He ordered that the evacuation be carried out as rapidly and as quietly as might be. It was rainy and windy after dark, but the boats moved back and forth between Brooklyn and Manhattan swiftly and almost silently. So great was the task for those who ferried the soldiers across the troubled waters between Long Island and Manhattan that many of the troops were still on the heights of Brooklyn at dawn. However, the storm that buffeted the American craft also kept Admiral Howe's ships out of the East River; and an early morning fog gave the Patriots more time in which to execute their retreat. At last General Howe learned that Washington was in flight, but too late to interfere. Even the American rear guard under Thomas Mifflin made its way to the boats before the British troops could attack. Almost as if by a miracle, Washington had saved most of the troops who had been stationed on Long Island. The bulk of the Patriot forces were momentarily secure on Manhattan.

Even so, General Howe had won an easy victory at very little expense. He had captured 1,097 Americans, including General John Sullivan and the Earl of Stirling, and hundreds of Patriots were slain or wounded in the fighting on August 27. The morale of those on Manhattan was low. If the British could swiftly overrun defenses so long prepared, how could they be repelled when they struck a second time? The American troops lost faith in their officers, and militia deserted by companies, almost by regiments. Fortunately for the Patriots, General Howe did not take quick advantage of the shock suffered by Washington's army. He did not put his troops in motion again for more than two weeks.

Meanwhile, Admiral Howe resumed his efforts to persuade the Americans to lay down their arms. His brother did not bother even to bury the Americans killed in the battle of Long Island; they lay where they fell for months after the struggle. However, the admiral talked to John Sullivan, expressed his affection for the Americans, and convinced that officer that the brothers were empowered to offer generous terms of peace to the Patriots. Sullivan was released to carry the good news to the Continental Congress. Regaining his freedom, he gladly performed that mission. The delegates in Philadelphia were not so gullible as Sullivan. There were undoubtedly many men among them who did not believe that the Declaration of Independence was decreed by the Deity, or that it was irrevocable. It is to be suspected that some would have been willing to cancel it, provided that American freedom within the British empire was assured. Nearly all of the delegates were educated men who knew that the affairs of men are chancy and unpredictable, that it may be prudent to take the good rather than vainly to seek the best. Certainly it would not do to refuse the admiral an opportunity to present his terms, if he had any to offer. To deny it to him would create suspicion among many Americans that their leaders were utterly unreasonable. Even the most violently anti-British delegates were willing to permit the admiral to submit proposals, for they knew that he could not offer concessions sufficient to weaken the Patriot will to resist. Accordingly, the Congress appointed a committee to meet the admiral and to listen to whatever he had to say. It consisted of Benjamin Franklin, John Adams, and Edward Rutledge. The three Patriots conferred with Lord Howe on Staten Island on September 11. He expressed his sincere desire to put an end to the war and his eagerness to please the Americans. After they had put down their arms, they could expect that Britain would be most generous. It was only too apparent to the three Americans that the Howe brothers could not even bargain until the Patriots had abandoned the struggle. They could not rely upon the admiral's sweet talk even for the safety of their own persons. Franklin, Adams, and Rutledge told the viscount that the Americans would accept nothing less than independence. Lord Howe continued his efforts to persuade the Patriots to put their trust in him, but it had become apparent to the most timid of them, in and out of the Continental Congress, that they must either place themselves at the mercy of Britain in order to obtain peace, or secure it by force of arms. They preferred to fight.

XVIII · *From Brooklyn to Princeton*

Although the Patriots rejected the pleas of Lord Howe, those who were stationed on Manhattan did not look forward with confidence to renewal of the contest with General Howe. Their morale remained shaky. Many of them lacked confidence in their generals, including Washington. Several of their officers were uneasy because they saw that the Patriot army might be trapped on Manhattan. If General Howe closed its avenue of retreat to the mainland—to Westchester—it would very likely be caught between British troops on the eastern bank of the Harlem River and British warships in the Hudson River. Washington was aware of the danger, but was reluctant to retreat. Was he equal to his tasks? A feeling developed in the Patriot army that he had erred on Long Island because of inexperience, that he might make further and even more grievous mistakes because of his lack of professional knowledge. General Charles Lee, fresh from victory at Charleston, was hurrying northward to join Washington. Some of Washington's officers hoped that Lee would appear in time to save the army. General Nathanael Greene rightly believed that it was dangerous to wait for Lee. On September 5 he urged Washington to evacuate New York, and also to burn the city, so that it would be of less value to the British. Adjutant General Joseph Reed gave the same advice to the Patriot commander in chief. Greene and Reed, knowing that the city could not be held and that it was rash to risk the army to defend it, proposed to accept the inevitable loss of New York and to deprive the British of the shelter that it could offer. However, their counsel was extreme, and the Continental Congress had spoken against destruction of the city, in part because the delegates hoped that the loss of the city would be only temporary. Others among Washington's advisers were less alarmed than Greene and Reed. On September 12 Washington decided to withdraw from the city and to concentrate on the northern end of Manhattan. He did not think it necessary to destroy the city, nor did he believe that he must retreat immediately to the mainland to assure the safety of his army. He wished to delay the advance of the British as long as possible, even at much risk. Before all of the Patriots left New York, General Howe struck.

Luckily for the Patriots, the British commander neither moved rapidly nor adopted the best tactics. General Henry Clinton again urged him to make use of Lord Howe's fleet, to land in force on the eastern side of the Harlem River, and to try to pin down Washington's army between the Harlem and Hudson Rivers. Such a movement would have compelled the Patriots to retreat; if executed swiftly, it might have led to the destruction of the American army. Had Washington been crushed against the Hudson, it is even conceivable that the Patriot cause would have collapsed. Howe was confronted by a splendid opportunity; he would never

269

have another that promised such great reward at such small risk. He did not seize it. On September 2, writing to Lord George Germain, he said that the war could not be won in 1776, that it would continue into 1777. He certainly did not hurry to put an end to it. He did not put his army in motion again until September 15, and then he directed its power against the southeastern shore of Manhattan. Two detachments of royal troops went ashore under the protection of the guns of the British fleet, at Kip's Bay and at Turtle Bay. They encountered feeble opposition, and they began to march westward across the island, and also northward. There were still many Patriot soldiers on the southern end of Manhattan. These might have been cut off. However, the slow advance of the King's troops permitted them to escape to the northward. The Americans offered very little resistance; they fled in panic, to Washington's disgust. Had Howe performed the flanking movement proposed by Clinton . . . As it was, Washington was able to establish himself on Harlem Heights. Indeed, in a series of skirmishes on September 16, Washington's men gave him a trifle of encouragement. They drove back Howe's advanced guard, and the British general made no immediate and serious effort to exploit his easy triumph.

Why William Howe moved so deliberately, so cautiously, when he possessed such great superiority, remains something of a puzzle. Did he wish to avoid shedding American blood in quantities, to avoid driving the Patriots to desperation, so that they would listen to his brother's arguments for a cessation of hostilities? Perhaps so. Admiral Howe himself, instructed to make full use of his fleet against the Americans, and in particular to intercept and seize their ships, did not ruthlessly execute his orders. In fact, although he did station some of his ships so as to cover several Patriot harbors, he waged a soft war on the water. He bombarded Patriot positions only when he was assisting his brother. More important to William Howe, one suspects, was the need to avert a major check by Washington. Even Henry Clinton, despite his championship of aggressive tactics, believed that a single Patriot victory would be most damaging to British arms. It would seem that General Howe wished to push back Washington at small cost, to create an impression of British invincibility, to destroy Patriot morale, and so to win the war. If so, he erred sadly.

For, as the result of his cheap triumphs on Long Island, the British general was deprived of much of his power to strike. Occupying New York, he had to keep it, to fortify it, to use it as a base, and to defend it, and was accordingly compelled to maintain a garrison of several thousand precious soldiers in the city. He also was forced to place a few troops on Long Island. He was not happy as the conqueror of New York. He found

Loyalists in the city, but too few to hold it while he went forward against the Americans. Nor did the burning of a part of the city—presumably set afire by Patriots—a few days after its capture improve the British general's spirits. On September 25, writing to Lord George Germain, he declared that it was too risky to advance again immediately against the Americans. He had received no assurance that the British army in Canada was marching southward; a body of 5,000 Hessians sent to assist him had not arrived; and he lacked offensive strength. Howe remained quiet in New York for twenty-six days, while the summer fled and autumn began.

Washington was thus given time to prepare against the next advance by the British general. He was unable to secure reinforcements. Indeed, ill supplied with tents, blankets, and other equipment, his army began to suffer from the cold on chilly nights. It continued to dwindle in numbers, and its morale did not rise. Nevertheless, declining to retreat even one mile more than was absolutely necessary, Washington undertook to hold northern Manhattan. He and his staff decided to place a large part of the Patriot army there, and to station troops to the eastward of the Harlem River to check a flanking movement by Howe. They also undertook to strengthen Fort Washington, on the northwestern side of Manhattan, and Fort Constitution, on the opposite bank of the Hudson, in order to prevent the British fleet from using that river—a mistake. They vainly hoped, by means of a boom and other obstructions stretched across the river, and by artillery fire from the forts, to bar Admiral Howe's ships, even though the *Phoenix* and the *Rose* had easily forced their way up the river in July.

On October 12 William Howe resumed the offensive. He had learned that long-expected reinforcements of British and Hessian troops were about to land at New York. They would increase his army to about 35,000 men. He was thus enabled both to hold the city and to take the field with the assurance that he would soon possess superiority over Washington in number as well as in quality of troops. Howe now attempted to do what Clinton had earlier urged, to pin the Americans against the Hudson. If they escaped him, they must retreat rapidly. Under cover of a fog, he passed through Hell Gate with the main body of his troops in transports supplied by his brother. He went ashore on Throg's Neck, from which a road ran northwest behind most of the American troops to Kingsbridge. But the Patriots had learned to guard against such a maneuver, and Howe had chosen the wrong spot to begin his encircling movement. Had he landed his men further to the eastward, he might indeed have cut off at least a part of the American army. Throg's Neck was virtually an island. To reach the mainland the British had either to use a causeway and bridge, or a ford. And both passages were watched by small detachments of Patriots. When a part of the British advance guard marched across the causeway, it was driven back by rifle fire; when other redcoats sought to make use of the ford, they too were repulsed. Then Patriot troops numbering perhaps 1,800 men advanced to defend the two approaches. It became apparent to Howe that it would cost him heavily to drive through to the mainland, and his camp equipment had not arrived. He remained quiet for six days on Throg's Neck, then made a second landing three miles to the eastward, at Pell's Point, a part of the mainland that offered no serious natural obstacles. Had he gone immediately to Pell's Point rather than to Throg's Neck, he would have had a much better chance to injure the Patriot army.

As it was, Washington learned that the British were moving, that he must flee from his own awkward position. The American general held a council of war on October 16. It was obvious that the troops stationed on Manhattan were in danger of entrapment. General Charles Lee, who had rejoined Washington, emphatically advised that the entire Patriot army withdraw to safer ground on the mainland. Others among Washington's officers were less alarmed. Washington decided to evacuate Manhattan, except for the fort named after him, and to concentrate at White Plains. He ought also to have abandoned Fort Washington, for the troops within it were left without support and exposed to British attack. But he did withdraw the bulk of his men on Manhattan in time. They began to move across the Harlem River on October 18, the very day that Howe went ashore at Pell's Point. Without sufficient transport, the Patriots marched slowly. A swift advance by the British from Pell's Point might still have interrupted the retreat of the Patriots as they straggled toward White Plains. However, Colonel John Glover, who had taken a leading part in the repulse of the British advance guard at Throg's Neck, as well as in the evacuation of Long Island, now added to his laurels. The British occupied Pell's Point at dawn on the eighteenth, but Glover, with about 750 men, resisted them throughout the day and permitted them to advance only a short distance from the water's edge. Perhaps the restraint imposed upon the British army by Glover convinced Howe that his flanking movement was too late to be successful. In any event, Howe made no strenuous attempt to execute it. He marched very slowly toward White Plains while the Patriots gathered there to oppose him. He did not reach that place until October 28.

At White Plains the Patriot army was in improved spirits. It had diminished to 14,500 men. But the morale of the Americans had been improved by the good showing they had made in the several skirmishes that took place after the capture of New York; by a few days of rest; by the arrival of food and drink; and perhaps even by the departure of many deserters. Moveover, the Patriot army was no longer seriously threatened with encirclement. Behind it were hills in which it could find at least temporary safety. Washington did not flee at Howe's approach. He had entrenched on fairly strong ground, with his right wing upon Chatterton's Hill, with the remainder of his troops stretched out to the eastward of the Bronx River. He did not even wait for the British to attack; he sent forward a division of about 1,500 men to retard their advance. The detachment was forced back by British and Hessian troops, but not before it had inflicted casualties, especially upon the Germans. Then Howe struck with power. He ordered 4,000 of his men to assail Chatterton's Hill, defended by 1,600 Patriots under General Alexander McDougall. Crossing the Bronx River, not without difficulty, Hessian and British infantry, supplied with artillery and assisted by a small body of cavalry, pressed forward. When a cannon shot struck an American militiaman, his regiment was barely restrained from flight. However, the bulk of the Patriot right wing stood firm for many minutes. One attack by the Hessians and another by the British were repulsed. Gradually, the Americans on Chatterton's were almost encompassed by their enemies. Before Washington could reinforce them, they were driven from the hill. Delaware Continentals held their ground long after their comrades had fallen back, then retreated in good order. Indeed, there was no rout. Howe acquired possession of the hill before nightfall, but Washington merely extended his line of defense to prevent a flanking attack from the hill.

The losses on both sides at White Plains were counted in scores rather than in thousands. Nevertheless, the battle was a great turning point, since General Howe soon afterward abandoned his stately and dignified pursuit of Washington's army and turned westward. Howe received reinforcements immediately after the fight for Chatterton's Hill. However, the Americans were now posted on strong ground. The British commander considered further strokes, but did not know quite what to do until the night of October 31. He then gave orders to Henry Clinton to mount an attack the following morning. He was too late. That same night, in a heavy rain, Washington fell back a few miles to North Castle. There, taking advantage of hilly terrain, he occupied a position where he could not be flanked, where he could very likely withstand frontal assaults. Howe did some thinking. It had become very doubtful that Guy Carleton would appear in New England—Carleton was still to the northward of Fort Ticonderoga, and it was not probable that he would risk marching into Yankeeland, since winter was near at hand. Was it worthwhile, then, for Howe to continue immediately his own attempt to push into New England? The British army now lay between General Washington and Fort Washington. Howe decided to march westward to exploit this advantage. He did not abandon the scheme to penetrate into New England. In fact, he also proposed to execute part of it, by sending General Henry Clinton with a small army to seize Newport before the onset of winter. He put his troops in motion on November 3. During the night of November 4 American sentries heard the rumbling from Howe's supply wagons. Were the British making ready for a new blow? In the morning the American army learned with relief that the royal troops had turned away and were marching toward the Hudson.

Washington and his generals were not quite so happy. What did Howe, "retreating" toward New York, intend to do? After a council of war on November 6 the American commander, concluding that it was necessary to cover the Highlands of the Hudson and New Jersey against British thrusts, divided his army and sent troops westward for those purposes. The remainder he entrusted to General Lee to prevent a British march into New England. Rather strangely, he and his advisers were apparently not then much alarmed for the safety of the American garrison at Fort Washington, although it was obviously exposed to attack. It was also useless to the Patriots as a means for controlling the Hudson. On November 7 three British ships made their way without difficulty up the river between that post and Fort Lee (earlier known as Fort Constitution).

Unfortunately for the Patriots, the officers responsible for the two posts were not fully aware that to try to hold Fort Washington was to invite disaster. Its commandant, Colonel Robert Magaw, believed that it could be defended for many weeks. If worst came to worst, he would be able to flee to New Jersey with its garrison, and even to carry off a large store of supplies collected within the fort. General Nathanael Greene, who maintained headquarters at Fort Lee and who was Magaw's immediate superior, was also deluded. Greene was to become one of the ablest commanders in the American army. Nevertheless, he agreed with Magaw. He said that the troops at Fort Washington were not "in any great danger," and that they could retreat to Fort Lee "at any time." But what if Lord Howe's fleet barred their way across the Hudson? Even if the admiral did not try to intercept the fleeing garrison, would the Americans be able to hold off assaults by the British army long enough to permit evacuation across the river?

Learning of the passage of the three British warships between the two posts, Washington by November 8 reached two inescapable conclu-

PLATE I

GEORGE III, by Gilbert Stuart.

PLATE II

Queen Charlotte, by Gilbert Stuart.

PLATE III

A nineteenth-century American conception of GEORGE WASHINGTON in classical guise. Statue by Horatio Greenough.

PLATE IV

WILLIAM PITT, First Earl of Chatham, by William Hoare.

PLATE V

JOHN ADAMS, by Joseph Badger.

PLATE VI

JEFFERSON in his fifties.

PLATE VII

(a) GENERAL CHARLES LEE.

(b) LORD NORTH,
by Rinke after Dance.

PLATE VIII

(a) LORD GEORGE GERMAIN,
from a portrait by
Sir Joshua Reynolds.

(b) CHARLES JAMES FOX,
from a portrait by
Sir Henry Raeburn.

PLATE IX

TRYON PALACE AT NEW BERN.
The last capitol of colonial North Carolina (restored).

PLATE X

FIRST NEWS OF THE BATTLE OF LEXINGTON, by William Ranney.
An imagined scene by a nineteenth-century American artist.

PLATE XI

(a) ADMIRAL RICHARD HOWE,
by J. Chapman.

(b) GENERAL WILLIAM HOWE,
by J. Chapman.

PLATE XII

(a) GENERAL GUY CARLETON,
from an engraving by
A. H. Ritchie.

(b) SIR HENRY CLINTON,
by J. Smart.

PLATE XIII

of the West Bank of the Hudsons River 3 Miles above Still Water, upon which the Army under the command of Lt. General Burgoyne, took post on the 20th Sep. 1777.

(Shewing General Frazer's Funeral.)

Published as the Act directs, Jan. 31, 1789, by William Lane, Leadenhall Street, London.

BURGOYNE'S ENCAMPMENT AFTER THE FIRST BATTLE OF FREEMAN'S FARM.

PLATE XIV

GENERAL FRANCIS PICKENS.   A partisan officer in civilian dress.

PLATE XV

CAPITULATION DE CORNWALLIS.

Wasington, Rochambeau, Lafayette — 19 Septembre, 1781.

A FRENCH VIEW OF THE SURRENDER OF CORNWALLIS.

PLATE XVI

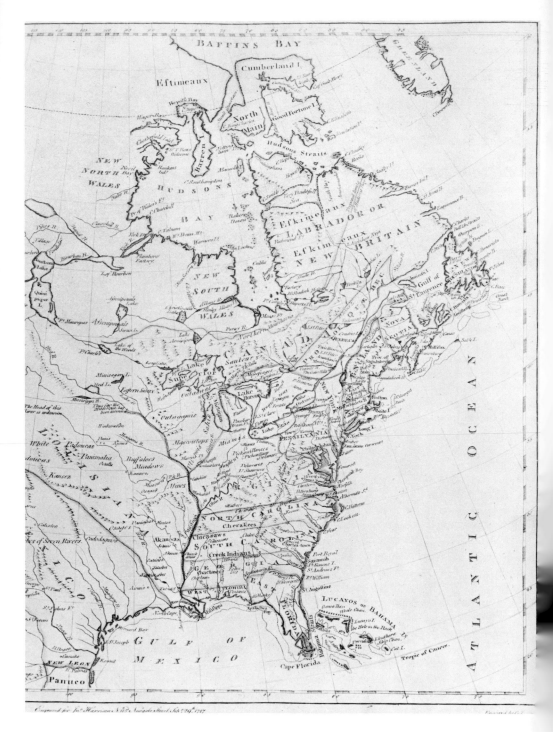

CONTEMPORARY MAP OF NORTH AMERICA.

sions—that the Patriots could not deny the lower Hudson to the British and that an attempt to hold Fort Washington was risky as well as useless. That day he wrote to Greene, "I am therefore inclined to think it will not be prudent to hazard the men and stores at Mount Washington, but as you are on the spot leave it to you to give such orders as to evacuating Mount Washington as you judge best." Greene continued to believe that the garrison on Manhattan was not in grave peril. Worried, Washington went to Fort Lee on November 12 to see Greene and to discuss the situation. But he did no more than talk about it. Greene believed he was unnecessarily concerned, and Washington in turn listened to him. The commander in chief did not order his subordinate to withdraw the garrison across the Hudson. Washington could not quite make up his mind, but continued to be anxious. He made a second visit to Fort Lee, and went with Greene and other Patriot officers to Fort Washington to inspect it. Then he learned that the British were moving to attack it. There was now nothing he could do but return to Fort Lee to wait for news of the result. The reports that he received were shattering.

As the Patriot commander in chief feared, William Howe had determined to take Fort Washington. Colonel Magaw had more than 3,000 men to defend it, but its works were unfinished. Howe knew that it was by no means impregnable. He had the opportunity to hit hard at the Patriots with very little risk of encountering a check. He began to move troops and artillery into position for assault during the night of November 14. The following day Magaw was summoned to surrender. He replied that he would fight to the "last extremity." On the morning of November 16, 8,000 British and Hessian soldiers advanced to the attack in four divisions, supported by artillery fire and also by cannonading from the frigate *Pearl,* stationed in the Hudson. Howe intended to make three assaults; the fourth division was merely to feign an attack. As it turned out, all four parts of the royal troops took part in the battle that followed. Magaw tried to defend the approaches to the fort. He did not have enough men to do it; on the other hand, the fort was too small to contain all of the garrison. The British and the Hessians had to climb rocks and penetrate through woods, and they suffered many casualtiees as they advanced. However, they drove forward in overwhelming force, penned Magaw's men within the unfinished fort, and compelled its surrender before the end of the day. The British and Hessians are reported to have had 78 killed and 374 wounded, the Americans only 59 slain and 96 injured. But the outcome was nothing less than disastrous for the Patriots. The British captured 2,607 American soldiers and 230 officers, together with all their weapons, large quantities of artillery, ammunition, tents, and other military equipment. The Americans had suffered a grievous blow.

It was quickly followed by another British stroke. With the detachment he had brought from North Castle, stationed at Hackensack, and the garrison at Fort Lee, Washington hoped momentarily to check the British if they tried to move into New Jersey. However, three days after the fall of Fort Washington, he reached the conclusion that he could not and ought not attempt to defend Fort Lee. Before the American commander could arrange for its evacuation, General Howe moved with unwonted speed to exploit his victory. On the night of November 19 he sent Lord Cornwallis with 4,000 men against Fort Lee. Cornwallis crossed the Hudson above the fort at dawn on the twentieth, and marched rapidly down the west bank of the river. Luckily for the Americans, Greene had put out patrols. One of them reported that Cornwallis was approaching. Given a little time, Greene hastily fled from the fort. Cornwallis pursued so swiftly that he took more than 100 prisoners, but Greene was able to join Washington with most of his garrison.

The Patriots were in distress. Their forces were dwindling and divided; their morale was lower than it had ever been before; the enlistments of some of Washington's troops would expire on December 1 and the rest could depart for home at the end of the year. Soon after General Howe turned westward from White Plains, Henry Clinton, assigned with a large detachment to an attack upon Rhode Island, had urged that he be sent instead up Chesapeake Bay toward Philadelphia, while General Howe pushed forward through New Jersey to the same city. The conquest of New England could be put off for a time, declared Clinton. Two thrusts against Philadelphia would have been difficult indeed for the Patriots to parry. However, an ally who was to be of the greatest help to them now came to their aid, winter. Admiral Howe insisted that it was necessary to take Newport, which offered the only harbor in the Northern Colonies suitable for his larger ships in cold weather. After the capture of Fort Lee, Clinton brought forward another scheme. He wished to lead his detachment, ready for embarkation, to Elizabeth or Amboy in New Jersey, to intercept Washington as he fled southward before Cornwallis. Again the Howes insisted that he proceed to Rhode Island. He did so, with four brigades of troops, at the beginning of December. He encountered very little opposition. Within a week Newport was safely in British hands. Clinton then hurried off to England, to see to it that his merits were recognized and rewarded in the imperial capital.

It was just as well for Washington and the Patriots that General Howe refused to send Clinton into New Jersey. For the Patriot general was unable even to check Cornwallis. Not yet thirty-eight years of age,

Cornwallis was young, vigorous, and bold. He pushed on from Fort Lee to Hackensack. Washington now had with him only 3,000 "much broken and dispirited" men. He fled to Newark, westward to New Brunswick. As he went, he called for aid. He urged Lee to come across the Hudson; he asked that New Jersey and Pennsylvania militia be sent to him. No help came immediately. At New Brunswick Cornwallis was hot upon Washington's heels. There the British pursuit briefly ceased, because Cornwallis had been ordered to stop at that place. Washington continued to retreat, to Princeton, then to Trenton. He collected all the boats on the Delaware River so that he could flee to the safety of its western banks. Joined at Trenton by Pennsylvania and Maryland militia, he turned about to face the British. They were advancing in overwhelming force. He fled once more, ferrying his army across the Delaware. As the last of his troops crossed the river, British troops appeared at Trenton, on December 8. They could not immediately follow, if for no other reason because they could find no boats to traverse the Delaware. The American army, such as it was, had survived.

For General Howe made no effort to cross the river. There was lumber available in and near Trenton with which to build boats. But Howe chose to go into winter quarters. He had, in fact, decided to put an end to hostilities for the year 1776 as early as December 3. That day he reported to Germain that he had done rather well. He had captured 4,101 Patriot soldiers during the campaign—the figure was low because it did not include hundreds of American officers he had taken. He had instructed Cornwallis to stop at New Brunswick because he intended that village to be his western outpost during the winter. Informed of Washington's weakness, Howe had resumed activity on December 6. Going to New Brunswick with troops from New York, he had personally directed the march of the British to the Delaware. But when he found that Washington had escaped beyond the river, the British general determined for the second time that he had done enough for 1776. The weather had been mild, but it might become harsh at any time. The Patriots were not to be despised. He wished to avoid a check at the Delaware. If he proceeded to Philadelphia without destroying his enemies, he would have a long and very vulnerable supply line across New Jersey from New York to Philadelphia, for the Americans controlled the Delaware River below their capital. He placed garrisons in western New Jersey in villages along that stream, and he returned to New York for the winter. He held New York, Long Island, and most of New Jersey.

Howe was not too pleased with his achievements, and Guy Carleton had even less reason to be happy. Carleton did not march into New

England; he did not reach the Hudson River; he did not even take Fort Ticonderoga. He was brought to a halt in a rather exotic way, not by American troops, but by American naval power.

Ordered by the Continental Congress in June 1776 to assume command of the army in Canada, General Horatio Gates went to his new appointment—and discovered that he had none. The remains of the Patriot forces that had served in Canada had retreated into New York, where General Philip Schuyler held sway. Joining Schuyler at Crown Point, Gates agreed to serve under him. There, on July 5, the two American commanders, with General Benedict Arnold and other Patriot officers, considered ways and means to check Carleton. Schuyler, on paper, had about 5,000 troops, but far fewer who were able to do duty. But he did possess some small armed ships on Lake Champlain. The Patriot generals decided to evacuate Crown Point, which was in ruinous condition; to concentrate their troops at Ticonderoga; to strengthen the "fleet" on Lake Champlain; and to entrust it to Benedict Arnold. The decision to withdraw from Crown Point was condemned by lesser officers and men under Schuyler. Retreat again? It was also censured by Washington, and by the Continental Congress. However, receiving reinforcements of militia who came forward as the menace posed by Carleton grew greater, Schuyler collected more than 6,000 men at Ticonderoga. Moreover, always a good supply officer, he brought up meat, flour, rum, clothing, and the thousand and one other things needed to feed and equip his men. He even managed eventually, despite vexing delays, to secure powder and shot for the many pieces of artillery that remained at Ticonderoga. He did all that could be done toward defending that place against Carleton. He could hardly have held it long against Carleton's greatly superior army, although he might very profitably have delayed the southward advance of the British general.

But the American army at Ticonderoga was not forced to fight in the summer or fall of 1776. Carleton could not move forward on Lake Champlain until he had cleansed it of "Admiral" Benedict Arnold's war craft. Carleton was therefore constrained to construct a fleet at the northern end of the lake to deal with Arnold. He began to do it. But Arnold and General David Waterbury brought in woodsmen, carpenters, and other artisans from near and far, who cut down trees and made new vessels to add to the Patriot flotilla. Carleton was thus forced to engage in a building race. He was able to dismantle three large vessels on the St. Lawrence, to transport them to the lake, and put them together again. He had the services of experienced workmen, and he won the contest. However, his squadron was not ready to sail southward from St. John's until

October 4. It was easily superior to the Patriot squadron, commanded by Arnold, in firepower, and Arnold's experience in naval warfare was confined to trading voyages between Connecticut and the West Indies. Carleton's fleet was manned by veteran seamen, that of the Americans mostly by landlubbers. Arnold did not even have skilled artillerists to discharge his guns. Nevertheless, with that cold courage which he always displayed, Arnold did not refuse battle. He had posted his nondescript fleet of two schooners, two sloops, and several row-galleys and gondolas near Valcour Island. He knew that he was outmatched—Carleton's fleet carried nearly twice as many guns. Nonetheless, when the British ships approached his position, on October 11, Arnold went out to fight. The shooting had hardly begun when one of his largest vessels went aground and was lost. But he carried on the unequal struggle throughout that day. By nightfall the Patriot flotilla was in a bad way. The British had not even used some of their ships. The Americans were almost out of ammunition, and their avenue of retreat southward was largely closed by the vessels of the victorious British. It seemed that Arnold could not avoid surrender. Instead, taking advantage of darkness and fog, he slipped past his enemies that night and fled. Carleton pursued, on October 12. He sank more than one Patriot vessel, and he captured others. Rowing and sailing, Arnold and the remnants of the Patriot squadron retreated to the eastern shore of the lake. There Arnold destroyed several of his craft rather than let them fall into the hands of his enemies. Only five of the sixteen vessels with which the Patriots began the struggle escaped destruction or capture.

Arnold lost the battle, and Carleton gained mastery of Lake Champlain. Nevertheless, Carleton had been held back for many long weeks, more by Patriots wielding axes and saws than discharging guns. His army, far superior to the forces collected by Schuyler at Ticonderoga, was compelled to wait for transport across Lake Champlain through July, August, September, and part of October. And it was too late, after the battle of Valcour Island, for the royal troops to move southward. Or so Carleton believed. He might have driven the Patriots from Ticonderoga before the onset of winter, but he could not expect to reach safe and comfortable quarters in southern New York or southern New England before cold and snow intervened. His army obviously could not spend the winter in northern New York at the end of a long and tenuous supply line from Canada. Was it worthwhile to proceed against Ticonderoga? He decided that the profit to be derived from an immediate attack upon the Patriots was too small to risk a check at that place. He withdrew his flotilla and his army to Fort St. John's. He would resume his advance in the following spring. It was fortunate for the Patriots that he chose to be sensible. The winter turned out to be an unusually mild one, and Carleton could very likely have moved down the Hudson.

Carleton did not need to worry about a Patriot counterthrust. He was not molested as he withdrew. And Howe might easily have placed his troops so that Washington would not have been able seriously to interrupt the repose of the main British army. However, pursuing the Americans to the Delaware, Howe became too confident. Patriot civilians were dejected. General John Cadwalader, an officer who rendered most faithful service under Washington, related that he himself was induced to complain "by the d-----d gloomy countenances seen wherever I go except among the soldiers." Hundreds of men in New Jersey abjured the American cause, sought and received pardon from the Howes, and took a special and solemn oath of loyalty to George III. The British general decided that, "the operations of this year being closed," he could safely maintain outposts on the Delaware during the winter, with New Brunswick serving as a base between them and New York. He told Lord George Germain that his "chain" of garrisons between New York and the Delaware was "rather too extensive," but he believed that none of his posts was seriously exposed to attack. He announced to his army on December 14 that it was to go into quarters. He placed large detachments at Trenton and Bordentown. Moreover, too confident and too much concerned for military honor, he put Hessian rather than British troops in those villages. Hessian officers claimed that they would be disgraced if the places of greatest danger were not entrusted to them. In consequence, the two garrisons were not composed of the most reliable troops in Howe's army. The Hessians no more feared Washington than did Howe. Colonel Johann Räll with 1,500 Germans was stationed at Trenton, Colonel Count Karl von Donop with about 2,000 Hessians at Bordentown.

Beyond the Delaware Washington seemed to be in desperate straits in mid-December. The Continental Congress, alarmed lest the British appear in Philadelphia, fled to Baltimore. Washington himself expected Howe to try to force his way across the Delaware. There were men, including officers, with Washington who had lost heart, who had lost faith in their general. But the American commander did not sink into despair. He now displayed that indomitable courage that ultimately brought to him the utter trust of his countrymen. He began to meditate upon a counterthrust against the royal army. Nor was his situation quite so alarming as it appeared to be. Many of the troops still with him were scheduled to depart for home at the end of the year, but others were joining him. His appeals for help were bearing fruit. Militia came up from Pennsylvania. A detachment of 1,200 men no longer needed to oppose

Carleton marched southward from Albany to join him. Moreover, the remains of the troops that had been left at North Castle under General Charles Lee came to his aid. After the capture of Fort Washington, Washington urged Lee to make his way across the Hudson. Lee moved slowly, in part because his men lacked shoes. Even after he had passed the Hudson, Lee loitered. Marching through the hills of northern New Jersey, he saw an opportunity to strike against Howe's line of communications, and so to bring Howe's advance toward the Delaware to a halt. His tactics were sound enough, but he ignored repeated requests from Washington to hasten into Pennsylvania. On December 13 Lee's army, reduced to 2,700 men, began to move westward from Morristown. That morning, Lee, having carelessly spent the night in a house at a distance from his troops, was captured by a party of British cavalry. John Sullivan then led Lee's army as swiftly as possible across the Delaware. By December 20 Washington had 6,000 men with him, and more were en route to his headquarters.

If Washington was to do anything, he must do it before the end of 1776, before his army again began to melt away. He had plenty of boats large enough to carry both men and small cannon. He had Colonel John Glover and his fishermen-soldiers to man the boats. He devised a plan for simultaneous attacks upon Trenton and Bordentown, with three Patriot contingents moving across the Delaware on Christmas night. He hoped to surprise the Hessians. He was able to execute only part of his scheme. Washington undertook personally to lead 2,400 men across the river above Trenton and to approach it from the east and southeast. General James Ewing, with Pennsylvania and New Jersey militia, was to go over the river below that place, and to prevent Räll from fleeing southward. He was also to try to hold back Count von Donop in the event that the German nobleman sought to go to the aid of Räll. Meanwhile, Colonel John Cadwalader, with Continentals and Pennsylvania militia, was to advance by way of Bristol and to occupy von Donop at Bordentown. Further, if Trenton fell, all the American forces, joined by still a fourth body advancing from Philadelphia, were to converge upon and destroy von Donop's garrison.

Washington's scheme was well contrived. With good fortune he might have destroyed both Hessian garrisons before help could come to them from New Brunswick. It was, however, executed only in part. Ewing found it impossible to get over the river, and Cadwalader did not cross it until late on December 26, so that he was unable to surprise von Donop. However, the approach of the militia from Philadelphia was discovered by von Donop and he moved southward to face them. Before he could retrace his steps and hurry to Trenton, that village was in American hands. It is no secret that Washington himself, with his contingent, made his way over the Delaware, through ice floes and in biting cold, during the night of December 25. He was conveyed across the river by his veterans from Marblehead; his troops were Continentals steeled by fighting and hardships. He and his men, landing above Trenton, marched as swiftly as they could toward that village. Räll was completely surprised at dawn. Confident in his own strength and in the weakness of the Patriots, he had not even bothered to build entrenchments. The Patriots were moving into the village in two columns before Räll was roused from his bed. He tried, too late, to form his men and to resist. After brief fighting, one third of the garrison managed to elude the Patriots and to flee toward Bordentown. Räll himself, mortally wounded, was captured with 1,000 of his men. Washington's losses were trifling. Moreover, the capture of Trenton persuaded von Donop to retreat. Informed of it by fleeing Hessians, he thought it prudent to take the remainder of the German troops eastward and out of Washington's reach.

Having gained such a brilliant triumph, Washington ought doubtless to have returned to the west bank of the Delaware, out of reach of the British, for they would almost certainly strike back in great force. He hesitated. Should he gather his troops on the eastern side of the river and seek further triumphs, or retreat? He cautiously returned to Pennsylvania. Then, becoming bold, he again crossed the Delaware, on December 30 and 31, and gathered about 5,000 men at Trenton. It may be said that he was rash, for the British had indeed decided that the campaign was not yet ended. The news of the fall of Trenton goaded Howe to action. Lord Cornwallis hastened from New York, thence to Brunswick, thence to Trenton, gathering troops as he went. On January 2 he approached the village with 6,000 troops. More were coming on behind Cornwallis. Withdrawing behind Assanpink Creek, Washington was suddenly in great danger. It was not likely that he could withstand British attacks. Nor could he hope to flee across the Delaware or along its eastern banks without suffering heavy losses. Cornwallis almost immediately opened hostilities. However, since darkness was near at hand, he decided to wait until morning before assailing the Patriots in great force. He did not take advantage of a magnificent opportunity. He ought to have expected the unexpected from a man who had marched through the night to take Trenton. But Cornwallis did not take special precautions to make sure that Washington did not flee during the night. After dark Washington and his generals considered their dangerous situation. What to do? They were told that there was a road by which the army could march off to the southward and thence eastward, around Cornwallis's position. In near-desperation the Patriot general, leaving campfires burning to persuade the British that their prey awaited destruction, marched his men quietly during the night around Cornwallis's army. When morning came, Cornwallis learned what had happened. He heard gunfire, from Princeton, behind him.

Washington not only escaped Cornwallis's clutches, but gained another victory, at Princeton, and forced withdrawal of the British from western New Jersey. At Princeton his army was confronted by three regiments of redcoats moving forward to join the British general. Greatly outnumbered, the redcoats offered stiff resistance. A bayonet charge threatened to crush the American vanguard. Cornwallis was pursuing as rapidly as possible. The Virginian rode forward among his men, rallied them under British fire, and routed the redcoats. Then he marched on to the east. Momentarily he considered an attack upon the British base at New Brunswick, but his men were exhausted. He had achieved enough, and it was now possible for him to take post in the hills at Morristown, where he would be relatively secure against British attack. He turned northward, and found safety in the hills. Howe decided that the British, because of cold and snow, could not molest the Patriots. Moreover, since Washington's army threatened the line of communications between New York and Trenton, he withdrew his troops into eastern New Jersey. Discovering that he occupied an excellent position, Washington remained at Morristown until the spring of 1777.

The American cause had survived the offensives of Carleton and Howe. The morale of the Patriots, severely shaken before Christmas of 1776, was restored. The British had sustained that severe check that Howe and Clinton had so earnestly sought to avert. Washington's victory at Trenton ended a long chain of British triumphs. The Patriot general reaped every possible reward from his brilliant attack upon the Hessians. Trenton was a great turning point in the war. It shook Howe and Lord George Germain. It enabled the Americans to look forward to the spring of 1777 with a steadier confidence. Joining the army as it fled from Fort Lee, Tom Paine had called upon his fellow Patriots in an essay entitled "The Crisis" to rally. "These are the times that try men's souls. The summer soldier and the sunshine patriot will, in this crisis, shrink from the service of their country; but he that stands it *now,* deserves the love and thanks of man and woman." The Patriots had refused to collapse. They would not again suffer from panic as they had in the autumn and early winter of 1776.

CHAPTER XIX

The Fall of Philadelphia

EVEN before Trenton William Howe had begun to consider what he ought to do in the campaign of 1777. He sent a plan of operations from New York to London. Then he put a second one in the mail for the imperial capital, then a third. General John Burgoyne hastened to London from Canada as soon as the British army in that colony went into winter quarters. There he offered his notions for 1777. They included a major role for Burgoyne. Henry Clinton arrived in London from Rhode Island. He desired recognition for his services, and an appointment that would give him an opportunity to display his genius. Lord George Germain, his colleagues, and George III considered. They gave Burgoyne the command of an army in Canada, instructing him to lead it to Albany and to put it at the disposal of Howe. They also endorsed a march into Pennsylvania by Howe with the bulk of his army. The conquest of New England was postponed. Howe did take Philadelphia. However, his triumph was an empty one. The American armies revived in the spring and summer of 1777. One of them dealt harshly with Burgoyne. Another, under Washington, though forced to abandon Philadelphia, continued to offer vigorous challenge to Howe until he went into winter quarters in the city of Brotherly Love.

Had the Patriots raised all the troops called for by the Continental Congress, Howe would hardly have dared to resume the offensive. For that body asked the states, in September 1776, to supply eighty-eight battalions of Continentals to serve for three years or the duration of the war. Moreover, on December 27 it gave Washington authority to enlist sixteen more battalions, together with 3,000 cavalrymen, three regiments of artillerymen, and a corps of engineers. The Congress desired to put about 75,000 men in Continental service. So many could neither be obtained, nor sustained.

In fact, before the battle of Trenton, Washington grimly wondered whether even a small part of the huge force contemplated by his superiors would ever appear at his camp. If fresh and numerous troops failed to join him, he warned, it would be useless to try to keep the field against the British. Nor, although Washington's victories at Trenton and Princeton lifted Patriot spirits, did many recruits come to Morristown during the early weeks of 1777. Congress offered, to every man who enlisted, a bounty of $20.00 and 100 acres of land at the end of his period of service. However, some of the states bid higher for men who would do duty only in the vicinity of their own homes. Besides, men were not eager to undergo hardships and dangers of winter quarters, where, they could believe, they were not needed. One thousand men who had taken part in the fighting of 1776 under Washington promptly re-enlisted, but his army dwindled away in the early weeks of 1777 at Morristown. Cold, occasional shortages of food, and an outbreak of smallpox assailed it. Fearing that Howe would take advantage of his weakness, the Patriot general had to call upon militia for short periods of service to present a semblance of strength. Fortunately, the winter weather that made the Patriots uncomfortable at Morristown also persuaded Howe that it would be unwise to execute a plan he had devised for an attack upon that place. The British and Hessians, too, shivered in New York. At New Brunswick royal troops, housed in cramped and chilly quarters, more than once received news that supplies of meat intended for them had been seized by Patriot foraging parties. Unmolested by the British, Washington's army sprang to new and vigorous life in the spring of 1777. By the end of May the Patriot general had no fewer than 9,000 Continentals with him at Morristown, and more were preparing to take the field. Before the end of the year about 34,000 men were enrolled in the Continental forces. They were supported by many thousands of militia.

The new Continental soldiers were not without experience or weapons. There was among them more than a sprinkling of men who had fought in 1775 and 1776. Henceforth Washington and other Patriot commanders would not lack reliable and hardened veterans. It is also true that the regiments of militia who served with them were steadier and more useful than the militia of the past, for they too had acquired some acquaintance with warfare and a measure of confidence—even though those troops never became truly reliable. Moreover, the Patriots, especially the Continentals, were much better equipped than they had earlier been. In 1775 and 1776 the Americans had imported military paraphernalia, especially gunpowder, from the European Continent and the West Indian possessions of France, Spain, and Holland; they had built "navies" and privateers that seized British transports carrying supplies; and they had begun to make gunpowder, bullets, cannon shot, and rough clothing. Even so, the Patriot forces had often suffered from shortages of ammunition, of uniforms, and of footgear as well as of food. During the retreat across New Jersey, as described, part of Washington's dwindling army had neither tents nor blankets for shelter against the cold; meanwhile, at North Castle, Charles Lee's men were unable to move to Washington's assistance for some days because they lacked shoes. Deficiencies were never permanently or entirely remedied. The Patriots did not possess that extraordinary ability to manufacture afterward manifested by their descendants. Moreover, the supply officers of the Continental army were usually unskilled in their duties and inefficient. However, in March 1777, "secret" aid began to reach the Patriots from Spain, and especially from France.

The ministers of young King Louis XVI of France had watched with pleasure the outbreak of the Anglo-American war, and they had seen an opportunity to gain revenge for the losses and indignities suffered by the Bourbons in the Seven Years' War, even to strike mortal blows against the British empire. The French foreign minister, the Comte de Vergennes, urged that France immediately put her revived fleets and armies in motion. Other advisers of the King at Versailles would not give their consent to such swift and forthright action. However, they were willing to do everything possible, short of waging war, to injure Britain. Accordingly, without even waiting for an official request for help from the Patriots, Vergennes arranged to give them powerful and theoretically clandestine assistance. His trusted agent, Caron de Beaumarchais, who was an adventurer extraordinary as well as a brilliant dramatist, established at Paris in 1776 the merchant firm of Roderique Hortalez and Company, solely to serve as a channel through which military necessities would flow to the Patriots. The company, nourished by gifts and loans from the French Crown and also by a present from Madrid, speedily began its work. Thus it was that two French merchant vessels unloaded thousands of muskets, scores of cannon, tents, blankets, uniforms, and other military gear in New Hampshire before fighting was resumed in 1777; and those ships were followed by others. During the remainder of the war the Continentals commonly carried muskets made in France; and they fired cannon from French arsenals, cannon sometimes stamped with the Bourbon fleur-de-lis.

The Patriot forces were thus much stronger in 1777 than they were in 1776. They needed all their power, for they were confronted by thrusts from Canada as well as an advance by General Howe against Philadelphia. Fortunately for them, the British failed to make the best use of the redcoats and their Hessian and Indian contingents. Indeed, the British committed a remarkable error in strategy that ultimately cost them an army. The divided command in North America encouraged them to make a mistake, and they did not fail to seize their opportunity. Too confident, too careless, too much separated by space and time, William Howe, John Burgoyne, Lord George Germain, and others made and executed plans for 1777 that brought disaster to Britain.

William Howe was certainly culpable. On November 30, 1776, at the time when Washington was in full flight in New Jersey, Howe wrote to Germain to recommend a plan of action for the next year. He reported that he had fewer than 20,000 men fit for service. He asked for 15,000 more troops, suggesting that they be procured from German rulers or Catherine the Great. With 35,000 men he would return to the strategy of 1776, would devote his army principally to the conquest of New England. He would post 8,000 men in New Jersey to hold off Washington; 5,000 as a garrison in New York; and 2,000 in Newport; he would send 10,000 up the Hudson River to meet at Albany the army that would advance from Canada, which he expected to reach that town in September; and he would put another 10,000 in motion from Newport against Boston. He then believed that the subjugation of the Yankees would quickly lead to the collapse of Patriot resistance, that British troops would be able to march even into the southernmost colonies in 1778.

That such strategy would have ensured the final defeat of the Patriots must remain doubtful. Nevertheless, concentration of effort against the Yankees offered promise of achievement. Moreover, Howe's plan was prudent in that it provided substantially for the safety of the army moving southward from Canada. Were its advance coupled with a northward thrust by Howe, the Patriots would have been hard pressed. It is not likely that they could have prevented a junction of the British forces at Albany. Accordingly, one must believe that Howe had devised a sound scheme for the year 1777. Moreover, he had enough strength to execute it, basically. For his report that he had fewer than 20,000 men was misleading. He had not lost 15,000 men since the landing on Long Island. By counting only private soldiers of his infantry and cavalry present and fit for duty—omitting sergeants, drummers, officers, and sick—he was trying to make it appear that his army was much weaker than it actually was. He was preparing an excuse for himself, in the event that he failed to accomplish much in 1777. He knew that Britain could not send him 15,000 more soldiers. He was doing what he could do to place blame upon his superiors, especially Germain, in the event that the British forces achieved little in the campaigns of 1777.

Having drafted a suitable design for the approaching year, Sir William—Howe was knighted for the victory he had won on Long Island—then swiftly proposed another which contained the seed of disaster. On December 20, after New Jersey had fallen so easily into British hands, that general's attention was directed toward Philadelphia. Dozens of Jerseymen had forsworn their Patriot faith and had solemnly renewed their allegiance to the Crown. Prominent Pennsylvanians were also joining the British, among them three members of the wealthy Allen family of Philadelphia and Joseph Galloway, so conspicuous in the First Continental Congress. Gazing across the Delaware, Howe suggested in a letter to Germain that his energies should be principally devoted in the early part of 1777 to the capture of the Quaker city. He believed that its Tories were strong enough to hold it, if he drove away Washington's army, if he provided the Loyalists with arms. He would defer "the offensive plan towards Boston . . . until the proposed reinforcements arrive from Europe." Howe was in an optimistic mood. Was he deceived by reports from the Pennsylvanians who had deserted from the Patriots? He proposed to lead 10,000 men across the Delaware; he would leave 4,000 soldiers in New York and 2,000 in Rhode Island for the defense of his bases; and he would place 3,000 men "to act defensively upon the lower part of Hudson's River to cover Jersey on that side," as well as to "facilitate in some degree the approach of the army from Canada."

Howe had not yet determined what he ought to do. He asked Germain for orders. The general was suggesting a design that he could probably execute with the troops he had—many more than he claimed to have, as he later admitted. If the Patriot forces were as weak and discouraged as they appeared to be, his second plan was not a bad one. But if the American forces revived, it was reckless. The British would profit little from the conqest of Philadelphia if the army moving southward from Canada was driven back. The loss of that army would be nothing less than disastrous, a fact of which Howe, anxiously seeking to avoid even a momentary check of his own force, was well aware. And it was evident that the army from Canada, if unsupported, must encounter difficulties under the best of circumstances. Howe assumed that it would not reach Albany before September. He knew that it must move through a rough and heavily wooded wilderness along wagon tracks and across unbridged streams. He knew that the British, striving to reach Montreal from the

288

south during the Seven Years' War, had been checked by inferior forces under the Marquis de Montcalm during several campaigns. He knew that Montgomery had found it most difficult to advance against Montreal in 1775, even though Carleton was then able to offer only weak resistance. In his second plan, promising little and late help to the British moving forward from St. John's, Howe did not properly provide for their safety. He would move southwestward from New York with the main body of his troops at the very time that the Canadian army would march toward that city. He proposed substantially to let that army advance without assurance of support. He was not taking into account a possible revival of Patriot power. He was too optimistic, and he was careless, in part no doubt, because that army was not under his command and would not be until it reached Albany.

Howe again demonstrated his lack of concern for realities and his eagerness to avoid responsibility on January 20, 1777. That day, in a "private" letter to Germain, he said that he would move against both Philadelphia and Boston—if the colonial secretary would send him 20,000 more troops. Howe could not have believed that Britain would be able to gather and to transport so many soldiers across the Atlantic in time to help him in the year 1777.

It is apparent that William Howe had not acquired foresight with his knighthood. Nor had Lord George Germain become broad-minded or wise. As early as August 1776—at a time when Guy Carleton seemed to have achieved all that could be expected of him—Germain decided to deprive that general of opportunity to win glory. He sent out to Canada a letter instructing Carleton to give the command of the army that was moving southward to John Burgoyne or some other suitable person. That decision could be defended on the ground that the junction of the two commanders in chief would cause trouble. Howe was not at all eager to serve under Carleton. But Germain speciously asserted that Carleton was needed at Quebec, that Carleton could not legally leave Canada. For what things of great importance? And why should any legal technicality be permitted to prevent Carleton from leaving Canada? The bearer of the letter was unable to deliver it because the ship which carried him could not break through ice in the Gulf of St. Lawrence. However, Germain was determined to strike at Carleton, and saw to it that the general received orders in the spring of 1777 to remain at Quebec. Precisely why the colonial secretary was so hostile to Carleton is not known. The two men were quarreling over patronage. Carleton wished to give an office in Canada to his younger brother, Germain desired to present it to one of his own favorites. But that small affair does not explain why Germain was hostile to Carleton. The general did harbor a grievance against Germain, who undoubtedly had played a large part in the making of the decisions of 1775 and 1776 which denied the office of commander in chief in North America to Carleton and also gave him a less important post than the one tendered to William Howe. Carleton was further offended because he was not authorized, with the Howe brothers, to negotiate with the Americans after they were defeated. Each of them, as a peace commissioner, received £5,000 per annum. Germain certainly had made no effort to please or to placate him. It is clear enough that Carleton had reasons for detesting the colonial secretary. His dislike was fully reciprocated, if only because human beings find faults in those they have injured. Let it be remembered that George III, although he permitted Germain to deprive Carleton of a chance to gain military renown, insisted upon recognition of the general's merits. Against the wishes of Germain, the King personally saw to it that Carleton received a knighthood as solace for the wounds inflicted upon him.

It was determined in London before Germain gave his opinion upon Howe's two plans, that John Burgoyne was to lead a British army from St. John's to Albany. Returning to the imperial capital from Canada, Burgoyne had eagerly solicited the appointment and had secured it. Then he lost it. Henry Clinton also turned up in London. He was unhappy because part of the blame for the British defeat at Sullivan's Island had been placed upon his shoulders. Clinton was never able to believe that his abilities and performances were properly rewarded. He wanted official recognition of his merits, and an opportunity to gain glory for himself. He was given a knighthood, presumably as a reward for his services in the battle of Long Island, but also to indicate that his superiors did not blame him for the British defeat at Sullivan's Island. Momentarily, it was also decided in London to place Clinton at the head of the army that would advance from St. John's. However, he finally and reluctantly agreed, instead, to accept a command under Howe in New York City. Assured that he would have his chance to gain fame, Burgoyne submitted his thoughts for the approaching campaign, in February 1777. He proposed to march from St. John's to Albany. Meanwhile, a smaller auxiliary contingent was to push eastward from Oswego and down the Mohawk River valley to the same place. At Albany Burgoyne was to place himself and both forces at the disposal of Howe. Burgoyne's plan was approved by King and cabinet. A cautious suggestion that the troops not needed for the defense of Canada be sent to New York by sea was set aside. Burgoyne, admitting that it would not be easy to force his way to Albany, was nevertheless sure that he would reach it. His masters shared his confidence, and their faith was not shaken by news of Washington's victories at Trenton and Princeton. Germain was so little concerned for the safety of Burgoyne's army that he failed to instruct Howe to act in such fashion that he would be able to rescue Burgoyne, in the event that the army from Canada encountered superior Patriot forces in the forests of northern New York.

Germain considered Howe's first plan in January 1777. He was then praising Howe for his achievements, and he expected the early collapse of the rebellion in America. He believed that the Patriots would not be able to recruit a new Continental army. He was somewhat upset when he observed that Howe claimed to have fewer than 20,000 men available for action in 1777. Writing to Howe, he correctly asserted that the general's claim was misleading. If he sent Howe 7,800 men, declared Germain, the general would have nearly 35,000 soldiers, counting only the rank and file. According to Germain's calculation, Howe still had with him about 27,000 troops, plus officers and others omitted in returns from the general. Even Germain's estimate was somewhat too low. Germain would not endorse Howe's first plan. He could not possibly raise 15,000 men to send across the ocean. Enthusiasm for the war had not risen in Britain, and the possible foreign sources of manpower had already been tapped. He did not insist, as he might well have done, that Howe already had enough men, with the help of the army from Canada, to conquer New England.

Germain was at least momentarily shaken by the news of the reversals encountered by the British at the end of the campaign of 1776. "The disagreeable occurrence at Trenton," he wrote to Howe on March 3, 1777, "is, I must own, extremely mortifying." He was disconcerted by "this unfortunate event." He informed the general that he would be able to send only 2,900 additional troops to New York—1,200 of whom reached that place in June, 1,700 in September. Nevertheless, Germain also carelessly gave his consent to Howe's second plan, that of December 20, conceived before the "unfortunate event" at Trenton. Why did he not insist that all of the available British forces in North America be concentrated against New England? That strategy, sound in 1776, had not lost its merits. It was obviously safer to use the two British armies there in one operation. Indeed, with New York City and the lower stretches of the Hudson firmly under British control, invasion of New England could be undertaken at relatively little risk. Moreover, the conquest of the Yankee country would bring rich reward. Were that stronghold of the Patriots subjugated, with the navigable reaches of the Hudson under British domination, the British would then be free to undertake further ventures. To be sure, the Yankees would offer strenuous resistance. Of course, Washington would do all that he could to assist them. Success was not at all certain.

However, it should have been evident to Germain as well as Howe that an advance by Howe against Philadelphia while Burgoyne made his way southward to Albany entailed greater hazards and promised much less reward—unless the Patriots were so weak that they could stand neither against Howe nor Burgoyne. The rout of the Hessians at Trenton, together with the well-known difficulties that would confront Burgoyne, should have been enough to alarm him. He could take no comfort from the fact that Howe vaguely proposed to put 3,000 men on the lower Hudson to "facilitate in some degree the approach of the army from Canada." And the expenditure of great effort and hazards in a march against Philadelphia—was there promise of commensurate returns? It would be pleasant, but not very profitable, to drive the Continental Congress from its lair. More serious, if the Patriot army was driven away from Philadelphia, would the Loyalists within the city be strong enough to hold it while Howe proceeded to other business? It had earlier been believed that the colony of New York contained many Loyalists, but they had certainly not joined the British in sufficient numbers to garrison New York City. Was there reason to believe that the Tories were stronger in Pennsylvania than they were in New York? Were not many of them members of the Society of Friends, prevented by conscience from taking up arms? Germain seems not to have recognized the shortcomings and dangers in Howe's second plan. He did not learn from experience at Trenton; he continued to be fundamentally optimistic; he accepted Howe's argument that an advance by land against Philadelphia was quite proper. He is hardly to be excused on the ground that he merely accepted the thinking of Howe, who presumably knew what he was doing.

It turned out that Howe conceived still a third plan that contained even less merit than his second one—and executed it. Before he learned that Germain had endorsed his scheme to move against Philadelphia by land, he decided to proceed against the rebel capital by way of Chesapeake Bay. Why he decided to approach Philadelphia from the sea and from the south is not entirely clear. Probably he was not eager to force his way across the Delaware River, where Washington would very likely bar his way. Moreover, he entertained hope that he might be able to cut the colonies in two at the Susquehanna River and push Washington, who would certainly try to defend Philadelphia, to the northward. The Patriot general, unable to flee southward, might be confined and destroyed somewhere between the Susquehanna and Hudson Rivers. General

The NEW JERSEY - PENNSYLVANIA THEATER

PENNSYLVANIA

NEW YORK

HUDSON R.

Morristown

Basking Ridge

New York

RARITAN R.

DELAWARE R.

SANDY HOOK

(New) Brunswick

SCHUYLKILL R.

Princeton

Trenton

Monmouth Courthouse

ASSANPINK CREEK

Whitemarsh

Valley Forge

Germantown

Bordentown

Paoli

Burlington

BRANDYWINE CREEK

Philadelphia

DELAWARE R.

Chad's Ford

NEW JERSEY

Wilmington

ATLANTIC OCEAN

CHESAPEAKE BAY

DELAWARE

MARYLAND

DELAWARE BAY

N

0   Miles   30

Charles Lee, as a prisoner of the British in New York City, had offered advice to his enemies, and had urged Howe to adopt such a strategy. Was Lee trying to prove his military ability to the British? Was he attempting to help them? Or did he seek, as he afterward said, to persuade Howe to do that which was least dangerous to the Patriots? The chances are that Lee did not intend to assist the British and that he exerted little or no influence upon Howe. Whatever was Lee's purpose, Howe did not expect to trap Washington—who merely withdrew westward when the British general captured Philadelphia.

On April 2, in a dispatch to Germain, Sir William described his third plan. He declared that he had 18,100 troops, not counting artillerymen, cavalrymen, or sick. It is apparent that he also omitted his sergeants and his commissioned officers, together with 3,000 Tories who had joined him, from this calculation—he continued to describe his army in such fashion that it might appear to be much less numerous than it actually was. He asserted that, without powerful reinforcements, the war could not be won in 1777. He now proposed to lead 11,000 troops against Phila-delphia by sea; to leave 4,700 men in New York City and its vicinity for the defense of the principal British base; to maintain another 2,400 in Rhode Island; and to place 3,000 Tories under the command of General William Tyron with orders to operate "upon the Hudsons River, or to enter Connecticut as circumstances may point out." It is clear enough that this scheme—even though Howe was able to muster many more men for these various assignments than he would freely admit—had even less merit than his second plan, for it would increase the geographical gap between the main body of Howe's army and the forces moving from Canada toward Albany. Howe might think that he had made no great change, that he had merely substituted one approach to Philadelphia for another. But he had virtually abandoned all chance of assisting Burgoyne, if that general ran into trouble, as events would prove.

Howe committed still another error. He did not flatly inform Burgoyne that the army advancing from St. John's must provide for its own safety. He did send a letter dated April 5 by sea to Carleton, which described his design. Carleton received it, and conveyed it to Burgoyne. In that message Howe said he could do little "to facilitate" the march of the army moving from Canada. But he also declared that he would place a corps on the "lower part of Hudson's river, sufficient to open the communication for shipping through the Highlands," a corps which might "afterwards act in favour" of the army advancing southward from Canada. He thus offered to Burgoyne a slender hint of possible help which he did not expect to extend.

294

In behalf of Howe, it must be pointed out that he did later consider the possibility that Washington would move against New York City or Burgoyne's army while he himself was en route to Pennsylvania. In July, before he embarked upon that adventure, he decided to leave a stronger garrison in New York City with Clinton than he had earlier planned. If Washington marched northward to attack Burgoyne, Howe believed that Burgoyne could defend himself. Moreover, if Washington took post on the Hudson in an attempt to bar Burgoyne's advance, Howe then intended to march to Burgoyne's rescue and to trap Washington between the two British armies. He also then thought of sailing up the Delaware River, so that he could follow Washington, in case of need. But it became apparent that Washington would seek to defend Philadelphia, and Howe, in the end, carried out his plan of April 2. He did not provide for the possibility that Burgoyne would encounter a strong American army on the Hudson while he himself faced another under Washington near Philadelphia.

It must also be remarked that Howe's third scheme, like his second one, was endorsed by Germain. A dispatch from the colonial secretary of May 18 not only gave his sanction, but asserted that "his Majesty entirely approves of your letter [of April 5] to Sir Guy Carleton." It is apparent, however, that Germain was somewhat concerned for the safety of Burgoyne's army. He expressed an ill-founded hope that Howe would complete his business in Pennsylvania "in time for you to co-operate with the army ordered to proceed from Canada, and put itself under your command." Certainly he should not have assumed that Howe could use the main body of his army in both Pennsylvania and New York. Whatever Germain thought, his dispatch reached Howe too late to have any effect. For a reason or reasons unknown, he did not receive it until August 16. Howe was then in Chesapeake Bay, en route to Philadelphia, and he was committed to his third plan. He informed Germain that he could not alter it. He had learned that Maryland and Pennsylvania were firmly dominated by the Patriots. Germain had not sent him sufficient reinforcements, and the general would have his hands full in Pennsylvania. The suggestion from Germain that he work together with Burgoyne after he had completed his tasks in Pennsylvania worried him. He would not finish them in time to transfer troops northward to the assistance of Burgoyne. He would not accept responsibility, in effect, for the safety of Burgoyne's army.

Germain was not the only person who felt qualms caused by Howe's intended advance against Philadelphia by sea. There were officers with Howe at New York who were satisfied with the general's scheme, among them his brother, Lord Cornwallis, and General James Grant—Cornwallis and Grant were personal friends of the commander in chief. But Sir Henry Clinton, unhappy with the secondary role assigned to him, sharply condemned Howe's plan and urged concentration instead against New England. Once again Howe declined to accept good advice from his troublesome subordinate.

Nor did anything happen after the first days of April to dissuade Howe from taking his ocean voyage. Many weeks were needed to assemble transports and supplies, and the general therefore had time to do some maneuvering and fighting before he sailed southward. Had he been able to strike severely at Washington's army, the situation might have been much altered. And Washington offered Howe an opportunity, of sorts. Toward the end of May, Washington led forth his revived army from Morristown and entrenched it at Middlebrook. The Patriot commander expected the British to advance by land toward the Delaware and Philadelphia, and intended to try to check their march. Howe immediately collected troops and went forth to engage Washington, attempting to induce him to commit his army to battle under conditions most unfavorable to the Patriots. The American general prudently refused to fight upon unequal terms. Howe then set a trap for Washington. If he could only persuade the Patriots to engage in such fashion and under such circumstances that they could not easily flee—Howe pretended to retreat toward New York. Washington was nearly snared. He left his prepared position, and followed the British into open country. Then Howe suddenly struck at the left flank of the Patriots. But Washington was alert. He swiftly and safely withdrew to Middlebrook. Washington declined to save Howe from himself.

Week after week of good weather for campaigning passed before Howe at last set forth from New York Harbor. Many scores of ships were needed to carry his army. On June 6 Howe declared that the war would not end in 1777, but that he expected to "strike deep" toward bringing it to a conclusion in 1778. On July 5, in a letter to Germain, he reported that "The embarkation of the troops is proceeding with the utmost dispatch." At last, on July 23, a British armada of more than 250 vessels, including warships under the command of Admiral Howe, set sail. Aboard the transports were about 19,000 troops. Six days later the huge fleet reached Delaware Bay. But it did not proceed up the Delaware River. Informed that the Americans had built forts to bar their passage up that stream, the Howes decided to proceed instead to Chesapeake Bay— even though it would eventually be necessary to clear the Delaware for a supply route to a British army established in Philadelphia. The brothers moved on slowly. The armada was plagued by storms and summer heat, and it was necessary to throw overboard many horses brought along for a contingent of cavalry and for transport that had died in confinement. The army did not begin to disembark at the northern end of Chesapeake Bay until August 25. The royal soldiers, all of them penned in the transports for a month, some of them for as much as six weeks, were white and weakened by the long voyage; and summer was on the wane. Moreover, Washington had come forward to bar their path to Philadelphia.

Washington was thoroughly puzzled by the departure of the Howes from New York. He had sensibly assumed that the main British army would move northward. For a time after the sailing of the great fleet he even believed that the British were trying to deceive him and that they would turn about and enter the Hudson. Then he wondered whether they were going to Charleston or to Philadelphia. He uneasily shifted back and forth in New Jersey until he learned that the British had entered Chesapeake Bay. It was a relief to him to hear that General Howe was actually advancing against the Patriot capital.

Not that the Patriot commander was confident of his ability to defeat Howe or to hold Philadelphia. But Washington believed that he could fight on nearly even terms, although he had dispatched a corps of riflemen under Colonel Daniel Morgan to the Hudson to help check Burgoyne. His army was equal to that of Howe in neither numbers nor discipline, but it was a far better army than any he had earlier led. Moreover, he could secure reinforcements of militia, in case of need.

The royal troops gained their land legs and marched northward. They foraged successfully for cattle, sheep, and horses. Well fed and equipped, they drove back American skirmishers and approached Brandywine Creek, which ran across their path to Philadelphia. There Washington, entrenched on the northern bank of that stream, had chosen to make a stand with about 11,000 men. A frontal attack by the British across the Brandywine could hardly have succeeded. Even if successful, it must have cost Howe dearly. It was therefore to be expected that the British general would undertake a flanking movement, as he did in the battle of Long Island. So he did, on September 11, sending a detachment to the westward and across fords above the American right flank. Not quite aware of Howe's intention, Washington learned that Howe had divided his army. He prepared to assault the British in front of him, but then prudently refrained from making such a ghastly mistake. Suddenly the British flanking force was marching down the northern bank. Surprised, Washington was attacked from two sides, and his avenue of retreat was threatened. However, his troops fought well enough to hold off the royal army until darkness intervened. Washington was able to fall back. He had lost perhaps 1,000 men, Howe about half as many.

Washington did not perform well on the Brandywine, and his army retreated in great confusion. But he was not downcast, nor were his men. The Continental Congress prudently departed from Philadelphia, to the interior of Pennsylvania, eventually to the village of York. Washington continued to try to defend the city. He could not both preserve his army and retain possession of Philadelphia. When Howe threatened again to move to the westward and around Washington's right flank—and so to pin the Patriots against the Delaware River—the Patriot general prudently withdrew away from the city. Howe then marched into it in triumph, on September 25. He had reached his goal.

Had he? A British officer observed that the entrance of the royal forces into the city was greeted with applause by women and children, with glum silence by its males. It quickly became apparent that Philadelphia contained many Patriots, some neutrals, and few who would bear arms for George III. Sir William sought to inspire its Tories by a show of strength. He was immediately forced to send part of his army down the Delaware River to help Lord Howe open the river to traffic—the army could not remain in Philadelphia without use of the Delaware as a supply line. That task was accomplished, not without cost to the British, for some Patriots who occupied forts upon the river offered stiff resistance. However, although General Howe therefore had fewer men, temporarily, to face Washington, he insisted upon displaying his contempt for the main American army. Posting 3,000 British grenadiers, his best troops, within the city, he placed the remaining 9,000 at Germantown to hold off Washington, should the American commander take the offensive. He did not expect Washington to attack, and he carefully refrained from building entrenchments at Germantown, for they would not be needed. He should have remembered the counterthrust the Patriot commander had delivered at Trenton.

Howe's recklessness very nearly brought disaster to Britain. Observing the careless arrangements of the British general, Washington struck. The royal troops at Germantown occupied strong ground, with their left resting safely on the Schuylkill River. There was a rather deep valley in front of part of their line, which was about three miles long. The grenadiers in Philadelphia were some seven miles away. Washington saw an opportunity to fight with the odds even, or actually in his favor. During the night of October 3 he quietly approached the British line at Germantown with 11,000 men in four columns. He ordered two of those columns, consisting of militia, to try to make their way around the royal troops and to assail them from the flanks and rear. He sent the other two, composed of Continentals, to make frontal attacks at dawn on October 4. Washington hoped to surprise his enemies. He did not quite succeed. The militia failed to execute their assignments. The Continentals, their movements covered by a fog, did surprise a British advance guard. However, part of that guard, retreating, offered brave resistance in a stone house belonging to the Chew family, about two miles from the main body of the royal army. The Patriots made a mistake. Instead of immediately assigning a detachment to deal with the surrounded British, both American columns spent some minutes trying to force the surrender of the house. Then they proceeded, but the noise of the engagement at the Chew house gave warning of their approach. The bulk of the British and Hessians, routed from sleep, had time to grasp their weapons and to form a solid line of defense. Even so, they were not fully prepared. Their line shook under the assaults of the Patriots, who broke through it at one point. Howe hurried from his headquarters between Philadelphia and Germantown to rally his men. The royal army was momentarily in great danger. Lord Cornwallis hastened forward from Philadelphia with the grenadiers to support the threatened army. Before he arrived, the tide turned against the Patriots. Their two columns collided and exchanged fire. The shooting at the Chew house, in their rear, also disturbed the Continentals. The Americans fell into disorder. The royal troops restored their line; then they took the offensive; and the Americans began a sullen and confused retreat. Cornwallis pursued them for several miles, but some of the Continental units were obviously prepared to resume the struggle, and he chose not to assail them. The Patriots were not routed; they quickly recovered both form and spirit. They had suffered more than 1,000 casualties. But Howe reported 535. The British had narrowly escaped defeat; they had won, at heavy cost that Howe could not afford, a barren victory.

For the American army, cheered rather than discouraged by the result of the battle of Germantown, regained its strength in camp west of Philadelphia. After his supply line on the Delaware River was opened, Howe once more took the field. Washington did not flee. Taking strong ground at Whitemarsh, he again offered to fight. Howe saw that success was doubtful, and he chose not to attack in force. Instead he retired to winter quarters in Philadelphia. Washington sought repose at Valley Forge.

It is well enough known that Washington spent a most trying winter at Valley Forge. In selecting that place for his camp he made an unfortunate choice, since it lay in a region that had been swept clean of cattle.

His men shivered in rude huts. Moreover, the American supply officers did not, perhaps could not, regularly send food or clothing to the army. Farmers preferred to sell cattle and grain to the British for hard cash rather than to accept depreciated Continental paper for their products. Foraging parties sent out by Washington were often unsuccessful. His men were twice threatened by starvation. Many of them deserted. Meanwhile, the royal troops were as comfortable as might be, only twenty miles away, in Philadelphia. It seemed that cold and privation might accomplish what Howe had failed to achieve, the destruction of the main American army. Appearances deceived. Hardened Continental veterans stubbornly refused to abandon their general. General Nathanael Greene, who had been a merchant before he became a soldier, assumed the duty of securing supplies and performed well. In the spring of 1778, the Patriot army revived after the winter at Valley Forge, just as it had in the spring of 1777 after its sufferings at Morristown.

Trying to maintain his army amidst harsh trials, Washington also endured personal censure while he sojourned at Valley Forge. He had won no victories in 1777. Men in and out of the Continental Congress condemned his performance. Why had he failed to hold Philadelphia? Why had he been defeated both on the Brandywine and at Germantown? He must be incompetent, declared men who did not understand the difficulties under which he labored. The man who had not hesitated to offer battle to the British, who was perhaps too eager to engage them, was assailed because he had not fought enough. A few of his critics, including General Thomas Conway, an Irish officer in the French army who had crossed the Atlantic to join the Patriots, sought the dismissal of Washington from his post as commander in chief. They proposed to put in his place General Horatio Gates, who had won laurels as the conqueror of Burgoyne. It is often asserted that a Conway Cabal was formed to elevate Gates at the expense of Washington. No good evidence has been found that any such combination ever existed. Certainly Conway had neither power nor influence. Gates, who entertained excessive confidence in his own abilities, was willing to succeed Washington. Washington and army officers who rallied to his support challenged his critics. One of his friends, General John Cadwalader, fought a duel with Conway and seriously wounded the French officer. Among those who sought the removal of Washington was Dr. Benjamin Rush, who had earlier been a member of the Continental Congress. Rush feared that Washington might become an incompetent dictator; without good reason, he admired Gates. James Lovell, a member of Congress from Massachusetts, was hostile to Washington and friendly to Gates; and it is to be believed that several of

Lovell's colleagues, including Samuel Adams and Richard Henry Lee, were at that time less than enthusiastic admirers of Washington. However, good sense prevailed in the Congress. No motion to relieve Washington of his command was offered. He retained the trust of his employers. Their faith in him would grow. Later in 1778 a British informant who was familiar with the Patriot leaders asserted that New England delegates in the Congress, together with Benjamin Franklin, desired to put Nathanael Greene in Washington's place. Franklin had then been in Paris for nearly two years; and it is most doubtful that either he or anyone else seriously meditated any scheme to set aside the Virginian after the Conway Cabal affair. Indeed, Conway himself, recovering from the wound inflicted upon him by John Cadwalader, later acknowledged that he had erred, and he paid tribute to Washington.

Strangely enough, even as the Patriot army wretchedly underwent hardships and Patriot politicians and officers wrangled over the record of Washington, the prospect for the Americans was bright. They had forced Burgoyne's army to lay down its arms, and France was about to enter the war as an American ally. On the other hand, if the British were physically comfortable in Philadelphia, their more thoughtful officers were not at all happy. And Sir William was thoroughly disgusted with the British military situation. As early as October 22, 1777, amidst rumors that Burgoyne's army had been completely defeated by the Patriots, Howe sent off a letter to London asking permission to resign his command. He and his brother had been friendly enough with Germain when all was going well for British arms in America. But Germain, preparing for a political storm that would come in England if the American rebellion prospered in 1777, had begun to attack the Howes. He employed "scribblers" who assailed them in English newspapers. Germain had long suffered from censure because of his behavior at Minden, and he would not accept responsibility for possible failure in America. There was, besides, a streak of meanness in the colonial secretary. Nor was Sir William Howe disposed to shoulder any blame for untoward events anywhere in America. His situation in Philadelphia was awkward. The Loyalists of Pennsylvania had not taken up arms in large numbers. When he called for Tory volunteers, offering at the time of enlistment a bounty of $5.00 and at the end of the war 50 acres of land, "where every gallant hero may retire, and enjoy his bottle and his lass," only 300 Loyalists responded. Asking leave to resign, he demanded, in effect, that a choice be made between him and Germain. One man must yield to the other. Lord North was reluctant to part with Howe, unless Jeffery Amherst consented to replace him, but Amherst had no desire to return to America. George III and the North ministry, without joy, at length decided to support Germain. On February 4, 1778, Germain wrote to Sir William to tell him that he was permitted to return to England and that he was to tender the supreme command to Sir Henry Clinton. Clinton arrived in Philadelphia on May 8. On May 21 Howe said farewell to his officers and embarked for England.

Before Sir William departed for home, he, together with his brother, was offered an astonishing tribute. There were younger officers in the army at Philadelphia who adored the general. Twenty-two of them subscribed £4,000 for a magnificent farewell party. They called it a "Mischianza." Included in the festivities were a regatta on the Delaware; a tournament in which British officers appeared as knights, serving as champions of seven Loyalist girls dressed in Turkish costumes; a splendid banquet; a dance; fireworks; and a supper at midnight. Conspicuous on the scene were two triumphal arches, one for the general, the other for the admiral. Sir William was assured in a message conveyed by fireworks that *"Tes lauriers sont immortels."* His laurels were actually few and evanescent.

William Howe was, of course, denounced by some Patriots as soon as he appeared at Boston. As commander in chief he was being increasingly condemned by the Americans. They claimed that he callously permitted brutal abuse of both Patriot civilians and Patriot prisoners of war, and their charges were not without substance. His troops, both British and German, did plunder noncombatants and did commit rapes. However, Howe did seek to restrain his men; he had several of his soldiers executed for looting and for ravishing females. He could have done more to protect helpless civilians. Yet it must be said in his behalf that it was most difficult to keep eighteenth-century professional soldiers under strict discipline, and that his army was guilty of fewer atrocities than would have been committed by a similar force in Europe. It is also true that the treatment accorded to Patriots who fell into British hands was not quite so vicious as the Americans said it was. In practice, Howe recognized the Patriots as belligerents. He did not execute captured Continentals or militia as traitors; he even exchanged prisoners, in the eighteenth-century style, with the Americans—an example followed by Sir Henry Clinton and other British commanders. Howe was specially censured because of the sufferings of Patriot captives in his notorious prison ships. Because of shortage of quarters and for reasons of security, he placed many hundreds of American prisoners in the *Jersey* and other vessels in New York Harbor. That they suffered from cold and even from lack of food, that they were abused by their guards, is undeniable. To be sure, the Continental Congress, obligated by the practices of the time to provide in part for the prisoners, neglected them for some time. Moreover, the British were themselves somewhat embarrassed during several months for lack of shelter and food. It is also true that the many complaints of the prisoners, including one that was both violent and profane from Ethan Allen, must be discounted. Nevertheless, it is clear enough that Howe neglected to see to it that the Americans housed in the ships were decently treated. Many of them died in captivity; others were finally released with shattered bodies.

The Patriots attacked Howe for immorality as well as cruelty. An American versifier, in May 1777, described a doubtless mythical scene in which Howe, accompanied by his mistress, presumably Mrs. Joshua Loring, Jr., addressed Tory troops about to set out upon a raid under General William Tryon:

> Without wit, without wisdom, half stupid and drunk
> And rolling along arm in arm with his punk,
> The gallant Sir William, who fights all by proxy,
> Thus spoke to his soldiers, held up by his doxy:
> "My boys, I'm a going to send you with Tryon,
> To a place where you'll get as groggy as I am . . ."

Francis Hopkinson, after the Patriots had sent kegs loaded with explosives down the Delaware River in a vain but noisy attempt to blow up British shipping, in January 1778, amused himself and others with "The Battle of the Kegs":

> "Sir William he, snug as a flea,
> Lay all this time a snoring;
> Nor dream'd of harm as he lay warm
> In bed with Mrs. Loring.
>
> Now in a fright, he starts upright,
> Awaked by such a clatter;
> He rubs both eyes, and boldly cries,
> 'For God's sake, what's the matter?' "

Loyalists and Englishmen also condemned Howe, long before he left America, for incompetence, gambling, drunkenness, and licentiousness. In January 1777, the *Middlesex Journal* of London published some biting doggerel:

> When Rome was urged by adverse fate
> On Cannae's evil day,

> A Fabius saved the sinking state
> By caution and delay.
>
> "Only one state!" replied a smart;
> "Why talk of such a dunce?
> When Billy Howe, by the same art,
> Can save THIRTEEN at once?"

Another English wag, in the spring of 1777, urged the general to leave his mistress and to take the field:

> Awake, arouse, Sir Billy,
> There's forage in the plain.
> Ah, leave your little filly
> And open the campaign.

In the summer of 1777 Nicholas Cresswell, a young Englishman who spent part of the war years in America, expressed astonishment that "a Negro-driver should, with a ragged banditti of undisciplined people, the scum and refuse of the earth," hold the British at bay. Howe must be a "lubber." Otherwise, how could he be "puzzled and plagued" by a mere "tobacco planter"? Howe was a "great chucclehead." Why did he not unmuzzle his "mastiffs," the British troops? They would quickly devour Washington "and his ragged crew." About the same time, the British Lieutenant Colonel Charles Stuart, never one of Howe's admirers, asserted that the general had won only "newspaper victories." The Loyalists, so pleased when Howe replaced Gage, later condemned Howe as well as his predecessor. In 1776, as Howe approached New York, the Tory poet Joseph Stansbury rejoiced:

> He comes, he comes, the Hero comes:
> Sound, sound your trumpets, beat your drums.
> From port to port let cannon roar
> Howe's welcome to this western shore.

In December 1777, Stansbury limned Howe as "The Carpet Knight" and declared that Howe preferred his mistress to Venus herself.

As the war continued, as the military prospect for the British faded, Howe was attacked ever more passionately by British partisans, especially by embittered Loyalists. Exiled and ruined in fortune, they ascribed their woes especially to that general. Most savage of all the assaults upon him was that delivered by Loyalist Thomas Jones in his *History of New York during the Revolutionary War*. Jones contended that Howe's supposed affair with Mrs. Joshua Loring, Jr., largely explained the failure of the general to crush the Patriots. He said that "as Cleopatra of old lost Mark Antony the world, so did this illustrious courtesan lose Sir William Howe the honour, the laurels, and the glory, of putting an end to one of the most obstinate rebellions that ever existed." According to Jones, the general was knighted as "a reward for *evacuating* Boston, for *lying indolent* upon Staten Island for near two months, for suffering the whole rebel army to escape him upon Long Island, and again at the White Plains; for *not putting an end to rebellion* in 1776, when so often in his power; for making such *injudicious cantonments* of his troops in Jersey as he did, and for *suffering* 10,000 veterans under experienced generals, to be cooped up in [New] Brunswick, and Amboy, for nearly six months by about 6,000 militia, under the command of an inexperienced general." Howe could have crossed the Delaware and could have brought the war to a conclusion in 1776, but did not, because "the General's favourites were not yet sufficiently enriched; the rebellion was to be nursed, the General to continue in command, and his friends, flatterers, mistresses, and sycophants, to be provided for." As Jones would have it, Howe might easily have driven the Patriots away from Morristown early in 1777, but "was diverting himself in New York, in feasting, gaming, banqueting, and in the arms of Mrs. Loring." The Tory historian declared that in the late spring of 1777 Howe "returned to New York, and after spending about a fortnight in dalliance with Mrs. Loring, while the troops were lying on board the transports crowded together in the sultry heat of summer, he went on board his brother's ship, and orders were given for sailing." Jones claimed that Howe was warned that Washington would attack at Germantown, that he gave no heed, that "upon the first alarm," he "was waked out of a sound sleep, having just returned from the faro table, not having been in bed above an hour." Concluded Jones, "Had the General been properly rewarded for his conduct while Commander-in-Chief in America, an execution, and not a mischianza, would have been the consequence."

It is apparent that the charges leveled against Howe by Jones—he also said some nasty things about Sir Henry Clinton and other British officers—are not to be taken at face value. There are some grains of truth in them. Howe was fond of his bottle of wine; condemning games of chance in orders to his troops, he himself did gamble freely. A middle-aged pleasure seeker, he set a good example for neither his officers nor his men. Evidence is ample that he engaged in dissipation at New York and especially during his stay in Philadelphia. Wrote a Hessian general stationed in the staid city of Brotherly Love, "We have parties and gamble, whereby every night 700 and 800 pounds are lost and won. Gen. Howe also gambles." Young officers, encouraged by the behavior of their chief, fell into debt. Some of them kept mistresses at Philadelphia in houses commandeered from their owners. One Loyalist, commenting upon the relations between British officers and Tory ladies of New York, declared, "I have drawn a curtain around wanton wives and daughters." He praised the character of Admiral Howe, but observed that "he is quite the contrast to a certain person." The Tory ladies of Philadelphia caught "scarlet fever" from British officers. It would appear that Philadelphia was much more than usually troubled by the social diseases while Howe resided there. Newspapers carried advertisements of Dr. Yeldall's "Antivenereal Essence," which was claimed to prevent as well as cure; of "Hannay's Preventive," imported from London and never known to fail when fairly tried; and of "Keyser's Pills," famous all over Europe for their efficacy against "a certain disease." The morals of the British and their friends in the Quaker city are also suggested by verse that appeared in the Pennsylvania *Evening Post* in February 1778:

AFTER SUPPER

'Twas ten o'clock; the cloth removed;
The servants all retreated;
Two tapers blaz'd; his fair beloved,
On Damon's knee was seated.

By love conducted, Celia's cheek
On Damon's bosom lay;
He gaz'd—he sighed—and wish'd to speak—
And knew not what to say.

His arms, twin'd round her taper waist,
Explain'd his wishful sighs;
And well were Celia's thoughts exprest—
They glistened in her eyes.

But soon these mutual looks of love
Their mutual silence broke;
And thus (his lips were seen to move)
The trembling Damon spoke:

"When will my Celia make me blest?
Oh when, my charmer! When?—"
The fair one leer'd, his hand she prest—
"Put out the lights—and THEN!"

XIX · *The Fall of Philadelphia*

All of which does not prove that Mrs. Joshua Loring, Jr., was to Howe as Cleopatra was to Mark Antony. If she was indeed his mistress—Howe is reported to have had at least two during his second sojourn in America—it is difficult to believe that his affair with her had much to do with his failure to crush the Patriots. Other more successful commanders have kept mistresses. There have even been great generals who were homosexuals, and at least one, the brilliant Narses, who was a eunuch. Moreover, there is some doubt that Elizabeth Loring actually was Howe's mistress. She was commonly believed to be such, at least from 1776 to 1778, by both Patriots and Loyalists. But public reputation does not necessarily coincide with private fact. Of Mrs. Loring and her husband, more later.

Sober historians of later times have offered opinions about Howe almost as bizarre as those of vengeful partisans of his own day. It has been suggested, not only that he was less than active, but that he and Lord Howe did not desire to crush the Americans, that they were secretly friends of the Patriots. While it is apparent that the brothers did not hate the Americans, it is equally clear that they tried to put an end to the rebellion. To be sure, they attempted to do it by mingling suasion with force. They did not wage a ferocious war. But they unquestionably gave their allegiance to Britain and the preservation of her empire. Moreover, honor required the Howes as English gentlemen to do their duty—and they felt the demands of honor. Still further, it should be remembered that the reputations and careers of the brothers were at stake. It is preposterous to say that they were covertly friends of the Patriots.

Admitted that General Howe was a failure as commander in chief—and that Admiral Howe did not gain glory in 1776 or 1777. Sir William never lost a battle in which he personally directed the royal troops. He won a series of victories over Washington. He gained little profit from his triumphs in the field. It may be said that he was not fortunate; it may be emphasized that his tasks were not easy ones. His deliberate and careful movements, intended to secure great advantages at little risk and at small cost, may be censured. But it is interesting that Germain, as late as January 1777, endorsed Howe's cautious maneuvers. They were consistent, it may be added, with the principles of warfare, at least with British principles of warfare, in the eighteenth century. British armies did not then move swiftly or audaciously. When Howe did take chances, before Trenton and Germantown, he paid for his temerity by defeat and near-defeat. Had he moved with the celerity demanded by many of his critics—some of them have urged that he should have kept or taken the field in the midst of harsh northern winters—he might have accomplished more than he did. He might also have encountered a check at the hands of the Patriots more serious than that inflicted upon the royal troops at Trenton.

Usually conventional and cautious in things military, Howe was not fitted for command in a most unconventional and unusual war. He lacked intellect. He had failed to fulfill the promise of his youth. As a young man he performed splendidly under direction. In his middle age he would have been a brave and useful colonel; but he would not have performed well as a general even in traditional European warfare. Not the least of his errors was his decision, careless, even though approved by Lord George Germain, to go off to Philadelphia in the summer of 1777, without providing for the safety of the army advancing from Canada. To be sure, that army was not under his control. But Howe played a principal part in designing a British disaster.

CHAPTER XX

Saratoga

OPPORTUNITY to win great glory came late to General John Burgoyne. Junior in rank to Carleton, Howe, and Clinton, he was their senior in years. He was fifty-five years of age when he took his place at the head of the army that was to move southward from Canada in 1777. Carleton was furious because he had been deprived of the command of that army. Clinton was also unhappy because he did not secure the appointment. It would have been his had he insisted. But it had been tendered to Burgoyne before Clinton could put in a personal and earnest plea for it in London. He was told that, if he wished, he could have the post. But would he not prefer to command at New York under Howe, with the assurance that he would succeed that general in the event that it proved necessary to find a replacement for Howe? Clinton, partly to avoid hurting Burgoyne's feelings, as he afterward said, reluctantly agreed to go to New York. His own chance to achieve enduring fame or to suffer lasting disgrace was thus postponed for a time—when it came, he encountered a harsh fate. Carleton, denied an important command after 1776, emerged from the War of Independence with a good reputation. Burgoyne's lot was even less happy than that of Clinton. He met irretrievable defeat; his troops were forced to ground their arms; he returned to England as a prisoner of the Americans; and his downfall precipitated the entrance of France into the war as an ally of the Patriots. George Bernard Shaw, in his play *The Devil's Disciple,* mistakenly placed Burgoyne in command of Continental troops. But Burgoyne has not been forgotten; he is well remembered as the British general who was compelled to capitulate at Saratoga.

The name of John Burgoyne ought to have been familiar to Shaw, for Burgoyne was a fellow playwright. He wrote, among others, one good play, *The Maid of the Oaks*. He was not without talent. He was a colorful man about London town, grown a little plump, rather than a soldier grimly devoted to military business when he first went to America in 1775. Nor did he then become a tardy but passionate student of strategy and tactics. He was gay, flamboyant, and confident—until he met disaster in the forests of New York. In youth he had eloped with and married a daughter of the Earl of Derby. He was a dandy, a convivial drinker, a gambler. He could be charming. He was a gentleman, a member of Parliament, and a cavalry officer, a man who indulged in much talk about the requirements of honor and who was fond of grandiloquent language. He had never held independent command of an army. His one claim to military fame arose from service in Portugal in 1762. English cavalry under Burgoyne had brilliantly charged and routed a Spanish detachment at Villa Velha. He would have no mounted troops with him in North America. Time and trial would demonstrate that he was not well qualified to lead infantry and Indians in the forests of New York.

In London in the early weeks of 1777 Burgoyne was confident of success. Guy Carleton, laying plans for the approaching compaign that he would have no opportunity to execute, asked for 4,000 additional troops. Burgoyne was willing to perform without important additions to the forces already available in Canada. He did not expect to make a mere triumphal march to Albany. He rather thought that he would meet stout resistance at Fort Ticonderoga, that he might be opposed by as many as 12,000 Patriots. Nevertheless, he did not anticipate that his army would be fundamentally endangered nor even that it would sustain heavy losses. He would reach his destination at Albany.

Back from London—he reached Quebec early in May—Burgoyne had to face Carleton. He had been critical of that general in London. Would not Carleton, ordered to remain in Canada, vent his spleen upon Burgoyne as well as Lord George Germain? Might he not even refuse to offer necessary help to his subordinate? Burgoyne was pleasantly surprised. Carleton was deeply angry, but he knew that his principal enemy was Germain, not Burgoyne. Had "Gentleman Johnny" not secured the command of the army that was to move southward, it would have gone to Clinton or to some general other than Carleton. Sir Guy promptly and haughtily submitted his resignation as governor of Canada to Germain in a letter that expressed his profound contempt for the colonial secretary. His wrath against Germain was almost unbounded. But he would not do less than his patriotic duty. He gave Burgoyne all possible assistance. At St. John's on June 13 Burgoyne raised a British flag over a relatively small but formidable force containing more than 8,000 redcoats and Hessians, about 150 French Canadians, some 100 Tories, and 400 Indian braves. The army was handsomely equipped with artillery. It contained many fine officers, including Major General William Phillips, second in command under Burgoyne; Major General Baron von Riedesel, senior among the German troops; and Brigadier General Simon Fraser, Lord Lovat. Shortly afterward, in warships and vessels of all sorts, including canoes, the army moved over the waters of Lake Champlain toward Fort Ticonderoga. Landing near the southern end of the lake on July 1, the royal army approached the fort on the following day.

Meanwhile, Lieutenant Colonel Barry St. Leger began to collect a motley force at Oswego. He arrived there on July 26 with about 900 men, among them British regulars, Hessians, Tory contingents of one sort and another, and French Canadians. At Oswego he met the Mohawk chief, Joseph Brant, with perhaps 1,000 Iroquois warriors. On the very next day St. Leger marched eastward toward the Mohawk River valley and Albany. The Patriots were to be attacked from the west as well as from the north—and they had to face bodies of Indians as well as European enemies.

For most of the Six Nations had finally cast their lot with the British. The Iroquois had remained almost completely neutral for two years. The Americans had anxiously and successfully urged them to remain quiet, and Guy Carleton had not sought their services. However, Lord George Germain now instructed Burgoyne and other British officers in North America to seek the help of the red men. The family of Sir William Johnson, having fled from the Mohawk Valley into Canada, exerted its powerful influence among the Iroquois. It was not too difficult to persuade most of them that the Americans, encroaching upon their lands, were their mortal enemies, that King George was their great and generous friend. Only the Oneida and some of the Tuscarora refused to assist the redcoats. They listened to American missionaries who warned them to keep apart from a quarrel that was not their own and to American emissaries who asked them to remain neutral or to assist the Patriots. In consequence, the Americans eventually obtained minor aid from the Oneida and Tuscarora; but Britain secured powerful and immediate assistance from the other four Iroquois nations.

Germain, with the consent of the North ministry, had callously or carelessly called for the enlistment of allies who would inevitably wage their own kind of specially savage warfare. To be sure, he stipulated that the Indians were to be employed only in contingents accompanying white troops and under the command of white officers. So, it was claimed, the familiar barbarities committed by the red men would be prevented. But Germain and his associates, if they knew anything whatever about America, were aware that the Indians, once engaged, would fight when, where, and how they wished, and that they could not be restrained from committing acts of cruelty against captives, against old men, against women, against children. So it had always been, whether the red men were allies of Britain, France, or Spain; and so it would be when they assisted the Americans. Nor was Burgoyne, with all his solicitude for his honor as a gentleman and officer, utterly averse to employment of the Iroquois. As he made his way toward Ticonderoga, he issued a proclamation that combined literary bombast with dire threats to the Patriots. He asserted that the Americans had established, at the expense of the Loyalists, "the completest system of tyranny that ever God in his displeasure suffer'd for a time to be exercised over a froward and stubborn generation," that they had resorted to "persecution and torture unprecedented in the inquisitions of the Romish Church," and that they had added "the profanation of religion" to "the most profligate prostitution of common sense." He warned the Americans who persisted in "unnatural rebellion" that he could turn loose Indians, "and they amount to thousands," to search out Patriots wherever they might hide. For vengeance wreaked by the warriors "in the phrenzy of hostility," he himself would "stand acquitted in the eyes of God and men." If the Americans did not put down their arms, they could expect "devastation, famine, and every concomitant horror that a reluctant but indispensable prosecution of military duty must occasion." He would have it that even the Hessians under his command were ardently devoted to the British cause. Shortly afterward, addressing Indian chiefs who accompanied his army, Burgoyne told them that they and their warriors must not shed Patriot blood, except in combat, and that they must not under any circumstances injure old men, women, or children. Did he expect them to fight like Eton gentlemen? He puzzled the chiefs and the braves. Did he, or did he not, wish them to strike at the Americans? To do him justice, he intended neither to execute his windy threats against the Patriots nor to permit his allies to wreak their customary barbarities. In consequence, he obtained little help from his contingent of Indians, but was condemned in both England and America for employing them. In fact, his empty threat that he would turn them loose actually steeled Patriot resistance. It was otherwise with St. Leger. He did not, perhaps could not, control his braves; and they committed numerous atrocities. But St. Leger did not reach Albany. Britain and her commanders earned shame for calling the red men into action against their own people, but gained little from using the warriors. So it was during the remainder of the war, everywhere in North America.

Preparing to meet the oncoming armies of Burgoyne and St. Leger, the Patriots encountered many difficulties. They actually had to raise and maintain three forces, for they had to guard the Highlands along the lower Hudson against a possible British advance from New York City while they struggled against Burgoyne and St. Leger. The British garrison of 3,000 troops in Rhode Island also caused some concern. Would it move aggressively? To raise and equip men to meet so many threats was an immense task. And it was not lightened by jealousies among the Patriot generals. For Generals Philip Schuyler and Horatio Gates were engaged in the early months of 1777 in a struggle for command of the army that would seek to check Burgoyne and St. Leger. Both men had their friends in the Continental Congress. New Englanders favored Gates, New Yorkers supported Schuyler. In the end, Gates was set aside, and Schuyler was entrusted with the command. He labored energetically in the late spring of 1777 to prepare against the onslaughts of the British, concentrating of necessity against Burgoyne.

But the Patriots were far from ready to meet Burgoyne as he approached Fort Ticonderoga. Schuyler was then at Albany, trying to gather men and supplies. There were no more than 3,500 Patriots, Continentals and militia, under Major General Arthur St. Clair at Ticonderoga as Burgoyne prepared to assault the fort. Schuyler then had no army to go to the rescue of the garrison. Nevertheless, the Americans—or rather, those not on the scene—hoped to hold Ticonderoga indefinitely, at least to check the advance of Burgoyne there for some weeks. The old fort had been renovated and strengthened; another had been erected on adjacent Mount Independence; and the two forts were connected by protecting works.

Burgoyne also expected to be sternly challenged at Ticonderoga, and he had brought with him scores of cannon to batter down its defenses; he rather thought that Ticonderoga was the chief obstacle in his path. He easily drove back the Patriots from their advanced positions. Suddenly, while the British general was gathering his troops, placing his guns, and arranging to surround the garrison, he learned that the Patriots had made a wretched mistake. They had neglected to fortify Sugar Loaf Hill, a lofty eminence from which cannon shot could be thrown down at both the American forts. The Patriots believed that artillery could not be dragged up that hill. Burgoyne sensibly sent one of his engineers, a Swiss in British service, to find out whether it was really impossible to make use of Sugar Loaf. The engineer made his way up the hill, reported that cannon could be transported to its crest, and that artillery fire would make both Ameri-

313

can forts untenable. On July 4 the British began to drag guns to the top. The following morning, to their dismay, St. Clair and his officers saw two pieces of cannon on the crest of Sugar Loaf. They knew that more would soon appear there. They immediately held a council of war. They agreed that the two forts could not be defended, that the Patriots must flee as soon as darkness came to conceal their movements. Toward night the Americans began to fire cannon, to cover the noise they made as they prepared to evacuate the two forts. The British speculated. Were the Patriots about to attack? Or were they making ready to flee? Burgoyne learned the following morning that they were in full flight. Ticonderoga was his, at trifling cost.

But St. Clair had averted disaster by his swift evacuation. Most of the American garrison escaped. The Patriots fled from Ticonderoga in two divisions, a smaller one by water under Colonel Pierce Long, a larger force by land under the personal command of St. Clair. An American flotilla carrying Long and his men was trapped by Burgoyne's fleet at Skenesboro (later called Whitehall). Long burnt part of his squadron; the remainder fell into British hands. Long led his men ashore. Joined by New York militia, he turned against the advanced guard of his pursuers, checked it in a skirmish near Wood Creek, then safely resumed his retreat. Meanwhile, St. Clair marched rapidly in summer heat toward Castleton, Vermont. On the night of July 6 St. Clair's rear guard, against his orders, camped at Hubbardton. It consisted chiefly of three New England regiments. Its officers did not bother to station sentinels to give warning of the approach of the enemy. The following morning British and Hessian troops, who had followed St. Clair with all possible speed, suddenly attacked the Patriot rear guard. Part of it fled immediately. However, the remainder, perhaps 600 in number, rallied and formed a line in thick woods and underbrush. In heavy fighting the royal troops advanced against the Patriot left, while the Americans moved against the British left. Then more Hessians reached the scene, and two charges by the Germans and the British disrupted the American line. The remainder of the American rear guard fled. The fight at Hubbardton was expensive to both sides. Altogether, the Patriots lost about 400 men. But nearly 200 of the royal troops were killed or wounded, and the remnants of the American rear guard escaped, and so did St. Clair, to fight on other days.

The easy British capture of Ticonderoga seemed to be a shattering blow to the Patriots. Was not Burgoyne's path southward now clear? John Adams, no soldier, wondered whether any American commander would hold his post until one of them was shot for neglect of duty. Some Americans even believed that St. Clair, who had once been a British army

314

officer, was guilty of treachery. It required a court-martial to prove that St. Clair, if he had displayed no genius, had bravely done his best. There were even suspicious Yankees who asserted that Philip Schuyler had been bought by the British, that he had connived with St. Clair to give them Ticonderoga. Gathering troops and moving northward to do what he could to check Burgoyne, Schuyler lost scores of men by desertion.

Correspondingly, Burgoyne was elated by his relatively inexpensive victory. Had he not been ordered to proceed to Albany, he might have invaded the valley of the Connecticut River and New England. He knew that he could expect no important help as he moved onward—he had been given the letter of warning of April 5 sent by General Howe to Carleton—but he was obviously confident that he would need no assistance. However, the British general soon began to encounter troubles, some of them provided by Schuyler. After the capture of Ticonderoga, Burgoyne had to cover only seventy miles to reach Albany. But they were long and tortuous miles over extremely bad roads that wound up and down, this way and that, through thick forests and across innumerable streams. Burgoyne made those miles even longer, for he advanced toward Fort Edward on the Hudson River by way of Skenesboro and Wood Creek rather than by a better route across Lake George. Probably he was trying to guard against Patriot attacks upon his flanks. Burgoyne was impeded by forty-two pieces of cannon—at first fifty-two—some of which he might have left behind. He also was embarrassed for lack of horses and oxen to move his cannon and his military gear. It is related that his personal baggage, including clothing, food, and wines, added to his problem of transport. Certainly Schuyler, unable to do battle for some weeks, did all that he could to impede the march of the royal troops. He had huge stones piled in Wood Creek; he had axemen fell thousands of trees across the roads that Burgoyne had to use; he even had streams diverted so that they would cross the path of the British. Burgoyne cleared away the obstacles with remarkable speed. Even so, his progress was seriously retarded. He did not pass Skenesboro until July 24, and he did not reach Fort Edward and the Hudson until July 29. After a short delay he moved another seven miles, down the east bank of the Hudson, to Fort Miller, immediately above the Batten Kill. There he stood still for many weeks, while the tide of war turned against him. He had to wait until his cannon and other gear could be brought forward. Before he moved again, his situation had become perilous, almost desperate.

It was not apparent to the Continental Congress, in midsummer, that fortune was deserting Burgoyne. Its members continued to receive disheartening news from the north after the fall of Ticonderoga. Schuyler, falling back as the British advanced, retreated down the west bank of the Hudson to Saratoga, then to Stillwater, then to the mouth of the Mohawk. As he withdrew, he sent gloomy dispatches to Philadelphia. His slender forces were insufficient to check Burgoyne; they were diminishing rather than burgeoning, as the British threat became ever more alarming; he expressed no firm resolution to fight to the last gasp; he seemed to assume that he was destined to meet defeat. Was he preparing excuses, the delegates asked themselves, for failing to halt Burgoyne? The New Englanders in the Congress urged that Horatio Gates be sent to replace Schuyler, and they had their way. Schuyler was dismissed from his command on August 4, and Gates assumed it on August 19.

Schuyler was far too pessimistic in his reports. His situation improved as he retreated to the mouth of the Mohawk. He was joined by Major Generals Benjamin Lincoln and Benedict Arnold, and by 600 Continentals from Peekskill. Moreover, as the menaces posed by Burgoyne and St. Leger became imminent, as the British approached their homes, the militia of New England and New York began to turn out in large numbers. Sent by Schuyler to threaten Burgoyne's left flank with contingents of Yankees, Lincoln soon gave Burgoyne cause to worry about the safety of his line of communications and supplies to Canada. The militia were all the more disposed to fight because of the brutal murder toward the end of July, of Jane McCrea, the fiancée of a Tory, by two of Burgoyne's Indian warriors. For fear of offending his red-skinned allies, Burgoyne refrained from attempting to punish the slayers. It seemed that he could not, perhaps would not, restrain the savages, that his threat to turn them loose against the Patriots was not an empty one. The Americans were only too familiar with the horrors of Indian warfare. They steeled themselves for a stern struggle. Yankees poured forth from their homes to rally behind that "damned Dutchman," Schuyler. Had he possessed equal determination, he would doubtless have become a great American hero.

The Americans stiffened, and won a most important victory, before Gates assumed command, at Bennington, Vermont. Moving slowly toward the Batten Kill, Burgoyne was urged by Baron von Riedesel to permit a raid into the Green Mountain country. He was told that horses, oxen, wagons, and food could be obtained there. The royal army especially needed horses, for it included German cavalrymen who had been forced to walk for lack of mounts. Burgoyne at length gave his consent to the adventure, and entrusted command of the expedition to Lieutenant Colonel Friedrich Baum. He is reported to have felt constrained to employ Baum and Hessian troops because the Germans formed the bulk of his left flank—they would be disgraced if a British officer and British troops were assigned to an expedition moving to the left of the royal army. Baum was given more than 700 men, including Germans, Tories, Canadians, British marksmen, musicians, and Indians, together with a few artillerymen and two cannon. He was to scour the Vermont countryside, and also to arrest prominent Patriots. He was to frighten as well as despoil the Vermonters, but he was not to risk heavy losses. Before Baum set out, he was informed that the Patriots had gathered supplies at Bennington, and that he was to move first against that village.

Advancing from Fort Miller on August 11, Baum soon encountered resistance by small parties of American militia. He brushed them aside. He also drove back 200 Patriots sent out by Brigadier General John Stark to check his progress. He was told that the 200 men were part of a force of at least 1,500 militia gathered at Bennington. Such was the fact. The threat posed by Burgoyne had roused New Hampshire to action, and that colony had sent Stark, a veteran of several battles, westward with as many men as could be raised. Baum resolved, despite his orders to avoid heavy losses, to engage Stark. Advancing toward Bennington, he was confronted not only by the New Hampshiremen, but by Green Mountain militia and Massachusetts troops. Stark commanded about 2,000 men; Baum, reinforced by 90 Tories, had about 800. Learning that he faced heavy odds, Baum decided not to attack; but he declined to retreat. He asked Burgoyne for help, entrenched upon a height above the Walloomsac River, and awaited attack by the Patriots. It came, on the morning of August 16. Stark sent two contingents around Baum's wings to assault the British rear. Baum, who knew no English, seems to have believed the flanking forces were bodies of Tories; he permitted them to take positions behind him without molesting them. Then the Patriots attacked him, almost simultaneously, in front and in back. The Canadians and Indians immediately fled; the Tories soon followed their example. But the Germans and British regulars fought desperately, for more than two hours. Twice the German cavalrymen, wielding heavy swords, charged and almost broke through the Yankee militia. However, the Patriots managed to withstand the onslaughts of the swordsmen; the royal troops began to run out of ammunition; and Baum fell, mortally wounded. The remains of his little army fled or surrendered.

The battle of Bennington was not yet ended. Late in the afternoon, Lieutenant Colonel Francis Breymann, sent by Burgoyne to support Baum, approached the field with about 650 troops, chiefly German. He had been delayed by rain, by the artillery that he dragged along, by the very formality with which his troops marched. Even so, Breymann might

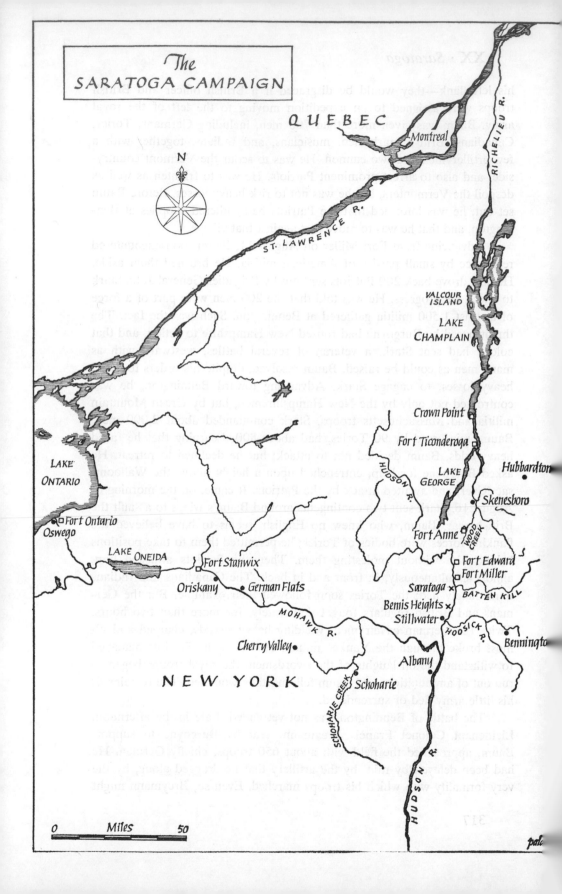

The
SARATOGA CAMPAIGN

QUEBEC

Montreal

N

ST. LAWRENCE R.

RICHELIEU R.

VALCOUR
ISLAND

LAKE
CHAMPLAIN

LAKE
ONTARIO

Crown Point

Fort Ticonderoga

Hubbardton

LAKE
GEORGE

Skenesboro

Fort Ontario
Oswego

LAKE ONEIDA

Fort Stanwix

Fort Anne

WOOD CREEK

Oriskany

German Flats

Fort Edward
Fort Miller

Saratoga

Bemis Heights

Stillwater

BATTEN KILL

HUDSON R.

MOHAWK R.

HOOSICK R.

Bennington

Cherry Valley

Albany

NEW YORK

Schoharie

SCHOHARIE CREEK

HUDSON R.

0   Miles   50

have been able to retrieve the day against Stark's men, for they were scattered, weary, and busy with looting. However, Stark had also called for aid, and 350 Continentals under Colonel Seth Warner appeared from Manchester in time to help Stark against Breymann. The intrepid Stark managed to reform part of his men. These, with the soldiers under Warner, engaged Breymann's troops, both armies arrayed in long lines, face to face. The fight was obstinate, but the royal troops, after exhausting their ammunition, at last broke and fled. Breymann, wounded, managed to escape in covering darkness with less than two thirds of his force. The Patriots won two victories in the battle of Bennington. They sustained about 70 casualties. More than 200 of the royal troops were slain, and about 700 were captured. Burgoyne had lost more than one tenth of his army in one shattering day.

Burgoyne received bad news that August from the west as well as from the east. The remnants of Breymann's force rejoined him, but Barry St. Leger did not appear, either in the camp of the British general or at Albany.

The British belief that St. Leger could sweep aside Patriot defenders and march down the Mohawk River to the Hudson was not unwarranted. Massively threatened by Burgoyne, the Americans would presumably be unable to concentrate against the smaller British army advancing from the west. Moreover, there were many Tories and neutrals in the valley of the Mohawk. It seemed that St. Leger's task was not formidable. His ferocious Indians would strike terror into the hearts of Patriot defenders, and his white-skinned contingents would do whatever formal fighting was necessary. St. Leger had enough cannon to bombard Fort Stanwix, the only fortified place in his path. It was believed that he would be able to capture that post without undue difficulty. If, by any chance, the Americans did move against him in force as he approached the Hudson, his army was of such a nature that he could easily and swiftly flee to safety.

The news that St. Leger was preparing to advance did indeed create fright among the Patriots of the Mohawk Valley. They knew that many of their neighbors would welcome the invaders, and they knew that St. Leger's Indian allies were both warlike and cruel. Nor could they expect loving kindness from the Tories who accompanied St. Leger—many of those being Loyalists had been driven from their homes in the valley by the Patriots. But terror may lead to desperate valor rather than spineless submission; and so it was among the Americans who dwelled along the banks of the pleasant river. On July 17 Brigadier General Nicholas Herkimer, a prosperous landowner of German descent who commanded the militia of Tryon County—that county covered the settlements of western New York—called for the arrest of all Tories and asked every male Patriot between the ages of sixteen and sixty to prepare to take up arms. Equally determined to fight, Colonel Peter Gansevoort and Lieutenant Colonel Marinus Willett, two brave Dutchmen, were renovating Fort Stanwix, which was in bad repair. Gansevoort commanded a regiment of New York Continentals in the fort, and Willett vigorously supported his efforts. Before St. Leger could reach that outpost, they had rebuilt it and made it defensible. Moreover, just as an advanced detachment of British troops and Indians on August 2 reached the fort, 200 Patriots slipped into it from the east. With about 750 men Gansevoort and Willett determined to hold the fort. They could hope for relief from Herkimer, even for help from Schuyler.

Moving rapidly, St. Leger surrounded Fort Stanwix on August 3 and demanded its surrender. But Gansevoort defied his threats; the fort was too strong to carry by assault; and St. Leger was compelled to besiege it. In the meantime, Herkimer collected about 800 men, together with 30 Oneida scouts, and marched up the river to relieve the American garrison. He sent messages to Gansevoort, urging that the defenders of the fort make a sortie when St. Leger divided his army to deal with the menace posed by Herkimer's advance.

As Herkimer had anticipated, St. Leger continued the siege with part of his force, sending all his Indians, together with Tory detachments, to check the relieving expedition. Six miles east of Fort Stanwix, near Oriskany, the Tories and Indians prepared an ambush for Herkimer. They took post on hills above a ravine through which he would march. The Tories would check his advance; the Indians would assail his men from both flanks. Herkimer fell into the trap. His Oneida scouts failed to warn him, and he led his men in column into the ravine. Suddenly they were assailed from three sides. The American rear guard fled, and the main body was soon surrounded. A crushing defeat for the Patriots, such as Major General Edward Braddock had suffered in 1755 at the hands of the French and their Indian allies, seemed only too likely. However, Herkimer, not an able commander, was a fighter. Mortally wounded, he rallied his men; most of them refused to succumb to panic; collecting in small groups, the militia stubbornly engaged their assailants in a bloody and chaotic fray. They stood their ground in a struggle that coupled hand-to-hand fighting with musket fire. A heavy shower of rain, making it impossible to discharge flintlocks, persuaded the combatants to rest for nearly an hour. When the battle was resumed, the Tories were strengthened by a detachment sent out by St. Leger. However, the militia had recovered from the shock of the surprise attack. Herkimer's men continued to exchange shot for shot and blow for blow. At length the Indians abandoned the sanguinary contest and withdrew, forcing the Tories to retreat with them to St. Leger's camp. Herkimer's men turned back. More than one quarter of them had been killed or wounded, and Herkimer himself was dead.

But the Tories and Indians also suffered losses at Oriskany. They sustained perhaps 150 casualties. Moreover, Gansevoort, in their absence, sent out Willett with 250 men to raid their campsites at Fort Stanwix. Before the British regulars could intervene, Willett carried into the fort all the movable gear belonging to the Loyalists and the warriors, including weapons, ammunition, clothing, and blankets.

Resuming the siege of the fort, St. Leger tried to frighten its defenders into surrender. He began to build approaches toward its wooden walls. He informed the officers of the garrison that he would take it. If they resisted further, he would not be able to restrain his savage allies when the fort fell. To avoid being massacred, the Americans should lay down their arms immediately. He received a firm and contemptuous reply from Willett. The garrison would not yield to a threat unworthy of a British officer. However, Willett, with a companion, then slipped through the besiegers to seek aid. The fort could not be held indefinitely.

Help was already on the way. Learning of the plight of the garrison at Fort Stanwix, Schuyler, just before he was replaced, boldly sent a relieving force from his own camp up the Mohawk—even though his army was still decidedly inferior to that of Burgoyne. Major General Benedict Arnold led 950 volunteers forward, and was soon joined by 100 militia. He began a rapid march toward the fort. He had reason to expect a desperate conflict with St. Leger. However, he reached the fort without fighting. On his way westward he devised a ruse that was astonishingly successful. The Patriots had captured a half-witted Tory engaged in recruiting his fellows, one Hans Yost Schuyler. He had been condemned to death. He was told that his life would be spared if he would go to St. Leger's army and report that Arnold was advancing with 3,000 men. The Tory accepted the offer, and set out with an Oneida warrior, who was to tell the same lie to St. Leger's Indians. The two unlikely agents performed their missions. St. Leger did not quite believe Hans Yost Schuyler, but his savage allies accepted the tale told by the Oneida. The losses they had suffered at Oriskany and the plundering of their camp by Willett had discouraged them. Despite the pleas of St. Leger, they fled through the forests toward Lake Ontario. He could not hope to maintain the siege without them. Disconsolately, he also retreated. The menace posed by St. Leger was removed. Making his way back to Canada, he set out to join

321

Burgoyne by way of Lake Champlain. He did not reach the main British army. Had he done so, he would have become a prisoner. Arnold entered Fort Stanwix amidst Patriot rejoicing, then promptly turned back to rejoin the army facing Burgoyne, now commanded by Horatio Gates.

Burgoyne knew, even before he learned of the retreat of St. Leger, that he would not easily reach Albany. From Fort Miller he wrote to Lord George Germain on August 20. He began to prepare a defense for himself, in the event that he met defeat. He said that he would remain at Fort Miller or fall back to Fort Edward, were it not that his instructions absolutely required him to proceed to Albany, even if his army were lost in the attempt. His orders did not peremptorily demand that he continue his advance at all costs. But the bulk of his army, including his British regulars, was still intact, and he continued to believe that he could drive on to his destination. Most of his Indian auxiliaries departed for home before September 1. However, having built a bridge across the Hudson, he crossed the river to its west bank on September 13 and 14 and resumed his southward march. So doing, he quite finally abandoned his chance of a safe retreat. He would win—or lose.

Horatio Gates was much less than a great commander, but fortune smiled upon him in the late summer and autumn of 1777. He inherited from Schuyler an army that was burgeoning. By September 12 he had with him at the mouth of the Mohawk more than 7,000 men, the majority of them tested Continentals. Moreover, the American militia were taking the field in thousands. The terrain through which Burgoyne had to make his way along the west bank of the Hudson also gave great advantage to Gates. Forested and uneven, it favored defense. Besides, Gates had a corps of riflemen whose power was vastly increased in that rough country. The riflemen would not be exposed to bayonet charges by the royal troops on open ground. Gates also profited from the help of brave and able officers, including Benedict Arnold and Daniel Morgan. To do Gates justice, it must also be said that, unlike Schuyler, he did not anticipate defeat. It must be added, to his credit, that he understood Burgoyne. He knew that the British general would attack, even under unfavorable circumstances. Gates wisely chose to go forward to meet the British army. He established his troops on strong ground at Bemis Heights. There his right was protected by the river, and his left by roadless woods. Hills and trees offered protection to his entire line, and it was strengthened by entrenchments built under the direction of Thaddeus Kosciusko. Gates was not without artillery to defend his fortifications. He patiently waited for Burgoyne to throw his army against the American line.

Burgoyne did what Gates expected him to do. On September 18 he camped three miles north of the American position. He was not properly informed of the arrangements made by Gates—scouts sent out by the British general were turned back by Patriot detachments that hovered about the royal army. Nevertheless, Burgoyne sent it into action on September 19. He ordered three attacks. Baron von Riedesel with 1,200 Hessians moved along the Hudson against the American right flank; Brigadier General James Hamilton with as many British regulars frontally assailed the American left wing; and Brigadier General Simon Fraser, with 2,200 British troops, Tories, and Indians, undertook to sweep around that wing. Burgoyne hoped that Hamilton and Fraser would be able to crush the Patriot left and force Gates to retreat from his entrenchments. Burgoyne himself accompanied Hamilton's column.

The outcome was most unfortunate for the British general. Benedict Arnold saw that Burgoyne intended to move against and around the American line on the west. He urged Gates to strengthen his left, and Gates did so, sending Morgan's riflemen to help hold off the British threats. What was even worse for Burgoyne, Fraser, pushing forward through forest, lost touch with Hamilton, became enmeshed in the woods, and took little part in the battle that followed. Hamilton was confronted by Morgan and his riflemen at Freeman's Farm. He drove back Morgan, but other American detachments came forward to check him. Freeman's Farm became the scene of a sharp struggle, in which Hamilton, beset by superior numbers, was worsted. He would have been routed had not von Riedesel at length come to his rescue. Burgoyne was forced to withdraw. He had suffered a severe defeat. The Patriot casualties numbered more than 300 men, but those of Burgoyne were nearly twice as many. He could not afford to lose those men; he could not replace them, whereas the Patriots could count upon reinforcements. Moreover, Burgoyne had gained no advantage whatever. He was still confronted by that strong American line. So ended the first battle of Freeman's Farm.

Patching up the wounds of his army as best he might, Burgoyne lay quiet for eighteen days. He entertained a vain hope that Gates would take the offensive. Burgoyne was rightly confident of his ability to repel an American attack. But Gates shrewdly and prudently declined to leave his entrenchments. Burgoyne also hoped, just as vainly, that Sir Henry Clinton would come up the Hudson to assist him. As the days passed, the morale of his troops and officers sank. On October 5 Baron von Riedesel and Simon Fraser advised Burgoyne to retreat toward Canada. The British general had been compelled to put his men on half rations. He might have saved a large part of his army by flight. Instead, he resolved to try again to break through the left of the American line. He planned to make a "reconnaissance in force" against it on October 7; if that maneuver succeeded, he would order his entire army into battle.

The "reconnaissance in force" led to the second battle of Freeman's Farm. In the morning of the seventh Burgoyne himself moved through the woods toward the American left wing with 1,500 British regulars, together with some 600 Tories and Indians. Gates was not surprised. Patriot patrols soon reported that the British were in motion. Advancing deliberately from Freeman's Farm, Burgoyne was attacked from both the left and the right by riflemen and Continental infantry. Then Patriot troops assailed his front. He was forced back to the British line. Benedict Arnold appeared on the scene, even though he had quarreled with Gates and had been deprived of command. Twice the Americans assailed the right flank of the British line, with Arnold furiously encouraging the Patriot troops. The second attack was successful. However, darkness intervened before the Americans could exploit their advantage. During the night Burgoyne withdrew his troops to temporary safety.

Although Burgoyne's army was not destroyed in the second battle of Freeman's Farm, it suffered a decisive defeat. The victory of the Patriots cost them about 150 men. The British lost perhaps 700 in killed, wounded, and captured; and General Fraser and Colonel Breymann were among those killed or mortally injured. Whatever faint hope of driving through to Albany Burgoyne had nourished before the struggle had vanished. The British general retreated with his beaten, depleted, and dispirited army to strong ground near Saratoga. That army, on the defensive and in good position, might still have been able to check an attack by Gates. But the Patriot commander refused to take an unnecessary risk. The American militia had come forward in overwhelming numbers. One way and another, more than 17,000 Patriots now opposed Burgoyne. Gates ordered detachments of militia to cut off the British avenues of retreat, especially Burgoyne's route to Ticonderoga. On October 12 the royal commander held a council of war with his remaining higher officers. He and they knew that Sir Henry Clinton had been able to put an army in motion up the Hudson toward Albany, but correctly concluded that it was too small to offer help, that it would reach Albany too late, if indeed it advanced so far. Burgoyne decided to flee toward Canada. Before his army could move, he learned that it was surrounded by swarming Patriots. He could hardly hope to cut his way through to safety. On October 13 he sent a message to Gates offering to lay down his arms upon suitable terms. Gates demanded a complete surrender. On October 14 Burgoyne informed Gates that he was prepared to sign a convention by which his army would put down its weapons, provided that his troops were permitted to embark for England under pledge never to serve again in North America.

Gates hesitated briefly. He knew that Sir Henry Clinton had broken through Patriot defenses on the lower Hudson, and that a British expedition was moving up the river toward Albany. He had sent the garrison of Fort Stanwix and other troops to do what they could to check the progress of that expedition. Was it not better to accept Burgoyne's offer rather than to insist upon an absolute surrender? Just possibly, Burgoyne might still escape his clutches. He accepted the terms proposed by the British general. On October 16 Burgoyne learned that the troops sent up the Hudson were indeed not far from Albany. Momentarily, he considered a resumption of hostilities. But his offer had been formally accepted, and it was too late for a gentleman officer to draw back. Moreover, there was no real hope that he would receive sufficient help in time to save his army. On October 17 at Saratoga the convention was executed—in part —with suitable military pomp and circumstance. The remains of Burgoyne's army, somewhat more than 5,000 men, put down arms in front of massive ranks of the victors. One Hessian observed that the American forces were not composed of old men, boys, and Negroes, that Morgan's riflemen were commonly six feet tall. Gates was polite to the crestfallen Burgoyne. Shortly afterward the British general at last reached Albany —as a prisoner.

Gates need not have been concerned lest he be assailed in force from the south. He could have insisted upon complete surrender of Burgoyne's army. When Howe sailed for Philadelphia, he left behind him in New York City more than 8,000 men, including Tories, together with 3,000 more in Rhode Island, under Sir Henry Clinton. It was Clinton's primary duty to defend the two British bases, and he hardly stirred during many weeks. In September he became somewhat alarmed lest Burgoyne be in trouble, and offered to make that diversion on the lower Hudson that Howe had promised. On September 24 a small reinforcement reached New York City from Europe. Ten days later Clinton moved up the Hudson with 3,000 men in transports escorted by a squadron of warships. Moving audaciously, he captured American forts in the Highlands erected to prevent passage of British ships. By October 8 the river was open. Clinton had executed the diversion. But it did not persuade Gates to weaken his army in order to protect his rear, as Clinton and Burgoyne had hoped. On the lower Hudson Clinton received a plaintive message from Burgoyne. The latter declared that he was in distress, and that he had expected solid help from the south. He even asked Clinton for orders. Clinton quite properly answered that he was obeying Howe's instructions, and that he could give Burgoyne no orders until that general reached Albany. Clinton could not believe that Burgoyne was desperate. However, he was informed by Major General Robert Pigot, who commanded in Rhode Island, that Pigot could easily hold his ground with 2,000 men and send an additional 1,000 troops to New York. Clinton then resolved to make at least another gesture in favor of Burgoyne. On October 13 he sent Major General John Vaughan with 2,000 men and a naval escort up the river toward Albany. If need be, Clinton would later supply further assistance. Vaughan came to a stop well below Albany on October 15. His pilots refused to proceed, because the river was too shallow to permit passage of his heavily laden transports. Vaughan—and Clinton—had to leave Burgoyne to his harsh fate.

Nor did it help Britain that the approach of Vaughan persuaded Gates to accept less than the unconditional surrender of Burgoyne, for the convention of Saratoga was violated by the Americans. Burgoyne's men were not permitted to go to England. Burgoyne soon began to complain that the Patriots were ignoring minor provisions of the convention. Sir William Howe found an excuse for breaking it. He claimed that he had been cheated by Washington in exchanges of prisoners. He would balance accounts. He planned, when Burgoyne's British troops embarked from New England, to bring them to New York for further service rather than to let them return to the British Isles. He was willing to let the Hessians who had served under Burgoyne proceed across the Atlantic. But Howe never had an opportunity to carry out his scheme. The Patriots also were dissatisfied with the convention. If Burgoyne's soldiers were allowed to go home, they could be used to replace garrison forces in Britain, thus enabling the British to send those troops to America. In this fashion at least some of the profits of the American triumph would be lost. Gates and Washington, like Howe, searched for excuses to break the convention. The Continental Congress did find reasons satisfactory to its members for keeping the army of Burgoyne in custody. The troops of the crestfallen general were led away to captivity.

The news that Burgoyne had laid down his arms at Saratoga shocked the British nation and shook the North ministry. It reached Paris together with reports that Washington's army had healthily survived the thrust by Sir William Howe into Pennsylvania. The advisers of Louis XVI of France learned for certain that the American rebellion was much more than a feeble insurrection, that the Patriots were formidable and dedicated to the cause of independence. The Comte de Vergennes insisted that the time had come, with the aid of the Americans, to strike heavily against proud and hated Britain. He had his way. France swiftly recognized the independence of the United States of America, entered into an alliance with the new nation, and then plunged into war against Britain, in 1778. In the following year Spain joined Britain's enemies. The War of Independence became an international struggle. The widening of the war almost assured American independence.

CHAPTER XXI

The American Federacy

IT is now time to turn from scenes of martial strife to arenas of political and social conflict, from the deeds of soldiers to the labors of American civilians. For, during the War of Independence, the Patriots formed an American federacy, creating thirteen states and a national government. Ideally, altruistic philosophers, generous-minded statesmen, and veteran politicians chosen by an informed and virtuous electorate ought to frame, or revise, the political institutions of mankind, in tranquillity and without haste. Neither the leaders of the Patriots nor their followers lacked blemishes. Moreover, compelled to construct a new order because of the destruction of British rule, the Americans faced that task in the midst of turmoil and battle. They were torn by jealousies and divisions among themselves. Nevertheless, they built well; they laid solid foundations for an enduring republic. They achieved political stability before the British armies and navy withdrew from their shores. The Americans of the Revolutionary generation created a liberal régime, one that was less oppressive than any other in the world. They executed social reforms of the first magnitude. So great were the changes made by that generation that some historians have been tempted to say that America underwent two revolutions in the third quarter of the eighteenth century. They have found an "external" one in the separation from Britain; they have seen an "internal" one within America. The word "Revolution" is often abused. The Americans of that era did not undergo a great domestic upheaval. They did not pass through a cataclysm such as that which began in France in 1789, such as that which commenced in Russia in 1917. They did basically reconstruct their institutions; they did advance, without excessive commotion, toward social equality and political democ-

racy—for white men. If one must affix a label to the domestic innovations
that came in America in the fourth quarter of the eighteenth century,
"Internal Reformation" is to be preferred to "Internal Revolution."

Whatever else may be said about historians, it can be asserted that,
like other scholars, they enjoy, or at least frequently engage in, scholarly
and hot contention. Tiring at last of one debate, they hasten into another.
They find it difficult to link sweetness with their own light and the vast
ignorance of their opponents. They might be more charitable, were they
to remember the results of intellectual contests among historians in the
past. Few of those quarrels ended in decisive victory for one party or
another. And often, alas, even the issue in such a struggle is now forgotten. Once upon a time, not so long ago, historians striving to defend the
powers of the American states against the authority of the central government vehemently asserted that the states were created before the nation, and that they had possessed, did possess, and of right ought to
possess, sovereignty. Other learned men proclaimed with equal force and
heat that the nation preceded its parts and that the central government
had possessed, did possess, and of right ought to possess, sovereignty.
The word "sovereignty" has not yet been satisfactorily defined, nor is it
likely to be. The use of it obfuscates, and it needlessly arouses national
and international passions. One cannot sensibly say that the states were
born before the central government, nor that the central government appeared before the states. All were, and still remain, projections of the
American body politic. They grew from that body together; they shared
power from the time when the Patriots overthrew British authority.

To be sure, the separate states acquired written constitutions before
the United States. The Patriots soon became dissatisfied with the Revolutionary régimes that blossomed in the colonial capitals during the
years 1774 to 1776. It was well that American executive committees
replaced royal and proprietary governors, that American conventions and
provincial congresses supplanted legislatures convened at the instance of
British executives. Nor was the transition, though attended by upheaval,
remarkably difficult. The lower houses of assembly in several colonies
merely transformed themselves by fiat into Patriot legislatures, and supplied the vacancies left by the departure of British governors. In some
colonies the Patriots were compelled to push aside existing assemblies
and to form others. Even when they created new legislatures, they followed existing patterns of election and procedure as far as circumstances
permitted. However, those new governments, even though they all arose,
phoenixlike, from the ashes of their colonial predecessors, were extra-
legal. Many of the Americans were accustomed to charters. Their leaders

subscribed to the compact theory. Was it not prudent—even necessary, in order to prevent the substitution of American tyranny for arbitrary British rule—to devise organic documents that would limit the authority of lawmakers, executives, and judges, that would protect the rights of the governed? The Patriots began to prepare fundamental written laws in several states for emergency, even for permanent use before the Declaration of Independence. A temporary constitution was adopted in New Hampshire on January 5, 1776, in South Carolina on March 26. Basic laws intended to endure were promulgated in Virginia on June 29. New Jersey also resolved, before the Declaration of Independence, to prepare basic laws that were to be observed into the indefinite future. The making of constitutions went on apace in the American states in 1776 and 1777. All of them put such a document into force long before the end of the War of Independence. Some of them were used as fundamental instruments of government for a half century. The written constitution, though not invented by the Patriots, became a special feature of the American political order, for they also soon established one for their nation. Moreover, the Americans used such documents successfully over many generations. They offered an example that was afterward copied in many parts of the globe. It is no secret that the sophisticated anthropoids who have dominated the earth for many centuries have achieved less than entire success in governing themselves. That they can control their primordial, their savage impulses under any sort of institution remains doubtful. Nevertheless, resorting to the device of the written constitution, the Americans of the Revolutionary age contributed handsomely to the art of government.

The Patriots also developed praiseworthy methods both for the making and for the adoption of such constitutions. The first of those instruments contrived by the Patriots were drawn by Revolutionary gatherings in hurry, in troubled times, even in the shadow of advancing British armies. They were prepared and put into effect by men much engaged in raising money, collecting troops, repressing Tories, and carrying on the everyday business of government. Late in 1775 the Continental Congress urged that no Revolutionary body undertake to draft a constitution unless that body was chosen by "a full and free representation" of the people in an election in which constitution-making was an issue. Most of the Revolutionary assemblies were authorized by Patriot voters to make constitutions. However, some constitutions were drawn by men not specifically permitted to act. In no state was the handiwork of the Revolutionary legislature submitted to the voters for approval or disapproval. Soon there was public outcry against such procedures. Was it right that fundamental law should be molded by men not specially and exclusively elected for that purpose? And ought not the voters to decide whether the product of the constitution-framers was satisfactory? And if they were not permitted to render a verdict by popular vote, ought not their will to be expressed through conventions specially elected by them to weigh the merits of those constitutions? Patriots who desired that their political institutions be made more truly representative and more democratic than they had been in the colonial time protested against the use of machinery that made difficult the expression of the popular will. As early as 1776 the voters of Concord town sturdily protested against the arbitrary imposition upon them of a political system limned by lawmakers of Massachusetts and intended to buttress domination of the state by its authors and their like. Had the plain men of Concord taken up their muskets on April 19, 1775, merely for the replacement of British masters by American ones? The Patriots in power in Massachusetts at first declined to give heed to the outcry from Concord. It was neither seemly nor safe to permit farmers, woodsmen, laborers, clerks, and sailors to participate directly in the drafting of ordinary law, in the taking of executive decisions. Why, then, should such less competent, such incompetent folk be allowed to play a role in the making of an all-important instrument of government, a difficult enterprise beyond the understanding and abilities of ill-informed and emotional men? Did the citizens of Concord desire mob rule, or anarchy? However, the vigorous complaint from that place was followed by others from many Massachusetts towns. John Adams, who had less than absolute faith in the ability and character of men lacking education and property, who did not, indeed, admire mankind in general, became alarmed. He and other leaders in the Bay State strove to persuade the Patriot rank and file that they ought gladly to accept direction from their superiors. Adams and his associates did not succeed. Similar attempts by similar leaders failed in the other states. Thomas Jefferson and many liberal-minded public men who harbored less fear of American humanity pointed out that the compact theory enunciated by the hallowed John Locke and the Declaration of Independence required that citizens—at least property owners and taxpayers—take an active part in the making of new political contracts. Gradually that argument won acceptance. Before the end of the War of Independence a constitution for Massachusetts was both prepared by a convention specially chosen for the purpose and endorsed in a special election. New Hampshire soon followed the example of Massachusetts. Thereafter the constitutional convention and the constitutional referendum became fixtures in the American political system.

Quarreling over the manner in which the organic laws of their states should be devised and adopted, the Patriots also engaged in hot debate concerning their content, with two striking exceptions. There was general consent that the form of government must be republican, for it would have been absurd even to think of a King for Connecticut, Maryland, Georgia, or any of the American commonwealths. Indeed, few Americans ever considered monarchy as desirable or possible for the nation as a whole after 1776. Agreed that they must have republican institutions, nearly all the Patriots also insisted that citizens be protected against state legislators, executives, and judges by the solemn promulgation of a Bill of Rights.

Many of the Patriots conceived that safeguards for the individual against arbitrary rule were actually more important than description of governmental machinery. Their leaders recalled the English Bill of Rights enacted by Parliament in 1689. It had barred various acts of tyranny in England. Surely the same bulwarks against despotism were needed, if less desperately, in America. Accordingly, every state formally declared that its people possessed various personal liberties that were inviolable. They were either listed in the state constitution or in a separate document that was considered to be as sacred as, even superior to, the state constitution. Not identical, those documents commonly required formal indictment of persons accused of crime, and declared that such persons were entitled to use of the writ of *habeas corpus,* reasonable bail, and trial by jury. Cruel and unusual punishments were forbidden, together with double jeopardy. Unreasonable searches and seizures of persons and property were prohibited. *Ex post facto* laws and the taking of private property for public use without compensation were barred. Such documents proclaimed the right of the individual to the possession of arms. The freedoms of the press, of petition, and of peaceable assembly were usually and specifically guaranteed. On paper, the Bills of Rights offered strong defenses against tyrannous governors, lawmakers, and magistrates. They did not, alas, put armor upon the individual that could not be penetrated. On the other hand, they offered weapons that lawyers and judges would use on behalf of vicious criminals. Even so, the protections given by those documents were essential to personal liberty. Together with the federal Bill of Rights, they have provided a large measure of freedom for the Americans against political and judicial abuse through many generations. The Patriots could not prevent every future invasion of personal liberty. Establishing as firm safeguards as they could, they inevitably consigned the task of maintaining and strengthening those protective devices to their successors.

While very generally agreed that they were opposed to despotism, especially of a British variety, the Patriots were by no means unanimously and utterly devoted to representative democracy. There were among them men who believed that the wishes of the mass—at least the desires of the white and masculine part of the mass—ought to dictate public policy. But there were many Patriot leaders—and followers—who placed much less than entire trust in the integrity and wisdom of ignorant and poor folk, who insisted that power must be wielded by propertied, educated, and superior men. In consequence, the making of the state constitutions was attended by acrimonious controversy.

The framers of those documents were often students of political philosophy as well as veterans in public affairs. Nor did they lack models. They were, of course, familiar with the systems of government that had prevailed in the colonies before 1775. They were not uninformed about the political order in Britain. They knew their John Locke, their Algernon Sidney, their William Blackstone, both from the writings of those scholars and from innumerable glosses upon those writings. Some of them were familiar, even too familiar, with *L'Esprit des Lois* of the French Baron de la Brède et de Montesquieu, that massive work which appeared in 1748 and which stressed the need for balanced government and separation of powers. Montesquieu, unhappily contemplating absolute Kings and Emperors on the European Continent, mistakenly conceived that Britain's limited monarchy was almost ideal, in part because he erroneously believed that legislative, executive, and judicial powers were distinctly compartmented in England. Misled by Montesquieu, some of the Patriots would insist upon excessively sharp divisions of authority. Very few of them had heard even the name of Jean Jacques Rousseau. It was perhaps just as well. The Patriots also had an opportunity to inspect specially prepared plans for state government. One was offered by Thomas Paine, who urged that each state establish a large unicameral assembly which should elect its own President and which should exercise virtually all authority not given to a national congress. Paine feared single and strong executives, independent and potent judges. Another scheme, presumed to be the work of Carter Braxton of Virginia, proposed a quite different system. It called for an elected lower house; an upper chamber composed of members chosen for life terms by the popular one; and a governor who would name all civil, military, and judicial officers. It is apparent that Paine preferred arrangements which would permit the mass to express its will, while the so-called Braxton design was intended to put power in the hands of the good and the few, to prevent "mob rule." A third model, carefully worked out by John Adams in his *Thoughts on Government* (1776) and widely circulated, was better drawn and far more influential than the other two. Adams insisted upon the need for two houses, a lower house elected by the voters, an upper chamber chosen by the lower one. These would annually choose a governor, who, with the consent of a privy council, would have a veto upon legislation. Experience might demonstrate that the governor should be directly elected by the voters. Judges were to be chosen by the legislature, and were to hold office during good behavior. County officers were to be elected by the voters. Adams desired a balanced structure. He would have a strong executive, but one checked by a council and secure in office for only a brief period. His bicameral legislature would enable the voters to voice their wishes, but would also permit the fewer able citizens to check the many less competent ones. Adams was a devoted republican, but he believed that the body politic ought to follow the leadership of educated men possessing both probity and talent—men like himself. He conceived that the suffrage should be confined to adult male owners of property. Mature but poor men, he thought, were no better fitted to vote than women or inexperienced youths.

The system fashioned by Adams was nowhere adopted in its entirety. It was offensive to many Patriots because it conceded too much authority to aristocrats and would-be aristocrats; it displeased other Patriots because it gave too great power to homestead farmers, shop owners, and mechanics. However, it did offer a storehouse of ideas that was rummaged by constitution-makers. Adams exerted more influence upon them than any other man.

The Patriots were indeed much divided with respect to their political goals. They had not formed an indivisible mass before the battle of Lexington and Concord. They all desired an end to British domination. They were nearly all republicans. So long as the War of Independence continued, they were also agreed that Loyalists must not be permitted to take an active part in public affairs. However, when they began to labor toward creating a new nation, they fell into three quarreling groups. One of these, the Conservatives, desired as little fundamental change as possible from the régime that had existed before the war. Led by planters, wealthy merchants, prosperous lawyers, and Anglican and Congregational clergymen, they believed that the power formerly wielded by the British ought to pass to American patricians—themselves—who had shared authority in the past with royal and proprietary officers. Those worthy, those superior, those experienced men ought to rule. The Conservatives desired restricted suffrage; bicameral legislatures; indirect election and long terms of office for members of the upper chamber; relatively powerful executives; high property qualifications for lawmakers and governors; and ap-

334

pointed and independent judges. They stood for sound money; they tended to defend established churches; they were averse to re-districting that would enable city mechanics and Western pioneers to voice their wishes more effectively. As the War of Independence continued, they increasingly favored the establishment of a strong national government, which, of course, they hoped to dominate. Among the Conservatives were Edmund Pendleton and George Washington of Virginia; the Rutledge brothers, John and Edward, of South Carolina; John Dickinson; John Adams; and sundry other prominent men less distinguished for character and magnanimity.

At sharp odds with the Conservatives were the Radicals, also known as the Democrats. The labels applied to them correctly indicate that they desired many and far-reaching changes. The mass of them was composed of plain and poor farmers, backwoodsmen, tradesmen, artisans, laborers, and clerks. But they were not without educated leaders, for lawyers, planters, and politicians such as Patrick Henry, George Bryan of Pennsylvania, and Thomas Person of North Carolina espoused their cause. The Radicals demanded representative democracy. To them, one white man was as good as another. Hence, all white adults ought to possess the suffrage, and the vote of a poor backwoods settler ought to have as much weight as that of a prosperous Tidewater merchant. The Radicals sought for unicameral legislatures, or for bicameral bodies in which the upper house was directly elected by the voters for short terms. They desired weak executives who could not become tyrants; they urged that judges be popularly chosen for short periods of office. They disliked established churches. Often, being debtors rather than creditors, they sought to improve their own condition by expanding the supply of paper currency. Even more than other Patriots, they were disposed to deal harshly with the Loyalists.

Between those Democrats and the Conservatives was a smaller body of moderates, the Liberals. These were men who detested domination by the sophisticated, propertied, and selfish few, but who doubted that all white males should immediately exert equal weight in public affairs. They would have a generous suffrage. Perhaps, in time, it would be safe, and even indispensable, to permit all adult males to vote. The Liberals disliked unequal electoral districts. They rather favored bicameral legislatures in which the lower house would have larger authority than the upper. They disliked strong executives and independent and arrogant judges. The Liberals were hostile to established sects; they desired religious freedom. Looking toward the future, they favored the founding and fostering of schools at public expense. As the mass of Americans became more enlightened, the suffrage could be expanded. The Liberals desired progress, and believed that it could be achieved. They sought to find a middle way. Their sympathies were with mass rather than class. As the years passed, they came to believe, with misgivings, that it was necessary to create a sturdy national government. Their leaders included broad-minded planters, lawyers, physicians, and newspaper publishers. Conspicuous among them were Thomas Jefferson, James Madison, Dr. Benjamin Rush of Philadelphia, and George Clinton of New York.

To classify the Patriots as Conservatives, Liberals, and Radicals is to establish divisions that are, in part, both arbitrary and inexact. Surely there were Patriots who gave little attention to public questions, who were largely indifferent. Besides, the loyalties and antipathies within the three parties were not uniform. John Adams may be described as a moderate Conservative—but were his views much different from those of Jefferson? Was he not closer to Jefferson than he was to many Conservatives? A Conservative might be a passionate enemy of an established church; a Radical might be merely a politician seeking personal gain by giving lip service to sentiments that he did not feel. Indeed, it is not to be doubted that all the principal men in the three groups were motivated to a lesser or greater degree by lust for personal power. Moreover, their allegiances and hostilities were not necessarily permanent. With the passage of time men wandered from one camp to another. Is it not true that human beings are fickle, inconsistent in ideals, inconstant in principle, irresolute in practice? The labels Conservative, Liberal, and Radical are useful; they are not precise and absolute descriptions.

In that struggle in the states the Conservatives enjoyed advantages. They possessed prestige and wealth; and they were often entrenched in office. They could vote, and their votes weighed more than those cast by backwoodsmen. Some of them, possessing property in several counties, could support several candidates. However, they were not uniformly victorious. The Tories, who would have been inclined toward the Conservatives, were not permitted to express their opinions. Moreover, standing forth as champions of the rights of mankind against the British, the Conservatives found it a trifle awkward to deny those rights to the humbler Americans. Since the thought often follows the word, it is even likely that some Conservatives who condemned the British for violating those rights came to believe that the wishes of their Patriot brethren ought not be entirely ignored. Besides, it was necessary not to alienate the Radicals utterly, so long as the War of Independence continued, for their help was needed to achieve military victory. The Radicals often secured the help of the Liberals. The contest was hot in some states. An armed clash between

Conservatives and Radicals in Philadelphia in 1779 resulted in the deaths of two men. There was commotion in Charleston five years later, and militia were called up to maintain order in that city. Generally, however, internal clash was a matter of words, votes, and political manipulation rather than gunfire or blows.

The results of the struggle in the states were various. The Conservatives were victorious in New York, Maryland, and South Carolina, the Democrats in Georgia. In Maryland the provisions of the constitution were largely dictated by wealthy planters and lawyers such as Charles Carroll of Carrollton, Edward Lloyd, William Paca, and Thomas Johnson. These men were determined that they and their kind should rule. Accordingly, they stipulated that the suffrage be exercised only by men who owned 50 acres of land or property worth £30, and they saw to it that eastern Maryland, where planters and merchants flourished, was overrepresented at the expense of the western part of the state, which was inhabited principally by homestead farmers. To make sure that the legislature would do nothing toward diffusion of wealth, they established a bicameral system. The members of the lower house were required to possess property worth at least £500, those of a senate property valued at £1,000 or more. Moreover, the senators were to be indirectly elected for terms of six years. Thus, though the governor in Maryland had little power, even though local officers were elected rather than appointed, the Conservatives established strong bulwarks against "mob rule." In Georgia it was otherwise. There the Democrats were unrestrained. They gave the suffrage to all men owning property worth £10, established a secret ballot, and imposed a fine of £5 upon qualified men who failed to use the franchise. They set up a virtually unrestrained unicameral assembly. Each of its members was required to possess 250 acres of land or £250. Local officers were to be elected, state officials to be chosen by the legislature. Juries were authorized to determine the law as well as the facts, and even to ignore laws that violated the constitution. Clergymen were barred from the legislature. In consequence, Georgia had majority rule for some years—until its government temporarily vanished in consequence of conquest of the state by British arms.

In the main, the new state constitutions provided for governments that were much more responsive to the people than the colonial régimes they replaced. In no state was the right to vote given to all white men—a constitution prepared for Vermont in 1777 called for manhood suffrage, but Vermont was not recognized as a state until 1791. Every state demanded that the voter possess property or pay taxes. The suffrage was less generously granted in the state of New York than it was in the colony of New York. However, most white men could qualify for the ballot in most of the states. Electoral districts were often redrawn so as to give greater, even due weight to the votes of men who lived in the interior. Colonial capitals on the seacoast moved westward, toward the centers of population. Elected executives superseded governors chosen by the Crown or by proprietors. The authority of the governor was greatly reduced. Indeed, in several states he was only a President, merely the head of an executive council—even many Conservatives who detested "democracy" preferred to put power in a senate rather than in a governor who might behave as had British appointees. A bicameral legislature was established in most of the states, the lower house responsive to the wishes of the mass, the upper one dedicated to the protection of property. Elected judges and sheriffs commonly replaced appointed magistrates and police officers. The new régimes in the states, if not democratic, were truly republican. Political privilege continued, but it was reduced. In some states the voters could still do no more at the polling place than to choose between two gentlemen whose politics were identical, two gentlemen who assumed that they need not be too concerned about the opinions or wishes of their constituents. But the time was not far distant when it would be necessary for men engaged in public affairs to govern their behavior in accordance with the desires of the voters. American aristocrats and would-be aristocrats lost power and prestige during the Revolutionary era. Their natural allies, the royal and proprietary governors, treasurers, secretaries, judges, and councilors vanished, together with many gentlemen and ladies who espoused the cause of Britain. Representative democracy would come in America, within a half century, at least for white male adults. It did not triumph with the Revolution, but the foundations for it inherited from the colonial times were solidified and enlarged.

The Patriots, of course, insisted upon making, together with the state constitutions, a national one. They obviously had to form some sort of American union to preserve their independence, if not to gain it. It was therefore necessary, in their opinion, to forge an organic instrument by compact. Such a document would give stability to an American national government. It could also supply protection against arbitrary and tyrannous action by such a government. As early as July 1775, Benjamin Franklin drafted a plan for a confederation that was to endure until Anglo-American troubles were solved—or so long as the Americans desired it to continue. At that time most of the Patriots believed that it was not yet necessary or advisable to create a formal union. However, the approach of independence persuaded the Continental Congress that the time had come to act. It will be recalled, indeed, that in June 1776 sentiment in that body for constitutional union was perhaps even more pervasive than desire for separation from Britain. Only five days after the submission of Richard Henry Lee's resolution of June 7 calling for confederation and foreign alliances as well as independence, a committee of five was formed to draw up a constitution for the yet-to-be United States. It was agreed that, to be effective, the document must be endorsed by all of those states. It was evident that a stable central government would be of great value in prosecuting the war against Britain, and it was hoped that some sort of union could be speedily established. A wave of nationalism was sweeping over the delegates.

The committee of five, in which John Dickinson was the principal figure while he remained in Congress, labored most diligently. It produced a plan which was laid before the delegates on June 12. However, that scheme, which was largely the handiwork of Dickinson, did not receive enthusiastic acclaim and swift sanction by the Congress. There were, of course, many men within it who insisted upon tinkering with the Dickinson plan—and Dickinson was not present to defend it. Besides, it was far from ideal. It would have concentrated large authority in the central government, with one remarkable exception. That government was not to have power to tax. Even so, many delegates scented tyranny in the Dickinson constitution. Men from the Southern States feared that it would enable the Northern commonwealths to dictate measures injurious to Southern interests. It pleased men of a Conservative cast, but it was disliked by members of a Radical complexion. Its provisions set state delegation against state delegation. The Congress began to amend the Dickinson document, and continued to make changes now and then over many months. Its members had to put aside the business to direct the war effort; and British invasions of New Jersey in 1776 and Pennsylvania in 1777 interrupted their deliberations. At last, in November 1777, the Congress submitted the result of its toil, the Articles of Confederation, to the several state legislatures for ratification.

If the Dickinson constitution was less than perfect, it cannot be said that the document sent to the states for their endorsement was superbly drawn. Their defects were by no means identical, but they were almost equally serious. The Articles called for a "perpetual" union and a weak central government that would consist largely of a unicameral Congress. That body was to have control over foreign affairs. It was granted power to make war and peace, to enter into treaties and alliances. It was also permitted to maintain an army and a navy. Further, it was authorized to coin money, to establish a postal service, and to manage Indian affairs.

339

However, it was denied power to tax, being compelled to rely upon the proceeds of requisitions upon the states, which were to contribute funds for national purposes in proportion to the value of privately owned and improved lands within their borders. The Congress was thus given an uncertain and fluctuating income, for it was not given authority to compel the several states to make their payments in full and without delay. It was declared that the Articles were to be "inviolably observed by every state," but those words were—words. Indeed, far too much power and prestige was conceded to the states. The Congress was not permitted to regulate commerce, whether foreign or internal, and the Articles asserted that the states were to possess "sovereignty, freedom, and independence, and every power, jurisdiction, and right" which was not expressly delegated to the national government. Moreover, voting in the Congress was to be by states, each of their legislatures to elect from two to seven members of that body; and the consent of nine delegations was required in matters of fundamental importance. Deprived of means to coerce the states, the Congress was also denied power to exert its will upon individuals, except for those in its employ. In the main, the Articles provided for a central government that would wield the powers formerly exerted by Crown and Parliament. The proposed Congress strongly resembled the extra-legal Congress which had been functioning since 1775. It would remain extra-legal until 1781.

Why did Congress turn away from the strong central government envisaged in the Dickinson plan? In part, no doubt, the framers of the Articles acted from ignorance, being unaware that the system they proposed was ill contrived to meet the needs of a nation. The spirit of nationalism, so evident at the time of the Declaration of Independence, had waned. Particularism was obviously a potent force—delegates jealously fought for the rights of their respective states. Men from the smaller commonwealths were alarmed lest the larger ones dominate a powerful central government. They successfully insisted that the vote of Rhode Island count for as much as that of Pennsylvania, that Delaware possess as much weight in national affairs as Virginia. Indeed, the Congress as a whole was permeated by fear of tyranny. It contained Radicals and Liberals who were especially alarmed lest the Conservatives acquire sway at the national capital. Who desired concentration of power there? Was it not John Dickinson and others of his kind? Certainly clash between the South and the North helped to persuade delegates from the Southern States that it was dangerous to permit power to pass into the hands of Northerners.

For that chronic and harassing conflict between South and North that was to vex the Americans during so many generations had begun. Even before the Dickinson document was formally considered by Congress, even before the signing of the Declaration of Independence, Edward Rutledge of South Carolina declared that "the idea of destroying all provincial distinctions and making everything of the most minute kind bend to what they call the good of the whole, is in other terms to say that these [Southern] Colonies must be subject to the government of the eastern provinces." Rutledge would not be ruled by Yankees, or by New Yorkers. It may be significant that it was Thomas Burke of North Carolina who successfully moved that the phrase asserting the "sovereignty, freedom and independence" of the states be inserted in the Articles. The Virginia delegation did not support Burke, but all the others from the South endorsed his amendment. It was especially pleasing to the men from South Carolina.

Sharing with delegates from other states a common fear of tyrannical rule from the national capital, the men from the Southern commonwealths—Maryland, Virginia, the Carolinas, and Georgia—quarreled strenuously with their Northern colleagues over another issue. The Dickinson draft proposed that the states donate to the common treasury on the basis of numbers, excluding Indians not taxed. This arrangement was the cause for heated debate toward the end of July 1776, even before formal signature of the Declaration of Independence. Samuel Chase of Maryland said it was most improper, because, in his opinion, Negro slaves ought not be counted. They were property, like cattle, rather than persons. He moved that Negroes be omitted from the calculations of numbers. John Adams objected to Chase's motion. He contended that slaves produced as much wealth as white laborers, hence that they should be taken into account. James Wilson of Pennsylvania took his stand with Adams. He claimed that the change urged by Chase would permit Southerners to gather in the profits of slavery, and would compel Northerners to bear a burden resulting from that institution. Benjamin Harrison pointed out that it was unfair to the Southerners to assume that slaves created as much wealth as whites. He urged that two slaves be considered the equivalent of one white. His compromise satisfied Southerners, but not many Northerners. John Witherspoon of New Jersey, who saw merit in Harrison's argument, suggested apportionment of requisitions upon the basis of the value of improved lands, the scheme that was eventually adopted by the Congress. Witherspoon's proposal was condemned by New Englanders. Their constituents, with their developed and well-kept lands, would be penalized for industry and thrift. Men from the South rallied behind Chase, and the contest became sharper. Thomas Lynch of South

Carolina asserted that it was idle to talk further about an American federation if Northerners refused to admit that slaves were property. Lynch and Edward Rutledge declared that they were taxed as such. Disclaiming any affection for the institution of slavery, Rutledge insisted that it would be unfair to consider Negroes as persons, since the profits from Northern merchant shipping, which would grow, were not to be taken into account. William Hooper of North Carolina disliked apportionment in accordance with population. His state had many people and comparatively little property. The Northerners declined to compromise. The Chase amendment was defeated by an almost completely sectional vote. Pennsylvania, New Jersey, New York, and the New England states opposed it; Delaware and four Southern states supported it. Georgia was divided.

But that decision was not final. Chase and other delegates from Maryland warned that their state would never approve the Articles unless altered. It was apparent that other Southern commonwealths would similarly balk. The Witherspoon formula was then reconsidered. The New Englanders continued to fulminate against it. The states had been asked to supply troops to the Continental army in proportion to their white population. Surely, it was only just to employ a formula based upon numbers, with slaves counted. However, the Yankees delegates pleaded in vain. It was necessary to settle the issue. At length, by another sectional vote, the Congress adopted the Witherspoon scheme. Five states, Maryland, Virginia, the Carolinas, and New Jersey, voted for it; the delegations from New York and Pennsylvania split; and only the four New England states cast ballots against it.

So that sectional quarrel ended in Congress, but it was revived and others developed when the Articles were examined in the state legislatures. Connecticut offered an amendment proposing a return to numbers, including slaves, as the basis for settling state donations for national needs. Other states, both Northern and Southern, urged minor changes in behalf of their respective regional interests. South Carolina requested major alterations. That state emphatically voiced sectional fears and asked for several basic amendments, in the main, no doubt, because of the efforts of William Henry Drayton.

Had he not died young, William Henry Drayton would be well known as a Patriot leader. A graduate of Oxford, a scion of a respected family, he had married an heiress, and had moved to the forefront among the aristocrats of South Carolina. Conceited and arrogant, he was also able, brave, and bold. He had dared to defend publicly the legality of the Stamp Act and of the Townshend duties. Then, reversing his course, he had joined the Patriots and had displayed executive ability and zeal in the American cause. He had become one of the principal leaders of the Patriots in his state. He saw numerous defects in the Articles of Confederation, and he offered a substitute constitution to the South Carolina legislature for its consideration. He flatly declared that there were in America a South and a North with opposed interests, and that those of the South must be constitutionally protected against Northern attack. He anticipated John C. Calhoun. The Articles, he said, gave too much power to Congress. And it would be wielded against the South, unless an unassailable barrier was raised against Northern aggression. He would deny to Congress "any power that can with propriety, be exercised by the several states—or any power but what is clearly defined beyond a doubt." Above all, he disliked the provision in the Articles which permitted Congress to make major decisions with the consent of only nine state delegations.

> When I reflect, that from the nature of the climate, soil and produce of the several states, a northern and southern interest in many particulars naturally and unavoidably rise; I cannot but be displeased with the prospect, that the most important transactions in congress, may be done contrary to the united opposition of Virginia, the two Carolinas and Georgia; states possessing more than one half of the whole territory of the confederacy; and forming, as I may say, the body of the southern interest . . . the honor, interest and sovereignty of the South, are in effect delivered up to the care of the north. Do we intend to make such a surrender?

Denying fear that "the north would abuse the confidence of the south," Drayton nevertheless demanded that all important measures adopted by Congress require the approval of eleven state delegations. Thus Congress would be prevented from declaring war, making peace, ratifying a treaty, or doing anything of great moment, without the consent of two of the four delegations from Virginia, the Carolinas, and Georgia.

Drayton was not the only Carolinian who anticipated clash between South and North and who sought to raise barriers for the defense of the South. The legislature of his state, in January 1778, set aside his personal constitution. However, it proposed many amendments to the Articles to protect Southern interests, among them a provision requiring the consent of eleven states in Congress for its more important actions.

But South Carolina was not yet prepared to enter into desperate struggle in defense of the South. Her amendments were rejected by the Congress, together with all others put forward by this state and that. Thereupon South Carolina ratified the Articles of Confederation, without

343

further complaint. After all, would the Congress for which it provided be able to do anything seriously detrimental to the South? There was little fear in the other Southern states that the Articles would serve as a vehicle for oppression by the North. Georgia, like South Carolina, vainly asked that clauses guaranteeing "all privileges and immunities of free citizens in the several states" to "the free inhabitants of each of these states" be altered so as to deny those "privileges and immunities" to Negroes. Neither Maryland nor Virginia nor North Carolina requested special protection for the South. North-South clash did not prevent establishment of a national government. But the stand taken by South Carolina, feeble as it turned out to be, was a harbinger of many and dangerous disputes to come.

Congress refused to make any changes in the Articles in the hope of securing early ratification by all the state legislatures. Accordingly, it rejected statesmanlike amendments submitted by New Jersey which would have given Congress authority to regulate maritime commerce and to levy import taxes. Those alterations would have improved the Articles enormously. Having its own tax funds, the Congress would have been able to make effective use of the powers vested in it. As it was, that body would suffer sadly from lack of a reliable supply of money.

Rather oddly—at least rather oddly in view of later events—ratification of the Articles was long delayed, until 1781, not by struggle between North and South, but because of contest over ownership and exploitation of the West, the vast region between the Appalachians and the Mississippi. The Articles were warmly condemned in Maryland, not because the citizens of that state feared aggression from the North, but because they were jealous of Virginia and Virginians. They cherished resentment against the Old Dominion because, like the people of all the smaller states, they dreaded domination by the large commonwealths, Massachusetts, Pennsylvania, and Virginia. An even more important reason for their distrust and dislike of Virginia and of the Articles was the fact that the Articles did not establish western boundaries for the states. Virginia and other states—Massachusetts, Connecticut, New York, North Carolina, South Carolina, and Georgia—claimed that their territories extended beyond the Appalachian divide, to the Mississippi, even, except for New York, to the Pacific Ocean. Soon after the beginning of the War of Independence a Maryland convention declared that the lands beyond the Appalachians, if they became American soil, must become the common property of all Americans. The Marylanders asserted, quite logically, that the region between the mountains and the Mississippi, if they became part of the American republic, would be won by the exertions and sacrifices of

344

all the Patriots. Hence, the Marylanders demanded that all the claims of the "landed" states be canceled by the Articles of Confederation. Thus the state pride of the Marylanders would be soothed, for the existing disparity between Maryland and Virginia in terms of size and population would not be increased. Besides, if Virginia did not control a large part of the West, if the West were placed under the authority of Congress, the Marylanders would enjoy equal opportunity with the Virginians to acquire lands beyond the mountain divide; they would not be forced to compete under handicaps with Virginians for land grants at the capital or at the county seats of the Old Dominion. Some Marylanders were motivated more specifically by desire for personal advantage. They were investors—among them Charles Carroll of Carrollton, Thomas Johnson, and Samuel Chase—in land companies which had been created to secure and to exploit wide stretches of trans-Appalachian lands in areas claimed by Virginia. Their Indiana, Wabash, and Illinois Companies were striving to establish unassailable titles to those lands, by purchase from Indians, by any and all means. And their efforts were severely cramped by the Old Dominion, which declared all their enterprises to be illegal.

The demand of Maryland, supported by other "landless" states, such as New Jersey and Delaware, was sharply denounced in Congress in 1776 by delegates from the "landed" states. The men from Virginia, swayed by pride in their state and the economic interests of the Virginians, and well aware that the Marylanders were moved by selfish interests, insisted that the south bank of the Ohio River, together with all that vast region between the Ohio, the Mississippi, and the Great Lakes afterward known as the Old Northwest, belonged to the Old Dominion by virtue of her charter of 1609. Maryland and her "landless" sisters won the first engagement, for the Dickinson draft substantially met their wishes. However, the men from the "landed" states later managed to alter the Articles of Confederation, before that document was submitted to the states, so that their claims were not injured. The "landless" states, except for Maryland, before long abandoned the quarrel, though reluctantly. However, Maryland refused to yield. That state flatly declined to endorse the Articles, unless the domains beyond the mountains were placed under the authority of Congress, unless the pretensions of the Maryland speculators were sanctioned. Virginia struck back, formally declaring that the claims of those speculators to Virginia lands were void. Further, in the spring of 1779, Virginia urged that the Articles of Confederation be put into operation by the twelve states that had approved the document. Maryland could go her own separate way, if she so desired. The Connecticut men in Congress found the proposal made by Virginia acceptable, but better judgment prevailed. It was most important that none of the states be omitted from the United States. Sentiment in Congress gradually veered. Ought not the "landed" commonwealths to make concessions? New York had the weakest claim to lands over the Appalachian divide—it was based upon a questionable suzerainty over the Iroquois nation, which claimed a doubtful suzerainty over tribes that lived to the westward. In February 1780, New York offered to abandon at least part of her pretensions, for the common good. In the fall of that year Congress asked the other "landed" states to do likewise. Virginia in particular was put to the test. Her response had far-reaching consequences.

The Virginians remained reluctant to abandon their hope of building a state empire beyond the mountains, even though much of that empire was actually in the possession of the British and their Indian allies. But the Virginians were neither utterly selfish nor completely lacking in vision. As early as November 1778, Richard Henry Lee expressed doubt that a vast Virginia stretching to the Great Lakes would be a healthy and truly republican state. Here was a reason of sorts for ceding all the lands north of the Ohio to the central government. But he offered a better one. Such a cession would promote the welfare of all the Americans. In 1779 the legislature of Virginia indicated that Lee was not the only man in the state who was willing to sacrifice for the common American good. That body declared that it might be wise "at a future day" to create new states beyond the Appalachians. Toward the end of 1780, Lee, Thomas Jefferson, James Madison, and Joseph Jones, displaying that generous statesmanship so frequently offered by the Virginians of the Revolutionary generation, urged that the Old Dominion make concessions to the "landless" states. That step was necessary in order to placate Maryland and to secure adoption of the Articles of Confederation and the establishment of an American union. Hence, on January 2, 1781, the Virginia assembly, continuing to declare that the private claims of Marylanders to lands beyond the Ohio were invalid, ceded to the United States the right of Virginia to the whole of the Old Northwest. Then Connecticut, reserving lands in that region for her citizens, presented her authority within it to the central government. It became clear that the "landed" states would yield to the wishes of the "landless" ones. Virginia would not countenance the special interests of Maryland speculators north of the Ohio, but Virginia would not discriminate against Maryland as a state or against her people merely because they were not Virginians. The legislature of Maryland responded generously to generosity. It would not demand that the claims of the Maryland land speculators be sanctioned as a price for endorsing the Articles. In February 1781, it formally authorized its delegates in Congress to declare that the thirteenth state had ratified the Articles. On March 1 Congress was able to announce that, after almost five years of labor and contest, the American confederation had been created.

Setting aside selfish personal desires, state pride, and sectional antagonism, the Americans had succeeded in forming a union. The Congress that met after March 1, 1781, looked very much like the one that existed before that day, but it had a constitutional basis. Events would soon demonstrate that the central government established by the Articles of Confederation was too weak to satisfy the needs of the American people. Indeed, vigorous efforts to strengthen that government began even before that constitution went into force. However, nearly two more years of war and five years of troubled peace passed before it was possible to make a stronger union under the Constitution.

The solution to the quarrel between the "landed" and "landless" states had far-reaching consequences. Ensuring the adoption of the Articles of Confederation, it also gave the central government authority over immense domains beyond the Appalachians. So it ultimately endowed that government with vast power. Moreover, after the British departed from the region, the Americans owned territories of imperial proportions in common. Thus was created a new bond among them. The importance of the Thirteen States was reduced; allegiance to the nation was immediately increased. Their common ownership of such extensive and rich lands in the valley of the Mississippi encouraged the Americans to strengthen their central government. If their union collapsed, what would become of those lands? Moreover, the many Americans who soon settled beyond the Ohio, and not long afterward across the Mississippi—and who were permitted to form new states—were much less moved by particularistic prides than were those who remained in the original Thirteen States. American nationalism was fortified. The rise of a relatively nationalistic West contributed to the preservation of the United States in the grinding trial of the Civil War.

CHAPTER XXII

Social Reform

CHANGES in America generated or fostered by separation from Britain were not confined to things political. The separation also offered opportunity for and gave impetus to social reforms that were both extensive and beneficial. It was not accompanied by profound economic overturn. However, the political and social innovations in America in the last quarter of the eighteenth century, considered together, were so impressive that one may not be surprised by the coming into historical vogue of the term "Internal Revolution." In the twentieth century historians and political scientists, observing, often unhappily, the rapid passage of power from state capitals to Washington, consoled themselves with the thought that the states would remain useful as laboratories in which political and social novelties could be tested before they were adopted for the nation as a whole. In the days of the Confederation, the central government lacked both power and money to do very much about domestic reform. However, the states were able to act, and they did. With some assistance from the central government they struck hard against religious discrimination and hereditary privilege. The Revolutionary generation also aimed blows at Negro slavery, sought to spread the benefits of education, and remodeled antiquated laws. The wide diffusion of property was encouraged, so that the typical white American family continued during many decades to be one that lived upon its own farm. Many benefits came to the Americans with, if not in entire consequence of, the severing of ties with Britain.

Among the splendid works of that generation were the measures it took to increase religious freedom. Although the Americans, on the whole, suffered less from persecution because of their faith, or lack of it, than any people in Europe, there was, it will be recalled, legal discrimination on the score of religion in one degree or another in every American colony at the beginning of the War of Independence. Even many of those who fled across the Atlantic so that they might worship God in their own fashion attempted to force other Americans to adopt their way and to see their light. Indeed, if one knows what lies beyond death, is he not obligated to teach his fellow men the truth, even to combining compulsion with persuasion? If he knows that they will suffer eternally because they kneel before a false God or none, because they are improperly baptized, because they erroneously celebrated the Lord's supper, because they fail to keep one or more of His commandments, is it not his duty to do whatever may be requisite to save them, even to torture and to destroy their temporal bodies in order to save their eternal souls? Happily, few Americans ever did combine utter faith and inescapable logic to reach that remorseless and bloody conclusion. They, or their forebears, came from parts of Europe in which the fury of religious persecution had waned. No one sect was dominant throughout the colonies. Except for a few Jews, the Americans were Christians, but of many varieties. No one of those Christian divisions could reasonably hope to destroy all the others in all the colonies. However, at the outbreak of the War of Independence, the Congregationalists were sufficiently possessed of zeal and numbers to maintain official churches in New Hampshire, Massachusetts, and Connecticut, and also to discriminate seriously against other Christians and non-Christians. The Anglican, or Episcopal, Church, though less firmly entrenched, was established by law in all the Southern Colonies. Its clergy and too many of its laymen believed that its power and privilege were specially sanctioned by God. Moreover, favor was given to orthodox Christians at the expense of agnostics, deists, atheists, Jews, and unorthodox Christians even in those colonies where no one kind of Christianity was legally exalted above the others.

Fortunately, most of the great leaders of the Revolutionary generation were devoted to religious as well as political liberty. Christian by inheritance and rearing, they declined in maturity to believe that the whole truth about man, about his eternal destination, about the universe, was to be found in revelations vouchsafed to certain persons among the Hebrews more than seventeen centuries before their own time. Nor could they concede the validity of elaborate and ingenious interpretations of the personality and mission of Christ offered by ancient Greek logicians, by St. Augustine, by Thomas Aquinas, by the papacy, by Martin Luther, by John Calvin, or by Anglican Archbishop William Laud. Much less could they accept a claim by any clergyman that he or his church provided the one and only avenue to personal salvation. In their old age Jefferson and John Adams exchanged opinions in a fascinating series of letters. Jefferson declared that he detested the Roman Church. Why, asked Adams, should the Virginian confine his loathing to that one church? All religious hierarchies, asserted Adams, were as vicious as orders of nobility.

The Enlightenment that spread over Europe in the eighteenth century crossed the Atlantic. It became evident to learned Americans as well as Europeans, in consequence of the discoveries of Isaac Newton, that the earth is a satellite of one sun among many, and that stars, planets, and satellites move in accordance with physical laws. How could elaborate Christian dogmas be reconciled with that new knowledge? They could not be, save by intricate casuistry. What, then, could a man who placed reliance in learning, in reason, believe? There had been among the Christians, from the time when they first appeared, men who did not subscribe to the abstruse doctrine of the Trinity, who looked upon Christ as a teacher of surpassing excellence, as an utterly splendid instrument of God, rather than as a divinity. The number of those unitarians was vastly increased as a result of the Enlightenment. Among them were Jefferson and John Adams, both of whom continued to believe in God and personal survival beyond death. Other learned men, deists, gave their allegiance to a Creator and Manager of the universe who might or might not be very much concerned about the destiny of a man, or even that of mankind. Agnostics appeared among the Americans, and doubtless even a few atheists, those people whose confident assertion that there is nothing divine or purposive in the universe is as dubious as the statements of those who know God, His history, His works, and His intentions in minutest detail. Among the Patriot unitarians and deists, in addition to Jefferson and John Adams, were George Washington, General Charles Lee, Thomas Paine, the mature Benjamin Franklin, and Ethan Allen. So it was that Washington, an Episcopalian in form, many times worshipped in Christ Church in Philadelphia, but did not take part in communion; so it was that he refers in his writings to the Creator and to Providence in Masonic and deistic language, but not to Jehovah, or even to Christ. Thus also can be explained the allusions in the Declaration of Independence, not to a God wondrously unveiled by the Scriptures, but to "Nature's God," a "Creator," and a "Divine Providence."

Heresy and discontent arising from the existence of religious privilege and tyranny were not confined to a few educated Patriots at the beginning of the War of Independence. Many of the less sophisticated Americans had become indifferent, had abandoned church membership, had ceased to attend services. Moreover, both clergymen and laymen of churches that suffered from legal discrimination were unhappy. In Maryland the Episcopalians were in a minority, but their church was supported by public funds. Roman Catholics, with Baptists and Quakers, contributed through taxes to maintain Episcopal clergymen in comfort; nevertheless, in a commonwealth founded by adherents of the Church of Rome, they could not legally hold office. Those who did not subscribe to the tenets of the Church of England were all the more discontented because its clergymen in Maryland were renowned for loose living rather than piety and good works. In Virginia, Presbyterians, Baptists, and agnostics alike were forced to help maintain Episcopal ministers who were less than devoted to Christ, less than solicitous for the welfare of their parishioners. In Massachusetts and New Hampshire the Congregationalists permitted some other Protestants to worship freely, and even excused them from paying taxes for the support of Congregationalist churches and clergymen. However, Congregationalism was firmly established. In Connecticut, too, a few Protestant sects were tolerated; but the orthodox Congregationalists of that commonwealth even discriminated against heretical congregations of their own sect. Anglicans who lorded it over other Christians in the South were themselves the victims of persecution in New England. The enmity harbored by the several sects toward each other enabled the enlightened Patriot leaders to move toward separation of church and state. Divisions among those sects, particularly the Congregationalists and Presbyterians, also served to weaken publicly supported orthodoxies. The Baptists, always stoutly opposed to linkage of church and state, steadily rallied behind the gentlemen who fought to establish religious liberty. In consequence, it was possible for reformers to destroy or weaken religious privilege in state after state. They engaged in many sharp struggles; they were not uniformly or completely victorious.

The Anglican Church was less able to defend its privileges than the Congregationalist one, in part because it was associated with Britain and Loyalism. Never firmly rooted in Georgia, it was swiftly disestablished in that state. The Georgia constitution of 1777 ordained freedom of religion—except for worship destructive of public peace and safety. That church was also quickly reduced to the level of others in North Carolina, where it had few clergymen and few adherents. However, the first constitution of North Carolina, proclaiming religious liberty, nevertheless illiberally denied public office to Roman Catholics, agnostics, and atheists. Nor could the Anglican Church long withstand the attacks of reformers in South Carolina. The establishment there was championed by aristocratic Low Country planters led by Rawlins Lowndes and Charles Pinckney.

They brought forward specious and irrelevant reasons for maintaining it. They could not convince the non-Anglican majority in the state that it was the duty of all South Carolinians to support the church of a minority. The South Carolina constitution of 1778 wiped out all religious privilege, save that public offices were denied to other than Protestants.

Nor were the Episcopalians strong enough in Maryland to ward off assault upon their entrenchments. Their church was deprived of its favored position over others by the Maryland Bill of Rights of 1776. But Maryland was nevertheless the scene of a struggle for religious freedom, for the Bill of Rights gave the Maryland legislature power to tax for the benefit of all churches, with a proviso that any taxpayer could stipulate that his contribution go to his own church or be used for the relief of the poor. This "general assessment" scheme possessed enticing appeal. Religion in all its varieties has been praised and defended in all ages and places as a prop for morality. Ought not the churches of Maryland to be assisted, so long as personal scruples were respected? The state legislature considered a bill for "general assessment" in 1785. Happily, it was looked upon by many in Maryland as a first step toward establishing all the existing churches, and it was decisively defeated. Religious freedom was firmly established in the state—except that belief in God was required of officeholders, a pernicious requirement that was not finally destroyed until the twentieth century.

It was in Virginia that the Anglican Church was most ardently defended—and attacked. Its communicants were more numerous than those of any other denomination, possibly forming a small majority in the state. Among them were many wealthy and influential planters. However, not a few of those aristocrats were deists. The Virginia Bill of Rights, solemnly adopted in the early summer of 1776, contained an article drawn by James Madison which forthrightly declared "that religion, or the duty which we owe to our Creator, and the manner of discharging it, can be directed only by reason and conviction, not by force or violence; and therefore all men are equally entitled to the free exercise of religion, according to the dictates of conscience; and that it is the mutual duty of all to practice Christian forbearance, love, and charity towards each other." Only those who are unfamiliar with the ability of theologians to divide the indivisible and to magnify that which cannot be magnified will assume that all of the Episcopalians of Virginia, displaying affection and generosity toward their fellow citizens, interpreted that trenchant statement as the death knell of the privileges of the Anglican Church. Not so, asserted the Episcopal clergy and many of their parishioners. Its true intent was merely to assure freedom of conscience to all Virginians. The several churches had not been made equal; in the state of Virginia the Episcopal sect must retain the position it had lawfully and rightfully occupied before 1776. Presbyterians, Baptists, Methodists, and Lutherans contended that their sects had been given equal status with the Episcopal Church. They found a leader in Jefferson, who returned from Congress in the fall of 1776 to do what he could toward improving the institutions of his beloved Virginia. No more fond of favor for Presbyterians or Baptists than he was of privilege for Episcopalians or Buddhists, Jefferson sought to persuade the Virginia assembly to deprive the Anglican Church of its special position. He could not muster enough votes to achieve his purpose. Edmund Pendleton and Robert Carter Nicholas formed a strong party of Episcopalians to check Jefferson. He was forced to accept a compromise. The non-Anglicans were relieved of various restrictions that had been placed upon them and from taxation to support the established church. Moreover, taxation of Anglicans for the maintenance of their church was suspended for a period of twelve months. Each year thereafter Jefferson and other reformers managed to continue that suspension, until 1779. In that year they finally secured the passage of a law which positively forbade the imposition of taxes for the benefit of the Episcopal Church, so, in effect, disestablishing it.

It seemed that Jefferson had won his battle, but he had not. In that same year, 1779, he failed to secure the passage by the Virginia assembly of a bill that specifically divorced church and state. Many of those who had been his allies turned against him. The seductive "general assessment" contrivance had appeal in Virginia as well as Maryland. Presbyterian ministers who had fought against privilege confined to the Anglican Church saw no evil in privilege for all the existing Christian churches. They abandoned their alliance with Jefferson. With the Anglicans they sought after 1779 the enactment of a law similar to that afterward proposed in Maryland. They gained powerful support. A rise in crime lent substance to their claim that the churches ought to be publicly assisted to prevent or to lessen decay in morals—as in ancient Rome men demanded that Jupiter be worshipped, not so much because they adored him, but because they believed that homage to the great god promoted virtue. The champions of "general assessment" eventually won the favor of Patrick Henry, George Washington, and the young John Marshall—of the orator, of the military hero, and of the man who would become a brilliant chief justice of the Supreme Court of the United States. "General assessment" could do no great harm; it would be socially valuable. And did it not offer a compromise that would put an end to exasperating contest over religion? The alluring scheme gained adherents. Led by

353

Patrick Henry, they secured an easy majority in the lower house of the Virginia assembly in 1784, and the passage of a bill, by a majority of two to one, to put it into practice. James Madison, with the help of Baptists and others, barely managed to defer final action. Alarmed, Madison embarked, with George Nicholas and Wilson Cary Nicholas, upon a campaign to sway public opinion against the measure. The Baptists ardently rallied behind them, also Presbyterian laymen. Madison artfully and successfully suggested to Presbyterian clergymen that the profits of "general assessment" would be reaped by the Episcopal Church. A mounting wave of petitions against the device poured into the assembly in 1785. "General assessment" was slain.

Then, at last, it was possible to resurrect and to pass the bill for religious freedom that Jefferson had brought forward in 1779. Madison, early in 1786, secured the enactment of the famous Statute of Religious Liberty. Long afterward Jefferson said that he wished to be remembered as the author of the Declaration of Independence, as the composer of the Statute of Religious Liberty, and as the founder of the University of Virginia. He was justly proud of the noble phrases of the statute. Its preamble, asserting that "truth is great and will prevail if left to herself," placed veracity above social expediency. The law proclaimed, in the peculiarly eloquent, dignified, and moving language characteristic of Jefferson's best writings, "that no man shall be compelled to frequent or support any religious worship, place, or ministry whatsoever, nor shall be enforced, restrained, molested, or burthened in his body or goods, nor shall otherwise suffer, on account of his religious opinions or belief; but that all men shall be free to profess, and by argument to maintain, their opinions in matters of religion, and that the same shall in no wise diminish, enlarge, or affect their civil capacities." Jefferson and Madison had won a splendid triumph.

No one acquainted with the New England of 1776 will be surprised that the reformers encountered stiff resistance when they assailed the Congregational establishments in Massachusetts, New Hampshire, and Connecticut, that their efforts were largely unrewarded until the eighteenth century had passed. To be sure, there was no Jefferson among the Yankees. But had one existed, he would have been frustrated. In those states, at the beginning of the War of Independence, the Congregationalists were easily dominant. Government supported the church, and Congregationalist clergymen defended government. Concessions had been made in all three of the commonwealths to Episcopalians, Quakers, and Baptists. They could legally secure exemption from taxes levied to maintain the official sect, could offer devotion to God in their own fashion. But

354

all other persons, of whatever religious stripe, were compelled to donate to the state church. Massachusetts, New Hampshire, and Connecticut officially subscribed to a modified form of "general assessment." However, the Episcopalians, Quakers, and Baptists found it most difficult to secure the exemption to which they were entitled by law. Congregationalist laymen holding civil offices often managed to deny petitions for exemption upon technical grounds; when they could not deny them, they delayed action as long as possible. There was even less religious freedom in Congregationalist New England than law required.

The system was challenged in the Massachusetts constitutional convention of 1780, and the basic document prepared by that body declared that "no subordination of any one sect or denomination to another shall ever be established by law." But that generous assertion—generous, that is, for Massachusetts—was largely nullified by others which permitted the legislature and the courts of the state to continue to deny equality to sects other than Congregationalist, and to discriminate against Episcopalians, Baptists, Quakers, Methodists, and Universalists. Only gradually and grudgingly did those who dissented from the old Puritan way gain parity with its defenders. The nineteenth century was well advanced before the ancient church of Massachusetts lost all special public sanction. A requirement long lingered that all officeholders be Christian. Religious enlightenment came tardily in Massachsetts, even though a minority felt the ferment of reform. Eventually, the state church, like all such creations, decayed internally. Massachusetts did gradually enter religious civilization.

So it was in New Hampshire and Connecticut. In those states the Revolution brought little immediate change. The ruling Congregationalists would not even offer lip service to the principle of equality among the churches. Congregationalists in pulpits and public offices, supported by laymen of their own religious cast, made a mockery of constitutional provisions and of laws that seemed to offer a measure of toleration. Their rivals continued to have the right to ask for exemptions from taxes levied to support the establishment; they were not legally denied the right to build their own temples of worship. In practice, their requests for their lawful rights were often thwarted. In Connecticut even many Congregationalists who were, or became, heretical, suffered at the hands of their orthodox brethren. The conservative Congregationalists gave ground as slowly and reluctantly in New Hampshire and Connecticut as they did in Massachusetts. Indeed, the old church managed to retain some of its privileges in those states even after they had been destroyed in Massachusetts. Its special position was not completely eradicated in Connecticut until the fourth decade of the nineteenth century. The Puritans who settled in New England in the seventeenth century sought religious liberty, but only for themselves. They and their descendants were loath to grant the same freedom to those they looked upon as heretics and pagans. At last, in New Hampshire and Connecticut, as in Massachusetts, the state church crumbled, as much from internal rot as from external assault.

In Rhode Island and the Middle States—New York, New Jersey, Pennsylvania, and Delaware—there was, happily, little need for reforming Patriots to struggle for change in the religious order. While the Anglican Church was established in four New York counties at the onset of the War of Independence, the arrangement was technical rather than actual. Indeed, its legality had never been recognized by the non-Anglicans of New York, who formed a large majority in the state. It was set aside without public commotion in 1777. Vestigial religious discriminations survived the Revolution even in some of those states. New Jersey continued to insist that officeholders be Protestant; Delaware demanded that its officials and legislators subscribe to the doctrine of the Trinity. Those political inequities injured few, and they did not permanently endure.

So it was that religious liberty substantially triumphed in the Thirteen States. It was also established in the territories beyond the Appalachians, not without contest. The device of "general assessment" had its champions, not only at state capitals in Maryland, Virginia, and New England, but in the Congress of the United States. In 1785 that body, preparing the fundamental Land Ordinance of that year, which prescribed policy regarding the sale of nationally owned lands on the far side of the mountains, considered a stipulation that a section in each township—one thirty-sixth of each such unit—be set aside "for the support of religion, the profits arising therefrom . . . to be applied forever according to the will of the majority of male residents of full age." Seventeen delegates endorsed the proviso; only six voted against it. Fortunately, it was defeated, because it did not secure the support of a sufficient number of delegations for passage. Two years later the Congress laid down a more liberal policy with respect to religion for the vast region north of the Ohio River in the Northwest Ordinance. That document declared that "Religion, morality, and knowledge, being necessary to good government and the happiness of mankind, schools and the means of education shall forever be encouraged." However, the ordinance also asserted that the people who might settle in the area and the new states that might be formed within it were never to deny certain rights to individuals without the formal consent of the national government, and that "No person, demeaning himself in a peaceable and orderly manner, shall ever be molested on account of his mode of worship or religious sentiments, in the said territory." The Congress, setting aside the ungenerous scheme of "general assessment" for the West, opened the way for religious liberty in the wide regions extending into the Pacific Ocean that afterward became parts of the American nation.

Despite all the progress made by the Americans toward religious freedom between 1776 and 1787, liberal-minded men continued to fear that religious tyranny would be revived by arrogant bishops, intolerant clergymen, and ignorant laymen passionately clinging to outworn dogmas. What person, knowing the propensity of man to persecute his fellows, will say that their alarm was groundless, even in America? Such men saw a grave defect in the federal Constitution of 1787; it did not forbid the formation of a national church. They demanded that it be altered so as to preclude the founding of such an instrument of tyranny. Liberal James Madison had the honor of presenting to Congress for that purpose a part of the first amendment to the organic instrument of 1787. Adopted in 1791, it proclaimed that "Congress shall make no law respecting an establishment of religion, or prohibiting the free exercise thereof." That provision was, in the twentieth century, construed by the federal Supreme Court to apply to the several states as well as the United States. Even so, all the ties between government and religion in America were not, and are not, cut. Christian sects and Christians in general—with notable exceptions, including most Baptists—continue to ask for special favor from political officialdom. They express their admiration for Thomas Jefferson, James Madison, and John Adams, but they do not possess the generous spirit and wisdom those men manifested toward religion. They do not permit worship of the Founding Fathers to interfere with their own religious and moral credos.

The Patriots who strove to terminate the sway of Kings and of arrogant and wily clerics could not fail to strike against dukes, viscounts, barons, and knights, against hereditary privilege, against both nobility and aristocracy. Jefferson asked, were not Europeans aristocrats, titled or untitled, born with spurs so that they might ride upon the backs of plain folk? Had they not united with monarchs and entrenched clergymen to abuse humbler Europeans, generation after generation? Escaping the clutches of British noblemen, the Patriots ought to make sure that they would not be replaced by American marquises and princes. They ought also to do everything possible to prevent the perpetuation, the growth, of the hereditary gentry that already existed in America.

It was not difficult to secure the legal destruction of titles of nobility. Very few Americans had been given such honors by the Crown. There were two American baronets, Sir John Johnson and Sir William Pepperell, both of them Loyalists. Titles were associated with a detested Britain, and they were disliked even by many American patricians who lacked special hereditary designation. Wealthy merchants and planters did not clamor for such distinctions. Indeed, it seemed rather unlikely in 1776 or in 1787 that any American government would undertake to found a hereditary caste. And yet—who could say that lust for membership in one did not exist, that it would never appear? Men—and women—have always sought recognition as superior persons, have tried to establish the eminence of their ancestors and the excellence of their descendants. Recalling that offices, including seats in upper chambers and places on the benches of justice, had become virtually hereditary in some colonies before 1776, several states, including Massachusetts and New Hampshire, constitutionally forbade the passage of office from one person to another by virtue of blood. In her Declaration of Rights of November 1776, Maryland asserted that "no title of nobility, or hereditary honours, ought to be granted in this state." A month later it was proclaimed with equal solemnity in North Carolina that "no hereditary emoluments, privileges or honors ought to be granted or conferred in this state." Pennsylvania similarly denounced titles of nobility in her Declaration of Rights of 1790. Georgia went so far as to deprive any individual who claimed to possess a title of the right to vote or to hold office. Other states would doubtless have acted, had it seemed necessary. However, there was no need after the Articles of Confederation went into force. That document declared that "no person holding any office of profit or trust under the United States, or any of them" could "accept of any present, emolument, office or title of any kind whatever from any king, prince or foreign state; nor shall the United States in Congress assembled, or any of them, grant any title of nobility." Those prohibitions were repeated in the federal Constitution of 1787, except that Congress might permit individuals to accept honors from foreign rulers or nations.

Were the Patriots of the Revolutionary generation unduly concerned lest there be hereditary honors in America? Many of them were passionately determined to prevent the creation of any sort of privilege on the basis of descent. Jefferson even sought to insert a clause in the Land Ordinance of 1784 to deny new states formed in the West the power to establish titles—Congress refrained from doing so, since the Articles of Confederation served as a sufficient prohibition. Ratifying the federal Constitution of 1787, Massachusetts and New Hampshire urged that it was unwise to permit Americans to accept foreign honors, even with the consent of Congress, and that the Constitution be accordingly amended.

When Congress, in 1791, considered a petition from the Baron von Steuben, it declined to recognize his title—not an unsuitable decision, since Steuben's claim to nobility was most dubious. After 1795, indeed, Congress required every alien seeking American citizenship to abandon claim to any hereditary dignity.

Even the creation of the Order of the Cincinnati immediately after the War of Independence caused furor. It was founded by Steuben and General Henry Knox, neither of whom was excessively modest. Membership in the order was confined to officers who had served in the American armies, to their eldest sons, to their eldest sons, and so forth. Those who entered the society were pledged "to preserve inviolate those exalted rights and liberties of human nature for which they had fought and bled." The King of Sweden discerned in the order a menace to his own authority because it was republican. He forbade Swedish officers who had fought in the American army to join the fraternity. It was condemned on far different grounds in America. Was it truly republican to restrict membership to officers? And was it not baneful to honor their male descendants in accordance with the principle of primogeniture? The order was vehemently denounced by Judge Aedanus Burke of South Carolina and by New England legislatures. Elected first president of the society, Washington asked Jefferson and Madison for advice. Was it pregnant with danger to republican institutions? They urged that hereditary membership be abandoned. He adopted their counsel. At the request of Washington, a national meeting of the Cincinnati set aside the provision for transmission of membership by blood. Chapters of the society in several states ignored the national rule. However, the Order of the Cincinnati, although it lingered into the twentieth century, never became a force of social or political consequence.

It was doubtless well that the Americans of the Revolutionary generation did nearly everything they could to destroy distinctions founded upon heredity. The Americans were not afterward uniformly devoted to social equality, even among persons of white skin. Prosperous men and women who coveted recognition of superiority for themselves and their progeny eagerly sought the acquaintance of English lords and French counts, even of bogus Balkan princes. They arranged for the presentation of their female offspring at the British court. Wealthy American parents gladly consented to marriages between their daughters and impecunious and unworthy European noblemen. Families that failed to secure prestige by such mismatches sought it by other means. Men and women longingly endeavored to secure entrance into *Social Registers,* into exclusive clubs, into societies of all sorts—and to keep out other persons. Social ranks did not disappear in the Revolution. The American gentry lived on, obviously in the Southern states, but also in the Northern ones. Eventually, it was largely submerged in an American plutocracy, though it continued to be set apart from the common herd by manners, education, beauty, or talent. The fortunes of families rose and fell, but a patrician order of sorts persisted in America. The hunt for royal or noble ancestors became a popular pastime in the republic. Oil heiresses of Oklahoma, daughters of steel magnates, and less prosperous and less conspicuous women of all parts of the United States gladly learned from professional genealogists that they were descended from Alfred the Great, from Charlemagne, from an obscure German princeling. Need it be said that American males similarly sought social credit upon the basis of descent rather than upon ascent gained by their own achievements? The lust for special recognition, for honors, for officers, for dignities of all kinds, earned or unearned, is not absent in *homo Americanus*. It is just as well that neither he nor his spouse can hope to secure a patent of nobility. On the other hand, men and women being what they are, it is doubtless necessary that they be permitted to indulge in less injurious forms of snobbishness. The clubs, fraternities, societies, and associations that have sprung up in such infinite variety in America offered them opportunity to do so. Those who are denied admission to Rotary International, to the Junior League, to Phi Beta Kappa, to the Masonic order, to the Social Register, to the Independent Order of Odd Fellows, to the Dames Descended from Cromwellian Clergymen, do not suffer like common folk separated by a gulf from their noble superiors. They may console themselves with the thought that they are valued for what they are by true Christians, authentic Jeffersonians, and devout Marxists.

Jefferson and other reformers were almost as keenly hostile to untitled aristocracy as they were to hereditary nobility. In Britain and Continental Europe the perpetuation of landed aristocracy was fostered by primogeniture and entail, those devices that more or less assured the passage of property from father to eldest son, generation after generation. At the time of the Declaration of Independence entail was permitted in every state except South Carolina. Owners of land could legally require that their property pass through a certain line of descent. They almost invariably stipulated that their estates be inherited by the eldest son, if any, in each generation. In Virginia even slaves could be entailed. Entailed property could not be sold or given away by its owner. Entails could be, and sometimes were, destroyed by special legal process in Virginia and Maryland, but, once established, they tended to endure. The device helped to maintain the wealth and power of a family. It favored the eldest son in each generation at the expense of his kin. More serious, it served to preserve property for one line of descent within a family, and so to assure to that line riches, social position, and political authority into the distant future. The principle of primogeniture, as it was applied in America, was somewhat less harmful, but had the same tendency. It, too, offered favor to the eldest son. In New York and the Southern Colonies he commonly received the landed estate of his father by will; he also received it if his father died intestate. In New England, Pennsylvania, New Jersey, and Delaware he was shown less partiality, being legally assured only of a double share in the estate of an intestate father.

The assaults of the reformers upon the two mainstays of aristocracy were uniformly successful, in considerable part because the two institutions were looked upon as British rather than American. Besides, they fostered, especially in the South, haughty families that were envied and hated. By 1786 every state had either forbidden entailment or rendered it innocuous. Primogeniture was everywhere abolished by 1792, and the children of a father who neglected to make a will became equals for purposes of inheritance. The consequences may not be precisely measured. But it is significant that Edmund Pendleton, the Conservative, fought desperately though vainly against Jefferson in Virginia in 1776 to maintain the right of entail; that primogeniture was destroyed in Virginia in 1785; and that many families in that state which had owned great estates at the beginning of the War of Independence were not lordly a half century later. One may not doubt that the destruction of entail and primogeniture contributed to diffusion of wealth, nor that it reduced social distinctions and political power derived from riches. To be sure, it did not forbid the passage of vast estates from parents to children to grandchildren, to distant generations. It remained possible for American clans possessing ability and prudence to become rich and to stay rich over long periods of time. Indeed, some of them, such as the Rockefellers, Fords, and Mellons, have not been impoverished in consequence of inheritance duties imposed by the federal government and the states in the twentieth century.

If the Americans moved toward political democracy and social equality during the Revolutionary generation, it is nevertheless true that they made no great and immediate changes in the economic order. The mass did not despoil the class; the rich did not become poor, nor did the poor become rich. There was, to be sure, expropriation of the property of numerous Loyalists—every state inflicted economic punishment upon the supporters of the King. However, the Loyalists were not all aristocrats; nor did their lands and homes uniformly pass into the hands of indigent

Patriots. In fact, most of the Loyalists, being prudent, cautious, or fortunate, escaped confiscation. Moreover, property seized by the states for political crime was usually sold at auction, and it was purchased by Patriot lawyers, merchants, planters, and army officers as well as homestead farmers and landless tenants. It is clear that in some cases the wide estates of Tory aristocrats were divided into farms owned by former tenants. It is reported that the lands of Loyalist James De Lancey of New York were distributed among some 275 persons, that those of rich Roger Morris were parceled among nearly 250 purchasers. In the main, however, there was no sharp class distinction between the Loyalist who lost his property and the Patriot who secured it. Amidst the military disturbances and economic derangements of war, including inflation, some Patriots—such as the merchant William Bingham of Philadelphia and the merchant Cabots of Massachusetts—moved up the economic ladder, while others slipped downward. However, such shifting was neither universal nor absolute. Nor did the Revolution bring swift and remarkable alteration of public policy concerning the sale of undeveloped public lands beyond the Appalachians. Had they been freely given in the form of homestead farms to landless Patriots, the economic consequences would indeed have been vast. Many Patriot soldiers were in fact given lands in the Mississippi Valley by the United States and some of the states in payment for their services. However, most of those lands were sold to, rather than bestowed upon, private persons. Often the terms of sale were such that poor men were unable to purchase; often they were acquired by speculators who exacted their profit when they in turn sold farms to tillers. American speculators replaced British ones. To be sure, there was some improvement in policy toward Western lands. American governments sanctioned neither manorial privileges nor quit rents. It was certainly not more difficult to acquire a homestead immediately after the War of Independence than it was in the colonial time. Moreover, after 1820, Congress arranged for the sale of wide stretches of public lands upon such easy terms that the acquisition of a farm in the West was not beyond the efforts of any industrious and thrifty man. After the passage of the Homestead Act of 1862, indeed, Congress gave farms to settlers as well as large grants to railroads. On the whole, the Revolution doubtless increased the opportunity of the landless to become proprietors of the soil. It does not follow that the Revolution brought in its train swift and massive overturn in the economic sphere. Its ultimate and indirect economic results we cannot measure; we may hazard a guess that they were enormous. But who can say with assurance that the continuance of the Americans within the British empire would necessarily have given great and special advantage to British—or American—exploiters that was utterly destroyed by the Revolution?

Certainly the destruction of British authority did not swiftly lead to the extirpation of the worst of all forms of tyrannies that existed in America in 1776—slavery. Considering the natural rights of mankind, and subscribing to the immortal propositions in the Declaration of Independence that "all men are created equal" and "that they are endowed by their Creator" with "life, liberty, and the pursuit of happiness," thoughtful and enlightened Patriots could not fail to condemn Negro bondage— and nearly all persons of African descent in America were slaves. Surely those natural rights were not given only to men of white, sallow, or brown skin, to Europeans and Americans of European descent. Ought such men to deprive their fellows of rights bestowed by the Governor of the Universe? When propagandists such as Dr. Samuel Johnson, defending British authority before 1776, censured the Americans as slaveowners and slavedrivers, they struck home. To be sure, they conveniently forgot that Britain and the British had fostered the slave trade from Africa and were responsible in large degree for the existence of Negro servitude, not only in North America, but in the West Indies. They preferred to remember that slavery did not exist in England—where there were very few blacks. Nearly all the prominent Patriots readily conceded that slavery was a vicious institution; and many of them, distressed that it should exist in a free America, urged that it be erased. Washington, Jefferson, Patrick Henry, Horatio Gates, Alexander Hamilton, John Adams, John Jay, James Madison, Henry Laurens—Northerners and Southerners alike— Conservatives, Liberals, and even Radicals more eager to improve the lot of poorer whites than that of the blacks—condemned Negro servitude. So did Philip Freneau, the principal American poet of the Revolutionary era, who wrote:

> O come the time, and haste the day,
> When man shall man no longer crush,
> When Reason shall enforce her sway,
> Nor these fair regions raise our blush,
> Where still the African complains,
> And mourns his yet unbroken chains.

Nor should it be forgotten that the Quakers were early, ardent, and special enemies of slavery.

The word "slavery" has a peculiarly ugly and sinister quality. The condition of a slave may be better than that of a serf, no worse than that of a legally free servant, tenant, or laborer. The sufferings of the Negroes in bondage in eighteenth-century America can be magnified. They, like the whites of their time, were less sensitive than their descendants. Even so, neither white nor black slaves have ever been contented with their status; and that of the Negroes in subjection in the America of 1776 was most unhappy. Born on the western side of the Atlantic and accustomed to the speech and ways of white masters and mistresses, the male slave might be a footman or a carpenter, the female a household maid. However, whether born on the North American mainland, in the West Indies, or in Africa, most Negroes in bondage performed manual labor, often in tobacco fields and rice and indigo swamps. They were scantily clad; their food was cheap and monotonous; their homes were cabins and huts. They were not usually allowed to marry legally; they were very generally denied opportunity to become literate; they could be, and were, sold as pieces of property, whether or not a sale resulted in the separation of husband from wife, of parents from children. If most of their masters and mistresses were humane, if some of them were lenient and gentle, at least a few of them were brutal taskmasters. Slaves were flogged into obedience. If a master slew his slave, his conduct might be condemned by his white neighbors; he would hardly be punished by a court of law. Slave women and girls could not deny their bodies to their masters, to the sons of their masters. Thus is explained in part the fact that the Negroes were moving biologically toward the whites. Mulattoes and quadroons were already common. Such persons did not acquire freedom because of the blood of whites in their veins. Mentally, they doubtless suffered more in servitude than did Negroes recently wrenched from Africa.

So obvious were the iniquities of the institution that it was quite easily destroyed in the Northern States—where there were few slaves, where slave labor was unprofitable, where there were few blacks, free or unfree. An anti-slavery society was founded at Philadelphia as early as the spring of 1775. Liberated, the slaves in the Northern States would pose no immediate menace, social, economic, or political, to the whites. Accordingly, Pennsylvania provided for gradual emancipation by a law of 1780. Three years later the highest court of Massachusetts construed a phrase in the constitution of that state, "All men are born free and equal," to mean that Negro servitude could not legally exist within its bounds. One way and another every state north of the Mason-Dixon line moved against slavery before the nineteenth century was well begun. By 1810 the institution was dead or dying everywhere north of that boundary.

Nor was it allowed to spread north of the Ohio River. In 1784

Jefferson sought the inclusion by Congress in its Land Ordinance of that year of a clause which would have prohibited slavery after 1800 in all the federally owned territories beyond the Appalachians. That bar against the extension of slavery was not, alas, erected. Jefferson could not secure quite enough support for the clause among delegates from the South to enshrine it in law. Three years later Congress did substantially prevent the spread of slavery into the Old Northwest, declaring in the Northwest Ordinance that "neither slavery nor involuntary servitude" was to exist in the region. No Southern delegate in Congress voted against that prohibition. There was no disposition among men in that body from the South to insist that slavery be legally permitted in an area where Nature herself forbade that it should flourish. Neither tobacco nor rice nor indigo—in the production of which the bulk of the slaves were engaged—could be profitably grown beyond the Ohio. Nor would Southern delegates defend slavery in principle.

However, Congress did nothing to hinder the advance of Negro bondage in the federal territories beyond the Appalachians and south of the Ohio. Moreover, the Southern states did not strike hard against the detestable institution. It not only continued below the Mason-Dixon line, but extended westward into Kentucky and Tennessee before the end of the War of Independence. Later its blight crossed the Mississippi, reaching even the high plains of Texas.

For it was no great feat to destroy slavery where it hardly existed, but a very different matter to strike at it where it flourished. Below the Mason-Dixon line, especially in South Carolina and Georgia, slave labor seemed to most white masters to be profitable. Besides, the children of the slaves had their value, one that increased as they grew to maturity. Would blacks in freedom perform the heavy, irksome, and even dangerous tasks they were forced to do as slaves, in the fields, in forests, in rice and indigo swamps? And was it not true that the Negroes could better withstand physical toil in the heat and humidity of Southern summers than whites? It was convenient to think so. Their labor was therefore all the more necessary to economic progress. Most whites did not doubt that the blacks were their physical inferiors, except in ability to do drudgery and to reproduce. They assumed that the blacks were intellectually and morally deficient, that the white race was hereditarily, even Biblically, superior. Moreover, would not the consequences of emancipation be most unpleasant for the whites, in regions where the Negroes were numerous? Where they formed a majority, as they did in some eastern counties of Virginia and in the Low Country of South Carolina, for example? Free, the Negroes might demand the right to vote, might insist upon social equality. They might even at some future time be able to dominate their former masters; it was to be feared that they would seek revenge for the wrongs that had been heaped upon them. Most of the Southern whites wished to have no tampering with slavery. Even those who disapproved of the institution were commonly reluctant to proceed against it, because of both the immediate and remote consequences of emancipation.

It was useless in the Carolinas and Georgia even to suggest to legislators that they act against slavery, as did a few New Englanders settled in Georgia's Darien. Once and again during the War of Independence it was urged in Congress that slaves be given their freedom in return for service in the Continental army. When the military fortunes of the Patriots were at lowest ebb, the whites of the far South denounced the scheme—and successfully. The larger the fraction of Negroes in the population, the greater was the disinclination of the whites to move against the institution.

It was not possible to hit hard at slavery even in Virginia, where the civilized Jefferson carried on so many campaigns against ancient abuses. Jefferson believed that slavery was abominable. He estimated that Negroes were not equal to whites in "reason" and "imagination." However, unlike many Americans of his and later times, he admitted that his guess could be erroneous—who can measure the hereditary abilities of one race as against those of another? Jefferson also saw clearly that mental endowment, or the lack of it, did not justify maltreatment of one race by another. Indeed, he realized that slavery injured master as well as man. Slaveowners accustomed to absolute sway over their human property tended to become both haughty and indolent. He feared that the blacks, freed, could not live in amity with the whites—they would not be able to forgive and forget the wrongs inflicted upon them and their ancestors by the whites. Accordingly, he favored liberty for the slaves together with their exportation to Africa. With George Wythe and Edmund Pendleton he drafted a bill which would have freed all Negroes born after a fixed date in Virginia and which would also have required their deportation. It was ready for consideration by the Virginia assembly in 1779, but Jefferson refrained from introducing it. It could not be passed. In 1782 Virginia did take one short step toward emancipation of the Negroes, giving permission to the owners of slaves to free them. In consequence, several thousand secured their liberty. However, that permission was later withdrawn. Most of the Virginians did not desire a numerous body of free Negroes in their midst; nor were they sufficiently concerned about racial troubles in the future to make the financial sacrifice necessary to export the blacks. Maintaining slavery, the Virginians did not massively attack the basic question of relations between the races; they consigned it to their descendants.

Even in Maryland it was not quite possible to give slavery a death blow. Charles Carroll of Carrollton and William Pinkney fought strenuously for emancipation. A bill for that purpose was defeated in the lower house of the Maryland legislature by a vote of 32 to 22 in 1785. But the champions of freedom for the Negroes in bondage were fewer and weaker than that vote seems to indicate. In a Baltimore newspaper in March 1789 "Benevolus" asked, "Why has the pride of American youth been immolated on the altar of Liberty, if all her sons are not to taste her blessings?" Nevertheless, it was only after a sharp struggle that Maryland, by a law of 1790, permitted manumission—private donation of liberty to slaves by their owners. As a result, many thousands of blacks were freed in the state. The slave population of Maryland actually declined before the Civil War—but Negro bondage continued in Maryland, and also in Delaware, where manumission was equally frequent, until the Civil War put an end to it.

Happily, although slavery survived and flourished south of the Mason-Dixon line, although it later spread far to the west, it was possible for the Revolutionary generation to destroy the oceanic traffic in slaves. That peculiarly vicious species of commerce carried on between Africa and America could not be defended by any truly humane person. Besides, it was to the immediate economic advantage of many slaveholders that the trade be terminated—scarcity of slaves would raise the value of their human property. And it was evident, even to whites who had no intention of freeing their slaves, that it was prudent, for their own safety, to restrict the growth of the Negro population. There were slave uprisings and rumors of slave insurrections in the South before the War of Independence. Accordingly, the colonial assemblies of South Carolina and Maryland restricted the brutal oceanic commerce in Negroes before 1775. The Virginia assembly sought to prohibit it, but a law passed for that purpose was set aside in England, partly because merchants of Liverpool, Bristol, and London desired to continue to make money from that sordid business. The traffic was barred by the Association in 1774, and the Congress resolved in April 1776 that "no slaves be imported into any of the thirteen United Colonies." There was no effort to revive it during the War of Independence.

Was it to be resumed? Delaware forbade the importation of slaves from abroad, in 1776; and state after Northern state, together with Virginia, soon followed her example. Maryland enacted a similar law in 1783; three years later, North Carolina put a stop to the trade by imposing heavy taxes upon it. Because the British carried off so many slaves from South Carolina and Georgia during the War of Independence, the planters of those states eagerly sought to replenish their stock of cheap labor after the close of hostilities. They insisted that the traffic be revived, and it was. However, Georgia restricted the commerce in 1793, and positively forbade it five years afterward. South Carolina barred it during the years 1787 to 1804, then permitted the entrance of Negroes from Africa, but not from the West Indies. At last the traffic was ended, except for occasional illegal importations, by federal law in 1808.

The reformers of the Revolutionary generation, believing that they could not secure the abolition of Negro bondage in the South, bequeathed an awesome racial problem to the Americans who came after them. Nor were they usually able—although they tried—to modernize criminal codes, to assure decent treatment of prisoners and insane people, to provide for orphans. They were checked by poverty, inertia, and ignorance. Criminal codes in the American colonies were much less severe than that of Britain. They were further softened in several states. Nevertheless, imprisonment for debt, branding and mutilation of persons convicted of crime, and capital punishment for a variety of offenses continued into the America of the nineteenth century. In fact, execution for crimes such as murder and rape persisted into the second half of the twentieth century.

Restrained to a large degree by lack of understanding among their fellow Patriots, reformers such as Jefferson, Madison, John Adams, Dr. Benjamin Rush, and George Clinton saw that education offered the brightest hope for a brighter future. They knew, indeed, that the American republic could hardly survive without formal instruction of the mass of its citizens. Adams asserted that the preparation of the Americans for their moral, civil, and political duties "ought to be the care of the public, and of all who have any share in the conduct of its affairs, in a manner that never yet has been practised in any age or nation." Jefferson developed a far-reaching plan for his dear Virginia. It called for the establishment of elementary schools at public expense in all parts of Virginia. It provided also for secondary schools and a state university, together with free tuition at those institutions for some poor but gifted students. Dr. Benjamin Rush and George Washington urged that a national university be founded.

Alas, during the War of Independence American schools, academies, and colleges suffered from political, economic, and military upheaval. Many of them closed their doors. Nor was it possible swiftly to restore them, to multiply them, to modernize them. Money was lacking; taxpayers were not eager to contribute for the education of the children of their poorer neighbors, were sometimes reluctant even to donate for the instruction of their own progeny; and many citizens were disposed to consign teaching to godly clergymen rather than to untrustworthy laymen. Many new institutions of learning were founded, but few were funded. Older ones were revived, but not regenerated. New free elementary schools, and even academies, did appear here and there, notably in Georgia. However, for all his zeal, Jefferson was unable to secure quick adoption of even part of his noble scheme of education in Virginia. That state finally made some provision for free instruction in reading, writing, and arithmetic in 1796. The University of Virginia did not make its appearance until 1819. Only four of the new state constitutions specifically pledged public support to education—and not uniformly to public education. Even so, the concept of instruction financed by tax money, long firmly established in New England, gained new impulse. Significant of an extraordinary adventure in education to come was the reservation of public lands by Georgia and by Congress for the building and maintenance of institutions of learning. Eventually, the Americans would do what John Adams said they must do—devote their wealth to education as no other people ever had done before.

Did the Americans, securing their independence from Britain, simultaneously execute an Internal Revolution? One of the most distinguished American historians of the twentieth century, Allan Nevins, a scholar not given to exaggeration, has said that the Americans did indeed carry through "a social and intellectual revolution" in the last quarter of the eighteenth century. Nevertheless, the phrase Internal Revolution—a dramatic one, at least to historians—is doubtless a trifle grandiose. But it is apparent that domestic change in that period was major. America became truly republican, and the shape of the democratic America that would be in the nineteenth and twentieth centuries began to emerge. It may be appropriate to think of a relatively rapid American evolution that began with the founding of the English colonies on the western shores of the Atlantic, one that proceeded with greater celerity in the era of independence than in any other. Whether or not one chooses to use the term Internal Revolution, it must be admitted that American institutions were not then perfected. The continuance of slavery was a grievous defect in the American body politic. Other faults in it persisted, and new flaws developed. Two centuries after the War of Independence the Americans had not reached Utopia.

CHAPTER XXIII

France Intervenes

ANCIENT injustices inherited from Europe were not so deeply entrenched in America that they could not be reduced, even destroyed, without convulsion. The Americans of the Revolutionary era were a fortunate people. They were well schooled in political warfare. They were led toward a better world by a galaxy of brilliant and talented men who had read widely about the art of government, who had gained experience in statecraft in innumerable civil contests at colonial capitals, in state legislatures, in governorships, in Congresses. They had much less experience in things military, but they learned about soldiering, and they produced generals who became increasingly proficient. Nevertheless, it long remained doubtful that their rebellion against Britain would succeed. They had their friends in Britain and on the European Continent who looked upon them as allies in a common cause of human liberty. Those partisans beyond the Atlantic were not sufficiently numerous, powerful, and active to assure the triumph of the Patriots. It was most desirable, quite possibly essential, that the Americans secure the assistance of European rulers who could put armies in the field and fleets upon the oceans. The Patriots could not expect that European Kings and their ministers of state would fondly adopt republican principles, would benignly applaud the new order that was emerging in America; but they had good reason to hope that the Bourbon monarchs of France and Spain, the traditional enemies of Britain, would seize the opportunity offered by the American rebellion to strike at their habitual adversary. After adopting the Declaration of Independence, the Congress sent emissaries to most of the courts of Europe to get whatever help they could. They were cordially received

370

only in Paris. The French ministry had decided to give aid to the Patriots even before they asked for it. However, France declined to offer more than clandestine assistance until the news of Saratoga, giving assurance that the Patriots were militarily potent, reached the French capital. Soon afterward, the youthful Louis XVI formally recognized the United States of America and entered into a treaty of alliance with the Patriots. War followed between France and Britain, beginning in June 1778. The entrance of France into the war changed its course, but did not bring swift triumph to the Americans.

No one familiar with the shifting friendships and hatreds of princes, presidents, and peoples can be amazed that the republican Patriots sought and obtained help from the Bourbon monarchies. In every age of human history tribes, city-states, nations, and empires have exchanged old allies for new ones. The annals of the human race are studded with treaties of perpetual amity quickly broken, with permanent alliances that endured but briefly, with conversions of presumably best friends into mortal enemies and of remorseless enemies into seemingly firm friends. In ancient Greece Athens fought against Sparta and Thebes; Sparta against Thebes and Athens; and Thebes against Athens and Sparta. Every powerful European nation has at some time been allied with all the others, has at some time engaged in hostilities against all the others. The chronicles of Asia and Africa similarly relate fluctuating concords and enmities. And the Patriots were of the *genus homo*. Even so, they were reluctant to seek the support of the Bourbons, absolute monarchs, detested Roman Catholics, and perennial antagonists. They made no effort to get it until after they had resolved to accept nothing less than complete separation from Britain. When they did ask for help, they found attentive ears in Paris— and even in Madrid. For there were men in Paris and Madrid, including ministers of state, who yearned to avenge the mortifying defeats and losses that France and Spain had suffered at the hands of Britain in the Seven Years' War.

After Britain reached a zenith of imperial power in 1763, informed Frenchmen and Spaniards respected, admired, and even feared Britain. They did not love her. Frenchmen long accustomed to think of their nation as the most powerful and the most civilized in the world would not accept British ascendancy. Both French and Spanish politicians eagerly watched and waited for an opportunity to bring Britain down, even to reduce her to a second-class power. As early as 1761, in the midst of military disasters on land and sea, Étienne François, Duc de Choiseul, the principal minister of Louis XV, began to prepare for the day when France would seek and secure ample revenge. A skillful diplomat,

Choiseul devised a defensive alliance between France and Spain—it did not help France or Spain in the conflict then in progress, but it would be useful at a later time. A brave soldier, Choiseul also undertook, with some success, to renovate the French army and navy. Among other improvements, the French began to fashion good muskets in relatively large quantities. He sought to make as much as possible of the scattered remains of the French empire, but he believed that it was unwise to make sacrifices to regain the territories beyond seas that France had lost to Britain. Studying British power, he concluded that it was derived from commerce rather than colonies. Accordingly, the lucrative traffic between Britain and her North American possessions was of the first importance. If the Americans became independent, might they not trade with France rather than England? When he learned that the Americans were restless under British rule, he sent agents across the Atlantic to measure the depth of their discontent. Would they rise in revolt? The reports he received were contradictory. He was never able to achieve his goal. He had secured and held office through the favor of Madame de Pompadour, the mistress of Louis XV. After her death in 1764, he lost authority and influence. So eager he was to strike at Britain that he urged his fellow ministers and his royal master to declare war against her in 1770. Spain and Britain were quarreling over possession of the Falkland Islands, barren and worthless islands in the distant South Atlantic. Spain, too, had regained vigor, under the leadership of King Charles III and several able ministers. Choiseul contended that the hour had come for France and Spain to attack Britain. But he could not convince his colleagues or his King that the time was ripe for action, and he was forced to resign from office. He never regained authority, yet his labors were not in vain. Four years later the old and indolent Louis XV died. He was succeeded at Versailles by the young and incompetent Louis XVI. As it happened, however, the new King soon chose for himself another able and experienced diplomat, Charles Gravier, Comte de Vergennes, as his foreign minister. Vergennes, like Choiseul, dreamed of an American rebellion that would give France opportunity not only to deprive Britain of much of her empire but to gain the vast benefits of trade with the independent Americans for France. Gifted with a subtle if not profound intellect, adroit, familiar with the wiles of courtiers and ambassadors, sufficiently unscrupulous in behalf of French interests, Vergennes was almost a great man.

Vergennes received with joy the news that Britain and her colonists had engaged on the battlefield. He had already been approached, indirectly, by Americans in London. They had suggested that, if Britain and her colonists came to blows, the Americans might be glad to have French help. He had cautiously refrained from displaying any interest in the suggestion. However, in the fall of 1775, learning that the Patriots were determined and able to fight, he quietly sent a special agent, M. Achard Bonvouloir, across the Atlantic to Philadelphia. Bonvouloir was to encourage the Patriots to continue the struggle; to inform them that they possessed the good will of France; and to tell them that they could freely make use of French harbors. Almost simultaneously, Vergennes entered into a close association with Caron de Beaumarchais for the purpose of supplying secret aid to the Patriots.

Beaumarchais was also aroused by the tidings of martial combat in America, and he too saw a chance for France to injure Britain. He is gratefully remembered for his splendid comedies, *The Barber of Seville* and *The Marriage of Figaro*. But Beaumarchais was much more than a playwright, being a man of many talents and diverse achievements, a man of the world. Born as plain Pierre Augustin Caron, the son of a watchmaker, he seemed to be destined for a quiet and bourgeois life. However, while still young, he devised an improvement for pocket watches, in consequence of which he received attention at the royal court of Versailles. Physically attractive, clever, witty, charming, and courageous, he made influential friends. He married above the station to which he was born, and was able to add "de Beaumarchais" to his family name, so becoming a gentleman. He performed well as a French secret agent in London. A bold and successful adventurer, Beaumarchais was not burdened by excessive scruple. He became an ally and remarkably useful tool of Vergennes.

In December 1775, Beaumarchais, undoubtedly with the support of Vergennes, formally urged Louis XVI to take advantage of Britain's distress. In a letter to the King he insistently advised the French ruler to seize a great opportunity. France ought secretly to send arms and even money to the Patriots. A self-made man, an *arriviste* who had not risen in the world with an unblemished reputation, Beaumarchais was aware that Louis XVI, lacking his own experience of that world, strove to behave as a man of honor. The King, Beaumarchais said, would be disinclined to aim a covert blow against a fellow monarch with whom he was officially upon terms of friendship. But the King must ignore any qualms that he might feel; he must place the welfare of the French state above all else.

The French monarch did not immediately accede to the wishes of Vergennes and Beaumarchais. However, they persevered, and they won allies at the royal court. A report from Bonvouloir, asserting that the Patriots were determined to fight, encouraged Vergennes to proceed. He pressed ever more vigorously for action. In March 1776, he sounded out the Spanish government concerning his project. Would Spain enter into it as a partner? He received the answer that he desired, from the Marques de Grimaldi, the Spanish minister responsible for foreign affairs. It would be wise, said Grimaldi, to give enough hidden help to the Patriots so that they could struggle with the British until both parties were exhausted—to the benefit of Spain and France.

Assured of Spanish participation in his scheme, Vergennes officially urged its adoption in the spring of 1776. He knew that execution of it entailed danger of open war with Britain; he was quite ready to accept that risk. Putting his proposal before his colleagues in the French ministry, he admitted that concealed aid to the Americans might indeed provoke a declaration of war from Britain. However, Spain would presumably be France's ally. The venture ought to be kept as secret as possible. Britain should be deceitfully assured that France harbored no sinister intent, and France should make no revealing commitment to the Patriots. France and Spain must prepare, and remain prepared, for war. What would be the profit for France? He expected that the Americans would, if militarily successful, form a republic or republics. They would not be powerful. It was to be feared, Vergennes argued, that reconciliation between Britain and the rebels would be followed by Anglo-American attacks upon the islands France still owned in the Caribbean Sea. The safety of those possessions would be enhanced by a Patriot triumph. Alone, the Americans would not be able, if they wished, to seize those colonies. Above all, Britain could be deprived of her rich trade with the Americans; it could be gained by France; and Britain could be deeply hurt at little expense.

The arguments advanced by Vergennes were, to a degree, sufficiently cogent. They did not appeal to Anne Robert Jacques Turgot, comptroller general of finances, who was an economist and a philosopher rather than a short-sighted politician. In a thoughtful state paper placed before his fellow executives Turgot pointed out that the scheme pushed by Vergennes and Beaumarchais hazarded too much for too little. Was there peril that the Anglo-Americans would in the future attack the French possessions in the West Indies? If so, that menace could be met when it appeared. Was it worthwhile for France to assist the Patriots? They must eventually win their independence in any event, for colonies were like leaves upon a tree that must fall in due season. Why should France expend treasure and perhaps become involved in war to achieve that which was already decreed? If Britain succeeded in crushing the American rebels, she would not be able to hold them in subjection even in the near future without maintaining large garrison forces among them. Moreover, Turgot contended, only too justly, France could not afford a war. The nation was heavily in debt. He was striving to find remedies for its financial ills. He correctly predicted that a war would drive France near to bankruptcy. Turgot also asserted that it was dishonorable to make a secret attack upon Britain, a charge that appealed to Louis XVI. However, all of the monarch's advisers, save for Turgot, rallied behind Vergennes. Turgot and the King reluctantly gave way. On May 2, 1776, Louis XVI officially gave his permission to Vergennes to proceed with his scheme. On June 10 he ordered that one million livres (equivalent to francs) be given to Beaumarchais toward executing it. The Spanish government soon presented a similar sum to that adventurer for the same purpose. Thus it was that France and Spain undertook to offer clandestine help to the Patriots, before they officially asked for aid, before an American emissary put foot upon French soil.

In an attempt to deceive the British, Beaumarchais had established the sham merchant house in Paris of Roderique Hortalez and Company. That firm bought muskets, cannon, gunpowder, blankets, tents, and other military accessories, and hurried them off to America. It even sent gold across the ocean. Its activities could not be hidden, nor could the fact that it was supported by the French government be completely concealed. In his haste to get shipments under way Beaumarchais even inserted among them cannon stamped with the Bourbon fleur-de-lis from French arsenals. Moreover, Vergennes and Beaumarchais consorted and consulted with Silas Deane, an agent of Congress who appeared in Paris in the summer of 1776 carrying orders to buy war matériel. Rumors spread through the city that France had committed herself to the Patriot cause. These encouraged adventurous military officers, including some in the French army, to seek out Deane and to offer their services to the Continental army. He engaged several of them, since they could supply special skills and experience. The British ambassador at Paris, Viscount Stormont, learned that both French officers and war materials were going aboard ships destined for American ports. He protested. Beaumarchais briefly put a stop to his operations, then resumed them more discreetly. Stormont continued to complain, but not so vigorously as to provoke war between Britain and France. Britain preferred to permit the French to offer help to the Americans rather than risk a struggle with the Bourbons.

The covert aid given the United States by France was most important. Through Beaumarchais the French Crown expended four million livres upon equipment for the Patriot armies during the years 1776 and 1777. Of special value was the gunpowder sent across the Atlantic. Together with powder bought by American merchants in European and West Indian ports, it ensured reliable supplies of ammunition for Patriot muskets, rifles, and cannon. Also useful to the Patriots were military technicians furnished by the French government, including Louis Le Bègue de Presle Duportail, who rendered splendid service and became the first chief engineer of the American army. The young Marquis de Lafayette, a captain in the French army, slipped away to America with the connivance of French officials, performed faithfully as a Patriot major general, and became a romantic and legendary figure among the Americans. Other French and foreign officers preceded and followed Duportail and Lafayette into the Continental army, including the Baron von Steuben, Thaddeus Kosciusko, the Count Pulaski, and others less distinguished. The help given by those men cost the Patriots many headaches, for they commonly demanded and secured rank above competent American officers. Lafayette became an American major general at the age of nineteen. It is not to be doubted, however, that those foreign officers, in the main, strengthened the Patriot forces. Beaumarchais's business operations also created troubles. Most of the supplies shipped across the Atlantic by Roderique Hortalez and Company were gifts from the Bourbon Kings of France and Spain. However, Beaumarchais afterward claimed that many shipments made by him were loans rather than presents, that he had expended his own funds in behalf of the Patriots. He and his heirs later asked for a payment of 3.6 million livres. At last the United States gave his heirs 800,000 francs to satisfy those claims. It is unlikely that he or they deserved so much, but the assistance that came to the Americans through him was, after all, almost beyond price to them.

It should not be forgotten that Spain contributed more than the million livres she in her turn gave to Beaumarchais. The Spanish government, lacking confidence in the discretion of Beaumarchais, prudently appointed its own agent, Don Diego de Gardoqui of Bilbao, to help the Americans. Gardoqui became the quiet and efficient Spanish counterpart of Beaumarchais. Through him Spain spent another million livres upon munitions and other military goods supplied to the Patriots. Moreover, Spain welcomed American merchants in her ports. Not that affection for the Americans welled up in the breasts of the royal ministers of that country. They continued to look upon the Patriots merely as instruments to employ against detested Britain.

It has been remarked that Viscount Stormont did not remonstrate too forcefully against the exertions of Beaumarchais, because France might respond with a declaration of war. Stormont, and his superiors in London, had good reason to be cautious. Vergennes favored secret help to the Patriots in the spring of 1776 only because he could not persuade his colleagues in office to wage open war against Britain. In strengthening the Patriots, he hoped to bring both France and Spain into contest with Britain. Turgot resigned from the French ministry, and Vergennes persuaded his fellows within it that France ought to strike—if conditions permitted. He sounded out Spain in the summer of 1776. The government of that country declared its willingness to fight, provided that Spain received Portugal and the Balearic island of Minorca as reward for her efforts toward victory over Britain. Vergennes was willing to pay that high price. However, before he could act, news of Patriot reverses, particularly of their defeat in the battle of Long Island, reached Paris. Fearing that the Americans might soon be subdued by British arms, he decided to wait until he could be sure that they would continue to resist the British forces. In July 1777 he again proposed that France and Spain take the field. He suggested the formation of a Franco-Spanish-American alliance, defensive and offensive, which would wage war against Britain until all of the allies agreed to make peace. Louis XVI gave his consent to the plan, but Spain balked. King Charles III had appointed a new foreign minister, the Conde de Floridablanca, an astute politician. Floridablanca was much averse to the creation of a powerful American state. He rightly calculated that such a nation might be hostile and more dangerous to the Spanish empire in the New World than Britain had ever been. He saw that a successful American republic would supply a bad example, not merely for the subjects of Charles III overseas, but for the Spanish people at home— they might be encouraged at some future time to believe that they could manage without a throne or a monarch. The perceptive Floridablanca persuaded Charles III to offer an alternative. Spain and France should seek to mediate between Britain and her rebellious colonists, to try to arrange a truce which would leave both combatants able to resume fighting, but not to molest Spain or her possessions beyond the Atlantic. Vergennes was disappointed. He was also discouraged by the news that Burgoyne had easily taken Fort Ticonderoga. He was once more forced to defer open hostilities against Britain.

But it nevertheless became ever more likely that France would commit herself to the Patriots, in some part because of the endeavors of Benjamin Franklin, who arrived in Paris early in December 1776. With Silas Deane and Dr. Arthur Lee, Franklin was instructed by Congress to try to secure official recognition of the United States and an alliance. After the signing of the Declaration of Independence Congress soon resolved to seek aid everywhere in Europe. As early as November 1775, that body had formed a "Committee of Secret Correspondence" to communicate with "our friends in Great Britain, Ireland, and other parts of the world." That committee had promptly established a correspondence with Dr. Arthur Lee in London and with Charles W. F. Dumas, a friend of Franklin, at The Hague. It was also largely responsible for the appearance of Silas Deane in Paris in the summer of 1776. However, so much averse to the French and Spanish were so many Patriots that Congress would not even permit American merchants, except by special license, to trade with France and Spain until April 1776. When it became only too apparent that Britain would rely upon force, when the Patriots resolved to separate from Britain, they also determined, in the summer of 1776, to ask for foreign help. They set aside the fear that they would fall under Bourbon hegemony. Driven on almost by necessity, Congress hurried off "militia diplomats"—men untrained in the art of international politics—to the courts of Europe, to Paris, Madrid, Berlin, Vienna, St. Petersburg, The Hague, and Florence. Franklin, Lee, and Deane were ordered to offer France commercial privileges and to promise that the Americans would never return to the British fold, in return for recognition by France of the American republic. The three commissioners were also instructed to pledge, in the event that France in consequence became involved in war with Britain, that the Patriots would not make a separate peace without six months' notice. Later, to strengthen the hands of the commissioners, Congress instructed them to play upon French fears that America might abandon the contest and also, if necessary, to promise territorial concessions to France and Spain—at the expense of Britain—in order to persuade the French King to act.

The American commissioners in Paris were an ill-assorted trio. Silas Deane, a Connecticut merchant, was sent abroad because he possessed commercial skill and elementary knowledge of the French language. It turned out that he was more devoted to money than to the American cause. He began to sell information to the British. Arthur Lee was a scion of *the* Lees of Virginia, a brother of Richard Henry Lee. He was faithful to the United States, moderately intelligent, and well-educated—he had been schooled at Eton and had studied both medicine and law in Britain. Unfortunately, he was windy, jealous, and quarrelsome. It seems that he was cursed with a persecution complex. He suspected that Deane and Dr. Edward Bancroft, secretary of the commissioners, were in British pay. His suspicions were only too well founded, but he could not offer evidence. Moreover, he condemned Franklin as an incompetent, as a self-seeker, if not something worse. Lee offended both Franklin and the Frenchmen with whom they dealt, and he gave little useful service. Franklin placed too great trust in Deane and Bancroft, but otherwise performed magnificently. It was he who carried the principal burden of the commission, who secured the good will of France, who obtained an alliance with that country.

Over seventy years of age when he landed in France, the Philadelphian was no longer young or vigorous. Permitting himself to be deceived by Deane and Bancroft, he could not match Vergennes in diplomatic skills. But he was nevertheless an almost ideal emissary. He was not so naïve as he appeared; he would not spend his fading energies upon lesser matters but devoted himself to the main chance. He had a vast reputation as a scientist and philosopher; he was a veteran and skilled propagandist; he had acquired the manners as well as the habits of a man of the world; he was witty, charming, and tactful; and he soon learned to stammer lucidly in French. From his home in Passy, a suburb of Paris, he carried on a brilliant campaign in behalf of the United States. He became an idol of the French capital and at the same time a seductive symbol of the American male, even of a nobler form of mankind to come. He created among influential French men and women, whose sentiments in turn affected those of the French ministry, a dense atmosphere of sympathy for America, and he thus made it easier for Vergennes to take action. He cordially consorted with fellow scientists, and he gained their support. A member of the Masonic Order, he hobnobbed with members of that fraternity. As a deist, he won the applause and affection of the aged Voltaire, who was himself almost a deity among French intellectuals. Voltaire and his followers adored Quakers and were inclined to classify Franklin as a Friend, or a friend of the Friends; Franklin did not indulge in critical comment upon the Quakers. Dressing plainly and wearing his own hair instead of a wig, Franklin seemed to be almost a man of Nature to the disciples of Jean Jacques Rousseau, who believed that civilization had corrupted the human race and that primitive man was innocent, honorable, and undefiled. The devotees of Rousseau were numerous in Paris and were to be found even at the royal court. The sophisticated American made no effort to convince them that he was other than they believed him to be. The opinions of women were also of importance in Parisian circles. Franklin cheerfully played the part of an elderly but assiduous gallant with them. He became the rage of Paris. Moreover, making friends among influential French men and women, he used his pen effectively against the British. One of his pieces of propaganda, an attack upon the British use of Hessian troops, aroused both mirth and sympathy for the Patriots. Franklin published a letter ostensibly written by a German ruler in which that princeling expressed the hope that his soldiers in British employ would fight to the death because he received more money for a slain trooper than for the services of a survivor.

If Franklin was able to win immense good will for the Patriots in Paris, not even he could persuade the men who governed France to make an alliance with rebels whose cause might be on the verge of collapse. Reports of the capture of Philadelphia by Sir William Howe restrained Vergennes. Then came news that Washington's army had performed creditably at Germantown, together with a report upon that army from the Baron de Kalb, the French officer serving under Washington. De Kalb, in a letter received in the French capital by November 24, declared that Washington's forces had not been seriously injured, that they were strong enough to withstand attack by Howe, that they would be able eventually to drive the British back into the Atlantic. Ten days later reliable information reached Paris that Burgoyne's army had been forced to put down its weapons at Saratoga. That startling news had a dramatic effect. It could no longer be doubted that the Patriots were able to fight.

But would they continue to fight? Vergennes was now ready to act, but he desired that Spain move with France. Before he could sound out the Spanish court, a British agent, Paul Wentworth, arrived in Paris from London. The news of Saratoga, causing rejoicing in Paris, had thrown London into gloom. The British government, aware that the entrance of France into the war could hardly be prevented, made a desperate effort to avert it. Wentworth, in conversations with Silas Deane on December 15 and 16, informed him that Britain would soon offer generous terms of peace to the Patriots. Wentworth urged that Deane and his fellow emissaries refrain from making any commitment to France. Vergennes doubtless learned quickly of the Wentworth enterprise. On December 17 he took the plunge, giving his promise to the American commissioners that France would formally recognize the United States of America, a step that must be construed as a hostile act in London, that must inevitably lead to war between France and Britain. France and America would become allies. He asked that America as an ally promise not to make a separate peace. Franklin, Deane, and Lee gladly agreed to sign such a pledge.

Vergennes kept his word, but several weeks passed before the government of Louis XVI acted officially. The terms of Franco-American agreements had to be worked out in detail and phrased in appropriate language. In the meantime, Vergennes was given reasons to draw back. The Conde de Aranda, the Spanish ambassador at Paris, heartily supported the French foreign minister, but his masters in Madrid, hastily consulted, just as positively declined to move openly against Britain. Floridablanca was as reluctant as ever to help create a strong American republic; and he and his colleagues were annoyed because Vergennes had committed himself—and France—to the United States without prior notice to Spain. They emphatically rejected pleas from Vergennes and Aranda that Spain seize a heaven-sent opportunity. Vergennes was given additional cause for concern by a growing crisis in central Europe. The Elector of the south German state of Bavaria had died, leaving no direct heir. It was likely that the Habsburg Emperor Joseph II would try to seize Bavaria, that he would be militarily opposed by Frederick the Great of Prussia, and that France, allied defensively with the Emperor, would be dragged into a struggle between the two German rulers. Vergennes refused to be diverted. He was so thoroughly convinced of the wisdom of his course that he was willing to act without Spain and despite danger of involvement in a war on the European Continent. On January 7, 1778, he secured formal approval of his policy by the French ministry and Louis XVI. The three American commissioners likewise steadily held their course. They rebuffed renewed entreaties from Paul Wentworth for delay. On February 6 they signed two treaties with France that went far toward assuring American independence.

In one of those treaties France formally recognized the United States of America, and received in return special commercial privileges that opened to French manufacturers and merchants a prospect of lucrative traffic with the Americans. The second compact created an alliance. In the event that Britain responded to French recognition of the Patriots by waging war against France, the allies were to fight and to make peace in full partnership. Neither was to make a truce or a treaty with Britain without the consent of the other. It was agreed that the paramount purpose of the alliance was to assure the independence of the United States. France pledged herself to protect American territory, not only as it was at the time of the alliance, but as it should be when hostilities ended. Further, France renounced forever all claim to Canada and the regions east of the Mississippi River that had passed from her hands into those of Britain in 1763. America, in exchange, guaranteed the French possessions in the West Indies, undertaking to help France defend them into the distant future. There could be no doubt that Congress would ratify the two treaties, so generous to the new American nation—unless Britain quickly offered the Patriots nearly everything that they desired.

The texts of the two treaties, Dr. Edward Bancroft afterward boasted, reached London within forty-eight hours after they were signed. But Britain did not immediately respond with a declaration of war against France. Indeed, the two rivals did not begin to exchange blows until more than four months had passed. Not that Britain failed to resent French meddling or was disposed to accept it without striking back. George III, Lord North, and their political allies were shocked both by the news of Saratoga and by the approaching intervention of France. They thought it to be advantageous for Britain to defer hostilities until the nation was better prepared to meet a crisis. Meanwhile, the North ministry began a desperate effort to conciliate the Patriots, to persuade them to make peace and to return to the empire.

George III, Lord North, and their followers continued to maintain their easy control of the British state after the Declaration of Independence. There was laughter in London in consequence of the King's speech at the opening of Parliament on October 1, 1776. In it the monarch was made to express the hope that, in view of the unquestionable intent of the Patriots to break free from the British empire, "we shall have unanimity at home." There was no closing of the ranks in Britain. Edmund Burke, Charles James Fox, and various Rockingham and Pittite politicians did not cease to condemn the policy and personnel of government. But they accomplished nothing. Parliament steadily supported the North ministry and the war effort, by majorities that ran as high as three to one. The ministry was buoyed up by news of victories of the royal troops in America—the defeats they encountered at Trenton and Princeton were shrugged off as unfortunate, but minor, events. The menace growing on the European Continent was not unrecognized. George III would not quite believe the alarming reports that reached London from Dr. Edward Bancroft and other British agents. He placed faith in deceptive official phrases of friendship that came to him from the French government. His advisers, more realistic than the King, hoped for final military victory over the rebels before France acted decisively.

In the autumn of 1777 several of the King's friends at last became gravely concerned. Declared Grey Cooper on September 12, "I have been anxious to the greatest degree for the fortnight past. I do not even know where Sr. Wm. Howe is gone." Cooper feared that Burgoyne's progress was "not so rapid or successful" as Burgoyne had promised that it would be. Lord North himself, even after learning of Howe's victory at Brandywine, expressed pessimism, on November 4. What should the King say about America to Parliament when it reconvened? "Shall we be very stout? or shall we take advantage of the flourishing state of our affairs to get out of this d----d war & hold a moderate language? . . . I am very melancholy notwithstanding our victory. My idea of American affairs is that, if our success is as great as the most sanguine politician wishes or believes, the best use we can make of it is to get out of the dispute as soon

382

as possible." As usual, however, North failed to assert himself against his determined colleagues and his King. That same month enemies of the ministry demanded in the House of Commons that Britain abandon her military efforts against the Americans and begin negotiations with them. A motion calling for such a change in policy was brilliantly supported by Edmund Burke, who flayed the ministry for its indefensible employment of Indian auxiliaries. But Lord George Germain asserted that the war was going well. The motion was defeated, 243 to 86. The ministry also easily won a vote of confidence from the House of Commons, 175 to 47. On December 2 the Commons again gave a handsome majority to government upon an American question, 178 to 89. That same day Lord Sandwich assured the House of Lords that all was well. The peers need not be alarmed lest France, or even France and Spain, should take advantage of the war within the empire. The British navy was ready for all emergencies. It was prepared to meet any sudden thrust by the French and Spanish fleets; moreover, it could overcome both in a protracted struggle. Sandwich's optimistic declaration could not immediately be disproved; the confident estimate offered by Germain was only too quickly demonstrated to be ill founded. On December 3 Germain was forced to admit that Burgoyne's army no longer existed. He had not received an official report about Saratoga, but the fact was undeniable.

Lords North and Germain were dazed by the news from America. Germain could talk of nothing else for several days. North wished to resign, but was persuaded to remain in office. What to do? Germain, momentarily depressed, said that it might be necessary to abandon all efforts to overrun the colonies, to resort to a war of blockade in order to wear down American resistance. Without encouragement from Germain or George III, North soon announced to the House of Commons, on December 10, that government would offer generous terms of peace to the Patriots. Otherwise, he had little to say to that body in the midst of a crisis. He even arranged to send members of Parliament home for the customary Christmas recess, from December 11 to January 20. Aging and ailing, the Earl of Chatham appeared in the House of Lords, protested against holidays-as-usual in such an anxious time, and urged a plan of action. He demanded an end to all efforts to reduce the Patriots to submission, because, if for no other reason, they must fail. The North ministry must go, and persons whom the Americans respected and trusted—including Chatham?—must propose peace to the Patriots and satisfaction of their every wish except independence. Britain must make ready for a war with France that would surely come. The Rockingham

Whigs also condemned North and his cohorts. But neither George III nor Parliament was ready to concede defeat in America or to acknowledge the impending war with France.

After the Christmas vacation the enemies of government resumed their assaults. They were gloomy and angry. To forestall war with France, Charles James Fox, the Duke of Richmond, and the Rockinghamites in general urged that Britain immediately recognize the independence of the United States. That measure, they asserted, would persuade France to avoid hostilities. Later, it would be possible to convince the Patriots that they should return to the British empire. But the followers of Chatham— in his absence because of illness—clung to his plan. And George III would not listen to a proposal that granted independence, even temporarily, to the Patriots. No Englishman, he declared in mid-January, could be "either bold or mad enough to treat on such a basis." The ministerial majority in the House of Commons sank, but the King would permit North to do no more than offer the Americans wide freedom within the empire, no matter what France might do. He still could not quite believe that his brother monarch at Versailles would stab him in the back. On February 17, exactly three years after the introduction of his Concilatory Resolution of 1775, North asked Parliament to repeal the Townshend duty upon tea, the Massachusetts Government Act, and the Prohibitory Act; to renounce power to tax the Americans; and to endorse the sending of commissioners across the ocean to "treat, consult, and agree" upon terms of peace. He did not go far enough to please the Rockingham faction; he went too far to satisfy true-blue Englishmen in Parliament who were disposed to make no fundamental concessions to the rebels, whatever might be the cost to Britain. However, North gained the consent of the imperial legislature, and hurried a ship across the Atlantic with the news that emissaries would soon appear in America with power to negotiate a liberal peace. But North was not the right man to make an offer to the Patriots, as Chatham had pointed out. North was also too late, and would give too little. That same February 17, pressed in the House of Commons concerning the threatening demeanor of France, North reluctantly admitted that "it was possible, nay too probable," that Louis XVI had extended recognition to the United States.

Lord North's new effort toward securing an accommodation was a belated half measure, almost certain to fail. Nor did he or his master or his colleagues see, even in early March, that they could not pursue a military policy in America that would both support the efforts of the British peace commissioners and provide assurance that the main British army would be safe from entrapment between the forces of

Washington and a powerful French fleet that might suddenly appear on the American coast. On the eighth of that month instructions were sent to Sir Henry Clinton. If he could, he was to bring Washington to battle early in the year 1778 and to defeat him. He would not receive numerous reinforcements. Troops would be sent to Quebec and to Halifax. If Clinton was unable to rout Washington, he was to stay in Philadelphia, or to evacuate that place, as he saw fit, and to concentrate for some months upon ravaging the American seaboard. Those orders were not inconsistent with the sending of peace commissioners across the ocean—Clinton would presumably pose at least a threat of sorts to the Patriots that might induce them to listen to the commissioners. But might he not be caught between the Patriots and a French fleet superior to that under the command of Lord Howe?

On March 13 the French ambassador in London threw down the gauntlet. He officially informed His British Majesty that France had recognized the United States of America. At last it was made cruelly evident to George III and his advisers that they must wage war upon France, and perhaps Spain. Lord North was stricken with panic. The American rebellion was too much for him to manage. He could not supply proper leadership in the greater struggle about to open, and begged permission to resign in favor of Chatham. That dynamic man might be able to repeat the triumph he had won in the Seven Years' War. But George III would not have the imperious Chatham as his first minister, whether or not the British nation needed him. North must stay in office. The King would consent only to an arrangement whereby Chatham served under North. Chatham would not act under North. The prime minister irresolutely remained in power—Chatham could not have helped much in any case, for he was soon to die. While those fruitless bargainings with Chatham proceeded, North and his colleagues suddenly realized that the army under Sir Henry Clinton and the fleet under Lord Howe were endangered. It was only too likely that a great French fleet would soon cross the Atlantic. Suppose that Lord Howe with his inferior ships stationed in Delaware Bay was penned in by French? Suppose that Clinton was cut off in Philadelphia by Franco-American forces? Was it not prudent to assume the defensive on the North American mainland and to strengthen the British forces in the West Indies, not only to protect British possessions, but to punish France by seizing the rich islands she still owned in that sea? On March 21 new and "most secret" orders signed by the King himself were hastily sent across the ocean to Clinton. He was to evacuate Philadelphia, to concentrate defensively at New York. If necessary, he was to withdraw to Halifax. Lord Howe was to cover his retreat.

So provision was made to protect His Majesty's forces in North America —but these new arrangements ruined whatever small chance of success the British peace commission had. Its members could hardly threaten the Patriots with dire punishment when the British forces evacuated Philadelphia, the one substantial gain achieved by British arms in the campaigns of 1777.

Did any very good reason remain, indeed, for sending out men to treat with the Patriots? It was, of course, possible that they would be favored by some unexpected turn of fortune. North persisted in executing the enterprise, without faith that the British emissaries would accomplish much. In April three commissioners, the young Earl of Carlisle, William Eden, and George Johnstone set off in the *Trident* for America. Would they have embarked had they known that Philadelphia was to be evacuated? The instructions of March 21 sent to Clinton were kept secret from them. The *Trident* entered Delaware Bay early in June—and encountered British war vessels and transports making ready to sail to New York. They learned to their despair and disgust that their mission verged upon the absurd. They went ashore at Philadelphia in gloomy mood.

The three British envoys received more bad news. Congress, in effect, had already given them its answer. Considering the papers that had been sent across the Atlantic from London to announce the coming of the commissioners, that body had unanimously resolved on April 22 that "the United States cannot with propriety hold any conference or treaty with any commissioners on the part of Great Britain, unless they shall, as a preliminary thereto, either withdraw their fleets and armies or else in positive and express terms acknowledge the independence of the said States." What was even worse for the British emissaries, the Congress had also received and acted upon the two treaties signed at Versailles on February 6. Carried across the Atlantic by Simeon Deane, a brother of Silas Deane, they had reached the Congress after it had adjourned on Saturday, May 2. On the following Monday the delegates swiftly, unanimously, and joyously ratified the two documents.

The three commissioners quite understandably cursed their lot. William Eden bitterly complained because he had not been informed, before he left England, that the British were abandoning Philadelphia. He had been deceived by his own employers. He also condemned the ignorance and stupidity of Englishmen who had tossed away a massive empire. "It is impossible," he wrote on June 15 to his brother in England, "to give you any adequate idea of the vast scale of this country. I know little more of it than I saw in coming 150 miles up the Delaware, but I know enough to regret most heartily that our rulers instead of making the tour of

Europe did not finish their education by a voyage round the coasts and rivers of the western side of the Atlantic." Three days later he declared that "It is impossible to see even what I have seen of this magnificent country and not to go nearly mad at the long train of misconducts and mischances by which we have lost it."

Eden afterward temporarily regained hope that America could be reunited with the British empire. But not because the commission in which he was the dominant figure accomplished anything. Its nominal head, the Earl of Carlisle, was both young and inexperienced in the affairs of the world. George Johnstone was a blunderer, a loquacious nuisance, and an inept intriguer. Viscount Howe and Sir Henry Clinton, who were technically associated with the British emissaries, were confronted by a military crisis and could not serve. Eden himself was sufficiently competent for his duties. However, it mattered little whether or not he and his colleagues were ideally fitted for their task, for they could not succeed. It is doubtless true that a few Patriots were willing to consider seriously a return to the empire, even after the signing of the French alliance. One such person was General Charles Lee, who was exchanged in the spring of 1778 for a British major general and who joined Washington's army at Valley Forge. There is a British document—quite possibly misrepresentative—which suggests that Philip Schuyler, after Saratoga, meditated upon opening a campaign for reconciliation with Britain. But the Patriots were very generally determined to persevere until they achieved independence. No prominent person came forth to urge that America would fare better within the empire, even if she could return to it upon her own terms.

Authorized to bargain with the Congress, with Washington, with any group of Patriots that might be willing to listen, the Carlisle commissioners were permitted to offer terms that would have been accepted gladly by almost all Patriots before the onset of hostilities. They could promise the Americans complete freedom, so far as their domestic affairs were concerned, also that Britain would render economic assistance to help restore American prosperity. They could propose that Americans enter Parliament, that British representatives appear in American legislatures, so as to secure unity among the estranged cousins. Britain would, of course, forgive all the offenses of the rebels. Washington would not listen to the pleas of the commissioners, nor would Congress. The body merely informed the British envoys of the decision it had reached on April 22. It had nothing to say to them until Britain conceded American independence or totally withdrew her armed forces. They could make neither concession. They had been supplied with secret service money. George Johnstone tried to cajole and bribe influential Patriots. His maneuvers were exposed, and the commissioners were ridiculed. They lingered on fruitlessly in America for many months, most of which they spent at New York. For they were compelled to leave Philadelphia with the British forces that evacuated that city in late June. They moved out of Delaware Bay just in time. On July 8 a strong French fleet that included eleven ships of the line, under the Comte d'Estaing, reached the entrance to the bay.

CHAPTER XXIV

Deadlock in the North

WHEN sailors upon French warships pulled up their anchors, when French soldiers took the field, the Patriots acquired the help of a powerful ally. Britain was forced to fight upon many land fronts and upon several seas. Her difficulties were increased by the entrance of Spain into the War of Independence as an ally of France at the beginning of the summer of 1779. After that time Britain had to protect her home islands against invasion, and to defend Gibraltar, Minorca, her possessions in India, her islands in the West Indies, her outposts in the Floridas, and other territories, as well as to carry on the struggle with the Patriots. The British state seemed to stagger under the assaults of its enemies. However, in a period of great peril, the British people rallied behind their King. They might not be united against the American rebels; they were much more willing, even eager, to contend against faithless France and perfidious Spain. Britain was, in the main, reduced to defensive measures. But her enemies were unable to concentrate all of their powers against her; her navy was able to meet almost all of the many threats posed by the French and Spanish fleets; and her troops, as usual, fought stubbornly upon the defensive, in adversity. Retreating from Philadelphia in the early summer of 1778, Sir Henry Clinton beat off an attack by Washington's army at Monmouth Courthouse in New Jersey. With Lord Howe, he concentrated at New York. They warded off a Franco-American menace in 1778. New York remained in British hands until the end of the war. The Patriots, even with French help, could not take that British stronghold. On the other hand, sending more and more troops into the Southern States, the British made no great effort to invade the interior of the Northern American commonwealths. The war in the North became one of blockade, raids, intrigues, and endurance. It slipped into uneasy stale-mate.

The army under Washington at Valley Forge emerged from cold shadows into bright sunlight in the spring of 1778. In February it was briefly threatened with dissolution. It was almost without food for a few days. Hundreds of men deserted to the British, and perhaps as many left the Patriot camp, with or without permission, to seek food and shelter elsewhere. But perhaps 5,000 Continentals dauntlessly endured cold and want. It will be recalled that General Nathanael Greene, who had not yet displayed brilliance as a field commander, demonstrated ability and zeal as a supply officer. As spring approached, meat, flour, whiskey, clothing, weapons, and ammunition poured into Valley Forge. A run of shad in the Delaware River permitted the troops to fatten upon fish. Men who had departed to regain health returned to duty, and with them came recruits. By May, Washington's army was again ready to fight.

It was, in fact, better prepared to confront the British than it had ever been. Washington had more than 13,000 men, and many of them were hardy veterans who had successfully withstood every danger and every hardship. Besides, his Continentals were now well drilled, and Washington's musketmen were now trained in the use of the bayonet. For the Baron von Steuben had appeared at Valley Forge and had success-fully undertaken to instill German efficiency in the army. Claiming that he was Frederick William Augustus Henry Ferdinand, Baron von Steuben, a former lieutenant general of Frederick the Great, and the owner of an estate in Germany, that officer was not a nobleman, was never more than a captain in Europe, and possessed broad acres only in his own fertile imagination. He was an egotistical poseur, an adventurer who sought to improve his lot in the New World. But he was also a hard-bitten soldier with a sense of humor. He could and did teach Continental officers and men how to advance, to retreat, and to turn with precision, how to wield their weapons in standard units and in unison. As inspector general in the late winter and spring of 1778 Steuben earned the lasting gratitude of the United States. The army that moved from Valley Forge in June of that year was more formidable, man for man, than any other Patriot force that had earlier taken the field. The value of the drilling done by Steuben was soon demonstrated, at Monmouth Courthouse.

The British decision to evacuate Philadelphia caused anger and con-sternation in that city. Army officers vainly clamored for an attack upon the Patriots at Valley Forge rather than a retreat to New York. Pennsyl-vania Loyalists who had publicly proclaimed their allegiance to Britain in assurance of royal triumph learned that the protection upon which they had relied was to be withdrawn. What was to become of them, their families, and their property? They were told that they must make their peace as best they could with the Patriots—or they must depart with the British forces. Many of them chose to flee rather than to face angry and vengeful Patriots. About 3,000 of them embarked in British transports, together with several thousands of Hessians, the least reliable of the troops under Sir Henry Clinton. The British did not possess enough shipping to carry away the entire royal army, its essential equipment, and the saddened Tories. Clinton therefore resolved to lead the bulk of his army, including his reliable British regulars, across New Jersey. He left Philadelphia on June 18.

Watching from Valley Forge, Washington was delighted to learn that the British were retreating. He had earlier expected them to resume the offensive, a conclusion fortified by brief appearances of British contingents outside Philadelphia. He quickly resolved to intercept Clinton in New Jersey. He hastily sent some of his Continentals into that state, called upon its militia for assistance, and set off after the British army. Burdened with military baggage, Clinton moved slowly. At Monmouth Courthouse, with Continentals at his rear and militia advancing against his flanks, he turned about, occupied strong ground, and defied his pursuers to attack him. Dozens of his Hessians had deserted upon the march, but Clinton still had with him nearly as many troops as Washington led. Washington was then faced by a momentous question. Should he assail Clinton? He had twice formally asked his generals that question. The majority of them had advised him not to risk a general engagement. They had pointed out that the British retreat was in itself a great victory for the Patriots. General Charles Lee, indeed, had argued that the Americans would do well to build a "bridge" for the British so that they might reach their destination. He contended that the Patriots could not overcome the British army, that a general engagement would very likely lead to a defeat which would destroy all the benefits gained from the British withdrawal. His counsel was prudent and sensible. It was also consistent, however, with a change in Lee's political beliefs. He did not desire to destroy the British army. One of the very first of the Patriots to demand a declaration of independence, he had come to believe that America would do well to accept freedom within the British empire—a fact that the impulsive Lee could not entirely conceal. Washington himself, supported by a minority of his officers, including the impetuous and reckless Anthony Wayne, was most reluctant to let Clinton escape without a struggle. The Patriot commander was always disposed to fight when the odds were not too heavy against him. He had not been able to win even one important victory over the main body of the British army in the field. He had been viciously and unjustly condemned during the preceding winter because he had not overwhelmed Sir William Howe in the campaign of 1777. On the other hand, Horatio Gates had been excessively praised for bringing about the downfall of Burgoyne. Washington commanded better officers and troops than ever before. Ought he not to send them into battle? Torn between conflicting advices, he resolved upon a middle course, to strike a partial blow at Clinton, but to avoid a general engagement under circumstances favorable to the British.

The result was other than either Washington or Charles Lee intended. Sending militia to threaten Clinton's wings, the American commander in chief ordered Lee, leading 4,000 men, to attack the British rear guard on the morning of the twenty-eighth, which turned out to be a torrid summer day. Washington held the rest of his army in reserve. Advancing across open country intersected by three ravines, Lee sent his men into action. He soon learned that he was opposed, not by a small rear guard, but by the main body of the royal army. Alarmed lest his men be driven back and trapped, Lee withdrew across the three ravines and occupied a defensible position. The Patriot artillery covered his retrograde movements. Coming forward, Washington condemned Lee for retreating, and the two men exchanged harsh words. Washington assumed command and repulsed British counterattacks, including a charge of British cavalry led by Clinton in person. Both sides were exhausted by their exertions in the intense heat and at last rested upon their arms. During the following night Clinton quietly left his lines and marched off toward Sandy Hook. It was not possible for Washington to mount another attack. Clinton, with most of his troops, safely reached New York, where he found Admiral Howe and the British fleet. Washington followed Clinton, and took up position outside the city.

The honors of the battle of Monmouth were about even. The casualties of the two armies were nearly equal, perhaps 300 men in each force. The British had driven back the Patriots; the Americans had withstood charges by the royal troops. The Patriots held the field of battle; the British army arrived at New York without excessive losses. Washington could take pride in the outcome. Charles Lee, however, was most unhappy. He had been censured by Washington on the battlefield in the presence of many officers. With characteristic vehemence he sent to the commander in chief a letter that was much less than polite and that demanded an opportunity to defend his behavior. Washington responded by ordering a court-martial of Lee, charging him with refusal to obey orders, unnecessary and shameful retreat, and disrespect toward his superior officer. Sure that his innocence would be established, Lee arrogantly and carelessly conducted his own defense. He neglected to call his best witness, a courier who could have testified that Lee was instructed to make a partial rather than a general attack. Even so, the testimony quite definitely cleared Lee of the charges, except for that of disrespect to Washington. But the judges were appointed by the commander in chief. Moreover, it was evident that, regardless of the evidence, Lee ought not to continue in service under Washington. Friends of the American commander were accusing the Englishman of treachery. Was there something in Lee's conduct at the trial which suggested that he had become less than utterly devoted to American independence? The judges softened the charges against him, but found him guilty and deprived him of power to command for a period of one year. Considering the record of the court-martial, the Congress long hesitated before ratifying the sentence. On the face of it, Lee could hardly be guilty, yet it would not do to exculpate him. His services had been substantial, but he had been insubordinate and creative of mischief. Unaware that Lee's political allegiance had altered, the Congress, wiser than it knew, at last endorsed the verdict. As the end of his sentence approached, Lee, continuing to protest against it, informed Congress that he would not serve again unless the stigma placed upon him by the court-martial was removed. Thereupon that body dismissed him from the Continental army. Having retired to a plantation that he had acquired in Virginia, the embittered officer virulently attacked Washington in letters and newspaper articles. He died obscurely in Philadelphia in 1782. His obvious and exasperating faults were forgiven him after his death, and he occupied a respectable place in the Pantheon of Patriot heroes for many decades. Then, nearly three quarters of a century after his death, the plan for military action he had offered to Sir William Howe in 1777 was revealed to the public. That he harbored treacherous intent remains doubtful. It is beyond question that Lee was endowed with intellectual powers; that he was a brave and hard-bitten soldier; that he was unstable, and sometimes half-mad.

Safely reaching the British base at New York, Sir Henry Clinton and Lord Howe were soon faced by a new threat. For the North ministry, demonstrating once more after receiving the tidings of Saratoga that it lacked political genius, also again offered proof that it contained no splendid strategist. Hostilities between Britain and France did not begin until June 16, when a French ship and a British one engaged in the English Channel. However, it was apparent during the two months preceding that combat that the French were preparing to strike. Alarmed lest they invade Britain, the ministry called militia into service, entrusted Sir

Jeffery Amherst with the task of repelling any French troops that might reach British shores, and collected a powerful fleet to deal with a somewhat smaller French one at Brest and to prevent the French from transporting an army across the Channel. The British navy, not very gloriously, withheld control of the Channel from the French.

But providing amply for the defense of the British Isles, George III, Lord North, and their associates failed to plumb the intentions of France and to meet a menace posed by a fleet under the Comte d'Estaing that had been collected at the naval base of Toulon on the Mediterranean coast of France. Vergennes and other servants of Louis XVI were not eager to mount an invasion of England; they intended rather to strip away Britain's colonies. They ordered d'Estaing to make ready for sea as rapidly and as quietly as possible, and to proceed across the Atlantic. Learning that the French admiral was preparing to move, George III and his advisers fell into confusion. Would d'Estaing join the French fleet at Brest, thus endangering British dominance of the Channel? Might not the Spanish fleet be added to that of France? They knew that the appearance of d'Estaing in American waters would pose a menace for the weaker squadron of Admiral Howe—and for Clinton's army. They resolved to run the risk of temporary Bourbon superiority in the Channel; they ordered Admiral John Byron to take a fleet to America to assist Howe; and George III himself went to the southern coast of England to hasten Byron's departure. Then they hesitated. Lord Sandwich and the admirals responsible for defense of the home islands wished to be absolutely sure that Britain was safe from invasion. Byron was kept in port. Then came news to London that d'Estaing had cruised through the Straits of Gibraltar, and that his course indicated his destination to be Delaware Bay. Byron was tardily ordered to proceed westward with all possible speed. He was further delayed by contrary winds. Moreover, en route to New York, his fleet was damaged and scattered by a storm—Byron, known as "Foul-Weather Jack" had a reputation for encountering unfavorable and high winds. Before any of Byron's ships could reach New York, d'Estaing appeared outside its harbor. The French admiral, reaching the entrance to Delaware Bay, had discovered that he was too late to interfere with the evacuation of Philadelphia, and had followed Admiral Howe to the British base at New York. He anchored outside its harbor.

Washington and d'Estaing saw an opportunity to strike a decisive blow. The French fleet, with eleven ships of the line, was easily superior to that of the British. Its ships were larger, and it possessed far greater firing power. Moreover, d'Estaing had with him 4,000 French troops. True, the British army concentrated at New York was superior in num-

394

bers to the combined Franco-American land forces. Besides, it had the advantage of entrenchments long since erected by the British for the protection of their American headquarters. But if the French admiral could break into New York Harbor and hold command of it long enough, Washington would be able to bring up militia from New England and perhaps even to force the surrender of the British army, cut off from supplies and from help by sea. The prospect seemed bright to Washington, so long compelled to fight on the defensive, so long permitted to take the offensive only at excessive risk. It was not so brilliant as it seemed, in that Clinton had sufficient force and could secure supplies to hold out for many months, until the British navy could come to his assistance.

Moreover, that bright outlook for Washington was clouded on the water as well as on land. For Richard Howe was now confronted by a crisis that brought forth his special talents. That admiral had failed miserably as a negotiator, and he had waged a soft and ineffective war against Patriot shipping and ports. But he was at his best when fighting against the Bourbons. He could not prudently undertake to force his way out of New York Harbor in order to engage d'Estaing, but he could prevent the French fleet from entering it in force. He resolutely prepared to stop d'Estaing if the French admiral tried to sail into the harbor. Thousands of seamen from British merchant vessels tied up at its docks volunteered for his service—they, too, were determined to do their part to meet the menace of the French fleet. Indeed, Howe and Clinton hoped that d'Estaing would venture to attack. "We should succeed at no time, if we can fail on such an occasion," declared the British admiral on July 11. Eight days later Clinton asserted, "We are all happy at the idea." The British placed a battery on Sandy Hook, then an island, to fire against the French warships, and Clinton sent infantry to defend it. Howe placed his war vessels on both sides of the passage into the harbor, arranging them so that they could discharge their guns from one side, then from the other, at the French ships.

The British were not put to the test. Their defenses and their evident eagerness to fight were enough to give any French admiral pause. D'Estaing, trained as a soldier rather than as a naval officer, was an extraordinarily brave man. He was not a Horatio Nelson. Even so, he might have put his fleet in motion, had it been possible. But he learned that his great warships—two of them carried eighty guns each—drew so much water that they could not cross a sandbar which lay athwart the entrance to the harbor. In vain, he offered a vast reward to any pilot who would guide his fleet over the bar. He could not get at his dangerous prey. Frustrated, he consulted with Washington. The two men regretfully concluded that it was idle to concentrate at that time against New York and that Franco-American forces should instead attack the British garrison at Newport.

Again the Patriots and the French encountered disappointment. The capture of Newport, with its garrison of at least 3,000 British troops under Sir Robert Pigot, would have compensated to a degree for the failure of the allies at New York. Success seemed almost assured when d'Estaing arrived off Newport on July 29. The Patriot General John Sullivan, placed in command of perhaps 10,000 Continentals and militiamen by Washington, soon occupied part of the island upon which Newport is located. Pigot could not hope to defend his post indefinitely against attack. But Admiral Howe came to his rescue. One warship from Halifax joined Howe, and another from Byron's scattered fleet. Howe still could not match d'Estaing in ships-of-the-line—the great battle craft of that time. He would not use that inferiority as an excuse for leaving Pigot to his fate. He rapidly followed the French admiral to Rhode Island, and challenged him. While the two fleets maneuvered for position, a storm came up that scattered both of them far and wide. There followed engagements between single ships which demonstrated that Howe's confidence was not ill founded. Three British vessels carrying 50 guns each fought against three French ones with 84, 80, and 74 guns, respectively, and held their own. D'Estaing collected his fleet off Rhode Island, but did not remain there. Howe, quickly refitting at New York and reinforced by the arrival of several ships from Byron's squadron, went in search of the French admiral a second time. He now commanded a fleet superior to that of d'Estaing, who prudently withdrew to Boston to clean and repair his fleet. General Sullivan was then compelled to retreat hastily in order to escape entrapment by the British.

The threat posed by d'Estaing had been fended off. Clinton suggested to Lord Howe that they turn the tables and jointly attack Boston and the French fleet before d'Estaing could return to sea. Howe displayed no interest in the proposal. Resigning his command in the western Atlantic, he went home in triumph. His brother, the general, returning from the war, had been graciously received by George III, but had otherwise been coldly treated by government and the British public. The admiral, espousing his brother's cause, haughtily expressed his contempt for those who had condemned his brother's conduct and his own. Upon landing in England, he did not bother to seek an audience with George III, but went directly to his country home. Later, in the House of Commons, accepting the praise that he so well deserved for checking d'Estaing, he pointedly remarked that his fleet ought not have been exposed to attack by d'Estaing. Sir William demanded an inquiry into his own behavior by the house. It was brief and inconclusive. Partisans of Lord George Germain,

Joseph Galloway, and other exiled Loyalists continued to assail the brothers. Sir William never again commanded an army upon the battlefield. But George III retained his special interest in his cousins and admired Lord Howe. The admiral was too valuable a man to remain indefinitely without command at sea. He was to serve again in two great emergencies, with his customary success in battle.

Had Sir Henry Clinton gone home with Admiral Howe, his reputation would have been better than it is; but he remained at his post. He asked Admiral Byron, who finally appeared at New York, whether that unfortunate seaman would take part in an attack upon Boston and d'Estaing. Finally, Clinton, lacking faith in Byron's abilities, abandoned that project. However, Byron sailed to Boston, but encountered another of those storms that plagued his career. His fleet was driven away by high winds. In his absence d'Estaing slipped out of Boston Harbor and set sail for the West Indies. The French admiral had sensibly decided that he could accomplish nothing, for the time being, on the coasts of North America. He left behind him many bitterly disappointed Patriots, not a few of whom ascribed the failures of the Franco-American forces at New York and Newport to his supposed deficiencies.

If d'Estaing achieved much less than the Patriots hoped and expected, it is nevertheless true that he gave the British forces in North America ample occupation in the campaign of 1778. And if his services brought no brilliant successes, the entrance of France into the war did immediately and positively assist the Americans. Their Congress could and did return to Philadelphia. Moreover, other benefits would come, for the North ministry, putting Sir Henry Clinton upon the defensive in 1778, had adopted a policy that would make it awkward and even dangerous for him to resume the offensive at a later time. Eager to strike back at France, to take from Louis XVI valuable Caribbean Islands that would compensate in part for the probable loss of Britain's colonies on the North American mainland, Clinton's superiors ordered him, in the spring of 1778, to send part of his army to the West Indies. He was also then instructed to attack Georgia, and if possible, South Carolina, when the approach of winter put an end to campaigning in the Northern American States. In the autumn of 1778 he executed those commands, sending a large detachment to the Carribbean to conquer the French island of St. Lucia and another to Savannah. Thus Clinton was deprived of men he needed, if he was to move out of New York in great force. Britain was committed to major operations in the West Indies and, as it turned out, to a venture in the Southern States that eventually acquired massive proportions.

For the assault upon Savannah was so easily successful that the

British were induced to commit more and more men to conquests in the far South. It was hoped in both London and New York, contrary to all experience elsewhere, that the Loyalists of Georgia would not only receive the royal troops as deliverers, but would take up arms in their own behalf. And were there not many Tories in South Carolina eager to fight, if they were given opportunity? Might not the appearance of British soldiers in the far South also encourage the Cherokee and Creek warriors to strike against the Patriots? Clinton sent 3,500 soldiers under Lieutenant Colonel Archibald Campbell to Georgia. They were assisted by 2,000 more who advanced northward from St. Augustine under General Augustine Prevost. The Patriots in the far South were not prepared to withstand the assaults of the two British contingents. They had not been seriously threatened for more than two years, since the battle of Sullivan's Island. Major General Robert Howe, who commanded the Continental forces in the South, had fewer men in Savannah than Campbell. That British officer landed near the town two days before Christmas and drove out the American garrison six days later. Then Prevost made his appearance. The British swept inland and captured Augusta on January 29, 1779. Georgia was in their hands. Sir James Wright came out from London to resume his duties as royal governor and to restore civil government. Presumably Georgia was regained for the empire. The British were tempted to invade South Carolina, and they soon did.

Thus it was that Britain, scattering her forces in North America and the West Indies, deprived Clinton of power to strike powerfully from New York. That policy ought to have been accompanied, as Clinton suggested, by the appointment of an admiral or a general to direct all the British forces in North America and the Caribbean Sea, a proposal that was afterward put forward by Admiral Sir George Rodney. However, Germain and Sandwich preferred to try to manage the war from London though separate commanders in the several theaters of conflict in the New World. What was even worse, so far as Clinton was concerned, was that his masters in the imperial capital failed to learn the most obvious lesson of the campaign of 1778, that British armies in North America would again be sorely threatened if the French should a second time achieve and hold naval superiority for a few months, or even for a few weeks, upon the American coast. Sending British naval squadrons hither and yon, they did not make sure that Clinton's men would not be again caught between the French and the Patriots. They did not even send an able admiral to replace Lord Howe. Early in 1779 Sandwich gave the command of the British fleet stationed at New York to one of his favorites, the old, half-sick, and incompetent Marriot Arbuthnot.

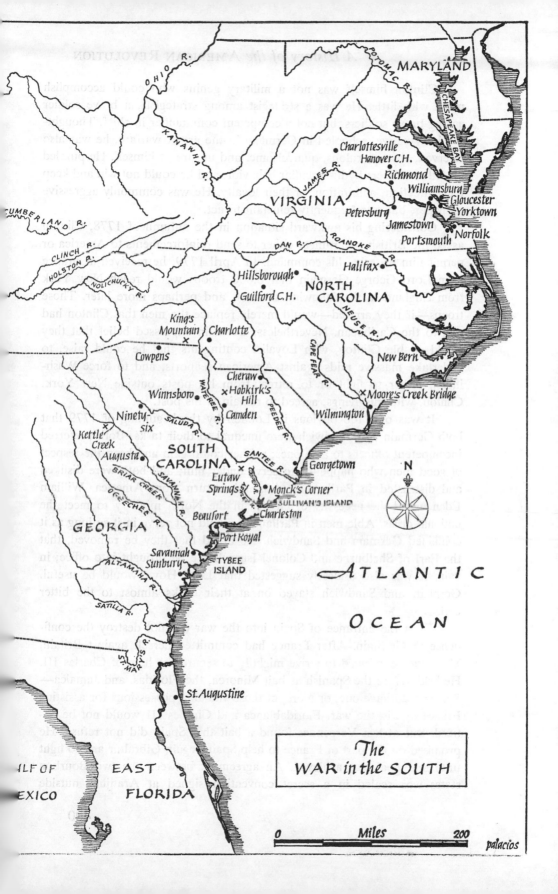

MARYLAND

OHIO R.

KANAWHA R.

POTOMAC R.

CHESAPEAKE BAY

CUMBERLAND R.

CLINCH R.

HOLSTON R.

NOLICHUCKY R.

Charlottesville
Hanover C.H.

JAMES R.

Richmond

Williamsburg

VIRGINIA

Petersburg

Gloucester
Yorktown

Jamestown

Portsmouth

Norfolk

DAN R.

ROANOKE

Halifax

Hillsborough

Guilford C.H.

NORTH
CAROLINA

NEUSE R.

King's
Mountain

Charlotte

CAPE FEAR R.

New Bern

Cowpens

Cheraw

Hobkirk's
Hill

WATEREE R.

PEEDEE R.

Moore's Creek Bridge

Winnsboro

Camden

Wilmington

Ninety-
six

SALUDA R.

SANTEE R.

Georgetown

Kettle
Creek

Augusta

SOUTH
CAROLINA

BRIAR CREEK

SAVANNAH R.

COOPER R.

Eutaw
Springs

Monck's Corner

ASHLEY R.

SULLIVAN'S ISLAND

Charleston

N

OGEECHEE R.

GEORGIA

Beaufort

Port Royal

Savannah

Sunbury

ALTAMAHA R.

TYBEE
ISLAND

A T L A N T I C

O C E A N

SATILLA R.

ST. MARYS R.

GULF OF

MEXICO

EAST

FLORIDA

St. Augustine

Miles

0   200

The
WAR in the SOUTH

palacios

Clinton himself was not a military genius who could accomplish much with little. He was a strategist among strategists, a brave soldier among brave soldiers, but not a competent commander in chief. Thoughtful, imaginative, schooled in Germany in the art of warfare, he was also reserved, shy, querulous, quarrelsome, and unsure of himself. He puzzled his fellow officers by his peculiar behavior, and he could not win and keep their affection, admiration, or their loyalty. He was commonly aggressive on paper, but was frequently reluctant to act.

Considering his awkward situation in the autumn of 1778, Clinton asked the British government either to send reinforcements to America or permit him to resign his command. In April 1779, he received assurance from Lord George Germain that 6,600 troops would reach New York from England in the following summer, and perhaps more later. Those troops—if they arrived—would merely replace the men that Clinton had sent to the Caribbean. Nevertheless, Germain expressed belief that they would enable Clinton, with Loyalist contingents that he could raise, to undertake massive raids against American seaports, and to force Washington either to fight or to retreat from his posts outside New York. Clinton, with misgivings, agreed to remain at his post.

It was only too obvious in London by the beginning of 1779 that both Germain and Sandwich were unequal to their tasks. Both preferred incompetent officers to able ones; neither could gain and keep the respect of good men who happened to serve under him; and both were disliked and distrusted in Parliament. After his return from America, William Eden urged the necessity of change in the North ministry to meet the national crisis. Able men in Parliament would not serve in it so long as it contained Germain and Sandwich. He urged that they be removed, that the Earl of Shelburne and Colonel Isaac Barré be brought into office; in vain. It was also uselessly suggested that Lord Howe would be useful. Germain and Sandwich stayed on at their desks almost to the bitter end.

Even the entrance of Spain into the war did not destroy the confidence of Germain. After France had committed herself against Britain, Vergennes continued to strive mightily to secure the help of Charles III. He held before the Spanish as bait Minorca, the Floridas, and Jamaica— Spain could have one, or more, of those valuable possessions for assisting France to win the war. Floridablanca and Charles III would not be enticed. But at last Vergennes found a bait that Spain did not refuse. He promised on the part of France to help Spain regain Gibraltar and to fight until that goal was achieved. An agreement between the two Bourbon states was sealed in a secret convention signed at Aranjuez outside

Madrid, in April 1779. Thereupon, Spain peremptorily asked that Britain accept her mediation in the Anglo-French struggle, or be subjected to Spanish attack. Britain, of course, rejected the demand; and Charles III began hostilities. Their Most Christian and Most Catholic Majesties proceeded to the execution of plans to invade England, and to invest Gibraltar.

If Germain continued to write confidently to Sir Henry Clinton, his country and his fellow ministers were shaken by the addition of Spain to the enemies of Britain. The threat of invasion of the home islands became real. Charles III insisted that Britain herself could be and should be conquered. Combining fleets, the French and Spanish should be able to seize control of the Channel; and a French army ought to defeat Britain's garrison forces without undue difficulty. Vergennes agreed that the attempt must be made. The domestic enemies of George III and Lord North urged that Britain abandon her efforts to reconquer her American colonies and concentrate against her traditional and formidable European adversaries. The British nation, they averred without contradiction, was in dire peril. Their proposal was defeated in the House of Commons. The King held firm. If the Thirteen Colonies were permitted to go free, Britain's West Indian islands would also soon be lost. Of what avail to safeguard England and not the empire? It was better to risk all; with God's help, contended the King sturdily, everything could be held by Britain and all that had been lost could be regained. Two Bedfordite ministers resigned, and were replaced, but North, Germain, and Sandwich, bolstered by the strong will of the monarch, carried on. The greatest peril posed by the Bourbons passed before the end of 1779. A combined Franco-Spanish fleet dominated the Channel for some weeks in the summer of that year, but it withdrew without accomplishing anything. Moreover, at the end of the year Admiral Sir George Rodney sailed to the relief of Gibraltar, destroyed a Spanish squadron en route, and completed his mission.

Even so, Britain increasingly felt the strain of the war. Her debt and her taxes were mounting. Nevertheless, Germain, at least officially, continued to express faith that the war in the New World could be won. It was obvious in 1779 that weak British garrisons in Mobile and Pensacola would be exposed to Spanish attack from Mexico, Louisiana, and Cuba, but he began to think about the conquest of New Orleans rather than defense of West Florida. He conceded in the summer of that year that the Patriots could not be crushed without massive help from the Loyalists. However, he hoped that General Prevost would be able to take Charleston. He admitted that the several enemies of Britain posed many difficulties for her. But, he wrote to Clinton, "Our cause is just, our councils firm and decided; and we trust that the zealous and able exertions of our officers will, under the Divine favour, be crowned with success." Later, in September of that year, toward influencing the Divine will, Germain urged Clinton to try to bribe members of the Continental Congress and American officers to betray their cause. Germain would cheerfully pay the cost —seduction of principal Patriots might bring as great gains as military triumphs. Clinton was already negotiating with General Benedict Arnold, and he was doubtless pleased to know that he could safely make most handsome promises to that treacherous man. He would have been much more pleased to receive heavy reinforcements so as to make sure that the Deity preferred the British to their American brethren.

General Washington did not believe that the Supreme Being favored George III or Germain. Emerging from winter quarters stretching from Connecticut to New Jersey in the spring of 1779, he was concerned lest Clinton should be greatly strengthened during the approaching campaign. However, he was not without confidence. His own army had suffered less than usual from cold and lack of food during the preceding winter. In October 1778, thanks to the French, it had received new uniforms and shoes. Washington's men, paid in rapidly depreciating Continental currency, received each month paper money that would buy very little. But they, too, were in good spirits that spring. Washington could not hope to stage a successful attack upon New York without French help; on the other hand, he could expect to check any army that Clinton might lead out of the city—if he declined to fight a decisive battle with the British under circumstances unfavorable to the Patriots.

Clinton entertained a slender hope that Washington might be enticed into a general engagement—had not Washington almost committed himself to such a struggle at Monmouth Courthouse? The Patriot commander was building forts at Stony Point and at Verplanck's Point, opposite each other below Peekskill on the lower Hudson, to hem in the British and to cover the approach to West Point from the south; Clinton planned to move against the two forts in the hope that Washington would come to the rescue of their small garrisons and accept battle on ground chosen by the British general. Clinton moved up the Hudson at the end of May with 6,000 men and easily captured the two posts. The seizure of Stony Point cost the British only one wounded soldier. But Washington, concentrating with 8,000 troops on the Hudson to check Clinton, prudently refrained from taking the offensive. He merely established himself farther up the river in order to protect West Point, where the Americans were building a strong fortress. Disappointed, Clinton turned back toward New

York. He consoled himself with the thought that he had acquired an outpost of "tolerable security" at Stony Point. He ordered that the defensive works begun by the Patriots be completed, and he placed within them a garrison of about 600 British and Loyalist troops. Stony Point was a lofty promontory, virtually an island; fortified, it would become almost impregnable. Besides, Clinton could quickly move to the support of its garrison.

Then Washington brilliantly struck back. Carefully surveying Stony Point, before its defenses were completed, he concluded that it could be carried by a surprise attack. He assigned "Mad Anthony" Wayne with 1,350 picked troops to the task. He chose the right man to lead the assault. The intrepid Wayne quietly approached the fort. He ordered his men to rely upon the bayonet, and led them forward in two columns in the night of July 15–16. Wayne himself was wounded, but continued to direct his men. They stormed the fort, killing sixty-three of its defenders and capturing the remainder. Wayne counted fifteen Americans killed, and eighty wounded. He demonstrated that the Continentals could perform superbly in the European style of fighting. He also won the respect of the British because his men mercifully gave quarter to the garrison as soon as it ceased to resist. Nor did Washington throw away the benefits of Wayne's splendid victory. He did not attempt to hold Stony Point; he permitted Clinton to put a new garrison in that place without challenge.

A month later Washington won another little victory that vexed Clinton, that displayed again the proficiency of the Continentals—and of Henry Lee, "Light-Horse Harry," who deserves to be remembered for more than fathering Robert E. Lee. At Paulus Hook in New Jersey opposite New York City was another British post, held by Major William Sutherland with more than 200 men. Light-Horse Harry secured permission to try to surprise the garrison. He succeeded. He struck before dawn on August 19; killed or captured all of the defenders, except for Sutherland and forty or fifty Hessians who obstinately held out in a blockhouse; and retreated with his prisoners before British reinforcements could intervene.

Washington had hoped to do more, much more, in 1779. Would not d'Estaing return from the West Indies and join the Patriots in an attack upon New York or Newport? But d'Estaing did not appear—he went instead to help the Patriots in the South. Washington at last went into winter quarters after an unusually quiet year.

If Washington was less than delighted by his achievements in 1779, Clinton was most unhappy. The reinforcements promised him by Germain came in August, but hardly more than half so many as the colonial secretary had pledged. Moreover, some of those troops were sick with fever when they arrived at New York, and they spread the contagion through Clinton's army. They were too few and too late to permit a thrust against Washington. Frustrated, Clinton asked permission to resign in favor of Lord Cornwallis, who had returned from England during the summer and who was eager to serve. He evacuated Stony Point, Verplanck's Point, and Newport, thus reducing his commitments near New York and securing men for active service in the far South. His attention was increasingly turning toward Georgia and South Carolina. Sir James Wright had told him that the British could not hold the territory they had conquered south of the Savannah River unless they seized Charleston. Clinton fancied that the capture of Charleston might bring about the collapse of the Patriots in South Carolina. Although he was well aware that the appearance of a French fleet on the American coast was only too likely, he sent more troops southward, thus providing a second and generous target for the French and the Patriots.

So enamored of the Southern adventure was Clinton that he went personally to South Carolina early in 1780. In his absence the Baron von Knyphausen, whom he had left in command at New York, advanced into New Jersey in force, but was checked by Washington and soon retreated to New York. Thereafter, the British army at New York substantially remained upon the defensive. In July, Clinton, having returned to his headquarters, was confronted by a threat and a great opportunity. A French squadron under the Chevalier de Ternay carrying 4,000 troops under the command of the Comte de Rochambeau appeared at Newport. Clinton hastily gathered troops on Long Island, and urged Admiral Arbuthnot to join him in an attack upon the French. But Arbuthnot believed that the venture could not succeed, and Clinton was forced to abandon it. When Admiral Rodney appeared at New York with a fleet that gave the British overwhelming superiority on the coast of the north Atlantic, the project was revived. However, Clinton had lost interest in it, and the French were allowed to remain at Newport. Their presence at once encouraged the Patriots and menaced the British.

Clinton turned away from Newport, at least in part, because he had hit upon another scheme that he fancied might win the war for Britain. His secret negotiations with Benedict Arnold, who had been given command of the American stronghold at West Point, were reaching a climax.

How it happened that Benedict Arnold turned traitor to the Patriots must remain to a degree inexplicable. Afterward, he said that the American alliance with France profoundly disturbed him and that he came to prefer reunion with Britain to a close association with the French. One may not believe that he was chiefly motivated by dislike and fear of the French. It has been suggested that he had been badly treated by his fellow Patriots and that he betrayed them in a moment of tempestuous passion. Since he was in clandestine correspondence with the British for sixteen months before he committed himself to them, it is obvious that his treachery was not the product of a momentary rage. True, he had not been promoted in the Continental army as rapidly as other and less competent officers. But he had reached the rank of major general, and he was esteemed, trusted, and defended by Washington. His progress upward had been somewhat delayed by Congress because that body had considered it necessary to award promotions in such fashion as to apportion them among the several states. Other Continental officers had similarly suffered disappointment. Some of them jealously resigned their commissions rather than accept inferior status they believed to be less than their due; none of them undertook to turn an American fort over to the British; not one of them even joined the British. The explanation of Arnold's conduct must ultimately be found in defects of character. Making his way forward in the world, he had not learned to be magnanimous. Brave and enterprising, he was also vain, mean, and mercenary. As a widower and commandant of Philadelphia, he had married a young woman, Peggy Shippen, of a Toryish family. He lived beyond his means in Philadelphia. It is to be suspected that his new wife encouraged him to think that his services had not been sufficiently appreciated by the United States and that his hostility toward Britain was unwarranted. In any event, Arnold did not merely change his allegiance and refuse further to serve the American republic. He offered to join the British and asked that he be compensated for the property losses which he would thereby sustain. Clinton agreed, and urged that Arnold give proof of his change of heart by assisting his former enemies. The American general at length undertook to help them capture West Point. Clinton made ready to sail up the Hudson and to take the fort.

But the conspiracy failed. The British general sent his deputy adjutant general, Major John André, a talented young officer, to see Arnold and to settle details for British seizure of the fort. Had the Clinton-Arnold scheme succeeded, Washington might have become a prisoner of the British, for it happened that he reached the vicinity of the fort at the moment of crisis. However, André was captured by Patriot partisans on his return journey. He carried incriminating papers, and the plot was exposed. Arnold barely made his escape to a British ship in the Hudson, and thence to New York. It is very doubtful that possession of West Point would have won the war for Britain. In any case, Clinton was compelled to abandon the enterprise. Moreover, the fate of John André gave him more cause for bitterness. André had changed into civilian clothes before he set out for New York. He thus became a spy. The Patriots offered to exchange him for Arnold, a proposal that the British commander had to decline. André was then sentenced to death by an American court-martial, and was hanged. Britain erected a monument in Westminster Abbey to the memory of that unfortunate young man, and George III made his younger brother a baronet. Clinton paid Arnold his price, £6,000, and gave him a commission as a British general. Washington and the Patriots generally were shocked by the treason of Arnold. But he was in no way indispensable to the American cause, and they grimly carried on the struggle against Britain. Efforts by Clinton to corrupt other prominent Patriots failed. Britain could not gain by bribery what she could not do by force.

Far more hurtful to Washington and his Continentals than the perfidy of Arnold were the hardships they suffered in quarters at Morristown during the following winter. Momentarily, in January 1781, the Patriot army there was threatened by dissolution. The usual deficiencies in food and shelter with which it was plagued in winter were accompanied by unusually harsh weather. The cold was so intense in New York that the oldest man could not remember its like. Seldom paid in money that would purchase anything—the Continental paper currency had become worthless—the troops became increasingly restless and desperate. Some clamored for discharge. They had enlisted for three years or the duration of the war, and they had served for three years. Their officers informed them that they had pledged themselves to do duty until the end of the struggle. They believed, not without reason, that they had been deceived. At last, about 1,700 Pennsylvania troops—many of them foreign-born—declined to obey their officers, and marched off to Princeton en route to Philadelphia to demand redress of their grievances from Congress. The upheaval was marked by the killing of two or three men. Other Continentals sympathized with the mutineers, and Washington conceded that the Pennsylvanians had good excuse for their behavior. Delighted by the news, Clinton sent emissaries to them to offer them full pardon and the pay they had not received. In return, they were asked only to march to New York. He gathered troops on Staten Island, with the intention of pushing forward into New Jersey to take advantage of the mutiny. But he again encountered disappointment. The Pennsylvanians listened to one envoy, then put him and his guide in the hands of Patriot officers, who hanged both men. The mutineers were not of the fiber of Benedict Arnold. They were promised redress, and returned to duty. Then New

Jersey Continentals mutinied, but they were surrounded by loyal New Englanders and reduced to obedience. Restlessness continued in the Patriot army. Disaffected men among the Continentals were discharged. Later, "Mad Anthony" Wayne executed a few Pennsylvanians who refused to obey orders. The crisis in the American army gradually passed, without benefit to the British.

Unable to subdue Washington by a powerful stroke, Clinton did seriously injure the Patriots by many small ones. To the continuing blockade of American ports and captures of American shipping by the British navy, he added raids against Patriot seaboard settlements. He was not a brute, and he was not fond of such warfare, directed more against civilians than against his armed enemies. But his masters in London expected, indeed ordered him to harry the coastal villages and towns held by the Americans, and he executed their will. In 1778 General Charles Grey raided New Bedford; General William Tryon soon afterward struck at New Haven; and, later, as a British officer, Benedict Arnold ravaged New London. A series of devastating incursions into those parts of Virginia adjacent to Chesapeake Bay began in the spring of 1779. Those forays, in which vengeful Loyalists joined British troops and tars, were hit-and-sail away attacks against which the Patriots could not properly prepare. The marauders, surprising the victims, overcame local resistance; seized whatever property they could carry off; burnt warehouses, vessels, and homes; and fled to their transports and safety when the Patriots gathered in force to oppose them. The raids, informing the American residents near salt water that neither they nor their possessions were safe, hurt the Patriots. Could they—and those who were not subjected to that cruel warfare—indefinitely endure the onslaughts of the British? The Americans did not yield; they found new cause to hate their enemies; they suffered increasingly from the distresses and strains of the struggle; but they fought on and on.

CHAPTER XXV

British Triumphs in the South

THE War of Independence began in New England, but the scene of vital struggle shifted westward and southward into New York, New Jersey, and Pennsylvania, then at length into the South. That region was long little molested by the British. For, if the Patriots north of the Potomac were subdued, those who resided in Virginia, the Carolinas, and Georgia must soon succumb to the onslaughts of the royal forces. Hence the acceptance by the British of defeat at Sullivan's Island and the retreat of the contingents of Lord Dunmore from Chesapeake Bay in 1776. The Southern Patriots had to fight the Cherokee after the early summer of that year, but otherwise were not required to defend their homes again until 1779. They struck hard against the Cherokee; they held the weak British garrison at St. Augustine in check; and they sent thousands of soldiers to the assistance of their Northern brethren. But then English failures on the Hudson and the Delaware persuaded the British to look elsewhere. Might it not be that warlike Loyalists, not too often found in New York and Pennsylvania and seldom in New England, were numerous in the Carolinas and Georgia? Before he returned to England, Sir William Howe, enlightened by experience, warned Lord George Germain that Britain must not rely upon securing powerful assistance from the Tories anywhere in America. A few would rise and take up arms when the presence of British troops permitted them to act. The rest would remain quiet. Nowhere, declared Howe, were the Loyalists so numerous and so devoted that they could hold a district conquered by the redcoats and Hessians. Nevertheless, Germain, preferring hope to information, continued to express belief that Tories would rally to the royal standard in regions where they had not yet had an opportunity to do so; and Clinton hoped against hope that they would join the royal colors in large numbers in the far South. After the capture of Savannah at the close of 1778, the British gradually increased their efforts in the South, and they won a series of smashing victories. In the late summer of 1780, indeed, British authority seemed to be again firmly established in South Carolina as well as Georgia.

Actually, there were, proportionately, more pugnacious Tories in the Carolinas and Georgia than in most parts of America. The Highlanders of North Carolina who rallied to the cause of the King in 1776 were not the only Scots in the South; and North Britons, whether of Highland or Lowland origin, were very generally loyal to the Crown. Not a few of the Scotch-Irish whose settlements stretched along the Piedmont from Virginia to Georgia were Tories, together with some settlers of German descent. Adherents of Britain were to be found almost everywhere south of Virginia; here and there they dominated communities in the interior. They were often willing to take up arms, but they formed only a minority. The majority of the numerous Scotch-Irish, in part because they remembered the ill treatment they and their forebears had received from Britain in Ulster, in part because they were Presbyterians, were ardent Patriots. Men of English and French Protestant descent also usually fought against the King. However, the Patriots were not numerous in South Carolina and Georgia, where the white population was thin. The two states were therefore peculiarly vulnerable to attack by the British. The Patriots of North Carolina and Virginia, as the British would discover, were far more formidable.

The reconquest of Georgia by Archibald Campbell and Augustine Prevost seemed complete at the end of January 1779. Indeed, the Patriot government of that state vanished, not to reappear until the end of the war. Georgia Tories in hundreds took up arms. Governor Sir James Wright was even able to call a Loyalist assembly into session at Savannah in 1780. But the capture of that town and of Augusta marked, not the end of the war in Georgia, but the end of the first phase of a long and arduous struggle that constantly spread northward. It was also a cruel contest, for the Patriots of Georgia, dispersed by superior force, fought on as best they could in small bands of partisans against their Tory neighbors. Some contingents of South Carolina militia followed their example. The partisans and armed Tories committed atrocities against each other. Ominously for the British, the partisans soon won a small but signal victory. About 700 North Carolina Loyalists marched to Georgia to join Lieutenant Colonel Archibald Campbell at Augusta. They plundered Patriots as they moved southward. They were intercepted at Kettle Creek by

South Carolina and Georgia militia led by Colonel Andrew Pickens, a redoubtable leader. They were defeated and driven back; less than half of them eventually reached Augusta. Of seventy captured by the Patriots, five, considered to be leaders of the Tories, were hanged at Charleston. They had committed no remarkable crime except that of taking up arms for the King. They would be avenged by the Tories, and reprisals would be inflicted upon the avengers, and so on, until long after the end of the war.

In the meantime, General Benjamin Lincoln replaced General Robert Howe, who had not performed superbly. Put in command of the Continental forces in the South, Lincoln was not a Southerner, but a Massachusetts man who had displayed zeal and a measure of ability in the Saratoga campaign. Lincoln remains a minor name immortal in medicine. Every now and then he fell asleep in broad daylight—he was afflicted by an uncommon syndrome to which his name has been attached by the physicians. It is not recorded that one of his involuntary naps led to a Patriot defeat. However, he was not a military genius, and he was not favored by fortune.

Lincoln hurried to South Carolina. Virginia and North Carolina sent militia to assist him, and he was able to collect 6,000 men, including 1,000 Continentals, for an advance across the Savannah River. He crossed it midway between Savannah and Augusta, but encountered defeat at Briar Creek and was forced to retreat. He moved forward a second time, against Augusta, but was again compelled to retrace his steps. For, as Lincoln moved westward, General Prevost boldly led 3,000 men northward against Charleston. He arrived outside that city on May 12, 1779, and demanded its immediate surrender. There were as many Patriot soldiers of one sort and another within the city as Prevost commanded, but it was doubtful that they could withstand the British troops. The civil authorities of Charleston temporized—Lincoln was surely coming to the rescue. They proposed that the city be declared neutral, possession of it to be determined eventually by the course of military events elsewhere. It was saved for the time being to the Patriots by the approach of Lincoln. Prevost, confronted by gathering and superior American forces, prudently withdrew. He carried off with him hundreds of Negro slaves, to the great distress of their owners. Leaving a garrison at Port Royal, he fell back to Savannah. There he remained quiet during many weeks of enervating summer heat.

Then it was the turn of the Americans to march against Prevost. Lincoln, Governor John Rutledge, and other Patriots had been greatly alarmed by the advance of the British general to Charleston. They wrote to Admiral d'Estaing, who had been busy in the West Indies for several months, begging him to come to their assistance. Washington wanted the French fleet to return to New York. However, d'Estaing, perhaps because he remembered only too well the discomfiture he had encountered at that place in the preceding year, sailed for the North American mainland, but to Savannah rather than New York. The French admiral brought with him 4,000 troops. He commanded a fleet that was even larger than that which he had in 1778 when he reached the mouth of the Savannah River early in September. He could not take his ships-of-the-line into the river because they drew too much water. They cast anchor. Four days later he sent smaller vessels into the river, and landed 3,500 soldiers. A few British warships fled upstream; others were sunk in the river to obstruct its passageway. On September 15 d'Estaing was joined by a special corps of Continentals, Count Casimir Pulaski's Legion. The following day d'Estaing sent a message to General Prevost demanding the surrender of the town. Prevost had fortified it, and he had perhaps 2,400 men within his lines. But many of them were Loyalists. About 800 of his best men were still at Port Royal under Lieutenant Colonel John Maitland. Lincoln was about to join d'Estaing with 1,350 Patriots. Prevost asked and obtained twenty-four hours in which to consider the French admiral's demand. He used that time to strengthen the defenses of the town and to mount more artillery. Maitland rapidly made his way from Port Royal through swamps and across tidal waters along the South Carolina coast into Savannah, adding strength and determination to Prevost's forces. Prevost defied d'Estaing and Lincoln to do their worst.

So strong were the lines established at Savannah by Prevost that the French and American besiegers decided that they must bring up guns from d'Estaing's fleet and make gradual approaches toward the British entrenchments. On October 4 they began to bombard the town from land batteries and French ships in the Savannah River. They moved closer to the British works. The artillery fire of the allies injured buildings in the town, but did not daunt its garrison. Prevost made two sorties but carefully refrained from making a major counterattack that might be costly. He conserved his forces so as to be able to ward off a massive attempt by his enemies to break through his defenses. It soon came. The French admiral would not even defer a general assault until after the outer works of the British had been captured. He had begun the siege in the belief that it would require no more than ten days. He was concerned lest his ships suffer from storm, and he was eager to put back to sea. It was possible that a British fleet would appear from the West Indies. D'Estaing and Lincoln laid plans for a general assault in five columns before dawn on

October 9. Their main attack was to be made against the Spring Hill redoubt, the key to the defenses of Savannah. There was delay, and daylight came before the allies moved forward. The royal forces were ready—it is reported, indeed, that an American deserter had informed the British of the plan of attack. Lieutenant Colonel Maitland occupied the Spring Hill redoubt with a body of British veterans. Three of the advancing columns were soon driven back; Count Pulaski, leading one of them, was mortally wounded. But a fourth and strong column, with help from another, swept on under murderous musket and cannon fire against the redoubt. The French and Americans almost carried it. South Carolina troops even penetrated it. However, Maitland's men drove them back with bullets and bayonets and forced them to retreat. Having displayed the utmost bravery, the allies were compelled to admit defeat. Their casualties numbered about 800; one of every five men who participated in the assault was killed or wounded. The British losses were perhaps 150.

Lincoln wished to continue the siege, but d'Estaing declined to pursue it further. He said that his fleet was too exposed to weather to remain longer on the Georgia coast. He put his troops aboard, and returned to the West Indies. Lincoln had no choice but to raise the siege. He marched off to Charleston. D'Estaing, as befitted a former soldier, had demonstrated great personal courage in the battle. However, he had combined three times with the Patriots, at New York, at Newport, and at Savannah; and the allies had been three times checked or defeated. The outcome of the siege of Savannah was most discouraging for the Americans. Were they to receive no direct and effective help from the French navy and army?

The British were correspondingly elated, and Sir Henry Clinton was persuaded to strike harder in the South. He was well aware that the French navy remained a threat. However, it had thus far failed to achieve much in North American waters. He could reasonably hope that the British admiralty would perform better in the future than it had in the past—that it would not permit the French to gain and keep naval superiority anywhere on the coast of North America. In any case, if he firmly established British sway over South Carolina and Georgia, the troops in that wide area would be able to defend themselves in the event that the French achieved temporary ascendancy upon the adjacent waters, until the British navy could come to their aid. In the absence of the French, it would not be difficult to send reinforcements and supplies by sea, save for the vagaries of the winds. To be sure, the Patriots of the North would send help to those of the South, by land. But it was possible to interrupt the passage of men, munitions, and food southward by sending British detachments into Delaware and Chesapeake Bays to raid and to cut Patriot communications.

So it was that Clinton set sail southward from New York in the last days of 1779 with about 8,000 troops, infantry and cavalry, together with heavy artillery, horses, and vast quantities of military gear in a fleet of transports guarded by Admiral Arbuthnot and a naval squadron. The voyage was neither short nor happy. High and hostile winds drove the British ships to the eastward. A transport carrying Clinton's artillery sank. All of his horses either died or were lost at sea. Patriot privateers captured some small vessels loaded with equipment for the cavalry, and one transport carrying Hessian troops reached harbor in England. The main body of the British armada did not put down anchor until the close of January, at the mouth of the Savannah River. Other ships gradually came into port. Sending to the Bahamas and elsewhere for artillery and powder to replace his losses in those essentials, Clinton moved slowly northward—en route he learned that his resignation had not been accepted, to the displeasure of Lord Cornwallis, who accompanied him and who had expected to succeed him. He occupied Seabrook Island south of Charleston on February 14. When it became evident that the Patriots would try to hold Charleston, he sent to New York for more men. Lord Rawdon accordingly joined him in mid-April with 2,500 soldiers, so that Clinton's army increased to 10,000 men. Meanwhile, the British general gradually approached Charleston. He cut off avenues of escape south of the city. On March 29, he sent picked troops in flatboats across the Ashley River. They occupied the peninsula between that stream and the Cooper River upon which Charleston was located, thus closing off exit to the westward. There was an American flotilla in Charleston Bay, but it was far too weak to challenge Admiral Arbuthnot's fleet. The Patriots sank most of their war vessels, together with merchant craft, at the mouth of the Cooper River and built a boom there. They hoped to prevent the British from entering it, and so to preserve a route by which, if necessary, they could flee northward. They could not defend the harbor. Eight British frigates sailed past the fort on Sullivan's Island, exchanged a few shots with its batteries, and anchored in sight of the docks of Charleston. The city was thus hemmed in upon three sides by the British forces.

The progression of the royal army and navy toward Charleston was not rapid, and the Patriots had time in which to gather strength and to decide what to do to meet the British threat. John Rutledge, governor of South Carolina, hastily sent a message to Havana to solicit the help of a Spanish fleet and Spanish troops, in vain. More to the point, he called the militia of the state into service; but the response was not enthusiastic. An epidemic of smallpox in Charleston in 1779 served many Carolinians as a reason for not entering the city; they wished to avoid that dreaded disease. However, about 2,500 militia gathered in Charleston, and 1,450 Continentals from North Carolina and Virginia rapidly marched southward to assist in meeting the British menace. As a result, General Lincoln commanded more than 5,500 men within the city as the British army closed in upon it. That he could hold it against attack by forces so superior to his own was certainly doubtful. He would have been wise to abandon the city quickly and to save his troops so that they might fight later under more favorable circumstances. However, conceiving that in the event of necessity he could retreat northward across the Cooper River, he decided instead to make at least a stand. There were about 500 Patriot troops, chiefly horsemen, at Monck's Corner, thirty miles above Charleston, under General Isaac Huger. They could protect the avenue by which he would fall back, if necessary.

On April 10 Clinton and Arbuthnot demanded the surrender of the city. Lincoln, of course, refused to yield it. But he soon became concerned for the safety both of Charleston and of his army. The Patriots had erected defenses between the Ashley and Cooper Rivers to hold off Clinton's army. However, it became apparent on April 13 that the city must fall, at least eventually. That day British land batteries and Arbuthnot's ships bombarded it, driving civilians and Patriot troops alike to shelter. The British shell and shot damaged and set fire to many buildings. Lincoln became alarmed, called a council of war. What should he do? At least one of his officers, General Lachlan McIntosh of Georgia, urged that the Patriot troops, or at any rate the Continentals, immediately evacuate the city, before they were surrounded. Civilians of Charleston desired that the soldiers remain to protect them. Lincoln hesitated.

The decision was made for Lincoln by the British Lieutenant Colonel Banastre Tarleton, who achieved sudden fame by closing the Patriot passageway to the north and to safety. Coming to America as a young cavalry cornet, Tarleton had displayed ability and had been permitted to raise a British Legion of Tory volunteers, a contingent that traveled on horseback and fought as either cavalry or infantry. He was a harsh, brutal, and vain man; he was also clever and audacious. The British Legion lost its horses on the long voyage from New York, but Tarleton, with characteristic enterprise, scrounged about and secured replacements. Supported by Major Patrick Ferguson and a corps of Loyalist riflemen, Tarleton suddenly attacked the Patriot cavalry under General Huger that protected Lincoln's escape route. Before dawn on April 14 the British

414

Legion burst into Huger's camp. Resorting to the bayonet, Tarleton's infantry dispersed the surprised Patriots, capturing more than sixty of them. The next day Lieutenant Colonel James Webster joined him with two regiments of British regulars. Tarleton and Webster placed their troops so as to bar retreat by Lincoln. Clinton sent more men to support them. Only a miracle, or a great stroke of fortune, could save Lincoln's army.

Neither the Divine nor chance intervened. Clinton's troops moved closer to the Patriot entrenchments covering the approaches to the city on the west. On April 19 and 20 Lincoln again held councils of war. He and his officers desired to offer a bargain to the British, by which the Patriots would turn over the city to them in exchange for unmolested withdrawal of the besieged forces. But civilians of Charleston, led by Christopher Gadsden, insisted that it could be defended, that it must not be surrendered without a struggle. On April 21, disregarding the pleas of the citizens, Lincoln proposed the bargain to Clinton and Arbuthnot. The British commanders were sure of their prey, and refused to let the American soldiers depart. Lincoln ordered a sortie against the British lines; it was successful, but it changed nothing. Marines and sailors from Arbuthnot's fleet landed on Sullivan's Island and captured its unresisting garrison. By May 8 the British were ready to begin a massive assault. Lincoln was now ready to surrender, provided that his Continentals were allowed to parade with the honors of war, that the militia with him were allowed to go free. Clinton and Arbuthnot would not accept those terms. In the evening of May 9 the besieged and the besiegers began an artillery duel that continued throughout the night. Amidst the din, fires broke out in several parts of the city. Its embattled civilians decided that they did not wish to continue to resist the British, and Lincoln surrendered on May 12. He and his Continentals became prisoners; the militia were also made prisoners, but were allowed to go to their homes upon parole—they could take no further part in the war unless they were released from their pledges.

The capture of Charleston was a very heavy blow for the Patriots and a great and inexpensive victory for the British. There had been little fighting. Not more than 100 men were killed on either side. However, 5,500 Americans fell into British hands, together with their muskets, artillery, gunpowder (376 barrels of it), ships, and all their military and naval gear. The fall of the city was the more disastrous for the Patriots in that many of their most ardent leaders in South Carolina became captives. No single event of the war cost the Americans more than their futile defense of Charleston. Clinton was jubilant.

So impressive was the easy capture of the city that all of South Carolina soon came under British control. On May 29 Banastre Tarleton gave notice to the Patriots that the strong arm of the King would extend far inland. A body of 350 Virginia Continentals had approached Charleston too late and in far too small strength to assist its defenders. Tarleton set out after them, pursued them almost to the boundary of North Carolina, attacked, and routed them. His men gave "Tarleton's quarter," continuing to kill helpless Americans after they had put down their arms and had hoisted a white flag. Other British detachments occupied posts stretching across and dominating the interior of South Carolina. Her Tories took up arms. With those who had come from New York with Clinton, they greatly strengthened the royal forces. In Charleston 200 men congratulated Clinton upon his conquest of the city. It seemed that British rule was permanently restored in the two southernmost American states.

Many of the Patriots of South Carolina fell into despair. Clinton offered protection to the persons and property of all those who would take a special oath of allegiance to George III. The alternative was threatened expropriation of plantations and Negro slaves, and even imprisonment of their owners. Dozens of Low Country folk, including members of the South Carolina aristocracy, among them Henry Middleton, once a president of the Continental Congress and Rawlins Lowndes, once a speaker of the colonial legislature of South Carolina, yielded to seeming necessity, forswore their allegiance to the Patriot cause, and solemnly pledged loyalty to the British Crown. Nor were the Patriots among the plain farmers of the South Carolina Upcountry all disposed to fight endlessly. Even Andrew Pickens, as brave an officer as might be, made his peace with Britain in a special personal bargain. So well entrenched were the British and their Loyalist allies that it seemed appropriate to ask William Bull, a respected South Carolina Tory who had served several times as governor, to return from England and to take office once more.

Soon after the capture of Charleston Clinton was forced to depart for New York. He consigned command of the royal forces in South Carolina and Georgia to Lord Cornwallis. Before leaving Charleston, he declared that "if a French or Spanish fleet does not interfere I think a few works if properly reinforced, will give us all between this and Hudson's River." He said, "I leave Lord Cornwallis here in sufficient force to keep it against the world, without a superior fleet shews itself, in which case I despair of ever seeing peace restored to this miserable country." The fleet would come, but not for many long months, and not to Charleston.

In entrusting Lord Cornwallis with the duty of reaping and preserving the fruits of the capture of Charleston, Clinton prudently warned that general against undertaking expensive and hazardous adventures. Above all, Cornwallis was to make sure that Clinton's conquests were not lost. His tasks were therefore primarily defensive. However, if those tasks proved to be easy and if it appeared that Cornwallis could expand British sway northward at no great cost or risk, then he was permitted to take the offensive. In view of the fact that Cornwallis would command in a theater distant from New York, he was also authorized by Clinton to correspond directly with Lord George Germain, so that the British colonial secretary might receive information about events in the South as rapidly as possible. Clinton gave the right instructions to the wrong man. It is true that he could hardly have offered the Southern command to any other British general. Cornwallis deserved it upon the basis of seniority. However, he was not upon terms of friendship with Clinton; he had expected to succeed Clinton, but had been disappointed. He still held a dormant commission as commander in chief that would become effective only when Clinton vacated his post. He was not fitted temperamentally for defensive duty; he was aggressive by nature. He was a younger version of Sir William Howe, but possessed far more energy than that general. A favorite of Howe, he did not remarkably surpass that officer in intellect. He was a general among soldiers, but only a soldier among generals. His status and the permission granted to him to correspond with Germain encouraged him to think and act without excessive concern lest he violate his orders from Clinton. A seed of disaster for Britain had been sown.

Cornwallis soon learned that there were glowing embers of rebellion in South Carolina; he—with Tarleton and embittered Loyalists—fanned them into flame. Unfortunately for the British, Governor John Rutledge was not in Charleston when it was taken. The legislature of the state could not and did not meet for more than two years. But Rutledge refused to bend the knee to Britain, kept out of the reach of royal forces, and called upon his militia officers to rally their men and to oppose the triumphant invaders. Several of them promptly responded, among them Thomas Sumter, Francis Marion, and Andrew Pickens. With Colonel Elijah Clark of Georgia and other leaders they collected small bands of devoted Patriots and began to assail and bedevil detachments of redcoats and Loyalists. When they were confronted by superior numbers they fled to safe hiding places in marshes and forests. Marion achieved fame as the "Swamp Fox." Pickens ultimately was the most valuable of Rutledge's officers, for he learned how to lead men in formal battle as well as forays. However, all of the partisans contributed to the revival of the Patriot cause. Their exploits harassed the British and vexed the local Tories. Their numbers and their zeal increased because Cornwallis attempted, not to placate, but to repress. He declared that all militia men who had taken the special oath of allegiance could be called into service against their fellow citizens. Moreover, he dealt harshly with Patriot leaders captured in Charleston who refused to subscribe to that pledge. He sent many of them, including Christopher Gadsden, into close and unhealthy confinement in St. Augustine. The South Carolinians must choose between King and Congress; if they failed to support the empire, they must suffer. Cornwallis drove many Patriots to greater exertions and sacrifices.

If many of the partisans were goaded into resuming the conflict, they were also encouraged to act by Washington and Congress. They were not deserted in the hour of their extremity. The Virginia and North Carolina Continentals captured at Charleston were followed southward by Maryland and Delaware Continentals, about 1,400 of the best troops in the American army. Led by the Baron de Kalb, they left New Jersey in April and arrived in North Carolina in June. There was much talk in Philadelphia and elsewhere at the beginning of the summer of 1780 about the disastrous loss of Charleston. A rumor spread that Congress was disposed to make peace with Britain, abandoning Georgia and South Carolina to the Crown. Congress scotched the rumor. It resolved unanimously on June 23, "That this Confederacy is most sacredly pledged to support the liberty and independence of every one of its members," and that all the Patriots would "unremittingly persevere in their exertions" toward "the recovery and preservation of any and every part of these United States that has been or may hereafter be invaded or possessed by the common enemy." Congress also sent southward, to replace the captured Lincoln, a general of great reputation, the victor of Saratoga, Horatio Gates. Had Washington had his way, its choice would have fallen upon General Nathanael Greene. However, that officer had not yet demonstrated ability to lead an army. Besides, as quartermaster general, receiving 1 per cent of the cost of all purchases for Washington's troops, Greene had made a profit for himself and was suspected, though without good reason, of being as much devoted to getting money as he was to the American cause. It was well known in Congress that Washington was jealous of the fame that Gates had gained by defeating John Burgoyne. Could not Gates perform in the South as he had in northern New York?

Horatio Gates accepted the command of the Continentals in the South, and rode to North Carolina. From his forced retirement General Charles Lee, aware, like Washington, that Gates was not a great commander, warned him that he was in danger of exchanging his Northern laurels for Southern willows. On July 25 he joined de Kalb at Deep River in North Carolina and assumed his new duties.

The situation faced by Gates was utterly unlike that in which he had won glory on the Hudson three years earlier. Then he had only to check the onward march of Burgoyne; then he possessed all the advantages of terrain; then his men, thanks to the efforts of Philip Schuyler, were fed and equipped for battle. At Deep River he discovered that the Maryland and Delaware Continentals, who would form the nucleus of his army, were in great distress. They—and the remains of Count Pulaski's contingent, which had effected a junction with de Kalb—had not eaten well for weeks. They had been reduced to the consumption of fruit and fresh corn, and were suffering from dysentery. North Carolina and Virginia militia were more or less ready to take the field. The Continentals were posted in a region that had produced Tories rather than beef or wheat. Only by an immense effort could food have been brought forward rapidly from Virginia, and there was no Schuyler to make it. Gates hoped that wagons loaded with provender would come to him. He was disappointed. He could hardly remain long where he was. He might have led his troops westward to Charlotte, a Patriot stronghold where at least some cattle and grain could be secured, thus deferring action until the Continentals and militia were fitted for it. But when could they be made ready? Was he not expected to go to the rescue of the South Carolinians and Georgians? He had been condemned because he had not attacked Burgoyne. He chose to be bold, to march southward against the British. If supplies did not reach his men from Virginia, they must live off the country. It was a decision worthy of a Napoleon, but Gates did not possess the genius of Napoleon. He moved forward on July 27. His immediate objective was the capture of a British post at Camden, South Carolina. There his troops could fatten upon a richer area—and British stores of food and rum.

As the Continentals made their way through almost barren territory toward Camden, they continued to suffer in the heat of a Southern summer. They managed to find a few cows; they were not relieved of dysentery. They grumbled, and their officers were also disgruntled. Why had Gates insisted upon marching through such a miserable country? But the general drove his men on. He was joined by 800 Virginia and 1,200 North Carolina militia who were in little better physical condition than the Continentals. At last, on August 13, the Patriot army camped only thirteen miles from Camden. Lord Cornwallis arrived in Camden that same day, after a forced march, with a body of British veterans. Lord Rawdon, the British commander at Camden, had learned of the approach of the Patriots, and had asked for help; and Cornwallis had responded with his customary energy. Gates was not aware of the presence of the royal general. Having learned that a British supply train was en route to the fort, he sent out Thomas Sumter with 100 Continentals and some militia to seize the convoy. The Americans needed those supplies.

Gates himself badly needed those reliable Continentals, but he did not know that he needed them. Still ignorant that Cornwallis was in Camden, he began a forced march toward it at ten o'clock on the night of August 15. He did not reach the British post. Cornwallis was not fond of being on the defensive. At the same hour he set out from the fort with 2,200 men to find and attack Gates. The two armies met, to the surprise of all concerned, in the early hours of August 16 at Saunder's Creek. They exchanged a few shots, then waited for daylight. In the meantime, Gates called a council of war. What should he do? He was advised to fight rather than attempt a hasty retreat. He commanded more than 3,000 men, about one third of them Continentals. He also had an advantage in position, for the two armies faced each other in a thin forest, with swamps on both sides of it and Saunder's Creek in the rear of the British. A defeat might have been disastrous for Cornwallis. The Patriots could depart, if necessary, without undue geographical difficulty.

Cornwallis was not concerned lest his retreat be interrupted. He intended to drive the Patriots before him. Nor did Gates display reluctance to engage. Placing his Continentals on his right flank, the American general ordered Virginia militia forming his left wing to attack. Meanwhile, Cornwallis sent troops forward to assail the Continentals. However, the militia moved forward in bad order, and he observed that they were vulnerable to counterattack. He concentrated against them, and they fled after brief resistance. In their flight they carried with them from the field many of the North Carolina militia, and Gates as well. De Kalb and the Continentals, with the remainder of the North Carolinians, were then exposed to assault from their left. Cornwallis struck hard at their naked flank as well as their front. They stood their ground for some time, inflicting heavy casualties. De Kalb enspirited them, but he fell, mortally wounded. At length, overwhelmed by swarming royal troops, the North Carolinians and Continentals broke and retreated. The Patriot army was routed. Pursued by Tarleton, the Americans fled northward in scattered contingents. They had met a crushing reverse. They had lost 600 men, the British perhaps half as many. Moreover, their defeat at Camden was compounded by another loss. Two days later Tarleton assailed and beat the detachment commanded by Sumter. And Gates added to the woes of the Patriots. He was brave enough. Nevertheless, borne back by the militia seeking safety in flight, he did not attempt to make a stand to cover the retreat of his army. Was he concerned lest he, the son of a servant, be captured and become the butt of British humor? He rode away on a fast horse to Charlotte. He arrived there, sixty miles from Camden, by nightfall on August 17, and went on to Hillsborough, North Carolina. There, ten days after the struggle at Camden, he was able to inspect the remains of his army, about 700 men.

The bold thrust attempted by Gates had failed miserably. He did not shake the grip of the British upon South Carolina. His own reputation was tarnished, and the morale of the Patriots also suffered. North Carolina was exposed to attack, and Cornwallis became a British hero. Moreover, the battle of Camden affected more than the reputations of commanders, more than the military status in the South. With the splendid British defense of Savannah and the capture of Charleston, Camden exerted influence in England.

It will be recalled that George III had successfully insisted, after the entrance of Spain into the war, that Britain should unremittingly struggle against all her enemies. But in the fall of 1779 the Marquis of Rockingham, the Earl of Shelburne, and Charles James Fox opened their annual campaign in Parliament against the North ministry and against the King. The war news, not so bad as it might have been, was not good. Ireland was restless. Her Roman Catholics were weighed down by many injustices; even her Protestants suffered from economic discriminations imposed by Parliament in favor of residents of England. Country gentlemen in Yorkshire—led by Christopher Wyvill, a devoted reformer, and Sir George Savile, a much respected politician—established an Association. It was to strive to destroy pensions and sinecures, to reduce the power of the monarch, and to reform the House of Commons. The price of wheat was very low, and taxes were high; plain farmers joined the Association in large numbers. It quickly spread to no fewer than twenty-eight counties, and it bombarded Parliament with petitions for change. If the country gentlemen in Parliament turned against the North ministry, it could hardly endure. In April 1780, the House of Commons passed by a vote of 233 to 215 a resolution introduced by John Dunning which declared "that the influence of the crown has increased, is increasing, and ought to be diminished." That forthright denunciation of George III was followed by the passage of another resolution which asserted that it was the duty of the Commons to remove abuses. But did gentlemen really desire the destruction of privilege, honesty in government, and a truly representative system? Was there not danger of going too far? Lord North successfully played for time; second thoughts persuaded many gentlemen that Association and reform smacked of America and revolution; they drew back. George III and his allies weathered the storm.

The King regained strength in June 1780 in consequence of his firmness in quelling the Gordon Riots in London. There was upheaval in the imperial capital, not because the monarch was an arbitrary ruler, but because Parliament removed certain restrictions that had been placed upon Roman Catholics. Lord George Gordon, a Protestant fanatic, raised a cry of "No Popery!" Mobs swept through the streets of London to protest against favor to the adherents of the papacy. They opened prison doors and let out scores of convicts. The rioters pillaged and burned, and city authorities could not restore tranquillity. At last the King personally assumed responsibility for the safety of the city. He ordered General Amherst to make unrestricted use of troops to subdue the rioters. The general did his duty. More than 400 persons were killed before calm resumed in London; but it did return. George III was not a Louis XVI. He gained credit for preventing anarchy. For what did his enemies stand?

Then, in the summer of 1780, came word to England of the capture of Charleston and the reconquest of South Carolina. George III and Lord North became almost popular. Was not Patriot resistance crumbling at last? At the beginning of September the monarch formally called for the election of a new House of Commons. He would have been forced to do so not later than 1781 by the Septennial Act, and he wished to take advantage of the change in British sentiment. In the ensuing election the King spent £100,000 in behalf of friendly candidates. He and his allies were victorious. They lost a few seats in the Commons, but retained an easy majority there.

The news of Camden arrived. It tended to confirm belief that the war was going well in North America, but also to exalt Lord Cornwallis at the expense of Sir Henry Clinton. Had not Britain at last found in the enterprising Cornwallis the man who could and would put an end to the American rebellion? He had disposed of the upstart Gates. Was he not the commander who could crush Washington?

CHAPTER XXVI

The Western Front

LITTLE has thus far been said in these pages about a most important phase of the War of Independence in America, the struggle of the Patriots with Britain's Indian allies. Nevertheless, it richly deserves narration, and not merely because blows delivered by the warriors, added to those struck by the British and the Loyalists, sorely tried the Patriots. Forced to fight upon a long Western front, they did indeed suffer immensely from the onslaughts of the Iroquois, the Shawnee, the Cherokee, the Creek, and other tribesmen. The frontiersmen, in small buckskinned bands, were compelled to struggle desperately to hold back onrushing Indians encouraged and supported by British money and British and Tory contingents. The assaults of the Indians from the west weakened Patriot defense against British and Tory attacks from the north, the east, and the south. Even Washington, sufficiently burdened with the task of keeping the field against the royal troops, was forced to think about the Indian menace and to send help to meet it. Whether or not America became independent, to a degree depended upon the outcome of hundreds of clashes between red men and white on the slopes of the Appalachians and on the lowlands adjacent to the Mississippi River. Moreover, the achievement of freedom would bring little ultimate benefit to the Americans and their descendants if they were driven back from the Mississippi Valley, if they should be confined to the regions between the mountains and the Atlantic. Possession of Trans-Appalachia, of lands as wide as, and even richer than, those upon the eastern side of the great ridge, was also at stake. If the American republic was to have a great and bright future, it must win those vast territories.

The Patriots were at last victorious on that Western front. At the beginning of the War of Independence they thinly occupied lands near the south bank of the Ohio River and river valleys in eastern Tennessee; otherwise, they had not established themselves in large numbers beyond the Appalachian divide; the immense stretches of woodlands and meadows between the Great Lakes on the north and the Gulf of Mexico on the south, between the Appalachians on the east and the Mississippi on the west, were still in very large part inhabited only by the red men. The flag of England flew over a few forts upon the fringes of that West. Upon European maps it was designated as British soil; the Indians primitively believed that it, or nearly all of it, was their own. Had it not always been thus? At the end of the war, the Spanish were again owners of St. Augustine and East Florida, together with Pensacola and Mobile. The British remained only in Canada—and in a few forts south of the St. Lawrence River and the Great Lakes which belonged to the United States, but which the redcoats had not yet evacuated. The Indians still resided within the interior of that West. But the Americans were firmly rooted in Kentucky and Tennessee. Their settlements had reached the Mississippi; their flag flew over the eastern bank of the great river. They would thrust forward toward the Rocky Mountains within twenty years, to the Pacific Ocean upon a wide front within another half century.

But if the future was so bright for the Americans, the outlook for those who dwelled in the backwoods, who were exposed to Indian attacks, was dark in 1775 and long remained somber. They could not hope that all, or even most, of the Indians would remain quiet. Border warfare with all its barbarities could hardly be avoided, if for no other reason because the lust of the Patriots for the lands of the aborigines did not vanish with the outbreak of the rebellion against Britain. The Indians, valuing the efforts of Britain, feeble as those efforts were, to protect their villages and hunting grounds, could not do otherwise than look upon George III as their distant but great and powerful friend; they correctly saw the Patriots to be their mortal enemies. Had Britain done nothing to stimulate them to take up arms, had her representatives merely ceased to try to preserve peace on the frontier, many Indians would nevertheless have gone to war—some actually did so without being incited. As it was, agents of Britain stirred up the warriors. The result was struggle far more bitter than any waged on the Atlantic seaboard. British troops in theaters of war east of the Appalachians seldom slew defeated Patriots who had put down their weapons, did not usually molest women or children. Loyalist contingents that served in those arenas, vengeful as those soldiers might be, did not habitually kill prisoners or inoffensive civilians. But the Indians followed their own rules of war, which sanctioned indiscriminate killing, the burning of cabins, and cruel torture of prisoners. The Patriots responded in kind. They might spare squaws and their children; they would not burn captives at the stake; but they put the torch to the homes of the red men, and they commonly gave no quarter to the warriors. The resolute Indian braves neither asked nor expected mercy.

Let it be remembered in behalf of the government of George III that it was not entirely responsible for the bloody contests that stained the American frontier. Let it be recalled that the French, the Spanish, the British, and their colonists had earlier incited Indians to attack whites, that they had bought scalps from their savage allies without inquiring whether a scalp came from a man killed in battle, from an unarmed settler, or from his wife or his innocent child. Nor should it be forgotten that the Patriots were the first to employ Indians, Stockbridge tribesmen of Massachusetts who served in the forces investing Boston—but who were neither numerous, savage, nor uncontrolled. Let it be added in defense of George III and his ministers that they felt forced to seek allies where they could find them. Let it be remembered that, when Lord George Germain ordered the seeking of help from the Indians, he stipulated that they be used in conjunction with royal troops and under the direction of royal officers—a safeguard against Indian brutalities that was largely useless. Britain did arm the red men and did successfully urge them to take the warpath against men, women, and children she claimed to be her own. The indictment against the King and his advisers in the Declaration of Independence, that they had "endeavoured to bring on the inhabitants of our frontiers the merciless Indian savages, whose known rule of warfare is an undistinguished destruction of all ages, sexes, and conditions," properly applied only to Lord Dunmore. The ugly charge anticipated the frightful fact. Unfortunately for the Patriots, British appeals for Indian help were only too successful.

To be sure, the British devils received even more than their due. A few days before the Declaration of Independence, the Cherokee warriors seized their muskets and tomahawks and assailed pioneer stockades and homes on the frontiers of the Carolinas and Georgia. Their onslaughts began soon after the repulse of the British at Sullivan's Island, before General Henry Clinton and Sir Peter Parker acknowledged defeat and departed. It was accidental that the Cherokee began hostilities almost simultaneously with the attack upon Sullivan's Island. But some Patriots would not believe that the long arm of coincidence had exerted itself. Other Patriots even offered "proof" that British agents stirred the Cherokee to action. They brought forward documents which demonstrated that Henry Stuart, a brother of Superintendent John Stuart, and Alexander

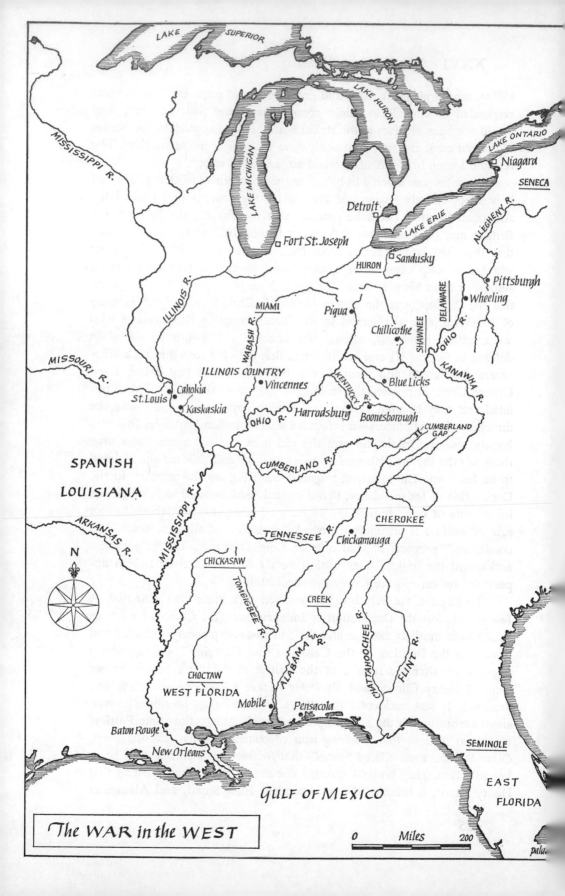

The WAR in the WEST

0   Miles   200

Cameron, the superintendent's representative for many years among the Cherokee, had successfully urged them to take up the hatchet. The papers were forged.

The Cherokee needed no goading. The white men, approaching both from the north and the east, were building their cabins closer and closer to the Cherokee towns. The deer upon which the Cherokee depended for sustenance were becoming scarce. If they were to survive, to live in their own way in their ancient hunting grounds, they must drive back the constantly encroaching whites. They could not be persuaded by John Stuart and his aides to wait until Britain should help them. Pouring out of their mountain valleys in the southern Appalachians, they struck savagely against the outlying parts of South Carolina and Georgia, wreaking havoc upon the borders of those states. They swept so far down into South Carolina that Ninety-Six, a fort well within the white settlements, became an outpost that received fleeing men, women, and children. The Cherokee indiscriminately killed whites and Negroes, Patriots and Tories. Unprepared, the borderers gathered in small forts to protect themselves and called for aid.

The Cherokee proceeded wih peculiar ferocity against the pioneers who had moved into the valley of the Little Tennessee River in and after 1768. More than once they had asked those settlers to depart, to leave the meadows adjacent to the Holston, Nolichucky, and Clinch Rivers; their demands had been uniformly denied. But the Cherokee did not surprise those settlements. The borderers were as prepared as might be. Near Eaton's Station on July 20 more than 300 warriors, led by Dragging Canoe, engaged 170 backwoodsmen in a bloody struggle at close quarters. The whites drove off the Indians. The next day the warriors, striking at dawn, tried to storm a stockade on the Watauga River near Sycamore Shoals. Its defenders were alert and repulsed the charge of the Cherokee. Nor could the warriors continue to besiege that place until it should be surrendered. The pioneers collected in ever larger numbers, and the Indians at length retreated to their mountain homes.

Then the whites struck back. Only sixteen years earlier, the Southern colonists had asked for and received the help of British regulars against the Cherokee. Now the Americans had to rely upon themselves. They were equal to the emergency. Georgia militia under Major Samuel Jack forced the Cherokee back. Then militia from the Carolinas and Virginia marched against them. Colonel Andrew Williamson and 1,500 South Carolinians guided by Catawba Indian scouts ravaged the easternmost villages of the Cherokee. They made one brief stand against Williamson, then fled. Meanwhile, General Griffith Rutherford led forward 2,500

North Carolinians into the heart of the Cherokee country. The Indians tried to check his advance, but were driven off. Simultaneously, Colonel William Christian collected Virginia militia and was joined by borderers from their settlements in eastern Tennessee. He marched against and swept through the Cherokee towns on the western side of the Appalachians at the head of 2,000 men. The Indians fled westward and southward. The Patriots burned their homes and devastated their fields. The Cherokee were routed. They were compelled to sign humiliating treaties of peace in 1777, in the late spring with South Carolina, in the summer with North Carolina and Virginia.

But the war went on. Dragging Canoe, a determined and dauntless foe, would not accept defeat. He retreated to the Chickamauga River with a few followers and continued the struggle. Gradually his band grew formidable, thanks to the British. For, although John Stuart and his aides did not instigate the Cherokee to take the field, they did what they could to enable Dragging Canoe and his adherents to persevere, also to persuade other Cherokee to resume the contest. In November 1776, Lord George Germain instructed Stuart to do everything possible to arm the Cherokee. Stuart accordingly supplied them with weapons and ammunition from Pensacola. Gradually the Cherokee regained strength and spirit. Dragging Canoe became so formidable that 900 Virginia and North Carolina militia under Evan Shelby undertook to destroy his colony at Chickamauga in 1778. They surprised and routed Dragging Canoe, but he retreated temporarily to Lookout Mountain and fought on.

It became ever more obvious to the Cherokee that they had nothing to lose by fighting. The whites were not content with the lands they had already taken from that tribe. Late in 1779 James Robertson and Colonel John Donelson founded Nashville with a party of pioneers, and other settlers put down there in the following year. The lust of the whites for land was boundless. In 1780, when many frontier riflemen were absent from their homes—they had crossed the Appalachians to assist their brethren hard-pressed east of the mountains by the British—the Cherokee gathered for another desperate effort. They fought in vain. John Sevier and 250 riflemen defeated and dispersed a band of the Indians on the French Broad River on December 8. Then Colonel Arthur Campbell came forward with 400 Virginians. Sevier's men joined the Virginians. Campbell drove through the western villages of the Cherokee. He captured and wrecked their capital, the "mother town" of Choté, and he carried off the records that the confederacy had begun to preserve in pathetic imitation of the whites. Small bodies of Cherokee raided South Carolina in 1781 and 1782, but were soon forced to flee. Dragging Canoe continued to fight from his stronghold at Chickamauga. He survived a punitive expedition led against him by John Sevier in 1782. Indeed, Dragging Canoe never did surrender to the Patriots. However, his fellow tribesmen had to bend to superior force; finally, in 1782, they bought peace from the Americans by ceding more of their precious and shrinking territory. At last, the power of the Cherokee was broken.

Furnishing the Cherokee with guns, tomahawks, and knives, John Stuart at first strove to moderate their ferocity by arranging to send white men with their war parties. However, the braves refused to fight in the paleface way, and Stuart's safeguard proved to be useless. In fact, some whites—being Tories—who went to war as allies of the Cherokee were more savage than the savages. Patriots saw in Indian raiding parties Loyalists painted and undressed like the warriors, saw them commit ghastly crimes against helpless prisoners. The malevolent outrages perpetrated by the Tories are more to be condemned than the innocent atrocities of the Indians. Stuart was compelled, in the main, to let the Cherokee wage war as they would. He might deplore their cruelties. He had an ugly duty to perform, but he executed it. From Pensacola, in fact, he beckoned more and more Indians to take part in the conflict. He urged the Creek, the Choctaw, and the Chickasaw tribes to sing their war chants and to go forth to battle. They, too, he said, were threatened by the onrush of the American frontiersmen. The Great King he served was their friend and benefactor, and he would help them to preserve their homes, their hunting grounds, and their freedom. He hoped and planned to send swarms of warriors against the Southern frontier.

Stuart was never able to create and mobilize such a formidable confederacy, which might have put in the field, with the Cherokee, as many as 10,000 braves. The unsophisticated Indians did not uniformly recognize that their independence was at least ultimately at stake. The Patriot settlements were not yet near the villages of the Choctaw; the far less numerous Chickasaw were not yet alarmed for their own safety. Even the Creek, long since angry because the pioneers were encroaching upon their lands, did not unanimously perceive that the Patriots were their mortal enemies. American emissaries pressed them to remain neutral. Stuart was not able to supply consistently from Pensacola the blankets, the powder and lead, the rouge paint that they needed; the Patriot envoys promised to furnish the goods desired by the Creek, and they sometimes fulfilled their pledges. The Creek, observing the chastisement meted out to the Cherokee by the Americans, had to consider the evil consequences of military defeat as well as the rich prizes of victory. The nation could not agree upon a policy. It then contained three parts. Two of them—the

Seminole, located in Florida, and the Upper Creek, concentrated in Alabama—joined the British. But the Lower Towns, lying closer to the Patriots, were largely under the influence of the Patriot George Galphin, an astute trader who exerted remarkable persuasive power among them from his headquarters at Silver Bluffs on the Savannah River. Galphin entreated them to remain quiet, and they listened to him. Even the Upper Creek refrained from taking up the hatchet until 1779, after Stuart's death at Pensacola. It was then too late for them to accomplish much. They went to the assistance of the British at Pensacola and Augusta in 1781 and at Savannah in 1782, but their great opportunity had passed. They, and all the Indian allies of Britain south of the Ohio River, received little help from England during the last years of the war. West Florida, including Mobile and Pensacola, had fallen to Britain's enemies.

It was apparent to thoughtful Patriots from the very beginning of the war that a sure defense existed against the southern Indians. If their supplies from Britain were cut off, they must either remain neutral or soon be subdued. Accordingly the Patriots meditated attack upon St. Augustine, to prevent the flow of arms to the Indians from that place. They failed to take St. Augustine, but their lack of success in East Florida was not too serious for them, since the British allies obtained arms chiefly through Pensacola and Mobile. If those towns could be taken, the Cherokee, Creek, Choctaw, and Chickasaw would be crippled. Two perceptive Patriots, Oliver Pollock, a merchant of New Orleans, and George Morgan, a veteran trader in the West, ardently urged that an army be sent down the Ohio and Mississippi Rivers to seize the two British bases. They were weakly held by redcoat garrisons. The Americans could thus not only bring the southern tribes to their knees, but also gain a rich province for themselves on the Gulf of Mexico and access to that body of water by way of the Mississippi. The Congress recognized the validity of the arguments put forward by Pollock and Morgan; but in the midst of many dangers, it could not provide the men. Nor was it within the power of any of the Southern states to mobilize such a force. In 1778 Captain James Willing offered evidence that West Florida was vulnerable. Moving down the Mississippi in a small armed boat, *The Rattlesnake,* with only twenty-seven men, he raided plantations in West Florida and wreaked heavy damage before he was driven away by its defenders.

But if the Americans were unable to mount an offensive against the colony, other enemies of Britain were strong enough to move against it, and did. The Spanish garrison troops in Louisiana were not numerous. However, Governor Bernardo de Gálvez, who ruled at New Orleans for King Charles III, was one of the many able men that monarch had taken

430

into his service. Lord George Germain might think that the British should undertake to capture that strategic spot. Gálvez did not wait to be attacked. Learning that his master had gone to war against Britain, he collected a small and heterogeneous army of Spanish troops, French Creoles, Americans, and Indians attached to Spain. He advanced eastward in August 1778, taking British outposts at Manchac, Baton Rouge, and Natchez. Early in the following year, assured of help from Cuba, he moved against Mobile by sea. Persevering despite storms that cost him both men and military gear, he attacked Fort Charlotte, the citadel of Mobile, in early March with 1,400 men. The garrison, under the British engineer Elias Durnford, consisted of only 300 troops, but a relieving army of 1,100 men sent out from Pensacola by General John Campbell, the commander of the British forces in West Florida, was approaching. Gálvez hastily ordered his soldiers to assail the fort, and it fell after two days of fighting, before the army ordered to the rescue of its garrison could reach Mobile. That army fell back to Pensacola. Gálvez then lacked power to proceed against Pensacola, the stronghold of the British on the northern shore of the Gulf of Mexico. Nevertheless, he clung to Mobile. He collected a large force at Havana, and sailed for Pensacola in October. The fleet carrying his troops was badly hurt and driven back by a storm. Again he collected ships and men. In March 1781, he appeared at Pensacola with a formidable and well-equipped army of perhaps 7,000 men and a strong naval squadron. General Campbell had done what he could to strengthen Fort George, the heart of the defenses of Pensacola. Within it he commanded about 1,600 men. He had also called to his aid hundreds of the Choctaw, Chickasaw, and other tribesmen. But the Indians could not materially help a garrison battered by artillery and invested by well-trained troops. Campbell was at last compelled to yield the fort, on May 9.

With the fall of Pensacola, West Florida came completely into Spanish hands. It was recognized to be Spanish territory by Britain at the end of the War of Independence. Soon after its close Spain began to support southern Indians against the United States—so rapidly do men change friends and enemies when it seems to be to their interest. However, Bernardo de Gálvez, without affection for the Patriot cause, did reduce the power of both Britain and the southern Indians during the last years of the war, and did therefore render important assistance to the Americans. Dragging Canoe might and did continue the struggle even after Britain and America had ceased to exchange blows; but that indomitable chief, for all his fortitude and constancy, was a nuisance rather than a menace to the United States.

What Pensacola in the lowlands of Florida was to the Creek and Cherokee, Niagara on the distant northern bluffs between Lake Erie and Lake Ontario was to the Six Nations. For Niagara was the depot of the warlike Iroquois after 1777, the source of supplies which enabled them to harry the frontiers of New York and Pennsylvania. From that place Chief Joseph Brant, a sophisticated Dragging Canoe, more than once went forth to battle against the Patriots. With him to war marched several thousands of warriors, contingents of Tories, and British regulars as well. Muskets, ammunition, and tomahawks reached Niagara from England by way of Quebec and Montreal and were distributed by British agents to eager braves. Because John Burgoyne would not permit the Iroquois to fight in their special way, they gave him little help; and the warriors who fought as allies of Barry St. Leger triumphed with him neither at Oriskany nor at Fort Stanwix. However, the Six Nations and their allies not only assisted Britain to defend Canada after 1777, but also poured down upon the border settlements of New York and Pennsylvania in raiding forces that severely punished the Patriots. The Americans responded by destroying the towns of the Iroquois, except for those of the Oneida and the Tuscarora who helped the Patriots or remained neutral. Before the war ended, the valleys of the Mohawk and Susquehanna Rivers were drenched with blood, and the power of the Iroquois, on the wane when hostilities began, was almost broken.

The Six Nations had much to lose and to gain in the war, for they were the most advanced—at least in the things valued by whites—of all the Indians who lived in the immense expanses between the Atlantic and the Pacific that afterward became part of the United States. Their confederacy was more stable than those of the Cherokee and the Creek. Their settlements, stretching from the Catskill Mountains to Lake Erie, resembled those of the whites with whom they were in contact. They lived in log houses, some with glass windows and fireplaces; they—or rather, their women, children, and old men—cultivated gardens and orchards; at least a few of the Iroquois had become Christians. Brave and proud, they had subjugated many of their Indian neighbors and had scourged French Canada. They had been potent allies of the Dutch when New York was still New Netherland, then of the English successors to the Dutch. But their numbers were diminishing as the War of Independence approached, and their lands were shrinking. The whites were advancing into their country from both the east and the south. So persuasive was the influence of a New England missionary, Samuel Kirkland, among the Oneida tribe that many of its warriors chose eventually to assist rather than to struggle against the Patriots. There were Tuscarora warriors who would not fight

432

for or against the Americans. But four of the Six Nations—the Mohawk, the Onondaga, the Cayuga, and the Seneca—listening to members of the Sir William Johnson clan and other British agents, recognized the Americans as their deadly enemies and committed themselves to alliance with Britain and war with the Patriots. Some of the Tuscarora joined them; the Oneida were few in number. In sum, the bulk of the Six Nations engaged in a struggle for existence.

The help of the Iroquois was accepted by General Frederick Haldimand, the man who succeeded Sir Guy Carleton as governor of Canada in 1778. Like Generals Gage and Howe, he was not overscrupulous about the cruelties of warfare as it was waged by Britain's forest allies. Even Sir Henry Clinton, who felt qualms concerning British raids upon American seacoast towns, was quite willing that Indians should attack the Patriots and so reduce his own difficulties. Haldimand feared that the Patriots would again march against Montreal and Quebec, that the French Canadians would follow the example of France and join the Americans. He had few British troops to defend Canada; in consequence, he was far more willing to make use of the Iroquois than he might otherwise have been. A Swiss-born professional soldier, he had served in America in the Seven Years' War, and he was no stranger to the fiendish malevolence of Indians inflamed by battle; nor was he ignorant that frontiersmen responded to Indian outrages in kind. But it was his duty to hold Canada for Britain, and he would not lose the colony because he was too fastidious about ways and means to hold it. He supplied British regulars, Tory contingents, and Iroquois alike at Niagara. With his support, the redoubtable Joseph Brant of the Mohawks and Colonel John Butler and his Tory Rangers went upon many a raid against the Patriot borderers.

It was Colonel Butler who struck the first great blow. He made his way at the end of June 1778 with 400 Tories and about 500 Iroquois into the valley of Wyoming in northern Pennsylvania. About 300 frontiersmen gathered under a Patriot colonel, Zebulon Butler, to oppose him. The American Butler tried to surprise the Loyalist Butler, failed, and was routed. No more than sixty Americans escaped. The others were killed upon the spot and scalped, or worse, were captured and later tortured and slain by the Iroquois. Resistance against the Loyalists and Indians seemed to be useless. The two principal forts in the valley surrendered in exchange for a promise that lives and property would be spared. The promise was not kept. Cabins and flour mills were burned; cattle were driven off; and surviving settlers fled. The beautiful valley was laid waste.

Two months later Brant—who as the brother of Molly Brant, for many years the mistress of the household of Sir William Johnson, had received the benefits of a white man's education, but had not lost the vigor of his forebears—struck at German Flats, a village on the Mohawk River. He led 150 Iroquois, and he was accompanied by 300 Tories. Surprised, the inhabitants fled into two small forts and a church. Brant did not attack them, but his followers put the torch to every house in the village and led away all the livestock they could find. They ruined the settlement. The Patriots exacted their revenge. A heterogeneous body of Continentals and riflemen gathered, marched against Unadilla, an Iroquois town fifty miles to the westward. They entered it without opposition on October 8—its occupants had fled—and destroyed it. Reprisal then succeeded brutal reprisal. In November Brant and 500 Indians, together with 200 Tory Rangers under the command of Captain Walter Butler, a son of Colonel John Butler, invaded Cherry Valley, fifty miles west of Albany. Its residents gathered in a strong stockade and successfully defied the raiders, who possessed no artillery. However, they killed or captured as many as fifty armed and unarmed inhabitants whom they trapped outside the fort. In July 1779, Brant struck the village of Minisink near the Delaware River, destroyed it, and carried off many prisoners. About 150 Patriots gathered and imprudently pursued him to the banks of that river. His followers were more numerous, and he was skillful in battle. He engaged the Americans and broke through a hollow square they had formed. His Indians slaughtered Patriots who had been wounded. Only thirty others managed to escape.

So grievously hurt by the punishing incursions of the Iroquois and the Tories from Niagara were the frontiersmen that they appealed to their fellow Patriots for rescue. They could not predict where their red and white enemies would strike, could not concentrate to meet them; nor could they gather in sufficient force to take the offensive. Washington considered their plight, in the last days of 1778. There was unquestionably a cure for their woes. The capture of Quebec or Montreal would cut the supply line of the raiders and would sooner or later reduce them to helplessness. The Patriots did not have strength enough to penetrate and to hold even a part of the lower St. Lawrence Valley. Even Niagara was too distant to strike. As an alternative, Washington decided that they could and must send forth expeditions to lay waste the Iroquois country. Early in 1779 Congress asked him to act. He arranged to send out Colonel Daniel Brodhead with 600 Continentals and militia against the western settlements of the Six Nations in the valley of the Allegheny River. Meanwhile, a much larger body of Patriots was to march into the very heart of the Indian confederacy. He offered command of the larger punitive force to Horatio Gates, who sensibly declined it, upon the scores of

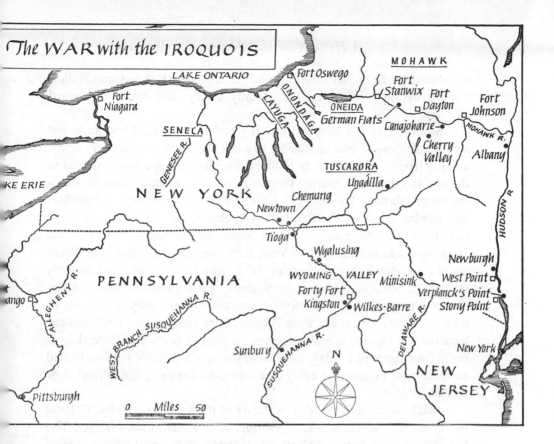

The WAR with the IROQUOIS

LAKE ONTARIO
Fort Oswego
MOHAWK
Fort Niagara
Fort Stanwix
Fort Dayton
Fort Johnson
ONEIDA
German Flats
Canajoharie
SENECA
GENESEE R.
CAYUGA
ONONDAGA
Cherry Valley
Albany
MOHAWK R.
TUSCARORA
Unadilla
NEW YORK
Chemung
Newtown
KE ERIE
Tioga
Wyalusing
Newburgh
PENNSYLVANIA
WYOMING VALLEY
Minisink
West Point
Verplanck's Point
Stony Point
ango
ALLEGHENY R.
Forty Fort
Kingston
Wilkes-Barre
DELAWARE R.
WEST BRANCH SUSQUEHANNA R.
Sunbury
SUSQUEHANNA R.
N
New York
Pittsburgh
0   Miles   50
NEW JERSEY
HUDSON R.

old age and ill health. Major General John Sullivan assumed the task. Washington instructed Sullivan to destroy the Iroquois towns, and also to seize and hold their inhabitants, men, women, and children, as hostages. He hoped that the warriors of the Six Nations, distressed by the destruction of their villages and alarmed for the safety of their families and friends, would abandon the struggle, or at least curtail their efforts.

Sullivan was given ample strength. He led forward more than 2,300 men, chiefly Continentals, from the Wyoming Valley on July 31, and he was met at Tioga, Pennsylvania, on August 22 by General James Clinton with 1,400 more Continentals. Sullivan had already begun his work. He had sent out a detachment that demolished the Iroquois town of Chemung. Moving forward from Tioga, Sullivan was confronted at Newtown on August 29 by Joseph Brant, Captain Walter Butler, and about 500 Iroquois warriors, together with hundreds of Tories and a few British regulars. Brant and Butler had built a breastwork of logs across Sullivan's line of match. They hoped to check the Patriots as they advanced in column and then to fall upon Sullivan's flanks. They were disappointed. Sullivan had prudently sent forward advance guards who reported the dispositions of the Indians and their white allies. The Patriot general

435

broadened his front and swept around the breastwork. Brant and Butler, assailed by superior power, fought only briefly, and then fled toward Niagara.

Sullivan's men were then free to wreak vengeance. They could not secure hostages—it was impossible to keep secret the march of an army, and the Iroquois sought safety in flight. But their villages were exposed to the axe and the torch. During the following month detachments of Patriots ranged through the villages of the Six Nations, burning all buildings and ruining gardens, cornfields, and orchards. Before Sullivan's army returned to Wyoming at the end of September, it had destroyed all the Iroquois towns in central New York save one, forty of them. The Patriots did not efface the dwellings of the hostile Iroquois with gentlemanly reluctance. Some of them, not surprisingly, perpetrated atrocities. Immediately after the battle of Newtown vengeful victors scalped a dozen of their slain enemies, and a New Jersey officer skinned two dead Indians from the waist down, to make leggings for himself and a friend. Participating in the erasure of a village near Lake Cayuga, a party of Patriots locked an old Indian woman and a boy in a cabin, set fire to it, and burned their victims to death.

While Sullivan devastated the heart of the Iroquois country, Colonel Brodhead, encountering little opposition, ravaged its western fringes. The Six Nations were grievously hurt. Their homes were gone; what was even worse, they were humiliated. They were accustomed to victory; never before in their tribal memory had their own settlements been invaded and blotted out. They might rebuild their homes; they might exact sanguinary payment from the Patriots; they were no longer invincible. The end of both their power and freedom was not far distant.

Long afterward, Americans concerned because the Indians in general and the Iroquois in particular encountered a harsh destiny, condemned Washington, Sullivan, and all the Patriots responsible for desolating the country of the Six Nations. Appeal ought not be made to a maudlin morality requiring one standard for the Iroquois (and their Tories and British allies), another and loftier one for the Patriots. In war, passions rise; in wars between Indians and whites, they led to many outrages.

The Iroquois did not meekly accept their sad fate. With their Tory and British friends they resumed their forays and prosecuted them with perhaps even greater vigor than they had exerted before the punitive expeditions of Sullivan and Brodhead. In May 1780, Sir John Johnson entered the Mohawk Valley from Crown Point at the head of 200 braves and 400 Tories. He killed or captured scores of Patriots, destroyed homes, slew or carried off horses and cattle, and retreated before the Americans could gather to strike at him. In August Brant hit settlements at Canajoharie on the Mohawk River. In September Johnson and Brant with about 1,000 raiders entered the Schoharie Valley, from the south, swept down it to the Mohawk, and marched westward up that river, doing immense damage. Engaged at Stone Arabia by Colonel John Brown commanding only 130 borderers, they killed Brown and one third of his men, and dispersed the remainder. General Robert Van Rensselaer with 1,500 militia attacked Johnson on October 19. The frontiersmen drove off Johnson's Iroquois contingent, and he was forced to flee. The British and their allies extorted retribution from the Oneida, who had given valuable assistance to Van Rensselaer. They razed the Oneida villages.

The gory contest continued. Washington was too weak and too busy elsewhere to offer more help. The incursions of the Indians and their white friends went on with little interruption until the fall of 1781. At length the defense of the Mohawk Valley was entrusted by the discouraged and desperate Patriots to Colonel Marinus Willett, the hero of Fort Stanwix. On July 1 at the head of 150 troops Willett met 200 Indians on the banks of the Mohawk and routed them with a bayonet charge. Late in October 1,000 Tories and Iroquois appeared on that river and sacked the village of Warrensbush. Willett attacked them with only 400 men and forced them to retreat after a sharp engagement. He pursued them and pounced upon them a second time. An Oneida warrior slew Walter Butler. His companions fled northward to safety.

At last the cruel war in the Mohawk Valley ended. News of Yorktown and of the making of an Anglo-American peace reached the valley and Niagara. The Tories and some of the Iroquois withdrew to Canada, where they long remained bitter enemies of the Americans. Attrition had so much decreased the military capability of the Six Nations that they could not again effectively challenge the Americans. Even though the British clung to Niagara long after the close of the war, the way had opened for the Americans to occupy the lands south of Lake Ontario and also the eastern shore of Lake Erie.

What was doubtless even more important, the Patriots more than held their own in the valley of the Ohio River. Of all the American pioneers, the most exposed to attack by the Indians were those who had settled in Kentucky immediately before 1775. That region became for them what it had been to the red men for generations, the "Dark and Bloody Ground." The settlements established by Judge Richard Henderson, and others, such as Boonesborough and Harrodstown, were thinly inhabited. But they survived and they grew. Indeed, they spread into central Tennessee and to the left bank of the Mississippi before the war ended. The Patriots even invaded the region between the Ohio River and the Great Lakes, and it became their own in the treaty of peace with Britain.

The Kentucky backwoodsmen were in special peril because their new homes were at a great distance from those of their fellow Patriots. They had two long lines of communication with the Americans east of the Appalachians, the Ohio River and a wagon track which ran through Cumberland Gap. At the beginning of the war the Kentuckians formed only a spearhead into the western forests; and the Indians to the southward and the northward were hostile and threatened both of their avenues to the east. Fortune favored them in one respect. Their most formidable antagonists, the Indian nations resident north of the Ohio River, were largely dependent upon distant Detroit for their arms, clothing, blankets, and liquor. Detroit was to them what Mobile was to the Chickasaw and Choctaw; Detroit could be supplied by the British only by way of the St. Lawrence, Lake Ontario, and Lake Erie. Accordingly, British agents could not easily nourish the war efforts of the Shawnee, Miami, Wyandot, Ottawa, and other tribes north of the Ohio. They did all that they could to encourage and maintain the enemies of the Kentuckians. The "Long Knives" possessed another advantage over the Patriots of New York and Pennsylvania in that belligerent Tories were far fewer at Detroit than they were at Niagara.

Nevertheless, the new villages and hamlets in Kentucky, indeed, all along the southern bank of the Ohio from Pittsburgh to Louisville, were shaken again and again by attacks of red men. Even during the first years of the war, the Kentuckians suffered from desultory and minor raids by the Shawnee from the north and the Cherokee from the south. Patriot agents passed across the Ohio to the villages of the Shawnee at Chillicothe and Piqua, circulated among their neighbors, attempting to persuade the warriors to make and keep peace. They failed in their errands. In 1777 it became apparent that bands of Indians would soon appear in force south of the river. The Patriots seized and held Chief Cornstalk of the Shawnee as a hostage. That ancient device was worse than useless. Cornstalk was murdered by cruel and foolish borderers. The Shawnee, the Miami, the Wyandot, and their allies poured over the Beautiful River. They relied upon the British at Detroit for help and they received it, from the hands of Lieutenant Colonel Henry Hamilton. That officer acquired the ugly sobriquet of the "Hair-Buyer." He was accused of buying Patriot scalps from the savage friends of George III. It may be that the accusation was not founded upon fact. It matters little whether or not he made such ghastly purchases; it was of great importance that he furnished the muskets, tomahawks, and knives that enabled the Indians to slay the frontier people, armed or unarmed, male or female, old or young.

Marauding parties of the red men struck hard across the upper Ohio in 1777 and across its lower stretches early in the following year. The obvious remedy, for the Patriots, was the capture of Detroit. In sending General Edward Hand to Pittsburgh, Congress authorized him to take the offensive, and if possible, to march against that town. In February 1778, Hand led forward 500 men toward a British outpost at Sandusky, but harsh weather persuaded him to turn back without accomplishing anything. Later in that year General Lachlan McIntosh, succeeding Hand, set forth with another expeditionary force that returned to Pittsburgh without achievement or glory.

But George Rogers Clark, at twenty-six already a doughty Indian fighter, successfully bid for fame that year. Virginia, firmly establishing her authority over Kentucky by 1776, entrusted the defense of the region to Clark. Like other Patriots, he saw that the capture of Detroit would reduce the striking power of the trans-Ohio tribes, might induce them to put down their weapons, to make peace. He secured funds from the Virginia assembly for an expedition that he would lead into Kaskaskia, Cahokia, Vincennes, and other villages in the Illinois country inhabited by a few hundred Frenchmen. He would establish a base in those villages. Then, if possible, he would move against Detroit. With 175 frontiersmen Clark floated down the Ohio River, then marched overland to Kaskaskia in the early summer of 1778. He and his men were half-starved when they reached that place. Luckily, they were not immediately confronted by armed enemies. There were no British regulars, Tories, or hostile Indians in Kaskaskia or in any of the neighboring villages. Most of their inhabitants welcomed the new allies of France. Clark had secured his base in the remote forests of the Old Northwest.

Clark was unable with his small force to proceed against Detroit, but he dealt with Henry Hamilton. Clark managed momentarily, with smooth and confident talk and with supplies sent up the Mississippi from New Orleans by Oliver Pollock, to placate the thousands of Indians who might have destroyed his little army. However, nearly half of his riflemen, their terms of enlistment having expired, went home. Hamilton decided to remove the menace posed by the Patriots in the French villages southwest of his headquarters. With 175 troops, chiefly Frenchmen, and more than 300 Indians, he appeared at Vincennes, garrisoned by a handful of Patriots, in December. They quickly surrendered. At Kaskaskia, Clark heard the news. Conventional prudence indicated that he should entrench and await attack by Hamilton, or even that he should flee to safety. He boldly chose to take the offensive. With 127 men, nearly half of them friendly Frenchmen, he marched 180 miles in seventeen raw midwinter days and appeared at Vincennes with hungry, weary men who were short of ammunition. Hamilton and his soldiers were quartered in a stockade called Fort Sackville that dominated the settlement. But Clark did not despair. He audaciously urged French inhabitants friendly to Britain to join Hamilton. He had his men march into the village in two columns, thus exaggerating the number of his followers. Fortune smiled upon him. Most of the Indians with Hamilton were impressed, and departed. Hamilton had sent forty men up the Wabash River to hasten forward supplies. Frenchmen who wished the Patriots well donated ammunition. Clark swiftly opened fire upon the fort. Hamilton had fewer than 100 men, but the stockade was well made and contained twelve cannon. However, the Patriot riflemen, shooting into the portholes, managed to kill or wound the gunners, and silenced the guns. In the morning of February 24 the American officer demanded that the fort be given up to him. To emphasize that he would not be put off with words, he had his men kill five Indians in sight of the garrison. As they entered Vincennes, the Patriots had captured the five braves—who were carrying American scalps. On February 25 Hamilton surrendered the garrison of seventy-nine men. Shortly afterward, the Americans also took the detachment Hamilton had sent out to bring in supplies. Clark sent the British officer under escort to Williamsburg, where Governor Thomas Jefferson kept him in close confinement for many months. He was lucky to escape the vengeance of outraged borderers.

Clark yearned to march on to Detroit, momentarily guarded only weakly; but he had neither men nor means sufficient to do it. Nor was he ever able to advance against that town. He laid plans for an expedition in 1780, again in 1781. His masters at the capital of Virginia endorsed his schemes, for they hoped not only to hit against the British and their Indian allies, but also to win the Old Northwest for Virginia. However, they could not offer him enough men or money or supplies to permit him to act. He was even forced to withdraw his riflemen from the Illinois country, because they were so much needed elsewhere. The French villagers in that region continued to acknowledge American sway over it; and they were not molested by the British. It turned out that Clark's occupation of Kaskaskia, Cahokia, and Vincennes was a permanent one.

Nevertheless, neither Clark nor any other Patriot found a way to stop the raids of Britain's allies, the Indians and the Tories, in the Ohio Valley. They increased rather than diminished after the entrance of the

Patriots into the Illinois country. The successors of Henry Hamilton at Detroit were not less active than he had been. Annoyed by thrusts of the Indians from the south, the Kentuckians suffered grievously as the result of assaults from the north. The Shawnee and Delaware in particular waged ruthless war against the borderers. In October 1779, Loyalists and Indians led by Simon Girty, a Tory most detested by the frontiersmen, surprised an American convoy on the Ohio River and killed fifty-seven men. In 1780 Colonel Henry Bird leading 150 Tories and 1,000 Indians, moved across the upper Ohio into the Licking River valley, captured two small forts, and carried away more than 100 prisoners, many of whom were slaughtered as Bird made his way back to Detroit. Clark struck back. In August 1780, he led 1,000 riflemen into the country of the Shawnee, destroyed their "mother town" of Chillicothe, and drove off Simon Girty and the Shawnee after a fierce struggle at Piqua.

But the conflict only became more bitter and more violent. Indians ravaging the Kentucky settlements killed scores of Kentuckians in 1781. Joseph Brant, appearing on the upper Ohio, surprised and wiped out a body of more than 100 Pennsylvania militia moving down the river. Even the news of the British surrender at Yorktown did not put an end to the fighting in the Ohio Valley. The Patriots massacred ninety Delaware who had taken no part in the war. In the spring of 1782 Colonel William Crawford led forward 300 men from Pittsburgh into the valley of the upper Sandusky River in an attempt to surprise the Shawnee and Wyandot. They were confronted by an equal number of Tories and Indians under the British officer, Captain William Caldwell, on June 4. After a sharp contest that continued into the following day, Caldwell was reinforced by a body of Shawnee, and the Americans were forced to retreat. More than fifty of them fell, and Crawford, captured, was tortured and killed by the savages. Two months later, Caldwell, Simon Girty, and a few other Tories, with 300 braves, attacked a stockade near Lexington, Kentucky. They were unable to force its surrender. Retreating, they watched for an opportunity to ambush frontiersmen who would pursue them. Their chance came, for 200 riflemen who caught up with them at the Little Blue Licks recklessly attacked them without waiting for other riflemen hastening forward. In a brief battle on August 19 the borderers were routed, and half of them were killed, wounded, or captured. Early in November Clark again invaded the Shawnee country, at the head of more than 1,000 riflemen. He met little resistance, and he burned six villages to the ground before he turned back. Then, mercifully, the sanguinary conflict in the Ohio Valley diminished. Word came that Britain and America had made peace, and British agents and Tories abandoned the contest.

The war in the distant West, like that on the frontiers of New York and Pennsylvania, closed without dramatic, without obviously decisive victory or defeat for any of the parties. Nevertheless, the Patriots gained all the fruits of triumph. They had not been forced back to the Appalachians; they had abandoned no ground they held at the beginning of the struggle. In fact, their settlements gained strength as it proceeded, for more backwoodsmen crossed the mountains and entered the Mississippi Valley even while it continued. The regions that afterward became the states of West Virginia and Kentucky were firmly occupied by the Americans when hostilities between America and Britain officially ceased. They had established footholds in the Illinois country. Moreover, they were entrenched in central as well as eastern Tennessee. For more than a decade after Britain had finally recognized American independence, Detroit, like Niagara, was held by a British garrison. The Indians north of the Ohio, trading with British subjects, at least tacitly encouraged by British agents, continued to make desultory raids. The southern Indians, similarly befriended by Spanish officials and British merchants in the Floridas, also remained restless and occasionally committed hostile acts. The American settlers beyond the Appalachians became unhappy because they did not receive military help from the Congress during about seven years after the finish of the War of Independence. A few of them turned to intrigues with their European enemies. However, during the next seven years a new and stronger American central government came to their rescue, crushed the Shawnee and their Indian allies, secured the withdrawal of British garrisons to Canada, forced the Spanish to open the Mississippi to backwoods traffic, and asserted American hegemony on the left bank of the Mississippi. Still another seven years, and New Orleans and all the colony of Louisiana became American territory. In 1803 the "empire of liberty" reached the heights of the Rocky Mountains. Only three years afterward, an American exploring party traveled overland to the Pacific. One of its two leaders was, fittingly, William Clark, a younger brother of George Rogers Clark.

CHAPTER XXVII

The War at Home

IF warfare in the West had its unique horrors alike for men, women, and children, it is also true that the struggle for American independence brought suffering to most of those involved in it, civilians as well as combatants. Word went to a wife in a remote valley in England's Cotswold hills that she had become a widow, to a mother in Glasgow that she had lost a son, to children in Normandy that they no longer had a father. If an American family lost none of its males, its members knew neighbors that had been less fortunate. The kin of the dead mourned for thousands rather than millions, but the quality of their grief was not thereby diminished. Maimed soldiers came home, and sick men who never regained health. If some Patriots profited from the war, it ruined others. A farmer was deprived of his horses, cattle, pigs, and poultry; the business, even the shop, of an artisan was destroyed. If an area was largely exempt from the ravages of armies and navies—few were entirely untouched—its residents at least suffered from a deranged economy and inflation. Instruction of the young was interrupted and the morals of their elders deteriorated in consequence of the reckless spirit engendered by the war. Specially injured by the conflict were Loyalists repressed by the Patriots, deprived of property and livelihood, and driven into exile. One ought not think that the Patriots achieved their freedom without making great sacrifices, undergoing many brutalities, bearing heavy and harassing strains. The lot of the Tories was much harsher. They, too, suffered, and the punishment inflicted upon the vanquished by the victors compounded their troubles.

The Patriots, being rebels against constituted authority, were, of course, legally subject to any punishment that Britain might inflict upon

443

them. Bearing arms against George III, they were guilty, according to British law, of treason. The death penalty could have been exacted of active Patriots who fell into British or Loyalist hands. Instead, from the very beginning of the struggle, the British treated the rebels in accordance with the rules of war, such as they were in Europe in the eighteenth century. They did not summarily execute Patriots captured while bearing arms. Too many Americans had weapons; and after the battle of Trenton they also had hundreds of Hessian and British prisoners whose lives could be taken in reprisal.

All of which does not mean that Patriots who became prisoners of the royal forces were handsomely, evenly gently, treated. True, the British did exchange captured officers rank for rank, in traditional European fashion, with the Patriots—they believed that they gained in such transactions—that a British captain was more valuable than an American one. However, Americans, whether officers or not, who spent months or years in British custody, underwent harassing trials. Many, indeed, did not survive confinement. They suffered from both heat and cold, from lack of food, from disease. In part, their hardships, their sufferings as prisoners, were unavoidable; in part, Congress, failing to provide certain necessaries, as custom then required, was responsibile for their privations. But their captors and keepers were callous. Notorious is the name of William Cunningham, who as a provost marshal had thousands of American prisoners in his care in New York. They were so numerous and the city was so crowded that hundreds of them were put aboard ships in the harbor. The *Jersey,* an old hulk, was the noisome and last home of many unfortunate Patriots. Ethan Allen, who survived a term as a captive, afterward charged the British with "murdering premeditatively (in cold blood) near or quite 2,000 helpless prisoners, and that in the most clandestine, mean and shameful manner." Allen, as already mentioned, was given to strong language and exaggeration. However, many prisoners sickened and died because Cunningham, a vicious grafter, "starved the living and fed the dead." It is mildly comforting to record that he was afterward found guilty of forgery in Britain, and that he went to the gallows for that minor crime.

War enhances the worst as well as the finest qualities of mankind. No army on campaign moves among hostile civilians, even among friendly ones, without committing depredations against property and crimes against persons. The hungry soldier, seizing and eating a chicken, does not eagerly seek its owner to pay him for it. For some soldiers the laws of war are those of the jungle. Lustful ones do commit rape, an atrocity of which the Indians, most exceptionally, were seldom guilty. On

June 29, 1776, before landing at New York, General William Howe ordered that any of his men guilty of plundering be executed "on the spot." He repeated that instruction on August 31. On September 6, however, he declared that the "present licentious behavior of the troops" was "a disgrace to the country they belong to." On September 10 his general orders recorded that John Deen and John Lusty, tried by court martial and "found guilty of having committed a rape are sentenced to suffer death." But the most severe punishments did not put an end to pillaging or to the molestation of females. Howe himself was not a model of military deportment. Nor was Sir Henry Clinton, who kept a mistress, as did—if scandalous report does not err—General John Burgoyne. It is to be suspected that Howe was not overly concerned about the peccadilloes of his soldiers. In any event, he could not entirely restrain them. After the battle of Long Island, the British army did not bother to bury the American dead, but both British and Hessian troops looted farms. If an owner protested his loyalty to George III, he might receive a requisition paper, worthless, for property taken. In the closing weeks of 1776 Howe's Hessians abused both Patriots and Loyalists in New Jersey. It was afterward remarked that marches of the British armies in the South could be traced by the mulatto children the redcoats left behind them. Need it be said that the Patriots, whether Continentals or militia, being human, were not all Galahads? When farmers in the vicinity of Philadelphia, in the winter of 1777-8, preferred to sell cattle and grain to the British for hard cash rather than to accept Continental paper money, foraging parties from Valley Forge forced them to accept the paper currency, gave them proof that their cattle and grain had been requisitioned, or simply carried off what Washington's army needed. The Patriots, of course, did not usually despoil their own people. They frequently compelled Tories to contribute foodstuffs; and some of them did not think that the wanton burning of the barn or house of an excessively ardent Tory was a criminal act.

The damages of war were not confined to the regions traversed by armies, bombarded by naval guns, or raided by red men. There were districts, such as the heart of New England, southern New Jersey, central Pennsylvania, and mid-Maryland, in which there was neither fighting nor devastation. But families everywhere in America felt the loss of protecting fathers and sons, of breadwinners. How many thousands of Patriots died in battle, in prison, of disease, of hardships, no one can say with assurance. Certainly those who fell in the field were only a fraction of the whole that died in consequence of the struggle—a Patriot soldier was much safer on duty with his regiment than he was in a British prison or in an American hospital. Nor can it be known how many men, ruined in health and spirit, returned to their kin as burdens rather than assets. Discharged veterans did not bring home with them large sums of money. Their pay was low. What the man in the ranks received per month, in the form of Continental currency, would purchase a bottle of rum in 1779. Later, many soldiers received grants of land as reward for their services. In the main, however, the Patriot troops who survived the war were meagerly compensated in cash and property. Their officers, as might be expected, fared better; the executive experience and prestige they gained in war frequently brought them lucrative civil posts.

The American economy was, of course, upset by the war. The farmer, the artisan, and the laborer might continue to sell their products and the use of their muscles as of yore; however, many of them found that their familiar channels of domestic trade were disturbed or destroyed. Those who produced naval stores and indigo ceased to receive British bounties. Fishermen, especially numerous in New England, were barred by the British navy from the Grand Banks of Newfoundland and even from waters adjacent to their homes. A busy traffic in small boats along the Atlantic seacoast was also interrupted by royal war vessels. In fact, all those engaged in maritime commerce, or even partly dependent upon it for a livelihood, acutely felt the economic impact of war. British markets for rice, fish, lumber, flour, and other raw materials were closed. Even more serious for the Patriots was the partial arrest of American overseas trade with the French, the Spanish, and neutral nations by the British navy. Seeking to go to familiar foreign markets and to reach new ones, merchant captains and their vessels, crews, and cargoes were frequently seized by royal warships.

To be sure, the British blockade was far from absolute. At every period of the war the Patriots could use dozens of harbors. The British admirals serving in American waters could not devote all their forces to guarding ports in the hands of the Patriots—they were compelled to assist the King's armies. It is even to be believed that Lord Howe deliberately neglected to strike at American merchant shipping. But the most zealous of naval commanders—they were eager to seize Patriot vessels and cargoes because of the prize money they would bring when sold—could not keep under close surveillance all the ports held by the Americans. A favorable wind, or a dark night, and a Patriot brig carrying stuffs that brought good profits was on her way to Haiti, Bilbao, or Nantes. Returning safely with scarce goods that were comforts and luxuries, that commanded very high prices, she might make a small fortune for her owner in one voyage. A merchant could lose one of every two ships he sent to sea and become wealthy nevertheless. So it was that the Cabot brothers of

446

Beverly in Massachusetts became prosperous enough to move to Boston and that the Cabots eventually joined its aristocracy. Thus William Bingham achieved opulence and was able to establish himself after the war in Philadelphia as the richest man in America. Fortunate captains of ships became merchants, and able seamen who served under them were at least employed.

There were other opportunities for Patriot captains, mates, sailors, and fishermen in the plethora of American navies that were founded in 1775 and after. Several of the states, together with Congress, undertook to build war craft. During the investment of Boston Washington collected a small squadron to intercept British transports. Some of those navies existed more on paper than in fact, and even that created by Congress was miniscule when compared to the British fleet which patrolled American waters. It was impossible for the Patriots to build enough ships-of-the-line and frigates to challenge that fleet. They tried, and they failed. However, Congress was able to make or procure several smaller vessels. A little squadron under Commodore Esek Hopkins raided Nassau in the Bahamas in March 1776. Two years later, that remarkable sailor of fortune, Captain John Paul Jones, made his way into the Irish Sea, spiked the guns of a fort at Whitehaven in England, and defeated and captured the British sloop *Drake*. In the autumn of 1779, commanding an old French merchantman refitted with forty-four guns and renamed the *Bonhomme Richard* in honor of Benjamin Franklin, Jones, accompanied by two French warships, appeared in the North Sea. There, on September 23, he engaged at close range the *Serapis,* a British warship of the same size as the *Bonhomme Richard*. Jones sustained such heavy fire that his ship sank on the following day, but he forced the surrender of the *Serapis,* and sailed away in her to France. He demonstrated that the Americans could hold their own, ship for ship, gun for gun, and man for man, against the British. He shocked the British with his successful raids in their home waters. Other American captains, such as John Barry, also performed most creditably. But neither the flamboyant and redoubtable Jones nor any of his fellow officers could offer battle to British ships-of-the-line, nor could they disrupt the British blockade of American ports.

Even so, the achievements of the infant American navy were not confined to the capture of the *Serapis* and a few smaller British warships. British merchant vessels offered numerous and lucrative quarry, the chance of gaining large sums of prize money. Accordingly, many American captains in public pay hunted them, and they were joined by scores of Patriot privateers. Indeed, privateering, offering opportunity both to strike at Britain and to make money, was so popular that it gave employment to thousands of American seamen. Among the men of Massachusetts who profited handsomely from it were John and Andrew Cabot of Beverly, Stephen Higginson, and Richard and Elias Hasket Derby of Salem. Their counterparts were to be found in New London, in Egg Harbor, New Jersey, in thriving Baltimore. More than 100 Patriot privateers preyed upon British shipping in 1778; three years later nearly 450 were in commission. The American navy destroyed or captured nearly 200 enemy vessels during the war, the privateers about 600. They inflicted heavy damage upon British shipping. Their assaults upon it, together with those of the French and Spanish, injured the British merchant marine so seriously that British insurance rates soared. The captains and crews of American ships both brought the war home to Britain and made personal profit. So many Americans went a-privateering that there were more of them engaged in that business in 1781 than there were Continentals with Washington.

If the warfare at sea presented opportunity to astute and enterprising merchants as well as bold captains and seamen, it nevertheless injured the American economy. In the large, the British were able to impose mercantile isolation upon the Patriots. Although they could feed and clothe themselves, and even make weapons and ammunition, they needed, or at least desired, many things that they did not produce—such as coffee, tea, sugar, molasses, wine, glass, paper, ironware, and fine clothing, along with military and naval gear. Such things became scarce, and their prices rose, to the benefit of merchants and those who successfully penetrated the British sea barricades. Here and there supplies of domestic produce, especially in areas where the armies were active, also became insufficient, and consumers had to pay more for them. In consequence the Patriots began to suffer early in the war from inflation, and they could find no remedy for it. Had they been largely dependent upon imports for their fundamental needs, the impediments to their maritime commerce erected by the British must have been destructive indeed.

The Patriots were galled, in fact, by two kinds of inflation, for they punished themselves with emissions of paper currency that lost value. Several of the states put forth paper money that depreciated, and the Congress, lacking revenue to meet constant and heavy expenses, printed it in large quantity. That body strove to limit the ever rising flood of cheap money. It asked the states, in 1777, to stop their printing presses; they did not comply. The Congress tried to restrain its own output, but could not. On March 1, 1780, nearly $200 million in Continental currency was in circulation. At that time Congress estimated that forty Continental dollars were worth one of the Spanish dollars upon which they were modeled.

Before the end of that year Continental currency lost all value whatsoever except for souvenirs. That paper was issued from necessity, and Benjamin Franklin pointed out that it took the place of taxation, the holders of the bills receiving less for them than they had given. However, the innocent and the patriotic suffered more from depreciation than the wary and the unscrupulous. It is doubtless true that no tax is truly equitable, but it is to be feared that inflation of the Continental money was a poor if necessary substitute for more conventional means of extracting moneys for public purposes.

The evils of inflation were compounded by laws requiring that cheap paper be accepted as legal tender, and even in small degree by forgery, for Tories contributed counterfeit bills to the generous supply of Continental currency. Special sufferers from the inflationary spiral were public servants and soldiers whose pay could not be rapidly increased so as to keep pace with soaring prices. Supplies of hard French and Spanish money, increasing rapidly toward the end of the war, fortified the American economy; they also advertised the weakness of Continental and state currencies; they were insufficient to meet the need for stable money.

Unable to reduce either shortages in goods or the flow of bad money, the Patriots inevitably turned their thoughts toward fixing prices and wages. Even before the end of 1776 representatives of the four New England states met at Providence to discuss the problem. They agreed that the Yankees ought not to rely passively upon the Divine Providence, that their states must enact rigid controls of both prices and pay. All of the New England commonwealths followed their advice. The Yankees offered a solution, if a rather dubious one, to the problems of inflation. In February 1777, the Congress suggested that other states might do well to follow their example. In fact, before the end of that year, the Congress urged that such controls be established everywhere from Maine to Georgia. In 1778 New York, New Jersey, and Pennsylvania did follow the example set by the New Englanders. But many Patriots, swayed by desire for profit as well as political doctrine, disliked the harsh remedy of fixation. It was "inconsistent with the principles of liberty to prevent a man from the free disposal of his property on such terms and for such considerations as he may think fit." Merchants insisted upon reaping all the profits that traffic would bear, and more. They engaged in that anti-social practice afterward called "black marketing." Later they did not even bother to conceal their violations of law. Workmen demanded and sometimes secured increases in wages. Public opinion did not support controls in such degree that they could be enforced. Even Congress, in June 1778, recommended that attempts to prevent rises in prices be abandoned. That same year a gathering of representatives from the New England states at New Haven urged that prices be set at 75 per cent above the levels of 1775—in vain. Inflation continued to the end of the war, and beyond, until scarcities vanished, until the printing presses ceased to pour forth paper that inevitably lost value.

If many Patriots suffered from ascending prices, few were seriously hurt by new taxes. The Congress could not impose them, and the states, with the exceptions of Massachusetts and Connecticut, preferred to pay the costs of the war from existing and future taxes together with, of course, paper money. Indeed, the burden of taxation was actually lighter during the war for some Patriots than it was before or after the conflict, since cheap paper currency was legal tender in several states. Both the central government and the states purchased extensively on credit, borrowed at home, and secured loans abroad. Much of the financial cost of the war was paid by the Patriots and their progeny, not without pain, in times of peace to come.

War brings out the finest qualities in men. Who does not admire the brave soldier, the staunch sailor? Afterward, the Continentals were venerated, justly, in America. But war also lowers some moral standards, alike for soldiers, sailors, and civilians. The struggle for freedom from Britain had its profiteers on the American as well as on the British side. It fostered hedonism among both the Patriot civilians and armed forces, though in lesser degree than might be expected. The newly prosperous often lived extravagantly. Speculation was encouraged. There were plunderers among the Continentals. However, neither they nor the Patriot militia became dissolute, in part no doubt because of lack of funds and opportunity. The American soldiers were remarkable, according to European standards, for their moral behavior. There were prostitutes in the ports to relieve Patriot sailors of their pay. The Continentals had their female camp followers. In general, the Americans, less ascetic than Indian braves, neither were nor became vicious or debauched. The Marquis de Lafayette wished to keep French troops apart from their American allies, so that the Americans would not learn the corrupt habits of French soldiers. In February 1778, Samuel Adams declared that the Patriots were undergoing an "inundation of levity vanity luxury dissipation and indeed vice of every kind," and that the consequences were worse than the destruction wrought by "the whole force of the common enemy." Adams and others in Congress were offended merely because Continental officers, after the example of the British, desired to engage in amateur theatricals. One must distrust the judgment of the Puritan Adams, who might be less than scrupulous in politics, but was otherwise very exacting with respect to standards of conduct.

One pernicious result of the War of Independence was the increased popularity of duelling. Private armed contests according to the code of honor were not unknown among the Americans before the war, since not a few of them claimed to be gentlemen and a few of those few believed that pistols or swords at dawn were the proper means for solving disputes with other gentlemen. The Yankees, more civilized over duelling than other Americans, resorted less often to the polite arbitrament of lead and steel. However, many Continental officers acquired nice notions of honor with their commissions; their counterparts among their British enemies followed the code duello; the foreign officers who joined the Continentals subscribed to it; Patriot generals, colonels, majors, captains, and lieutenants issued and accepted challenges to private combat. In 1777 General Lachlan McIntosh killed in gentlemanly fashion young Button Gwinnett, a signer of the Declaration of Independence from Georgia. McIntosh thus created a scarcity of Gwinnett's signature that long endured, to the dismay of later Americans who sought to collect the autographs of all the men who put their names upon the Declaration. General John Cadwalader, serving as a champion of Washington, forced General Thomas Conway to the field of honor and wounded him so badly that Conway almost died. The gallant young officer John Laurens, as a defender of Washington's honor, fought General Charles Lee after the battle of Monmouth and injured him. Then both General Anthony Wayne and the Baron von Steuben demanded satisfaction from Lee, but accepted verbal explanations in lieu of the privilege of shooting or stabbing him. It was his status as a retired officer and a gentleman that led Alexander Hamilton to go to the duelling ground at Weehawken in 1804 with Aaron Burr, despite the fact that Hamilton had recently lost a son in personal combat. The killing of Hamilton, followed by indictments against Burr for murder, brought duelling into disrepute everywhere in the Northern states. However, the barbarous custom continued for a time among military men, lingered longer among Southerners, and persisted in the Wild West, in the form of ungentlemanly and deadly contests with six-guns, into the twentieth century.

If the war brought many trials to the Patriots, the sufferings of their internal enemies, the Loyalists, were far greater. The Tories did not escape the afflictions visited upon the Patriots; at the same time they became the prey of their neighbors, their former friends, even of their kin; at last tens of thousands of them became exiles. Of every 100 colonists in 1775, two or three did not become—or at least ceased to be—Americans, many because they were formally banished, others because they were persecuted beyond endurance.

For the Patriots, despising passive Loyalists, hated active ones. The rancor which they harbored against the Tories was deep-seated. Washington, normally neither hotheaded nor passionate, condemned them in strong language. Franklin employed the most severe terms about them, and he never fully forgave his son William for espousing the cause of the empire. Other Patriots cursed them at length and with fervor in general, and abused individuals in particular. Loyalists who took no part in public affairs, who kept quiet, might suffer only economic and social ostracism, might even escape the unwanted attention of the Patriots. Those who made known their opinions by word or deed encountered very different treatment. Brutal champions of American freedom in Massachusetts daubed the house of Tory Edward Stow with faeces and feathers in May 1770, repeated the performance on the following July 5, and covered it with whale oil and feathers on July 9. Early in 1774 a Massachusetts mob seized Jonathan Malcolm, a tidewaiter, ripped off his clothing with such force that he had an arm broken, covered him with tar and feathers, and paraded him about for hours, punctuating their marching with beatings of the unfortunate official. Another Massachusetts mob burned the house of Peter Frye in Salem in October 1774, and a third one rode Daniel Dunbar upon a sharp rail in 1775. It is reported that Filer Diblee of Connecticut, his family being plundered four times by the Patriots, collapsed under the strain, "took a razor from the closet, threw himself on the bed, drew the curtains, and cut his own throat"; that Millington Lockwood of Connecticut, wounded in the head by the Patriots, went insane and drowned himself. In Augusta, Georgia, Thomas Browne, a Loyalist who refused to keep quiet, who publicly defended Britain, was coated with tar and feathers at the beginning of the war. Later as one of the successors of John Stuart, Browne instigated Indian attacks upon the frontiers of Georgia. Who will utterly condemn that maltreated man for seeking barbarous revenge?

Such brutal acts of private enterprise did not cease after 1775, because earlier mob members were presented with abundant opportunities as soldiers to vent their feelings upon the royal forces. Moreover, American legislatures and civil officers struck officially and oppressively against their domestic enemies. The Patriots detested the Tories because they were formidable. But they were also swayed by spiteful jealousies, by less than holy passions, and by lust for Loyalist property. Patriots who had not been able to secure royal or proprietary offices envied Loyalists who had obtained those dignities, with the salaries and fees attached. Congregationalist and Presbyterian clergymen and laymen dominated by narrow dogma and sectarian malevolence eagerly hit at Anglican rectors who were themselves less than generous-minded and who stood for the King.

Patriot tenants took advantage of an opportunity to break free from liberal as well as extortionate Loyalist landlords. Patriot debtors aimed blows with pleasure at Tory creditors. Many Patriots hoped to pay for the war by seizing and selling Loyalist estates and shops at auction; and not a few of them sought to become owners of Tory lands and businesses at small cost to themselves.

The primary reason for persecuting the Tories, to be sure, was that they were formidable, not in themselves, but as allies of Britain and the royal forces. Although they were not sufficiently numerous to hold their own against the Patriots in any state, or any large area, they formed a substantial minority everywhere, except in New England and Virginia. Proportionately, there were probably more of them in New York and Georgia than in the other American commonwealths. How many were they, in all? No one can say with assurance. Attempting to borrow money in Holland, John Adams said they made up no more than a tenth of the population; he was then trying to persuade Dutchmen that the Patriots would be able to pay back loans. On another occasion he estimated that nearly one third of the whole was Tory. Joseph Galloway once contended that the Loyalists comprised the great bulk of the population, four fifths of it, even nine tenths. The number of Loyalists was often exaggerated at the time, by Tories seeking to encourage British action, by Patriots alarmed and striving to goad their fellows to make greater efforts. Altogether, the Loyalists very likely formed one fifth to one fourth of the colonists. Perhaps one person in ten was neutral, or nearly neutral. If these fractions are approximately true—they cannot be remote from reality—the Patriots were not an aggressive minority, but a militant majority. Had such not been the case, the rebellion must have failed, since the Tories were not less vigorous, less soldierly than the Patriots.

For the American adherents of the King, taking the field somewhat tardily, because they did not at first believe their services were needed, supplied more and more fighting men for the cause of the Crown. They took the field as militia; some enlisted in regiments of British regulars and in the royal navy; many carried weapons in specially created regiments and corps of "provincials." It has been conjectured that as many as 50,000 Loyalists wielded arms for the empire; they can hardly have been fewer than 30,000. In the last years of the war Tory units containing, at least on paper, more than 10,000 men, formed an important fraction of the royal forces; they were especially active, determined, and redoubtable in the campaigns of 1780 and 1781 in the South.

Nor were the contributions of the Tories in behalf of the King confined to military service on the Atlantic seaboard. It will be recalled that they stimulated Indians to take up arms and that they took part in raids upon the American frontiers. They supplied information to the British; they acted as spies; they guided royal troops. They concealed foodstuffs from the Patriots and sold them to the British. A committee of Loyalists at New York sent out privateers to hunt down Patriot merchant vessels. New Hampshire Tories forged several million dollars of Continental money. Loyalist editors published newspapers and propaganda in behalf of Britain, notably at New York, Philadelphia, and Charleston; and Loyalist pamphleteers and poets railed at and satirized the Patriots. The squibs directed against the Patriots as a body and as individuals by the clever and witty James Rivington in his New York newspaper made them squirm, although Washington may actually have chuckled over the propaganda put forth by Rivington, for there is reason to believe that the printer was also a spy for the general.

As early as January 1776 the Congress urged the Revolutionary régimes in the several colonies to begin formal repression of the Tories, to prevent them from speaking or writing against the American cause. In November 1777 it asked the states to seize and sell the property of the Loyalists and to lend the proceeds to the Congress for the support of the war effort. The state governments needed no spurring. They moved as zealously and as quickly against the friends of the King as Congress could desire. They rapidly deprived the Tories of freedom of speech and press. Moreover, they soon resorted to the oath of allegiance as a most effective device to ascertain, to curb, and to punish the Tories. The oath was uniformly couched in such terms that a firm and scrupulous adherent of the Crown could not subscribe to it. Cautious and timid Loyalists took the solemn pledge to evade penalties imposed upon those who declined to take it, but the stouter Tories commonly refused to offer solemn homage to a cause they detested. Thus identified as enemies, they were trapped. Those who would not execute the oath were fined and stripped of citizenship, the suffrage, and the right to hold office. In some states they were denied access to the courts. There were states in which refractory physicians, lawyers, and teachers were not permitted to practice their professions. Some non-signing Loyalists were forced to pay taxes three times those imposed upon their Patriot neighbors. Hundreds of laws cramped and harassed the Tories in diverse ways.

But such penalties were minor compared to those which were inflicted upon Loyalists designated by the Patriots as traitors, they being usually defined as persons who had accepted a British commission, had served in the royal forces, or had encouraged others to enlist in those forces. Every one of the states passed laws which declared their property

454

to be forfeit, in part or *in toto*. Such Loyalists might be imprisoned; they were commonly banished. If expelled Tories failed to leave, or returned to their homes, they were subject to execution. In consequence, thousands of Loyalists, preferring exile to prison or death, departed. Often they were given no opportunity to defend their conduct, being simply condemned by name in legislative acts. Even individuals who were British-born, who could not reasonably be classified as colonists, were thus mulcted of lands, houses, and goods. There were Patriots who protested against expropriation of the Tories, but in vain so long as the war continued. The taking of the estates of the Loyalists was even justified by the specious contention that they had supplied false information and encouragement to tyrannical British ministers before the battle of Lexington and Concord. One cannot be impressed by that flimsy excuse. The Patriots in general were determined to subdue their domestic enemies and to force them to pay as much of the cost of the war as possible; and individual Patriots sought cheaply to acquire Tory patrimonies. Patriots who condemned confiscation as immoral and unwise were answered by "A Sentry" in the Maryland *Gazette* of March 3, 1780. "Good God! What is this state come to . . . we cannot take the property of our enemies to pay our taxes, when, if it was in their power, they would take our lives." A week later "A Maryland Officer" went to the support of "A Sentry" in the same newspaper. "Let the assembly give it to us, and all the devils in hell shall not take it from us." Tory property worth millions of pounds was seized by the Patriots.

The American states ceased to press punitive laws against the Tories soon after the close of the war. In fact, within a decade most of them softened or removed penalties imposed upon the adherents of the King. Were the Loyalists harshly treated? A few of them were formally tried and executed, at least ostensibly because they had committed offenses against military law. Some others who had carried arms were killed without trial by enraged Patriot partisans, usually because they had committed—or were believed to have perpetrated—atrocities. A minority of Tories lost part or all of their property. When it is considered that the War of Independence was, insofar as the Loyalists and Patriots were concerned, a civil war, one may conclude that the colonists who supported the empire, according to European standards of the eighteenth century, were not remarkably abused. It is nevertheless ironic that the Americans who asserted the sanctity of the rights of mankind violated the rights of Loyalist mankind, necessarily—and unnecessarily.

Even neutrals suffered at the hands of the Patriots. There were many Tories, such as Peter Kemble of New Jersey, General Gage's father-in-law, who were respected and liked, who lived quietly, who escaped serious injury. But the most inoffensive Tory might incur the wrath of the Patriots, for they were inclined to classify neutrals with their enemies, to assume that those who were not with them were against them. It has been suggested that perhaps one tenth of the colonists committed themselves neither to King nor to Congress. Included in that fraction were the majority of the Quakers. A few of the Friends rallied to the Patriot cause, some even taking up arms in its behalf. More of them doubtless preferred allegiance to Britain above American Independence. It was difficult, of course, for the Patriots to separate Quaker neutrals from Quaker enemies. Was not the follower of George Fox and William Penn who consorted with the British in Pennsylvania, who sold his cattle to British commissaries rather than to American ones when the Continentals were half-starved, an adherent of the Crown? There was clamor in Pennsylvania against the Quakers before the war. It grew during the conflict. Leaders among them were singled out, removed from their homes, and detained at a safe distance from the British forces. Two Pennsylvania Quakers who had served as guides for Sir William Howe were executed by the Patriots amidst great commotion.

Ardent Patriots, lukewarm Patriots, neutrals, moderate Loyalists, stout Tories—none of them were unaffected by the war.

CHAPTER XXVIII

The End of the War

THE war went on and on. All those engaged in it became weary. Britain fought tenaciously against her diverse enemies, and it seemed that victory might at last go to the least exhausted of the combatants. But Lord Cornwallis insisted upon taking the offensive in America. He was permitted to concentrate a British army in Virginia. The French and the Americans had three times failed to trap a British force between a French fleet and an allied army. They tried once more, and their perseverance earned them a stunning triumph over Cornwallis in October 1781. The war then drew rapidly toward a close in the American theater. Although it continued furiously elsewhere for some months, the downfall of Cornwallis signaled the achievement of independence by the United States.

It will be recalled that the paramount duty of Lord Cornwallis, under the orders given him by Sir Henry Clinton in the late spring of 1780, was to defend the conquests made in the South by the British commander in chief. Clinton desired that Cornwallis refrain from undertaking expensive and hazardous adventures. However, Cornwallis was permitted to take the offensive, if he did not thereby seriously risk the loss of those conquests. Should the Patriot forces opposing him become feeble, he was also authorized to move northward into North Carolina and into Virginia. Clinton then optimistically thought that Cornwallis might be able to push as far along the coast as Baltimore. But if the Patriots offered much resistance, Cornwallis was to hold Charleston, to act on the defensive, and to send troops he did not need to Clinton. It was possible for him to act aggressively, to obey the letter of his instructions, and to violate their spirit. He did not fail to seize his opportunity. Even

457

before the battle of Camden, he decided that it would be difficult to retain mastery over South Carolina so long as the Patriots could use North Carolina as a base for mounting attacks upon his forces. "I see no safety for this province but in moving forwards as soon as possible," he informed Clinton, urging that Clinton assist him by sending an expedition from New York to the Chesapeake to create a diversion in the rear of the Patriots under Horatio Gates. Cornwallis did not intend to spend his energies in hunting down guerrillas like Sumter, Marion, and Pickens in South Carolina and in fending off Patriot attacks from North Carolina. He proposed to destroy his distant enemies. The partisans, deprived of hope of help, could then be wiped out.

The easy victory won by Cornwallis at Camden encouraged him to march into the interior of North Carolina. Bringing up additional troops, he moved northward from Camden on September 8 at the head of an army that was far superior to the shattered forces Gates was trying to revive at Hillsborough. Brushing aside small bodies of Patriots that sought to obstruct his march, Cornwallis occupied the village of Charlotte, southwest of Hillsborough, on September 25. He remained there until October 14, and then retreated, not because Gates confronted him in overwhelming strength—Gates had not moved from his camp—but because of a growing danger posed, surprisingly, by Patriot backwoodsmen to his rear.

As usual, when the British advanced far into the interior, the American militia took the field in impressive numbers. As Cornwallis advanced, Major Patrick Ferguson, leading a Loyalist corps containing perhaps 1,200 men, moved forward from Ninety-Six in South Carolina. He was to disperse any small forces of Patriots that he might encounter, to collect Tory volunteers, and to join Cornwallis at Charlotte. But Ferguson did not reach that place. Pursuing, Ferguson suddenly became the pursued. Riflemen from the hills of North Carolina and Virginia, even frontiersmen from the Watauga settlements, converged upon him at Gilberttown in North Carolina late in September. Colonel Isaac Shelby and Colonel William Campbell of Virginia, Colonel Benjamin Cleveland and Colonel Charles McDowell of North Carolina, and the redoubtable border fighter, Colonel John Sevier, issued the call to arms and set out to find Ferguson. The backwoodsmen increased in number as they approached Gilberttown, and it became evident to Ferguson that he could not stand against them. He fled rapidly southward and then eastward, sending an appeal to Cornwallis for help as he went. He could not elude his enemies. About 900 of them were mounted, and they followed him closely. It became evident that he would soon be surrounded by swarming militia. He therefore established his force on the level summit of King's Mountain in South Carolina in the hope that he could hold out until relief came from Cornwallis. Sending out about 200 men to forage, he was busily engaged in preparing to defend his position when the mounted riflemen appeared at the foot of the hill, on October 7. They did not wait for the militia on foot to join them. Dismounting and attacking from three sides, they climbed the hill. When the Tories fired at them, they took cover behind trees and brush, then resumed their ascent. Some of Ferguson's men were armed with home-made bayonets. They drove back one body of Patriots as it drew near the summit, then another, but they suffered from rifle fire and they could not hold off all the frontiersmen. The backwoodsmen gained the summit, and they shot at the Tories from all sides. Some of them tried to surrender. Ferguson would not let them hoist the white flag, fought on until resistance was hopeless, and was killed when he tried to escape by cutting his way through the Patriots. His men then began to lay down their arms. The frontiersmen continued to fire at them, killing some of them even after they had sat down weaponless in token of surrender. Remembering the slaughter of helpless Patriots by Tarleton and misdeeds of Ferguson's men, they exacted a cruel revenge before their officers could restrain them. Ferguson's force was destroyed. Only the foraging party he had sent out earlier managed to flee to safety. More than 150 of the Loyalists were killed; the remainder, including many wounded, were captured. Even after the heat of the battle had passed, the Patriots displayed blood lust. They hanged nine Tories supposedly guilty of atrocities.

King's Mountain was a crushing defeat for the royal forces. Tarleton, sent out by Cornwallis to the relief of Ferguson, was much too late to help him. He brought the news back to the British general. The militia were rising all about Cornwallis. He lacked supplies, and he reluctantly gave the order to retreat. Racked by fever, he rode southward in a wagon to Winnsboro, South Carolina, while his men beat off attacks by militia. They camped at Winnsboro and rested.

Reposing and recovering his health in South Carolina, Cornwallis had time to think. Except for waging guerrilla warfare, the Patriots remained quiet. He had been forced to fall back without striking a blow at the American army under Gates; in fact, he was still more than 150 miles away from that army when he began his retreat. It was clear enough that the numerous militia of North Carolina and Virginia were not to be despised when fighting in their own country and in their own way. The name of Banastre Tarleton no longer aroused terror among the Patriots; fighting against the Americans in several small engagements, Tarleton had been sometimes victorious, sometimes defeated. Cornwallis might well have concluded that he should remain on the defensive. He could rather easily maintain his supply lines. If the Patriots managed to gather enough strength to assail him, he could choose the ground upon which to fight, and he could be confident of the result. Had he followed that course, recommended by Clinton, the Patriots could hardly have shaken the British grip upon South Carolina and Georgia. At least they would not have been able to strike effectively without powerful assistance from the French; and it was doubtful that even French help would have served to dislodge the royal troops in the far South.

But Cornwallis, as we have seen, disliked the prudent defensive. War of attrition was not to his taste. His instinct was to attack his enemies, and his pride had been injured. If he could move against the army under Gates, if he could muster enough men to secure equality with the Patriot army in terms of numbers, why could he not repeat his triumph at Camden? He was given an opportunity to strike a second time into the interior of North Carolina, and he seized it. Sir Henry Clinton had not been pleased to learn about the first advance of Cornwallis into that state. However, he had undertaken to make the diversion in Virginia requested by the earl. The departure of an expedition to Chesapeake Bay was delayed, but Major General Alexander Leslie entered it on October 20 with 2,500 men. Leslie was instructed to establish a base, to raid Richmond and Petersburg, to get in touch with Cornwallis, and to follow his orders. Clinton intended that Leslie remain in Virginia. However, he permitted Cornwallis to do as he pleased, and Cornwallis arranged to bring Leslie's troops into the Carolinas. He thus acquired enough men both to defend the posts held by the British in South Carolina and Georgia and to take the field with a strong army of 4,000 British regulars, Hessians, and Loyalists. Moreover, Clinton offered him additional encouragement by sending 2,000 more men to the Chesapeake under Brigadier General Benedict Arnold. The turncoat was ordered to establish a base at Portsmouth, Virginia, to raid into the interior of the Old Dominion, and so to interrupt the flow of Patriot supplies southward and to give the Virginians military business at home.

Before Cornwallis could move, the Continental forces in North Carolina acquired new leadership. Daniel Morgan appeared at the camp of Gates. Disappointed because he had not been promoted to the rank of brigadier general, Morgan had resigned from the American army and had gone home in 1779. He had another reason for remaining quiet, for his health was uncertain. He suffered from rheumatism and also from hemorrhoids. But he was needed, and he returned to duty despite his psychic and physical difficulties—Congress soon removed his mental trouble by making Colonel Morgan a general. Then General Nathanael Greene came southward to replace Gates. It was apparent after his defeat at Camden that Gates was not equal to arduous command in the South and that he ought to be replaced. Congress therefore asked Washington to name his successor, and Washington immediately chose Greene. On December 3, at Charlotte, with befitting ceremony, Gates turned over his army of 1,500 men to Greene, who was kind to his unfortunate predecessor. The crestfallen Gates traveled northward. In Richmond the Virginia assembly thanked him for his efforts. He responded by declaring his devotion to the Patriot cause. Later he returned to duty upon Washington's staff, married a wealthy Virginia heiress, and comfortably spent his old age in New York City. Some historians, superfluously seeking to exalt Washington, have dealt harshly with other Patriot generals, Gates especially. They have given him little or no credit for Saratoga, have magnified his defeat at Camden. No informed scholar has ever questioned his loyalty to the United States.

Nor has any historian condemned Nathanael Greene, a favorite of Washington, for incompetence. He was not a great commander; he never won a major victory over the British. But, laboring under many difficulties, he proved to be more than a match for Cornwallis and other British commanders in the South. He was thoughtful, methodical, steady in adversity, and cautious in prosperity. He won the respect and trust of his officers and men. It is unlikely that any other Patriot general could have accomplished more than he did in the theater of war of the Carolinas and Georgia.

Greene did not strive to be brilliant, to crush his opponents by sudden and swift strokes. Rather, encouraging the Patriot partisans to continue to harry detachments of the royal forces, he at first sought merely to develop a stable and sturdy army that could hold Cornwallis in check. He foresaw that supply would be his greatest difficulty. As he traveled southward to assume command, he urged Patriot officials in Delaware, Maryland, and Virginia to do everything possible to send him food, clothing, and ammunition—his army could not live well upon the lean countryside of the Carolinas. Despite his efforts, his men often suffered from severe shortages. Similarly, Greene studied the territory in which he would serve, had maps of it made. He observed that it was traversed by many rivers; he had boats built that could be carried on wheels and wagons, that enabled his army to move swiftly over those streams. But if Greene was systematic, he was not a slave to military convention; he was energetic; when it seemed necessary, he was audacious.

461

Indeed, Greene adopted a bold course immediately after he succeeded Gates. His small army was growing. His hungry and thirsty men soon devoured all the cattle and drank all the rum available in any area where they camped. It would be much easier to obtain nourishment for them if the army were divided into two parts and stationed in regions where food and drink were relatively abundant. Accordingly, he sent Daniel Morgan with about 600 men to the westward of the Catawba River. He himself took post with some 1,100 troops at Cheraw Hill in upper South Carolina, some 140 miles to the eastward. There Greene received valuable reinforcements, Light-Horse Harry Lee and his Legion, together with 400 Virginia militia. He also received splendid news from Morgan.

Dividing his army, Greene knew that one part of it might be destroyed in the absence of the other. He relied upon the ability of his troops to retreat rapidly in case of need, and he had faith in Daniel Morgan. The trust that he placed in that officer was well founded. Moreover, Cornwallis, somewhat puzzled by the unorthodox strategy of Greene, made a mistake. Ready to advance at the beginning of 1781, he sent out Banastre Tarleton, on January 2, to crush Morgan's contingent, while he himself moved northward. Having dealt with Morgan, Tarleton was to rejoin the main British army. Remembering the fate of Patrick Ferguson, he might well have refrained from detaching Tarleton, but he put confidence in that officer.

Tarleton moved with his customary celerity. He set out with 1,100 men, including his own Legion, British infantrymen, 50 British cavalrymen, and some Tory militia. He took with him two small cannon. It was not necessary for him to pursue Morgan very far. Reinforced by Patriot militia, so that his numbers were almost equal to those of Tarleton, Morgan was not unwilling to fight. Retreating before Tarleton on January 15 and 16, the American general established his army at the Cowpens in South Carolina and awaited the onslaught of the royal troops. He imprudently chose ground from which he could not easily retreat, for a creek ran athwart part of his rear. Greene would hardly have approved the location chosen by Morgan. But he could not otherwise have found fault with his subordinate. Morgan knew that Tarleton would attack frontally, and he was well aware that his own militia, being riflemen, would in all probability run for safety when they were exposed to a British bayonet charge. He made his arrangements accordingly. He would not have another Camden. His army was located in an open wood. He placed reliable Maryland and Delaware Continentals, together with some of his militia accustomed to battle, in a line across a low hill. Behind them he put

462

Colonel William Washington, a cousin of the general and a veteran officer, with two small bodies of cavalry. He stationed two lines of riflemen in front, carefully instructing them so that they would not disrupt his other troops by a helter-skelter retreat. They need not fear a charge by royal infantry or cavalry. They were to fire twice, choose officers for targets, aim low, do as much damage to the enemy as possible, and flee around the left wing of the Continentals. Their horses were tied behind the Continentals, and they could ride off, if they chose. Morgan's plan was better executed than he could have hoped. Tarleton came up on January 17 and hastily attacked. The riflemen beat back one British charge with deadly fire, then fled as directed. Colonel Washington drove off British dragoons who pursued them. Sure of victory, Tarleton drove against the main American line, and was repulsed by Morgan's veterans. Tarleton brought up reserves, and charged again, against their right flank. They turned to face him, beat back their assailants, and took the offensive. The retreating riflemen, having traversed the rear of the American position, came up to strike at the British left. Colonel Washington hit the royal troops upon their right flank. They broke and ran. Tarleton escaped with 140 horsemen, but more than half of his army was killed or captured. His fearsome reputation was gone, and he rejoined Cornwallis as just another good cavalry officer. Daniel Morgan rejoiced. He had "whupped" Tarleton.

Morgan had achieved much more than a brilliant and useful little victory. Cornwallis had suffered "a very unexpected and severe blow." He determined to retrieve the loss inflicted upon his army, to pursue and destroy Morgan's force. He still had more than 2,500 men, perhaps even 3,000. Morgan fled northward, with Cornwallis following him. The British general, failing to catch his prey, destroyed his tents, his rum, and all his heavy baggage so as to move faster. He could not come up with the rapidly moving victors of Cowpens. Greene ordered the contingent at Cheraw Hill to fall back into North Carolina, brought together the two parts of his army, and took post at Guilford Courthouse. Cornwallis continued to advance. Greene was almost strong enough to offer battle, but he prudently refrained. He would not fight when the odds favored Cornwallis. Was not battle precisely what the British general wanted? Greene resolved to retreat further, to draw Cornwallis after him, even into Virginia. The British would lose strength, the Patriots would become stronger. With Cornwallis close behind, but checked briefly again and again by the American rear guard, Greene made his way over the Dan River in mid-February in the boats he had sagaciously built when he assumed command. Cornwallis could not easily cross the swollen stream.

Greene would gain recruits in Virginia. The British commander had lost 250 men in the pursuit, and his supplies were running low. He had no choice but to fall back. Reluctantly, he reversed his steps and made his way to Hillsborough.

One disappointment after another came to Cornwallis in North Carolina. Assuming the pose of a conqueror—had he not driven Greene from the state?—he called upon its Loyalists to join him. They began to gather, but soon decided that it was imprudent to show themselves. Assured that he would be reinforced by Virginians and North Carolinians, Greene returned from the Old Dominion. He sent out mobile troops from Virginia to suppress the Tories. Light-Horse Harry Lee surprised a body of 400 Loyalists who had collected under Colonel John Pyle, killed many of them, and dispersed the rest. Thereafter Cornwallis had to rely upon the troops he had brought with him. He soon exhausted the resources of Hillsborough and moved westward. Meanwhile Greene's army grew so big that its commander judged it safe to offer battle. With at least 4,500 men—all but 500 of them, to be sure, were militia—Greene took post at Guilford Courthouse on March 14. At last Cornwallis had the chance to meet Greene in formal combat that he had so long sought, but he no longer had enough men to be confident of victory, no more than 2,000 that he could lead into battle. However, his army, largely composed of veteran British regulars and Hessians, contained as fine soldiers as could be found. He did not refuse the challenge. On the morning of March 15 he boldly attacked Greene. The American general had substantially adopted the tactics employed by Morgan at Cowpens, placing his militia riflemen in two forward lines, with his Continentals forming a third one and with Colonel Washington and Light-Horse Harry Lee covering his flanks. Again the deadly fire of the riflemen shattered ranks of the royal troops, but they bravely re-formed, drove many of the militia from the field, and engaged in a desperate struggle with the Continentals. The outcome became uncertain. Greene might have won a decisive victory by a counterattack with all of his remaining troops; on the other hand, the cost of defeat would be heavy. At length, with his reserves covering his retreat, he withdrew from the field. Cornwallis had gained his victory. But was it victory? Almost 100 of his men were killed, more than 400 wounded; Greene's losses, except for decamping militia, were smaller. Cornwallis did not have strength enough to pursue the Americans, to reap profit from his triumph. In fact, his army was so weakened that he could not safely stay in the interior of North Carolina. He led what remained of it eastward to Wilmington, and thence to—Virginia and disaster.

Greene, not Cornwallis, took the offensive after Guilford Courthouse. When the British general marched eastward, the Patriot commander moved southward. It was obvious that he intended to attack the British posts in South Carolina and Georgia, and it is equally clear that it was the first duty of Cornwallis to go to the rescue of the British detachments scattered over South Carolina and Georgia and, above all, to protect the British base at Chaleston. Indeed, on the defensive, with short supply lines, the Earl would doubtless have been able to hold the Patriots indefinitely at bay in the far South. But Cornwallis, at Wilmington, engaged in some thinking, an activity in which he did not excel. He had become, he said, "quite tired of marching about the country in search of adventure." Nor was he much interested in standing upon the defensive in South Carolina and Georgia, duty or no duty. In fact, he concluded, Britain gained nothing from Clinton's defensive warfare "mixed with desultory expeditions." Could not the war be won by battle in Virginia? It might be worthwhile, he fancied, even to evacuate New York in order to concentrate upon an offensive in Virginia. He had been authorized to go into that state—after he had subjugated North Carolina. He knew that he was in favor in London, and he ignored his instructions—or should one say that he interpreted them to please himself? He marched northward from Wilmington with his 1,600 men, effected a junction at Petersburg on May 20 with other British forces sent to Virginia by Clinton, and assumed command. His thinking was confused; he had no plan, which, if executed, must lead to the downfall of the Patriots; nor could he be sure that he would be given enough troops by Clinton to act aggressively on a grand scale. It seems not to have occurred to him that he was again "marching about the country in search of adventure," nor that he might be trapped by a French fleet dominating Chesapeake Bay.

With the departure of Cornwallis, Greene was able to proceed effectively against the British forces that remained in South Carolina and Georgia. Commanded by Lord Rawdon, they numbered about 8,000 men, and they were sufficiently formidable to offer stout resistance to Patriots frequently suffering from lack of food and clothing. However, Greene called upon the Patriot partisans for help, received it, and began to reduce seven forts that ringed Charleston and Savannah. Light-Horse Harry Lee and Francis Marion captured one of those posts, Fort Watson, on April 23. Lord Rawdon advanced with 1,500 troops to protect his garrisons, and attacked Greene two days later, at Hobkirk's Hill, near Camden. Greene had as many troops, but was worsted after a hard-fought battle and forced to retreat. However, Rawdon prudently withdrew toward Charleston, and Patriot contingents took five more of the British outposts in the spring of 1781. Greene himself undertook to seize the last of them, Ninety-Six. As usual, he encountered defeat and gained the fruits of victory. A Loyalist garrison bravely held out in Ninety-Six for a month, until Rawdon, having received reinforcements, came forward to compel Greene to raise the siege. But Rawdon, realizing that Ninety-Six could not be held indefinitely, ordered its evacuation on July 3 and fell back toward Charleston. Three months after the departure of Cornwallis for Virginia, the British conquests in the far South had shrunk to Wilmington, Charleston, Savannah, and the districts adjacent to those places.

The shrewd and resourceful Greene never had the pleasure of driving the British out of South Carolina or Georgia. They clung tightly to their footholds. He remained unfortunate on the battlefield. At the end of the summer of 1781, having collected 2,300 men, including many veterans, he advanced toward Charleston. He did not have enough strength to take that place; he could not even invest it. With a force equal in numbers Colonel Alexander Stuart, successor to Lord Rawdon, faced Greene at Eutaw Springs on September 8. The Patriot general attacked; his tactics were sound; his tried and true Continentals behaved with their customary gallantry; his militia conducted themselves well. Stuart's troops fought with equal courage. The tide of battle swayed back and forth in a bloody struggle. At last the royal soldiers broke and fled. But victory continued to elude Greene. Pursuing, Greene's Continentals entered the British camp, found rum, and celebrated their triumph. While they rejoiced, their enemies re-formed their ranks. The royal troops returned to the fray, drove back the Americans, and forced Greene to retire from the field. However, they won glory without profit. Greene sustained many casualties, but the British losses were much heavier. More than 800 of Stuart's men were killed, wounded, or captured. Moreover, Stuart had no choice but to retire toward Charleston.

After the hard-fought battle at Eutaw Springs the bulk of the British remained within their lines at Charleston and Savannah. Greene's troops —and the Patriot partisans, no longer compelled to hit and run—hovered about the two British bases. They were too exhausted to strike. At last, after the end of fighting in Virginia, Continentals from the Middle States came to help them. Their services were not needed, for the end of the war was in sight. The British then evacuated Wilmington. When at last the forces of George III left Charleston, Greene, his troops, and the partisans joyfully entered the city. Soon the guerrillas entered into a debate with the Continentals and militia who had come southward to fight the British. Greene's men claimed that victory had been achieved largely through their efforts. The partisans contended that they had made a large contribution. There was credit enough for them to share. Another debate had already begun, among the British. Participants in it sought, not to divide glory, but to apportion responsibility for a crowning disaster at Yorktown.

Sir Henry Clinton, in New York, was shocked when he learned that Cornwallis had assumed command in Virginia. He had indeed authorized that general to move northward—provided that Cornwallis marched as a conqueror. He had not intended to concentrate large forces in Virginia, nor to make it a major battleground. He had sought to establish an easily defensible base on Chesapeake Bay; to punish the Patriots by raids from that base into the interior of the state; and to interrupt the flow of supplies southward to the army commanded by Gates and Greene. Benedict Arnold, sent to the Chesapeake with a small force by Clinton, was no less energetic as a British general than he had been as an American one. He had fortified a post at Portsmouth, and he had ravaged the Virginia countryside as far westward as Richmond. But Clinton had learned that it was dangerous to keep troops in Virginia. Arnold had not found a strong place on the shores of Chesapeake Bay that could easily be defended against attack by sea. Moreover, Arnold had twice been threatened with encirclement. In February 1781, ships from the French squadron at Newport had sailed for Virginia, but had turned back. In March a small French naval detachment seeking to enter Chesapeake Bay had been defeated in battle by Admiral Arbuthnot and had been drawn back to Newport. But Clinton had been given cause for worry. He had felt compelled to send more troops to Virginia, and he had placed the British forces there under the command of General William Phillips. However, he remained concerned lest the French establish themselves in superior force in the Bay. Admiral d'Estaing had appeared in American waters in 1778 and again in 1779, and the French squadron at Newport had posed a threat in 1781. Clinton feared that the French would make a great naval effort before the end of that year.

Putting together the contingent he had brought from North Carolina, Arnold's detachment, and the men brought to Virginia by Phillips, Cornwallis had more than 7,000 men when he assumed command at Petersburg. What was he to do with them? Clinton declared, "my wonder at this move of Lord Cornwallis will never cease. But he has made it, and we shall say no more but make the best of it." However, the British commander in chief and his aggressive subordinate continued to disagree, and they made at last the worst of it.

Cornwallis, clinging to his belief that Virginia was the key to the war and that a large army was necessary to secure the key, displayed his usual energy in the late spring of 1781. The raids of his predecessors in command in Virginia had aroused alarm among the Patriots, and they were

467

gathering to oppose the British. The Marquis de Lafayette, sent south-ward by Washington with 1,200 Continentals, had taken command of the Americans. He had been joined by Virginia militia, and 800 more Conti-nentals under General Anthony Wayne were en route from Washington's army. But Lafayette was far too weak to challenge Cornwallis. The Brit-ish general advanced beyond Richmond, destroying tobacco warehouses and a Patriot supply depot. He sent out Tarleton to raid, early in June, and Tarleton made his way as far as Charlottesville, driving Governor Jefferson and the Virginia legislature into ignominious flight. Then Corn-wallis turned eastward and marched to Williamsburg. Reinforced by Wayne's Continentals and riflemen from western Virginia, Lafayette fol-lowed him at a safe distance.

Cornwallis was seeking an ideal spot for a base. At Williamsburg on June 26 he received instructions from Clinton. The British commander in chief had learned that a powerful French fleet had left Brest in March and that it would doubtless eventually appear on the coasts of North America. He therefore resolved to prepare for an emergency. He proposed to con-centrate his troops in New York, leaving only a small force in Virginia to defend the base that Cornwallis planned to build. If the menace posed by that fleet could be warded off, he even hoped that the Patriots, exhausted, might in consequence lay down their arms. He therefore urged Cornwallis to find and fortify a strong place on Chesapeake Bay. Cornwallis should then lead the bulk of his troops to New York, by sea or by land. If he moved northward by land into Pennsylvania, Clinton would march from New York into New Jersey to meet him.

It is to be doubted that even a fourth failure by the French navy to help the Patriots would have led to the collapse of their cause. The resources of the Americans were strained. It is not likely that they would have yielded to an enemy holding only a few spots on their seacoast. Nevertheless, Clinton had intelligently devised a sound plan to meet an approaching emergency. But he did not execute it. He offered ideas, not orders, to Cornwallis. He even said that Cornwallis could keep in Virginia all of the troops there, if the Earl really needed them to build and protect a British base.

Cornwallis declined to execute the wishes of his superior. He mis-read them, deliberately, it would seem. He informed Sir Henry that the establishment of a base required that he keep all his troops in Virginia. More than 7,000 men? If he could not have all of them, he said, there was no reason for maintaining any troops in Virginia. Accordingly, the Earl told Clinton that he would lead them to Portsmouth and prepare for their voyage to New York. He asked permission to return to the Carolinas, and began to march toward Portsmouth, followed by Lafayette. At the James River he tried to trap the young Frenchman. Pretending to send almost all of his troops across that stream, he hid most of them in woods on its north bank, behind his rear guard. He hoped that Lafayette would commit himself to an assault upon his rear guard and expose the Patriot army to a crushing counterattack. Lafayette fell into the snare, but Cornwallis was unable to close it, because the approach of darkness gave Lafayette opportunity to fall back to safety. The British general proceeded on his way—and then retraced his steps.

Clinton should have let Cornwallis send his troops to New York, should have permitted that general to go back to the Carolinas, where he might have been useful. However, on June 27 the British commander in chief received a dispatch from Lord George Germain telling him that he should have been more active in the Chesapeake in the past, that he ought to be more aggressive there in the future. Clinton had long been contemplating resignation from his post; Cornwallis would doubtless be his successor; his superiors in London seemed to endorse the views of Cornwallis rather than his own. Against his own better judgment he hastily sent added instructions to his refractory subordinate. Cornwallis was not to sail back to the Carolinas. He must return with his troops to the peninsula between the James and York Rivers. He was urged to establish a principal base at Old Point Comfort and a smaller one at Yorktown. Clinton would be pleased to have Cornwallis send part of his forces to New York. But again, if that general believed that he needed all of his soldiers, he could keep them. Cornwallis was to have his own way. He sent none of his men to New York; he led his army to Yorktown; there, finding what he thought to be a location superior to Old Point Comfort, he at last began to fortify, early in August. Lafayette hovered just beyond his reach. Cornwallis built a trap, not for Lafayette, but for himself. He erected protective works not only at Yorktown, but also at Gloucester on the northern side of the York River. He remained at Yorktown until he became the quarry of overwhelming French and American forces.

For the Patriots and the French at last managed to combine their efforts successfully. The Americans, war-weary, eagerly sought to achieve more than a successful defensive in 1781. The Congress dispatched a special emissary to Paris, Colonel John Laurens, to urge that France send another fleet. The plea was supported by Washington, Rochambeau, and Lafayette. Laurens, with Benjamin Franklin, who had become the first American minister to France, presented it to a sympathetic Vergennes. France, too, was feeling the strain of war, but the ministers of Louis XVI determined to make a great effort. Admiral François Joseph Paul de

Grasse was ordered to take a powerful fleet of twenty warships to the West Indies, to proceed into North American waters in the summer, and to join the Patriots and the French forces in Rhode Island in a common enterprise against the British. He set sail from Brest across the Atlantic in March without molestation by the British home fleet. The news that de Grasse was on his way westward delighted Washington and Rochambeau. They met at Wethersfield, Connecticut, in May to lay plans for the time when de Grasse should appear. They agreed that the capture of New York should be the objective of the French and Americans. Accordingly, Rochambeau moved his army, about 5,000 men, from Newport to positions near those occupied by Washington outside New York. The Patriot general also arranged to raise New England militia for the hour of action. New York was a tempting target. Were it taken, the British could hardly continue the war in America. But Rochambeau was well aware that an attack upon the long-entrenched British in New York was not at all certain to succeed. When Cornwallis concentrated in the Chesapeake, the French general entreated Washington to alter his objective. The chances of taking Cornwallis's army were much better than those of forcing a surrender of New York by Clinton. Under pressure from Rochambeau and other French officers, Washington reluctantly agreed. The French minister to the United States, the Chevalier de la Luzerne, together with Rochambeau and Washington, sent messages to de Grasse urging him to come to Chesapeake Bay and to bring troops with him. The French admiral responded. He would reach the bay in August, and he would have with him more than 3,000 French regulars. He did precisely what he said he would do. He arrived at the entrance to the bay on August 30.

Meanwhile, Washington undertook to prevent the escape of Cornwallis by land. Learning in mid-August that de Grasse was sailing for the Chesapeake, he urged Lafayette to do everything possible to hold Cornwallis at Yorktown. Then, leaving a small force under General William Heath outside New York, he marched southward with Rochambeau, 2,000 Continentals, and Rochambeau's French troops. At the same time the French squadron at Newport set out for Virginia—the allies were determined to secure superiority on both land and sea, to crush Cornwallis. Washington's army marched through Philadelphia before Clinton could act. The British commander did not swiftly become alarmed for the safety of Cornwallis. He had been assured from London that the British navy would check de Grasse. He believed that de Grasse was bringing only part of his fleet into North American waters, and he fancied that the French admiral might be sailing for New York. He continued to believe for many days that his own forces and those of Cornwallis were quite safe. He might have assailed Heath's scanty army in the absence of Washington. To what avail? Heath would retreat and would be reinforced by New England militia. Clinton meditated but did not make an attack upon the French fleet at Newport, presumably exposed by the departure of Rochambeau. Then, at last, he learned of the mounting threat to Cornwallis and began to take part in an effort to rescue him.

The French and American troops moved into position against Cornwallis with the same precision that the French navy had displayed. French money smoothed Washington's march southward. At the beginning of September de Grasse put ashore the troops he had brought with him from the Caribbean. They joined Lafayette outside the entrenchments of Cornwallis. That general then learned that his army was in great peril. He was surrounded by land and sea. Should he rely upon the British navy to save him? Or should he drive through the allied troops and flee by land? He could hardly escape by land without suffering severe losses, because his army must march for hundreds of miles in hostile country and under attack to reach safety, whether he moved northward or southward. He chose to wait for the navy to expel the French fleet from the Chesapeake and to relieve him. Soon the allied troops became too strong for him to try to break out. Washington's army marched into Baltimore and Annapolis. There it embarked in transports efficiently provided by de Grasse, and was carried through the Chesapeake to the camps of the allies outside Yorktown. Cornwallis was then faced by a well-equipped and powerful army of about 16,000 men, half of them French, nearly all of them veterans. Moreover, contingents of Virginia militia were at hand to support the American and French regulars. If Cornwallis was to escape capture, he must indeed be delivered from the sea.

British politicians and admirals added their own mistakes to those of Cornwallis and Clinton. The British navy was not too weak to deal with de Grasse. It could muster enough warships to fight him upon equal terms; it possessed a special advantage, in that the British had learned how to protect their ships against barnacles with copper sheathing and could therefore remain at sea longer than French vessels. However, de Grasse—like d'Estaing in 1778—was permitted to cross the Atlantic in the spring of 1781 without molestation. His departure did not cause immediate alarm in London. Lord George Germain was then hopeful that rebel resistance in Virginia would soon collapse. Early in April, with the approval of Germain, Lord Dunmore was actually preparing to leave for Virginia to resume his interrupted duties as royal governor. It was assumed at the British capital that Sir George Rodney, who commanded a fleet in the West Indies, would check de Grasse and see to it that the

471

French admiral did no damage either in the Caribbean or elsewhere. The advisers of George III did not share the alarm expressed by Sir Henry Clinton in that same April. He declared that the success and even the safety of British troops in Virginia depended upon a "decided naval superiority." "Every precaution," wrote Clinton, should be taken "to give me at least timely notice of the contrary being likely to happen, as my ignorance of such an event might be most fatal in its consequences." In June, becoming somewhat more concerned about the safety of their forces in North America, the British war ministers sent warships, but only three of them, off to New York to reinforce the fleet stationed there.

Admiral Rodney performed no better than his superiors in London. Avaricious and conceited, he was a lucky man rather than an able one. Maneuvering against de Grasse in the Caribbean, he learned before the end of July that the French admiral was about to sail northward. It was Rodney's obvious duty to follow de Grasse, at least to send sufficient help to the small British fleet at New York so that it could hold its own against de Grasse—and the French squadron at Newport. He failed to act decisively. He chose to believe that de Grasse would leave part of his fleet to protect the French colonies in the West Indies against British attack; but de Grasse boldly set off with all of his ships, twenty-eight of them. Ill, Rodney himself sailed for England. Before he left, he ordered Admiral Sir Samuel Hood to proceed northward with fourteen ships. He sent two more to Jamaica on convoy duty and suggested to Sir Peter Parker, who commanded these, that Parker order the two, and four others stationed at Jamaica, to sail for North America. Unaware that the six war vessels would be badly needed in Chesapeake Bay, Parker did not start them off in time to be of service in the approaching crisis.

Thus it was that Sir Thomas Graves, who had succeeded Admiral Arbuthnot at New York, had to do what he could to rescue Cornwallis in the face of French naval superiority. He had only seven ships-of-the-line; with those brought into New York by Hood on August 27, he had nineteen fit for sailing. He was not aware that he could not match the power of de Grasse, nor was Hood. But the Newport squadron was already at sea, headed for the Chesapeake, and it was clear enough that Cornwallis was in danger. The two admirals went to the mouth of the bay, and found de Grasse within it. He came forth to fight. The fleets engaged on September 5. Graves was not a great admiral who could overcome heavy odds, and Hood was unable to infuse genius into Graves. In a less than desperate encounter de Grasse damaged five of the British ships and secured the advantage; and the British, after some futile maneuvering, went off to New York to prepare for a second effort. Returning to the bay, de Grasse found the Newport squadron at anchor. Its commander, the Comte de Barras, had slipped into the Chesapeake while Graves and Hood were busy with de Grasse. The French fleet in the bay had become almost too powerful to attack; the fate of Cornwallis's army was virtually sealed.

The Americans and the French had Cornwallis in their clutches, and they would not let go. The fortifications he had erected at Yorktown and secondarily at Gloucester did not constitute a Gilbraltar. His positions could be carried, and the allies had all that was necessary to break down resistance, including artillery, trained gunners, and engineers. Cornwallis knew that he could not resist them indefinitely. Even before they attacked, he wrote to Clinton that "If you cannot relieve me very soon, you must be prepared to hear the worst." Washington, with Rochambeau and the other French officers faithfully executing his orders, established lines opposite the British entrenchments on September 28. French and American troops under General de Choisy took post outside Gloucester to hem in a British garrison there and to prevent escape by Cornwallis through Gloucester. The bulk of the allied army encamped opposite Yorktown. Cornwallis promptly abandoned weaker fortifications about the village, and withdrew into his strongest positions. The allies moved forward into the works deserted by the British general. They began to bombard Yorktown with heavy artillery, and they built two entrenchments by means of which they could approach close enough to storm British defenses. They easily beat back a sally intended to disrupt their preparations. On October 15, in night attacks, they captured two key British redoubts. It became evident to Cornwallis that he could not hold out much longer against overwhelming force. He laid plans to lead his men across the York River, to break through the forces of General de Choisy, and to flee as best he might. A storm interrupted the preparation of boats on the river. There never was any real hope that a large part of hs army could make its way to safety. The hour drew near, if help from New York did not promptly appear, when he must yield.

The relief for which Cornwallis hoped did not come. In New York Sir Henry Clinton collected 7,000 men for an attempt at rescue. But he could accomplish nothing without the British fleet. Admiral Graves repaired his ships and obtained reinforcements. The days passed. Graves could not gather strength to match that of de Grasse. At last, on October 17, he set sail southward with a fleet no more than two thirds the size of that commanded by the French admiral. With Graves went Clinton and transports carrying the troops gathered by the general. How were Graves and Clinton to force their way into the Chesapeake and to extricate

Cornwallis? It was not necessary for them to answer those difficult questions. Before they reached the mouth of the bay, they received news that their mission was in vain, that Cornwallis had surrendered. They returned in dejection to New York.

It became impossible for Cornwallis to continue to resist on October 16. The artillery of the allies pounded his entrenchments, and his guns could not reply for lack of ammunition. On the following day the British general offered to lay down his arms, with stipulations. He asked that his troops be permitted to go to England under pledge that they would not serve again during the war against either America or France. Washington demanded a complete surrender. Cornwallis had no choice but to comply. On October 19 he signed papers that put his army, together with British sailors at Yorktown, more than 8,000 men, in the hands of Washington. At two o'clock in the afternoon, the defenders of Yorktown filed between lines of French and American troops to lay down their weapons. The ceremony was solemn, but not without a touch of humor. The Comte de Barras attended on horseback in behalf of de Grasse. He was not accustomed to horses. When his steed stretched to vent himself, Barras cried, "Good heavens! I believe my horse is sinking!" So says another French officer who was present. The French and British troops were resplendent in their uniforms; Washington's veterans, shabbily dressed, nevertheless looked like the fine soldiers that they were. Cornwallis did not appear to present his sword to Washington, as custom required. He claimed to be indisposed, and he commissioned General Charles O'Hara to act for him. Washington insisted upon proper protocol and made a gracious gesture. He referred O'Hara to General Benjamin Lincoln, who had been compelled to give up his own sword at Charleston, who now had the pleasure of receiving the symbol of surrender from O'Hara. Meanwhile, a British band played a song, "The World Turned Upside Down." Or was it "The King'll Come Into His Own Again," a song which seems to have had the same music?

The King did not come into his own again. The royal troops at Gloucester, together with Banastre Tarleton, also put down their weapons, and were sent off to prison camps with their comrades from Yorktown. The rejoicing Washington meditated another blow against the British. He asked de Grasse to join him in an attack upon New York or Charleston. The French admiral replied that he was needed in the Caribbean and sailed away. Washington marched northward and resumed his vigil at New York. De Grasse had done enough. He had superbly performed his part in what Rochambeau afterward called the "miracle of the blockade and capture of Cornwallis." The surrender of that general ultimately brought an end to the war. There was skirmishing in the Carolinas and Georgia after Yorktown, and also border warfare in the Ohio Valley. But the news of Yorktown at last moved Britain to abandon all effort to crush the rebellion in America.

In New York Charles Stuart, the son of the Earl of Bute, observed the approaching end of the long train of events which his father had helped to put in motion. He did not exaggerate when he described reports of the surrender of Cornwallis as "some of the blackest tidings ever received from this country." Frederick Smyth, a Loyalist at New York, glumly recognized the futility of continuing the struggle. He commented that the only active British officers were desk men under Clinton who drew handsome profits from official business. Cornwallis, on parole, appeared at New York and then proceeded to England to make his excuses for the disaster he had encountered. He succeeded beyond his deserts. He managed to secure new military appointments, and he afterward won glory in India, where he was not confronted by backwoods riflemen, Daniel Morgan, Nathanael Greene, or Washington. Surveying the wreck of his hopes, Clinton disconsolately recognized that the end had come. For a time Clinton feared that even New York would fall to the Patriots and the French. There was, he said, "no judging in what multitudes the neighboring populous provinces" would "pour out their warlike militia" against his base. Returning to England in 1782, he engaged Cornwallis in a bitter war of words which he did not win. He could not convince the British public that he was not largely responsible for the stunning defeat inflicted upon forces under his command. There was no new and splendid career for him. He wrote a history of the war to justify his conduct that remained unpublished until the twentieth century. It is sufficiently apparent that most of the blame for that crowning disaster must be apportioned among Cornwallis, Clinton, Sir George Rodney, and their superiors in London. In their behalf, it must be said that their mistakes cost so dearly because the actions of Patriots and the French were constantly attended by good fortune. It is not too surprising that a patriotic nineteenth-century American historian, George Bancroft, could see in the chain of events that led to Yorktown the moving hand of the Deity.

The competent historian must not profess to plumb the intentions of that Governor of the universe to whom the leaders of the Patriots appealed, nor to understand the purposes of any other Divinity. Nor must he yield to the temptation to indulge in false drama. There have been persons who have looked upon the struggle at Yorktown as one that must bring either victory or final defeat to the Patriots. Such was not the fact. The Patriots did not commit all their power against Cornwallis; nor is there any reason to believe that, failing to capture his army, the American troops gathered in Virginia must have fallen prey to their British antagonists. If defeated, they could have fallen back, as they had so often been forced to do. One may not say that they were incapable of fighting on indefinitely. It should be remembered that the tides of battle in 1781 were running against Britain before Cornwallis was trapped at Yorktown. Had he escaped, the Patriots might well have won a war of endurance. As it was, the capture of his army brought the war to a quicker and merciful end.

CHAPTER XXIX

The Peace of Paris

AFTERWARD, French historians described Yorktown as a victory won by the French with American assistance, and not without good reason. If so, the profits of it were nevertheless gained by the Patriots rather than by their allies. Britain could thereafter raise no more regiments to send across the Atlantic; it became evident in London that the Americans could not be subdued. Lord North, Lord George Germain, and the Earl of Sandwich were driven from power, and George III was compelled to replace them and other ministers who had supported the war effort in America with men determined to make peace with the Patriots. British forces that remained in America were ordered to do no more than defend themselves. The war died down in America. Generals Washington and Greene found it difficult to muster strength enough to attack New York or Charleston; later, it became obvious that it was unnecessary for them to continue hostilities, since Britain had no desire to keep only the two cities. The war between Britain and the Bourbon monarchs continued furiously for many months in 1782. In the meantime British, American, French, Spanish, and Dutch diplomats began to bargain at Paris. At long last they framed a treaty of peace that was not utterly unacceptable to any of the warring parties. Its principal beneficiary was the American republic, which was not only officially received into the family of nations but was formally endowed with territories that assured a bright future to the Patriots and their progeny.

It is reported that Lord North, learning of the surrender of Cornwallis, cried, "O God! It is all over!" That North uttered those words may well be doubted; that he lost all hope of victory is beyond question. George III and Lord George Germain once more demonstrated that they were made of more stubborn stuff than the prime minister. The King would not admit defeat. The war must be pursued in America, he declared, "though the mode of it may require alteration." As usual, North bent to the strong will of the monarch. Germain sent out instructions to New York regarding the new "mode." Conceding that the "fatal issue of the Virginia campaign, and the loss of so fine a body of men" must alter British military policy in America, "for no more regiments or corps can be sent from this country," he said that there could be no more "inland" campaigns in America. Accordingly, the burden of the war must be assumed by the navy. The army, recruiting as many Loyalists as possible, should assist the navy to distress the Patriots. But even Germain had no faith that the new system would achieve anything of importance. To replace Sir Henry Clinton, who was permitted to resign his post, Germain proposed to name General James Robertson, a desk officer and a man in his dotage, whose only virtue was that he had testified in behalf of Germain when the minister was attacked by Sir William Howe in the House of Commons.

George III was able to persuade Lord North to carry on. At last, however, Parliament turned against the King and his ministry. The British politicians—Rockingham, Edmund Burke, Shelburne, Charles James Fox, and others—who had so long contended in vain against government vehemently renewed their denunciations. The country gentlemen in the House of Commons who had supported the ministry for so many years, who had begun to waver as early as 1779, now deserted in increasing numbers. As early as December 12, 1781, Thomas Powys, one of them, bitterly likened the status of the British empire to that of the Romans in fatal decline. The majority of the ministry in the Commons sank to 41 before the Christmas holidays. The war news continued to be bad. It became apparent that Britain could not successfully struggle against all her enemies. Early in 1782 North was able to muster a majority of only 19 in the Commons. The desperately unpopular Germain could not remain in office. His resignation was announced on February 11; he was forced from office by George III, who recognized his constancy, though hardly his achievements, by making him Viscount Sackville. On February 22 a motion to abandon all efforts to coerce the Americans was defeated in the Commons by only 1 vote. Five days later a similar motion received a majority of 19. But George III would not unequivocally promise to refrain from further military action against the Patriots. Accordingly, to force the hand of the monarch, Sir Henry Seymour Conway, on March 4, moved that "this House will consider as enemies to his Majesty and this country, all those who shall endeavor to frustrate his Majesty's paternal care for the ease and happiness of his people, by advising, or by any means attempting to further prosecution of offensive war on the continent of North America, for the purpose of reducing the revolted colonies to obedience by force." That decisive pronouncement was carried without a division in the Commons. Lord North did not even waste energy in a useless attempt to defeat the resolution. Then his enemies demanded the resignation of North and of the ministry that had so long sought to subdue the Americans. The King tried to stem the tide, to reconstruct and to strengthen the ministry, in vain. Told that he must accept a new one, led by the Marquis of Rockingham, with authority to offer as much as independence to America and to undertake removal of corruption in Britain, the King talked of abdicating. He did not make such a spectacular gesture. He yielded; North resigned on March 20; and Rockingham returned to power on March 27.

Aristocratic eighteenth-century British politicians being what they were, Rockingham holding office was much less eager to cleanse the Augean stables of British politics than Rockingham condemning Lord North. He destroyed some sinecures and withdrew some unearned pensions. He did not lead Britain toward political democracy. He did fundamentally alter Britain's American policy. Reshuffling the duties of cabinet members, he entrusted colonial business to the Earl of Shelburne, European affairs to Charles James Fox. He and his colleagues sent Sir Guy Carleton off to New York to replace Sir Henry Clinton; Shelburne commissioned Richard Oswald to go to Paris to negotiate with Patriot commissioners gathering in that city; and Fox ordered Thomas Grenville to proceed to the same place to bargain with the French and Spanish. Becoming commander in chief in America at last, Carleton was instructed to remain on the defensive. Indeed, if he was attacked in great force, he was to capitulate. He was to try to secure the consent of the Patriots for unmolested transfer of his army to places where they could be employed against the French and Spanish. Rockingham, Shelburne, and Fox still hoped to persuade the Patriots to accept less than independence; to drive a wedge between them and the Bourbons; and to concentrate the forces of Britain against her ancient European enemies. At New York Carleton managed to persuade himself that it was still possible to convince the Americans that they ought to remain in—or return to—the British empire. But he was unable even to secure an arrangement with the Patriots which would permit him without hindrance to embark his troops for service against France or Spain. The Americans, seeing that a trap had been laid for them, declined an immediate advantage which they could secure only at the price of betraying their French ally. Carleton stayed on at New York as a caretaker until peace was made. The efforts of the British emissaries at Paris to separate the Patriots from the Bourbons merely gave the American commissioners an advantage which they successfully exploited for the benefit of the United States. They enjoyed a most favorable bargaining position, especially since Britain had foresworn any attempt to use military force against the Patriots. Authorized by the Congress to negotiate, Benjamin Franklin, John Jay, John Adams, and Henry Laurens secured for them nearly all that they could reasonably ask.

It was not difficult for the British to instill distrust of Spain among the Patriots, for they had long been at odds with that country. Charles III and Floridablanca had not become friends of the republic emerging in North America. Spain had entered the war for her own purposes; had not made an alliance with the Patriots; had not even recognized the independence of the United States. Alarmed lest a strong American republic offer a disturbing example to the Spanish colonies in the New World, fearing future American expansion southward, the government of Charles III sought to create a situation in which a weak American republic counterbalanced British power beyond the Atlantic, to the profit of Spain. Floridablanca preferred, indeed, that the struggle between Britain and America end in an uneasy truce, with the Patriots denied full recognition as a nation. As the war proceeded, he and his royal master had taken steps to cramp the Patriots. They feared for the safety of Louisiana; they saw that the Patriots desired East and West Florida, and they looked upon the Mississippi River as an avenue which the Patriots might use to penetrate into the Spanish dominions. The conquest of West Florida by Bernardo de Gálvez was for them a blow against the Americans as well as the British. They were disposed to make much of the success of a raiding force of Spanish militia from St. Louis that captured a British post at St. Joseph in southwestern Michigan and held it for one day. They wished, if possible, to secure the eastern part of the Mississippi Valley for Spain, to establish the Appalachians as the boundary of the United States on the west.

That the interests of the United States clashed with those of Spain was recognized by the Congress as early as 1779. At that time, hoping that the war would soon be brought to a successful conclusion, the Congress resolved to entrust John Adams with the task of negotiating a treaty of peace, and to send John Jay to Madrid to seek an alliance with Spain. The delegates wanted for the United States all of North America east of the Mississippi and Canada as well. But it was clear that Spain would certainly not enter into an alliance with a nation that sought to establish itself on both the Mississippi and the Gulf of Mexico. Accordingly, in August of that year, the Congress determined to insist that American territory extend to the Mississippi on the west but only to the latitude of 31° between the Mississippi and Chattahoochee Rivers on the south. On September 17 the Congress authorized Jay, in exchange for an alliance and a promise from Spain of free navigation of the Father of Waters, to guarantee possession of both Floridas to Spain in the event that the dons took them from the British. Jay was also to seek a loan and a treaty of commerce.

Reaching Madrid early in 1780, John Jay was not welcomed. Floridablanca received him informally, and lent him money so that he had funds which permitted him to remain in Spain for more than two years. But the minister treated Jay as a nuisance rather than an emissary of importance. He would not enter into serious discussion with the Patriot. However, during 1780, he did carry on lengthy talks with Richard Cumberland, a British special agent, about terms of peace and the future of the Patriots. He proposed that Britain offer them, not independence, but a truce, with the British retaining control over the territories held by the royal forces—in effect, New York, Long Island, Wilmington, South Carolina, and Georgia. Receiving new instructions from Philadelphia, Jay raised the price that America would pay for a Spanish alliance; as an added inducement, the Patriots would renounce the right to navigate the lower Mississippi through Spanish territory. The offer was generous, but Floridablanca unwisely rejected it. Then Jay, realizing that the Congress had bid too high for an alliance that the Patriots did not need, withdrew the proposal. He went from Madrid to Paris in May 1782 a much wiser man. He had learned that Spain desired neither a strong nor a friendly America. He had also become aware that France would not lend powerful support to the Patriots when their interests clashed with those of Spain.

The Patriot leaders at home also came to realize that they could not rely upon France to sustain them in quarrels with Spain. The Comte de Vergennes sought to please both his allies rather than to favor either. Even before the entrance of Charles III into the war, when Vergennes sent Conrad-Alexandre Gérard across the Atlantic as the first French minister to the United States, he informed the Spanish court that Gérard would defend the interests of Spain with as much zeal as he would assert those of France. He ordered Gérard to pretend that France was not solicitous in behalf of Spain, but nevertheless to do what he could toward securing the Floridas, Jamaica, and a share in the Newfoundland fisheries for France's European ally. Vergennes at the same time assured the Congress that France was waging war exclusively for the benefit of the United States. In America Gérard went beyond his instructions to please Spain— in obvious assurance that Vergennes would not condemn his activities. To persuade that country to declare war upon Britain, he urged that the Patriots offer Spain a barrier region along the eastern bank of the Mississippi. Thus the Patriots could increase the difficulties of Britain, the common enemy of the United States and France. It was awkward for Gérard that in the alliance of February 6, 1778, France had guaranteed the territories of the United States. He explained away that difficulty; he claimed that the French pledge did not apply until the American boundaries were laid down in a peace treaty, an argument that did not satisfy every member of Congress. After Charles III had declared war upon Britain, Vergennes himself came forward to defend the pretensions of Spain in North America. He instructed the Chevalier de la Luzerne, who succeeded Gérard at Philadelphia, to insist that the Patriots recognize the right of Spain to both the Floridas and to urge them to concede to Spain a barrier territory along the eastern bank of the Mississippi. Eager as the Patriots then were to please France—they were profoundly grateful for French help—the Congress resented his interference and insisted that America must stretch westward to the great river. Vergennes further irritated the Patriots by suggesting that they should not press Britain hard with respect to fishing rights off Newfoundland—at a time when he was asserting claims for Frenchmen on the Grand Banks.

As the war proceeded, Vergennes became even less solicitous for the welfare of the Patriots. His first duty was to France, and he was prepared, if necessary, to force heavy sacrifices from the Patriots in order to save the French state. By 1780 France was staggering under the financial strain of the war. He could not patriotically ruin his own country so that the Americans might achieve all their wishes; nor would he execute promises made to the United States by France in their treaty of alliance at destructive cost to France.

In certain respects the war went well for France in 1780. In that year the League of Armed Neutrality, inspired and encouraged by Vergennes, made its appearance, and The Netherlands entered the struggle as a foe of Britain. The League, to which all the great powers and most of the smaller ones of Europe eventually subscribed, sought to limit the exercise of British sea power. After 1778 British warships searched and expropriated the vessels of neutrals carrying enemy and contraband goods. That practice exasperated the nations bordering upon the Baltic Sea. Led by Catherine the Great, they agreed to formulate a code of neutral rights on the sea and to use collective force, if necessary, to defend those rights. The growing list of European states that joined the League emphasized the unpopularity of Britain on the European Continent. So hostile was the behavior of The Netherlands as a neutral that Britain declared war against that country. Because Holland had helped the Patriots, the French, and the Spanish, was threatening to join the League, and had laid plans to build a fleet, Britain began hostilities against the Dutch in December 1780.

But the League of Armed Neutrality never came to blows with Britain, and The Netherlands injured Britain less as a belligerent than as a non-contestant. From the very beginning of the war Dutch merchants sold munitions to the Patriots. The tiny Dutch colony of St. Eustatius in the West Indies became a busy depot at which, despite protests from Britain, the Americans exchanged their produce for cash, ammunition, and goods of all sorts. Also, Dutch vessels carried shipmasts from the Baltic to French and Spanish ports, where they were much needed. Waging war against the Dutch, who possessed no powerful navy, the British seized scores of Dutch merchant vessels, interrupted the sea traffic of the Dutch, and captured St. Eustatius. Holland was thus deprived of ability to offer much more than loans of money by Dutch bankers to the Patriots and the French.

Moreover, Vergennes was beset at home in 1780 by Jacques Necker, who had been placed in charge of French finances and who ardently sought to make peace with Britain. Himself a banker, Necker knew that France was not too far from bankruptcy. With the tacit consent of the Comte de Maurepas, who presided over the French ministry, Necker secretly suggested to Lord North that it might be possible to put an end to the war by the establishment of a truce in America, with the Patriots and the British both holding the ground they occupied. The overture made by Necker was flatly rejected in London, for George III would not discuss with the perfidious and interfering French either a treaty of peace or a truce between Britain and the Americans. The venture by Necker into diplomacy thus failed. Besides, he lost favor at the French court early in 1781, and Vergennes retained control of the foreign policy of Louis XVI.

But Vergennes himself came to believe during that winter that it might become necessary for France to accept the plan for a truce proposed by Spain and Necker. France had solemnly promised to continue the war until the Americans had gained their independence. He preferred to keep that pledge. Nevertheless, the exigencies of his own country might force him to seek release from it. He would not ask the Patriots to make "so painful" a sacrifice for the sake of France. But could not France consent to such a truce if it were urged by neutral nations? Early in 1781 Catherine the Great and Count Kaunitz, the foreign minister of Austria, offered their services. They offered to serve as mediators and to arrange for a peace conference at Vienna. In the following summer, Vergennes conferred at Paris with John Adams, who at the time was commissioned to make peace on behalf of the Patriots. Would Adams consider a truce? Only if the British forces were withdrawn from the Thirteen States. Would he go to Vienna? Only if Russia and Austria first recognized American independence. Vergennes abandoned the scheme. He knew that George III would resist European interference in Britain's colonial affairs; besides, he had not abandoned hope for military victory over Britain.

The maneuvers of Vergennes taught Adams, who might be duped by a fellow Yankee but not by a wily Frenchman, not to place excessive faith in France, just as those of Floridablanca instructed Jay to be on close guard against Spain. But the Congress, despite mounting evidence that Vergennes was much less than altruistic, continued to rely upon the friendship and generosity of "the great and good ally." In June 1781, that body, deciding that it was prudent to assign the duty of negotiating peace to a commission rather than to an individual, appointed Adams, Jay, Franklin, Jefferson, and Henry Laurens as its representatives. They were instructed to insist only upon independence. For the rest, in accordance with the expressed wishes of Vergennes and the Chevalier de la Luzerne, they were told "to make the most candid and confidential communications, upon all subjects to the ministers" of France, to "undertake nothing" without their knowledge and consent, "and ultimately to govern yourselves" by their advice and opinion. The Congress was too trustful.

Fortunately for the United States, Benjamin Franklin, though not so suspicious of the French and the Spanish as Adams and Jay, was no less determined that America become independent and that her territories extend to the Mississippi. For, as it turned out, Franklin was the principal spokesman for the peace commission over several months. Afterward he received strong support from Adams and Jay. Jefferson, unhappy and disturbed because of the illness and death of his wife, declined to serve. Henry Laurens was captured on the Atlantic by the British and was kept prisoner in the gloomy recesses of the Tower of London for many weeks. Finally released at the urging of Franklin, he emerged too late to offer much help. Moreover, he was ill and shaken by the death of his son, Colonel John Laurens, in battle. Jay arrived in Paris from Madrid on June 23, and Adams, busy at The Hague in an attempt to borrow money, did not reach the French capital until October 26.

Franklin was less concerned than his colleagues about the maneuvers of Vergennes and Floridablanca because he had learned his way through the devious paths of diplomacy. He did not doubt that he could match the representatives of Britain, France, and Spain in wiles and artifices, and he had reason to be confident. He talked informally during many weeks in the spring and early summer of 1782 with Richard Oswald, an old friend, and with Thomas Grenville, who also approached Franklin on behalf of the British. Oswald and Grenville sought to persuade Franklin that France was an unreliable ally, that the ties between Britain and America were too strong to be completely sundered. Seeking to divorce America from her ally, they suggested that the Patriots negotiate separately with the British. Vergennes did not object to such bargaining, provided that its results were incorporated in one treaty of peace. Accordingly, Franklin agreed to separate talks, from which the Americans must gain. Moreover, despite the instructions of Congress, he did not bother to inform Vergennes about the nature of those discussions or to ask the advice of the French foreign minister. Nor was he overswayed by appeals from Oswald and Grenville for a settlement founded upon ancient and enduring links between Britain and America. He said that America could not abandon her alliance with France. The bonds between Britain and America had been broken. He himself retained a measure of fondness for Britain. Toward regaining the respect and affection of all the Americans, Britain should begin by offering them both independence and liberal terms of peace. Time might then bring resurrection of some of the political ties that had been sundered, Franklin hinted. The Philadelphian asked for all possible benefits for the United States in a manner as pleasing to the British agents as the situation would permit.

The conversations at Paris did not immediately bear fruit. Indeed, little progress was made until Shelburne became prime minister, as the result of the death of Rockingham on July 1. Jealous of Shelburne, Charles James Fox left office, and Shelburne thus acquired complete control over the negotiations with the Americans. He was more reluctant to concede independence to them than was Fox; on the other hand, he could be large-minded on occasion and he was an old friend of Franklin. Shelburne sent Alleyne Fitzherbert to Paris to replace Grenville, and the talks between the British and American emissaries—John Jay having joined Franklin—proceeded. Franklin described to Oswald the terms which Britain should offer the Patriots. They included recognition of American independence, generous boundaries for the new nation, and fishing rights for the Americans on the Grand Banks. Britain would do well, said Franklin, to accept blame for the War of Independence, to pay for destroyed Patriot property, to cede all of Canada to the United States, and to propose freedom of trade between Britain and America. The demands and requests that Franklin softly voiced shocked neither Oswald nor Shelburne. But the prime minister knew that the British politician who acknowledged American independence would suffer censure at home, even though he was forced to do it largely because of the shortcomings of others. The tide of war, except in North America, seemed to be turning against France and Spain, in favor of Britain. He would have been reluctant in any case to concede absolute separation between Britain and America, even as a step toward their ultimate reunion. He was willing to enter into official bargaining with the Patriots, but he declined to recognize American independence until peace should be made between all the combatants in the war. The British would deal with "any commissioner or commissioners" of the "colonies or plantations."

That decision, conveyed to Franklin and Jay early in August, disturbed them. Why should Britain defer admission of American independence? They consulted Vergennes, who declared that it mattered little whether formal recognition was granted soon, or late, in the treaty of peace. The two Americans became alarmed. Did Vergennes sincerely desire independence for the Patriots? They decided to demand British recognition, to make sure that the French minister would not seek to barter away American freedom for the benefit of France of Spain.

Jay was specially fearful lest Vergennes turn away from, or even against the Patriots. Through August and into September he was engaged in conversations with the Conde de Aranda, the ambassador of Charles III to the court of Louis XVI, about accommodation of Patriot and Spanish claims in North America. The suspicions of Spain and of France that he had developed at Madrid became stronger, with good reason. In talks with Jay, Aranda at first insisted that Spain must receive at the peace not only the Floridas, but much of the region between the Appalachians, the Great Lakes, and the Mississippi. The Americans were to be limited on the west by a line running southward from the western end of Lake Erie—a line which would have put some of the new American settlements in Kentucky and Tennessee under the flag of Spain. Jay insisted that the United States must extend to the Mississippi above latitude 31° and that American citizens must have free use of the Mississippi to its mouth. Aranda asked Vergennes to help settle the dispute, and Vergennes offered the services of his secretary, M. de Rayneval, as a mediator. The Spanish ambassador and Rayneval then prepared a "compromise" which they claimed to be satisfactory to Vergennes. They proposed that the region between the Ohio and the Great Lakes remain in British hands, and that an Indian reservation under Spanish hegemony be established to the westward of a line running from the mouth of the Cumberland River to the eastern boundary of West Florida. When Jay learned on September 9, that Rayneval had left Paris for London upon a secret mission, he drew the proper conclusion. It was evident that Rayneval was to ask the British to endorse the "compromise," which would erect British, Spanish, and Indian barriers against American expansion.

Jay and Franklin would not be hoodwinked. They, too, could approach the British. They informed Richard Oswald, and Shelburne, that they were prepared to withdraw their demand for immediate recognition of American independence, provided that Oswald was formally instructed to bargain, not with the "colonies or plantations," but with "the United States of America." Indicating that the Americans would not continue the war for the benefit of Spain, that they must have access to the Grand Banks fisheries, regardless of the wishes of France, and that their territory must stretch to the Mississippi, Jay and Franklin hinted that if necessary to protect American interests, they would make a separate peace with Britain. To ensure British cession of Trans-Appalachia to the United States, they offered free commercial access to it, by way of the St. Lawrence and the Mississippi, to all British citizens.

Meanwhile, on August 29, Shelburne and his cabinet had most reluctantly decided that they must ask Parliament for permission to concede American independence immediately. Shelburne was now able, if he accepted the bargain offered by Franklin and Jay, to defer formal independence, to drive the Americans apart from the French, and to gain advantage for Britain. He did not fail to seize his opportunity. He gave Rayneval a cool reception. On September 19 the British cabinet agreed to empower Oswald to treat with "the commissioners appointed by the colonys, under the title of Thirteen United States."

Then the negotiations between the Patriots and Oswald proceeded rapidly. Franklin and Jay informed Vergennes that they were treating formally with the British emissary, but neither asked his advice nor told him about the progress of the discussions. They disobeyed their instructions from Congress to consult with and to follow the advice of Vergennes because they could not trust him to defend American interests. By October 8 the three men had finished the draft of a preliminary treaty which was to become final upon the conclusion of one between France and Britain. America was to become independent, with boundaries substantially those sought by the Patriots. However, Franklin and Jay were forced to abandon the Patriot dream of converting Canada into a fourteenth state. Canada was to remain British; its frontier with the United

States was described in much the same fashion as was afterward established, except that Ontario was to be American. The Patriots had to accept that arrangement in order to get Trans-Appalachia; they were compelled in addition to concede free commercial use of the Mississippi to British subjects. The Americans were to have ready access to the Grand Banks fisheries. The British were to withdraw their forces from the American republic "with all convenient speed." The draft also contained a far-reaching provision which granted equal rights in navigation and commerce throughout the territories of both countries to both British and American citizens. That stipulation would have taken Britain and America far along the road to British reconciliation and friendship.

But Shelburne refused to endorse the agreement, and the bargaining went on. The fortunes of battle continued to turn in favor of Britain, against France and Spain. The British were holding their own in India and more than their own in the West Indies. Minorca had fallen to their enemies early in 1782, but Gibraltar was holding out against powerful Franco-Spanish forces. Indeed, in September its garrison beat off a final massive attack by the Bourbons. Shelburne asked for concessions from the Patriots. He sent Sir Henry Strachey to Paris to join Oswald and to urge that the Americans accept a less generous northwestern frontier, promise that the private debts of Americans to British citizens would be paid, and pledge compensation to the Loyalists for their losses. Moreover, Shelburne the statesman felt forced to become Shelburne the politician. He believed in freedom of trade, but he knew that Parliament would refuse to alter the Navigation Acts in favor of the Patriots. Accordingly, he instructed Oswald and Strachey that the clause in the draft treaty establishing the equal rights of the British and the Americans in commerce and navigation in both countries must be deleted.

Joined by John Adams, Franklin and Jay opened talks with Strachey and Oswald on October 26. The American commissioners continued to ignore Vergennes. They were determined to make sacrifices, unless too much was demanded of them, to secure a treaty with Britain. They consented to a revision of the American boundaries which placed all of Ontario in Canada. They also agreed in a secret article to an extension of West Florida northward of latitude 31°, in the event that Britain retained that colony—a pledge that America was not required to fulfill, since West Florida became Spanish territory in 1783. They guaranteed the payment of debts owed by Americans to British citizens—a promise which the United States afterward kept by paying obligations neglected by some Americans. But the Patriot emissaries would not engage to compensate the Loyalists for their losses. Franklin was specially averse to any concession that would benefit the colonists who had rallied behind the King. At length, the spokesmen for the Patriots gave their consent to a clause which required the Congress to recommend earnestly to the states that they indemnify the Tories. They offered enough so that the British cabinet gave its approval to the preliminary treaty. It was formally signed on November 30, 1782.

The Patriot diplomats had won a great triumph, for the war between Britain and her European enemies was rapidly drawing to an end; and the treaty of November 30 was certain to be included in the approaching general peace. They had secured not only independence, but boundaries for America that left "little to complain of and not much to desire," as they reported to the Congress. They had defeated the determined effort of Spain to keep Americans away from the Mississippi. The concessions they were in consequence forced to make to Britain over the Mississippi Valley proved to be of little importance. The Spanish in West Florida did not constitute a formidable barrier against later American expansion. The Patriot commissioners failed to secure Ontario; but the United States had never had any good reason to claim that region.

Benjamin Franklin had the task of informing Vergennes that he and his colleagues had made the preliminary treaty without consulting the French foreign minister, a duty that was all the more delicate in that it was necessary for Franklin to ask at the same time that France guarantee payment of a loan then being negotiated by the Patriots. Vergennes did not hide his displeasure. He was disposed to look upon the Americans as clients of France; the Patriot commissioners had ignored him; and Jay and Adams had not bothered to conceal their distrust of him and his agents. He sent a gentle and polite complaint to Congress, and made another to Franklin. He was not shocked by the behavior of the commissioners; they labored for America as he did for France. He could have defended his own less than liberal conduct toward the Patriots and his concern for Spain in the negotiations as necessary because of the distress of his own country. Franklin offered a soft apology, subtly suggesting that it would be prudent for France and America to conceal their disputes from Britain. Vergennes courteously allowed himself to be propitiated. What good for France could come from recriminations? He also made it possible for the Patriots to borrow six million livres.

The Anglo-American treaty did not take effect until the autumn of 1783. Similar preliminary agreements were made by Britain with France and Spain on January 20, 1783, and a general armistice was proclaimed. However, the final peace was not established until September of that year. There was time for Britain to make a last effort to wean the Patriots away from France and to persuade them to turn back toward Britain. It was made by Charles James Fox, who combined with his old political enemy,

Lord North, to overthrow Shelburne and to force his way into a new British ministry—Shelburne was held responsible for the losses suffered in consequence of a war which he had neither begun nor lost. It was obvious that the Franco-American alliance had passed its bloom. Fox sent to Paris David Hartley, a friend of Franklin and a devoted advocate in England for the Americans in peace and war. Hartley urged the Patriot commissioners to consider a defensive military alliance with Britain. He also proposed that maritime commerce between Britain and America be unrestricted, except that American ships be denied the privilege of carrying to Britain goods not produced in the United States—a proviso intended to soothe many in Britain who wished to apply the Navigation Acts against the Americans as foreigners. It was both too late and too early for such arrangements, upon which might have been built an enduring concord between the two countries. The Patriots could not honorably enter into an alliance with Britain, since they were still committed to France. Moreover, despite the fact that France had assisted them for her own purposes, many Americans were grateful to France. A sentimental attachment to that nation long persisted in the United States. On the other hand, the Patriots could not, even before the War of Independence was officially ended, consider Britain as a friend. Indeed, hostility toward the mother country was harbored by many Americans for generations. Conversely, many British detested the Americans in 1783 and long continued to be enemies of the republic. Shelburne, Fox, and Hartley were eager to repair as best they could the deep wounds of political and military struggle, but they and their like were in a minority. Fox was no more able than Shelburne to persuade the British cabinet and Parliament to tear down for the benefit of the Americans the barriers exerted by Britain to protect and enhance her maritime commerce. Even as Hartley was making his proposals in Paris, Britain closed her ports in the West Indies to American shipping. Franklin and his colleagues could do no other than tell Hartley that his mission was in vain.

The Peace of Paris was signed on September 3, 1783. Its principal beneficiary, unquestionably, was the United States. Spain, unable to secure the return of Gibraltar, did regain Minorca and obtained both of the Floridas, together with other minor concessions. France, profiting little territorially from her immense exertions, had to derive her chief satisfaction from the heavy blow she had struck at Britain. Revenge cost France dearly. She did not get the overseas trade of the Americans—it reverted into its familiar channels with Britain after the war. The expense of the war severely injured French finances, in a dubious state even before the conflict, and so contributed to the onset of the great Revolution that began in that country in 1789. Britain was beaten, but emerged from the war in better condition than her European rivals. She had lost the most valuable of all her overseas possessions. But Britain would build a new empire upon the remains of the old. The Americans, no longer legally forced to buy from and sell to the British, became again the best customers of Britain. British merchants were able to undersell French ones, and could offer credit that their competitors could not or would not extend to the Americans. Economics regained for Britain the trade that politics had lost. The Britain that George Grenville claimed to be in deep distress in 1763 survived the War of Independence, and a doubling of her national debt. The continuing Industrial Revolution in England gave strength to the nation. Even the long wars that began with France in 1793 and continued for more than twenty-two years did not reduce Britain to bankruptcy. Britain brought down Napoleon, became the greatest power in Europe, and long continued to dominate the oceans.

American independence had been recognized by The Netherlands in 1782, and America definitely became a member of the family of nations in the following year. But it was doubted for some years by European enemies, including Kings and aristocrats, that the new republic would survive. They happily magnified every American difficulty. The Americans would end in anarchy if they did not accept monarchy or a dictatorship. Staying on in Paris, Benjamin Franklin pointed out that even the sun has its spots, and predicted once more a brilliant future for America.

Franklin saw the solid substance beneath appearances of weakness in the republic. All his fellow countrymen did not share his faith. It was difficult to get together a quorum in the Congress in 1784 to ratify the treaty of peace. Even before the end of the war, while American diplomats in Paris were reaping the benefits of military triumph, there were serious troubles at home. As peace approached, Washington's Continentals became restless. They were better fed and clothed than they had been before Yorktown, but their pay remained in arrears. Both officers and men became alarmed lest they be sent home without pay or prospects. The officers wanted half pay, which they had been promised in accordance with the British system. A delegation of officers went to the Congress in Philadelphia in the winter of 1782–3 to ask that provision be made for the Continentals. They were put off. Some delegates even proposed that their demands be merely referred to the states. Officers and troops alike became embittered. Were their sacrifices to go unrewarded? In March 1783 an anonymous officer, probably Major John Armstrong, Jr., urged, in the Newburgh Addresses to the army, that they take justice into their own hands. Washington had difficulty in soothing the spreading discontent. However, at length, the Congress undertook to give the officers full compensation for five years in lieu of half pay, and Robert

Morris, superintendent of its finances, found enough money in the treasury to offer the private soldiers three months' pay. The Continentals were at last satisfied, but not before some Pennsylvania troops—who had done little fighting—so bedeviled the Congress that it fled from Philadelphia to Princeton.

The mood of the Continentals was such in the spring of 1782 that Colonel John Lewis Nicola was inspired to suggest to Washington that the general should accept an American crown. Nicola declared that there were other officers who agreed with him that Washington ought to become King, and such may well have been the case. Certainly there were still some Americans who subscribed to the monarchical principle. It is well known that Alexander Hamilton asserted his belief in limited monarchy in 1787 and later. In 1787 the Baron von Steuben, who obviously did not properly assess the temper of the Americans although he had chosen to make his home among them, ludicrously addressed Prince Henry of Prussia, asking him whether he was interested in mounting an American throne. Washington was astonished by Nicola's proposal. No man knew more about the sufferings of his men; no one was more familiar with the weakness of the Congress, than Washington. He was well aware that the Articles of Confederation were defective, that America needed a stronger central government. But the suggestion that he should become a King—or even a dictator—he rejected utterly. He was not an egotistical Napoleon, grasping for power. He was not a democrat. He was a man of honor who would not stoop to conspiracy, who had given his allegiance to the American republic. "Let me beseech you, then," he wrote to Nicola, "if you have any regard for your country, concern for yourself or posterity, or respect for me, to banish these thoughts from your mind." Nicola was finally silenced.

The time came, as winter approached in the year 1783, when General Guy Carleton evacuated New York and Washington entered the city with his troops. He remained there only briefly. On December 4 he bade farewell, amidst tears, to the officers who had borne so many trials with him. Proceeding to Annapolis, where the Congress was in session, he resigned his commission as commander in chief. He had served at the head of the Continentals eight years, six months, and eight days. He declared that he was taking "leave of all the employments of public life." He went on to his beloved home at Mount Vernon. But the government of the republic for which he had fought so long needed basic reform. He would help to improve it, and he would be called back into service as the first magistrate of a grateful nation.

CHAPTER XXX

The Fate of the Loyalists

THE treaty signed at Paris required that Congress "earnestly recommend" to the American states that they rescind all the laws they had enacted to punish the Loyalists. The men who devised that provision knew that the states would not comply immediately, fully, or unanimously. So it turned out. Massachusetts quickly undertook to cleanse its statute books, to permit Tories to mingle once more as equals with the Patriots. However, most of the American commonwealths moved less rapidly; penalties imposed upon the Tories survived in a few cases for more than a decade. Like the diplomats, the Loyalists were well aware that all was not forgiven in the treaty of peace. If the Revolution contained an element of Genesis for the Patriots, it was Exodus for many of the Loyalists, including both men and women who could not safely return to their homes and Tories who preferred to begin life anew outside the United States and under the British flag. At the end of the war there was a massive departure of Loyalists, a large part of them men who had fought for the empire. The new nation lost tens of thousands of worthy and talented persons. They and their descendants, who inherited their virtues and who proudly added to their sacrifices for Britain, gave vitality to the British empire. Most of the Tories remained in the American republic and were ultimately so utterly absorbed that they and their progeny could hardly be identified even at the distance of fifty years after the Declaration of Independence.

How many Loyalists left the United States is not and cannot be precisely known. It has been said that they numbered as many as 100,000; that figure should probably be cut in half. It is estimated that 1,100 left Boston in 1776, that as many as 32,000 departed from New

York with General Guy Carleton at the close of the war, that several thousands more then sailed away from Charleston. To these large bodies must be added those who fled singly, by twos and threes, and in small groups, before, during, and after the conflict. The Tories began to seek safety in flight as early as 1774, scattering in all directions. There were dozens of them in England as early as 1775. Others made their way to Halifax, Montreal, Niagara, Detroit, St. Augustine, Pensacola, Mobile, the Bahama Islands, and British possessions in the West Indies. A large contingent eventually began life afresh in England; the bulk, perhaps 38,000, settled in Canada; a few established themselves permanently in various other British colonies.

What sort of people were the exiles? Romance fostered by their children and grandchildren has it that they were virtuous, educated, prosperous, mannered gentlemen and ladies who gallantly and faithfully sacrificed everything but life itself for Britain; that they were hardly of the same breed as the Americans from whom they separated. That myth spread from Britain and especially from Canada to the United States and acquired vogue even among the progeny of the Patriots. But assuredly the Loyalist exiles were of the same blood and flesh as the Patriots. All the disparate elements in the American colonial population were to be found among them, and in much the same proportions, with two exceptions. There were Negroes among them, but only a few; there were Scots among them, relatively many. The Scots, indeed, were so Toryish that the state of Georgia denied admission to immigrants from North Britain by a law of 1782. Persons of Dutch and German descent, especially those who had not felt so fully the influence of the American environment, left with Loyalists of English, Welsh, Irish, Swiss, French, and mixed European ancestry. The Jews supplied devout Loyalists as well as devoted Patriots.

Nor does it appear that the exiles were better educated or more talented than the Patriots. True, merchants, lawyers, physicians, and Anglican clergymen were comparatively numerous in the ships that carried off Loyalists. Together with royal and proprietary officials, they formed a body of learned and able men whose departure injured America intellectually. On the other hand, teachers, Congregationalist and Presbyterian clergymen, and planters (who were so often college and university graduates), contributed proportionately few persons to the Tory exodus. In the Loyalist migration were informed and respectable politicians, such as Thomas Hutchinson of Massachusetts, William Bull of South Carolina, and Sir James Wright of Georgia; the Reverend Dr. Samuel Seabury of New York; Benjamin Thompson of New Hampshire, a spy for General Gage before the war, a favorite of Lord George Germain, a cavalry officer, and ultimately, with the title of Count Rumford, a distinguished scientist; and General Sir John Stuart, a son of the Indian superintendent, who won fame by defeating a Napoleonic army in Sicily in 1806. One may expand this list by adding the names of other well-known men, such as Joseph Galloway and William Franklin, neither of them truly remarkable for ability. William Franklin, a courteous gentleman, resembled his father physically, but lacked his diverse and prolific genius. It is also possible, by loose use of the words "Loyalist" and "exile," to insert the name of the famous artist from Massachusetts, John Singleton Copley. He went to Europe before the war to study painting, not to evade unwelcome association with the Patriots. He was devoted to art rather than to politics, and remained in England so that he might more successfully pursue his profession. Ironically, he executed his finest portraits in America, before he studied in Italy and England. There is greater justification for inserting Benedict Arnold as a belated Loyalist. But America lost little by the departure of Arnold; and it may be more appropriate to place him in his own special category. It requires no great space to enumerate the men of talent who left America as a consequence of the War of Independence, and very little to mention those who possessed genius. To be sure, the careers of the Loyalist exiles were interrupted; and they did not have the opportunities in Britain, in Canada, in the West Indies that would have come to them in their old homes. Even so, it is a striking fact that almost all of the great men of the Revolutionary generation born in the New World were Patriots, among them, to mention only a few, Washington, Franklin, Jefferson, John Adams, Madison, and John Marshall.

But if those who fled from America did not include the majority of her gifted people, were they not nevertheless her propertied aristocrats, despoiled by their economic and social inferiors? Were not the devoted Loyalists those who had, the Patriots those who had not, but would have? Such was the belief of many Tories at the time, and of less than careful historians since. A Georgia lady put it that in the Revolution "everywhere the scum rose to the top." Declared Tory Judge Samuel Curwen of Massachusets in 1780, "those who five years ago were the *'meaner people'* are now by strange revolution, become almost the only men of power, riches and influence." He commented unhappily that "The Cabots of Beverly, who you know, had but five years ago a very moderate share of property, are now said to be by far the most wealthy in New England." It is indeed likely that the exiles were, in the average, somewhat richer, somewhat more socially dignified, than the Patriots before the war. But the difference cannot have been great. If wealthy merchants and lawyers were relatively numerous among the Loyalists, rich planters were very generally to be found in the Patriot camp. The expatriates included, not only a contingent of gentry, but many persons from the humblest echelons of the colonial society, plain farmers, tenants, servants, barbers, mechanics, Indian traders, jewelers, shoemakers, saddlers, and laborers. Moreover, the exiles left behind them many who enjoyed wealth and superior social status before the war, who continued to look upon themselves as select. On balance, men who sought to rise in the world were more likely to be Patriots; on the other hand, those who had much to lose would tend to be Loyalists. But there was no sharp and clear cleavage between lordly patricians and aspiring plebeians.

It would similarly be erroneous to assume that the exiles were uniformly persons of the highest morals. The descendants of Benedict Arnold have performed most worthily as Britons; one may not praise Arnold himself for his steadfast devotion to principle. Nor is it in order to make much of the merits of William Goodgion of Georgia, who took an oath of allegiance to the Patriot cause and another to George III, who served as a member of a Patriot assembly in Georgia and also in the royal forces. British commissioners who investigated his conduct said that he was "guilty of impartial treachery to both countries." Another Loyalist, who did not leave the United States, but doubtless would have been an exile had he not died at Charleston in 1780, compiled an equally odd record. The Reverend John Morrison, a Presbyterian clergyman, was suspended from his church at Peterborough, New Hampshire, in 1772 because he was "dangerous alike as the companion of either sex." He served with the American militia until the day after the battle of Bunker Hill, then deserted and joined the British army.

Certainly the outcasts and fugitives included persons who became Loyalists solely to keep property. There were shrewd colonists who found a way to avoid confiscation, whether the Patriots were victorious or the British. Two business partners quietly agreed that one of them should be a Patriot, the other a Tory, and arranged to put their possessions legally in the hands of the partner who was on the side of the victors. Brothers entered into similar compacts, and husbands and wives. There is reason to believe that members of the prosperous Lloyd and Gardiner families of New York's Long Island and of the wealthy Dulanys of Maryland entered into such pacts. Participants in those schemes could, of course, justify them upon the ground that expropriation was unjust and vicious, whether executed by the Patriots, the British, or the Loyalists. Need it be said that many others, less astute, believed that their property could be sufficiently safeguarded by embracing the royal cause, since they believed that Britain would crush the rebels? Ample evidence exists that such persons were numerous among the exiles. Their failure to predict the outcome of the war cost them dearly.

The forces that moved those who suffered so much for Britain were, of course, various and mixed beyond precise dissection. Historical simplicities are commonly eccentricities, occasionally mendacities. It is apparent that some of the exiles, being royal and proprietary officials, were true to their beef and their wine, that others were swayed by expectation of office. Colonists who were born in Britain, who were recent comers to America, usually adhered to the King. Richard Montgomery, Horatio Gates, and Thomas Paine, joining the Patriots, were exceptional. Few persons born in Scotland became Patriots. Colonists who had served in British regiments in the Seven Years' War were usually—and understandably—ardent Loyalists. One cannot be surprised that clergymen of the Anglican Church, so intimately associated with the Crown, so firmly supported by Parliament, gave fervent allegiance to Britain. It is clear enough that some warm Tories adhered to the mother country because they feared that the triumph of the Patriots would be followed by social leveling and detestable democracy. Among the exiles were men who urged the need for an American nobility. Mystic fidelity to the King had its influence. Many devout Loyalists believed that the government of Britain was ideally constituted, that Britain was the home of true liberty.

Heterogeneous in ancestry, birthplace, occupation, religion, and social status, and character, the Tory exiles were also disparate in politics. For some of them, those who were bound to Britain by powerful ties of emotion, neither King nor Parliament could do serious wrong. But the majority of the expatriates, including the intellectuals among them, did not admit the King, his ministers, or Parliament to be omnipotent or omniscient. It is a striking fact that needy Loyalists asking financial help from Britain commonly made sworn statements in which they denounced the Stamp Act as unconstitutional and as responsible for their own sad experiences. They were faithful to Britain despite her sins; they cherished political philosophies not remote from those to which the Conservatives among the Patriots subscribed; and more than a few of them at last concluded that they had erred in making sacrifices for Britain and the empire, that they loved America more than the mother country, that they could be happy only in the United States.

If it be true that the cleavage between the Loyalist fugitives and the Patriots was based in only minor degree upon differences in ancestry, wealth, class, breeding, or education, it is not to be doubted that such differences were even smaller between the Patriots and the Tories who remained in the United States, since it was the active and aggressive

Loyalists, in the main, who went into exile. So, too, political divergence between the Patriots and the stay-at-home Tories was less sharp. Moreover, it should not be forgotten that the expatriates were only a glamorous minority of a minority. Thus it was that most of the Tories, staying in the United States, accepted the new order without endless regret, without gnawing bitterness. It is a striking and most informative fact that there was no Loyalist revolt within the American republic after 1783. There were Tories who never left it, but who never gave it their allegiance. They were few; they were oddities. Mingling with the Patriots and their progeny, the majority of the Tories and their descendants were absorbed into the American body politic.

The ultimate reconciliation of the stay-at-home Tories and Patriots included the reunion of families that had split apart. For the War of Independence did indeed set son against father, and brother against brother. General John Stark had a brother who was a Loyalist, and a nephew who served with the Patriots, then with the British. Of three sons of John Lovell of Massachusetts, two were Tories and one was a member of the Continental Congress. There were Massachusetts Winslows, Saltonstalls, Quincys, and Lorings who were Loyalists, and Winslows, Saltonstalls, Quincys, and Lorings who were Patriots. Of the five sons of David Ogden, Sr., of New Jersey, himself a Loyalist, three agreed with him in politics, but two were rebels. He had a brother who favored independence. The Patriot Captain William Howard of New Jersey was married to a female adherent of Britain; he dared to put a sign over the mantel in his home, "No Tory talk here." Edward Telfair of Georgia was a Patriot; his brother William was a Loyalist. Charles Price, holding an office in Savannah at the beginning of the war, stood for the empire; he had a son who fought and died for American independence.

Let it not be thought that the Tory exiles as a whole soon forgave the Patriots or quickly became friends of the United States. If their fellows who remained at home accepted, more or less graciously, their less than wretched lot in the new nation, many of the expatriates nourished an abiding hostility toward America which they transmitted to their offspring. They became more British than the British, in part because the loyalty of the bulk of the American Tories was confirmed by the generosity of the British government, which protected them against want and helped them to begin new lives. Many of them, until the end of the war, were fed and sheltered by the British forces in America. Others, who went to England, received temporary pensions that cost the mother country as much as £70,000 per annum toward the end of the war. Moreover, Britain did not display her gratitude by giving merely monetary help. Loyalists were tendered military and civil appointments, especially in Canada. They were given grants of land and transported to new homes in Nova Scotia and other parts of Canada. After the war Britain opened her purse strings to pay permanent pensions to Loyalists who had been deprived of office and to compensate all those who had lost their property. More than 5,000 persons presented claims to a British commission created to consider their cases. They asked for £8 million. The commission, setting aside unwarranted requests and reducing others, liberally distributed almost £3.3 million among 4,118 Loyalists. Exiles possessing influential friends among the British who could testify for them fared better than others, since claimants were generally unable to produce deeds or other legal proof of ownership of property. Nevertheless, the commission did its best, to the credit of the British state.

The three fourths of the exiles who settled in Canada, despite the hardships they underwent as pioneers, fared better, on the whole, than those who put down in Britain. Most of them were emigrants from New England and the Middle States. Establishing themselves in the Maritime Provinces and later in Ontario, they encountered and survived the same trials that so many of their ancestors had successfully endured in the seventeenth century. They built new colonies in Canada, and they counterbalanced the French population of Quebec. With later emigrants from Britain, they and their descendants formed an English-speaking majority in Canada. Thus they served to confirm the verdict of the Seven Years' War against the continuance of Canada in the French empire. The presence of the Loyalists and their offspring also militated powerfully against annexation of Canada by American penetration. The enmity harbored by the exiles in Canada against the Patriots persisted, and it was nourished by the War of 1812. It was imbibed by their descendants, who proudly called themselves United Empire Loyalists. Those English-speaking Canadians long looked to Britain for protection against the American republicans, and they continued for many generations to offer a special devotion to Britain and the British empire. Eventually they ceased to fear American military aggression and joined with the French Canadians to cut all political ties between Canada and Britain. Two centuries after the War of Independence the Canadian nation was riven by sharp conflict between its English-speaking and its French-speaking peoples. It seemed possible that the progeny of the Loyalists and the Patriots—becoming ever more closely associated, economically, militarily, and culturally in the twentieth century—might be politically reunited by common consent. In any event, the rancor stemming from the War of Independence, that had so long existed, had by then largely vanished.

The afflictions and troubles of the Tories who carved new homes for themselves in Nova Scotia, New Brunswick, Prince Edward Island, and Ontario were not trifling. Gazing southward across the borders of Canada, men and women who had fled from the sweets of Canaan to harsh frontiers longed to return. A Loyalist woman, after disembarking in Nova Scotia, wrote, "I climbed to the top of Chipman's Hill and watched the sails disappear in the distance, and such a feeling of loneliness came over me that though I had not shed a tear through all the war I sat down on the damp moss with my baby on my lap and cried bitterly." Joseph Stansbury, a Loyalist poet who settled in Nova Scotia, yearned to go back to Philadelphia. He was not permitted to resume life there, where he had made many enemies, but he was allowed to establish himself in New York. However, most of the Loyalists in Canada learned to be content, even happy. In regions almost unoccupied they were able to create a new society that was largely their own. They remained in a North America that was familiar to them; they were not forced, as were the Loyalists who settled in Britain, to adjust themselves to a society beyond the Atlantic in which they were a small minority, in which they were strangers.

The Tories who put down in Britain did not undergo, to be sure, the physical trials imposed upon those who went to Canada. They suffered from more subtle sorrows. With exceptions, they had little reason to complain against the British government; public men in Britain, who knew or learned their history, valued their fidelity, regretted that their sacrifices had been in vain, pitied their lot, and strove to help them. But they were not welcomed as brethren by the British whose hearts were with the Patriots; British folk who were indifferent alike to George III and George Washington were as little interested in American Tories. Many among the British who supported the war against the Patriots, but who did not know about the constancy and contributions of the Loyalists to the empire, looked upon them as unwelcome strangers, even as suspect colonials.

Thus the inevitable pangs of people driven from their familiar firesides were magnified. Establishing themselves in and near London and Bristol, the first of the exiles to reach England—very few Tories went to Ireland or Scotland—impatiently waited for a report that the rebellion had collapsed so that they could return home. Collecting in clubs and coffeehouses, they exchanged stories of their adventures, scanned the newspapers, and queried newly arrived refugees about the course of the war and the condition of their relatives and friends. Those who brought money with them, those who soon secured support from the British treasury, lent funds to the others. Hopes of going home soared and fell. At last came the end of the war, a flood of fleeing Tories, and the certainty that the Patriots had triumphed. It was then necessary for the Loyalists to recognize that they were indeed exiles and to act accordingly. Many older people who could not resume their occupations subsisted upon grants of money from government; younger ones began new lives as best they might. Gradually most of the exiles, losing their special identity, merged into the British people.

There was much unhappiness among the expatriates. It was not possible for men and women who had lost so much, perhaps everything but life, because they had stood for the empire, to accept without heartache the cool treatment they commonly received in Biitain. Had they spent themselves and their substance for union with a people who ignored them, who looked upon them as alien, who considered them to be inferior? Had they erred when they committed themselves to Britain? They longed to see again the rocky hills of New England, the pleasant meadows of New Jersey, the tall pines of North Carolina, the low Sea Islands of Georgia. In nostalgic memory America acquired added majesty and new loveliness.

The Britain to which the Tories fled was not like the Britain that many of them had conceived in imagination. They found the nation that had sought to extract stamp and tea taxes from the Americans to be, despite the strains of war, rich. They discovered that the wealth of Britain was most unevenly distributed, that it was a splendid country for opulent members of the nobility, for propertied ladies and gentlemen, even for successful merchants, that it had little to offer to Americans who lacked both capital and substantial income. One Loyalist who had migrated from England to America shortly before the War of Independence was harshly reminded that plebeians were not valued in his native land. Richard Davis, a baker by trade, had acquired two offices in Georgia; he had, in fact, become clerk to the chief justice of the colony. Remaining faithful to Britain, he lost his posts and asked that he be compensated for his sacrifice. Many other Tories did receive such an indemnity. However, the British commission that considered the claims of the Loyalists, sufficiently sympathetic when weighing the petitions of ladies and gentlemen among the exiles, scorned Davis. It declared that "he got into situations created by the war which he had no right at any time to have expected," that he came "with a very bad grace" to ask for compensation, and that "He will probably be able to get his bread in this country by following his old trade of baker which is much more fit than to be clerk to a chief justice." It was not right or seemly for a mere baker to rise in the world. Davis should have joined the Patriots, most of whom would not have held

501

it against him that he had once earned his livelihood by kneading dough and cutting pastries.

Even Loyalists born in America who were not plebeian in their own land learned that they were outsiders in England. Jonathan Sewell of Massachusetts wrote to a friend in the New World that he could "have no idea what a noble country this is for a gentleman—every thing is upon an immense scale—whatever I have seen in my own country, is all minia-ture, Yankee-puppet-show." Sewell said that "the wealth of this country is truly astonishing, but unless a gentleman can get his share of it, he has no business here." Judge Samuel Curwen of Salem in the same state asserted that England "is, or might be, a paradise of delights for those who enjoy a full purse, and are by education and habit formed to relish its delights, amusements and pursuits." Curwen found it difficult to make acquaintances among the English, for they were "too proud or reserved." The Reverend Jonathan Boucher, an English-born Anglican clergyman who had sojourned in Maryland, declared that the Bishop of London and the Archbishop of Canterbury were "cold and formal, and seem to think they do wonders, when they give you a dinner." Boucher decided that he was "fit only for America," where "I have some character and note—here every body I see eclipses me." He lamented that he had "all to begin again." Boucher was young enough to start a new career. But many of the gentry among the exiles were too old to regain in England the status they had enjoyed in America; and other younger gentlemen could not over-come the handicaps imposed upon them by sudden poverty. The offspring of the expatriates often did well, but they themselves were usually disap-pointed. Resenting real and fancied slights, they unhappily shifted about from lodging to lodging, wandered from one vain hope of preferment or fortune to another. Samuel Curwen met George III and described him with less than worshipful enthusiasm as "tall, square over the shoulders, large ugly mouth, talks a great deal, and shows his teeth too much; his countenance heavy and lifeless, with white eyebrows." Peter Oliver of Massachusetts denounced the King's British subjects. "We are obliged," said he, "to put up with every insult from this ungrateful people the English without any redress."

Even that stout and distinguished champion of the empire, Thomas Hutchinson, learned that most faithful service could be forgotten. When he arrived in London in 1774, he was received by George III; the King's ministers called upon him; and he was tendered an honorary degree by Oxford University. He was even offered a baronetcy, but refused it be-cause he lacked funds to live in the style suited to the title—and govern-ment did not give him enough income to permit him to accept it. His advice was eagerly sought. But he received less and less attention from the British in high places as his political value waned. Eighteen months after his arrival, he wrote, "We Americans are plenty here, and very cheap." He was no longer young. His thoughts turned increasingly, "day and night," to the Massachusetts that he loved. "New England is wrote upon my heart in as strong characters as Calais was upon Queen Mary's," he declared. He hoped that he would return home, "live and die" among his former neighbors, and "I trust, recover their esteem." "I had rather die in a little country farm house in New England than in the best nobleman's seat in Old England," he asserted. Snob, excessively diligent officeseeker, and poor politician Hutchinson might be, but he was devoted to his native country. He never saw it again. He did not forgive his Patriot enemies; he sanctioned British employment of Indian warriors against them. He died in 1780 and was buried, not in Boston, or near his home in adjacent Milton, but in London.

Nathaniel Hatch, another Massachusetts officeholder, encountered an even sadder fate. Uprooted, he consorted with other exiles in London. One night he joined some of them in a gay party. The following morning, depressed, he killed himself.

Elizabeth Lloyd, stepdaughter of Nathaniel Hatch, also encountered tragedy. The opinion has been cited already that she was a profligate courtesan, the *femme fatale* of the War of Independence, that General William Howe devoted himself as excessively to her as Mark Antony gave his attention to Cleopatra, and that Howe in consequence lost America for Britain as Mark Antony lost the Roman empire. Certainly she began life most respectably, for she was of the prominent Lloyds of Lloyd's Neck, Long Island, and Boston. She was descended from other dignified colonial families, and she married, quite conventionally, Joshua Loring, Jr., of Massachusetts, a good-looking, pleasant young man with prospects, whose father had commanded a naval squadron on the Great Lakes under General Jeffery Amherst during the Seven Years' War. The outlook for the attractive couple was bright before the outbreak of the war. They had children, and they prospered. Joshua Loring had connections and a gift for making friends. After a period of service as an officer in the British army, he entered the British customs service. He secured an appointment as surveyor of the woods in New Hampshire, and early in 1775 he bought the post of sheriff in Suffolk County, which included Boston. But the young Lorings were Tories, and their comfortable little world was destroyed by the war. The husband, trapped in Boston after the battle of Lexington and Concord, lost his employment and his property; the wife, who happened to be outside the city on April 19, lost a child during the investment of the city.

The Lorings were among the 1,100 Loyalists who fled to Halifax with Howe's army. But they accompanied Howe to New York, and both Patriot and Loyalist tongues began to wag. Joshua Loring, with a brother-in-law, had formed a company to sell wine and rum to the royal officers and troops. Howe gave the company his favor. Moreover, he presented Loring an appointment as commissary of prisoners with a salary of £1 per day, with other perquisites. Loring was accused by Ethan Allen, probably without justice, of making money by cheating prisoners in his care. Allen called him a smiling "monster." But Alexander Graydon, a Continental officer who was for a time in the care of the commissary, afterward declared that he had no complaint to make; and the Patriot General Gold S. Silliman asserted that when he was a prisoner of the British in 1779, Loring treated him "with complaisance, kindness, and friendship, that ought never to be forgotten by me." It became common talk that he was rewarded by Howe because he was an uncomplaining cuckold, that Mrs. Loring was the mistress of the general. Afterward, the Loyalist historian, Thomas Jones of New York, called her the "Sultana," claimed that she squandered large sums in gambling, and said that Howe neglected to win the war because he was more interested in her than in achieving victory. She was contemporaneously and ribaldly assailed in Patriot prose and verse. She went to England in 1778, and her husband joined her there at the end of the war. They settled at Reading in England and had more children. When Joshua died in 1789, Elizabeth, with a recommendation from Howe, was given a temporary pension that she continued to receive until 1831. The descendants of the Lorings regained status for the family in England and have rendered valuable service to their country.

It is not to be believed that Sir William Howe seriously neglected his duty because of Elizabeth Loring or any other lady in America. Was she his mistress? The common talk may have arisen from fact. It is possible that the highly respectable young wife, shaken by the loss of her child and many troubles and surrounded by loose-living British officers, succumbed to the hedonism of war. But it is quite likely that the Lorings were merely indiscreet, and that they were the victims of scandalmongers. It is probable that neither Thomas Jones, an embittered Tory who was determined to find a scapegoat in Howe, nor the Patriots who derided Howe and the Lorings, knew those persons intimately. In a history of her family a daughter of Joshua and Elizabeth Loring relates that Howe had met Joshua at the siege of Havana in 1762 and that the two men then became good friends. There are still in existence at least two letters written to Elizabeth by her husband during the war in which he expresses a warm affection for her. In any event, the Lorings survived the war; the gossip died down; and they contributed to Britain, in their descendants,

504

high-ranking naval and army officers, together with at least one bishop of the Anglican Church.

There is no record indicating that the Lorings ever seriously considered a return to America, and it is unlikely that they did so. It was otherwise with a number of Loyalists who had perhaps suffered less in America than they, but who were not happy or even content in England. Such persons often joined their fellow Tories in Canada; some were interested in a scheme that was never executed for founding a Loyalist refuge in Australia; a few so yearned for their firesides in the United States that they chose to go home. As late as 1793, despite his successful career as a scientist on the eastern side of the Atlantic, Count Rumford said that he expected soon to go back to America. He did not actually return. But other exiles ultimately chose to cast their lot with the new republic. More of them would have done so, had they been assured that they would be civilly received within it. However, immediately after the war, Tories who went back to their homes risked abuse. A few who reappeared in South Carolina and who were believed to have been guilty of atrocities were lynched; and a Connecticut Loyalist, who neglected to find out whether he was welcome, was half-lynched. Gradually, political passions waned among the Patriots, and it became possible for Loyalists to secure a cool though still not warm reception. Exiles who could not become British, who learned at last that they were and could be no other than American, wandered back across the Atlantic—Judge Samuel Curwen to Massachusetts; Peter Van Schaack and the Reverend Samuel Seabury to New York; Stephen Kemble, an officer in the British army and a brother-in-law of General Gage, to New Jersey; Governor John Penn and the Reverend Jacob Duché to Pennsylvania. Van Schaack declared that he would be as "good a subject of the new government as I ever was of the old," and lived on as comfortably as might be to old age in his old home. Judge Curwen, on the other hand, returning to Salem, was never quite happy.

Samuel Curwen was a victim of divided loyalties. As an expatriate he gradually turned against the British, but he never gave full allegiance to the new order in America. One of the first of the exiles to reach England, he was already sixty years of age. He soon became uneasy in "this country of aliens." Subsisting without pleasure upon a British allowance, he became bored and homesick. He found the privileged in England to be frivolous, the poor to be sullenly indifferent to the course of the war. His Yankee pride was piqued by British expressions of contempt for the Americans. He came earnestly to wish that "the despised Americans may convince these conceited islanders, that without regular standing armies

our continent can furnish brave soldiers and judicious and expert commanders." He was annoyed to hear Englishmen speak of "our colonies,
our plantations," as if they were merely the property of Britain and the
superior British. He received the news of the surrender of Cornwallis, a
heavy blow to "this haughty America-despising people," with mixed feelings. After the end of the war he went down to the Thames to see
merchant vessels flying American flags. He learned that if he returned to
Salem, he would not be molested, that the British treasury would continue
to pay him his pension even if he went back to Massachusetts. But, going
home, he discovered everything to be changed. He was tolerated, not
welcome. He was no longer a person of importance in his native country.
Curwen considered removal to Nova Scotia. But being an old man he
stayed on in Salem, never quite adjusting to the new scheme of things,
until his death. The colonial world in which he had occupied a comfortable niche was gone, and he could find no satisfactory substitute for it.

It has been suggested that the new order, into which Curwen could
not fit, in which so many thousands of Loyalists had no part, was defective because the departure of so many responsible, respectable, and law-
abiding persons left a gaping wound in the American body politic. If the
exiles were not remarkable for talent, were they not people who had
specially contributed stability to colonial society? Did not the triumph of
the Patriots, if it brought liberty, also encourage contempt for established
and worthy institutions, for government, for churches, for courts? Was
not America's lynch law derived, even in name, from illegal attacks by
Patriots upon Tories? It is evident that the Americans, long after the
Revolution, were indeed less obedient to law than the British or the
Canadians; that they were generally less respectful of authority; that they
were, despite their remarkable kindness and gentleness in their treatment
of each other, more addicted to personal violence. It must remain doubtful that the Revolution in general, that the exodus of the Loyalists in
particular, inflicted grievous injuries upon American society. Certainly
the Americans of the Revolutionary generation destroyed many abuses,
and they created a new régime that endured, that won the respect and
envy of peoples over the globe.

CHAPTER XXXI

The Forging of the American Union

DURING and immediately after the War of Independence their enemies often predicted that the Americans would come to ruin, that they would slip into anarchy. Certainly, even after they had secured their freedom from Britain, they had to face a most difficult question. Could they establish an enduring national government that would assure internal peace and prosperity, and at the same time provide for their common defense? The most discerning men among the Patriots saw serious defects in the Articles of Confederation even before that constitution went into force, and its shortcomings were recognized by men of affairs before the end of the war. It became obvious to them that the central government lacked both sufficient power and proper machinery to wield power. But was it possible to find suitable remedies? And could the widely scattered Americans, with their allegiances to Thirteen States, with their diverse economies, with their varying social structures, with their fears of tyranny, be induced to accept those remedies? Both of those questions were answered in the affirmative. The Constitution was superbly devised in 1787 and became the basis for an enduring union in the following year. The Founding Fathers, have been amply, if properly, praised. The merits of the Americans as a whole, who peacefully debated the contents of the Constitution, who often understood its splendid qualities, who insisted that a Bill of Rights be added to it, who accepted it, have not been sufficiently applauded. The years immediately following the end of the War of Independence were once described as "the critical period" of

507

American history, one that came to an end with the ratification of the Constitution. One may not endorse such a fulsome phrase. The lot of the Americans was by no means desperate during those years. It is nevertheless true that they overcame many civil difficulties and that the founding of the new and stronger union under the Constitution not only assured that the benefits of independence would not be lost, but that they would be inherited and enlarged by later generations of Americans.

The peace of 1783, with all its gains for the Americans, did not bring with it instant prosperity. It required time to mend the damages and disruptions of war. The Southern planters had lost thousands of slaves who were employed by the British as military laborers until the end of hostilities and then carried off to the West Indies, to a new bondage. Those Americans who had been assisted by the Parliamentary bounty upon naval stores and indigo lost that special benefit from British rule. Northern merchants seeking to revive American maritime commerce—a Yankee ship appeared in the Thames flying an American flag even before the signing of the treaty of peace—learned that Britain's mercantilist restrictions injured foreigners more than British colonists. American ships were barred in 1783 from British ports in the Caribbean. If markets in Holland, Germany, and France were now open to Americans, it was also true that Americans could not buy manufactured goods on credit in those countries as they were accustomed to do from the British. At the same time, British creditors insistently demanded payment of debts contracted before the war, alike from American merchants and planters. As soon as the war ended, American merchants made extensive purchases of British goods in the hope of making swift and handsome profits. The Americans bought nearly £3.7 million worth in 1784, but Britain imported things Americans valued at only £750,000. A shortage of currency aggravated every economic difficulty. Gradually, the American merchants found new markets, including some in distant China. But the years 1785 to 1786 were marked by a commercial depression. American maritime commerce did not again reach the high level it had attained before the war until 1788.

The economic condition of the Americans at that time cannot be measured precisely by sales and purchases of goods abroad. Few of them were utterly dependent upon commerce or industry for a livelihood, and few of them lacked food or shelter in the bad times of the mid-1780's. Nevertheless, it is evident that Americans on the land as well as those in cities and towns were distressed for lack of cash. They rose in revolt in Massachusetts. Many of the states were striving to reduce the debts they had incurred during the war, and raised taxes toward that end. Farmers whose property was endangered because they could not pay their debts or taxes begged for stay laws that would permit them to defer payment. A demand for the familiar panacea, the issuance of paper money, arose, and seven of the states resorted to the printing press, despite the pleas of creditors and others who feared the effects of circulation of cheap money. The additions to the supply of money in fact proved to be beneficial. In Massachusetts the legislature refused to act to relieve embarrassed farmers, and they took up arms to defend their homes and lands. Bands of them closed many courts in that state in the autumn of 1786. The insurrection soon collapsed in eastern Massachusetts, but it continued into the following winter in the western part of the state, under the leadership of Daniel Shays, a Revolutionary officer. With hundreds of followers Shays threatened to seize a national arsenal at Springfield. Governor James Bowdoin called into service militia who beat back an attack upon the arsenal by Shays and 1,200 of his followers on January 26, 1787. Four of his men were killed. Pursued by militia in overwhelming force, the Shaysites fled and dispersed. The Massachusetts legislature then took some steps to remove the causes for discontent.

The Congress voted to raise troops to assist in putting down Shays's Rebellion, but did not actually collect and put them in motion. Such was the usual behavior of that body so long as the Articles of Confederation endured. It could display wisdom, as it did in framing the Northwest Ordinance. But the central government was fundamentally feeble. It lacked a strong executive and courts that could enforce its will. The authority vested in the Congress by the Articles was insufficient for the needs of the nation. Moreover, the Congress was often unable to exercise the powers it did possess, because of lack of funds. It was compelled largely to depend for money upon requisitions sent to the states—and the states, burdened with local troubles, did not uniformly and promptly send their full quotas. In 1785 New Jersey flatly refused to supply any money whatever. The income of the central government was in consequence both inadequate and uncertain. It was hard pressed to meet its current obligations; it was unable materially to reduce its debts contracted during the War of Independence; without loans from Dutch bankers who had farsighted faith in the United States as well as keen eyes for profit, the nation would have been threatened by bankruptcy.

Such a government could defend neither the maritime commerce of the Americans nor their frontiers; it did not command the respect of foreign rulers; it could not frighten Indian chiefs. When John Adams arrived in London in 1785 as the first American minister to Britain, he was received in gentlemanly fashion by George III; and he and his wife

Abigail were welcomed by Lord and Lady Effingham, old and faithful friends of the Americans. But British officers of state soon let the republican Mr. Adams know that he and the government that he represented were not of much consequence in Britain. They did not bother even to send an envoy to America. Britain failed to withdraw troops stationed in forts on the southern side of the frontier between Canada and the United States, so violating the peace treaty of 1783. Adams urged that the forts be evacuated. He was told that they might be—when the Americans paid their debts to British merchants. Jefferson, replacing Franklin as the American minister in Paris, was given a gracious reception, but he accomplished little there. He vainly tried to form an international expedition against the Barbary pirates of North Africa, who were preying upon American commerce. Instead, the Congress was forced to pay tribute to the pirates, as did all the European nations. Spain sent an envoy to the United States, Don Diego de Gardoqui. He let the Americans know that they were not to be given treaty rights to use the Mississippi after it entered Spanish territory, and that a quarrel between Spain and the United States over the northern boundary of West Florida must be settled in favor of King Charles III.

For lack of money, the Congress let die the little navy it had created during the War of Independence. What was much worse, it could maintain but few troops. It was therefore unable to offer protection to Western frontiersmen exposed to Indian attacks encouraged by both the British and the Spanish. A few unhappy settlers in Kentucky and Tennessee wavered in their allegiance to the United States. Might they not do better by creating independent nations beyond the Appalachians, by seeking the friendship of Britain or Spain? Momentarily, it seemed possible that the Americans would permit themselves to be divided by the mountain range.

The remedy for many of the ills of the new nation was obvious. Given a substantial and reliable income, the central government would be able to deal with both foreign and domestic enemies. In fact, the device by which funds could readily be secured—duties upon imports—was also obvious. Accordingly, there were several efforts in the early 1780's to amend the Articles of Confederation so that such levies might be imposed. But that constitution could not be altered without the unanimous consent of the thirteen state legislatures; and it proved to be impossible to secure approval of the change by all of them. The Congress then considered, in 1786, amendments which would have given it power to compel the states to honor the requisitions of the central government. But it was only too clear that the several legislatures would not endorse that

510

scheme, and it, too, was abandoned. The requirement that all alterations in the Articles of Confederation be ratified by all the states was a formidable barrier against necessary constitutional reform. Was there no way in which it could be achieved?

Far-reaching changes in the American federacy did become possible. In September 1786, delegates from five states attended the Annapolis Convention, called to consider ways to encourage the free flow of commerce within the nation. Only twelve men were present, and they could do nothing immediately to achieve the purpose for which they had met. However, among them were Alexander Hamilton and James Madison. The two men saw an opportunity. They secured the issuance of an invitation to all the states to send delegates to a convention at Philadelphia, in May 1787, that should discuss, not merely problems of internal trade, but all matters necessary "to render the constitution of the federal government adequate to the exigencies of the Union." It was evident that the framers of the invitation desired much more than a few changes in the Articles of Confederation. But no fewer than five states soon named delegates, and the Congress, in February 1787, cautiously gave its approval to the convention, "for the sole and express purpose of revising the Articles of Confederation and reporting to Congress and the several legislatures such alterations and provisions therein." Then seven more states commissioned delegates to the convention. Rhode Island, the smallest of them, declined to participate.

What had happened to persuade nearly all of the legislatures to accept the invitation from Annapolis? To be sure, the defects of the Articles of Confederation had become only too apparent. Doubtless, the economic depression then passing—blame for it being placed upon government, as usual in America—influenced men to seek political change. Unquestionably, the Shays Rebellion exercised an effect—was it not necessary to prevent anarchy, to endow the central government with sufficient authority to maintain internal order? It was prudent to act toward warding off the establishment of restrictions upon internal trade by the states, some of which were displaying the particularistic jealousies that had existed among the colonies; it was desirable to place foreign commerce under national control, so that it might be protected and encouraged by a single and strong government. There were other reasons behind the swelling demand for constitutional change. The Conservatives among the Patriots had suffered many defeats in their contests in the states with the Radicals and Liberals. Many of them desired a strong central government and hoped to dominate it. Some of them owned certificates of indebtedness issued during the War of Independence by the national régime in payment for goods and services. Faith in the ability of Congress to redeem the certificates had waned, and they had lost most of their value. But would not a new and solvent central government pay the debts of the United States in full, so rewarding those who had lent to the nation when it was in distress—and others who had foresightedly purchased certificates at prices far below their face value? Those certificates were not important to most of the Conservatives, but the latter very generally desired constitutional provisions that would prevent the passage of stay laws and the issuance of cheap and unsupported paper currency by the states.

During the nineteenth century a myth developed among the Americans, to the effect that the Constitution framed by the federal convention that met at Philadelphia was the work of altruistic genuises, the so-called Founding Fathers. Worshiping the Constitution as Europeans looked up to Kings and Emperors, they venerated the men who made it. Its authors would have been surprised by such adulation; they well knew that they were not selfless demigods. In the twentieth century several scholars, observing that they were in fact planters, merchants, and lawyers, have contended that they primarily sought economic benefits for their class, perhaps even for themselves as individuals. One must set aside such crass economic determinism. Nor may one accept without cavil another contention offered by some twentieth-century historians to the effect that these men, being of the Conservative camp, devised an organic instrument which enabled the Conservatives to execute a counterrevolution, the equivalent of the Thermidorean reaction in France in 1794. The American Revolution and the French Revolution of 1789 were different in origin, in development, and in consequences.

Admittedly, the men who appeared at Philadelphia in the late spring and early summer of 1787 were persons of means, merchants, lawyers, and planters rather than mechanics, plain farmers, and teachers. But was it not almost inevitable that such men, being the best educated Americans and those most experienced in public affairs, should be chosen by the state legislatures? Does it follow that they were not interested in the economic advance of poorer and less sophisticated Americans, that they were not genuinely concerned for the establishment of order at home, for national defense? Surely they had in mind their own interests, their own desire for power, but they could not forget that their own well-being was ultimately, even immediately, intermingled with the welfare of the humbler Americans. It will not do to contend that George Washington, who presided over the convention, and James Madison, who was the principal architect of the Constitution, were mere selfish Conservatives. It is well to remember that Benjamin Franklin, old, experienced, and no lover of aristocrats, sat in the convention and endorsed the document; that Thomas Jefferson, no champion of privilege, examining it in far-off Paris, concluded that it was generally satisfactory. Let it not be said that Washington, Madison, Franklin, and Jefferson were hoodwinked by astute and sinister conspirators. In the main, the delegates displayed an enlightened, a generous selfishness.

The men in the convention numbered fifty-five, the majority being lawyers. More than half had attended college. Most of them were experienced public servants. There was much talent among them, and some genius. Presiding, Washington, neither fluent nor subtle, said little about the many questions faced by the convention; dignified and sober, he reminded the delegates by his very presence that they were Americans who must do their duty. Nor did Franklin seek to dominate the gathering; tired, he amiably encouraged younger men to toil. Alexander Hamilton, Revolutionary officer and brilliant young lawyer, was a member, but attended only a few sessions. He made no secret of the fact that he believed limited constitutional monarchy to be the ideal form of government. So he deprived himself of opportunity to participate in the work of the convention. John Dickinson was present as a representative of Delaware. He had little to say. James Wilson and Gouverneur Morris of Pennsylvania talked frequently, as did Elbridge Gerry of Massachusetts and George Mason of Virginia. Wilson, a thoughtful lawyer, helped to solve several problems. Morris was a one-legged and amorous snob who steadily asserted the superiority and wishes of a man of wealth; he could write good English, and it was he who eventually put the Constitution into good form. Mason was solicitous for the protection of personal liberty and Southern interests. John Rutledge and Charles Cotesworth Pinckney of South Carolina also appeared as champions of the South. They were generous-minded aristocrats who would not let unworthy suspicions of Northerners prevent the creation of a stronger central government. Roger Sherman and Oliver Ellsworth of Connecticut most usefully helped to make two compromises that settled two grave disputes in the Convention. But it was the Virginia delegation, led by the modest and shy scholar James Madison, that principally supplied both vision and leadership. Absent were Jefferson and John Adams, busy in Paris and London. Also absent were Samuel Adams and Patrick Henry. Jefferson and John Adams could have offered important contributions. Samuel Adams and Henry did not see pressing need for constitutional change; with ability to sway men, they did not possess constructive intellect.

The convention was not open to the public. Its sessions were secret, and there was no effort to keep a precise record of speeches. Its affairs were not conducted as if it were a New England town meeting. Its procedures could be described as undemocratic; but they proved to be beneficial. Delegates could speak neither to the gallery nor to the Americans generally. They were thus encouraged to eschew loquacity and oratorical display. Moreover, not committing themselves publicly and prematurely to absolute positions upon the many questions they faced, the delegates were better able to make concessions in order to achieve agreement. Even so, the convention encountered many troubles; at times, it seemed likely that it would adjourn without result. Tempers frayed in the humid heat of a Philadelphia summer. The delegates did not finish their work until September.

The convention made rapid progress in its first sessions. It reached two fundamental decisions before June 19. It formally resolved that the American federation must be basically altered, that America must have a stronger central government. Toward that end, it also determined to prepare a new constitutional instrument to replace the Articles of Confederation. Its members could have amended that document so as to achieve their goal, but the result would quite surely have been an unseemly hodge-podge containing contradictory statements. They wisely chose to begin anew; they did make use of many suitable phrases from the Articles.

But the delegates soon also demonstrated that they were human rather than semi-divine. The Virginians, arriving early at Philadelphia, had time to concoct the "Virginia Plan" for a new federal system, which they presented to the convention. Madison was doubtless its principal author. It was furiously debated in June and early July, partly because it would have vested vast power in the central government, partly because delegates from the "small states" saw in it arrangements that would enable the "large states," Virginia, Pennsylvania, and Massachusetts, to rule the nation. The Virginians proposed a bicameral Congress, which was eventually established in the form of the House of Representatives and the Senate. Seats in the lower house were to be apportioned in accordance with population; it was to choose the members of the upper chamber from lists of names submitted by the states; and the Congress was to elect the executive. The central government was to be virtually the judge of its own powers and was to have authority to coerce the states. It is evident that the Virginians proposed to instill excessive vigor in the central régime, especially in the "popular" branch of the legislature. Such a concentration of power would have made ratification of the new Constitution impossible; the protests against it of the men from the "small states," such as New Jersey and Delaware, were quite justified. But did they have good reason to fear that the representatives of the three largest

American commonwealths in the lower house would combine to dominate the republic? So they believed. Gunning Bedford of Delaware hinted that he would prefer the restoration of British authority to dictatorship by Virginia, Pennsylvania, and Massachusetts. William Paterson of New Jersey offered the "New Jersey Plan" as a substitute for that brought forward by Virginia. It called for retention of the unicameral legislature under the Articles of Confederation, with its voting by states; for giving Congress power to tax and to regulate interstate and foreign commerce; for the vesting of executive authority in a plural body chosen by the Congress; and for a national Supreme Court. The scheme advanced by Paterson had obvious merits, and parts of it were eventually inserted in the Constitution. It did not give the central government enough muscle; it reserved too much power to the states.

All attempts to soothe fears of the "small state" men lest the "large states" control the union failed. Madison cogently pointed out that men in Congress in the past had not voted in accordance with the size of the commonwealths from which they came, that they would not do so in the future. They would assert economic, social, and sectional interests that ignored state boundaries. It was to be expected that men from Massachusetts and New Hampshire would vote alike, that representatives from Georgia and South Carolina would see eye to eye. He did not err, but his opponents refused to recognize the inescapable logic of his argument.

If the convention was to continue, it was necessary to find a middle way between the Virginia and New Jersey schemes with respect to the form of the national government. It was found, with the delegates from Connecticut supplying impetus. Hence the so-called "Connecticut Compromise," which called for a House of Representatives composed of members from districts established in accordance with population and a Senate containing two persons from each of the states, chosen by their legislatures, with a safeguarding proviso that no state could be deprived of its "equal suffrage" in that body without its consent. The "small states" were thus assured that their supposed special interests would have protection in the Senate. An ironic result was that a people that had revolted against taxation without representation were most unequally represented in a Senate that could not initiate a tax bill, but could amend or even refuse to pass one. Afterward, populous New York had no greater voice in the upper chamber than sparsely inhabited Nevada. Two persons in it from thinly settled Alaska had status equal to that of two others from a heavily tenanted California.

Resolving the dispute over the form of the national legislature, the Connecticut Compromise also opened the way for a more suitable description of the powers of the central régime. The men from the "small states," satisfied that they would not be overwhelmed by their big neighbors, became less fearful of concentration of authority at the nation's capital. On the other hand, Madison and other champions of the Virginia Plan came to realize that the powers of the central government must not be described in general and generous phrases that would permit it to do almost as it willed. A constitution endowing it with such potence could not obtain the assent of the American people; moreover, it became increasingly obvious that such a vast grant of authority was quite unnecessary to meet their needs. Accordingly, it was at length decided to list the powers of the central government, making substantial additions to those wielded by Congress under the Articles of Confederation, and also to impose certain specific limitations upon the central government. It was thus possible to enlarge its authority in quite precise language, and at the same time to erect some safeguards against unwarranted expansion of that authority.

The quarrel between the "large states" and the "small states" arose principally from thoughtless jealousies. But controversy between North and South, which also threatened to disrupt the convention, had its origins in fundamental differences. It became ever more apparent during the War of Independence that the nation contained two quite distinct regions with clashing interests. It was recognized that the boundary between Pennsylvania and Maryland, the Mason-Dixon line surveyed in 1767, also divided the one region from the other. The term "Southern States" came into common usage to designate collectively Maryland, Virginia, the Carolinas, and Georgia. Before the Constitution was adopted, the area covered by those states began to be called "the South." The "Northern States" and "the North" made a complementary appearance. The South—with its warmer climate, special agriculture, Negro slaves, agrarian society, and planter aristocracy—was increasingly opposed to a North that contained few slaves, few large estates, and comparatively fewer aristocrats, that was burgeoning in commerce, that was beginning to develop infant industries. It will be recalled that William Henry Drayton of South Carolina was actually concerned lest the Congress under the Articles of Confederation became an instrument by which the North would dominate the South. There was much bickering between spokesmen for the two regions in that Congress. In 1779 they quarreled acrimoniously when they discussed the terms of peace they would seek to obtain from Britain. New Englanders urged that it was of the first consequence to secure fishing rights on the Grand Banks; Southerners, on the contrary, would have it that it was essential to acquire free navigation of

516

the Mississippi. Indeed, whether or not Congress should exert pressure upon Spain to open the river to American shipping was a subject of warm dispute throughout the 1780's. Southerners desired that America move vigorously; Yankees were reluctant to act. Trying to select a permanent site for the national capital, the delegates divided upon sharp sectional lines. So irritated were both Northerners and Southerners that there was serious talk of separation on both sides of the Mason-Dixon boundary in 1785 and 1786.

The mistrust which Southerners harbored against Northerners was not shared by Washington, who was a steady and devout nationalist. He would not even speak of his Virginia as a Southern state. He did not fear that the North would in stupid selfishness seek to dominate the South or the republic. No man knew better than the former commander in chief the need for a central government that could provide for defense, that would give stability and strength to the union. He had not fought for two or three or thirteen nations. But other delegates from the South were concerned lest their region be submerged in the union, lest its interests be set aside in favor of Northern ones. Even Madison, who was determined to give the central government very large powers, jealously and zealously sought to safeguard Southern interests. John Rutledge and Charles Cotesworth Pinckney were of the same mind as Madison. George Mason, though he thoroughly detested the oceanic traffic in slaves, was nevertheless a tenacious champion for the South. He would not consent to sacrifices injurious to his region for the sake of national unity. There were many in that region who felt as he did. Was it possible to create a strong central government and at the same time to satisfy the Southerners in the convention—and was it possible sufficiently to please the Southerners generally so that the Constitution could be put into force?

There was no struggle over Negro slavery in the convention. Much as many members desired its abolition, an attempt to give Congress power to proceed against it must have made adoption of the Constitution impossible. Northerners did not assail the institution, and Southerners did not feel compelled to defend it. The problem of slavery and the more massive one of relations between whites and blacks were left to the states and to the future. But were slaves to be counted when seats in the House of Representatives were apportioned in accordance with population? Congress was given power to impose direct taxes. Were slaves to be numbered with whites when such levies were imposed? Southerners urged that Negroes be considered equal to whites for the purpose of representation, but not for the purpose of taxation. Northerners insisted that slaves ought to be counted as persons with whites so far as taxation was concerned, but not with respect to representation in the Congress. Tempers flared on both sides. The inconsistent stands taken by champions of the two sections finally led to an inconsistent but acceptable compromise suggested by Madison. It was agreed that five slaves were to be counted as equal to three whites for both purposes.

Spokesmen for the two regions quarreled even more strenuously about the authority to be vested in the Congress over external taxation and commerce. There was general agreement that the central government must impose import duties; the proceeds from them would supply it with a substantial and reliable income. But should it be empowered to tax exports? The products sent to sea from the South, principally tobacco, rice, wheat, and indigo, were far more valuable than those shipped from the harbors of the North. Southerners insisted that duties upon exports would be inequitable, that the Congress must be forbidden to enact such levies. Besides, many Southerners envied the Yankees because they profited from maritime trade, a branch of traffic in which Southerners were not active. They demanded that the Congress be denied power to pass laws that would favor American at the expense of foreign shipping. They wished to prevent the Yankees from securing a monopoly of the carrying trade between Southern and foreign ports. How they would be hurt by such a monopoly is not quite clear—Washington later asked why they were so eager to defend the carrying trade of the British, competitors of the Yankees and enemies of the United States. Delegates from South Carolina and Georgia wished to place still another restriction upon the authority of the Congress over maritime commerce. Planters in those states desired that the slave trade with Africa and the West Indies be allowed to continue so long as South Carolina and Georgia desired— there was still a shortage of slave labor in the deep South. Northerners opposed all three of the demands made by the Southerners. They sought to vest in the Congress full authority to tax external commerce, to pass navigation acts that would strike at the British, and to put a quick and final end to the oceanic traffic in human bodies. After acrimonious debate, with delegates from Connecticut and South Carolina leading the way, a compromise was arranged. It was agreed that the Congress should have power to regulate foreign commerce; it might impose import, but not export duties; it could proceed against the oceanic trade in Negroes, but not until the Constitution had been in force for twenty years. The bargain was quite satisfactory to John Rutledge and Charles Cotesworth Pinckney, who thereafter ardently fought for the Constitution. It was most offensive to George Mason, who declined to affix his signature to a document he believed to be hostile to Southern interests.

518

The convention toiled over other questions. After much wavering, it decided that the nation must have a single and powerful executive. At last, in September, it finished its work. Only forty-two of the delegates were present when the Constitution became available for signature; only thirty-nine put their names upon it. The signers did not believe that the political instrument produced by the convention was ideal; the delegates performed better than they knew. Despite its shortcomings, including failure to provide for political parties, the Constitution provided for a federal system superbly fitted to the needs of the Americans at that time. Moreover, amplified and altered by amendments, by decisions of the Supreme Court of the United States, by Congressional statutes, by custom, the Constitution continued in force generation after generation. The achievement of its framers has been justly lauded.

The Constitution provided for a system in which the central government would have sufficient authority to be described as both federal and truly national. Like those of the states, it was to rest upon the people, and was to be able, within specific limits, to enforce its will upon the people. Its powers were listed, and it was restricted by special prohibitions. Together with the powers vested in it by the Articles of Confederation, it was permitted to impose import duties and internal taxes; to regulate interstate and foreign commerce; to issue currency—a privilege denied to the states; and to maintain an army and navy. It was to consist of three branches, the bicameral legislature that arose from the Connecticut Compromise; an executive dominated by a President, indirectly chosen by an electoral college or by the House of Representatives and endowed with a veto upon Congressional bills, command of the armed forces, and other powers; and an independent judiciary consisting of a Supreme Court and other lower tribunals. "Checks and balances" were inserted to prevent undue expansion of the authority of any one of the branches at the expense of the others. The Constitution had one very serious defect. Its framers did not insert in it a Bill of Rights to protect the citizen against tyrannical exercises of national authority. Did they believe that it was unnecessary to provide for such contingencies, since that authority was confined to specific grants of power? Probably so. It is also likely that Conservative-minded members of the convention were not eager to defend personal rights against the Congress, the President, or federal judges.

It will be recalled that the convention, preferring to make a new Constitution rather than to try to revise the Articles of Confederation, declined to be cramped by instructions from the old Congress. Nor would the makers of the Constitution submit it, as required by the Articles, to the thirteen state legislatures for approval, a procedure that would almost certainly prevent its ratification. They boldly ignored the Articles and asked that their handiwork be considered, not by the state legislatures, but by state conventions. Moreover, they declared that the Constitution was to be in force as soon as nine of those conventions endorsed it—they hoped to secure the approval of more than nine, and of all the larger states. They did not intend that their labors be wasted because Rhode Island refused its consent. Did they commit an act of usurpation? Certainly judgment of the Constitution by state conventions containing men specially elected to consider it was more democratic than decision by state legislatures. Moreover, the delegates could argue with some cogency that ratification by all of the states was an absurd requirement. The old Congress inspected the Constitution. Some of its members pointed out that the method of adoption was unconstitutional with reference to the Articles of Confederation, but Congress sensibly sent the document to the states for decision.

Some scholars have condemned the procedure by which the Constitution was endorsed, assailing it as undemocratic. They have contended with good reason that it would have been defeated, had it been submitted to plebiscites in the several states. It is possible, however, that it would have received a majority in a nationwide plebiscite. In any case, the procedure was truly republican, and decision by state conventions—their members chosen by persons qualified to vote in their respective states— was extraordinary neither then nor later. It was just as well that the judgment was made by men far more acquainted with political philosophy and constitutional complexities than the voters who chose them. Scholars have also said that the Constitution did not win favor among city workmen and farmers of the interior, that it appealed especially to wealthy planters, lawyers, and prosperous men of business. Such was indeed the case, but enough of the poorer and less sophisticated Americans approved of it so that it could be ratified. No one could afterward demonstrate that they erred because they rallied behind Washington and Madison, John Rutledge and Roger Sherman, James Wilson and John Dickinson.

The champions of the Constitution had the better arguments, and they used them in convention after state convention during the closing weeks of 1787 and the first six months of 1788. They also debated with enemies of the Constitution in newspapers and pamphlets, in the state legislatures, and at meetings of the voters. Three of them, Alexander Hamilton, James Madison, and John Jay, wrote in behalf of the Constitution the famous series of essays called *The Federalist,* which appeared in many newspapers. It is a part of semi-sophisticated American folklore that *The Federalist* was largely instrumental in facilitating the adoption of the Constitution. But the essays were abstruse and dull; neither Hamilton nor Jay nor Madison could write with the persuasive power of Tom Paine or of Jefferson; they assuredly did not sway opponents of the Constitution in the South, for the authors made no great effort to answer objections to the instrument that were peculiarly Southern. *The Federalist* did later become useful to public men and students as a gloss upon the Constitution, but it was not decisive in 1787 or 1788. However, the Federalists, as the friends of the Constitution are known, were able to point out in speeches and in print that the document called for a suitably strong central government, but not for the reduction of the states to helplessness; that the President and the Congress would be responsible, directly and indirectly, to the voters; that the national government would be able to attain solvency, encourage commerce, promote prosperity, and defend America against both foreign and domestic adversaries. It would give the nation dignity and compel respect. Such appeals, directed to pocketbook, patriotism, and pride, were most difficult to refute. Moreover, Washington gave his blessing to the Constitution, and he would in all likelihood become the first President under it. The case for ratification was all the more convincing because the opponents of the Constitution, the Antifederalists, led by Patrick Henry, Richard Henry Lee, and George Clinton of New York, were divided among themselves. Some of them desired to maintain the Articles of Confederation without change; some were willing to accept the Constitution with massive amendments; others were disposed to endorse it with a few alterations.

But if the Antifederalists were not united, if they had the weaker arguments and inferior leadership, they drew strong support from the camp of the Radicals that had fought against the Conservatives in so many battles in the several states. Some Liberals also joined them, and they vehemently assailed the Constitution, its champions in general, and its makers in particular. They asserted that the friends of the Constitution were trying to create a "consolidated" union, a national régime that would be both all-powerful and tyrannical. They claimed that the rich and the well-born—the Conservatives—intended to use the Constitution as a vehicle to establish themselves as masters of the republic. They castigated its architects because they had failed to insert in it a federal Bill of Rights. Was not that omission in itself sufficient proof that its authors secretly nurtured designs against liberty? To such contentions the Antifederalists in the South added another, that the Constitution, despite the concessions obtained in the constitutional convention by the Southern delegates, was an instrument that would enable the North to injure Southern interests, indeed, to rule the South.

In the Northern states the most potent argument against the Constitution was that it did not contain a Bill of Rights. The conventions of Delaware, Pennsylvania, New Jersey, and Connecticut gave their approval without serious struggle. Endorsements by Massachusetts and New Hampshire were also obtained by the early summer of 1788, but only because the Federalists solemnly promised that they would support the addition of a Bill of Rights immediately after the new government came into being. By June 21, six Northern states had acted favorably, but New York was still wavering and the legislature of Rhode Island had not even bothered to arrange for a convention.

In the meantime, three Southern states, Georgia, Maryland, and South Carolina, had endorsed the Constitution. Thus it had the approval of nine states. But its fate was by no means decided. A new union without New York, Virginia, and North Carolina could hardly succeed. Moreover, there was especially vigorous and sharp hostility to the Constitution in both Virginia and North Carolina. South Carolina, impelled by John Rutledge, Charles Cotesworth Pinckney, Charles Pinckney, and the planter aristocracy of that state, had ratified despite a passionate warning from Rawlins Lowndes that "when this new Constitution should be adopted, the sun of the Southern states would set, never to rise again." There were many in Virginia, notably Patrick Henry and George Mason, who agreed with Lowndes. Moreover, it became apparent that North Carolina would follow the lead of Virginia. Whether or not the Constitution was to be much more than an exercise in political theory was therefore settled in Virginia.

The contest in Virginia was not decided until June 25. Before her state convention met, Patrick Henry so vehemently demanded amendments which would protect the South against Northern aggression that Washington came to suspect that Henry desired to form an independent Southern confederacy. In the convention Henry denounced the Constitution with his customary force and fervor, and he was joined by William Grayson and other notables. Henry correctly predicted that the national government, if not constitutionally prevented, would eventually move against Negro slavery; he argued well for the necessity of changes in the Constitution; but he also found many trivial faults in it. Grayson would not have a national régime that possessed a navy—it would be used against the South. James Madison, supported by John Marshall, Governor Edmund Randolph, Edmund Pendleton, and George Innes, quietly and patiently demolished most of Henry's objections. It was possible to say that his fears for the South were quite unfounded, because the South, extending into Kentucky and Tennessee, was at that time expanding more rapidly than the North. Light-Horse Harry Lee almost savagely assailed Henry. Lee rudely expressed an opinion that the orator was stupid and condemned him for posing as the great champion of liberty. Lee reminded the convention that he himself had fought for liberty, and he invited comparison of his record with that of Henry. He declared that the "people of America, sir, are one people. I love the people of the north, not because they have adopted the Constitution, but because I fought with them as my countrymen." Proclaimed Lee, "In all local matters I shall be a Virginian: in those of a general nature, I shall not forget that I am an American." Washington, not present at the convention, would not have engaged in a personal attack upon Henry. But everyone in that assembly knew that Lee otherwise expressed the sentiments of Washington. And there could be little doubt that Washington would be the first President under the Constitution. No one could believe that he, devoted as he was to the American nation, would take part in oppressing his fellow Virginians. At last, promising to labor for the passage of a federal Bill of Rights, Madison and his cohorts won a narrow victory.

It then became certain that the Constitution would go into force. Feeling against it was strong in New York. Alexander Hamilton, who did not admire it, but fought for it as an improvement over the Articles of Confederation, was its principal champion in the New York convention. He managed to defer a vote upon it until news came that Virginia had given her assent. With the Federalists promising that they would not struggle against the addition of a Bill of Rights, New York responded to the news, endorsing the Constitution by a majority of three. A convention in North Carolina voted against it. But that state could not flourish as an independent nation. In 1789, after it had become quite certain that a federal Bill of Rights would indeed become part of American fundamental law, a second convention in North Carolina gave assent. Sentiment against the Constitution was so ardent in Rhode Island that a convention did not meet until 1790, many months after the new national government had come into being. Having no other choice, the smallest of the states at last entered the new union.

Forging that union, the Founding Fathers did not offer solutions to all the troubles of the Americans. They did not try to arrange for the abolition of slavery. Negro bondage, a huge dark blot upon the American scene of liberty, continued, and at last supplied burning issues that led North and South into the bloody Civil War. Had the Founding Fathers striven to destroy slavery, the Constitution must have failed of adoption. They achieved all that could be expected of mortals in their time and circumstances. The political abilities and virtues displayed by the Americans generally in connection with the making of a sturdy federal republic have not received so much praise. It ought not be forgotten that they, too, demonstrated political wisdom. Debating the merits of the Constitution, the Federalists and Antifederalists did not resort to armed force. There was minor tumult in Pennsylvania and New York; a defender of the Constitution in North Carolina acquired two black eyes; no one was seriously injured during the protracted contest. The opponents of the Constitution demanded and later secured, in 1791, the passage of the Bill of Rights, a much needed addition to it. Moreover, they gracefully accepted defeat and took their part in the new régime. Many of them learned to revere the document they had so fervently assailed.

To the surprise of no one, Washington was unanimously chosen by the electoral college as the first President under the Constitution. The republic acquired a chief magistrate who towered above Kings and Emperors. The great man rode from Mount Vernon to New York in the spring of 1789 to assume his duties. His progress northward was a triumphal procession. His Continentals, officers and men, came forth to hail him as he passed their homes. At Trenton, scene of his brilliant victory clutched from crushing defeat, he was paid a touching tribute. A banner proclaimed that he had saved the mothers, that he would protect their daughters. In New York, before a concourse of spectators, he stiffly and modestly took the oath required from the President by the Constitution, "I do solemnly swear that I will faithfully execute the Office of President of the United States, and will to the best of my Ability, preserve, protect and defend the Constitution of the United States." Never was a political oath more superfluous.

In that first election under the Constitution, the Conservatives secured control of the Congress. They befriended merchants, creditors, and speculators, but they did not destroy the political and social gains of the Revolution. Their sway at the national capital was not absolute and did not long endure; twelve years later they peacefully abandoned power there to Liberals led by Thomas Jefferson. The Constitution was not a device that enabled a selfish few to dominate the many. It was, rather, the crowning innovation, the consummation of the Revolution. In the eyes of Europeans and others, it was a radical document. Under the Constitution the American nation acquired added vitality; its government was able to destroy hindrances to economic advance, to protect American rights upon the oceans, to expand the territory of the United States, to give military protection to its citizens. Sanctioning the Constitution, the Americans confirmed the far-reaching reforms of the Revolution and opened the way for many more wholesome changes to come.

ESSAY UPON AUTHORITIES

IT will be apparent to scholars specializing in the period of the American Revolution that this volume is based upon a wide variety of materials, including manuscripts and published documents as well as magazine articles and books by historians. Adequately to describe the primary sources for the era would be an immense and tedious task, and it will not be attempted in this brief essay upon authorities. Indeed, it is not possible even to mention more than a small fraction of the writings of the scholars. Moreover, the author, referring to this contribution but not to that, has inevitably slighted the achievements of many worthy, even splendid, students of the Revolution. He must beg forgiveness because he is cramped both by space and by his own limitations in learning and viewpoint. He has emphasized recent writings.

The difficulties that confront the author of a bibliographical essay upon the age of the Revolution have been augmented in recent years by a revival of activity in the field. During the decade of the Great Depression relatively few scholars devoted their energies and talents to America and Britain in the third and fourth quarters of the eighteenth century. Since World War II there has been a rising flood of learned articles and books that threatens, as the bicentennial of the Declaration of Independence approaches, to overwhelm even the specialist in the field of the Revolution.

Not surprisingly, there is now no one satisfactory history of the Revolution as a whole—this volume, it is hoped, will serve toward closing that gap. The classic history of George O. Trevelyan, retaining its literary charm, does not satisfy the demands of modern scholarship, nor does the unfinished *Founding of the American Republic* by Claude H. Van Tyne. The history of the Revolution offered in William E. H. Lecky's *England in the Eighteenth Century* is outdated. The account of the Revolutionary period by Edward Channing, in the third volume of his *History of the United States,* is judicious, but incomplete and antiquated after the passage of a half century. Eric Robson, *The American Revolution* . . . (London, 1955), is a Namierite attempt to deal with both England and America that could not succeed because of the premature death of its author. Esmond Wright, *Fabric of*

Freedom, 1763–1800 (New York, 1961), written by an Englishman, contains more factual errors than may be permitted to an American author. *The Birth of the Republic, 1763–89,* by Edmund S. Morgan (Chicago, 1956), is sound, but very brief. It almost omits things military. The most recent Marxian interpretation of the Revolution is offered by Herbert Aptheker. Dan Lacy has offered an accurate and very dry analysis of the convulsion in *The Meaning of the American Revolution* (New York, 1964). For a recent discussion of interpretations, one may go to Edmund S. Morgan, "The American Revolution: Revisions in Need of Revising," *William and Mary Quarterly,* third series, XIV (1957), 3–15.

Writings dealing with Britain in the first quarter century of the reign of George III have thrown much new light, not only upon that country, but upon Anglo-American relations. The extreme partisan and Whiggish view of Britain and America put forward by George O. Trevelyan and others of his persuasion is now discredited, so completely that George III has recently been described as a true Whig, so thoroughly that the historical pendulum may swing toward an equally untenable Toryish outlook. The works of Lewis B. Namier, notably *The Structure of Politics at the Accession of George III* (London, 1929, 2 vols.), *England in the Age of the American Revolution* (London, 1930), and (with John Brooke) *The History of Parliament. The House of Commons 1754–1790* (New York, 1964, 3 vols.), have exerted profound influence, adding fundamentally to our knowledge of the British political system as it was in the era of the Revolution. Disciples and critics of Namier have built upon his work, clarifying and refining his conclusions. John Brooke has contributed a clear and important analysis of *The Chatham Administration 1766–1768* (New York, 1956), and Ian R. Christie has similarly described *The End of North's Ministry 1780–1782* (London, 1958). Christie has also offered a helpful study of *Wilkes, Wyvill and Reform. The Parliamentary Reform Movement in British Politics 1760–1785* (New York, 1962). Other recent and useful books about eighteenth-century British politics and politicians are: Archibald S. Foord, *His Majesty's Opposition 1714–1830* (New York, 1964); George Rudé, *Wilkes and Liberty: A Social Study of 1763 to 1774* (New York, 1962); Eugene C. Black, *The Association: British Extraparliamentary Political Organization 1769–1793* (Cambridge, Mass., 1963); Lucy S. Sutherland, *The City of London and the Opposition to Government 1768–1774* . . . (London, 1959); John Norris, *Shelburne and Reform* (New York, 1963); and Charles R. Ritcheson, *British Politics and the American Revolution* (Norman, Okla., 1954). One result of recent revisionism is a much more favorable estimate of George III, expressed, among others, by Richard Pares in *King George III and the Politicians* (Oxford, 1953) and by Herbert Butterfield in *George III, Lord North and the People 1779–80* (London, 1949) and *George III and the Historians* (London, 1957). There is no satisfactory biography of George III, admittedly a difficult subject. The student may consult J. Steven Watson, *The Reign of George III*

526

1760–1815 (Oxford, 1960). Also lacking are sound biographies of George Grenville, Lord North, the Earl of Halifax, Lord Mansfield, and the Earl of Hillsborough. There is room, in view of recent scholarship, for a new study of William Pitt, Earl of Chatham. George H. Guttridge has analyzed *The Early Career of Lord Rockingham, 1730–1765* (Berkeley and Los Angeles, Calif., 1952). Lewis Namier and John Brooke, *Charles Townshend* (New York, 1964), portrays Townshend in colors even darker than those used by filio-pietistic American historians. The attempt by the authors to psychoanalyze "Champagne Charley" is frothy. Pauline Maier, "John Wilkes and American Disillusionment with Britain," *William and Mary Quarterly,* third series, XX (1963), 373–95, is informative. B. D. Bargar, *Lord Dartmouth and the American Revolution* (Columbia, S.C., 1965), is generous in its estimate of Dartmouth. For the Earl of Sandwich, one may go to George A. Martelli, *Jemmy Twitcher: a Life of the Fourth Earl of Sandwich, 1718–1792* (London, 1962). Gerald S. Brown, *The American Secretary: The Colonial Policy of Lord George Germain 1775–1778* (Ann Arbor, Mich., 1963), is too kind to Germain. Alan Valentine, *Lord George Germain* (New York, 1962), deals harshly with him. Concerning British political thought one should also consult Caroline Robbins, *The Eighteenth-Century Commonwealthman: Studies in the Transmission of English Liberal Thought from the Restoration of Charles II until the War with the Thirteen Colonies* (Cambridge, Mass., 1959); H. Trevor Colbourn, *The Lamp of Experience: Whig History and the Intellectual Origins of the American Revolution* (Chapel Hill, N.C., 1965); George H. Guttridge, *English Whiggism and the American Revolution* (Berkeley and Los Angeles, Calif., 1942); and Harvey C. Mansfield, *Statesmanship and Party Government: A Study of Burke and Bolingbroke* (Chicago, 1965). James T. Boulton, *The Language of Politics in the Age of Wilkes and Burke* (Toronto, 1963), reminds us that British politicians were addicted to rhetoric. Two more studies of eighteenth-century Britain, dealing with her society and political system, G. E. Mingay, *English Landed Society in the Eighteenth Century* (Toronto, 1963) and J. R. Pole, *Political Representation in England and the Origins of the American Republic* (New York, 1966), should be consulted.

Several studies of executive offices in London help the student to understand the workings of the British government, among them, Mark A. Thomson, *The Secretaries of State 1681–1782* (Oxford, 1932); Margaret M. Spector, *The American Department of the British Government* (New York, 1940); Dora Mae Clark, *The Rise of the British Treasury: Colonial Administration in the Eighteenth Century* (New Haven, Conn., 1960); and Franklin B. Wickwire, *British Subministers and Colonial America 1763–1783* (Princeton, N.J., 1966). It may be suspected that the Wickwire volume ascribes somewhat more expertise about America to subordinate officials than they possessed, and that they exerted less influence than is claimed for them. Arthur H. Basye, *The Lords Commissioners of Trade and Plantations, 1748–*

527

1782 (New Haven, Conn., 1925) and Oliver M. Dickerson, *American Colonial Government, 1696–1765* (New York, 1939), continue to be useful for an understanding of the Board of Trade.

The most judicious analysis of the fundamental reasons for American discontent is that offered by Charles M. Andrews in *The Colonial Background of the American Revolution* . . . (New Haven, Conn., 1924), a brief but illuminating work. Unfortunately, Professor Andrews was unable to complete his masterpiece, *The Colonial Period of American History* (New Haven, Conn., 1934–8, 4 vols.), which covers only the seventeenth century and English commercial policy. Robert R. Palmer, *The Age of the Democratic Revolution: A Political History of Europe and America, 1760–1800* (Princeton, N.J., 1959–64, 2 vols.), Hannah Arendt, *On Revolution* (New York, 1963), and Jacques Godechot, *France and the Atlantic Revolution of the Eighteenth Century, 1770–1799* (New York, 1965, English translation) cover the relationship between the American and French Revolutions.

There are many accounts of the origin and development of the Anglo-American contest during the years 1763 to 1775. Lawrence H. Gipson, *The British Empire Before the American Revolution* (New York, 1936–, 13 vols. to date), exhaustively covers the history of the empire during the quarter century before the Declaration of Independence. The author of that massive work does not claim that it is magisterial. Ransacking a multitude of sources, he has devoted much space to North America. Striving to be impartial, Professor Gipson, an American, is, one feels, somewhat too kind to British politicians who sought to assert dominance over America, such as Charles Townshend; overly disposed to accept the notion of the rightful supremacy of the King in Parliament; and somewhat too critical of the claims and behavior of the colonists. Few persons will read all of *The British Empire Before the American Revolution*, written in a monographic style. The scholar delving into problems handled by Professor Gipson will ignore his work at his own peril. Gipson's *The Coming of the Revolution, 1763–1775* (New York, 1954) has the merits—and defects—of his larger work. An older book concerning the same period by John C. Miller, *Origins of the American Revolution* (Boston, 1943), is better balanced, studded with contemporary quotations, and readable. For the beginnings of the Revolution, George L. Beer, *British Colonial Policy, 1754–1765* (New York, 1907), retains value, but the best account is that by Bernhard Knollenberg, *Origin of the American Revolution, 1759–1766* (New York, 1960). Mr. Knollenberg suggests that the change in British policy that led to Revolution began before 1763. In *Mitre and Sceptre* . . . *1689–1775* (New York, 1962) Carl Bridenbaugh asserts somewhat too emphatically the importance of discontent in America stemming from fear of the Anglican Church. Allen S. Johnson has described "The Passage of the Sugar Act" in *William and Mary Quarterly*, third series, XVI (1959), 507–14. For the relationship between the American colonies and the West Indies one may consult Richard Pares, *Yankees and Creoles* . . . (Cambridge, Mass.,

1956). Dora Mae Clark, "George Grenville as First Lord of the Treasury," *Huntington Library Quarterly,* XIII (1950), 198–224, is helpful concerning Grenville's attitude toward the British army in America. Edmund S. and Helen M. Morgan, *The Stamp Act Crisis* . . . (Chapel Hill, N.C., 1953), deals in scholarly fashion with British policy and especially with American reaction. The Morgans have little to say about British activity concerning the West. Robert D. Meade, *Patrick Henry: Patriot in the Making* (New York and Philadelphia, 1957), gives Henry all the credit he deserves. The well-known work of Clarence W. Alvord, *The Mississippi Valley in British Politics* . . . (Cleveland, Ohio, 1917, 2 vols.), is a pioneer but outworn study. For British policy on the West, one may consult John R. Alden, *John Stuart and the Southern Colonial Frontier* . . . *1754–1775* (Ann Arbor, Mich., 1944); Jack B. Sosin, *Whitehall and the Wilderness* . . *1763–1775* (Lincoln, Neb., 1961); Thomas P. Abernethy, *Western Lands and the American Revolution* (New York, 1937); and Francis S. Philbrick, *The Rise of the West, 1754–1830* (New York, 1965). The classic account of the Indian uprising of 1763 is contained in Francis Parkman, *The Conspiracy of Pontiac* . . . (New York, 1905, 2 vols., and other editions). The most accurate history of the Indian war is to be found in Howard Peckham, *Pontiac and the Indian Uprising* (Princeton, N.J., 1947). The history of the new British colonies may be found in Charles L. Mowat, *East Florida as a British Province, 1763–1784* (Berkeley and Los Angeles, Calif., 1943); Cecil Johnson, *British West Florida, 1763–1783* (New Haven, Conn., 1943); and A. L. Burt, *The Old Province of Quebec* (Toronto and Minneapolis, 1933). There is some information about General Thomas Gage and the part played by the British army in the Stamp Act crisis and later Anglo-American troubles in John R. Alden, *General Gage in America* . . . (Baton Rouge, La., 1948), and also in John Shy, *Toward Lexington: The Role of the British Army in the Coming of the American Revolution* (Princeton, N.J., 1965). For the background of the Currency Act of 1764, see Joseph A. Ernst, "Genesis of the Currency Act of 1764: Virginia Paper Money and the Protection of British Merchants," *William and Mary Quarterly,* third series, XXII (1965), 33–74. Jack P. Greene and Richard M. Jellison, "The Currency Act of 1764 in Imperial-Colonial Relations, 1764–1776," *William and Mary Quarterly,* third series, XVIII (1961), 485–518, is most helpful concerning a subject that has been too long neglected. The attitudes and behavior of the American merchants in the Stamp Act crisis and the crises that followed are portrayed in the highly detailed study by Arthur M. Schlesinger, *The Colonial Merchants and the American Revolution, 1763–1776* (New York, 1918). Professor Schlesinger's *Prelude to Independence: The American Newspaper War upon Britain, 1764–1776* (New York, 1958) is, unfortunately, slender. The making and adoption of the Townshend policy cannot be understood without consulting the biography of Townshend by Namier and Brooke, mentioned above. For John Dickinson, one may consult David L. Jacobson, *John Dickinson and the*

Revolution in Pennsylvania, 1764–1776 (Berkeley and Los Angeles, Calif., 1965). Oliver M. Dickerson, *The Navigation Acts and the American Revolution* (Philadelphia, 1951), contends somewhat too vigorously that vicious execution of the Navigation Acts by British officers was a potent cause of colonial discontent after 1764. Carl Ubbelohde, in *The Vice-Admiralty Courts and the American Revolution* (Chapel Hill, N.C., 1960), deals cautiously with his subject. For the British customs service in America, one may go to Thomas C. Barrow, *Trade and Empire* . . . (Cambridge, Mass., 1967). Bernard Donoughue, *British Politics and the American Revolution: The Path to War, 1773–75* (New York, 1964), is most valuable for the crisis that began in 1773. Benjamin W. Labaree, *The Boston Tea Party* (New York, 1964), is a thorough study.

For the political thought of the colonists one should begin with Bernard Bailyn, *The Ideological Origins of the American Revolution* (Cambridge, Mass., 1967). Reference should also be made to Clinton Rossiter, *Seedtime of the Republic: The Origin of the American Tradition of Political Liberty* (Chicago, 1953), and Louis Hartz, *The Liberal Tradition in America* . . . (New York, 1955). Randolph G. Adams, *Political Ideas of the American Revolution* . . . *1765–1775* (Durham, N.C., 1939), retains value. Edmund S. Morgan has written cogently about "The Puritan Ethic and the American Revolution," in *William and Mary Quarterly,* third series, XIV (1967), 3–43. For intricate Anglo-American constitutional argument, the student may commence with Charles H. McIlwain, *The American Revolution: A Constitutional Interpretation* (New York, 1923), Robert L. Schuyler, *Parliament and the British Empire* . . . (New York, 1929), and Charles F. Mullett, *Fundamental Law and the American Revolution, 1760–1776* (New York, 1933). Jack P. Greene, *The Quest for Power: The Lower Houses of Assembly in the Southern Royal Colonies, 1689–1776* (Chapel Hill, N.C., 1963), sheds new light, not only upon the political experience of the Americans, but also upon local quarrels that contributed to American discontent. Leonard W. Labaree, *Royal Government in America* (New Haven, Conn., 1930), explains in detail how Britain looked upon and directed the royal governors.

The volume of propaganda emitted during the years 1763 to 1776, much of it pseudonymous and anonymous, was massive. Philip Davidson, *Propaganda and the American Revolution, 1763–1783* (Chapel Hill, N.C., 1941), serves as an introduction to the subject. Fred J. Hinkhouse has written about *The Preliminaries of the American Revolution as Seen in the English Press, 1763–1775* (New York, 1926). Bruce I. Granger, *Political Satire in the American Revolution, 1763–1783* (Ithaca, N.Y., 1960), Robert R. Rea, *The English Press in Politics: 1760–1774* (Lincoln, Neb., 1963), and Solomon Lutnick, *The American Revolution and the British Press, 1775–1783* (Columbia, Mo., 1967) are useful. John C. Miller has informed us about *Sam Adams: Pioneer in Propaganda* (Boston, 1936). For the activities of Benjamin Franklin, one must consult Verner W. Crane's splendid work, *Benjamin Franklin's Letters to the Press, 1758–1775* (Chapel Hill, N.C., 1950) and his *Benjamin Franklin and a Rising People* (Boston, 1954). For the work of other colonial agents in England, one may go to Ella Lonn, *The Colonial Agents of the Southern Colonies* (Chapel Hill, N.C., 1945); Jack P. Sosin, *Agents and Merchants: British Colonial Policy and the Origins of the American Revolution, 1763–1775* (Lincoln, Neb., 1965); Michael G. Kammen, "The Colonial Agents, English Politics, and the American Revolution," in *William and Mary Quarterly,* third series, XXII (1965), 244–63; and Nicholas Varga, "Robert Charles: New York Agent, 1748–1770," in *William and Mary Quarterly,* third series, XVIII (1961), 211–35.

The author desires to mention here certain other special studies which throw light upon the colonies before the War of Independence: Alice M. Baldwin, *The New England Clergy and the American Revolution* (Durham, N.C., 1928); Arthur C. Bining, *British Regulation of the Colonial Iron Industry* (Philadelphia and London, 1933); Carl Bridenbaugh, *Myths and Realities: Societies of the Colonial South* (Baton Rouge, La., 1952); Arthur L. Cross, *The Anglican Episcopate and the American Colonies,* (New York and London, 1902); Emory Evans, "Planter Indebtedness and the Coming of the Revolution in Virginia," *William and Mary Quarterly,* third series, XIX (1962), 511–33; Jack P. Greene, "Landon Carter and the Pistole Fee Dispute," *William and Mary Quarterly,* third series, XIV (1957), 66–9; Jack P. Greene, "The Gadsden Election Controversy . . .", *Mississippi Valley Historical Review,* XLVI (1960), 469–92; Richard M. Gummere, *The American Colonial Mind and the Classical Tradition . . .* (Cambridge, Mass., 1963); Alan Heimert, *Religion and the American Mind: From the Great Awakening to the Revolution* (Cambridge, Mass., 1966); Brooke Hindle, *The Pursuit of Science in Revolutionary America, 1735–1789* (Chapel Hill, N.C., 1956); David S. Lovejoy, "Rights Imply Obligations: The Case against Admiralty Jurisdiction," *William and Mary Quarterly,* third series, XVI (1959), 460–84; Albert E. McKinley, *The Suffrage Franchise in the Thirteen English Colonies* (Philadelphia and Boston, 1905); Joseph J. Malone, *Pine Trees and Politics: The Naval Stores and Forest Policy in Colonial New England, 1691–1775* (Seattle, 1965); Richard L. Merritt, *Symbols of American Community, 1735–1775* (New Haven, Conn., 1966); Abbot E. Smith, *Colonists in Bondage: White Servitude and Convict Labor in America, 1607–1776* (Chapel Hill, N.C., 1947); Thad W. Tate, "The Coming of the Revolution in Virginia: Britain's Challenge to Virginia's Ruling Class, 1763–1776," *William and Mary Quarterly,* third series, XIX (1962), 323–43; Moses C. Tyler, *The Literary History of the American Revolution, 1763–1783* (New York, 1941, reprint), an older work that remains standard; Gordon S. Wood, "Rhetoric and Reality in the American Revolution," *William and Mary Quarterly,* third series, XXIII (1966), 3–32; and Louis B. Wright, *The Cultural Life of the American Colonies, 1607–1763* (New York, 1957).

531

The best general accounts of the period of the War of Independence in America are John R. Alden, *The American Revolution, 1775–1783* (New York, 1954), John C. Miller, *Triumph of Freedom, 1775–1783* (Boston, 1948), and Claude H. Van Tyne, *The American Revolution, 1775–1783* (New York, 1905). John R. Alden has also given special attention to the South in *The Revolution in the South, 1763–1789* (Baton Rouge, La., 1957). Willard W. Wallace, *Appeal to Arms* . . . (New York, 1951) and Howard H. Peckham, *The War for Independence* . . . (Chicago, 1958) offer military histories that are sound and brief. Christopher Ward, *The War of the Revolution* (New York, 1952, 2 vols., John R. Alden, ed.), is vivid, contains much interesting detail, is largely devoted to the American side of the war upon land. Other military histories of a popular nature are those by Bruce Lancaster, *From Lexington to Liberty* . . . (Garden City, N.Y., 1955); George F. Scheer and Hugh F. Rankin, *Rebels and Redcoats* (Cleveland and New York, 1957); and Lynn Montross, *Rag, Tag and Bobtail* . . . (New York, 1952). Piers Mackesy, *The War for America, 1775–1783* (Cambridge, Mass., 1964), is largely based upon British records, insufficiently accurate on detail of events in America, and devoted, not very successfully, to defense of George III, Lord George Germain, the Earl of Sandwich, and others who directed the British war effort. Older studies that supply background about the British army are Sir John Fortescue, *A History of the British Army* (London and New York, 1899–1930, 13 vols.) and Edward E. Curtis, *The Organization of the British Army in the American Revolution* (New Haven, Conn., 1926).

There are some fine modern studies of phases of the war. Descriptions of the beginning of the conflict which retain their usefulness are Allen French, *The Day of Concord and Lexington* (Boston, 1925) and *The First Year of the American Revolution* (Boston, 1934). Bruce Bliven, Jr., has described the *Battle for Manhattan* (New York, 1956). Alfred H. Bill's *Campaign of Princeton, 1776–1777* (Princeton, N.J., 1940) and *Valley Forge: The Making of an Army* (New York, 1952) are readable. Leonard H. Lundin, *Cockpit of the Revolution* (Princeton, N.J., 1940), carefully narrates warfare in New Jersey. Alexander A. Lawrence, *Storm over Savannah* . . . (Athens, Ga., 1951), offers an excellent account of the siege of Savannah. H. L. Landers, *The Virginia Campaign and the Blockade and Siege of Yorktown, 1781* (Washington, 1931), may be consulted with profit; also Harold A. Larrabee, *Decision at the Chesapeake* (New York, 1964). Carl Van Doren, *Secret History of the American Revolution* . . . (New York, 1941), covers the Arnold-André conspiracy and reveals the blackness of Arnold's treason. See also James T. Flexner, *The Traitor and the Spy* . . . (New York, 1953). Carl Van Doren, *Mutiny in January* . . . (New York, 1943), covers the collapse of order in Washington's army early in 1781. M. F. Treacy, *Prelude to Yorktown* . . . (Chapel Hill, N.C., 1963), deals with the Southern campaigns of Nathanael Greene. Some light upon minor American officers is to be found in Herbert T. Wade and Robert A. Lively, *This Glorious Cause: The Adventures* of *Two Company Officers in Washington's Army* (Princeton, N.J., 1958). For the history of the private soldier, one may go to Joseph P. Martin, *Private Yankee Doodle* . . . (Boston and Toronto, 1962, George F. Scheer, ed.). Benjamin Quarles has covered *The Negro in the American Revolution* (Chapel Hill, N.C., 1961). There is, unfortunately, no complete and modern history of the American navy in the War of Independence. Reference may be made to Gardner W. Allen, *A Naval History of the American Revolution* (Boston, 1913, 2 vols.) and to Edgar S. Maclay, *History of American Privateers* (New York, 1899).

For special studies of the British side of the war and British commanders, in addition to those mentioned above, one may begin with Troyer S. Anderson, *The Command of the Howe Brothers in the American Revolution* (New York, 1935). Based largely upon unpublished British documents, that volume marked a great advance in scholarship on British operations and remains useful. There is no good biography of Sir William Howe. A sophisticated study of the role played by Viscount Howe in the Revolution, by Ira Dempsey Gruber, should soon be in the press. A preliminary report upon part of his findings is offered by Professor Gruber in "Lord Howe and Lord George Germain: British Politics and the Winning of American Independence," *William and Mary Quarterly,* third series, XXII (1965), 225–43. There is as yet no satisfactory biography of General John Burgoyne, nor is there a truly scholarly history of his campaign of 1777. William B. Willcox has made most valuable contributions on British operations during the later years of the war in various magazine articles, in his edition of *The American Rebellion: Sir Henry Clinton's Narrative of His Campaigns, 1775–1782* . . . (New York, 1954), and in *Portrait of a General: Sir Henry Clinton in the War of Independence* (New York, 1964). Professor Willcox does not magnify the virtues of Clinton. Critical of Lord Cornwallis, he is sufficiently kind to that commander. There is no good biography of Cornwallis. The reputation of Sir Guy Carleton, once rated too highly by Whiggish historians, has suffered at the hands of A. L. Burt, notably in his article, "The Quarrel Between Germain and Carleton: An Inverted Story," *Canadian Historical Review,* XI (1930), 202–22. Professor Burt does not make it clear that Carleton had good reason to detest Germain, a fact of which George III was well aware. Robert D. Bass, *The Green Dragoon: The Lives of Banastre Tarleton and Mary Robinson* (New York, 1957), is impressionistic but interesting. Paul H. Smith, *Loyalists and Redcoats: A Study in British Revolutionary Policy* (Chapel Hill, N.C., 1964), deals with the history of Loyalist troops in the war. William M. James, *The British Navy in Adversity: A Study of the War of Independence* (New York, 1926), has lost value.

Biographies of Patriot commanders contain much useful material concerning the war. Essays on several American commanders are to be found in George A. Billias (ed.), *George Washington's Generals* (New York, 1964). The best life of Washington, though not a magisterial one, is that by Douglas

S. Freeman *et al., George Washington: A Biography* (New York, 1948–57, 7 vols.). Samuel W. Patterson's study of *Horatio Gates, Defender of American Liberties* (New York, 1941) should be replaced. Bernhard Knollenberg, *Washington and the Revolution* (New York, 1940), makes clear the need for doing justice to Gates. John R. Alden, *General Charles Lee . . .* (Baton Rouge, La., 1951), does not say that Lee was a whole-souled and abused Patriot. The best of the biographies of Nathanael Greene is that by Theodore Thayer, *Nathanael Greene: Strategist of the American Revolution* (New York, 1960). The complex Greene deserves further study. George W. Kyte has contributed "Victory in the South: An Appraisal of General Greene's Strategy in the Carolinas," in *North Carolina Historical Review,* XXXVII (1960), 321–47. Concerning Greene's achievements, see also Hugh F. Rankin, "Cowpens: Prelude to Yorktown," *North Carolina Historical Review,* XXXI (1954), 336–69. Willard Wallace, *Traitorous Hero . . .* (New York, 1954), is a judicious and readable study of the life of Benedict Arnold. The best book about *General Von Steuben,* that by John M. Palmer (New Haven, Conn., 1937), should be replaced by a more exhaustive and more critical study. R. Don Higginbotham has written well about *Daniel Morgan: Revolutionary Rifleman* (Chapel Hill, N.C., 1961). George A. Billias, *General John Glover and His Marblehead Mariners* (New York, 1960), is interesting and useful. Broadus Mitchell, *Alexander Hamilton: Youth to Maturity, 1755–1788* (New York, 1957), gives Hamilton too much military credit. The second volume of Donald Gerlach, *Philip Schuyler and the American Revolution in New York, 1733–1777* (Lincoln, Neb., 1964–, 1 vol. to date) will enable us to see Schuyler in clearer light. North Callahan has contributed *Henry Knox, Washington's General* (New York, 1958). There is no modern biography of Baron de Kalb, and those we have of Anthony Wayne and Light-Horse Harry Lee are semi-popular. Louis Gottschalk, in *Lafayette Joins the American Army* (Chicago, 1937) and *Lafayette and the Close of the American Revolution* (Chicago, 1942), destroys much romance, offers a cool and judicious account of Lafayette as an officer in America. A history of the French army in America during the War of Independence is much needed. Some information about it can be gleaned from Lee Kennett, *The French Armies in the Seven Years' War . . .* (Durham, N.C., 1967).

For the war in the West reference can be made to John Bakeless, *Background to Glory; The Life of George Rogers Clark* (Philadelphia, 1957), a lively biography; John Bakeless, *Daniel Boone* (New York, 1939); John D. Barnhart, *Henry Hamilton and George Rogers Clark in the American Revolution . . .* (Crawfordsville, Ind., 1951), a volume which is not unkind to Hamilton; John W. Caughey, "Willing's Expedition down the Mississippi, 1778," *Louisiana Historical Quarterly,* XV (1932), 5–36; Randolph C. Downes, *Council Fires on the Upper Ohio* (Pittsburgh, Pa., 1940); Carl S. Driver, *John Sevier, Pioneer of the Old Southwest* (Chapel Hill, N.C., 1932); Dale Van Every, *Men of the Western Waters* (Boston, 1956), a popular history; Philip M. Hamer, "John Stuart's Indian Policy during the Early Months of the American Revolution," *Mississippi Valley Historical Review*, XVII (1930–1), 351–66; James A. James, *The Life of George Rogers Clark* (Chicago, 1928), a sober work; James A. James, *Oliver Pollock* (New York, 1937); Kathryn M. Mason, *James Harrod of Kentucky* (Baton Rouge, La., 1951); Thomas E. Matthews, *General James Robertson, Father of Tennessee* (Nashville, Tenn., 1934); Milo M. Quaife, *The Capture of Old Vincennes* (Indianapolis, Ind., 1927); Howard Swiggett, *War Out Of Niagara . . .* (New York, 1933); and Samuel C. Williams, *Tennessee during the Revolutionary War* (Nashville, Tenn., 1944).

A convenient compilation of factual information on the War of Independence is offered in Mark M. Boatner (ed.), *Encyclopedia of the American Revolution* (New York, 1966).

There are many studies of the Loyalists in this and that colony-state and several of the Tories as a whole. The familiar book about them by Claude H. Van Tyne, *The Loyalists in the American Revolution* (New York, 1902), has become almost outworn. It has been replaced in part by William H. Nelson, *The American Tory* (Oxford, 1961). Wallace Brown, *The King's Friends . . .* (Providence, R.I., 1966), offers interesting statistics and sidelights about the Loyalists from an analysis of petitions to the Crown for compensation. Other studies of the Tories are Julian P. Boyd, *Anglo-American Union: Joseph Galloway's Plans to Preserve the British Empire, 1774–1788* (Philadelphia, 1941); Arthur G. Bradley, *United Empire Loyalists . . .* (London, 1932); Richard D. Brown, "The Confiscation and Disposition of Loyalists' Estates in Suffolk County, Massachusetts," *William and Mary Quarterly*, third series, XXI (1964), 534–50; Robert O. De Mond, *Loyalists in North Carolina during the Revolution* (Durham, N.C., 1940); Lewis Einstein, *Divided Loyalties: Americans in England during the War of Independence* (Boston, 1933), an interesting book which, among other things, offers a reminder that the War of Independence was less than total; Alexander C. Flick, *Loyalism in New York during the American Revolution* (New York, 1901); Harold B. Hancock, *Delaware Loyalists, Papers of the Historical Society of Delaware*, new series, III (Wilmington, Del., 1940); Isaac S. Harrell, *Loyalism in Virginia . . .* (Durham, N.C., 1926); Edward A. Jones, "Loyalists of New Jersey in the American Revolution," *Collections of the New Jersey Historical Society*, X (1927); Leonard W. Labaree, "Nature of American Loyalism," *Proceedings of the American Antiquarian Society*, new series, LIV (1944), 15–58; Robert S. Lambert, "The Confiscation of Loyalist Property in Georgia, 1782–1786," *William and Mary Quarterly*, third series, XX (1963), 80–94; Adolphus E. Ryerson, *Loyalists of America and Their Times . . .* (Toronto, 1880), an older book reflecting the viewpoint of descendants of the Loyalists; Lorenzo Sabine, *Biographical Sketches of Loyalists of the American Revolution* (Boston, 1864, 2 vols.), offering clues to the history of many Tory worthies; Wilbur H. Siebert, "Dispersion of the American Tories," *Mississippi*

Valley Historical Review, I (1914), 185–97; Wilbur H. Siebert, Loyalists of Pennsylvania (Columbus, Ohio, 1920); Wilbur H. Siebert, Loyalists in East Florida, 1774–1785 (Deland, Fla., 1929, 2 vols.); W. J. Sparrow, Knight of the White Eagle: Sir Benjamin Thompson, Count Rumford of Woburn, Massachusetts (New York, 1966); Harry B. Yoshpe, Disposition of Loyalist Estates in the Southern District of the State of New York (New York, 1939), an important work which offers valuable information on the nature of the purchasers of forfeited Tory property; Oscar Zeichner, "Rehabilitation of Loyalists in Connecticut," New England Quarterly, XI (1938), 308–30; and Oscar Zeichner, "Loyalist Problem in New York after the Revolution," New York History, XXI (1940), 284–302.

There has been much writing about the Declaration of Independence, including Carl L. Becker, The Declaration of Independence . . . (New York, 1922), a minor classic that has substantially withstood scholarly assault; Julian P. Boyd, Declaration of Independence . . . (Princeton, N.J., 1945); Edward Dumbauld, The Declaration of Independence and What It means Today (Norman, Okla., 1950); Herbert Friedenwald, Declaration of Independence (New York, 1906); and John H. Hazelton, Declaration of Independence . . . (New York, 1906). For the immediate background of the Declaration, one may consult Curtis P. Nettels, George Washington and American Independence (Boston, 1951). The student may begin an examination of the many writings on the Mecklenburg Declaration of Independence with William H. Hoyt, Mecklenburg Declaration of Independence (New York, 1907).

Edmund C. Burnett, The Continental Congress (New York, 1941), remains the standard work concerning that body. Merrill C. Jensen, The Articles of Confederation . . . (Madison, Wis., 1940), deals cogently with the struggles over the provisions of the first constitution of the United States. Herbert B. Adams, Maryland's Influence upon Land Cessions to the United States . . . (Baltimore, 1885), covering the attitude of Maryland toward the Articles of Confederation, retains interest. For Southern attitudes toward that document and the Constitution of 1787 one may consult John R. Alden, The South in the Revolution, 1763–1789 (Baton Rouge, La., 1957), and John R. Alden, The First South (Baton Rouge, La., 1961).

General histories of the period of the Confederation that may be consulted with profit are Andrew C. McLaughlin, The Confederation and the Constitution, 1783–1789 (New York, London, 1905), an older study which has been attacked but not entirely discredited by revisionists; Merrill Jensen, The New Nation: A History of the United States During the Confederation, 1781–1789 (New York, 1950), a thoughtful book that portrays the postwar era in brighter colors than those used by McLaughlin; and Forrest McDonald, E Pluribus Unum: The Formation of the American Republic, 1776–1790 (Boston, 1965), which offers original and stimulating views concerning various questions disputed by scholars. For that period reference should also be made to E. James Ferguson, The Power of the Purse: A History of

American Public Finance, 1776–1790 (Chapel Hill, N.C., 1961).

There has been much controversy over the making and ratification of the Constitution of 1787. There are many respectable accounts of the federal convention, including those offered in Max Farrand, *The Framing of the Constitution of the United States* (New Haven, Conn., 1913); Carl Van Doren, *The Great Rehearsal* . . . (New York, 1948); Clinton Rossiter, *1787: The Grand Convention* (New York and London, 1966); and Catherine Drinker Bowen, *Miracle at Philadelphia: The Story of the Constitutional Convention* . . . (Boston, 1966). The economic and social motivation of the Constitution is analyzed with vigor in Charles A. Beard, *An Economic Interpretation of the Constitution* (New York, 1913), a pioneer but incomplete study. Beard's views are strenuously attacked in Robert E. Brown, *Charles Beard and the Constitution* . . . (Princeton, N.J., 1956). The student should also go to Forrest McDonald, *We the People*: *The Economic Origins of the Constitution* (Chicago, 1958). The best general study of the enemies of the Constitution is Jackson T. Main, *The Antifederalists*: *Critics of the Constitution, 1781–1788* (Chapel Hill, N.C., 1961). One recent book concerning the struggle over ratification within one state, Linda G. DePauw, *The Eleventh Pillar: New York State and the Federal Constitution* (Ithaca, N.Y., 1966), deserves attention. Reference should also be made to Jackson T. Main, *The Social Structure of Revolutionary America* (Princeton, N.J., 1965); Richard B. Morris, "The Confederation Period and the American Historian," *William and Mary Quarterly*, third series, XIII (1956), 139–56; Richard B. Morris, "Class Struggle and the American Revolution," *William and Mary Quarterly*, third series, XIX (1962), 3–29; and Cecelia M. Kenyon, "Republicanism and Radicalism in the American Revolution: An Old-Fashioned Interpretation," *William and Mary Quarterly*, third series, XIX (1962), 153–82. More attention should be paid to the Bill of Rights. Robert A. Rutland, *The Birth of the Bill of Rights, 1776–1791* (Chapel Hill, N.C., 1955), Irving Brant, *The Bill of Rights: Its Origin and Meaning* (Indianapolis, Ind., 1965), and Edward Dumbauld, *The Bill of Rights and What It Means Today* (Norman, Okla., 1957), serve as introduction to the subject.

For political, social, and economic change in the several states, one may recommend, among much valuable work, William W. Abbot, *The Royal Governors of Georgia, 1754–1775* (Chapel Hill, N.C., 1959); Wilbur C. Abbott, *New York in the American Revolution* (New York, 1929); Oscar T. Barck, *New York City during the War for Independence* . . . (New York, 1931); Charles A. Barker, *The Background of the Revolution in Maryland* (New Haven, Conn., 1940); Carl L. Becker, *History of Political Parties in the Province of New York, 1760–1776* (Madison, Wis., 1909), a pioneer monograph that retains value; Anne Bezanson, *Prices and Inflation during the American Revolution*: *Pennsylvania, 1770–1790* (Philadelphia, 1951); Paul F. Boller, Jr., "George Washington and Religious Liberty," *William and Mary Quarterly*, third series, XVII (1960), 486–506; Carl and Jessica Bridenbaugh, *Rebels and Gentlemen* . . . (New York, 1942); Carl Bridenbaugh, *Cities in Revolt* . . . (New York, 1955); Robert E. Brown, *Middle-Class Democracy and the Revolution in Massachusetts, 1691–1780* (Ithaca, N.Y., 1955); Robert E. and B. Katherine Brown, *Virginia, 1705–1786: Democracy or Aristocracy* (East Lansing, Mich., 1964); Philip A. Crowl, "Maryland during and after the Revolution . . .," *The Johns Hopkins Studies in Historical and Political Science,* series LXI, no. 1 (1943); Harry A. Cushing, *History of the Transition from Provincial to Commonwealth Government in Massachusetts* (New York, 1896); Elisha Douglass, *Rebels and Democrats* . . . (Chapel Hill, N.C., 1955); Robert A. East, *Business Enterprise in the American Revolutionary Era* (New York, 1938); H. J. Eckenrode, *Separation of Church and State in Virginia* . . . (Richmond, Va., 1910); H. J. Eckenrode, *Revolution in Virginia* . . . (Boston, 1916); Lucile Griffith, *Virginia House of Burgesses, 1750–1774* (Northport, Ala., 1963); Hugh B. Grigsby, *Virginia Convention of 1776* (Richmond, Va., 1855); Oscar and Mary Handlin, "Revolutionary Economic Policy in Massachusetts," *William and Mary Quarterly,* third series, IV (1947), 3–26; Edward F. Humphreys, *Nationalism and Religion in America, 1774–1789* (Boston, 1924); J. Franklin Jameson, *The American Revolution Considered as a Social Movement* (Princeton, N.J., 1926), a seminal rather than definitive study; Gustav A. Koch, *Republican Religion* . . . (New York, 1933); Charles A. Lincoln, *The Revolutionary Movement in Pennsylvania, 1760–1776* (Philadelphia, 1901); Charles L. Lingley, *Transition in Virginia from Colony to Commonwealth* (New York, 1910); Mary S. Locke, *Anti-Slavery in America* . . . (Boston, 1901); David S. Lovejoy, *Rhode Island Politics and the American Revolution, 1760–1776* (Providence, R.I., 1958); Robert McColley, *Slavery and Jeffersonian Virginia* (Urbana, Ill., 1964); Richard P. McCormick, *New Jersey from Colony to State* (Princeton, N.J., 1964); Bernard Mason, *The Road to Independence: The Revolutionary Movement in New York, 1773–1777* (Lexington, Ky., 1966); Richard B. Morris, *Government and Labor in Early America* (New York, 1946); Richard B. Morris, "Primogeniture and Entailed Estates in America," *Columbia Law Review,* XXVII (1927), 24–51; Curtis P. Nettels, *The Emergence of a National Economy, 1775–1815* (New York, 1962); Allan Nevins, *The American States during and after the Revolution, 1775–1789* (New York, 1924), a storehouse of information and particularly seminal on the "Internal Revolution"; Richard J. Purcell, *Connecticut in Transition* (Washington, D.C., 1918); J. Paul Selsam, *Pennsylvania Constitution of 1776* (Philadelphia, 1936); E. W. Sikes, *Transition of North Carolina from Colony to Commonwealth* (Baltimore, 1898); Reva C. Strickland, *Religion and the State in Georgia in the Eighteenth Century* (New York, 1939); Charles S. Sydnor, *Gentlemen Freeholders: Political Practices in Washington's Virginia* (Chapel Hill, N.C., 1952); David Syrett, "Town-Meeting Politics in Massachusetts, 1776–1786," *William and Mary Quarterly,* third series, XXI (1964), 352–66; Theodore Thayer, *Penn-*

sylvania Politics and the Growth of Democracy, 1740–1776 (Harrisburg, Pa., 1953); Richard F. Upton, Revolutionary New Hampshire (Hanover, N.H., 1936); Thomas J. Wertenbaker, Father Knickerbocker Rebels: New York City during the Revolution (New York, 1948); and Otto Zeichner, Connecticut's Years of Controversy, 1750–1776 (Chapel Hill, N.C., 1949).

The standard work upon international relations connected with the American upheaval is Samuel F. Bemis, Diplomacy of the American Revolution (New York, 1935). One should also consult the latest work on the subject by Richard W. Van Alstyne, Empire and Independence: The International History of the American Revolution (New York, London, Sydney, 1965), for a different approach. Other works of value concerning international relations are Samuel F. Bemis, Hussey-Cumberland Negotiation and American Independence (Princeton, N.J., 1931); Julian P. Boyd, "Silas Deane: Death by a Kindly Teacher of Treason," William and Mary Quarterly, third series, XVI (1959), 165–87, 319–42, 515–50, a fascinating study which suggests that Dr. Edward Bancroft mercifully put his friend Deane to death; Weldon A. Brown, Empire or Independence . . . 1774–1783 (Baton Rouge, La., 1941), a volume which covers the Carlisle Commission; Edward S. Corwin, French Policy and the American Alliance of 1778 (Princeton, N.J., 1916); Henri Doniol, Histoire de la participation de la France à l'établissement des États-Unis d'Amérique (Paris, 1884–92, 6 vols.); Gerald S. Graham, British Policy and Canada, 1774–1791 . . . (New York, 1930); George H. Guttridge, David Hartley, M.P., An Advocate of Conciliation, 1774–1783 (Berkeley, Calif., 1926); John Franklin Jameson, "St. Eustatius in the American Revolution," American Historical Review, VIII (1903), 683–708; Elizabeth S. Kite, Beaumarchais and the War of Independence (Boston, 1918, 2 vols.); Carl L. Lokke, France and the Colonial Question . . . 1763–1801 (New York, 1932); Claude-Anne Lopez, Mon Cher Papa: Franklin and the Ladies of Paris (New Haven, Conn., 1966), which deals with a subject of enduring interest; Rafael Sánchez Mantero, "La misión de John Jay en España (1779–1782)," Anuario de Estudios Americanos, XXIII (1966), 1389–1431; John J. Meng, Comte de Vergennes: European Phases of His American Diplomacy . . . (Washington, D.C., 1932); Richard B. Morris, The Peacemakers . . . (New York, 1965), a lively account of the negotiations of 1782 to 1783; James B. Perkins, France in the American Revolution (Boston, 1911); Paul C. Phillips, The West in the Diplomacy of the American Revolution (Urbana, Ill., 1913); Charles J. Stillé, "Beaumarchais and the Lost Million," Pennsylvania Magazine of History and Biography, XI (1887), 1–36; Kathryn Sullivan, Maryland and France, 1774–1789 (Philadelphia, 1936); and Claude H. Van Tyne, "French Aid before the Alliance of 1778," American Historical Review, XXXI (1925), 20–40.

In addition to those mentioned above, there are many other biographical studies which throw light upon the Revolutionary era, among them Catherine

D. Bowen, *John Adams and the American Revolution* (Boston, 1950), a readable book; Page Smith, *John Adams* (Garden City, N.Y., 1962, 2 vols.); Ralph V. Harlow, *Samuel Adams* (New York, 1923); John Pell, *Ethan Allen* (Boston, 1939); Kate M. Rowland, *Life of Charles Carroll* . . . (New York, 1898, 2 vols.); E. W. Spaulding, *His Excellency George Clinton* (New York, 1938); Jules D. Prown, *John Singleton Copley* . . . (Cambridge, Mass., 1966, 2 vols.); William M. Dabney and Marion Dargan, *William Henry Drayton and the American Revolution* (Albuquerque, N.M., 1962); Edward P. Alexander, *James Duane* . . . (New York, 1938); Aubrey C. Land, *The Dulanys of Maryland* (Baltimore, 1955); Verner W. Crane, *Benjamin Franklin, Englishman and American* (Baltimore, 1936); Carl Van Doren, *Benjamin Franklin* (New York, 1938); Gerald Stourzh, *Benjamin Franklin and American Foreign Policy* (Chicago, 1954); John W. Caughey, *Bernardo de Gálvez in Louisiana, 1776–1783* (Berkeley, Calif., 1934); George Washington Greene, *Life of Nathanael Greene* (New York, 1867–71, 3 vols.); Francis V. Green, *General Greene* (New York, 1893); Nathan Schachner, *Alexander Hamilton* (New York, 1946); Herbert L. Allen, *John Hancock, Patriot in Purple* (New York, 1948); Frank Monaghan, *John Jay* (New York, 1935); Marie Kimball, *Jefferson* . . . (New York, 1943–, 3 vols.), interesting upon Jefferson's cultural pursuits; Dumas Malone, *Jefferson* . . . (Boston, 1948–, 3 vols. to date), the best life, so far as it goes, of Jefferson; Samuel Eliot Morison, *John Paul Jones, A Sailor's Biography* (Boston, 1959); Friedrick Kapp, *Life of John Kalb* (New York, 1870); M. Haiman, *Kosciuszko in the American Revolution* (New York, 1943); David D. Wallace, *Life of Henry Laurens* . . . (New York, 1915); Burton J. Hendrick, *The Lees of Virginia* (Boston, 1935); Irving Brant, *James Madison* . . . (Indianapolis and New York, 1941–61, 6 vols.); Albert J. Beveridge, *The Life of John Marshall* (Boston, 1916–19, 4 vols.), which should be replaced; Kate M. Rowland, *Life of George Mason* . . . (New York, 1892, 2 vols.); Robert A. Rutland, *George Mason, Reluctant Statesman* (Williamsburg, Va., 1961); Kenneth R. Rossman, *Thomas Mifflin and the Politics of the American Revolution* (Chapel Hill, N.C., 1952); Clarence Ver Steeg, *Robert Morris: Revolutionary Financier* . . . (Philadelphia, 1954); Paul A. W. Wallace, *The Muhlenbergs of Pennsylvania* (Philadelphia, 1950); Reginald Lucas, *Lord North* (London, 1913, 2 vols.), a study that is mentioned only because it has not been replaced by a better one; Moncure D. Conway, *Life of Thomas Paine* (New York, 1892, 2 vols.), an outworn biography that has not been superseded; Robert L. Hilldrup, *Life and Times of Edmund Pendleton* (Chapel Hill, N.C., 1939); David John Mays, *Edmund Pendleton* (Cambridge, Mass., 1952, 2 vols.), a superior biography; Marvin R. Zahniser, *Charles Cotesworth Pinckney* . . . (Chapel Hill, N.C., 1967); Charles C. Pinckney, *The Life of General Thomas Pinckney* (Boston, 1895); Albert von Ruville, *William Pitt, Earl of Chatham* (London, 1907, 3 vols.); Basil Williams, *Life of William Pitt* (London, 1913, 2 vols.); Kate M. Hotblack,

Chatham's Colonial Policy . . . (London and New York, 1917); Elizabeth S. Kite, *Brigadier General Louis Lebègue Du Portail* . . . (Baltimore, Philadelphia, London, 1933); H. J. Eckenrode, *The Randolphs* . . . (Indianapolis, Ind., 1946); John F. Roche, *Joseph Reed, A Moderate in the American Revolution* (New York, 1954); Esther Forbes, *Paul Revere and the World He Lived In* (Boston, 1942); Brooke Hindle, *David Rittenhouse* (Princeton, N.J., 1964); Jean Edmond Weelen, *Rochambeau* (Paris, 1934); George T. Keppel, Earl of Albemarle, *Memoirs of the Marquis of Rockingham* (London, 1852, 2 vols.); Nathan G. Goodman, *Benjamin Rush* . . . (Philadelphia, 1934); Richard M. Barry, *Mr. [John] Rutledge of South Carolina* (New York, 1942), a semi-popular book; Roger S. Boardman, *Roger Sherman* (Philadelphia, 1938); Friedrick Kapp, *Life of Major General Frederick William Von Steuben* (New York, 1959, 2 parts); Anne K. Gregorie, *Thomas Sumter* (Columbia, S.C., 1931); Charles Martyn, *Life of Artemas Ward* (New York, 1921); John Cary, *Joseph Warren* . . . (Urbana, Ill., 1961); John C. Fitzpatrick, *George Washington Himself* (Indianapolis, Ind., 1933), which claims too much for its subject; Rupert Hughes, *George Washington* (New York, 1926–30, 3 vols.), an unfinished life that retains interest; Bernhard Knollenberg, *George Washington: The Virginia Period, 1732–1775* (Durham, N.C., 1964), the most scholarly study of Washington before he became commander in chief; James T. Flexner, *George Washington: The Forge of Experience, 1732–1775* (Boston, 1965), covering Washington's youth in greater detail; Dudley W. Knox, *The Naval Genius of George Washington* (Boston, 1932); Nathaniel W. Stephenson and Waldo H. Dunn, *George Washington* (New York, 1940, 2 vols.); and L. S. Mayo, *John Wentworth* (Cambridge, Mass., 1921).

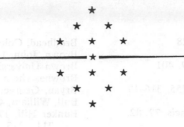

INDEX

John R. Alden was born in Michigan in 1908, and attended the University of Michigan, where he received his A.B. (1929), M.A. (1930), and Ph.D. (1939). He taught at the University of Nebraska (1945–55), then transferred to Duke University in 1955, where he has been chairman of the Department of History (1957–60), and was appointed, in 1963, James B. Duke Professor of History. He has also taught at the University of Chicago, the University of Michigan, and Columbia University. Among his many academic honors is the Albert J. Beveridge Prize of the American Historical Association (1945) and a Guggenheim Fellowship (1955–6). Mr. Alden was invited to be Commonwealth Fund Lecturer at University College, London, in 1960, and Donald Fleming Lecturer at Louisiana State University in 1961. He makes his home, with his wife and daughter, in Durham, North Carolina.